Communicating through
letters and reports

*[You learn more by thinking about what you're
doing than by simply thinking or simply doing.]*

Communicating through letters and reports

C. W. Wilkinson

Professor of English and Chairman (emeritus)
Business and Technical Communication Courses
University of Florida

Peter B. Clarke

President, Arcus Company

Dorothy C. Wilkinson

Assistant Professor of Business Communication
College of Commerce and Business Administration
University of Alabama

Eighth Edition   1983

Richard D. Irwin, Inc.
Homewood, Illinois   60430

ISBN 0-256-02935-0
Library of Congress Catalog Card No. 82–82479

Printed in the United States of America

2 3 4 5 6 7 8 9 0 D 0 9 8 7 6 5 4 3

Preface

Note to teachers and students (in and out of school):

This Eighth Edition of *Communicating through Letters and Reports* represents a major evolutionary step in the growth of the book. We have gone beyond the usual updating to include information not only on how to meet current business communication problems but also those which will be current in the near future. Teachers familiar with this book will find that the basic content and teaching aids follow the spirit of the successful previous seven editions. So do this edition's improvements and additions.

Our main purpose is still to help you improve *your* business communications, to speak and write effectively and efficiently. Our philosophy is still to emphasize successful presentation of messages through effective use of our remarkably flexible language.

Basically, we have:

1. Thoroughly updated every part of the book to take into account the technological and methodological changes in the way business operates and communicates.
2. Painstakingly revised our own style for conciseness and readability and nonsexist wording.
3. Emphasized a management point of view throughout.
4. Revised examples and cases to reduce the prevalence of retail-oriented material in favor of industrial, wholesale, institutional, and government (all levels).
5. Added four completely new sections on *(a)* writing a readable style, *(b)* using nonsexist language, *(c)* communicating with nonnative speakers of English, and *(d)* writing proposals (as new Appendix D).
6. Inserted numerous sections on various aspects of international business communication, added cases based on international business communication problems, and added a completely new appendix on this subject (Appendix C).
7. Rewritten and rearranged the report writing section to give the subject a fresh treatment and better organization.
8. Added study and review questions and exercises as new features at the end of each chapter.

9. Placed the case series (all new) in Appendix E to keep from unduly lengthening chapters.

10. Adopted a more attractive, inviting, and functional format and typography.

11. Further expanded the *Teacher's Guide* by including more helpful information on teaching and the textbook. You will also find a large number of additional new cases as well as some material which you might wish to continue using from the previous edition of the textbook.

If you are teaching *Communicating through Letters and Reports* and do not have the *Teacher's Guide,* you should obtain one from your Irwin representative or by writing the publisher direct. If you are familiar with earlier versions of the *Guide,* you will find the new edition different and much more complete than in the past, with a wealth of materials to make your job easier.

Students and teachers of college courses in communicating through letters, through reports, and through combinations of the two will find the book easily adaptable to varying standards and student abilities. By attention to only the major principles and the easier questions, exercises, and cases, freshmen and sophomores of average ability can use the book effectively. By attention to all the refinements and the more difficult cases, upperclassmen in our best universities will find it among their most challenging texts.

Note to students

In learning anything as complex as preparing superior letters, reports, and oral presentations—or managing people who do—you need instruction in *principles,* then *illustrations,* and finally *practice* in applying the principles. Accordingly, the first four chapters (Part One) present what we consider to be the basic principles applicable to all business letters. If you go no further, you will have a sound fundamental concept of the appearance, language, style, and psychology of tone and persuasiveness for effective business letters and memos.

For more detailed analysis and application, the next eight chapters (Part Two) show you how to handle your letters and short memos functionally according to three basic plans: good-news, disappointing, and persuasive messages. Though the book presents analyses and examples of inquiries, replies, orders and acknowledgments, claims, adjustments, credits, sales, job applications, requests, and collections, the emphasis is not on such specific types. As you read through the book, you will see the fundamentals applied in the many illustrations.

Four chapters (Part Three—completely revised) cover all important aspects of writing reports, including their importance, nature, definition and classification, preparation, and appropriate style.

Part Four presents the basic principles of effective oral business communication in the main kinds of situations (reports, interviews, conferences, and dictation).

All of the illustrations are from actual business letters, memos and reports, or based on actual situations. But because even comparatively good business letters that go through the mail may not serve well as textbook illustrations, we have sometimes edited them beyond merely changing the names of companies, products, and individuals. And in some instances, we have written our own illustrations. We are fully aware, however, that the perfect letter never has been and never will be written.

Having studied the principles and seen them illustrated, you can then make the principles stick in your mind (and thus make their application habitual) by putting them to use in working out selected cases from the many given at the ends of chapters. The ample number and variety of cases allow selection to fit your interests, abilities, and desired emphasis.

The situations and problems embodied in the cases come from our collective experiences in business and industry, from our reading, and from other sources. We have endeavored to make them as realistic and up-to-date as possible. Indeed, most of them are problems actually faced by real people recently. In a few instances we have the actual letters these people wrote, and have included them in the *Teacher's Guide*.

Preparing and presenting *perfect* business letters, reports, or oral communications is next to impossible for all of us. Doing even *good* ones does not just come naturally to most. If you are content to do them as many *are* done, instead of as they *should* be, you will gain little or nothing from studying this book. But with a concentrated effort to improve, you can learn to present superior ones.

Please remember, however, that this book is not a dictionary, formula book, or cookbook to follow blindly. Your aim should be thoughtful consideration of principles for use in creating your own original work rather than slavish imitation of textbook models. You should learn and follow the *principles* illustrated, *not the wording* of the illustrations.

Likewise, the checklists (a special feature of this book) are thought starters rather than thought-stopping rules to follow blindly. They are summary reminders of points about the particular kind of communication under discussion, not formulas for or straitjackets on it. They do *not* mean that all the points discussed earlier about a kind of message and summarized in a checklist are applicable to every one of that general class. Thoughtful consideration of a point in a checklist will quickly tell you whether the point is applicable to your particular problem, but ignoring the lists will frequently lead to omission of important points; and slavish following of a list will often lead to inappropriate contents. Hence, when used properly, the checklists can help you produce better messages, help teachers to mark student shortcomings quickly, and thus help you to see where you went wrong.

From our own business experience, from the many people in business and industry we have talked and worked with, from thousands of articles in business magazines, from associating with many other teachers on the job, through long and active membership in the American Business Communication Association (including a charter membership, three terms as president, and at least one in almost every job in the association), from widely varied consulting work, and from college students and business people we have taught, we have learned much about business communications and effective ways for teaching people to improve theirs. We have brought together and modified what we have learned through many years of experience. And we have contributed our own ideas.

In studying this book, then, you learn what we think is the best that has been thought and said about communicating in business through the years. By learning its suggestions, you can improve your own effectiveness as a business communicator.

C. W. Wilkinson
Peter B. Clarke
Dorothy C. Wilkinson

Contents

Checklists

About the Cases in this Book

For clear, quick, and easy case identification and cross-referencing, we have used the following efficient numbering system:

1. *All the cases in each chapter carry sequential numbers, though subdivisional headings in Chapters 5 and 7 divide them into categories.*

2. *For cross-references elsewhere in the book, we use double numbers (such as 5–12, meaning Case 12 in Chapter 5).*

3. *Appendix E provides supplementary cases in eight series. Each series carries a Roman numeral I-VIII, and the related cases in each series carry capital-letter designations. At appropriate places we therefore refer to these supplementary cases of the same kind by cross-references such as "Appendix E: I, A; VIII, A, D" (meaning Case A of Series I in Appendix E and Cases A and D in Series VIII are three more similar cases).*

The cases in this book are disguised and sometimes slightly modified real situations. Mostly they are from among the more difficult communication situations of business. Most names of firms and individuals, however, are fictitious for obvious reasons.

We have tried to give you the basic information needed without complicating details. You are expected to fill in details from your own imagination. But you are not to go contrary to the statements or implications in the cases, and your imaginary details must be reasonably likely.

The writing in the cases is intentionally not good—nor is the order of points the best—because you would learn nothing from copying from us. So beware of copying our sentences and clauses. Put your ideas in your own words.

Letters and memos

[*Through your letters you quickly reveal the kind of polite person or stinker you are.*]

part 1

Why study letter and memo writing?

The main reasons you should study letter writing are:

1. You are almost certain to write many business letters and memos during the rest of your life, regardless of the kind of work you do. Letters and memos are the most common forms of written communication for managing business affairs, and everybody has business affairs to manage.
2. Your degree of failure or success in managing many of those affairs will depend on whether you write ordinary letters and memos or really good ones.
3. All too often the untrained, unthinking business writer writes bad letters and memos. Usually the procedure is to follow the bad writing style, the bad tone, the ineffective psychology, and even the messy or old-hat appearance of bad ones received or read in the files.
4. Through systematic study and practice you can learn to write good letters and memos and thus greatly increase your chances of success in handling your personal business or business affairs on a job.

The importance of effective business writing is increasing, too. Continuing rapid changes since the mid-1960s in the technology of word processing are speeding up and making cheaper the processing of information. Word processing machines have incorporated microcomputers to gain text-editing capabilities and then joined with minicomputers to produce complete word processing/data processing systems that are within reach of even the smallest offices and businesses.

What, then, does the spread of word processing mean to business communication and, more important, to teachers and students of business communication? Contrary to some popular expectation, the business letter and memo are very much alive and active.

Letters will still be the preferred means of communication between organizations for a good many years to come. Their format may change slightly: letters produced by quality computer printers will become acceptable and letters transmitted through the sender's telephone to the receiver's CRT screen (a TV-like screen) are becoming more popular. But whether a letter or memo is on a computer print-out, an electronic screen, or whatever else comes along, *it will still be a letter or memo*. The devices of style and interesting, clear, inconspicuous writing will still be important. Positional emphasis works on a

CRT screen as well as on a letterhead; and whether a reader reads from an electronic display or a piece of paper, deadwood phrases and incorrect spelling and grammar will still defeat the purpose of a message.

Perhaps the biggest change computerized data/word processing systems have made is an increase in the flow of information. As the amount of information communicated by words increases, the more necessary it becomes that people write clearly, concisely, and correctly. Employers already put a high premium on people who can capably communicate in English.

In the next few years, as computerized data/word processing becomes a common part of the American office, we can look forward to an increased emphasis on writing that quickly and effectively communicates the message—exactly what *Communicating Through Letters and Reports* teaches.

Other things you learn

In learning to write better letters and memos, you will also learn some principles of practical psychology that will enable you to get along better professionally and socially with other people.

When you improve your ability to write clear, concise, persuasive, and natural English (which *is* the desirable language of business), you gain accuracy and naturalness in phrasing anything else you have to write or speak.

Through your study of letters and memos you will get further insight into the ways of the business world: practices used in getting people to buy; handling orders, gaining and refusing credit; making collections; adjusting claims; and selecting employees.

You will learn how to save time and money on business writing. As a good business writer, you can often write one letter to settle a business transaction that would require two or three from an untrained writer. By using form letters and form paragraphs, you can cut down on costs when the form message will do the job. When, however, you have situations requiring individual letters, you will recognize them and know better than to waste money on forms.

You will also be able to dictate or write the necessary individual letters and memos more rapidly because you will have gained the self-confidence that comes from knowing how to tackle a job. You will write freely and effectively the letters and memos you *have* to write and the many others you *should* write.

Perhaps most important of all, you will realize that every letter and memo you write is an item in your overall public relations—and you will try to make each one win, instead of lose, friends.

Letter volume and costs

According to a recent report, the U.S. Postal service handled 74.9 billion pieces of first-class mail and 35.1 billion pieces of third-class (business) mail.

Since about 86 percent of first-class mail (or 64.4 billion pieces) also is business, that is a total of 99.5 billion pieces of business mail the Postal Service handled in one year. If we accept the First National Bank of Chicago's latest figure of $6.76 (though Dartnell pays $7.11) as the estimated cost of preparing a business letter (materials, time, equipment) and take 60 cents as the average cost of preparing each direct mail piece, we come up with a total year's expenditure for business letters and direct mail of $456.4 *billion* (64.4 billion pieces × $6.76 plus 35.1 billion pieces × $0.60). That's BIG business—big enough to justify considerable attention to its efficiency!

Letter advantages

When you consider the advantages of letters, you see why people in business write so many and spend so much money on them. Despite the cost of a letter, it is often the most economical way to transact business. You can't go far (not even across town, if you figure your time and traveling expense) or talk much by long distance during business hours or say much in a telex for the cost of a letter. But for that money you can put your message in a letter and send it anywhere in the country and almost anywhere in the world.

Even if you do talk to another person, you do not have a written record, as you do if you follow the almost universal business practice of making a copy of your letter. Because a letter and its answer can make a written contract, letters often replace personal calls and telephone calls even when the two parties are in the same city.

Telex, Teletype, and facsimile transmission provide written records of communications and have the added advantage of being virtually immediate, though only people with access to the systems can receive messages. But their cost makes them impractical unless a company can make heavy use of them. This fact generally restricts their use to large organizations with numerous locations.

Still another advantage of letters is that both the writer and reader can handle a letter at their most convenient times. Therefore, it can get by receptionists and secretaries many times when a telephone call or a personal call cannot. Moreover, the reader usually gives it full attention without raising partially considered objections and without interruption, a decided psychological advantage.

Emphasis in business

When executives began to realize how much letters cost, how important letters and reports are to the smooth operation of their firms, and how few of their employees were capable writers, many of them started training and correspondence control programs. At General Electric, Westinghouse, Southern Pacific, Marshall Field's, the New York Life Insurance Company, and the big mail-order houses (Montgomery Ward, Spiegel's, and Sears, Roebuck), to mention only a few of the leaders, such programs have demonstrated the economy and efficiency resulting from improved correspondence. Even these firms, however, prefer to hire people who can already write rather than train them on company time.

A frequent question in employment interviews and inquiry letters to professors, therefore, concerns the ability of college graduates to do such writing. An applicant who presents evidence of ability to write good letters, memos, and reports becomes a favored applicant for nearly any job.

Emphasis in schools

Many of the executives who are aware of the importance of good letters and memos are graduates of the few schools that have taught business writing since early in the 1900s. These business leaders are the main reason why today in the majority of respectable colleges and universities literally thousands of students are studying and practicing how to write more effectively for business. Without exception, surveys by such organizations as Delta Sigma Pi, the American Assembly of Collegiate Schools of Business, and the American Business Communication Association have confirmed the high regard of former students for the work.

Common misconceptions

Yet some people—mostly for lack of information—do not respect even university work in business writing. They sometimes think courses in letter writing are merely about letter forms. Although this is a part of the course, it is only a small part (less than 2 percent of this book).

You may even hear the mistaken idea that students of letter writing learn the trite, wordy, and nearly meaningless expressions so common at the beginnings and endings of letters untrained writers usually prepare. Actually, you learn to write naturally, concisely, and clearly, to take care of business without beating about the bush, and to end letters when you are through—without wasting first and last sentences saying nothing.

Still others think that in the study of letter writing the emphasis is on high-pressure techniques and tricks and gadgets. Just the opposite is true. In drawing on the findings of psychologists, we are not advocating that you attempt to *manipulate* or outsmart your reader in sly, unethical fashion. The intent of the writer toward a reader should always be morally and ethically proper. Our intent is to help you write acceptable things in an acceptable way more likely to convince your reader of the legitimacy and the attractiveness (or soundness) of your proposal or position.

You may hear that letter writing is "just a practical study." It certainly is practical, for the ability to write good business letters is useful. But it is also a cultural study because its primary purposes are the development of (1) your ability to maintain pleasant relations with others and (2) your language effectiveness.

Why the high regard for business writing?

One of the reasons why courses in business writing have found increasing favor with students, recruiters, executives, and college administrators is that they are blends of the cultural and the practical.

The business correspondent writes to an individual for a definite, practical purpose—and must write with the same exactness as other good writers. The purpose is not, however, entertainment (or self-expression in purple passages and deathless prose). *Action* is usually the goal. Letter and memo writing is partially a study of probable or estimated human *reaction* as a basis for securing the desired *action*. Since the quality of persuasion is more important to the business writer than to most writers, a good knowledge of practical psychology is essential.

The good business writer must learn to do more than just sell goods and services. Successful handling of claim, adjustment, credit, and collection letters requires learning tact, patience, consideration of the other person, a necessarily optimistic attitude, and the value of saying things pleasantly and positively instead of negatively. These are the reasons why you can expect more successful social and business relations with other people after a thorough, conscientious, and repeated analysis and application of the principles of good letter and memo writing in this book.

Furthermore, the good business writer must learn to be concise, interesting, and easy to follow—to hold a reader's attention. For reasons of courtesy a listener will bear with a long-winded, dull, or unclear conversation—maybe even ask for explanations. But the reader of a letter or memo feels no such obligation. The good writer therefore edits carefully to phrase ideas more effectively in writing than in talking.

In conversation one can cushion the effect or shade the meaning with the twinkle of an eye, inflection of the voice, or gesture of a hand and can adjust and adapt the presentation according to the listener's reaction. With far less chance of failure a speaker can get along by "doin' what comes naturally." The letter or memo writer has no such chance to observe the effects of the first part of a presentation and adapt the last part accordingly—and therefore must learn to *foresee* the reader's reaction all the way through. This situation requires more thorough knowledge of practical psychology, more preliminary reader analysis, and more careful planning of messages and phrasing of thoughts than in oral communication.

Such reader analysis, planning, and editing establish good habits of expression—habits which carry over to the spoken message. This fact is the reason we say that you will learn to talk better if you learn to write better. It is also the reason we say that, in learning to write effective letters and memos, you will learn to do a better job of writing anything else you have to write.

Art, science, or skill?

The use of the language—in clear, concise adaptation to one's readers so that they can absorb the message with the least amount of effort and the greatest amount of pleasant reaction—is an art. Several generations of business writers have shown that the proper language for business in general and for letters and memos in particular is just plain good English. Though it is more concise and more precise, it is neither more nor less formal than the conversational language of people who read most letters and memos.

Good business letters and memos are also the result of a conscious use of principles which have evolved since the turn of the century. No one would claim that business writing is an exact and thoroughly developed science, but prominent business writers who have experimented with letters and memos for over 80 years have given us a near-scientific framework of empirical principles as a starting point. Though some of these principles have not undergone exact scientific testing, they have taken a great deal of the speculation out of letter and memo writing. We can therefore approach business writing with considerable knowledge of what good writing principles are and when, where, and how to apply them.

Summary

In studying letter and memo writing, you not only learn how to get the desired results from the many you will have to write. You will also get a greater understanding of people and how to influence them, an increased facility in the use of language (both oral and written), a more thorough knowledge of business practices and ethics, and a resultant confidence in yourself.

As you may have noticed in the preceding explanations, effective letter and memo writing depends on achieving the desired reader reactions. Furthermore, achieving those effects depends on making a careful analysis of the reader's likely reactions to the appearance, the style, the goodwill element, and the appropriate persuasion in your messages. Those are the topics of the next four fundamental chapters.

Appearance:
What the reader sees

Just about everybody has to write business letters and memos. Most people consider themselves "pretty fair" writers, too. Actually, however, the statement "Anything done by everybody is seldom done well" is as true of business writing as it is of any other activity.

If you do write good business letters and memos, you can answer yes to these questions:

1. Is their appearance pleasant and unobtrusive?
2. Is your writing style interesting, clear, and inconspicuous?
3. Do your letters and memos reflect basic goodwill?
4. Does your writing follow good persuasion principles?

You and any other business writer should apply these four tests because

—A pleasant and unobtrusive (undistracting) appearance, giving the first impression the reader gets, is important. If the appearance is bad, you start off with one strike against you.

—Your letter or memo may establish a favorable first impression yet fail completely because its language is dull, vague, inaccurate, difficult to follow, unnatural, or full of errors.

—Even with good appearance and style, your message can fail if it reflects poor tone and/or fails to reflect a desire to be of service to the reader.

—Your letter or memo may be appropriate in appearance, easily readable because of its clear and natural style, and pleasant because of its good tone and service attitude, yet fail because it does not follow good psychology or does not stress benefits to the reader.

With all four desirable qualities—good looks, good style, goodwill, and appropriate persuasion—your letters and memos will accomplish their purposes in most instances.

To explain and illustrate these four essentials of any good letter or memo is the function of Part 1 of this book. To show how the principles apply in various kinds of letters and memos is the main function of Part 2.

We do not believe you can write the good business messages you are capable of without understanding each of these four essentials. For that reason we ask you to read extensively before you start writing; and for the same reason no letter or memo cases appear until the end of Part 1.

The appearance of an individualized letter or memo is like a person's appearance: Since it is not the most important thing, the less attention it attracts to itself, the better. The wording, a desirable tone reflecting goodwill, and the persuasive qualities are more influential than the looks of a letter in determining its success or failure. Just as some listeners will reject the messages of speakers who do not come up to expected standards of appearance, however, so will many readers reject a written message that calls attention to its format and thereby distracts from the content.

A personalized (individualized) letter sent by first-class mail will nearly always get a reading. Flashy designs and lavish colors are like yelling at a person whose attention you already have. Even worse, if it is either too messy or too gaudy, or if it violates the conventions of letter form, the appearance distracts the reader's attention from the important feature—your message.

Direct mail/marketing (sales) letters are sometimes justifiable exceptions. Because they are frequently unpersonalized mass mailings, they often must struggle to get read at all. In striving to capture attention, their writers may use computer-simulated personalization, cartoons, gadgets, bright colors, important-seeming messages on the envelopes, and other gimmicks. Except for such direct mail, however, the physical letter should serve only as a vehicle for your message. The reader should not notice it since it would distract attention from the message.

A memo, by its nature, should never need to work for a reader's attention. A neat, clean, conventional appearance is always the goal.

STATIONERY

The first thing your reader will notice if it is inappropriate is your stationery. The most common business stationery—and therefore the least noticed—is 20-pound white bond with some rag content in 8½ by 11-inch sheets. Variations acceptable under appropriate circumstances include heavier and lighter paper, different sizes, and various unobtrusive colors and shades.

Paper heavier than 20-pound is more expensive, too stiff for easy folding, and too thick for clear carbons; and lighter than 20-pound is too flimsy and transparent for letters. (If used, carbon copies are usually on very light paper because it is cheaper, takes less file space, and allows a greater number of clear carbon copies.)

The main off-standard sizes are Executive or Monarch letterheads (7½ by 10½ or 11 inches, used mainly by top executives) and half sheets (8½ by 5½ inches, used most frequently in intracompany memos or notes).

Though white is the standard, only the rainbow and your sense of appropriateness to your kind of business set the limits for color variations. Some tests have shown that colored papers sometimes produce better results in sales mailings. If you are sending out large mailings, however, you may be wise to run your own test on a small sample to see what color works best for that particular situation.

Paper with some rag content is more expensive than all-pulp paper, but it gives the advantages of pleasant feel, durability, and resistance to yellowing. The plasticized papers on the market usually claim to be easily erasable; but they have a "hard" feel, may be somewhat transparent, and are given to smudges. With the use of white-out products to facilitate typing corrections and the advent of word processing, the erasable papers have found only a limited market in business and industry.

Whatever your choice of paper for letter and memo sheets, be sure you use the same quality and color for envelopes and second pages.

The acceptable variations in stationery allow you to reflect the personality of your business, just as you select clothes appropriate to your personality. The big points are appropriateness and inconspicuousness. In selecting paper for your letterheads, then, you should have a good reason before choosing something other than 20-pound white bond, 8½ by 11 inches. Anything else may distract the reader's attention from your message.

LETTERHEAD

The main trend in letterheads for many years has been toward simplicity. Letterheads once took up a good part of the sheet with slogans, names of officers, and pictures of the firm's plant and product. Good modern letterheads usually take no more than two inches at the top and may occupy just a corner. They use wording, design, color, and graphic techniques to convey the necessary information and communicate a desirable image of the firm represented.

The minimum content is the name, address, and telephone number of the firm, including area and ZIP codes. Sometimes an added trademark or slogan indicates the nature of the business. Firms doing much nationwide or international business frequently give a toll-free telephone number and/or an address for cablegrams or telex.

Recent years have shown a marked movement toward the use of color in stationery. This trend is partly the result of increased acceptance of colored paper and color printing and partly from heightened awareness of the role of letterheads as representatives of a company. Firms wishing to present a modern image are turning to carefully designed graphics, such as the imaginative use of special colors and blind embossing. Good designers, however, are careful to avoid garish combinations and tasteless designs.

PLACEMENT ON THE PAGE

Even with appropriate paper and a well-designed letterhead, you can still spoil the appearance (and thus distract from the message) unless you place the letter on the page properly. Two methods are in common use: the standard-line plan and the less-popular picture-frame plan.

Standard-line plan

The standard-line plan of placing a letter on the page saves time and money because the typist or word processor operator does not have to reset the margins for letters of varied length. Typewriters set to the company's standard line (usually six inches, 60 spaces of pica type or 72 of elite) give all letters the same side margins. The top margin is about the same as the side margins, and the bottom margin is about one and a half times as wide. By varying from the standard spacing between letter parts (more or less between the date and inside address, for example, or three spaces instead of two between paragraphs), you can adjust letters of differing lengths for proper height or just float the letter in the middle of the page.

Memos almost always use the standard-line plan, in keeping with their intended saving of time and money.

Picture-frame plan

Typing a letter so that it looks like a picture framed by the white space around it takes a little more time than the standard-line method because you have to set the marginal stops according to your estimate of each letter's length. With patience, however, it enables you to fit long and short letters to the page in more conventional fashion.

The idea is that a rectangle drawn around the typed letter (not including a printed letterhead) should look like a picture framed in the marginal white space. You determine the width of side margins according to your letter length and make the top margin about the same. The bottom margin will take care of itself automatically. It should be about one and a half times as long (deep) as the other margins, as illustrated later in this chapter.

In gaining experience, a typist soon learns where to set a typewriter's marginal stops for letters of various lengths. If you're just starting to gain the experience, however, you might well try this general plan. For short letters (100 words or less) leave about 2-inch margins at the top and sides. For long letters (over 250 words) leave at least 1-inch margins. Split the difference for middle-length letters.

Word processors make using the picture-frame plan much easier. Once a letter is in the machine's memory, an operator can quickly configure it with any desired margins. In only a minute or two the operator can print out versions with different margins to see how they look if appearance is important enough to justify the extra time and effort. But even with word processing, the standard-line plan is by far the more popular.

POSITION AND SPACING
OF LETTER PARTS

Standard parts

The usual business letter has six standard parts. *As a general rule, single space within parts and double space between parts*. But note exceptions as they come up in the following explanation.

The conventional *heading* or first part of a letter on paper with no letterhead (illustrated later) usually includes the sender's address (but not name) and date. It establishes both top and side margins because it is the first thing on the page, and the end of the line going farthest to the right sets the margin. It may appear on the left, too, in a pure block form. Such a heading is usually three lines but often more. Thus it affects the number of words you can fit into a given typewriter setting.

Increasingly, writers are moving the sender's address to below the signature or title. This is a logical place for it and leads the reader to begin reading with the important part of the message, the content.

On printed stationery you can write the dateline as a unit with the letterhead or as a separate part. As a unit with the letterhead, place the typed-in date for best appearance according to the design of the printed part. Usually it retains the balance by appearing directly under the center of a symmetrical letterhead; often it rounds out one that is off balance. As a separate part, it fixes the upper right or left corner of the letter. Thus it is the *first exception* to the general rule of double spacing between letter parts.

The *inside address* includes the title, name, and address of the person to receive the letter, including the ZIP code. The beginning of the address establishes the upper left corner of the letter if the date is a unit with a printed letterhead. Otherwise, it begins at the left margin, two to six spaces lower than the dateline. So it is the *second exception* to double spacing between letter parts. (*Warning:* Be careful to spell names right and to use proper titles. People do not like seeing their names misspelled or with the wrong title. Standard practice calls for some form of title—professional, honorary, or courtesy—in *front* of *other* people's names, even when a professional or position title follows.)

The *salutation* or friendly greeting, the third standard part, begins at the left margin a double space below the inside address and ends with a colon (:) or no punctuation whatsoever. The wording must match the first line of the address, disregarding any attention line. If you address an individual, the salutation must fit (usually *Dear* plus title and name); if you address a firm or other group, you must choose an appropriate salutation.

Since a salutation is the first indication of the formality of a letter, you should give some thought to the implications of how you greet your reader and how you match the tone of your salutation in the complimentary close.

Until recent years that obligation gave letter and memo writers little problem more than knowing whether to address a woman as Miss or Mrs. The main forms for letters addressed to persons are (in descending order of formality, with appropriate complimentary closes):

```
Dear (appropriate title          Yours truly (or)
plus surname)                    Sincerely yours

Dear (surname or given           Sincerely yours (or)
name)                            Cordially yours

Dear (given name,                Cordially (or) Regards
nickname, or such more           (or some more familiar
familiar term as                 phrasing, as long as in
originality produces and         good taste)
good taste allows)
```

In line with the trend toward informal friendliness of business letters, most business writers use the person's name in the salutation when they can and match the friendly tone with some form of *sincerely* or *cordially*.

In recent years, however, new developments have made more difficult the problems of (1) addresses and salutations to women and (2) salutations to mixed-sex groups and business firms. Since the abbreviation "Ms." (or simply "M.") came into our language to solve the earlier problem of how to address a woman of unknown marital status, many women have come to dislike it. But—many other women dislike the old forms of Miss and Mrs. (even when right, according to past practice); and most rightly resent the use of "Gentlemen" for a firm or group involving even one woman.

Of course if a woman has given you her preference (as she should—see "signature block" later), you would use it. Beyond that we can give you only some not-completely-satisfactory guidelines to choices for handling the two problems.

1. For addressing women when you don't know their preferences of courtesy title, you can (a) continue the standard forms of a few years ago (Miss or Mrs. when you know and Ms. or M. when you don't), though you may thereby antagonize some women; (b) skip the title and explain why (thus in a way asking the lady's preference—particularly desirable if the correspondence seems likely to continue); (c) use the AMS (Administrative Management Society) Simplified form or a variation of it, which omits both salutations and complimentary closes (illustrated later) but does not help you on inside or outside addresses; (d) (if you're on a comfortable first-name basis) use only the first name in the salutation.

2. For salutations to mixed-sex groups and business firms, you can (a) use the AMS Simplified form (probably your best choice); or (b) use "Ladies and Gentlemen" when addressing a mixed group (though we don't like it except when making a speech). We do not subscribe to "To whom it may concern" or "Dear Sir or Madam" (old hat and too formal; and many women do not like to be thought of as madams). Dodging with "Dear Business Executive" or ". . . Owner" is like running into a river to dodge a pothole.

The *body* or message of the letter begins a double-space below the salutation. Usually you single-space within paragraphs and double-space between, though for the standard-line layout in very short letters you may use double-spacing within and triple-spacing between paragraphs. Since the body is all one part, regardless of the number of paragraphs, the standard double-spacing between paragraphs is a *third exception* to the general rule of spacing. In any case, the number of paragraphs affects the fit of a letter to a given typewriter setting. A letter of 250 words in seven paragraphs, for example, will take at least four more lines than the same number of words in three paragraphs. Yet you should not overlook the chance to improve readability by such means as keeping paragraphs short and itemizing points when helpful.

The *complimentary close* (worded appropriately according to the descending scale of formality illustrated above) goes a double space below the last line of the body. It may begin at the center of the page, in line with the beginning of a typed heading, in line with the dateline used as a separate part, at a point to space it evenly between the center and right margin of the letter, or (in full block) flush at the left margin. The most common forms employ one of three key words—*cordially*, *sincerely*, and *truly*—each ordinarily used with *yours*. Juggling the order of the key word and *yours* or adding *very*—as *Yours truly, Yours very truly, Very truly yours*—makes little difference. The key word is the main consideration.

Proper form for the *signature block* depends on whether the letter is about your private affairs or company business where you are an employee. In writing about your own business, space four times below the complimentary close and type your name. The typed name is important for legibility—and consideration for your reader. Then pen your signature above it.

If you're writing about company business and the company is to be legally responsible for the letter, however, the company name should appear above the signature. That the letter is on company stationery makes no difference. So if you want to protect yourself against legal involvement, type the company name *in solid capitals* a double space below the complimentary close; then make the quadruple space for your signature before your typed name. You also give your title on the next line below the typed name or, if there is room, put a comma and your title on the same line with your name. Thus you indicate that you are an agent of the company legally authorized to transact business.

```
Very truly yours,                    Sincerely yours,
ACME PRODUCTS, INC.                  LOVEJOY AND LOEB



John Y. Bowen                        (Miss) Phyllis Bentley, Treasurer
Comptroller
```

Because the possibility of legal involvement is usually remote, many writers prefer to omit the company name from the signature block in the hope of gaining a more personal effect through a letter from an individual instead of from a company. If you feel that way, you can set up the signature block as follows:

Cordially yours,   Sincerely yours,

H. P. Worthington   *Phyllis B. Hudson*

H. P. Worthington   (Mrs.) Phyllis B. Hudson
Assistant Public Relations   Treasurer
Manager

Before you do, however, we suggest that you (1) get official agreement to bail you out of any legal involvement and (2) remember that some readers feel greater security in dealing with a company instead of an individual.

Women's signatures bring up a special problem. Note that in all the men's signatures illustrated, no title precedes the names. Without some indication, however, the person who answers a woman's letter does not know what courtesy title to give her. (For help on how to solve this problem, see our discussion of salutations.) As a matter of consideration, a woman should indicate how she wants to be addressed—the way Miss Bentley, who became Mrs. Hudson, did in the preceding examples.

Special parts

Besides the six standard parts of a business letter, you will often find use for one or more of seven widely used special parts.

You can use an *attention line* in a letter addressed to a company if you want a certain individual to read it but don't know the person's name. "Attention: Purchasing Agent" or "Attention, Purchasing Agent" will do the job. In either position, flush at the left margin or centered, put it between the inside address and salutation with a double space above and below. Remember, however, that *an attention line has no effect on the salutation, which relates to the inside address instead*.

A *subject line* may save words by telling your reader quickly what the letter is about or referring to former correspondence for necessary background. It usually appears at the left margin a double space below the salutation; but when space is a premium, it may appear centered on the same line as the salutation. To make it stand out, either underscore it or use solid capitals. The informal "About" is increasing in use. And more and more correspondents omit the word *Subject* or its equivalent. The position and wording make clear what the subject line is.

Initials of the dictator and the typist often appear at the left margin a double space below the last line of the signature block. The trend is toward omitting the dictator's initials because of repetition from the signature block; but if used, they come first (usually in unspaced capitals), separated from the typist's by a colon, a diagonal, a dash, or an asterisk. A good method that saves times is to lock the shift and type CRA:MF or just write all in lowercase as cra/mf. Some writers place the typed name here and omit it from the signature block.

An *enclosure notation,* a single or a double space below the identifying initials (or in their place), is a reminder to the person putting up the mail to actually make the enclosure. Sometimes offices use an asterisk in the left margin at the line in the body referring to the enclosure. You may spell out Enclosure or abbreviate it Encl. or Enc., followed by a number indicating how many enclosures or by a colon and words indicating what the enclosures are.

Copy designations (carbon- or photo-) are useful when other persons need to know the contents of the letter. The names of people to receive copies appear after CC (or Cc or cc or just Copy to) at the left margin, a single or double space below the initials (or the enclosure notation). If you don't want the addressee to know others are receiving copies of the letter or memo, you can type Bc and the names on the copies only, to indicate "blind copies." Occasionally you may see PC (photocopy) or XC (Xerox copy).

Postscripts are rare in business today in the original sense of afterthoughts. Rather than reveal poor planning, the modern business writer would have the letter typed over, or in informal correspondence might add a handwritten note. (Incidentally, some research evidence suggests that such notes actually increase pulling power—probably because they give a letter or memo a more personal touch.)

The main use of postscripts now is as punch lines. Since they have the advantage of the emphatic end position, writers often plan them to emphasize an important point. The well-planned postscript that ties in with the development of the whole message and stresses an important point is effective, especially if handwritten.

When you do decide to use a postscript, it should be the last thing on the page, a double space below the last of the preceding parts. The "P.S." is optional; position and wording clearly indicate what it is.

Second-page headings are essential for filing and for reassembling multipage letters that become separated. Since pages after the first should be on plain paper, even when the first page has a printed letterhead, for identification they should carry at least the addressee's name, the date, and the page number, typed down from the top the distance of the side margin something like one of the following:

```
        Mr. C. R. Jeans            —2—          March 21, 19—
```

or

```
        Mr. C. R. Jeans
        March 21, 19—
        Page 2
```

or (for speed and equal acceptability)

```
       Mr. C. R. Jeans, March 21, 19--, page 2
```

The body of the letter continues a triple or quadruple space below this.

FORMS OF INDENTION AND PUNCTUATION

The main letter forms in use today are semiblock and block with mixed or open punctuation. The example letters (Figures 1–1, 1–2, 1–3, and 1–4) explain and illustrate them as well as other correct but less popular forms. Those pages are integral parts of the explanation; so you should read them thoroughly as well as look at them.

As you read and observe them, points you should keep in mind are:

1. The two big trends in letter form continue to be toward simplicity and time-saving.
2. All consistent forms are correct, but the outmoded indented form and closed punctuation and the AMS (formerly NOMA) Simplified form tend to call attention to themselves and to characterize their users.
3. In studying letter writing, you should learn all widely used current forms, with their advantages, disadvantages, and dangers; but you should realize that if you go to work for a company, you should use your employer's preferred form unless and until you can persuade the company to change.

ADDRESSING THE ENVELOPE

For those people who open their own mail, the envelope makes the first impression. The envelope should be of the same quality as the letterhead stationery, with the return address, including the ZIP code, printed in the upper left corner in the same design as the printed letterhead. For unprinted envelopes, type the return address in the same place.

Proper form for the main address on envelopes has changed considerably in recent years. To speed up and economize on mail handling, the Postal Service has moved steadily toward machine sorting of mail—LSM (letter sorting machine) and OCR (optical character recognition) handling. How you address your letter will determine its handling—and the difference could determine whether it goes out in today's mail!

1. Traditionally, the main address—blocked the same as the inside address, and with the ZIP code—should go in the lower half of the envelope with the beginning and ending points of the longest line equal distances from the edges.

2. The envelope in Figure 1–5 would also qualify for LSM handling by using the ZIP code number and the required two-letter state abbreviation from the official list found on page 25.

Figure 1–1   Block form, standard-line layout, mixed punctuation

arcus co.
5800 North Kilbourn Avenue
Chicago, Illinois   60646   **(312)545-0974**

November 12, 19--

Professor Tsugihiro Okuda
Oita University
700 Dannoharu
Oita City 870-11, Japan

Dear Professor Okuda:

Here is a letter laid out in the popular standard line plan and in
block form with mixed punctuation. It is the most popular format today
for business letters in America.

Ideally, all the letters an organization sends out should be typed with
the same margins (standard line). This practice can mean a real saving
in time, especially if the organization has centralized word processing
or a "typing pool."

Whatever the length of the letter, the margins remain the same. The
typist or word processor operator simply "floats" the letter between
the letterhead and bottom of the page for the best appearance.

This letter uses a standard line of about 6 inches (margins set at 15
and 85, elite type). And since I used a word processor, I was able to
take advantage of the justification feature to even the right-hand
margin.

All the elements of the letter begin at the left margin, doing away
with the need to set and use tabs (another saving). The punctuation
may be mixed (as in this letter) or open (none after the salutation and
complimentary close).

The basic idea, Professor Okuda, is to attain a successful blend of
economy and acceptable appearance.

Cordially,

Peter B. Clarke
President

Figure 1–2   Block form, picture-frame layout, open punctuation

R I C H A R D   D.   I R W I N · I N C.

1818 RIDGE ROAD · HOMEWOOD, ILLINOIS 60430   TELEPHONE: (312) 798-6000

November 12, 19--

Lightning Software Company
154 June Street
Alpena, Michigan 49707

Attention: Manager of Office Services

This letter is in block form (no indentation), open punctuation (nothing after the salutation or complimentary close),
and picture-frame layout.

Though picture-framing a letter takes additional time, some
people feel the resulting appearance is worth it. With a
good word processing system, however, the task is simple.
(We used one to prepare this letter.)

Note that all the elements of the letter begin at the left
margin. This plan is a big time-saver since the typist or
word processing operator does not need to set and use tabs
and remember which elements to tab. This layout tends to
give the letter a "modern" look and is quite acceptable
today.

Sincerely yours

RICHARD D. IRWIN, INC.

Mrs. Jean Cauthen

Mrs. Jean Cauthen
Manager, Office Procedures

jc/fv

Figure 1–3   AMS Simplified form, standard-line layout

THE UNIVERSITY OF ALABAMA
Graduate School of Business
College of Commerce and Business Administration
University, Alabama 35486

MANAGEMENT AND MARKETING

Telephone: 205/348-6183   Telephone: 205/348-6090

November 12, 19--

Professor Tsugihiro Okuda
Oita University
70 Dannoharu
Oita City 870-11, Japan

LETTER FORMATS IN THE U. S. A.

You are right on all three points, Professor Okuda. Different business people in
the U. S. do use different letter formats. Three or four formats are the main
ones. Others you have seen (probably illustrated in some of the older books in
your library) are largely old forms that most American writers have dropped in
favor of more efficient modern ones.

Of the main forms in use today, I prefer the one I am using here--called the AMS
Simplified because of its efficiency. You will notice it has several characteristics.

This letter has no salutation or complimentary close, the most immediate differences between this and more conventional layouts. Dropping those two parts saves
time, avoids the possible embarrassment of mishandling a salutation, and presents
an "efficient" look to most readers.

Everything begins on the left margin--the AMS form rules out all indentation,
even for itemizations. You use a standard line of your choice (I have used a
left margin of 10 and a right margin of 90, and elite type). Since I used a word
processor for this letter, I could justify the right-hand margin automatically.

The date is two lines above the inside address and is independent of the letterhead. Where a salutation would go in other forms, you insert a subject line in
all capitals. Then you work your reader's name into the first sentence. All the
other elements of a letter--signature block, typist's initials, and so on--you
locate in the conventional manner.

This letter layout has been around for many years under several names. Though
some feel it lacks the warmth of a conventional layout, you may find it useful.
You may, however, prefer one of the other modern U. S. formats I have illustrated
in the enclosed letters.

C. W. Wilkinson

cww:ab
Enc. 2

Figure 1–4 Plain paper, semiblock form, standard-line layout, mixed punctuation

            46 Guild's Woods
            Tuscaloosa, AL 35401
            November 12, 19--

Professor Tsugihiro Okuda
Oita University
700 Dannoharu
Oita City 870-11, Japan

Dear Professor Okuda:

    For personal rather than company business you might consider using this semiblock form with standard-line (six inches) layout, indented paragraphs, and mixed punctuation. As you can see, this letter demonstrates some differences from the other example letters.

    Instead of a letterhead you use plain paper, typing your address and the date at the top, either aligned on the left margin or, as shown here, at the same tab as the complimentary close and signature block.

    Mixed punctuation means you do not punctuate after the elements of the inside address but do punctuate after the salutation and close.

    Whether you indent your paragraphs is optional.

    The complimentary close and signature block begin at the middle of the page. Any notations (like the "Enc." below) appear double-spaced below the signature block and on the left-hand margin.

            Cordially yours,

            Dorothy C. Wilkinson
            Dorothy C. Wilkinson

Enc.

    One variation of this layout that has found favor lately is to make the sender's address part of the signature block rather than putting it at the top of the page and to place the date beneath it.

Official list of state abbreviations

Alabama	AL	Montana	MT
Alaska	AK	Nebraska	NE
Arizona	AZ	Nevada	NV
Arkansas	AR	New Hampshire	NH
California	CA	New Jersey	NJ
Colorado	CO	New Mexico	NM
Connecticut	CT	New York	NY
Delaware	DE	North Carolina	NC
District of Columbia	DC	North Dakota	ND
Florida	FL	Ohio	OH
Georgia	GA	Oklahoma	OK
Guam	GU	Oregon	OR
Hawaii	HI	Pennsylvania	PA
Idaho	ID	Puerto Rico	PR
Illinois	IL	Rhode Island	RI
Indiana	IN	South Carolina	SC
Iowa	IA	South Dakota	SD
Kansas	KS	Tennessee	TN
Kentucky	KY	Texas	TX
Louisiana	LA	Utah	UT
Maine	ME	Vermont	VT
Maryland	MD	Virginia	VA
Massachusetts	MA	Virgin Islands	VI
Michigan	MI	Washington	WA
Minnesota	MN	West Virginia	WV
Mississippi	MS	Wisconsin	WI
Missouri	MO	Wyoming	WY

3.   For the faster OCR handling, you must follow additional specific requirements for the main address, as explained and illustrated in Figure 1–5 on a No. 10 envelope (4⅛ by 9½ inches):

a.   Single space, capitalize everything, omit all punctuation, use block style. No proportional spacing of characters, no italic or script, do not spell out any numbers. All address information must be in the last three lines with the street address or box number immediately above the city-state-ZIP code (which should be the last line). If the ZIP code will not fit, it may go on the left margin immediately below the city and state. Put a minimum of two and a maximum of five spaces between the state and the ZIP code. The full state name is preferable for OCR, but the two-letter abbreviation is acceptable. Put apartment numbers, suite numbers, etc. on the same line as the street address if possible. For mail addressed to a foreign country, follow the same rules. Include the postal delivery zone number (if any). The name of the country must be the last item in the address.

b.   Put nothing to the left, right, or below the address, which must begin at least an inch from the left edge and be more than half an inch from the bottom. Any codes should be part of the address and immediately above the addressee's name.

Figure 1–5   No. 10 envelope addressed for OCR handling

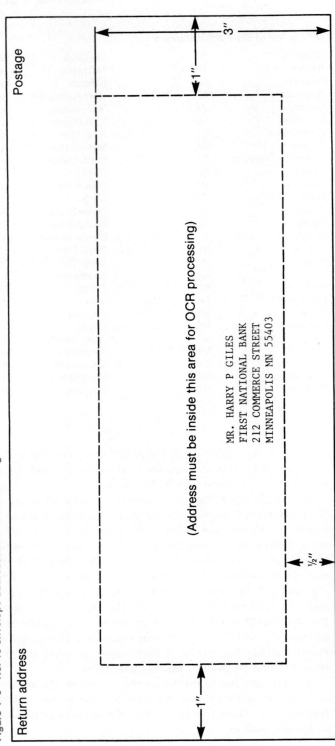

Return address

Postage

(Address must be inside this area for OCR processing)

MR. HARRY P GILES
FIRST NATIONAL BANK
212 COMMERCE STREET
MINNEAPOLIS MN 55403

3"

1"

1"

½"

c. Use both the ZIP code and the full state name or two-letter state abbreviation.

d. Keep typewriter or printer type clean and ribbons fresh so as to provide clear, crisp impressions.

Enjoying the economies of window envelopes (largely through typing the addresses only once) requires folding the letter so that the inside address shows through the window without showing any other part. For OCR handling, window envelopes must follow additional rules (for which see your postmaster).

INTEROFFICE MEMORANDUMS

The business letter is still the main form of written communication *between* companies and individuals or other companies. But interoffice memorandums (commonly called memos) now replace many letters as message carriers, especially *within* companies.

Memos first came into widespread use largely to combat the high costs of producing business letters. Since the major cost of a letter or memo is the time spent in composing and dictating, however, about the only cost savings in memos today come from not using expensive letterheads, envelopes, and postage and from the easier job of typing them (despite the simplified letter forms previously discussed).

The main reasons now for using memos are:

1. The situation does not justify the expense of a letter.
2. Face-to-face communication is not possible or not desirable.
3. The information is too complex for oral commnication.
4. One or both parties desire a written record.
5. The receiver asks for a written communication as a way of providing time to think about the problem or obtain additional information before responding.

For anyone in a medium or large company, memos will be the most common form of written communication with other people in the firm, especially those in other locations and including those both above and below you on the organization chart. What they know about you and how they think of you will depend on how you communicate with them—in short, by your memos.

Early in your career, especially, your only contacts with higher echelons in your organization will likely be the reports and memos you send up. Further, as you progress in your career, you will have to demonstrate your abilities as a manager—often by the memos you send down to your subordinates directing their activities. And finally, in dealing with your peers, you will find memos are important tools in establishing and maintaining your position.

Memos vary widely in format, from simple handwritten "From the desk of . . ." notes to carefully designed forms with interleaved carbon copies and provisions for assuring an answer and proper filing. But since they usually go from one person to another in the same organization, memo messages are less formal than letters. Whether handwritten or typed, they share with letters the single purpose of communicating information in writing so as to effect an action.

Memos have conventional, stylized headings (Figure 1–6). The universal elements are a date line, a "To" line (addressee's name with courtesy title— and job title unless known to all who get copies, or in a very informal message), a "From" line (writer's name—and identifying position title unless known), and a "Subject" line. (Leaving plenty of room to make the subject clear and precise is a good idea. The more comprehensively you describe the subject here, the less you will have to say in the body to introduce it and identify it before you can say anything of significance.)

The body begins two or three lines under the Subject line and continues until you've said what you need to, which may take three lines or thirty pages. No salutation or complimentary close appears, though when needed three other items may. When the memo needs authentication, the writer signs or initials it next to the From line, or underneath the body, following personal or company preference. A typist's initials may appear at the bottom as on a letter. If copies are to go to other people (Figure 1–7), the typist may also type a copy designation and the names of receivers.

Notice these details in the two memos: One is on an ephemeral topic to one reader; so efficiency pointed to a quick, handwritten memo. The other went to many people; so it was photocopied in sufficient number. Since some of its readers would not have known who R. F. Noonan was, he gave his official title. The other writer would have wasted time even with a full signature. The careful phrasing of subject lines in both indicates the contents concisely. Itemization seemed helpful in one but would have served no purpose in the other, and the writers used it accordingly.

Because memos are usually less formal than letters in both format and language, some writers give them inadequate attention. That is a mistake, and it can be a very bad one. *Just about everything we say in this book about letters also applies to memos.* Whether your memos will accomplish their purpose depends on the writing style, their organization, the principles of successful business communication we discuss in the first two parts of the book, and even their appearance. Memos deserve care in preparation just as letters do, for they are important to your company's success, and yours.

Though the interoffice memos we discuss here are not exactly the same as the memo reports discussed in Chapter 13, the similarities may make it worth your while to look there. You will find more details on form and a checklist.

Everything we say here and elsewhere in this book applies to "electronic mail" as well as to the conventional kind. Whether your reader sees your message on a CRT (video) screen or on paper, the four tests of a good letter or memo outlined at the beginning of this chapter still apply, as do all the techniques of clear, concise, readable writing.

Figure 1–6   Typical handwritten interoffice memo

UNIVERSITY OF FLORIDA

DATE *Jan. 20*

MEMO TO: *Andrea*

FROM: *CWW*

SUBJECT: *Work for today*

Since I have an appointment downtown during your working hours, please

1) record the grades of the attached papers in my grade book.

2) check the revised class lists against my rolls and return the lists to the Registrar with proper notation).

3) get the Congressional Record, vol. 88, Part 9, from the Library and copy Congressman Hill's comments on p. A-1486, and

4) make a table showing percentages, by class and major, of students on the E#255 lecture lists (both lists in one table).

Figure 1–7 Typical multicopy memo

January 19, 19--

```
TO:        All Occupants of Business Administration Building

FROM:      R. F. Noonan, Building and Utilities Department

SUBJECT:   Interruption of Electrical Service
```

The electricity will be off in your building on Tuesday, January 21, from 8 a.m. to 4 p.m.

We will provide temporary electric service for lights only in departmental offices.

All electricity will be off for approximately one-half hour from 8 to 8:30 a.m. and again from 4 to 4:30 p.m. for connection and removal of the temporary service.

ADAPTATIONS FOR INTERNATIONAL BUSINESS COMMUNICATION

Though most of what we say about international business is in Appendix C, the differences in letter formats and formalities seem more appropriate here. Even though you can get by with most of the U.S. practices we have explained, you can improve your relations with people of different cultures by making a few minor adaptations in the appearance and cordiality of your letters.

In other countries business stationery varies from onionskin to heavy parchment-like paper in white or light colors—generally in 8½ × 11″ size but often on legal-size or metric-size paper. Thus your present letterhead will serve well, though onionskin or very thin paper can reduce the cost of overseas airmail postage.

Besides the company name, type of business, and address, many international firms include their trademark, name of bank or banker, and cable, telephone, and telex numbers in their letterheads. Sometimes import and export registration numbers also appear. In the absence of a letterhead your overseas business friends will generally follow the suggestions we gave earlier for the format of personal letters—and you can do the same.

In keeping with their more formal style and stronger expressions of cordiality, your international business friends use most of the special parts we do except for postscripts and enclosure notations. A frequent one is a request for confidentiality—the Italian *Riservata* (or, for strictly confidential, *Riservatissima*).

International firms usually address the reader by name (if known) or by a job title (Dear Vice President) or a general (though usually sexist) salutation: Gentlemen, Dear Sir(s), ... You can fairly safely follow your usual practice for salutations; but be a little more formal, preferably by selecting an expression from the receiver's language.

The French use *Monsieur, Madame,* or *Mademoiselle,* and (to a company) *Messieurs,* but never *Cher Monsieur* or *Chere Madame* unless acquainted with the reader personally.

In Italy *Egregio Signor* precedes the name for a gentleman and *Gentile Signora* for a lady (or sometimes only *Signor* or *Signora*). Spanish writers use *Muy señores nuestros* when writing a company or group of persons, but to a particular person they use *Muy señor mio* or *Muy señor nuestro.* For obvious reasons we can't illustrate salutations of each country, but these examples give you a little taste and show you the wide variation.

You can safely use American-style complimentary closes by making them a little more formal (unless you know the reader).

To an older person or superior the French prefer *Veuillez agréer, Monsieur (Madame, Mademoiselle);* but you will also see added phrases like *l'expression de mes (nos) sentiments distingués* or *sentiments dévoués.* When a Spaniard does not want or need a reply, the ending is *Atentamente;* but when a reply is required or requested, then *Atentamente, quelamos en espera de sus grata noticias, suyos afmos. ss. ss.* or *Pendientes de sus noticias, cuya urgencia agradeceremos, nos reiteramos de ustedes afmos. ss. ss.* In Italy for a friendly letter, writers use *cordiali saluti.* Other endings are *Vogliate gradire i nostri distinti* (or *migliori saluti*) or *Distinti saluti* (but not *Migliori saluti* or *Vi salutiamo distintamente*).

QUESTIONS

1. Of the letter formats explained and illustrated,
   - *a.* Which is your preference for use with printed letterheads? Why?
   - *b.* Which is your preference for plain paper? Why?
2. How, if at all, might you vary your answers to the preceding questions for
   - *a.* Some kinds of readers?
   - *b.* Some topics?
3. Do you agree that the four tests given for a letter or memo are
   - *a.* Clear?
   - *b.* Valid?
   - *c.* Adequate?
   - *d.* Justified by the explanation?
   - *e.* Listed in the best order?
4. Which appeals to you more, standard-line or picture-frame layout? Why?
5. Which appeals to you more, block or semiblock identation? Why?
6. Which appeals to you most, closed, open, or mixed punctuation? Why?
7. In our list of the standard parts of a letter, which (if any) have you never seen in use? Do you now feel that we should or should not have listed it (or them)?
8. In our list of the special parts of a letter, which (if any) have you never seen in use? Do you now feel that we should or should not have listed it (or them)?

(All the cases for the first four chapters are at the end of Chapter 4 and of Part 1 because we think you should cover all four basic tests of a good business message before trying to write one. We urge you to read the first four chapters quickly but thoroughly so that you can put all the basic principles to use even in your first letter or memo.)

Style: What the reader reads

2

[Transmission of ideas and enthusiasm is essential to great accomplishment.]

Let's assume that you have set up your letter or memo as suggested in Chapter 1 and it has passed your reader's first test—eyeballing test for appearance.

For its second test, ask yourself: *Is it written in interesting, clear, and inconspicuous style?*

If it is so uninteresting that it isn't read, you've obviously wasted your time.

If it is interesting but not clear, you've probably confused and annoyed your reader. You may therefore get no response—or have to write again.

And if your style is conspicuous because of something unexpected, inappropriate, or incorrect, it distracts your reader from *what* you've said (by calling attention to *how* you've said it) and causes doubt that your facts and reasoning are any more reliable than your writing. Both weaken your message.

HOW TO THINK ABOUT YOUR WRITING

Your first step toward assuring that your style is interesting, clear, and inconspicuous is to think about it. When you realize that how you say it vitally affects how your reader gets your message, you are taking your first step in thinking properly about your writing. Remember our title-fly slogan: "You learn more by thinking about what you're doing than by simply thinking or simply doing."

Thinking about your style means not taking anything about it for granted. For example, consider articles. They have considerable effect on what words mean. Too many definite articles make writing complicated and confusing. By making everything specific, they obscure what should be specific and thus turn strong phrases and sentences into weak, generalizing ones.

Most people use too many articles (*a, an,* and *the*). Next time you write something, go over it and mark every article. Then see how many of them you can omit. If any of your words or phrases can stand alone without articles, omit those articles.

Please don't misunderstand us. We are not against using articles. Without them, English would be rough and awkward; and it would not adequately communicate specificness. We have made them our example because *we want you to think about your writing, to consider whether everything you put on paper is necessary.* If you think, you can write well without using articles at all, as we have done so far in this chapter.

Real thinking about your writing requires thinking about it *in context*. Words, phrases, clauses, or whole sentences that would be all right in one situation may be bloopers under different circumstances. For instance, a letter acknowledging an order you're filling might well end with "We appreciate your business and hope to continue serving you, soon and often." Because of context, however, it was not good when an unthinking tombstone manufacturer used it.

Even perfectly good words, phrases, clauses, or sentences may misfire if you don't think about what they mean in their context, including their *sequence*. We've given you examples in the exercises at the end of this chapter; but here's one more for now (the heading on a statistical table): "U.S. Population Broken Down by Age and Sex."

HOW TO WRITE INTERESTINGLY

Depend mainly on content

In writing for business and industry, you should depend on content, not style, to arouse and hold your reader's interest. After all, the purpose is not to entertain. Usually you have an inquiry or other indication that your reader is interested in your general subject. Skills of style are unnecessary to get a reading.

If bare facts have insufficient appeal to get your reader's attention, you can make them both interesting and persuasive if you *show how those facts point to benefits for the reader* (you-attitude; **YA** in Appendix F). In writing about a product, for example, merely giving the physical facts (size, shape, color, and/or material) may be dull. But if you interpret the facts as providing reader benefits (psychological description; **PD** in Appendix F), the content is more interesting: "Made of aluminum, the Gizmo is light and rust-free—you don't need to paint." And if you write so that the reader imagines successfully using the product and enjoying its benefits (dramatized copy: **DC** in Appendix F), the content is even more interesting.

A good message can become dull, however, if poorly presented. Wordiness, indefiniteness, triteness, pompousness, monotony, and difficult reading are the most common offenders. By replacing these with their opposites, you will speed up and clear up your message—and that's all you can expect style to contribute to making your letters interesting.

Put the emphasis where it belongs (Emp and Sub in Appendix F)

Since content is the greatest means of gaining interest, the big ideas of your message deserve the major emphasis.

Though you may use minor mechanical means of emphasis (underscoring, capitalizing, itemizing, using two colors), your four primary means are (1) position, (2) space, (3) phrasing, and (4) sentence structure.

The most significant ideas need to appear in the emphatic beginning and ending *positions* of the letter or memo, of your paragraphs—even of your sentences.

In addition, you write more about points you want to stress. If you write ten lines about the efficiency of a dishwasher and two lines about its convenience, by *space* you emphasize efficiency more than convenience.

As a third major means of emphasis, you should select concrete, specific words and *phrasing* to etch welcome or important ideas in your reader's mind. When an idea is unwelcome or insignificant, choose general words that merely identify, not stress. *General:* "The typewriter needs several new parts and . . . ." *Specific:* "Your versatile IBM Memory Typewriter will . . . ."

Because an independent clause carries more emphasis than a dependent one, you can also stress or subordinate ideas through your choice of *sentence structure.* An important idea calls for statement in one independent clause (a simple sentence). Sometimes, however, you have two equally important and closely related ideas; so you should put the two independent clauses together in a compound sentence. If you have two related ideas of *different* importance, a complex sentence of one independent and one dependent clause divides the emphasis properly. You may have noticed, for example, that we merely named (parenthetically in a dependent clause) the minor mechanical means of stressing ideas. The four primary means, however, we first itemized; then we gave each a separate paragraph of discussion and thereby emphasized them by independent-clause statement and by means of space.

In messages carrying ideas which the reader will welcome, then, use those ideas to begin and end the messages. They usually should begin and end paragraphs. They should take up most of the space. Their phrasing should be specific. And they should enjoy the benefits of independent instead of dependent construction. Conversely, you should embed unwelcome or unimportant ideas in a middle paragraph, cover them just enough to establish their meaning, and strip them of the emphasis of concrete, specific words.

Controlling emphasis in your writing is a technique you can put into immediate successful use—in the next piece of writing you do. We recommend that you work first on emphasis by position, since that technique is effective and easy to use. At first you will have to think about getting important ideas at the beginnings and ends of your letters and paragraphs, but you will be surprised how quickly this procedure becomes almost automatic . . . and how it will improve the effectiveness of your writing.

The letter and memo samples in this book use the principles for appropriate emphasis and its opposite—subordination. Two special points, however, deserve your attention right here:

1. You may be inclined to write something the reader already knows. If it serves no purpose, think about your writing and omit it. But if you need to say it (for emphasis or as a basis for something else you want to say),

put it subordinately. That is, do not put it in an independent clause: not "Summer will soon be here . . ." but "Since summer will soon be here, ..."

2. When you need to refer to an enclosure or other part of your message (say a graph), word your reference to emphasize what to do with, look for, or get from it. Don't emphasize that it is enclosed: not "Enclosed is (or worse, "please find") . . ." but something like "You'll find further details of construction and users' satisfaction in the enclosed pamphlet."

Here's a test of whether you're on the right track: To *de*-emphasize a word like *enclosed,* be sure you use it as an adjective before the thing enclosed (the pamphlet) and not as the verb of the sentence. (See **Emp2** in Appendix F.)

Write concisely but completely (**Conc** and **Dev** in Appendix F)

Every word you can spare without reducing the effectiveness is wasteful if it remains. Too many words stretch interest to the breaking point. But if you leave out necessary information and vivid details to achieve brevity, you fail to develop enough interesting ideas to hold or persuade your reader. You therefore face the dilemma of length.

A first step in the solution of that dilemma is a clear *distinction between brevity and consciseness*. Brevity is mere shortness. Sacrificing completeness because of a mistaken notion about the importance of brevity is a common mistake. Writing a letter or memo lacking necessary information (and therefore lacking interest and persuasion) is poor economy. Either it is waste because it produces no result, or both you and your reader have to write again. Even people who say a letter or memo should be brief do not want to make decisions without all the pertinent information.

What these people really want—what you want—is conciseness, making every word contribute to your purpose. A 50-word letter is brief; but if you can write the message in 25 words, the 50-word letter is not concise. A 400-word letter is not short; but if all the words contribute to the purpose, it is concise. So if you need three pages to cover all your points adequately, use that much space. Conciseness comes not from omitting details that contribute to clearness, persuasiveness, or interest but from writing all you should say in as few words as possible.

Experience and long practice may teach you to write complete and concise first drafts. While gaining that experience, however, you will do well to follow four guidelines for conciseness.

1. Avoid expressing ideas that don't deserve to be put into words. Since only you know your topic and your purpose as you write, you are the only one who can cut out everything that has no bearing on them.

2. Don't waste words saying what the reader already knows. For an example of both poor and proper handling of things the reader knows, compare the following two versions of a heating engineer's report to an office manager.

You'll notice that the first is flat, wordy, dull, and even insulting because it tells the known in independent clauses. The other is interesting, concise, and polite because it implies two knowns (you asked us/we have done) and uses a *subordinate* clause for the necessary statement of the other known.

Poor	*Improved*
Three days ago you asked us to investigate the problem of discomfort among your office workers. [Assumes that the reader has a short memory.] We have made our study. [Obviously, since you're reporting results.] Too low humidity is apparently the main cause of your trouble. Your building is steam-heated. [Doesn't the reader know?] Therefore our solution is to	Too low humidity is apparently the main cause of your workers' discomfort. Since your building is steam-heated, your solution is to . . . .

To show the reasoning behind your suggestion, you do need to mention the steam heat; but the subordinating *since* implies "Of course you and I know this, but it has to go in for completeness of logic." When you have to establish something the reader knows, or when the reader probably knows it but you can't be sure, give the information subordinately—as the "Since . . ." does.

3.   As a general principle, in answering a recent letter or memo, don't waste words to say "I have your letter of . . ." or to tell what it says. Obviously you got the message or you wouldn't be answering it; and starting to discuss the same subject will remind your reader adequately. Instead of

You asked us to let you know when the new model of the Clarion radio came on the market. It is obtainable now.

you can say the same thing with

The new Clarion radio is now available.

That clearly implies that you got the letter and the idea of "You asked us to let you know."

Of course, if the inquiry is not recent, or if somebody other than the original inquirer may handle your answer (as often happens in big organizations), you may need to refer (by topic and date) to the communication you are answering. Even then a subject line will save words and allow the emphatic first sentence to say something important.

Rather than this	*You might better write*
On February 20 you inquired about our experience with Mr. James H. Johnson. We are glad to tell you about his work for us.	Mr. James H. Johnson, about whom you inquired on February 20, was a steady, conscientious bookkeeper here for 18 months.
Johnson was a steady, conscientious worker during the 18 months he kept books for us.	

Under no circumstances do you need to waste words as in the following:

Permit me to take this opportunity to thank you for your letter which I have just received. In reply I wish to state that we shall be very glad to exchange the electric water heater in question for a similar one in a larger size in accordance with your request.

Through *implication* you can reduce that wordy beginning to

We'll be glad to exchange your water heater for a similar one in a larger size.

In most refusals you can save words and your reader's feelings by eliminating the negative statement of what you won't do and concentrating on what you will do. You thus imply the negative idea and gain not only conciseness but interest and acceptability. For illustrations, see "Positive Statement" late in Chapter 4.

4. If your first draft contains any wasteful expressions, revision should eliminate them as well as *deadwood phrases* (those which contribute nothing).

Consider the following incomplete list of offenders, in which a line blocks out the deadwood or the concise statement follows in parentheses:

free gifts
lifelong native
shot fatally three times
long period of time
is at this time
at a price of $50
important essentials
enclosed herewith
remember the fact that
held a meeting (met)
main problem is a matter of cost
your order for a cultivator was shipped
in the opinion of Mr. Johnson (thinks)
that is the situation at this time (now)
the X plow is quite different
   in character

falsely padded expense accounts
during the course of the evening
engaged in making a survey
the color of the X is blue
until such time as you can
in regard to (about, regarding)
in the development of (developing)
in this day and age (today, now)
the soldering process proved to be of an
   unsatisfactory nature
the general consensus of opinion among
   most students is that (most students
   think that)
the trouble with the light was
   that it was too dim
in the state of Texas

made the announcement that (announced)

for the purpose of providing (to provide)

at an early date (soon) [if you have to be indefinite]

decide at a meeting ~~which will be held~~ Monday

eliminate needless words ~~that may be present~~

~~there is~~ only one point ~~that~~ is clear, ~~and that is~~

the price was higher than I expected ~~it to be~~

the workers ~~are in a position to~~ (can) accept or reject

neat ~~in appearance~~

at ~~the hour of~~ 4:00

eight ~~in number~~

circular ~~in shape~~

throughout the ~~entire~~ week

~~at a~~ later ~~date~~

during ~~the year of~~ 1984

costs ~~the sum of~~ $10

came ~~at a time~~ when

at all times (always)

in the event that (if)

put in an appearance (came)

during the time that (while)

these facts ~~serve to~~ give an idea

if ~~it is~~ possible, let me have

~~according to~~ Mr. Johnson (says)

arrived at the conclusion (concluded)

Often you can avoid such clutter by changing a clause to one word:

—all the people who are interested in (interested people)

—buying new machines which are expensive (buying expensive new machines)

—using processes that are outmoded (using outmoded processes)

—saving work that does not need to be done (saving unnecessary work)

Perhaps the worst form of clutter, however, combines wasted words with clichés, as in the following.

Poor	Better
If we are not mistaken	We believe
In accordance with your request	As requested
We would therefore ask that you kindly investigate	Please investigate
We now have a letter from our Sparta office advising that	Our Sparta office writes that
Which is in connection with	Regarding
A check in the amount of	A check for
We wish you would furnish us with	Please send us
We are not in a position to	We cannot
Let us hear from you in regard to	Write us about
Your early attention to this matter will be greatly appreciated	Please act promptly on this
They bring out the point that	They point out that
Will you please arrange to send	Please send
We should like to ask whether you have received our shipment of	Have you received our shipment of
Upon consulting our records, we find that your order reached us on	Your order arrived on

Write vividly: Avoid indefiniteness

Even good content concisely stated can be uninteresting, however, if your reader gets only an inactive or fuzzy mental picture. You therefore need to use five techniques to write vividly:

1. Write about people in action as the subject or object of many sentences.
2. Use active rather than passive voice most of the time.
3. Use concrete rather than abstract language.
4. Use specific rather than general words.
5. Give enough details to make the picture clear.

1. Most things happen because people make them happen. The interesting, natural, and clear way to write about those happenings, therefore, is to talk about those *people in action.* That is why we suggest that you make people the subject or object of most sentences.

Since each reader is most interested in personally related things, interest in your letter will depend on how you put that person into the picture as the main actor. "You can save 30 minutes at dinner time with a Pronto pressure cooker" is more vivid than "A Pronto pressure cooker saves 30 minutes at dinner time." (For psychological reasons, if a point is a criticism and hence unpleasant, however, make your actor a third person or your message impersonal, rather than accuse. See **Accus** in Appendix F.)

2. Consistent use of people as subjects will help you to write in *active rather than passive voice.* The passive "30 minutes at dinner time can be saved" lacks the vividness of the original because it omits the all-important *who*. Besides, passive constructions are usually longer, weaker, and fuzzier than active ones (**Pas**). Excessive use of "to be" verbs, *(be, is, am, are, was, were, been, being)* usually produces flat writing, partly because it leads to a passive style. If the basic verb in more than half your sentences derives from *to be,* your style will seem flat.

"There are" and "It is" beginnings (**Exp**letives) delay the real idea of the sentence and frequently force a writer to use the unemphatic passive voice. The sentence "There are 1 million people in Cincinnati" is not so vivid as "One million people live in Cincinnati." "It was felt that . . . ." becomes more vivid when rephrased as "We felt . . . ." (See **Exp** in Appendix F.)

You can eliminate most passives and expletives if you will *think*—that is, conscientiously try to use action verbs. People live, run, eat, buy—in short, act. They do not just exist, as indicated by *is, was, were, have been.* The price of stock *creeps up, rises, jumps, zooms*—or *plummets.* For vividness (and for economy) good writers make their verbs do a big share of the work. The more action you can pack into your verbs, the more specific and concrete you can make your writing.

When you use active verbs and cut out passives and expletives, through your show of self-confidence you gain another desirable style quality—*force*. You appear more confident by standing up and being counted, by taking responsibility for what you say—instead of dodging, hedging, or hiding behind language evasions. A cowardly writer will hide behind passives, expletives, and little toothpulling qualifiers:

It is believed that you might do well too . . . . (Who believes? Not sure, huh?—"might?" Hedging your bets?)

A mistake has been made in your accounts that . . . . (Who made it? Hiding behind a passive, huh?—like a scared kid hiding behind mother's skirt.)

Other little qualifiers, like *might,* which rob sentences of their strength, are *often–frequently–sometimes, most–some, may–perhaps–maybe–probably,* and their ilk. Before using any of them, ask yourself, "Do I need the word to avoid the risk of exaggeration or am I a timid or cowardly writer?" Certainly you don't want to appear so meek, timid, and cowardly as the person who asked the old elevator operator to "Please take me to the ninth floor—if it's not out of your way!" Neither, however, do you want to come across as an overconfident, unreliable, cocksure, arrogant exaggerator by too ready use of the categoricals like *the only way, always–never, everywhere–nowhere, everybody–nobody,* and *best–worst.*

3. When you **use concrete rather than abstract language,** you give your reader sharper mental pictures. When you write *superiority, efficiency,* and *durability* in telling about a product, your words are abstract; they give only hazy ideas. To make the picture sharp and lively, give the evidence back of the abstraction. If you think your product is of highest quality, you must have reasons for thinking so. To establish the idea of superiority in cloth, for instance: Thread count? Number of washings before fraying? Tensile strength? Resistance to shrinkage and fading?

In job applications you need to put across the ideas of your sociability, initiative, and dependability. But just claiming that you have those abstract qualities will make you look more conceited than competent. You can both avoid the conceit and present concrete, convincing evidence, however, by citing leadership in specific activities and offices held in organizations, ideas and plans you originated, attendance records, and completed projects. Thus you give active, vivid evidence of these qualities and convince your reader.

4. You further eliminate haziness and dullness when you **use specific rather than general words.** An investment, for instance, may be a stock (common or preferred), a bond, or a piece of real estate. The closer you can come to picturing the special type of thing named, the more specific and hence the more vivid your writing is.

Take the verb *walk* as another example. Does a person amble, trudge, skip, or one of the 50 or more other possible ways of walking? When you are inclined to write *contact,* do you mean write, go see, telephone? You present a sharper picture if you name the specific action.

5. Even when you are specific and concrete, unless you **give enough details to make the picture clear,** you will fail to be vivid. Specifications for a house may call for painting it, for example; but unless they tell the kind of paint, how many coats, and what colors, the painter does not know what to do. You need to flesh out skeletons to bring them to life, even if it sacrifices some brevity.

Comparisons can help you explain the unknown or variable in vivid terms of the known. *Slowly* becomes sharper if you say "about as fast as you normally walk." "A saving of 2 percent when paid within 10 days" becomes more vivid if you add "$3.30, or a free box of Lane's choice chocolates, on your present invoice of $165."

Write naturally to avoid triteness and pomposity (Nat in Appendix F)

All kinds of trite expressions and jargon dull interest and put the reader to sleep. We even call them "bromides" ("flat, commonplace statements," Webster says) because bromides are sleep-inducing medicines.

Unfortunately too many people in business learn all they know about writing from the bad letters and memos they receive and thus continue an outmoded, inappropriate, and unnatural style. Like parrots, they use expressions unthinkingly. One person meeting another on the street would not say, "I am glad to say that we have received your letter of March 14, and in response we wish to state that . . . ." A good business writer would not write it either, but more likely, "Those tonnage figures for April were just what I needed," or "Your suggestions about the committee memberships helped a lot in my decision. Thanks." The first is slow, vague, roundabout, and stilted; the others are clear, direct, and natural.

Pompous writing (puffed-up, roundabout, and big-wordy) is as dull and confusing as the use of bromides. Why many people write "We will ascertain the facts and advise accordingly," when in conversation they would say "We'll find out and let you know" is a mystery. A Washington blackout order during wartime originally read: "Obscure the fenestration with opaque coverings or terminate the illumination." A high official who wanted the message understood revised it to read: "Pull down the shades or turn out the lights."

Stuffed-shirt writers use a phrase or clause when a well-chosen verb would express the idea better. For example: "Smith raises the objection that . . ." instead of "Smith objects that (or objects to) . . . ." One writer stretched a simple "Thank you" to "I wish to assure you that it has been a genuine pleasure to have been the recipient of your gracious generosity."

Good writers avoid bromides and pompous wording to make letters and memos natural. Common advice is "Write as you talk." Don't, however, take that advice literally. The informal style appropriate to letters and memos is more precise and concise than good conversation. What the advisers mean is that you should not stiffen up, use big words and trite expressions, or get involved in complicated and formal sentences when you write letters. Rather, let the words flow out naturally and informally with the general tone and rhythm of the language actually used by people rather than stuffed shirts.

Write like this	*Not like this*
Many people	A substantial segment of the population
Know well	Are fully cognizant of
Object	Interpose an objection
Wait	Hold in abeyance
Carry out the policy	Effectuate (or implement) the policy
As you requested	Pursuant to your request

Before, after	Prior to, subsequent to
Get the facts	Ascertain (secure) the data
Ask the defendant	Interrogate the defendant
Find it hard to	Encounter difficulty in
Big difference	Marked discrepancy
Begin (or start)	Initiate (or institute)
Complete (or finish)	Consummate
In the first place	In the initial instance
Haste makes waste	Precipitation entails negation of economy
Make unnecessary	Obviate the necessity of
Think of	Conceptualize
Here is	Enclosed please find
Now	At this point in time
About	With regard to
Because	Due to the fact that
Soon	At an early date
Consider	Take under consideration

Vary sentence pattern, type, and length

Unvaried sentence pattern, type, length, or rhythm causes many a reader's mind to wander. Though much necessary variety will come naturally from writing well, revision can enliven your style by removing a dull sameness.

The normal English sentence pattern is subject-verb-complement. Most of your sentences should follow that sequence; but if all of them do, they produce monotony. Particularly noticeable are series of sentences beginning the same way, especially with *"I"* or *"We."* (One critical lecturer stressed the point by laughing at such "we-we" letters.) The following list suggests possible variations of sentence beginnings:

With a subject:
>   A simple way to key returns is to use different return
>   envelopes with the several letters being tested.

With a clause:
>   Because human beings are unpredictable, you cannot
>   rivet the sales process to a formula.

With a phrase:
>   For this reason, you should test to find which letter
>   pulls best before making a large mailing.

With a verb:
>   Should you find that all pull about the same, you have
>   the usual dilemma!

With correlative conjunctions:
>   Not only the lack of funds but also the results of
>   continual overcrowding and busing in elementary and
>   secondary schools will continue to lower the caliber
>   of work in American colleges.

With an adverb:
> Ordinarily, students like courses in business communication.

With a verbal:
> Allowing plenty of time, the student started the report early in the semester.

With an infinitive:
> To be a successful business letter writer, a student must be able to lose selfishness in contemplation of the reader's problem.

With adjectives:
> Congenial and cooperative, Dorothy worked many nights until midnight when we faced a deadline.

Proper emphasis of ideas is the main reason for varying sentence type, but the variation also avoids monotony and retains interest. Choosing sentence structure in terms of needed emphasis (as explained earlier) will nearly always result in enough variety to prevent monotony.

Sameness of sentence length (and to some extent, paragraph length) can become as monotonous as unvarying sentence pattern and type. Together they produce an interest-killing rhythm characteristic of a childish style. Children's books often put both listener and reader to sleep—but business writing should not. For that reason business writers need to learn an easily readable style without limiting themselves to a child's monotonous short-word vocabulary and unvaried short, simple sentences.

HOW TO MAKE YOUR WRITING CLEAR

The strongest rebuke a reader can give a writer is "I don't understand; what do you mean?" Conciseness helps clarity as well as interest because your reader avoids the job of separating the important from the unessential, and vividness helps by giving a sharp picture. But other more important aids to clearness are

1. Making your writing easy and interesting to read.
2. Planning for unity, coherence, progress, and proper emphasis.
3. Using accurate wording, punctuation, grammar, and sentence structure.

Make it easy and interesting to read

Your responsibility as a writer is to present ideas interestingly enough to get a reading and clearly enough for your reader to understand with the least possible effort. As the difficulty of understanding an idea increases, people are more inclined to lose interest and skip it. Any time your reader has to back up and reread or has to slow down to understand, you may arouse disgust and be ignored or misunderstood.

In promulgating your esoteric cogitations or articulating your philosophical or psychological observations, circumspectly eliminate platitudinous ponderosity. Studiously manipulate your communications to manifest clarified conciseness, compact comprehensibleness, coalescent consistency, and a concatenated cogency with intelligibility and vivacity but without rodomontade or thrasonical bombast. Sedulously eschew polysyllabic profundity, pompous prolixity, psittaceous vacuity, and vapid verbosity.

Considering your Gunning Fog Index is the first step toward clear writing. In that step we are fortunate because about 40 years ago several writers became fed up with the difficult-to-read style then becoming prevalent. Rudolph Flesch's Ph.D. dissertation (*Marks of a Readable Style*, Columbia University, 1943)[1] presented three tests for measuring how easy to read and how interesting a piece of writing is:

1. Average sentence length (preferably fewer than 19 words).
2. Average word length (preferably fewer than 150 syllables per 100 words).
3. A liberal percentage of human-interest words and sentences (references to people by name or other clear means).

Robert Gunning soon supported and slightly modified Flesch's advice.[2] Before long, Professor Seashore of the University of Iowa zeroed in on how the length of paragraphs affects readability—and advised us to keep 'em short and well organized.

Though many others have written on readability, these three have covered all the significant factors; and Flesch and Gunning have given us formulas for *testing* our writing. Flesch's reading ease formula is the only one that involves human-interest, but that important factor is difficult to figure and impossible to score objectively. For that reason and because Gunning's Fog Index matches the school grade level for which the material is easy reading, the Gunning formula enjoys wider use. Gunning also warns us not to write by formula but to (*a*) test our writing occasionally by the formula and (*b*) revise both the copy that doesn't pass the test and our future writing style—using as guidelines the results of the test and the 10 principles explained in his book.

Because we think you will want to (and should) take Gunning's advice, here is the procedure for figuring your Fog Index. Thus you can quickly learn how to adapt your writing to the abilities of your readers. You'll also see that the factors which lead to a favorable index are the things we teach in this book, especially in this chapter.

Figuring the Gunning Fog Index is a simple, three-step process.

1. Find the average sentence length (ASL) by
   a. Taking several representative 100-word samples, counting anything with space around it as a word—including figures.

---

[1]Revised and published in 1946 by Harper & Row as *The Art of Plain Talk* and in 1949 and 1974 as *The Art of Readable Writing*.
[2]In *The Technique of Clear Writing*, McGraw-Hill, New York, 1952—revised in 1968 and 1973.

     b. Counting the sentences involved in the samples, stopping in each sample with the sentence ending nearest the 100-word point.

     c. Dividing the total word count by the sentence count. The result is the first factor in the formula—the average sentence length.

2.   Find the PHW (percentage of hard words—three or more syllables) in the total sample—not including capitalized words (proper names), combinations of easy words (like *afternoon, businesslike, bookkeeper*) or verb forms made into three syllables by -*ed* or -*es* endings (*dribbled, enriches*).

3.   Add number 1 above (the average sentence length) and number 2 (the percentage of hard words) and multiply the sum by .4. For example suppose you have ASL 19 and PHW 14 = 33 × .4 = 13 (Fog Index and grade level). Then the material is properly adapted to college freshmen but too difficult for people with less reading ability. If the figures had been 24 + 16 × .4 = 16, a reader would need college-senior reading ability.

Using words your reader understands is important in making your writing easy to read. You will usually be wise to choose the more commonly known of two words. Uneducated people will understand you, and educated readers will appreciate your making their job easy. Small words can say all the things you want to say. If you have 50 percent more syllables than words, your writing requires more reader effort than it should.

For an example that illustrates what it advises about clear writing, we quote a man well known for his way with words, Arthur Kudner: "Big, long words name little things. All big things have little names, such as life and death, peace and war, or dawn, day, night, hope, love, home. Learn to use little words in a big way; they say what you mean. When you don't know what you mean, use BIG words . . . . That often fools little people."

Keeping your sentences reasonably short and direct will also help to make your writing easy to read and hence clear. An average of 17–20 words is a healthy one for readability. But you need not avoid sentences of 4 or 5 words— or (occasionally) 40, if necessary for presenting an idea exactly.

If the average length is not too much above 20, smooth sequence of thought and directness are more important than the word count. To avoid involved, indirect sentences, look at the punctuation. It cannot make a bad sentence into a good one. If you have to punctuate a sentence heavily, you will be wise to rephrase it more directly. Sometimes the best solution is to break it up into two or three sentences.

Using short, well-organized paragraphs will also help clarity and readability. The usual pattern of letter and memo paragraphs is a topic sentence followed by supporting or developing details. But if one sentence says all you need to on the topic, start the next topic—in another paragraph. Padding one with needless stuff or covering two topics in it because some composition books ban single-sentence paragraphs is *baaad* writing.

Frequently a single-sentence paragraph is highly desirable to give an idea the emphasis you want!

Especially in letters, long paragraphs are uninviting and hard to read. First and last paragraphs of more than four lines and others of more than eight are likely candidates for breaking up.

Making frequent personal references (names of people and pronouns referring to them) also helps make your writing interesting and readable. Since you and your reader are the two persons most directly involved in the actions, desires, and benefits you write about in letters, most of your pronouns will be "you"—or "you" understood—and "I" or (when clear) "we." (If you're ever tempted to use *we* without clear meaning, however, remember what Mark Twain once said: "The only people entitled to use the indefinite *we* are kings, editors, and people with tapeworms.")

Itemizing key points and tabulating significant figures can help to make your whole letter, memo, or paragraph clear and easy to read. For instance, if your topic sentence mentions three big advantages in using XYZ Wafers, the three will stand out more clearly and emphatically if you number them and list them on separate lines.

Progressing at a proper pace also affects the readability of what you write. Pace is simply the frequency with which you present ideas. The speed of reading is unlikely to vary much; but readers cannot assimilate several ideas that come too quickly and will become bored and inattentive if they come too slowly. Inexperienced writers often make the mistake of presenting snippets of undeveloped ideas too rapidly, one after the other, in an effort to be brief. What they achieve is a loss of reader comprehension because of hazy ideas too fast for the reader to figure them out. Further, too fast a pace leads to curtness and a brusque, unfeeling tone.

Plan for unity, coherence, progress, and proper emphasis

If you are answering a letter or memo, underscore points in it to be covered. In any case think your answer through before you start to write or dictate. You can't plan anything more than a simple message by just thinking as you write. Clear writing is usually the product of a three-step process which stresses organization and coherence.

1. The preliminary planning step requires specific answers to four questions:

   a.   What effect do I want to produce? Decide specifically what you want to happen. Otherwise you cannot achieve one of the main objectives of organizing—unity. Good organization should result in a oneness by showing how every part relates to the general theme.

   b.   Who is the reader? Until you make a clear estimate of what your reader is like, you cannot apply the principles of adaptation (in Chapter 4).

   c.   What facts and ideas must I present to produce the desired effect on this kind of reader? List not only points of positive interest but probable reader objections to overcome.

   d.   What is the best order of presenting the items listed?

You can organize well only by answering specifically all four of the preliminary-planning questions. In preparing a nonroutine message, usually you need to spend about 40 percent of your total preparation time on preliminary planning.

2.   The second step is continuous, fast writing. You follow your preliminary plan and *keep going*. Write the entire piece without stopping. Only that way will you be efficient (using only about 20 percent of the time) and get the natural coherence that comes from following a chain of thought straight through.

3.   In the third step (using about 40 percent of your time) you revise for tone (Chapter 3) and conciseness, coherence, and correctness (Chapter 2). You may also need to reorganize a bit by shifting words, sentences, or whole paragraphs into better position. But usually the main work on organization through revision will be a few changes in wording for better coherence. You may find that all you need to strengthen coherence is some transitional words like *and, but, for, because*, and the variants of each (see **Coh** 3 in Appendix F).

Although you should not leave out any necessary bridges between parts, the fewer you can use and still make the sequence of thought clear, the better. Try especially to avoid overformal and slowing references like *the latter, the above-mentioned*, and *namely*.

Use accurate wording, punctuation, grammar, and sentence structure

Conventions, not rules, establish proper usage of words, punctuation, and grammar. The important thing is to use them with the exact meaning the reader attaches to them. To that purpose, we have provided a list of frequently misused words under **D** in Appendix F.

Remember, too, that words and sentences sometimes change meanings according to what precedes and succeeds them. For instance, a would-be secretary brought laughs when the last two sentences in an ad for a job read "No bad habits. Willing to learn." Similarly, the following last two sentences advertising a big dog for sale brought more laughs than prospective buyers: "Will eat anything. Loves children." (For proper word relations, guard particularly against the errors discussed in **Mod** 1 and 2 in Appendix F.)

The difficulties of accurate expression stem partly from the way words pick up related meanings (connotations, in addition to their denotations or dictionary meanings). Consider the difference between *cheap* and *inexpensive* or between *house* and *home*. And note that *hope, trust*, and *if* can suggest doubt. "You claim" or "you say" even suggests doubt of the reader's truthfulness.

The words you use should give not only the general idea but the precise idea quickly. If you say *soon* or *later*, your reader doesn't know just when you mean. If you say *checks, notes, stocks, etc.*, nobody can tell whether you mean to include bonds. (Etc. is clear only in such statements as "I am particularly interested in the odd-numbered questions, 1, 3, 5, etc." But it then becomes unnecessary, as it usually does when it is clear.)

A large vocabulary enables you to choose the precise word to give the exact idea. But if you don't use judgment to stay within the reader's vocabulary, you will sometimes use words that leave the reader in the dark or slow up the pace. For example, you may be inclined to write *actuarially*, but most readers will get the meaning more quickly if you write *statistically*.

Punctuation marks, like words, mean only what a reader takes them to mean. They can help by breaking your sentences into thought groups if you follow the conventions (**P1–P13** in Appendix F). But if you use a system of your own and your reader interprets according to the standard system, you mislead just as if you used words in unfamiliar ways. For instance, if you put up a sign to mean

No Parking: Reserved for Our Customers

you will certainly mislead people if you write:

No Parking Reserved for Our Customers

Like faulty wording, faulty punctuation not only confuses but distracts the reader's mind from the key idea. You've surely seen the laughable highway sign "Slow Men Working."

Fortunately, the system of English punctuation is well established (by convention, not by rules), and most readers know at least the main parts of the conventions. Unfortunately many people who know how to *read* most punctuation marks do not know the conventions well enough to use the marks precisely *in writing*. If you have any doubts about the following main troublesome areas of punctuation, see the symbol **P** in Appendix F for explanation and illustration:

No comma before *and* or *but* connecting two-part (compound) subjects, verbs, or objects (**P1**).

Semicolon between independent clauses except with strong conjunction (**P2**).

Comma after all dependent clauses at the beginnings of sentences and with nonessential ones elsewhere (**P3**).

Comma to separate coordinate adjectives (**P5**).

Pair of commas around a parenthetical expression unless you want to deemphasize by parentheses, emphasize by dashes, or avoid confusion with other commas by using parentheses or dashes (**P4, 7**).

Hyphen between words used as a single modifier of a following noun (**P8**).

So-called errors in grammar and sentence structure also mislead readers. They also slow up reading and produce indefiniteness, disrespect, and distrust. The statement "You should not plant strawberries where tomatoes have grown for several years" will mislead readers if you mean "Wait several years before planting strawberries where tomatoes have grown." And the dangling participle in "Smelling of liquor, the officer arrested the reckless driver" (**Mod. 1**) did lead to a police officer's being questioned about drinking on duty.

Faulty grammar can confuse too—though often only temporarily. Most readers will understand despite wrong verb forms like "He come to my house at 10 P.M.," the wrong choice between *lie* and *lay,* and shifts in number like "The Acme Company is located in Chicago. They manufacture . . . ." Those same understanding readers will, however, notice the bad English, become amused and/or sympathetic, and lose respect for and confidence in the obviously ignorant or careless writer. All these reactions are *distractions from the message* because the style calls attention to itself—becomes conspicuous.

HOW TO KEEP YOUR STYLE INCONSPICUOUS

A reader's starting point of interest is what you say, not how you say it. In a well-ordered sentence, a reader will receive no jolt. Your style, therefore, becomes noticeable and distracting only if you do something unexpected with it. Simplicity and naturalness are good guides on the right road.

If you make your style too flowery, formal, or stiff for the situation, or if you make it too flippant and familiar, it will distract from your message and arouse doubts about your sense of appropriateness. (An obvious striving for such style is a sign of immaturity.) If you violate any of the conventions of word choice, spelling, punctuation, sentence structure, or grammar, your unconventional practice will both distract and cause your reader to doubt your general knowledge and ability. For instance, if you cause the reader to say, "Why, that writer can't even spell," the *even* strongly implies "So of course I can't depend on such a person to know anything else either."

The two main ways a writer does something unexpected with style and thus draws undue attention to it are

1. Choosing the wrong level of usage for the situation.
2. Violating any of the more common conventions of word choice, spelling, punctuation, grammar, or sentence structure.

Any of them will distract the reader and weaken the impact of the important thing—your message.

Choose the right level of usage for the situation

The appropriate level of language, like proper dress, is a highly variable thing. What is effective in one situation may not be suitable in another just as a tuxedo is out of place for a day in the office or a weiner roast, blue jeans for a formal party, or a bathing suit for church.

The first step in choosing the right level of usage is to think about the situation in the light of five communication factors (sometimes called the communication formula):

1. A writer (or speaker) who has
2. A particular message to communicate through
3. A medium (letter, memo, report) to

4.   A definite readership (or audience) for
5.   A definite purpose (in business, a *practical* purpose—not entertainment).

If any of the factors change, the situation shifts so that a formerly good sentence may become bad, or vice versa. Still, many thoughtless writers almost ignore the last two factors—readership and purpose. Only in view of all of them can you classify the situation and choose the appropriate level of usage.

Having classified the communication situation, you can take the second step by considering the nature of the different levels of usage. Some linguists/philologists have distinguished as many as seven levels, but a more functional modern classification names three: formal, informal, and illiterate.

Informal English is the most useful for letters and memos and for most other kinds of functional speaking and writing today. In it, the emphasis is more on being functional than on being elegant. Its general tone is that of the natural speech of educated people in their usual business and social affairs. In its written form it is more concise and more precise than normal conversation; but its vocabulary, phrasing, sentence structure, and grammar are essentially the same as in good conversation among educated people. That—rather than a literal interpretation of the words—is the meaning of the often-heard advice that you should write as you talk.

But informal English is a broad category, ranging all the way from a style which verges on formal English to that which verges on the illiterate. When informal English approaches the formal, it does not allow slang, shoptalk, contractions, or omission of relative pronouns and other connecting words. It may use generally understood allusions, figures of speech a little more complex than similes, and words and sentences that are somewhat long. Some misguided writers insist on the highly questionable requirement of impersonal style (no pronouns referring to writer or reader) for reports and research papers at this dignified-informal level of usage.

Near the deep end of the informal level of usage is what we call "familiar-informal." Its whole attention is on content and to heck with style. It's OK if you're writing to somebody you know pretty well or if the two of you have lots in common. In using it you have to assume that you don't need to show that you know English. As in this paragraph, it uses contractions, a light touch, and rather simple sentence structure and words. If you want to use some slang and shoptalk, you just let go. Its value is its freshness, vividness, emphasis, and naturalness. The danger point, which this paragraph flirts with, is that it will be abused in an attempt to be clever and thus will call attention to itself.

Formal English is characterized by precision and elegance of diction, sentence structure, and grammar. Like the person dressed in formal clothes, it often appears stiff and unnatural, more to be admired for its appearance than for any function it may perform. It admits of no contractions, ellipses, or indignities of any kind. Of necessity, it uses many everyday words; but by design it includes many in the *précieuse* category. Like the person of high society, it sometimes chooses its associates with more attention to their paternity than to their practicality. As a consequence, its words are frequently somewhat rare and long, with histories traceable back to the first word families of Old French or Latin. It is often fraught with abstruse literary and historical allusions, perhaps to impress the reader with the writer's erudition or skill with bons mots. Rather than concerning itself with facilitating the reader's comprehension, it employs lengthy and labyrinthine sentences and paragraphs more fanciful than functional, more rhythmical than reasoned, more literary than literate, more artificial than accurate, and more absurd than acceptable. Following an unsound belief that they are thereby being more objective, its writers often strive for an impersonal style and bring forth a mountain of words from a molehill of an idea, or a diarrhea of words and a constipation of ideas. Its worst misguided practitioners—some lawyers, sociologists, engineers, and politicians, apparently hoping to achieve dignity (and defending their practices by claiming that they achieve precision)—frequently abuse formal English by carrying it to the ridiculous extremes of the too technical, the pompous, and the flatulent (commonly called "gobbledygook" or "bafflegab").

Abused formal English has no reason for being. Even in its best sense, formal English is nearly always unsuitable for business writing. It calls attention to itself as inappropriate in all but the most formal occasions.

The illiterate level of usage is the third one of them three we dun named. It ain't got no bizness in bizness. Ya see, folks who reads letters spects you ta right right. If'n ya writes wrong, he shore sees ya errors and knows ya ain't eddicated so he thinks ya don't know nuthin else neither if ya cain't get yer rightin right.

An easy way to choose the appropriate level of usage for a situation is to ask yourself which type of dress would be most suitable if you were going to see your reader and talk your message. If the answer is formal dress, choose formal English or dignified–informal. If the answer is an everyday business suit, use the broad middle ground of informal English. If the answer is sport clothes, use familiar–informal.

Follow the conventions

You have already seen how following the conventions of wording, punctuation, sentence structure, and grammar affects clarity. But violations of those and other conventions have an even more important bearing on keeping your style inconspicuous. If you go contrary to the conventions (something your reader doesn't expect of an educated writer), you distract attention from your message *and* lose the reader's respect and confidence in you. After all, if a writer has not learned the fundamentals of the native language, knowing anything else of importance or value seems unlikely.

Even in the following first paragraph of a letter from a hotel manager to an association president, you know what the writer means, despite poor sentence structure; but you are distracted and you can't hold much respect for the manager or the hotel.

```
Your recent convention over with and successful, we
are wondering if since then you have decided on the
next year's meeting city, and you jotting down on the
margin of this letter the city and dates selected,
this will be indeed appreciated.
```

From this, don't you get the impression that the sloppy language probably means the hotel might not be a very well run, clean place to stay?

Spelling is probably the most exactly established convention in the English language. Though the dictionary spells a few words two ways, it lists most of them in only one way. Because of this definiteness, spelling has acquired more importance in the minds of most people than it deserves for any confusion from bad spelling. Most readers (even relatively uneducated ones) will notice your errors and look down on you for them. And that is a big part of total communication. So unless you are willing to appear uneducated, you had better learn English spelling.

Because it is so unsystematic, you'll find no easy way. Consider yourself fortunate if you have learned to spell by observing the words you read and by listening closely to their pronunciation. If you have not used these methods, you should start now; but don't assume that pronunciation is always a safe guide. (You will find some helpful guidelines, however, under **Sp** in Appendix F).

Poor *word choice* that is close enough to meet the basic requirement of clarity is usually not so noticeable as misspelling, but it may be distracting and even degrading. Among the thousands of possible bad choices, the pairs listed under **D**iction in Appendix F give the most trouble. If you are unsure of any of the distinctions, look up the words; any educated reader will notice if you confuse them.

Variations from *standard punctuation* may lead to misunderstanding, but more frequently they distract and retard the reader. If you have trouble with punctuation, study the material under **P** in Appendix F.

Grammar and sentence structure are so closely related that you should consider them together. They have a definite bearing on clarity (as previously explained), but they have more significance in terms of making your style inconspicuous. Most of the troubles come from

—A writer's having heard uneducated people speak unconventionally, particularly family and fellow workers. (Solution: Observe the skills of effective writers and speakers, study writing, practice.)

—Simple carelessness (Solution: Proofread and revise.)

—Trying to use big words and complicated sentence structures before mastering them. (Solution: Remember that they are unnecessary to dignity or effectiveness; write simply, at least until you can use more involved structures precisely and clearly.)

—Following some misguiding "rules of English." (Solution: Learn what the true conventions are according to language scholars, ignore misguiding "rules" and unjustifiable restrictions on the language, and give your attention to the more important aspects of good style—interest, clarity, inconspicuousness.)

Here is a realistic interpretation of some points that language scholars make in contradiction to statements of some less well-informed people:

—A split infinitive is undesirable only if it is awkward or unclear.

—*And, but,* and *so* are good sentence beginnings if they deserve the emphasis they get there. The same applies to *however* and other transitional words, but some people object only to *and, but,* and *so*.

—Prepositions are perfectly good at the end of sentences if you want them to have the emphasis they would get there.

—One-sentence paragraphs are perfectly good. The ban on them is nonsense. Often a one-sentence paragraph, especially the first or last in a letter, is just what you need.

—Passive voice is usually undesirable because it is weak, wordy, and awkward; but it still exists in the language because it is useful in some situations (to avoid direct accusations, for example). To ban it completely is high-handed.

—What some people still call colloquial expressions and slang are important and useful parts of the language; when the situation calls for the informal level of usage, they can improve language effectiveness.

—Many words have varied meanings when used alone; but if the context makes the interpretation readily clear and definite, to ban use of these words or to limit them (*while* or *since,* for example) to one use is unrealistic and lordly.

—The distinctions between *shall* and *will* are almost completely gone except in formal English; *will* is much more widely used.

Appendix F covers some common violations of the conventions and gives suggestions for avoiding criticism.

HOW TO HANDLE TWO NEW LANGUAGE PROBLEMS

Two language problems which have long existed are now demanding serious consideration: (1) sexist communications and (2) writing in international business. Both are important exceptions to the generally good advice to "follow the conventions" of the English language.

Avoid sexist language

For efficiency in language (and no doubt partly as a reflection of the attitude of male dominance) English has never developed universal- or dual-sex personal pronouns. Conventionally, English-speaking people have blithely used the male forms *(he, his, him)* when the sex of the person referred to was unknown or the intention was to include either or both sexes. Recent improvements in the attitude toward women are therefore running into a language problem.

Largely through the efforts of organized women's groups, most reputable speakers, writers, and publishers are learning and practicing ways to circumvent the sexist convention and make the language give women fair recognition.

Though we can't explain all the how-to's in this book (which is largely about something else), here's a list of the main ways:[3]

—Shift to the plural, where pronouns are the same form for both sexes.

—Phrase (or rephrase) errant sentences to avoid the need for third-person singular pronouns. *The* can often replace them.

—Identify the individual involved; then refer back with the appropriate pronoun. (By this means you'll also enhance your style through specificness and gain human interest by picturing a person in action.) Remember, however, that some of both females and males are of high station in life and some of low; so keep a balance. Otherwise you will show sexism by stereotyping one sex regularly in high-station activities and the other in low.

—Use gender-free terms (suitable in some cases) and other means to avoid the word or syllable *man* in many expressions also involving women: *sales representative* (or, in a store, *salesclerk*) instead of *salesman; police officer* instead of *policeman; mail carrier* instead of *mailman* or *postman*. The names of job categories are nearly all gender free: professor, secretary, manager, lawyer, plumber, doctor, teacher, minister, accountant, farmer, banker, retailer . . . . *Person* may serve the purpose in some places like *chairperson* and *salesperson*. (But beware of using laughable constructions such as *personager* and *unpersonned*.)

You can even more easily desex some female terms like *hostess, waitress, actress*, and *drum majorette* by simply omitting or changing the female-designating ending. In their basic forms, these words all include both sexes. Many similar words do too—but check an up-to-date dictionary to be sure. You can also (at the expense of a few words) change the phrasing to the *person serving/ waiting on; performing* or the *performer; leading the band*. But

—Try to avoid doubling as a solution (*she or he, she/he,* or the reverse).

—Ignore (or try to educate) those people who object to the word or syllable

---

[3]Though we do not agree with everything said in it, the best and fullest treatment of the subject is Bobbye Sorrels Persing, *The Nonsexist Communicator*, Communication Dynamics Press, East Elmhurst, N. Y., 1978.

man where they think it means (but does not) only a male person: *man* or *mankind* (in the original and still first-listed meaning of "all humans," as in "Man does not live by bread alone"); and in words like *manual, manufacture, manipulate,* and even *manure.*

—See Chapter 1 for suggestions on the special problem of courtesy titles in addresses and salutations.

As you see, the main solutions to the sexist-language problem lie in (1) being fair-minded and alert to it and (2) adapting the language we have.

Adapt language in international business

Since you will likely be involved to some extent in the booming international business and its relevant communications—now estimated at $1.3 trillion a year and growing at 20 percent yearly—you will need help.[4] With our limited space (in a book largely about something else) and our limited knowledge of only four foreign languages, we cannot hope to make you competent in the other 3,000 or more languages and dialects; but we can give you some background and helpful hints.

Again an exception to the generally good advice to follow the conventions of English, the international language problem also has its best solution in adaptation. Also similarly, this language problem almost always remains to some extent despite the half dozen or more means people use to solve it. Usually the writer, an employee, a special interpreter, or a friend knows the reader's language (including its sociological reflections); or the reader may know the writer's language or use someone who does.

The trouble is that unless both writer *and* reader are *native* speakers of the same language, misunderstandings may occur. Even professional interpreters rarely know all the nuances and idioms of languages other than their native tongues.

You see, then, that we can again give you some helpful guidelines. We have done so (along with some cultural differences and other aspects of international business) in Appendix C.

(All the cases for the first four chapters are at the end of Part 1 because we think you should cover all four basic tests of a good business message before trying to write one. We urge you to read the first four chapters quickly but thoroughly so that you can put all the basic principles to use even in your first letter or memo.)

(Since you will remember the principles of good style better if you practice them while concentrating on them alone, however, you may profit by working through at least some of the following exercises.)

---

[4]R. Hal Mason, Robert R. Miller, and Dale R. Weigel, *International Business* (2d ed.), John Wiley & Sons, New York, 1981, p. 9.

EXERCISES

A. Determine what is not good about the following "sentences" and rewrite them or be prepared to discuss them, as your teacher directs. Some of them have more than one thing wrong. You may also benefit from finding (in Appendix F) the appropriate symbol(s) for criticism of each and reading the discussion of the symbol(s).

1. After eating lunch the meeting came to order.
2. Neither the operators nor the supervisor have had much experience with the Textwriter.
3. Sarah is not sure who's pen she found, but she thinks it was your's.
4. Although many of my friends are painters, I do not enjoy it.
5. The parole board decided that Jones was mentally ill after listening to three psychiatrists.
6. By signing the enclosed forms, your beneficiary may be changed.
7. The executives decided that the simplest solution was for each to have their own garage key.
8. The sales manager wrote many of his memos while sitting in restaurants on the backs of menus.
9. Remember that as the dictator you are responsible for errors, not the typist.
10. The income of a western farmer is often higher than an eastern manufacturer.
11. Our M-798 carries a lifetime guarantee, the National Luggage Dealers Association approval, and come in four beautiful colors.
12. Only having two parts, the screen will give full protection while being light weight.
13. I would like to refer you to Dr. John Smith my college advisor Professor Raymond my instructor in chemistry and the reverend Bill Dudley the pastor of my church.
14. Originally a means of entertainment only, the Church was quiet late in accepting the organ (long considered a pagan device).
15. It was found that there are 12 main reasons why goods are returned. The most significant of these being almost entirely customer faults. These 12 reasons are . . . .
16. Included in the shipment are three one ounce packages and one sixteen ounce package.
17. As a recognized authority in Business Communications, the faculty of our Department solicits your assistance and expertise in evaluating the research contributions and qualifications of Dr. X for promotion . . . .
18. Incidently, our faculty is particularly interested in the value of his research . . . .
19. It is our policy that the completed promotion dosier is assembled jointly by myself and the candidate, with the latter having primary responsibility for its composition . . . .

20. Shirts, socks, and shoes must be worn to be served.

B. As an exercise in properly handling passives, study the subject (look it up in the Index and under **Pas** in Appendix F); then rewrite the following passage from a company's managment report, changing all passive sentences to active and all active ones to passive.

A report was drawn up and reviewed when a change was needed. Rearrangements were made. Even the largest division was rearranged so that each employee was given knowledge of all the tasks involved. Throughout the four-year program, a running account of the costs and savings in each department was kept by the company to determine net gains. Workers found their work to be more challenging and much more interesting after the change.

C. Without looking at the following 10 words (printed upside down), get somebody to pronounce them for you to spell (in writing). Then check them against the spelling tips (under **Sp** in Appendix F) to understand why the spelling of each is as it is.

babies' preferences, disastrous.
received, traveling, sloping, valleys, fifty-five, monkeys, changeable, (Most)

D. Rewrite in modern language.
   1. In reference to your request for an instruction booklet, please find same attached hereto.
   2. We trust you will send check in full payment at your earliest convenience.
   3. We beg to advise that there is a balance due of $23 in the above-captioned account in your name.
   4. Enclosed herewith is a draft in the amount of twenty-three dollars ($23).
   5. Your order of recent date for a catalog will be sent under separate cover.

E. Rewrite more vividly and specifically.
   1. Telephones are now available in color.
   2. Chicago has many advantages as a convention site.

Goodwill: How the reader feels

3

[Disagreements come from lost accord.]

No business firm or individual intentionally drives away customers or friends by creating ill will or by seeming indifferent. For lack of conscious effort and know-how to build goodwill, however, many people in business *do* drive others away.

Proper *tone* and *service attitude* are the methods of winning and retaining friendliness and confidence—that is, goodwill or disposition to return to you because you treat people well. Good business communication can help to produce that positive disposition by developing a friendly, confident feeling through proper tone and service attitude.

The same situation exists in international business relations, though language and sociological differences sometimes make intended tone and service attitude harder to communicate accurately. For these reasons the charter members of the American Business Communication Association started a continuing exchange of friendly international relations. Now, after 40-plus years of mutual cooperation, the association has more than 100 members in 20 other countries (especially Canada and Japan). A Canadian (Dr. Rennie Charles) has served a term as president, and the association is considering a name change to reflect its intercultural interests and activities.

Careful attention to goodwill is one of the reasons Japan's and China's international business has grown so well in recent years. Specifically, many Japanese professors and business executives are members of both the Japan Business English Association and the American Business Communication Association. Some have addressed our annual association meetings. Others have studied under our direction at our U.S. universities, visited in our homes, and asked for names and addresses of other U.S. business people and professors who might be interesting and helpful. They are all much interested in communicating the favorable tone and service attitude that contribute to the smooth flow of business.

TONE

[Beware of those who fall at your feet; they may be reaching for the rug.]

No doubt you have heard someone complain, "It isn't *what* he said—it's

63

the *way* he said it!" Inflections and modulations of voice, facial expressions, hand gestures—all affect the tone of a spoken remark. The point applies in writing too. If you want your writing to build goodwill, you *will make a conscious effort to control the tone*.

Basic to a desirable tone is a balance of personalities (writer's and reader's) acceptable to both. Without an attitude of mutual respect, you will have difficulty achieving the other qualities necessary for good tone—courtesy, sincerity, and proper gratitude.

Acceptable balance of personalities

As a good business writer you will need to subordinate your own wishes, reactions, and opinions. You can, however, overdo the suggestion "Make it *big you* and little me." Anything you say that looks up to or down on the reader will throw the relationship off balance.

Undue humility usually backfires. No reader expects a writer to be so humble as in the following.

```
I'm sorry to ask a busy person like you to take
valuable time to help me, but without your help I do
not know how to proceed. Since you are a world
authority on . . . , and I know nothing about
it . . . .
```

Flattery also causes readers to question the sincerity of some writers, especially obvious flattery in an attempt to get the reader to do something.

```
Your keen discrimination in footwear shows in your
wise summer-stock order of the ninth.
                    --
Your eminent position in commercial aviation, Mr.
Pogue, is the subject of much admiration.
                    --
When an Atlanta girl marries, she immediately thinks
of Rich's, the merchandising cynosure of the South!
```

Instead of gaining favor, the writer loses face and the reader's faith.

Passing deserved compliments or giving credit where credit is due, however, is something else—the good manners of anybody except a boor. So when you want to indicate your sincere awareness of the reader's position or accomplishment, avoid the smell of flattery by making the compliment subordinately.

Obvious flattery	*Better*
You are receiving this questionnaire because you are an authority on heat treating.	As an authority in heat treating, how do you think the passage of HR-724 will affect waste disposal?

Now the compliment gets such a light touch that it may give a faint glow of satisfaction, and consideration of the question precludes unfavorable reaction.

As you see, handling a compliment subtly is frequently a question of inserting a complimentary phrase in a statement intended primarily to accomplish something else:

```
How, in your opinion, will passage of HR—724 affect
waste disposal?

                              —

After successful experience in the field, would you
say that any single area of preparation is more
important than others for effective public relations
work?
```

More frequent than undue humility and flattery, however, is a writer's implication of too much self-respect and too little for the reader. Lack of respect usually reflects itself in (1) condescension ("talking down" to the other person), (2) preachiness (*didacticism* is another word for it), and (3) bragging.

Condescension implies that the writer feels superior to the reader and shows little respect. No one wants to be considered a nobody and looked down on or talked down to.

Yet, in attempting to be bighearted, a business executive insulted a reader with "The machine is probably not defective, but a firm of our standing can afford to take it back and give you a new one." In the same category are "I am surprised that you would question the adjustment procedure of a firm like Blank's" and "You are apparently unaware of the long history of satisfactory customer relations at Blank's." Even "We shall allow you to" has condescending connotations not present in "We shall be glad to" or "Certainly you may."

A particular danger lies in writing to children, who are not lacking in respect for their own ways of looking at things. When the secretary of a boy's club requested that a department store manager contribute some boxing gloves to the club, the manager answered: "When you grow up to have the heavy business responsibilities I have, and you're asked for contributions by all kinds of charitable organizations, you'll understand why I cannot make a donation to your club." And to make matters worse, the manager began the next sentence with "You are probably unaware . . . ." The boy's vocabulary failed him, but what he tried to express was "That pompous ass!"

A condescending attitude even crops up in job applications in statements like "You may call me at 743–4601." The implication is the writer is permitting the reader a privilege when just the opposite is true. An applicant is in no position to appear so aloof.

Repeated use of such phrases as "we think," "we believe," and "we suggest" often appears to be condescension. Such a sense of superiority is almost certain to erect a barrier of incompatibility or cause a sputter like "Well, Bigshot, I can think for myself!"

Preachiness (didacticism), an extension of condescension, is undesirable because, when you tell your reader what ought to be done, you imply reader ignorance or incapability and thus suggest your superiority. The juvenile-sounding marketing lecture in some letters to retailers is one of the most frequent offenders:

> The only way for you to make money is by offering your customers merchandise that has utility, good quality, and an attractive price.
>
> ---
>
> It's time for all dealers to get in their Christmas stock!

The reaction to such preachy statements will likely be an emphatically negative "Don't tell me how to run my business!"

A flat and obvious statement (see **Obv** in Appendix F) is frequently irritating because it implies stupidity, even though the writer's intention is good:

> Selecting the best available personnel for the various operations is one of the most important things you do. Therefore you should . . . .

Even sales writers and job applicants are sometimes flat, obvious, and preachy:

Flat and preachy	*Better*
Tax time will soon be here . . . that means sifting through piles of clients' records, endless mathematical computations, long hours filling out tax forms. A good tax program for your computer can save you all that trouble.	For those hectic months just before tax time, a comprehensive, proven tax program for your computer can help you organize clients' records, automatically figure taxes, and produce filled-out, ready-to-mail tax forms––all more accurately and with far less time and trouble than you now have to take.
The business cycle is changing from a seller's market to a buyer's market. You are going to need a strong force of good salespeople.	Now that business is shifting from a seller's market to a buyer's market, you're probably thinking about the strong force of good salespeople you'll need to meet competition.
Do you want Ferguson's to keep growing and keep getting better?	Good service at the right prices is not the only reason Ferguson's has

```
Of course you do!

That's why you should
employ only those who
want to move steadily
forward and push
Ferguson's on to even
greater heights.
```

```
grown as it has over the
last five years. The team
of Ferguson men and women
has been equally
responsible.
```

As you see, careful phrasing can eliminate most of the irritation due to preachiness—and the psychological browbeating in the third example (**BB** in Appendix F). Often the key is to subordinate information that is obvious or known to the reader but must, for a reason, be included. Put it in the middle of a paragraph, preferably in a phrase or dependent clause.

Bragging is another undesirable extension of the writer's ego. Conscious use of superlative wording ("newest," "latest and greatest," "outstandingly superior," "final word") is a flagrant and obvious way to make your reader react unfavorably—and not believe you. Even experienced writers sometimes annoy readers with undesirable—and almost always unsupported—references to size of company, efficiency of operations, or quality of product, like:

```
We could never have become so big, successful, and
prestigious if we had not always . . . .
```

—

```
Even in a firm as large and as well run as Bowen and
Bowen, such incidents are bound to happen
occasionally.
```

—

```
You are unfortunately a victim of routine made
necessary by the vastness of an institution so well
operated as the White Sands Hotel.
```

A desirable balance of personalities between reader and writer (eliminating undue humility, flattery, condescension, preachiness, and bragging) will help to improve the tone of your writing; but it will not assure courtesy, the second element in desirable tone.

Courtesy

[Kindness is the oil that reduces friction between people.]

Being courteous is being considerate of the other person's feelings through exercising patience and tact. But often one's immediate, emotional, or unthinking reaction is an impatient or tactless expression. For that reason, one famous lecturer regularly suggests the use of a "soaking drawer"—a special drawer in the desk to put nasty-toned letters and memos overnight, for revision the next day.

The idea is good. Courtesy often requires a cool, conscious effort to be understanding and forgiving, to anticipate another's likely reaction, and to avoid offense. Sleeping on a nasty message can provide the better conditions. Besides that, correspondents need to keep in mind the major causes of discourtesy and to respect a French proverb which says "To speak kindly does not hurt the tongue."

Anger is almost certain to cause loss of both friendliness toward you and confidence in you. Most people have a good deal of self-respect and confidence in the wisdom of their decisions. An attack on them produces a wave of anger and self-defense. Such sentences as the following are almost sure to produce that result:

```
We cannot understand why you are so negligent about
paying bills.
                            --
What's going on in the office at your place?
                            --
We certainly have no intention of letting you get away
with that!
```

Crude slang or profanity, especially if in a display of heightened feeling, is likely to be interpreted as anger, whether or not it is intended as such. Don't use either. (And don't try to be coy and cute with quotation marks for questionable slang—or dashes in words that are obviously profanity.)

Petulance (peevishness or fretfulness) is simply anger in a modified degree. Here is how a woman scolded an interior decorator: "When do you expect to return my furniture? You've had it now for more than two weeks. That ought to be long enough to do a little upholstering job." A calm request that the work be finished as soon as possible because of the need for the furniture would probably bring just as quick action, and it would leave the upholsterer in a better mood to do a good job.

Both anger and petulance are the result of impatience and unwillingness to accept the responsibilities of successful human relations.

Accusations, on the other hand, are usually the result of insensitivity to how another person will react to a remark. You cannot cultivate tact (skill in dealing with others without giving offense—or, as somebody said, the ability to get your point across without jabbing anybody) without a deep and almost constant concern for the feelings of others. The sensitive, thoughtful person knows that people do not like to be reminded of their carelessness or ignorance—and that they will react unfavorably to the person who insists upon reminding them.

The other person may not always be right; but if you are going to keep the greatest friendliness (goodwill), you will remember not to call attention to errors if you can avoid doing so—or, when necessary, to do it with the least likely offense *(in impersonal style or by implication)*.

Accusing
Much as we dislike doing

Revised, better
Since we want you to be

so, we shall have to delay your purchase order number B—33084, dated June 26.

You neglected to specify which insulation you want on the wire.

Kindly check our specifications and this time specify whether you want shielded or unshielded wire.

We have enclosed an envelope for your convenience.

entirely satisfied with the wire you ordered June 26 (your purchase order B—33084), please tell us whether you want shielded or unshielded insulation?

Shielded insulation is a little more expensive, but it meets all regulations——including the new FAA RMS—625/4.

Just check the appropriate box on the enclosed reply card and sign as authorization. As soon as we receive it, your wire will be on its way.

The revised version has far better tone and is thus more likely to retain the goodwill of the reader. It eliminates the accusation and the unfavorable reminder in the underlined words of the original, the sarcasm the reader would probably read into *kindly,* and the pompous-sounding reference to the enclosure. You could practice the same technique if speaking with the customer.

The contrast between the two versions of that letter points to an important principle in business communication: *When you have sincere compliments to give, personalize them for full effect; on the contrary, when you are inclined to point the accusing finger, shift to impersonal, passive, or other unaccusing phraseology.*

Unflattering implications are usually the result of tactlessness combined with suspicion or distrust. The collection correspondent who wrote, "When we sold you these goods, we thought you were honest," implied an unfavorable idea of much greater impact than the literal statement.

The adjustment correspondent who says, "We are investigating shipment of the goods *you claim* you did not receive," need not be surprised to receive a sharp reply. Similarly, "*We are surprised* to receive your report" and "*We cannot understand* why you have had trouble with the Kold-Hold when other people like it so well" establish by implication semiaccusing doubts of the other person's reasonableness, honesty, or intelligence.

And the sales writer who begins a message by implying doubts about a reader's alertness can expect few returns from the letter:

Alert hardware dealers everywhere are stocking No-Flame, the fire-resistant . . . . Are you prepared to meet the demands of your home-building customers?

In similar vein the phrases "Do you realize . . . ?" and "Surely you are . . ." immediately suggest doubts that the reader or listener measures up on either score.

Such lack of tact is usually unintentional. Most people, however, do not question whether it is intentional; the result is ill will.

Sarcasm, on the other hand, is generally deliberate. And it is extremely dangerous in business correspondence. The smile which accompanies friendly sarcastic banter cannot find its way onto paper; unfriendly sarcasm is sheer malice. It is the direct opposite of the attitude necessary for a tone of goodwill because it shows a lack of respect for the other person and a deliberate attempt to belittle. The sales manager sending the following memo to a group of employees falling short of their quotas would build no goodwill:

> Congratulations on your magnificent showing!
>
> We're only $50,000 short this week.
>
> How <u>do</u> you do it?

The United Way leader who included the following in a public report could hardly expect future cooperation from the people indicated:

> The ABC employees, with an assigned goal of $800, magnificently responded with $452. Such generosity should not go unmentioned.

Sarcasm should never be used in business writing. It's too risky. The moment of triumph is short-lived; the loss of friendship may be permanent.

Curtness, born of impatience and a false sense of what constitutes desirable business brevity, reflects indifference and thus seems discourteous. The woman who received the following letter promptly labeled the manufacturer sending it as a boor:

> We have your request for our booklet and are enclosing same.
>
> Thanking you for your interest, we are . . . .

A poor letter like this, reflecting such lack of interest, destroys much of the favorable impression made by even a good booklet.

This writer might very well have helped to convert a casual inquiry into a sale by taking the time to show interest in serving with a letter like the following, with its good service attitude, positive and specific resale material, and action ending (all of which we discuss later):

> Here is your copy of Siesta's booklet <u>Color at Mealtime</u>.
>
> When you read it, you'll understand why we say that in Siesta you can now have handsome dinnerware that is sturdy enough for everyday use yet surprisingly inexpensive.

No photography, however, can do justice to the
delicacy of some Siesta shades or to the brilliance of
others.

Your friendly local dealer will be glad to show you a
selection of Siesta. Unless the stock is complete, the
dealer will be glad to order additional colors for
your examination.

See your dealer soon and start enjoying Siesta's color
at mealtime.

You can find Siesta in Omaha at (name and address of
dealer).

This letter adapts easily as a form letter with only the last line and the inside
address and salutation individually typed.

Stereotyped language is another mark of discourtesy because it suggests
indifference. And nobody likes to be treated in an indifferent, routine way.
Writers of messages like the following jargonistic disgrace can expect little
feeling of friendliness from their readers:

We have your letter of the 19th and in reply wish to
state that the interest on your mortgage is now
$361.66.

We trust this is the information you desired, and if
there is any other way we can oblige, please do not
hesitate to call upon us.

Since stereotyped language is primarily a question of style, see **Nat** in Appendix F for fuller discussion and more examples.

Untidy physical appearance is another factor affecting the apparent courtesy of letters and memos. Sleazy paper, poor placement, strikeovers, messy
erasures, dim or clogged type, poorly matched type and processed material,
and penciled signatures are like trying to gain an audience's respect when
you're dressed in an old tweed suit and they are in formal wear . . . and your
socks don't match!

In putting your best foot forward through courtesy, however, you must be
careful not to trip up. Overdone attempts to be courteous may seem insincere
and thus destroy the third element in desirable tone.

Sincerity

[*Don't stretch the truth; it snaps back.*]

When a reader or listener feels the first flashes of doubt, with an unex-
pressed reaction of "Well, I'll take that with a grain of salt," confidence in the
writer or speaker wanes—because of apparent insincerity.

Sincere cordiality is entirely free of hypocrisy. It is unwillingness to exaggerate or fictionalize upon the true state of a situation. Inappropriate cordiality (usually unbelievable and sometimes distasteful) is commonly the result of effusiveness, exaggeration, or undue familiarity. (Flattery and undue humility often sound insincere; but in our opinion they relate more closely to the balance of personalities discussed in a preceding section.)

Effusiveness means gushiness. It is excessive politeness, which often *is* insincere and always *sounds* insincere. "Overdone" means the same thing. You sound effusive simply because you've used too many and/or too strong adjectives and adverbs:

```
We are extremely happy to place your name on our list
of highly valued customers who have open accounts with
us, and we sincerely want you to know that we have
hundreds of most loyal employees all very eager and
anxious to serve you.
                          --
Your excellent choice of our fine company for the
establishment of an open account we consider a
distinct compliment to the superb quality of our
merchandise and outstanding service. And we are
genuinely happy about it.
                          --
I was exceptionally pleased to note your name on this
morning's list of much-appreciated new charge
customers.
```

The plain fact is that in a business relationship such highly charged personal reactions do not exist—and business people know it. Phrases like "do all we can" and simply "happy" or "pleased" are appropriate because they are believable.

Furthermore, the coy quality of the following endings is unrealistic in a business situation—and therefore unbelievable:

```
We do hope you'll come in soon. We can hardly wait!
                          --
Don't forget to come in soon. We'll be looking for
you!
                          --
Simply note your color choice on the enclosed card,
mail it to us--and then sit back with an air of
expectancy.
```

In avoiding effusiveness, you'll do well to watch especially overused words like *very, indeed, genuinely, extremely, really,* and *truly*—which begin to gush in a very short time.

Exaggeration is stronger, and therefore even more destructive of sincerity. The person who wrote, "Work is a pleasure when you use these precision-made tools," appears to be overstating the case to a carpenter-reader. And the writer of the following, if around to overhear, should be prepared for an emphatic *"Bull!"* when a retailer-customer opens the letter:

> New customers, happy and eager to buy, will surely
> applaud your recent selection of 4 dozen Tropical
> Holiday shorts.
>
> Especially made for the humidity of Macon, these
> garments will lead tennis players for miles around to
> tell their friends that "Thompson's has them!"

Superlatives and other forms of strong wording are among the most frequent reasons why so many letters sound insincere. The trite "more than glad" is nearly always an insincere attempt to exaggerate a simple "glad." And "more than happy," if translated literally, could mean only slaphappy. The classic illustration is the misguided "What could be finer than . . . ?" Any reader can and usually does supply at least one quick answer of something which seems finer than the product or service mentioned.

Exaggerated wording is nearly always challenging. Few things are actually *amazing, sensational, revolutionary, ideal, best, finest,* or *perfect.* Simple, accurate, specific statements of quality and value not only avoid the impression of insincerity; they are often more forceful than the general superlatives made nearly meaningless by years of misuse. If you describe products or services in terms like the following, you are inviting negative responses toward yourself and your firm:

> Want Amazing Protection
> That Can <u>Never</u> Be Canceled?
>
> Here is a really magnificent opportunity. Imagine a
> health and accident policy that can never be canceled.
>
> --
>
> This new mower is revolutionary in build, style,
> performance, and customer appeal. Amazing, of course!
> Here is your golden opportunity! A sensational
> solution to your spring sales problems!

Undue familiarity also causes people to lose favor. Sometimes it crops out merely because the writer or speaker is uncouth. The reader or hearer may feel sympathy for the person who does not know how to act with people—but will not likely have the disposition to return for more uncouthness.

Undue familiarity results from (1) calling the reader by name too frequently or writing or speaking in too informal language to a stranger and (2) making references to subjects which are too personal for business discussions. For an obvious purpose the writer or speaker pretends a closeness of friendship or an overweening interest which does not exist. Like other forms of pretense, it brings resentment. In the following letter giving information on home insulation to a college professor, the jocularity doesn't just fall flat; it boomerangs!

> Just set the thermostat and relax. That's all you have
> to do, Professor Eckberg. Pick up your book and settle
> down in a cozy chair. The Mrs. won't be continually
> warning you to get your old sweater, or nagging you to
> keep turning up the thermostat, or to put another
> blanket on the cherubs.
>
> Yes, Professor Eckberg, Isotemp will guard over your
> household. Take a gander at the statistical table in
> the folder, Modern Insulation for Older Homes. This
> table shows that out of every 8,000 cases of
> respiratory diseases, 6,536 occurred in uninsulated
> homes—over 75 percent from the very type of home
> you're now living in!
>
> Didn't you say you spent over $1,500 for fuel last
> year, Professor Eckberg? That's a lot of money out of
> a professor's salary; and as you said, "Even then the
> place wasn't always warm."
>
> If you fill in and return the enclosed card, we will
> send Mr. Don Diller, our Milwaukee representative, to
> answer any of your questions. Incidentally, Professor
> Eckberg, Mr. Diller is a graduate of the University of
> Wisconsin with a degree in heating engineering. He may
> be the guy who slept through half your classes six
> years ago, but somewhere he learned how to make your
> home more comfortable and reduce those high fuel
> bills. Then the Mrs. can buy that fur coat she's been
> nagging you about for when she goes outside, where it
> is cold!

Such diction as *cherubs, gander,* and *nagging* might be all right in breezy conversation with an old friend and perhaps in a letter to the old friend, but certainly not in a letter to someone the writer does not know. Using the reader's name four times in such short space furthers the impression of fawning. And the assumptions and references to family relations and activities are typical of familiarity that breeds contempt. These spring from insincerity, but they are discourteous in the truest sense and thus destructive of goodwill.

Gratitude

In business communication as in social relations, proper handling of deserved gratitude is a significant point in the tone of relationships. When people extend favors, they expect to receive some recognition; and everybody except the self-centered, boorish, or inept gives it. Probably because of early training, most of us have little trouble showing gratitude properly in face-to-face relations; but in business writing the what, when, and how seem to be problems for many.

To help, we offer the following suggestions:

1. When the reader has already done you a favor—
   a. Don't begin with "Thank you . . ." unless that is your most impor-
      tant or most likely acceptable point. Instead, go ahead with your
      message and
      (1) Let the overall pleasant spirit show your good feeling without
          wasting words saying "Thanks . . ." explicitly, or
      (2) Tuck the expression in a subordinate position and word it to
          give due (not overdue) emphasis.
   b. If you feel that you must begin with gratitude, be sincere (don't gush
      or exaggerate) and word your expression to relate naturally to what
      follows—perhaps as a "buffer" (explained in the next chapter).
2. When you want to show gratitude for future favors (asked for or hoped
   for)
   a. Don't express it in the present tense ("I appreciate") or in unquali-
      fied future indicative mood ("I will appreciate . . ."). Either way
      presumes that the reader will do as you ask, and you have no right
      to be so presumptuous.
   b. Either
      (1) Qualify the future indicative with an "iffy" or questioning re-
          quest ("I shall appreciate it if you will . . ." or "Will you please
          . . . ?), or
      (2) Use the future conditional ("I would appreciate your . . .").

See the Index for help on handling gratitude in special situations.

SERVICE ATTITUDE

In addition to a desirable tone as a means of maintaining goodwill, good
business communicators show that their concern extends beyond making a
profit or other purely selfish interests. They're like the very successful business executive who said that the difference between the average person and
the exceptional person usually lies in three words—"and then some." The top
people, he said, "did what was expected of them—and then some. They met
their obligations and responsibilities—and then some. They were good friends
to their friends—and then some. They proved themselves dependable in an
emergency—and then some . . . ."

A business organization obviously must make profits if it is to exist; both
reader and writer accept that premise. To deny it is to fly under false colors.
The answer is neither to deny nor to affirm; just don't talk about it! Instead,
let your messages remind others of your thoughtfulness and genuine desire to
be of service—to meet your obligations, and then some—through:

1. Resale material on the goods and/or the house.
2. Sales promotional material on other goods (in some cases).
3. Special-occasion messages.

Resale material

Often you need to assure a customer of the wisdom of an earlier choice of goods and services—or of the house (business firm) chosen to do business with—and thus stress satisfaction. In *keeping the goods sold,* resale material helps keep unfilled orders on the books, fosters repeat orders, and forestalls complaints. It is an effective device in meeting competition.

As applied in business to goods and services, *resale* means favorable talk about something the customer has already "bought"—that is by purchase, practice, or approval, although it may not yet be delivered. Most buyers would feel better about the product upon reading the following resale idea woven into an acknowledgment of an order:

```
The Henshaw electric boudoir clocks you ordered on
March 1 (eight at $22) are our fastest-selling models
in this price range. Because they are accurate as well
as beautiful, they make excellent gifts.
```

One of the most prestigious restaurants in Austin, Texas, helps promote its fine dinners by sticking this little sign into the skin of each baked potato served:

```
For goodness sake Don't skin me! I've been rubbed,
tubbed, and scrubbed. I'm clean as a whistle . . . and
a lot tastier. You may eat me skin and all—for I'm an
Idaho Potato—baked and served the XXX way.
```

The woman receiving the following would most likely feel much more secure in her choice of a dress—and thus happier with the dress as well as the company that sold it to her:

```
You'll stay fresh, neat, and comfortable in your 100
percent Visa polyester blue separates from Meredith
Palmer.
```

A prosperous TV dealer promotes the main line by delivering, with each set sold, a bouquet and this note:

```
A red, red rose and congratulations . . . on your
selection of a new XXX. Be assured it will provide the
finest in beauty and entertainment for years. Enjoy it
with pride.
```

Such material is *most effective when it is relatively short and when it is specific.* Tell a customer buying a shirt, for instance, that

```
It will launder rapidly and easily because of the no-
iron finish.
```

or

```
The seams are double-lockstitched for long life.
```

or

> Made from long-staple California cotton, your
> Pallcraft shirt will give you the wear you expect from
> a shirt of this quality.

But don't try to tell *all* these points in a resale passage. And for your own greatest effectiveness, don't try to get by with a lame generality like "Pallcraft shirts are a good buy."

Used most frequently in acknowledgments, resale material on the goods may also appear in certain credit, collection, and adjustment messages, as you'll see later.

Resale material on the house consists of pointing out customer-oriented policies, procedures, guarantees, and special services sometimes called "the little extras" (the "and then some's") a good firm (the "house") provides its customers—retail, wholesale, or industrial. Resale is especially helpful in the beginning of a business relationship. But any time you add a new service, improve an old one, or expand a line is an appropriate occasion to tell customers about the firm's continued attempt to give satisfaction. The following excerpt from a message to a dealer is typical:

> Along with your shipment of Lane candies are some
> display cards and window stickers which you'll find
> valuable aids in bringing these delicious candies to
> the attention of your customers. Our Advertising
> Department will regularly furnish you with seasonal
> displays and will be glad to help you on any special
> display problem in connection with the sale of Lane's.

Retail stores often write their customers about lounges, lunchrooms, and personal shoppers, to mention only a few such samples of resale on the house:

> You are welcome to use Rosen's air-conditioned
> lounging and rest rooms on the mezzanine, the fountain
> luncheonette on the first floor, or the spacious
> parking lot right behind the store. It is absolutely
> free to customers shopping at Rosen's, whatever the
> size of your purchase.

Resale passages are the writer's (or speaker's) attempts to confirm or increase the buyer's faith in goods, services, or the firm in which committed interest already exists. Sales promotion material (on new and different goods or services) seeks to promote interest in *something else* the firm can supply.

Sales promotion material

For a number of reasons, sales material about related products is desirable in some acknowledgment, credit, collection, and even adjustment messages. The most obvious business reason is that regardless of what you try to market, you must constantly seek to sell more of it to more customers all the time. In terms of communication, however, *the most significant reason is the concrete demonstration that the firm desires to be of further service*. A third function of sales promotion material is that it can end a message naturally and easily, with emphasis on further service. The following example illustrates the point:

```
We shipped your carpenter's tools, as itemized on the
enclosed invoice, by parcel post this morning. They
should reach you by October 15. Thank you for your
check, which covers all charges.
```

Resale
```
The Crossman level with aluminum frame is stronger and
weighs less than wooden ones, and it will remain
bright and true. The tempered steel used in the Flex-
Line tape is permanently oiled; so you can be sure it
will easily and rapidly unwind and rewind every time
you use it.
```

Sales promotion
```
When you receive the fall and winter catalog we're
sending separately, turn to page 126 and read the
description of the Bradford 6½-inch electric handsaw.
To enjoy the savings in time and energy this efficient
piece of equipment offers, use the handy order blank
at the back of the catalog.
```

You'll need to observe three precautions in the use of sales promotion material:

1.   Above all, it should reflect *the desire to be of service* rather than the desire to sell more goods. It is low-pressure sales effort, comparable to the way a salesclerk, after selling a woman a pair of shoes, may casually pick up a matching or complementary purse and say, "Perhaps you'd like to examine this purse, which goes with your shoes so well." Only after the customer displays an interest in the suggested item does the salesclerk begin a real sales talk. If another sale results, that's good. But if not, it's still good: most customers are pleased because of the demonstrated interest in their welfare or happiness.

If, however, the insatiable sales appetite of "I want to sell you more" shows through selfish, greedy terminology, you neither promote sales nor please the customer. When emphasis is on *what we want* rather than *what you get,* the effect is unfavorable, maybe even repellent. When emphasis is on *order* instead of *service,* Greedy Gus overtones are almost inevitable:

Greedy Gus original	*Service-minded revision*
```We also sell attractive summer purses, silk and nylon hosiery, and```	```The summer purses and costume jewelry shown on pages 29 to 32 of the```

```
costume jewelry to              accompanying catalog have
complete your excellent         also sold well for many
line of goods. We are           of our other customers—
sending you our catalog.        and we think would for
And we hope to fill many        you. We'll be glad to
more orders for you.            handle your order for
                                these items on the same
                                terms as this one.
```

2.   *Appropriateness* is also a factor. When a woman buys a suit, a natural item to call to her attention is a blouse. A man buying a suit may be interested in matching or blending shirts, ties, or shoes. But to tell a purchaser of heavy-duty truck tires about the good buy you now have in refrigerators or the buyer of a washing machine about your special on tires would be questionable most of the time. Such suggestions appear to be dictated by the greedy desire for further sales rather than by an eagerness to render service. Almost always, *sales promotion material should be on items related to those under consideration*.

3.   Before using sales promotion material, consider also *the kind of message* you are writing. A message requiring further action on the reader's part needs final emphasis on that action, not on sales material. In acknowledgments, for example, you can use sales promotion endings to good purpose when you are sending the goods as requested, but not when additional action by the customer is necessary.

Also, although you might use such material in an early collection mailing to a good customer, it is decidedly inappropriate as soon as your message shows concern over the account. And in adjustments you may safely use sales promotion material to end a full-reparation message, because you can be fairly sure the customer is going to be pleased; but its use in a compromise or a refusal is usually questionable.

Both resale and sales promotion material help to sell more merchandise, but they are even more effective as goodwill builders because they imply positively and emphatically the general statement "We are eager to serve you well."

Special goodwill messages

To demonstrate continuing interest in the customer and the desire to serve, special goodwill letters also subtly use resale material on the goods and the house, and sales promotion material. Many business people refer to them as the "letters you don't have to write—but should." Since the customer does not expect them, since they usually bring something pleasant, and since your reader knows you do not have to write them, they are doubly welcome and thus greater builders of goodwill than some other types.

Because they are of great variety in function and occasion, and because you can write them with greater understanding and skill after studying some other kinds of business messages, however, we treat them in greater detail in Chapter 6. Suffice it to say here—before we take up some other kinds of business communications—that your study of special goodwill messages will reinforce the central theme of the preceding chapters: consideration for the other person.

(All the cases for the first four chapters are at the end of Part 1 because we think you should cover all four basic tests of a good business message before trying to write any kind. We urge you to read the first four chapters quickly but thoroughly so that you can put all the basic principles to use from the start.)

QUESTIONS

1. Besides quality, selection, convenience (closeness), and price, on what other bases do you choose the places where you buy food, clothing, shelter (unless your own home); meals out, snacks and drinks, entertainment; transportation vehicles (and service on them)?

2. Be ready (on request) to cite a specific instance of some business person's *(a)* not keeping a proper "balance of personalities" with you, *(b)* lack of courtesy, *(c)* lack of sincerity, *(d)* lack of proper gratitude, *(e)* lack of service attitude.

3. Conversely (to 2), cite an instance of good *(a)* balance, *(b)* courtesy, *(c)* sincerity, *(d)* gratitude, *(e)* service attitude.

4. What are the two best ways to convey necessary faultfinding (accusing) to another person in a letter or memo?

5. Assuming no confusion in translation, what, if any, differences (from your reactions) might have come in the 2 *(a)*–*(e)* and 3 *(a)*–*(e)* situations if you had been French? German? Israeli? Pakistani? Japanese?

6. How, if at all, would you change your answers to 1 and 4 if applied to the various nationalities in 5?

7. Name three of the five common errors that can prevent an acceptable balance of personalities.

8. Why is stereotyped language a mark of discourtesy?

Persuasion: What the reader does

4

[Knowledge or skill without justice is cunning, not wisdom.]

In business you're nearly always trying to sell something—whether it's a product, a service, or an idea. Your business communications, therefore (unless just reporting information), try to produce an action or a reaction which may soon lead to an action.

If you are going to be successful in that mission, you'll want to make conscious use of five principles which have proved helpful in getting the desired response:

1. Planned presentation in the light of your objective.
2. You-viewpoint interpretation.
3. Adaptation—even personalization when possible.
4. Positive statement.
5. Success consciousness.

PLANNED PRESENTATION

You can make your job of beginning a letter, memo, or talk simple if you will classify it according to one of the following three probable reactions of your readers or listeners—whether domestic or intercultural:

1. Will they welcome it? That is, does it say things they will be glad to hear or at least not unhappy to hear? Does it take action they have requested? Does it request action they are prepared to take? (A–plan)
2. Will the basic message displease them? Does it contain bad news? (B–plan)
3. Or does it request action they are probably not already willing to take? (C–plan)

According to subject matter, you can list hundreds of different kinds of business letters, memos, and talks. For determining your beginning and later development of points, however, you need to decide whether your message contains good news or neutral information (A–plan), disappointing information (B–plan), or persuasion intended to motivate the reader to action (C–plan).

Good-news or neutral messages

Most A–plan letters and memos say or imply yes. They include favorable replies to requests, acknowledgments in which you can ship goods as ordered, adjustments fully complying with the reader's request, credit approvals, and the like. Since you are doing what the reader wants you to do, *the first sentence should contain the big idea*. That is what the reader most wants to know. Then you follow up with necessary details in order of relative importance or natural sequence. Frequently messages of this kind (including oral ones) end with a short punch line recalling the benefits of the good news in the beginning, as suggested by Figure 4–1.

Figure 4–1   A–plan (good-news and neutral) messages

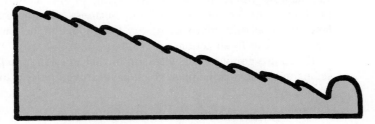

Letters, memos, and talks which merely seek or transmit business information follow the same basic order. Among them are inquiries and replies about job or credit applicants and facts about an organization, its personnel, or its products. All these are neutral situations (neither very pleasing nor displeasing), readily taken for granted. The messages should therefore have the same directness and dispatch as the following yes letter (replacing a packaging-machine part damaged in transit):

> Your new lower rack sensor unit, shipped by UPS Blue
> Service this morning, should be at your door about
> June 12.
> The same kind of thick padding carefully protecting
> your new sensor unit in the heavy-duty corrugated box
> will be standard for all our future shipments of
> fragile articles so that they will arrive in the same
> perfect condition in which they leave our plant.
> And now will you take a moment to assist us in
> recovering for the sensor unit from the Postal
> Service? Just sign the enclosed notification forms and
> return them with the original sensor unit. Of course
> we will reimburse you for returning it.
> Your Cary Can-packer will soon be operating
> efficiently again--in time for the cherry harvest.

*   *   *   *   *

A note of caution is in order here, however: In A–plan messages to people whose native language is not English (particularly Latinate and Oriental people), *the desirable directness must not rule out their conventional expressions of courtesy, politeness, and cordiality*.

Disappointing messages

B–plan messages—those that say no or "yes, but . . ." (that is, modified refusals)—should not be direct. If you have to tell someone that you can't give the booklet requested, that you can't fill an order as specified, that you can't extend credit, that you can't offer the requested job, or that you can't make the adjustment desired, you have a situation which is goodwill-killing—if you blurt out the disappointing information immediately. You can do better.

We assume that you are a fair-minded person who does not act high-handedly or arbitrarily but have good reasons when you refuse anything. In most cases you can show that some of your reasons are beneficial to the other person— as when a mother refuses her child something for the child's good as well as (sometimes even *rather than*) her own. The following psychology of refusing therefore depends on your having good reasons, as does any satisfactory refusal.

You know that when you refuse anybody anything considered due, disappointment and frustration develop unless you give justifying reasons (not just excuses or no explanation at all). You know further that if you begin with the refusal, you will at least disappoint (maybe even anger) that person. You also know that an angry person is not a logical one. So even if you did give good reasons *after* the refusal, they would fall on an illogical mind, where they would not take effect.

But if you start pleasantly and give justifying reasons *before* a refusal, your logical reasons fall on a logical mind. Your good reasons can therefore convince the other (logical) person that you *are* justified—and to accept your refusal without irritation because you show the justice of it. This psychology directs you to a rather specific plan for all refusals.

To soften the effect, you try to catch favorable interest in your opening remarks with *something from the situation on which both of you can agree*. Effective business communicators use this kind of pleasant beginning (commonly called a "buffer") for two reasons: (1) to suggest that they are reasonable persons who can see two sides of the question and (2) to set the stage for a review of the facts in the case. A good buffer will therefore be

—Pleasant, usually agreeing with something the other person has said.
—Relevant, thus quickly showing the subject.
—Equivocal, avoiding any implication that the answer is yes or no.
—Transitional, carefully worded for a natural movement into the explanation.

This word of caution about buffers is due, however: In being pleasant and agreeable, be careful about the third point and do **not** say something that later seems contradictory. A buffer inconsistent with later statements loses its effectiveness.

After you establish compatibility, you analyze the circumstances sympathetically and understandingly, giving the reasons why you can't do what the other person wants you to do. *Only after you have tactfully prepared the way with these justifying reasons do you want to reveal or even imply the disappointing news.* You further attempt to soften the blow by such subordinating means as embedding the refusal, giving it minimum space or time, and positive statement when you have to state it. But better, you can usually make the refusal clear by implication. Certainly you do not want to stress it—and if you are communicating with a Japanese person, you go even further with these subordinating devices to convey a negative message gently.

Graphically, your procedure looks like the line in Figure 4–2. The following positive refusal illustrates the strategy:

Your comments, Professor McGinnis, on the effectiveness of the "More Business" series are helpful to us at Read's who worked on these practical guides for users of direct mail.

When we first planned the booklets for our customers, we had in mind a checklist for a business using direct mail extensively rather than a thoroughgoing treatment suitable for a textbook. Accordingly, we set our quota for noncommercial users at a low figure——partly because we did not expect many requests.

Since the series has proved so popular with our customers, we have for over a month been distributing our limited copies only to commercial users, although we are glad to make available what we can to educational institutions.

Perhaps you can use the extra copy——sent to you this morning by parcel post——as a circulating library for your students. Two or three days' use should be ample for most of them, and they're perfectly welcome to copy anything they care to.

Figure 4–2   B–plan (disappointing) messages

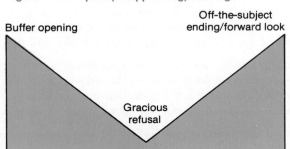

Will you give us the benefit of your suggestions for
making the series more extensive and helpful after you
have had an opportunity to test its teachability more
thoroughly?

Persuasive messages

For even the third basic kind of situation, the C–plan, starting need not
be difficult. Just figure out something you can offer that the reader or listener
wants, needs, or at least is interested in. Preferably it will be a promised or
implied benefit, thus catching attentive interest from the start. You then develop your message in concrete pictures of the benefits available for complying with your suggestion. After enough evidence for conviction, you are in a
psychological position to ask for the action you want. Figure 4–3 illustrates
the plan.

Prospecting (cold-turkey) sales and application letters, executive memos
calling for improved operations, persuasive requests, and some collections
follow this pattern, as in the following persuasive request for a confidential
manual:

How often have you received——even from well–educated
people——letters that are not worth your attention?

As a public relations director and an employer, you
are of course interested in this problem. And I, as a
teacher of business communication, am too. Here at
Harwood we're turning out a thousand students each
year who are better trained in writing effective
letters and memos than the usual college graduate.
We'd like to be sure, however, that we're up–to–date
in giving them what business wants.

Quite likely, you know, some of these students will
some day be writing for companies like yours. Wouldn't
they be better prepared if we stressed the ideas that
you have emphasized in your recent correspondence
manual? Both the students and business firms would

Figure 4–3   C–plan (persuasive) messages

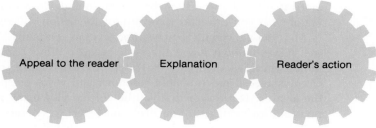

benefit from your letting us have a copy for our
teaching files. Of course, we'd handle the material
with whatever confidence you specify, and we'd be most
grateful for this practical teaching aid.

But the ones especially benefiting from your sending a
copy would be the students and business firms like GE.
Will you send us a copy today?

The planned steps in all persuasion are here. You get attentive interest
quickly by promising or mentioning a prospective benefit, give explanation
backing up that promised benefit, forestall or minimize any objections you
can foresee, and confidently ask for the action you want.

YOU-VIEWPOINT

*[People wrapped up in themselves are usually small
packages.]*

The you-viewpoint or you-attitude is a state of mind: always bringing out
and emphasizing the benefits to the other person resulting from your suggestion or decision and subordinating or eliminating (but not denying) your own.

Of course, it isn't pure unselfishness. When you try to sell something,
obviously you are trying to make some money; but you don't need to put that
idea into words. When you attempt to collect, obviously you want—maybe
even need—the money; you don't need to put that idea into words. When
you apply for a job, obviously you either want or need work to earn some
money; you don't need to put that idea into words. Both parties involved
assume all these ideas. Putting them into words merely sounds selfish, wastes
words, and helps your cause not one bit.

Nor is the you-attitude a question merely of politeness, courtesy, or good
manners. The business reason for you-viewpoint presentation is that it gets
results. *When you show that you are aware of and are doing something about
another person's needs or problems, your suggestion will get a favorable reaction.* In other words, you can get the action you want if—and only if—you
show benefits worth the cost and trouble.

So in C–plan messages (asking for action the other person is not already
motivated to take) you show by central theme and wording that you are thinking of what you can offer in return for the action you request at the end.

The you-viewpoint requires imagination, certainly. The old story of how
the village half-wit found the mule is apt ("Why, I just thought, 'If I was a
mule, where would I go?' "). The ability to visualize someone else's desires,
circumstances, and probable reactions and write or speak in those terms is
the answer. It requires that you be able to play many roles. When you communicate to managers, you *are* a manager; to doctors, you *are* a doctor; to
merchants, you *are* a mercchant—and you try to see things through *their*
eyes.

Phrasing helps, it is true. You are more likely to communicate in terms of another person if you use more *you's* and *your's* than the first-person pronouns *I, me, mine, we, us, our*. But if you apply that test alone, the sentence "We want your check" has more you-viewpoint than "We want our check," when obviously neither has any. The you-attitude sentence might well read, "To keep your account in the preferred-customer class, please send your check for $142.63 today." Whether you say "sending *us* your check" or not is immaterial, except that it wastes a word. What *is* significant is that the *you*-viewpoint is there.

We-viewpoint	*You-viewpoint*
We are shipping your order of August 20 this afternoon.	You should receive the Janus 8-inch floppy diskettes you ordered August 20 no later than Tuesday, August 25.
We have spent six years making Janus diskettes fast-selling.	Back of your Janus diskettes are six years of successful testing and improvement. Because we verify every sector on every disk, you will virtually never get a "Bad sector on A:DOS" error.

Making your reader or listener the subject or object of most sentences will help you keep you-viewpoint interpretation too. As you've already seen in the discussion of writing interestingly (in Chapter 2), psychological description and dramatized copy are *effective because they keep the reader involved and show that you have the you-viewpoint*. The only way to get it in the first place, however, is to subordinate your own reactions to those you estimate are the other person's and to show that attitude clearly by your wording.

An example of well-intentioned writing that is fundamentally bad (because writer dominated) is the conventional thank-you beginning: "Thank you for your order of June 2 for . . ." and "We are grateful for . . . ." Even worse is the selfish "We are glad to have your order for . . . ." All three emphasize the personal reaction of the writer rather than something the reader is interested in knowing. The same is true of the common, and weak, speech openings "I'm glad to be here . . ." and "Thank you for . . . ."

If you agree with a request or can fill an order, an opening like the following has more you-viewpoint because it is something your reader wants to know:

Your suggestion of getting the general manager's help on our planning is in effect. I've made the arrangements.

––

```
Your . . . should arrive by prepaid UPS no later than
Friday, June 7.
```

If you can't do as suggested or make shipment, a favorable comment is a better example of you-viewpoint than the selfish statement of pleasure from the implied compliment or upon the receipt of another order—or a disappointing statement about not now getting the ordered goods.

```
Having our chief accountant in on our planning session
would indeed be a good idea if she were not already
committed to an out-of-town assignment at the time.
```

When the reader has done you a favor and your main message is appreciation, some form of thank you may be one of the best beginnings you could use. In other situations, in place of the conventional "Dear Mr. Miller," the salutation "Thank you, Mr. Miller!" has directness and enthusiasm which are heartwarming. The first paragraph may then concentrate on a more significant point:

```
Those articles about palletization which you suggested
contain some of the best information I've been able to
uncover.
```

But doesn't the statement of the significance you attach to your reader's contribution adequately establish your appreciation, without wasting words with "Thank you"?

We do not mean to imply that an expression of gratitude is out of place (see "Gratitude" in Chapter 3). But we do want to stress that (1) You usually have something more important to put in the emphatic beginning position and (2) Besides, you can accomplish the same "Thank you" function with some statement which will place more emphasis on your reader—where it should be!

ADAPTATION

The preceding remarks concerning planned presentation and you-viewpoint apply whether you're writing a memorandum, making a speech, or sending a special or form letter. The closer you can come to making your reader or listener nod in agreement and think "That's what I want to hear," the greater your possibilities for a favorable reception.

When you can make the other person also think "That sure fits me," you have an additional advantage. Successful adaptation gives the feeling that you had the one person specifically in mind.

Even in addressing a large number of people, you will usually have identifiable common characteristics (of geography, age, educational level, vocation, or income status, for example). By thinking about them, you can adapt your persuasion points, language, and style and make references to circumstances and events recognized as fitting by each member of the group.

Adapting talking points

In adapting talking points (or theme), you simply *seek out and emphasize those reasons you believe will be most influential in causing the particular receivers to take the action or reaction you want*. Specifically, you would try to sell a typewriter to a secretary on the basis of ease of operation, to an office manager on ease of maintenance and durability, but to a purchasing agent on the basis of long-range cost. The lawn mower which you would sell to a home-owner because of its ease of handling and maintenance, you would sell to a hardware dealer because of its salability and profit margin. A car may appeal to one person on the basis of economy, power, or dependability of operation; to another the appeals of appearance and comfort may be stronger.

Accordingly, you adapt your talking points for increased persuasiveness. This is a fairly simple procedure when you are dealing with one person and is entirely possible in a group if you study the characteristics common to all people involved.

Adapting language and style

You adapt language and style, in general, in the light of the other person's age, educational level, and vocation (which influence social and economic position). As years, education, professional and social prestige, and financial status increase, you are safer in using longer sentences, uncommon words, and more formal language (but remember the discussion of readability in Chapter 2). Sometimes you will want to use the specialized terms of vocational classes such as doctors, lawyers, and insurance people. Although some of these terms are too specialized for a general audience, to specialists they convey the impression that you understand their special problems. The application of this suggestion means that when you write or talk to doctors, references to patients, laboratories, diagnoses, and the like help; to a person in insurance, prospects, premiums, and expirations are likely referents.

Referring to common experiences

Better adaptation than language and style, however, are references to common experiences. A reference to vocation, to a geographical factor, to some home and family status—in fact, to any activity or reaction you can be reasonably sure your readers or listeners have experienced—rings the bell of recognition and makes them feel that very definitely you are talking to them and about their conditions.

In a letter to college students, for instance, the following reference would almost universally bring positive (and in most cases humorous) recognition:

```
When your teacher talks on . . . and on . . . and on
. . . (even when it's two minutes past the
bell!). . . .
```

To parents:

> When your child yawns, turns over, and <u>finally</u> goes to
> sleep.

To school superintendents:

> . . . to reduce the necessary and healthy noise of
> active adolescents when they're changing classes.

To anyone who is or has been a secretary:

> An hour's transcription to get in the night's mail——
> and at five minutes to 5:00!

Any of the preceding phrases could go into a form or an individualized message. The more specifically you can phrase these references to make them pinpoint one person, however, the more effective your adaptation will be.

Personalizing

The starting purpose of specific adaptation is, of course, to further the impression that you have prepared the message for the individual. To heighten the feeling of friendliness, business communicators sometimes use names or other individualizing references in a few of the sentences. At about the middle, much as you use a friend's name in conversation—or near the end in the same way you frequently use a person's name in ending a conversation—such references as the following help to give the impression that your message is for one person rather than a group:

> You'll also appreciate the lightness of the
> Multimower, Mr. Allen.
>
> ——
>
> Your Dallas Luminall dealer will be glad to call on
> you and answer any other questions you may have, Mr.
> Bowen.

In individually typed messages the placement of the name presents no problem; in forms, try to put the name at the end of a line (as in the preceding examples) so that typing in the reader's name is easy, regardless of length.

Lest we overemphasize the effectiveness of this name-calling, however, we point out these shortcomings and dangers:

1. It is a somewhat mechanical process and probably the least effective means of adapting.
2. In typing names on forms, you may do more harm than good unless you match type perfectly. Of course if you can afford a word-processing machine, it can do the job.
3. And, as you saw under "Undue familiarity" in Chapter 3, using a person's name too frequently (as many computerized letters do) may do more harm than good by seeming unctuous and fawning.

You can also increase the feeling of friendliness in letters by the wording of your salutation and complimentary close (as explained in Chapter 1). Of far greater significance, however, are adaptation of talking points and lifelike references to the reader's activities. The following letter answers the lady's questions in a sound sales presentation and enhances the persuasiveness of the message with special references (such as to the housekeeper and the power failure mentioned in her inquiry) that could apply to no one but the reader:

Dear Mrs. Jackson:

The Stair-Traveler you saw in the June <u>Home and Yard</u> will certainly make daily living easier for you and your faithful old housekeeper. You can make as many trips upstairs and downstairs as you care to <u>every day</u> and still follow your doctor's advice.

Simply sit down on the bench (about the same size as a dressing-table stool) and press the button. Gently and smoothly your Stair-Traveler takes you upstairs at a rate just a little faster than ordinary walking. Should the electricity fail in Greenbriar while you're using your Stair-Traveler, automatic brakes bring it to a gentle stop until the current comes on. Then you just press the button to start it again.

Folded back against the wall when not in use, the Stair-Traveler's simple, straight lines of mahogany will blend in well with your antiques. Your Stair-Traveler will be right at home on your front straight stairway, Mrs. Jackson. It will be more convenient for you there, and the installation is simple and economical. Notice the folded Stair-Traveler on page 3 of the booklet I'm sending; it looks somewhat like a console table.

To explain how simple and economical installing your Stair-Traveler can be, Mr. J. B. Nickle, our Memphis representative, will be glad to call at a time convenient for you. Will you use the enclosed postcard to let him know when that will be?

Such specialized references do increase costs when they mean writing an individualized message rather than using a form. But many times you must if you are to get the job done. Even in form paragraphs and entire form letters, however, you can make some adaptation to the reader's situation.

You can find out a great deal about your reader through letters to you, your credit records (including credit reports), sales representatives' reports, and the like. Even a bought or rented mailing list contains the names of people with some common characteristics of vocation, location, age, sex, finances, and buying and living habits. You won't make your message do all it could do if you don't use these common characteristics to adapt it according to talking points and endow it with the marginal pulling power of known references to familiar events, activities, places, or persons.

POSITIVE STATEMENT

Your letters, memos, and oral communications have greater prospects for success if you focus on positive ideas too—because people respond more favorably to a positive prospect than to a negative one.

Saying the cheerful, positive thing that people want to hear rather than the unpleasant or unhappy, negative thing is really just an extension of you-viewpoint. It comes from staying optimistic yourself and superimposing a positive picture on a negative one, thus at least subordinating the negative idea. Translated into business communication procedures, *it is stressing what something is rather than what it is not, emphasizing what the firm or product can and will do rather than what it cannot, leading with action rather than apology or explanation, and avoiding words that convey basically unpleasant ideas.*

Test after test of both advertising copy and letter copy has demonstrated the wisdom of positive statement. That is why years ago successful copywriters warned against the denied negative (and today's writers still issue the same warning). That is why the effective writer or speaker will make the following positive statements rather than their negative counterparts:

Negative	*Positive*
The Binks industrial spray nozzle is not the usual gobs, splotches, and runs painter everybody hates.	The Binks industrial spray nozzle paints continuously and evenly at the coverage its operator chooses and sets it.
We are sorry that we cannot furnish the club chairs by August 16.	After checking with the Production Department, we can definitely assure you your club chairs by August 29.
We cannot ship in lots of less than 12.	To keep down packaging costs and to help customers save on shipping costs, we ship in lots of 12 or more.
I have no experience other than clerking in my father's grocery store.	Clerking in my father's grocery store for three summers taught me the value of serving people courteously and promptly.

A special form of negativism is the challenging question which invites a negative answer. Although it contains no negative wording, "What could be finer than an XYZ dishwasher?" will elicit, among other answers, "A full-time maid!" Such questions, along with the apparently harmless "Why not try a Blank product?" get people out of step with you and, because they invite a negative response, are deterrents to the success of your suggestion.

Keeping your messages positive also means deliberately excluding negative words. You can't be "sorry" about something without recalling the initial unhappy experience. You can't say "unfortunately" without restating some gloomy aspect of a situation. Nor can you mention "delay," "broken," "damages," "unable to," "cannot," "inconvenience," "difficulty," "disappointment," and other negatives without stressing some element of the situation which makes people react against you rather than with you. Even a "however," after you've been talking pleasant things, will surely give a kind of sinking feeling.

For all these reasons the effective writer will say "ABC Dog Biscuits will help keep your dog healthy" instead of "ABC Dog Biscuits will help keep your dog from getting sick." It's just a question of *accentuating the positive, eliminating the negative where possible, and otherwise subordinating it* (see **Emp** and **Neg** in Appendix F).

SUCCESS CONSCIOUSNESS

Success consciousness is the confident attitude that your reader or listener will do what you ask or accept the decision you present. To reflect this attitude, guard against any phrasing which suggests that you may not get the action you want.

Success consciousness is your own conviction that your explanation is adequate, your suggestion legitimate and valuable, and your decision the result of adequate evidence and logical, businesslike reasoning. Thus assured yourself, you are not likely to say something which suggests that you are unsure of your ground. The sales writer who says

> <u>If you'd like</u> to take advantage of this timesaving piece of equipment, put your check and completed order blank in the enclosed envelope and drop it in the mail today. . . .

would be better off not to remind the reader of the option to reject the proposal. Simply omitting the phrase *if you'd like* establishes a tone of greater confidence. The one word *if* is the most frequent destroyer of success consciousness.

Likewise, when tempted to say

> <u>Why not</u> try a sample order?

you should remember that the suggestion is stronger with the elimination of *why not.* It has not only the disadvantage of suggesting that you are not sure but also the distinct disadvantage of inviting consideration of reasons for not doing what you want.

Hope and its synonym *trust* are second only to *if* as destroyers of success consciousness. In proposing an adjustment, the sentence

```
We hope you'll approve of our decision.
```

gains success consciousness (and thus better response) when reworded:

```
With this extension of your contract for our
professional personnel-screening services, you can
continue to select only high-quality employees in
these critical times.
```

By assumption (implication)—by definitely omitting the doubtful-sounding expression—the seller seems to say, "Of course, you and I realize that this is what you want."

In refusals something like the following sentence sometimes appears in an otherwise well-written message:

```
We trust you will understand our position.
```

Usually, however, it appears in a poor one. And it is most frequently the result of inadequate explanation. The writer seems to despair of giving an adequate explanation and to hope that the reader will figure out one. If you find yourself feeling that way, go back and see whether your explanation is adequate. If so, omit such a sentence; if not, revise your explanation so that it is convincing—and substitute some positive, confident statement for the weak-kneed expression.

Even in simple replies the problem arises with such a sentence as

```
We hope this is the information you wanted.
```

The implications of doubt disappear quickly and easily with

```
We're glad to send you this information.
```

This principle of success consciousness applies in all types of business writing and speaking, but it is most significant in sales situations—and especially in the action ending.

A word of caution against high-pressure presumptuousness is in order here, however. To omit a reference to an alternative is one thing; to imply that no alternative exists is quite another! The job applicant who so boldly and confidently asks

```
When may I come in to see you?
```

gives the impression that the prospective employer has no alternative but to set up an interview. Such presumptuousness may irritate—at a critical time. Rephrased like the following, a request for an interview would strike most people favorably:

```
Will you give me a convenient time when I may come in
and tell you more about why I believe I am the
aggressive sales representative you're looking for?
```

The proper degree of success consciousness requires careful wording, particularly at the end. Basically, you need to consider what your purpose is.

Sometimes you want someone to take no overt action on the topic—as in most B–plan messages and some A–plans. In that case you may end with a pleasant comment or further support for something said earlier (thanks or resale, for example), with an off-the-subject comment (usually a pleasant look to the future, perhaps sales promotion material), or with something else pleasant. Certainly you want to avoid suggesting inadequacy of treatment and such jargon as "Please do not hesitate . . ." or "Feel free to . . . ." And in B–plan messages guard particularly against referring back to the trouble you've supposedly cleared up.

At other times you are asking for action that is simple, easy, and likely—as in most A–plan messages (no strong reader resistance). Here a subtle reference to or suggestion of that action is most appropriate:

```
I shall appreciate your answers to . . . .

You are cordially invited to . . . .

When you send in your check for the $27.50 now due,
please . . . .
```

In C–plan letters, memos, and talks you are asking for action the reader or listener may be at first reluctant to take. The force of your push for action—to overcome resistance—must therefore continue to the end. Here particularly, such words as *if*, *trust*, and *hope* show a lack of success consciousness that is self-defeating.

As you see, each of the three situations requires a quite different ending. You will do well, therefore, to keep in mind the principle of success consciousness as you study the discussions, illustrations, and checklists for different classes of business messages throughout this book.

One important general point deserves your attention here, however: Even though the earlier part of the letter, memo, or talk may have indicated a desired action, you need to *refer to, suggest, ask for, or push for that action at the end*.

EXERCISES

1. Give an instance of a politician's (preferably presidential) use of success consciousness—whether effective or ineffective and whether justified or patently pretended.
2. From the many points you would like to get across to varied people, cite one in positive-statement form (and provide a less positive statement for comparison).

3. From your own experience, provide an example of effective or ineffective adaptation; then tell how it might have been (for better or worse).

4. From your own experience, tell an instance in which you or somebody else used or ignored the you-attitude; then tell how it might have been (for better or worse).

5. From your own experience, tell an instance where you or somebody else applied or ignored the principles of planned presentation in
   a. A good-news message.
   b. A bad-news message.
   c. A situation calling for persuasion.

6. Give any evidence or reasoning (not speculation) you can that any of the principles in this chapter might not work equally in some other culture.

Rewrite for you-attitude, positive aspect, and goodwill.

7. You cannot join our mutual fund until you contribute a minimum of $500.

8. If your correct name is Lou V. Harwood, you may complete the enclosed Request for Correction of Name, and return it with your contract for endorsement.

9. We do not send receipts of payment because of the extra work involved and because your canceled check serves as a receipt.

10. We regret that we neglected to answer your letter sooner. Unfortunately, we did not have all the necessary information.

11. We cannot quote you a price on the installation of air conditioning until our engineers have submitted an estimate.

Applications of Part 1 principles

A. From a current magazine, book, or newspaper find a passage (or passages) using sexist language in at least five sentences. Rephrase the sentences to eliminate the sexism and submit your work in a form that shows clearly the original and the revision.

B. For the second paragraph under the section **Make it easy and interesting to read** (middle of Chapter 2):

1. Figure the Fog Index.
2. Rewrite it as best you can.
3. Figure the Fog Index on your rewrite.

C. Which is better and why?

1. *a*. I am enclosing a copy of the news release that appeared in the *Decatur Star* on May 16, 1975. I am also enclosing a copy of the release we sent to them to be published. As you will note, they changed it quite a bit.
   b. The enclosed news release and a copy of the release we sent the *Decatur Star* differ specifically in . . . .

2. *a*. As you requested, I am sending you notification of the profit made by the Springfield City Board of Education Lunchroom Division on the summer program this year. We cleared $46,691.92.
   b. After paying all bills, the Springfield City Board of Education Lunchroom Division cleared $46,691.92 on the summer program this year.

3. *a*. Please thank your Bachelor Living Class for the delicious meal they prepared. The food was absolutely delicious and beautifully prepared.
   b. Please thank the members of your Bachelor Living Class for the delicious meal they prepared and served. I especially enjoyed the sour-cream yellow squash casserole.

4. *a*. On Friday, December 10, 1982, the Order Department employees will have a Christmas party at the Golden Corral, 2926 McMillan Road, 7:00 P.M. Each employee may bring one guest, and each person should bring a $5 gift. All persons will pay for their own meals.

b. On December 10, 1982 (Friday night) the order department employees will have a Christmas party at the Golden Corral, at 2926 McMillan Road at 7:00 P.M. Each employee may bring one guest. Each person should bring a $5 gift that is useful and can be used by anyone. Each person will pay for their own meal.

5. *a.* The company cafeteria served meals to the following groups in conjunction with the company's image-building program:

b. This letter will certify that the company cafeteria served meals to the following groups in conjunction with the company's image-building program:

D. As a practice exercise, set up one of the following letters in acceptable format, content, and wording as directed by your instructor:

1. *Letterhead:* Allis-Chalmers, Box 512, Milwaukee, Wisconsin 53201. *Inside address:* Aubrey Macklin, 2319 Bitter Creek, Austin, Texas 78744. *Signature block:* Sincerely yours, Robert B. Wilkinson, Counsel and Director, Patent Law Department. *Subject:* Re: T-post Setter/Puller Attachment for Farm Tractor. *Body:* In accordance with our standard procedure, your letter has been stamped "Received (date), Allis-Chalmers Patent Law Dept." and is being returned herewith without copies being retained by us. Thank you for your recent letter pertaining to the above subject. We ask that you sign and return one copy of the enclosed Form 2972–5 with each unpatented idea submitted. If you have an issued U.S. patent, please send us a copy or advise the number so we may order a copy. Our company is always interested in reviewing new ideas. Like most companies, we have a standard policy for receiving disclosure material from nonemployees and I am enclosing a copy of a leaflet which explains this policy. We will see that appropriate people in our company have an opportunity to study your disclosure and advise you of their decision as promptly as possible. We appreciate your thinking of Allis-Chalmers.

2. *Letterhead:* Florida Farm Bureau Insurance Companies, Post Office Box 730, Gainesville, FL 32601. Use current date. *Inside address:* Dr. Paul R. Gregory, 1125 Northwest 61st Place, Gainesville, FL 32603. *Signature block:* Sincerely yours, Harold McCallister, Vice President. *Body:* Your Better Letters course was excellent. Just how much practical application our graduates are making of what they learned remains to be seen. At your convenience, please review the enclosed letters. We would appreciate your evaluation of them, and your comments on improvement, or the lack of it.

3. No letterhead, but instead use a *heading* that includes the sender's address (606 Queens Road, Indianapolis, IN 46220) and the current date. *Inside address:* Mr. Andrew Blackweld, Teacher of Vocational Agriculture, Newberry High School, Newberry, Indiana 44714. *Signature block:* Sincerely, Joseph M. Knight. *Body:* Are you finding it is hard to get enough money to operate your land laboratories effectively? Even with the high cost of agricultural products and the country's constant requests for explanations, many agricultural teachers

feel that their school boards do not allocate enough funds to operate their labs. I feel that most board members simply do not know very accurately either the costs of operating a good school lab for vocational agriculture or the educational values that can come from one. By answering the enclosed short questionnaire, and having your students do the same, you may help me relieve this problem. The questionnaires will help me to write a better report to the county school board concerning the value of land laboratories relative to their cost. Only I will see the returned questionnaires. You can be certain that what you say will be held in the strictest of confidence. But, if you have no objections, I would like to be able to quote you. Please answer the questionnaire and add any other thoughts you may have. When finished, just put them in the enclosed stamped envelope and drop it in the mailbox. You will be doing yourself, your fellow teachers, and your students a great service. Since the final report is due the last week of May, the information would be most helpful if you would return it by May 12.

4. *Letterhead:* Lyon's Building Supplies, Berry Road, Olathe, Kansas 66061. *Inside address:* George P. White, Chattahoochee Brick Company, Atlanta, GA 30305. *Signature block:* Sincerely yours, Joseph Morrison Young, President. *Subject:* Requested confidential information about Paul Rhodes. *Body:* Since Rhodes came here as an accountant and assistant business manager 18 months ago, he has advanced until he is now plant manager. Paul is a hard worker and very eager to succeed in everything he attempts. Sometimes he drives himself into a tense condition, but he always seems to thrive on the challenge his job offers him, and I am sure that in a larger plant like Chattahoochee he would be confronted with enough challenge to satisfy him. Also Paul and his wife want to live in a larger city where they can enjoy all the cultural opportunities a city has to offer. Although at Lyon's Paul has no opportunity to sell, saleswork probably wouldn't be hard for him because he does enjoy people, is impressive looking, and is persistent. All of our employees like Paul—even our truck drivers, for whom he has to plan very strict budgets. In many ways I would hate to lose Paul, but I know he wants larger horizons.

How to win the reader's approval and motivate action

part 2

Neutral and good-news messages

5

Though people use the telephone for many of the simpler kinds of neutral and good-news messages discussed in this chapter, they are also, using more and more letters and memos. For efficiency in handling varied situations as a manager, employee, or individual conducting your own business affairs, therefore, you need the skills and techniques to write the messages well.

As you learned in Chapter 4, messages that give what the receiver wants should do so in the opening phrases. The emphasis should be on speed, specificness, completeness, and conciseness. Inquiries, favorable replies, credit approvals, and adjustment approvals are typical of A–plan, direct-style messages.

Routine claims also should be direct, since they are reports most firms welcome as means for improving service.

Similarly, in courtesy exchanges of information about job and credit applicants (where regardless of whether the information is favorable or unfavorable to the applicant, it is what the inquirer wants to know), the message should begin directly with a key point.

Most of the communications you're likely to prepare in doing business internationally will also be direct exchanges of information. Often they will be by Telex or short covering letters (such as inquiries or replies) supplemented by standardized forms (like those shown in Appendix C) for establishing credit, quoting prices and terms or conditions, and invoicing shipments. Of course they should be clear, concise, and specific—and preferably in the language of the receiver—as explained in Chapter 2. Most of them should also be direct, as explained here.

DIRECT INQUIRIES

Any firm that wants to stay in business welcomes inquiries about products, services, operations, and personnel. The possibility of making a sale will motivate a reply concerning the firm's products. An inquiry about routine operations will get a reply out of simple business friendship. Requests for information about job and credit applicants get ready answers because giving such information is established business courtesy based on the principle of reciprocity.

In no case would the attitude toward such inquiries be negative; if it is not one of eagerness to comply, at least it is willingness. In a direct inquiry you therefore have no problem of motivating a response. Your problem is making clear exactly what you want, so that the willing responder can give you the necessary information with as little expenditure of time and energy as possible. Resolve this problem by beginning directly and being specific and concise.

About products. Requests for catalogs, price lists, descriptive folders, and other information about products and services should be direct, specific, and brief—as in this interoffice memo:

```
What day in October will you schedule the annual R & D
Plans Board meeting? I want to be sure both my
department heads will be free to attend.

Will we meet in the main conference room at
headquarters as we did last year?
```

Notice the direct question and the specific phrases "What day in October" and "in the main conference room."

The following letter to a resort hotel is another good example of desirable directness and specificness:

```
Please send me descriptive material about your
accommodations, recreational facilities, and rates.

My wife, 16-year-old daughter, and I are planning a
two- or three-weeks' stay in the South this fall and
are considering the Edgewater Gulf.
```

Without the second paragraph, the writer would get much more information than needed, and that only in general terms. With the second paragraph, however, the hotel can give the necessary basic information *and* only the special information that would interest this family group.

A specific paragraph indicating special interests would help even more:

```
My wife and I are primarily interested in the golf
facilities and in dinner dancing; our daughter insists
that she be able to ride horseback every day.
```

Out-of-the-ordinary questions involving special conditions require detailed answers for satisfaction. Because they also require explanation before the reader can get a clear picture, they are better set out in expository paragraph form, as in the following:

```
Where will the World Business Communication Convention
meet this year, and when? I believe Professor Arvind
M. Velankar of Pune, India, said that the meeting
would be in Tokyo in November.

Since I'll be spending all of November in Japan, I
could easily be a part of the meeting and even present
```

```
a paper on some of the problems we face in
intercultural communication. I presented such a paper
at the American Marketing Association last April in
New York. Do you have any provisions for paying for
papers?

With all the cutbacks for travel, I'll not have much
spending allowance. What will be the costs for the
registration fee and a hotel room for one person?
```

An inquiry should start with a direct question or identification of the subject *before* explanations of why you ask. A question commands more attention than a statement; the reader sees the reason for the explanation; and such an arrangement nearly always saves words.

About people. Similarly, *personnel inquiries* should begin with the key question and follow with necessary explanations and specific questions:

```
SUBJECT: INQUIRY ABOUT JAMES R. SULLIVAN

While Mr. Sullivan worked under you as a part-time
instructor in marketing, did he show an aptitude for
selling? Was he naturally friendly and able to get
along with faculty and students alike?

We are considering him for the job of sales manager in
the North Ohio territory. Since he listed you as a
former supervisor, we would welcome your comments.

As sales manager he would have to supervise the work
of two junior sales representatives in this territory.
We are particularly interested, therefore, in your
evaluation of his leadership ability.

We would appreciate your giving us this and any other
confidential information that will help us come to a
decision and shall be glad to help you in the same way
when we can.
```

Direct credit applications—those where no question exists about the desirability of the account—are just as simple and concise as other direct inquiries. A telephone call or a direct-style letter immediately phrasing the request and giving the necessary information is appropriate:

```
Will you please open a charge account in the name of
          Mr. or Mrs. J. T. Tolloway
          76 Idlewild Drive
          Dallas, Texas 75221

We have just moved here from 27 Crescent Drive, Denver
80202.

Stores with which we have had accounts for about five
years in Denver are the White House, Foleys, J. P.
Price & Co., and the Town and Country Shop.
```

> I am employed as a supervisor at the L. B. Price
> Distributing Company where I earn $30,500 annually;
> Mrs. Holloway is not employed.
>
> The Merchants National Bank handled our checking
> account in Denver. Our local bank is the First
> National.

Despite having given enough information of the kind usually required for credit extension or refusal, however, the inquirer need not be surprised to receive an application form. Most merchants have standard forms which they require all charge customers to fill in to complete a contractual agreement. In fact, a telephone call or visit to the credit department giving the same information or asking for the form might serve the purpose just as well.

Requests from business firms of national reputation, with solid capitalization and unquestioned ratings, are also direct and simple. Information about such firms is readily available from any number of credit sources. They can assume acceptability of their credit; so the application for it may be only by implication. By telephone, Telex, or letter from an authorized agent (usually a purchasing agent), an order might contain no more than the following:

> Please ship subject to your usual terms 6 dozen Samson
> 10-inch locking plier wrenches.

If the receiver might not readily recognize the company name, adding a note like "We are listed in Dun & Bradstreet" or "We have done credit business with . . ." would be proper.

Credit inquiries from one business house to another are as direct, concise, and specific as those about products. Because they ask for the same kind of information over and over again (explained later under "Credit Approvals"), in most instances they should be forms. The following form inquiry is typical, with a time-saving space for the answer(s):

> Will you please give us the confidential information
> requested below?
>
> In applying for credit with us, the applicant gave us
> your name as a reference.
>
> We would appreciate the courtesy. Any time we can
> return the favor, please call on us.
>
> Applicant: John Y. Bowen
> Length of time sold on credit _____
> Credit limit (if any) _____ Credit terms _____
> Current amount due _____ Past due _____
> Highest credit extended _____ Most recent credit ____
> Paying habits _____
> Remarks _____

When, however, special circumstances arise which the form does not cover, you'll need to write a special letter. Like any direct request, it should get right down to business:

```
SUBJECT: CREDIT INQUIRY ABOUT MR. H. F. GREEN,
         GROCER, VINITA, OKLAHOMA
```

Will you please send us a confidential summary of your credit experience with Mr. Green?

Naturally we'd like to have the usual items which reveal his buying and paying habits.

But since we learned from one of the companies here in McAlester that Mr. Green buys a large part of his supplies from you and that he has given your name as a credit reference very recently, we'd like to have your explanation of why he did not list your firm when he applied for credit with us.

We shall appreciate your help and shall be glad to assist you in the same way any time we can.

When you ask your reader to give information about people, as in inquiries about job and credit applicants, both of you face a special problem—*compliance with the libel and other laws*. You have a duty to help protect your information source. Of course, truth is the most important protection, but truth alone is not complete protection in some states.

You can help by making the reply what lawyers call a *privileged* communication. You show that you have an interest to protect, and you promise to keep the information confidential.[1] As a matter of courtesy but with no legal significance, you say that the inquiry was authorized (if true). Otherwise, inquiries and replies about people are the same as those about other things.

Perhaps you noticed that the preceding examples expressed appreciation and offered to return the favor. Especially when asking people to do things without any obvious benefit to themselves, courtesy demands just that. Usually the best way is in connection with your request for specific reader action (generally the last paragraph). But don't be presumptuous or jargonistic about it by using the lazy "Thank you in advance." Instead, express it in first person, future tense—as those writers did. And if *shall* or *will* sounds too presumptuous or imperious, change to *should* or *would*. To be sure you do it properly, see "Gratitude" in Chapter 3.

You can increase your chances of getting an answer, or a faster answer, if you can justifiably ask for it by a certain date. (People are inclined to put

[1]You go ahead and promise confidentiality despite the fact that you can't keep the information confidential under certain conditions. The Fair Credit Reporting Act empowers the subject of such a report to see what was said to whom and by whom if the information bears on a turndown for credit, insurance, or employment.

DIRECT INQUIRY CHECKLIST

1. Get this message under way quickly.
   a. A subject line may help by showing the nature of the inquiry, but don't depend on it (or any other heading) for coherence or as the antecedent for any pronoun.
   b. Make your question(s) specific (not just "some information" but "what sizes . . .").
   c. For a fast opening, imply ideas or refer to them subordinately.
      Slow, plodding:
      "Will you please give us some information about Travis Brannon? He reports that . . . ."
      Fast-moving:
      "What would be your reaction if Travis Brannon, your former assistant, walked into your office trying to sell you . . .?"

2. Be careful about the form and wording of the questions.
   a. Ask directly for information; don't hint. "I should like to know if . . ." is wordy and slow. "What does the . . ." is faster.
   b. Word questions to get what you want—not just yes or no when you need an explanation. Avoid questions phrased to suggest a certain answer, too broad questions (". . . any information you have"), and double-barreled questions (". . . whether . . . and, if so, . . .?").
   c. If you want to run a series of questions, itemize (tabulate); but provide explanations the reader needs for pointed answers.

3. Cover at least all the basic questions to which you want answers.
   a. Ask the minimum number of questions to get the information.
   b. Arrange questions in the most appropriate order.

4. Express gratitude cordially in first person, future tense: "I would be grateful (or appreciate)" eliminates the awkwardness and wordiness of "It will be appreciated if . . ." and the presumptuousness of "Thank you in advance." If appropriate, offer to reciprocate.

5. At the end, confident and positive reference to the reader's next action makes a coherent summary to the entire message, leaves your reader clear as to what you want done, and stimulates action. For a surer, faster response, justify and ask for an answer by a certain date.

6. In inquiries about people, establish the privileged aspects.
   a. Be sure your explanation shows you have an interest to protect.
   b. Promise confidential treatment of the information.
   c. If the inquiry is authorized, say so (for courtesy, not legal reasons).

things off—especially if the benefit is not obvious and immediate.) Therefore you should consider justifying and end-dating:

```
Because Mr. Sullivan wants our decision by the end of
the month, we would especially appreciate your answer
by the 25th.
```

Getting credit information on potential overseas buyers may be a little more difficult, but you have various sources that will help you.

1. You can request the names of the customers' banks and the names of other companies (references) with whom they have done business nationally or overseas.
2. Your own bank may be able to help through its correspondent banks here and overseas.
3. The *World Traders Data Reports* (U.S. Department of Commerce) supply sales information, financial references, and trade references.
4. Dun and Bradstreet's International Division publishes reports.
5. The Export-Import Bank of the United States has free information.
6. The Foreign Credit Interchange Bureau (FCIB), a subsidiary of the National Association of Credit Management, has bulletins on foreign markets and economic conditions, credit interchange reports, worldwide collections service, and consultation services.

The most important considerations to keep in mind about direct inquiries are to get started in a hurry, to be as specific in your questions as you can, and to explain enough (but only enough) for your reader to answer well and easily. The accompanying Direct Inquiry Checklist will help you with most of your inquiry problems, although it is not a prescription, a coverall, or a cure-all.

None of the checklists in this book are. And they are especially not outlines. If you try to use the appropriate checklist as an outline, you will simply not be able to come up with a good message to handle the particular situation. Instead, use the checklists for what we designed them for. First, draft your message. *Then* use the checklist to make sure you have covered everything you should have and said everything appropriately (though we realize that not all points apply to every case).

FAVORABLE REPLIES

Any company or person desiring the goodwill of others replies to all reasonable inquiries—and does so promptly. If a delay is necessary, some explanation should go quickly indicating the reason and approximately when to expect a complete answer:

> Your request for information about robotization is one for Mr. J. S. McConnough, our industrial engineering specialist, who will be in Denver for another 10 days.
>
> Shortly after he returns to the office, he will write you.

The situation appears to contain no possibilities of sales but, as in the case of any inquiry, represents at least a good opportunity to make a friend. Proper handling might well lead to a sale.

Because some inquiries ask only for assistance, whereas others readily indicate a potential customer (and a quite different reply), we divide this discussion into (1) replies to inquiries without apparent sales possibilities (including reports dealing with personnel and credit applicants) and (2) replies to inquiries with sales possibilities (often called invited sales messages).

Replies without sales possibilities

When someone asks you something, you say either yes or no—in an A–plan or a B–plan reply. For all practical purposes an undecided, noncommittal response like "Well, I'll think it over" is a refusal and needs to be handled in the B–plan inductive style (reasons before conclusion). This section deals only with good-news (A–plan) replies; refusals and modified refusals come later (Chapter 7).

In favorable replies without sales possibilities, particular points to watch are the direct beginning, completeness of coverage, and (when appropriate) resale.

Direct beginning. The fundamental principle in all A–plan replies is to say yes immediately and thus gain increased goodwill, as well as save time and words. Your compliance is the point of greatest interest—of far greater interest than any expressions of your gratitude. When you can do what somebody has asked you to do, begin by doing it or with a statement indicating that you will do it.

The direct beginning can also establish many ideas by implication, thus shortening your message:

> We are glad to send you these last three annual reports of National Reaper, Inc. and to add your name to our mailing list to receive future copies as they come out, around March 1 each year.

The direct beginning also establishes a cheerful, ungrudging tone and eliminates pompousness. Observe the difference between the following slow, grudging, jargonistic original and the revision:

Indirect, wordy, grudging	*Direct, compact, cheerful*
We have your request for our <u>HOW</u> book.	Here is your copy of the <u>HOW</u> book.
It was prepared primarily for material–handling engineers, and so we were not prepared for the numerous requests we have received from schools. We are sending you one, however, and hope you	We prepared it after extensive research by our material–handling engineers with the help of consultants and plant workers who specialize in material–handling methods. We're sure

Indirect, wordy, grudging	*Direct, compact, cheerful*
will find it helpful.	you'll find it useful in the classroom.
If there is any other way we can be of assistance, please do not hesitate to call on us.	

Note that the revised version not only begins directly but makes comments on the book showing it is something special. In such situations, where you send helpful information, you have every reason to enhance the desirability of what you've done and to offer to do more (unless you specifically do not want to). Also note that the direct beginning makes unnecessary any reference to the inquiry and saves space.

Completeness of coverage.   Obviously, you need to take up every question in an inquiry. When you fail to do so, extra correspondence results (or your reader marks you as careless, indifferent, or ignorant). At times, of course, you can't answer—because you don't know, or because you can't reveal the information. In either case simply tell your reader so, but don't ignore the question.

When questions call for strictly factual answers, when the inquiry tabulates questions and leaves space for answering, your job is easy. When the answers must be evaluative and expository, your job is sometimes not so easy.

The following personnel report answers a typical inquiry about the subject's selling ability, personality, cultural background, character, and integrity. Note the effect of *embedding* the necessary negative in the middle and interpreting it along with a positive characteristic of the applicant. Note, too, that the reply is not a recommendation but a *personnel report* of the writer's experience with and evaluation of the applicant—as it should be.

SUBJECT: CONFIDENTIAL REPORT ON TRAVIS BRANNON

Mr. Brannon is a careful, accurate worker with lots of initiative. And he makes friends readily.

I got to know Travis quite well while he made two A's in my courses, Sales Management and Public Relations, and later when he graded papers, had conferences with students, and did clerical jobs as a student assistant. His questions in class and in conferences showed a keen understanding of business problems and a calm, practical approach to their solution. And his term reports showed solid, serious, yet original business thinking.

Impressed with his scholastic performance, his friendliness and ability to get along with people, and his obvious wide range of interests, I asked Travis to be my assistant. Then I particularly liked the

quickness with which he caught on to assigned jobs and
the willingness and accuracy with which he did a job
every time it came up after I had explained it to him
only once. On many small jobs and some not so small he
went ahead and did what was necessary without being
told.

As he demonstrated ability, I let him do more and
more. And he accepted the added responsibility and
authority with obvious delight. As a result of such
unbridled enthusiasm, I occasionally had to change a
grade or contradict what he had told a student in
conference. When that happened, he was noticeably
silent for a few days; then he apparently forgot the
incident and became his cheerfully helpful self again.

I must say, Mr. Parks, that I never had to lower a
grade Travis gave a student. I never had one single
reason to suspect that any student had an inside track
with him. He was completely trustworthy with
examinations, grade records, and the like.

Perhaps the most noticeable things about Travis were
his eagerness, his efficiency in making use of all his
time, and his general alertness. These qualities,
though they sometimes led him to interrupt conferences
with students and colleagues, stood him in good stead
with students and faculty alike.

I feel sure that if Travis walked into the office of a
college professor on almost any campus, the reaction
toward him and your company would be favorable.

In most cases giving information about a credit applicant, all you'll need to
do is look at your customer's record and fill in the blanks provided on the
inquiry. But when some atypical factor presents itself (or when the inquiring
firm does not provide blanks), you'll need to write a special message.

In addition to the standard information you may need to incorporate explanations of the effects of local conditions on the size and timing of purchases
or on paying habits. And of course, any unusual question—like the one about
Mr. Green—requires special attention. Since it is usually the reason for the
special letter, it often merits the beginning position, like this:

SUBJECT: CREDIT REPORT ON MR. H. F. GREEN

I suspect that Mr. Green did not list us as a
reference for fear we would retaliate. About a month
ago he was a little miffed when we guessed wrong on
one of his vague orders--and he told us so.

Our relations have always been satisfactory, however,
from our point of view. Since we started doing
business with Mr. Green in August, 1977, we've been
safe in allowing him credit up to $700 several times.

He has a yearly account of about $4,000; his monthly
purchases vary from $30 in the summer to $700 in the
fall. When crop money in the fall spurs payments, Mr.
Green generally takes advantage of our 2/10 EOM
discount. With only a few exceptions, he has paid his
net bill by the 30th. On the two occasions that we had
to press him for collection, he paid up promptly.

Right now is the slack season in the farming regions;
so Mr. Green has let ride his May and June accounts
totaling $700.30. Of this amount, only the May bill of
$382.40 is now overdue. Since, on June 16, he sent in
his $366.60 check in payment of his April account, we
know that Mr. Green pays his bills as soon as he gets
his money. A retired farmer who still owns three
farms, he is the sole owner of his modest store.

I am glad to send you, at your request, this
confidential letter about Mr. Green.

Completeness of coverage does not, however, mean recommendation. Note
that neither the earlier personnel report nor the credit report recommends
the applicant—as they should not—and hence that such letters should not be
called "letters of recommendation."

But in replying about people, completeness *does* require covering the legal
aspects. You could get into trouble by sending damaging information without
meeting the obligations of doing so. Conversely, if you play it straight you
need have no fear.

Legally and morally you are on safe ground only if your report meets the
requirements of a *privileged* communication. First, *don't volunteer information; send it only if requested by somebody with an interest to protect,* and
subordinately make that clear. Beyond that you owe the inquirer, the person
reported on, and the state *the truth as you see it (including your evaluations
and opinions), good faith to avoid misleading or malice, and reasonable care
to be right about facts.*

The accompanying Favorable Reply Checklist summarizes the most important points to keep in mind as you write replies complying with a request
which has no sales possibilities. It applies equally to overseas personnel reports but not credit reports.

The usual method of assuring payment when exporting is to get a letter of
credit (issued by a bank at the importer's request). Your international banker
will check out the foreign bank. A U.S. bank can confirm a letter of credit
and thus guarantee payment. For an example see Appendix C.

Replies with sales possibilities

Failure to answer inquiries and requests of the types we have been discussing will mark you as uncooperative and probably lose you lots of goodwill

FAVORABLE REPLY CHECKLIST

1. Make your opening show that you are doing as asked.
   a. When you are saying yes, sending something, or giving information, do so immediately!
   b. The most effective way to show that you're glad to do something is to do it immediately: not "I am very glad to tell you . . ." but "Henry Benton, about whom you inquired, has served us well as . . . ."
   c. Don't emphasize the obvious: "This is an answer to . . ."; "Concerning your inquiry . . ."; "We have received . . . ."
   d. Consider using a subject line to get you off to a fast start.

2. Completeness, specificness, and correctness are essential.
   a. Answer every question—direct or implied—of the inquiry. Scant, skimpy treatment implies that you are unwilling to extend an ordinary courtesy or that you are dubious.
   b. You want to evaluate when evaluation will be helpful. But do more than editorialize with "fine," "splendid," "excellent." Give specific evidence. In a personnel report, for instance, tell things the applicant did, work habits, personality.
   c. Be careful of the facts; avoid malice or carelessness.

3. Tone is all-important.
   a. In a personnel report:
      (1) Remember that you are reporting, not recommending.
      (2) Beware of superlatives, for accuracy and believability.
   b. Don't do anything grudgingly or parade your generosity.

4. You often have negative material to handle.
   a. Be honest; don't ignore the shortcomings and mislead.
   b. Watch space, word choice, and position to avoid overemphasis on either favorable or unfavorable points.
   c. When you must restrict the use of what you give, be definite—but place the negative in the middle.

5. Remember the libel laws when writing about a person.
   a. Label the information confidential.
   b. Indicate that it has been requested.
   c. Subordinate these ideas in the beginning or ending statements.

6. When sending something tangible, add a few enhancing words.
   a. Make them short.
   b. Make them as specific as you can.

7. End graciously and confidently.
   a. Your expression of willingness—more appropriate here than in the beginning—nullifies any possible curt impression.
   b. Don't suggest inadequacy: "I hope" or "If this is not . . . ."
   c. Omit bromides: "Please do not hesitate" or "Feel free to."

and a good many sales; but failure to answer inquiries with direct sales possibilities is business suicide.

When someone inquires about your goods or services, clearly an unsatisfied need or desire exists and the inquiry implies that you might satisfy it. You have an *interested,* potential customer—a prospect. *If* you give satisfactory information and treatment, you'll probably have a real customer.

Your selling job here is certainly much easier than in the usual sales letter (as discussed in Chapter 8) because the inquirer is already interested and has practically invited you to send a sales letter. You probably spend a lot on advertising to get people into this mood. So don't just sit there!—or just punch a button telling your office machinery to spit out another copy of some form letter that answers three unasked questions, ignores three asked ones, and answers three others.

Although you will be able to write better invited sales letters after studying special sales techniques in Chapter 8, we take them up here because they are the most significant kind of reply any business firm sends—industrial, wholesale, or retail; domestic or international. They are more than goodwill builders; they are sales builders. Accordingly, they draw heavily on the principles discussed in Chapter 4.

In answering an inquiry with sales possibilities, you have no problem securing attentive interest. Your problems are to start favorably, answer all questions, subordinate unfavorable information, handle price positively, and stimulate action.

Getting started positively.   When a prospective customer writes you the equivalent of "Tell me more," the thing the reader most wants to know is the information requested—as specifically as you can give it. That is far more interesting than any of your expressions of pleasure or gratitude.

But in most cases involving a detailed inquiry, you will want to check the importance and nature of the questions before framing your reply. Some you can answer with more positiveness than others. The most important one you can answer favorably should be your start:

> With your Pow–R–Pac you will feel safe even when traveling alone at night on the country roads you spoke of.
>
> ––
>
> In making the Rover bicycle you saw advertised in <u>U.S. Youth</u>, we use lightweight, high-grade steel of the same quality used in motor bikes.

Such positiveness stimulates enthusiasm and increases the desire to read further.

Answering all questions.   In some instances you cannot give the requested information. For example, the letter about the Stair-Traveler (Chapter 4) could not give cost details because installation varies according to the placement of the machine in a particular home. The visit of the representative (clearly referred to) would have to clear up that point. But *if you cannot supply an answer, do not ignore the question*. Such action only leads to irritation, disgust, or (worse) suspicion. Indicate that you are supplying the information some other way or that you are getting it.

Most of the time you can give all the requested information, even though it runs to considerable length. The following reply to a request for more information about reconditioned Lektrasweeps is good. It has you-viewpoint and positiveness, and it answers every question (though answers about the motor, repairs in the home, and a trial period had to be partly unfavorable).

> The reconditioned Lektrasweep you asked about has the following attachments: a 6-inch upholstery brush, a 6-inch lampshade brush, a 12-inch prober, and a plastic blower attachment, in addition to the standard 12-inch rug brush.
>
> These are the same attachments that come with vacuum cleaners costing $40 to $80 more. Were we to include a 1-hp. motor (necessary only for spraying attachments), the price would have to be considerably higher. Since most users want their Lektrasweeps for cleaning purposes only, we eliminate the spray attachments and thus are able to give you a good low-cost cleaner operating efficiently on a ½-hp motor.
>
> I believe we have the machine you'll find convenient for your cleaning. The quiet operation of the motor is especially desirable in small living quarters, and the brown crackle finish will resist nicks and scratches and clean easily. Another convenience is the 20-foot cord, <u>which enables you to clean an entire room from one wall plug</u>.
>
> The Lektrasweep guarantee protects you against mechanical failures of the vacuum cleaner for a full two years. If any parts fail because of defective materials or workmanship, specially trained service personnel at the central plant in Cleveland will put your Lektrasweep in service again and return it to you within a week. Although we consider all sales final (another of the economies resulting in the low price of your Lektrasweep), as long as the machine shows evidence of proper care, as explained on the written guarantee, we absorb the charges for servicing and new parts and return your Lektrasweep charges prepaid. The few returns to the central plant have been handled to the customers' satisfaction.
>
> Next time you're in Madison, come in and let us demonstrate a Lektrasweep. After a thorough test of

> its effectiveness in picking up dust, lint, and other
> particles from rugs, upholstery, and walls, you'll see
> why we are so confident of the Lektrasweep.
>
> To get your Lektrasweep before you can come to
> Madison, use the enclosed order blank and reply
> envelope to send us your payment and instructions. You
> can be enjoying easy Lektrasweeping the day after we
> hear from you.

This was a particularly difficult reply because so many of the questions had to be answered with limitations, reservations, or an implied no.

To get full value out of the replies about Lektrasweeps and Roanoke lamps (next example), you need to look at each a second time. Both effectively illustrate two aspects of you-viewpoint especially important in all sales writing—including the answers to product inquiries:

1. *Psychological description.* Except in the first paragraph about the Lektrasweep, every time the writers give a physical fact about the product, they *tell* and *emphasize* a resultant benefit. As you look again, see how many more pieces of psychological description you can find like the italicized part of "... 20-foot cord *which enables you to clean an entire room from one wall plug.*"

2. *Dramatization.* The most effective kind of sales writing gets the reader to imagine actually using and enjoying the benefits of the product. Where else in the two letters can you find dramatized copy like "You and Mrs. Baines will agree that the Roanoke is a handsome, efficient lamp when you place a pair in your own living room"?

For further help on answering all questions, see the second group of form enclosures later in this chapter.

Subordinating unfavorable information.   Only a very poor sales writer would have started the Lektrasweep reply with

> No, the Lektrasweep does not have a 1-hp motor.

or even with

> The Lektrasweep is equipped with a ½-hp motor.

Another example will more firmly implant the reasons for positive handling of unfavorable information in invited sales. The inquiry asked whether

1. The Roanoke lamp was three-way.
2. The shade was of parchment or paper.
3. The shade was available in a design.
4. The lamp was weighted to prevent tipping.
5. The base was real brass or an alloy.
6. A pair could be returned for full refund if they didn't fit in with the 18th-century living room.

Answers to all but question 5 contained negative information. Here is one way of handling this inquiry to turn it into a sale despite the unfavorable circumstances:

> Yes, the base and standard of the Roanoke lamp you saw in <u>Home and Yard</u> are of solid brass, which will blend in tastefully with almost any style of 18th-century furnishings.
>
> For durability and ease in cleaning, the 10-inch shade is lightweight metal. Either the forest green or the royal red shade will contrast effectively with your drapes, and the quarter-inch gold bands around the top and bottom give the Roanoke lamp a distinction which most of our customers prefer to a design.
>
> The white lining of the shade and the milk-white bone china reflector enable the single 150-watt bulb to give you good reading light—10 foot-candles within a radius of 8 feet, which is more than the minimum recommended by the American Institute of Lighting. Then, too, the indirect lighting reflected from the ceiling is pleasant for conversational groups.
>
> To make the Roanoke more stable than other lamps of this size and shape, our designers put six claw feet instead of the usual four on the base and thus eliminated the necessity for weighting. Claw feet, as you know, are characteristic of much 18th-century design.
>
> You and Mrs. Baines will agree that the Roanoke is a handsome, efficient lamp when you place a pair in your own living room. Should you decide to return them within 10 days of our shipping date, we will refund your money less shipping charges.
>
> Use the enclosed order blank and envelope to tell us your choice of color. Include with the order blank your check or money order for $80 (including shipping charges). Within five days after we hear from you, you will be enjoying your Roanoke lamps, which will give you good lighting at a moderate price and will make appropriately decorative additions to your living room.

The letter wisely begins and ends with positive ideas and, as positively as circumstances permit, establishes the negative answers of "No, the Roanoke is not three-way; it is not weighted; the shade is not available in a design; no, the shade is not parchment or paper; we won't refund *all* your money if you return the lamps." It does so through the usual means available to any writer: embedded position and positive statement (see **Emp** in Appendix F).

Handling price.   When you have a genuine bargain, a real price reduction—one which the reader will recognize as such—that information may be the best lead you can choose for your message.

Most of the time, however, you are trying to sell at an established price. And most of the time you are writing to someone who wishes the price were less! For these reasons, good sales writers attempt to minimize the effect of price by one or more of several methods:

—Introducing price after presenting most of the sales points.

—Stating price in terms of a unit ("$1.67 a wrench" rather than "$20 a dozen").

—Identifying the daily, monthly, or even yearly cost based on an estimated life of the product ("10 cents a night" for a good mattress sounds much easier to pay than "$182.50").

—Suggesting a series of payments rather than the total (an alumnus is more likely to contribute "$10 a month for the next year" than to contribute "$120 next year").

—Comparing the present price with the cost of some product or activity the reader accepts readily. ("For the price of six cigarettes a day your child can have better schools" was the punch line of an ad promoting a school-bond drive. Likewise, a sales writer sold air-conditioned sleep for the price of a daily Coke.)

—Associating the price with a reminder of the benefits to be gained.

The first and last of the suggestions you can always apply. You may want to use the others as indicated by the following varying factors.

In general, the higher the income bracket of your readers, the less desirability for applying the techniques.

The higher the price and the less familiar your readers are with your product or service, the greater the desirability for minimizing price in one or more of these ways. Minimizing price has more effect on consumers than on dealers or business or industrial customers.

Often you will be able to omit direct price talk because a sales representative will handle it in a face-to-face interview or because you need more information before determining price. Sometimes you can shift the burden of price discussion to an enclosure. But *when you are trying to close a sale, you must identify what it is going to cost and help your reader justify the expenditure.*

Securing action.   Having convinced your reader that your product or service is worth the price, you want to get action before a change of mind, before forgetfulness defeats you, before the money goes for something else—before any of the things that could happen do happen.

A word of caution here, however: The bromidic, high-pressure, general expressions like "Act today!" "Do it now!" "Don't delay!" are more likely to produce reactions ranging from indifference to disgust than the favorable reaction you seek.

Instead, in all persuasive messages, your good action ending:

—Makes clear the specific action you want your reader to take.

—Clears up any question about how to take the action.

—Makes the action easy (and makes it sound as easy as possible).

—Supplies a stimulus to action, preferably immediate action.

On finishing your letter, your reader should know just exactly what you want done. In invited sales it's to send in an order or take some step in furthering the sale, such as to invite the visit of a sales representative, make a visit to a demonstration or salesroom, or try out the product. The psychological urge is stronger if you *name the explicit action* rather than resort to the vague "Let us hear from you soon" or any of its equivalents.

At times you may have to name two actions and ask the reader to take one or the other. If you possibly can, avoid doing so. Some folks faced with a choice resolve their dilemma by doing nothing.

Facilitating devices—order blanks, order cards, and postcards or envelopes already addressed and requiring no postage—remove some of the work in taking action. References to them—*preferably directing the reader to use them*—reassure your reader that what you are asking is simple, requiring little time or effort.

Moreover, through careful wording, you can further this impression. "Write us your choice" suggests more work than "Check your choice of colors on the enclosed card." "Jot down," "just check," "simply initial" are examples of wording that suggests ease and rapidity in doing something. Wording like this will help to reduce some of your reader's reluctance to take action.

The final suggestion for a good action ending—that of supplying a stimulus to action—is a matter of either threatening your reader or promising something. Remember a stimulus is motivation—a reader benefit! Talk of limited supply, price rises after a certain date, introductory offers for a limited time, premiums, and the like is all very well *provided it is true* and *provided it is specific*, so that the reader is likely to accept it.

In many circumstances you have nothing you can use as a stimulus but the desirability of your product or service. You *always* have that, however. In the final analysis your reader buys for what the product contributes to life; when you ask for money, mention *again what benefits will result*.

Such a stimulus comes appropriately as the ending idea. This placement has decided psychological value too, for it emphasizes the service attitude—rather than the greed stressed if you end with dollars and cents talk or the mechanics of ordering.

Desirably, the stimulus is short—often only a phrase, at most a short sentence, restating the theme. The Stair-Traveler letter, for example, could have ended effectively with

```
Mr. J. B. Nickle, our Kansas City representative, will
be glad to call at a time convenient for you. Fill out
and mail the enclosed postcard, and he will come to
```

INVITED SALES CHECKLIST

1. Get started in a hurry!
   a. The direct, specific, favorable answer to one of your reader's main questions is the surest way of maintaining interest.
   b. At least give a good sales point if no answer can be affirmative.
   c. "Thank you for"—while perfectly nice—is unnecessary and slow.
   d. Keep out the selfish sounds like "We're glad to have . . . ."
   e. Do not begin with an answer containing negative information.
   f. You don't need to work for attention; you already have it.
2. Arrange points for natural coherence and favorable information at the beginning and end (even of paragraphs as well as the whole). Embed touchy points.
3. Answer every question, stated or implied, or explain why.
   a. You need specific statements for conviction.
   b. Avoid denied negatives. If a product isn't something, what is it?
4. Psychological description (you-viewpoint) is good selling.
   a. Put the product to work in the life of the reader right from the start, and let reader-use sentences (dramatization) predominate throughout to give a visual image of benefits.
   b. Depict reader possession and/or participation instead of mere mechanical you-beginnings.
5. Consider using an enclosure for details, economy, and pictures.
   a. Don't mention it too early.
   b. Don't emphasize that you have enclosed it; what the reader is to do with it or get from it is what counts: not "Enclosed you will find a folder," but "Read on page 2 of the enclosed folder . . . ."
6. Adaptation is easy here; the inquiry gives you cues.
   a. Maybe use the name one time beyond the salutation.
   b. Work in a reference to home town, firm, or organization.
   c. Refer casually to a commonplace action or event characteristic of the reader's job, community, area, or economic status.
   d. Fit your style to the person's way of life.
7. Try to cushion the shock of price when you have to state it.
   a. Use the appropriate method(s) of minimizing price.
   b. Make price and payment method clear, or give a reason.
8. In a full-fledged four-point action ending (what to do, how, aids to easy action, stimulus to promptness) confidently ask the reader to take the action you want (preferably order, if fitting).

```
your home and explain how simply and economically your
Stair-Traveler can make your daily living more
pleasurable.
```

For other examples, reread the endings about the Roanoke lamp and the Lektrasweep.

Invited sales are persuasive (C–plan) presentations. You should therefore apply all the points discussed in Chapter 4. The accompanying Invited Sales Checklist summarizes the most significant points from it and the discussion here.

ROUTINE TRANSMITTAL MESSAGES

A frequent written communication is the routine transmittal letter or memo. Often people in a firm send information or material to other people either in their company or with other companies. This information or material usually has a short cover letter or memo which carries the address, announces what is enclosed, and identifies the sender.

These short notes do not strictly fall into the category of favorable replies, since generally no question arises about your compliance with the request, if there is one. The reason we talk about this routine type of writing is that for most young people early in their careers, such messages are their primary (and maybe only) contact with upper management. Such writing deserves some care.

The routine transmittal message should be short. Though you may sometimes need to explain what you are sending, you do not need to spout eloquence over simply sending information. In any case, do not be trapped into using the old-fashioned "Enclosed you will find" or "Attached is" beginnings. Much more natural and direct beginnings are "Here is the information on . . . ." or "This is the material you asked for . . . ." Custom within your firm will dictate whether you need to mention the date of your reader's request, but any file number or other formal identification should appear in the first sentence or a subject line.

After announcing that the material is here (which should be pretty evident), quit unless you have something else relevant to say.

What your note can go on to say after the initial announcement is interpretation of data you've dug up, or suggestions or questions on what to do with the information, that you're sending more information than your reader expected, or that the information is dated, perhaps, or not yet complete, or whatever the situation calls for. Keep this second part of your message short and direct; and resist the temptation to add an ending offering further assistance. If your reader does need more information, you'll hear about it! And anyhow, you should have sent all the information in the first place.

FORM ENCLOSURES, LETTERS, AND DOCUMENTS

Invited sales messages (and various other kinds) do take time and therefore money. Unless a firm has practically unlimited money and trained personnel, it will have to use form messages some of the time for speed and economy in handling inquiries with sales possibilities.

Form enclosures and letters can decrease the cost of correspondence by cutting time needed for dictation, transcription, handling, and filing—despite the best of office equipment. The closer you can come to completely eliminating one or more of these steps, the more you can save. The big problem is to determine when you can save enough in costs to justify the loss in effectiveness.

Before you can decide, however, you need to know the potentials of forms.

Enclosures

Three classes of *form enclosures* deserve your attention:

1. Forms which are the basic reason for the mailing.
2. Forms which give supplementary information.
3. Forms which aid the reader in responding.

Since the *first group* are the key things in the envelopes (checks, requested pamphlets, brochures, and the like), they deserve to come to the reader's attention immediately. In some cases they may properly be the only thing necessary. In most situations, however, you should *make something of them* by saying something about them—even if for no reason but goodwill. You've already seen earlier in this chapter the reasons and approaches for comment when transmitting requested booklets. Similarly, simple and typical covering letters (often forms themselves) beginning something like the following could hardly help making their readers feel better:

> Here is your current quarterly dividend check (our
> 200th without interruption, raised to 50¢ a share this
> time) and our thanks for your continued confidence in
> Rushman.
>
> —
>
> The enclosed check paying for your services as
> consultant carries with it our thanks for the good
> advice you gave us.
>
> —
>
> This check will tell you more clearly than words that
> when we guarantee satisfaction with Acme products or
> your money back, we mean it.

Unlike the first group of form enclosures, the enclosures in the *second group* are *not* the basic reason for writing but are *helpful to give additional details* and thus avoid unduly cluttering and lengthening the main message. Most frequently useful in sales letters as brochures and detailed price lists, they also help in job application letters (as résumés) and in answering various inquiries about products (as installation, operating, and repair guides).

As supplements, these informative enclosures do not deserve mention until late in the message—usually the next-to-last paragraph, *after* the key points and *near enough to the end* that the reader will finish before turning to the enclosure (perhaps never to return). As with the first group, the important thing to say about these enclosures is *not* their mere existence—*not* "We have enclosed . . .," and certainly *not* "Enclosed please find . . ." (the reader has probably already found)—but what the reader should get from them.

```
As you'll see from the enclosed brochure, . . .

                        --

The illustrations and explanations on pages 3 and 4 of
the enclosed installation guide will answer, better
than I can, your questions about wiring the two
thermostats in combination.
```

The *third useful group* of form enclosures (reader aids in replying) naturally deserve mention only in the ending—where you ask for action. Order blanks and reply or return cards and envelopes (usually stamped and addressed—but *not* properly called "self-addressed," unless you insist on being trite, jargonistic, illogical, and wordy) can often help you get an answer when the reader might not go to the trouble necessary without them. As in referring to other form enclosures, the point to stress is *not* the idea that they are enclosed but the suggestion that the reader use them.

If you'll use the word *enclosed* as an adjective instead of a verb, you'll probably put the emphasis where it belongs in referring to all three classes of form enclosures, like this:

```
By filling out and mailing the enclosed reply card
promptly, you . . . .

                        --

Sending in your order today on the enclosed form will
bring you . . . .
```

Form letters

Although most readers like the implied extra consideration of the individual letter, few business people will object to a form letter *because* it is a form but only if it seems to give them less attention than they desire. New customers and those writing you about important affairs are most likely to feel that way. Anybody, however, will rightly object to a sloppy form or a form message which does not contain the necessary information. And many people will object to a form which tries to masquerade as an individualized message but fails because of discrepancies in type, faulty alignment, or inept wording. The undisguised form, however, can successfully carry its message in many situations, especially those involving numerous similar inquiries to which you will give similar replies, somewhat like the following:

```
As I'm writing this letter,
The Richmond U.S. Government Money Market Trust
```

Is paying your fellow members xx.x% on their investments. This was the average net annualized yield for the 7-day period ending on September 8, 198-.

If you really want to hold your own against inflation, compare what this investment is giving other members with what your own checking and savings accounts are presently giving you. Of course, with a bank account and savings certificate your principal is insured and the investment has a fixed return. A money market fund investment is not insured and the return fluctuates. The Trust, however, invests exclusively in securities issued or guaranteed by the U.S. government.

The Trust has three beneficial features:

1. Free check redemption. Your money is available simply by writing a check to redeem your shares. The minimum amount of any check redemption is $500.
2. You pay no sales charge when you put your money in. You pay no charges when you take your money out.
3. The Trust will invest your money exclusively in securities that the U.S. government issues or guarantees—the safest security investments.

The chances are that your present checking and savings account dollars are not giving you as much inflation-fighting muscle as you would have with a U.S. Government Money Market Trust investment. Don't let one more day go by before you act on this situation. You can invest with as little as $500, but the larger your investment, the greater your return. The sooner you act, the sooner your dollars will be doing more for you.

You have the prospectus giving you important details about the Trust, the expenses and charges, who manages it, and more. Complete the application and write your check for this powerful new way of fighting inflation. Use the enclosed postage-paid envelope.

Even the signature of this letter is printed. Thus a reply which would cost several dollars if individually handled runs to no more than 50 cents. And the firm gains extra goodwill by answering promptly.

You can print *strict form* messages by the thousands at low cost. And you can adapt them in talking points and references even to a large mailing list. They can answer an inquiry (or order), express gratitude, convey some evidence of service attitude, and look forward to future business relations, as in the following postcard acknowledgment:

```
We will give your recent order our immediate careful
attention and follow your shipping instructions
exactly.

You may be sure we appreciate this opportunity to
serve you and shall be happy to do so when you again
decide to order computer supplies.
```

But completely printed letters have limitations. Personalizing is impossible. And if you print the body and then insert individual inside addresses and salutations, you will have greatly increased costs and likely discrepancies between the two types. Unless you sell only one product or have a different form for each product, you can't include resale talk on the goods, although you can for the firm.

Fill-ins enable you to be more specific than you can be in a strict form. For example, the strict form above could read like this as a fill-in (the filled-in parts are in parentheses):

```
Today we shipped you (400 MRP118520SD 20-pocket
Microfiche Reference Panels @ $3.15, 6 TPZ11854BL
blue 4" capacity Trapezoid Ring Binders @ $26.35)

as ordered on (purchase order no.)

via (UPS)

Thank you for your order and for giving us this
opportunity to prove that MagiComp is your fastest and
most complete source for all your computer supplies
and accessories.
```

But even if you do a good job of matching print and type in a preprinted fill-in like this by using word processing equipment, in most instances the irregular spacing calls attention to the fact that the message is a form fill-in. More sophisticated equipment can type out the entire form, picking up the fill-ins from data about the order already on record.

International business communication, for example, makes much use of forms. The usual method of assuring payment when exporting is to get a letter of credit (issued by a bank at the importer's request). Your international banker will check out the foreign bank. A U.S. bank can confirm a letter of credit and thus guarantee payment. For an example see Appendix C.

What we have said can apply to form paragraphs as well as to whole letters or memos. The procedure is to write an excellent paragraph covering each frequently recurring point in the firm's correspondence. Usually half a dozen ending paragraphs and a dozen beginnings will cover most situations. Other paragraphs will be about the various products of the company. Each company correspondent and each typist then gets a book of the coded paragraphs to type manually to record for use in word processing equipment.

A dictator could code a letter simply 13, 27, 16, 42. That would mean a four-paragraph letter made up of those standard paragraphs in that order. If no ready-made paragraph covers what should be in the second paragraph, dictation would be "13, special, 16, 42," followed by the wording for the special second paragraph. If the same point comes up frequently enough, the firm should prepare a good paragraph for it and put it into the correspondent's book.

Because such paragraphs get frequent use, they should get careful preparation so they are better than most people would write quickly under the pressure of dictation. Obviously, the same advantage applies to an entire form message.

Even if you spend 30 to 50 hours on one message, when you send it to a thousand people, dictation time and transcription time are only a fraction of the time individual messages would require. Thus forms cut correspondence costs, reduce the burdensome human aspects of the ever-increasing correspondence problems of management, and expedite replies to people who want information quickly.

Certain *dangers* exist, however. *The greatest is the tendency to use a form when it simply does not apply.* When a person asks if Sure-Clip tee-nuts can withstand temperatures up to 2,400°F, answering that "Sure-Clip tee-nuts are specially finished to resist corrosion and be compatible with a wide range of ferrous and nonferrous metals" is nice but doesn't answer the question.

One good solution, if a form does not answer one of the specific questions, is to add a postscript. If you cannot answer all questions by adding a little to an existing form, you need to write an individual message.

Another danger is in broadcasting that the message is a form with such references as

> To all our customers:
>
> Whether you live in Maine or California. . . .

In a letter or memo the personal touch pays off. The wording of even a form letter, then, should *give each reader the feeling that it fits.* And remember that in every test ever made, the form letter that makes no pretense of being anything else results in more returns than the imperfectly disguised form, whether the slipup is due to poor mechanics or inept wording.

The suggestions made about forms in this chapter should help with *any repetitive writing situation, whether it is one involving replies to inquiries, acknowledgments of orders, sales, credit, collections, or adjustments.* So except for occasional incidental references pointing out the ease or wisdom of form treatment in a particular situation, the remainder of this book deals with individualized, personalized messages because:

1. You can learn more about communication principles and their application that way.
2. As a result of such specific study and practice, you will write much better forms when you need to.
3. In most circumstances calling for a letter or memo, an individualized copy will do a more effective job for you than a form.

Short note replies

In an effort to expedite many day-to-day answers to inquiries (and reduce correspondence costs), many executives turn to the short note reply (SNR). One leading copying-machine manufacturer in its advertising explains this way:

1. Just jot a personal note on the margin of the letter you received—no wasted time in dictation.
2. Insert the letter and a sheet of copy paper into a copying machine.
3. In just four seconds you have the letter ready to mail back to the sender—plus the copy for your files.

Certainly most readers will appreciate the thoughtfully fast answer. The practice seems to be gaining favor—rightly so, in our opinion.

ORDERS

Buying and selling by mail has long involved much more than just the big mail-order houses. It includes mail sales through large department stores; national marketing of seasonal and regional produce like fruit, game, syrup, and candy; farmers' orders for various supplies, machinery, and replacement parts; office equipment and supplies from manufacturers and distributors; and even industrial tools and materials.

To overcome the disadvantage of buying without seeing, feeling, and trying the product, sellers by mail usually provide pictures and full information (in both small and large catalogs), and they offer guarantees and return privileges and provide necessary installation, operation, and service manuals.

Since sellers by mail usually supply well-designed order blanks and addressed envelopes with their catalogs, the only problems connected with writing an order appear when you do not have the blanks and must write a letter. Though increasingly sellers offer ordering through toll-free 1–800 telephone numbers (often with credit card payment), still millions of order letters go through the mail. Furthermore, even if you never write one, the best way to learn how to order is to study order letters.

But an order is probably the easiest kind of letter to write. The reader is in business to sell goods; so if you clearly specify what you want and make satisfactory plans to pay for it, you'll get an answer. A poor order letter may, however, bring results different from what you really want.

The basic requirements for an order letter, as you can see from almost any order blank, are five (which will serve as a checklist for order letters):

1. Make them orders, not just hints. The *acceptance of a definite offer to sell* or *an offer to buy* is contractual. The usual beginning for an order is therefore "Please send me . . . ."
2. Describe the goods adequately. Although the catalog number alone usually identifies except for color and size, give four or five clean-cut columns of information:

a. Quantity desired.

b. Catalog item number, if any, and catalog page number.

c. Name of product and as many details as are appropriate, such as model, color, size, material, grade or quality, pattern, finish, monogram initials.

d. Unit price.

e. Total price for the designated quantity of the item (column *a* times *d*).

In the absence of a catalog, to supplement the inexact information you may need to explain more fully by telling how the product is to be used, and in some cases by sending drawings.

In ordering replacement parts for machines, be sure to give the name and model number of the machine and the name and number of the part. Frequently, you can find the number on the part itself if you have no parts list.

3. Write a separate, single-spaced paragraph for each item, with double spacing between paragraphs.

4. Make clear how you expect to pay—perhaps most likely, in personal orders, by giving your name and your card name, number, and expiration date. If you have not established credit but want goods charged, you should provide credit information with the order.

If you want neither credit nor COD shipment (which costs you more), several methods of remitting are open to you: check, money order, certified or cashier's check, or bank draft.

Regardless of how you remit, refer to the remittance in the order and tell its form, amount, and intended application.

5. Be sure the *where* of shipment is clear—especially for a shipment to an address different from yours, as when sending gifts—and also the *when* and *how* unless you want to leave them to the seller.

The following typical order illustrates the five points:

```
Please send me the following items listed in your
current spring and summer catalog:

1  60 C 6587L   Glass casting rod, Model 162,
                extra light action,
                5 ft. 8 in.  . . . . . . . . . . $18.95

1  60 CP 6302   Pflueger Summit reel,
                Model 1993L  . . . . . . . . . .  33.75

2  60 C 6846    Cortland "Cam-o-flage" nylon
                casting line, 10-lb. test,
                100-yd. lengths @ $4.30 . . . . .  8.60

      Total . . . . . . . . . . . . . . . . . . $61.30
The enclosed check for $69.63 covers the price, sales
tax, and parcel post charges.

As I plan to go fishing a week from next Saturday
(June 26), I will want the equipment by that time.
```

STANDARD ACKNOWLEDGMENTS

Acknowledgments should be an effective means of increasing goodwill and promoting business. A person who orders from you evidently has a favorable attitude toward your firm and its goods. Your job in acknowledging the order is to keep it that way by giving satisfaction.

A buyer expects to get the product quickly and to be appreciated—or to get a prompt and reasonable explanation. To give less is to make a customer for somebody else. (According to a U.S. Department of Commerce survey, seeming indifference is responsible for at least 67 percent of lost customers.)

Frequently a correspondent who handles a large volume of orders, however, comes to look upon them as routine matters and answers accordingly. Doing so overlooks two things: (1) The individual customer usually sends comparatively few orders and does not look on them as routine at all; (2) A routine acknowledgment seems like indifference.

Justifying reasons (strikes, impossibility of always estimating demand accurately, as well as incomplete orders from buyers) may prevent a seller from filling some orders promptly, or at all. But no reason justifies not acknowledging orders promptly and appreciatively. To that purpose most large-volume sellers-by-mail use forms to acknowledge all but unusual orders. The following fill-in forms let a large department store acknowledge quickly (fill-ins underscored here):

> Thank you for your letter ordering <u>a ladder</u>.
>
> We're processing your order now, and you should receive the shipment promptly.
>
> —
>
> As you requested, we have sent <u>the pocket calculator</u> to <u>Mrs. M. W. Colby</u>.
>
> Thank you for calling on us. We try to make our service convenient. Order from us again when we can serve you.

Neither does the seller have much excuse for not doing more than the minimum the customer ordinarily expects. A large order—or even a small first order from a new customer—is an opportunity to cement a lasting business relationship through a well-written acknowledgment.

Clearly *the standard acknowledgment* of an order you can fill immediately is a good-news letter. The beginning should be a direct answer to the reader's biggest question—what you are doing about the order. Tell immediately the *when* and *how* of shipment, preferably timed and worded to indicate that it's on the way, and identify what it includes, the charges, and (here or later) the financial arrangements if necessary. (But remember that you are sending goods, not an order, which is what you received.) The approximate arrival date is also desirable, not only as a convenience to the customer but also for the psychologically favorable effect of helping the reader imagine actually receiving and using the goods.

Give the date and one or more of order number, relisting, or a general naming of the class of goods, or list them on an attached invoice or shipping list and refer to it in the letter.

To a new customer, a hearty welcome, resale, and a forward look are even more important than to an old customer; and service attitude and appreciation are important to every customer.

The middle section of a standard acknowledgment is the place for financial details, resale talk of more than phrase length, and explicit evidence of your service attitude. For instance, in acknowledging dealers' orders, you might talk about having your sales representative set up window and counter displays, offer free envelope stuffers (small promotional pamphlets about your products for the dealer to send to customers), or describe your radio, TV, and magazine ads that call customers' attention to your products and help the dealer sell more.

Encouragement to future ordering (just preceded by any appropriate sales promotion material) is almost invariably the best ending for the standard acknowledgment. The accompanying Checklist for Standard Acknowledgments outlines the previous points.

Here's an example of how the parts go together for an effective personalized acknowledgment covering all points specifically:

> You should receive your eight cases of Tuff Paper towels in time for Friday afternoon shoppers; we sent them by prepaid express this morning.
>
> The $3.27 voucher attached to this letter is your change after we deducted $76.80 charges and $4.93 express from your $85 check.
>
> Thank you for your order. We're glad to serve you with this first shipment of paper products.
>
> You'll find these Tuff Paper Towels have a fast turnover, Mr. Ford, because homemakers like the way they soak up grease, dust off spots, and save cloth towels from many dirty jobs. And you'll like their attractive small packaging that takes up a minimum of display and shelf space. Your markup figures out at exactly 29 percent.
>
> For more information about Tuff Paper dishrags and window washers, colorful shelf paper your customers will like for their pantries, and other paper products every household needs, look in the enclosed booklet. Notice that each article carries the usual Tuff Paper margin of profit.
>
> Perhaps you'd like to take advantage of our regular terms of 2/10, n/60 on future orders. If so, we'll be glad to consider your credit application when you fill in and return the enclosed form.

CHECKLIST FOR STANDARD ACKNOWLEDGMENTS

1. Of greatest interest to the customer is complete, accurate shipment.
   a. Emphasize the good news (sending the goods—not an order) in the first sentence, preferably also indicating method, arrival time, and use.
   b. Clearly identify the order by one or more of date, number, reference to the goods by name—perhaps a complete listing.
   c. If you list, tabulate—in the letter if short; on a referred-to invoice or shipping list if long.
   d. Clear up any uncertainty about payment details.
   e. Appreciation (and a welcome to a new customer) may come early in the letter but probably will fit better near the end—if not adequately implied.

2. Resale is part of acknowledgments to reassure the reader.
   a. Make it specific and short.
   b. Adapt it to your product and reader (consumer versus dealer).

3. Service attitude, especially important to new customers, may help with others.
   a. For a consumer: delivery schedules, free installation, maybe credit possibilities (invite application without promising approval).
   b. For an industrial customer: full stock, quick shipment, custom or special capabilities, maybe credit.
   c. For a dealer: sales and service representatives, manuals, displays, and advertising aids and programs (mats, envelope stuffers, etc.).
   d. If you talk advertising, give publications and radio or TV stations, amount of space or time, schedules; and emphasize how the advertising promotes sales: "Your customers will be asking for . . . because of the full-page ads running . . . ."

4. Sales promotion material can indicate service attitude and build sales.
   a. Keep it appropriate—usually on seasonal or allied goods.
   b. You-attitude and specificness are essential in sales promotion.
   c. Emphasize your service to the customer—how the suggested product might help—not your selfish desire to sell more, as implied by "Our product . . . ," "We also make . . . ," or "We'd also like to sell you . . . ."
   d. Emphasize reader action when referring to enclosures.

5. Look forward to future orders.
   a. If sales promotion is the basis, suggest specific, easy action.
   b. If resale talk is the basis, continue in terms of reader satisfaction rather than suggest that something will go wrong.
   c. Guard against bromides and greedy wording as you close.

> And when you order, if you want window and shelf
> displays to help you sell, just say so. Then watch
> Tuff kitchen paper products bring Altoona customers
> into your store for frequent repeat sales.

The trouble with this kind of acknowledgment is that it is costly. To be specific on all points, to adapt the message to an individual, and to make it persuasive require an average-length, individualized letter. But when the prospect of numerous future orders depends on the letter, to do less is foolish.

In many cases, however, a form can serve as an acknowledgment (especially for small orders from established customers), as we illustrated in the discussion of forms. The Tuff Paper situation could be handled in a form message like this one (which, incidentally, *could* serve for acknowledging a repeat order):

> You should receive the Tuff Paper products you ordered
> in just a few days; they are already on the way.
>
> Thank you for your order. We are glad to serve you in
> this way.
>
> You'll find that Tuff Paper products have a fast
> turnover; homemakers like them for many messy
> household cleaning jobs.
>
> You will like their attractive packaging that takes up
> a minimum of shelf and display space. And the sizable
> markup!
>
> Read the enclosed booklet for more information about
> Tuff Paper dishrags, window washers, colorful shelf
> paper, and other paper products every household needs.
>
> Use the handy order blank and business reply envelope
> in the back of the booklet when you want to order the
> additional Tuff Paper products your customers will be
> asking for.

If the situation is one in which specificness would add to the effectiveness of an acknowledgment, a fill-in rather than a strict form could serve. For instance, you could add a postscript of special material to the preceding.

Forms of any kind, however, can go sour from overuse. If, for instance, the buyer above orders Tuff products weekly, blindly sending the same letter week after week would shortly have the undesired opposite effect of convincing the buyer that you take such business for granted. If you have a situation where someone may repeatedly get the same form letter, you would be wise to revise it periodically to keep it fresh and effective.

The situation will govern whether to use forms and, if so, which kind. Pinching pennies by dashing off personalized letters that are just a little too short to be adequate, or resorting to forms that don't do the job, is poor economy. The result is comparable to throwing out *almost* enough rope to reach a drowning person. If you are going to write a personalized letter, make it a good one. Its cost does not increase in proportion to length. A question you should always answer before cheapening your correspondence is whether you lose more in results (including goodwill) than you save on costs.

CREDIT APPROVALS

In naming what they commonly call the four C's of credit—the bases for evaluating individual as well as corporate credit applicants, domestic or international—credit specialists name character first, followed by capacity, capital, and conditions.

Character is honesty. It is one's good word. In business it is living up to the spirit as well as the letter of the contract. In credit, it is meeting obligations as one promises to do.

Capacity is the ability to earn the means for payment.

Capital is the already available money behind the debtor. It may be cash, land, buildings, machinery, securities, patents, and copyrights, to mention the most common forms. It could as a last resort furnish the money for payment in the event of reversals.

Conditions (plural) has two parts. One is general business trends. The other is special or local conditions or the trends of the debtor's business as shown in its comparative financial statements.

Because these four C's—especially the first two—are reflections of "personal" qualities of an individual or business, credit communications are open to negative possibilities. When you question honesty, earning ability, or judgment, you are treading on potentially dangerous ground. With tact, patience, and a positive attitude, however, communications about credit can be goodwill builders.

One of the fundamental concepts that will help you to write successfully about credit is this: The credit privilege has to be *earned;* nobody hands it out indiscriminately or gives it away. For that reason you should not talk about *granting* credit. More appropriate terminology is *approval* or *extension* of credit.

On the basis of one or more of the four C's an individual or firm merits credit. For many, character is the primary reason. They may earn little, and they may have little or no capital, but they pay their bills and thus earn the right to credit. And this is the bedrock of credit extension.

Anticipating those who may be unable or unwilling to pay is one of the primary functions of the credit manager. To hold down losses from bad debts, the credit officer evaluates applicants' credit records and estimates their financial stability in the light of general business ups and downs.

But approving only gilt-edged applications will seriously curtail sales. Accordingly, a credit manager must be sales-minded, and well informed about the firm's goods, to help build customer confidence and increase sales.

Since marginal risks are vital for profitable operations, evaluating and encouraging borderline cases must get careful attention. For both the firm and its customers the credit manager is part counselor, part sales promoter, and part detective.

When the information you receive about an applicant is favorable, you will of course approve the application and set up the account. Because of the sheer weight of numbers, most credit approvals are form messages like the following:

THE J. P. BOWEN COMPANY

Is pleased to open a charge
account for you and welcome you to
our family of regular patrons

Such a notification sent promptly is certainly better than nothing. Yet it falls far short of what a good credit message can do to strengthen the credit relationship, promote goodwill, forestall collection problems, and stimulate sales.

Establishing the basis for credit

In credit approvals you may take advantage of the simple, obvious psychology of praise or approval. If you place a customer on the credit list because of a prompt-pay rating, you should say so. Hearing about the good rating encourages the customer to maintain that rating. The same is true for some reflections of favorable capacity or capital positions.

The reference should not be lengthy; in fact, the best way is to subordinate it in the extension of credit or the explanation of terms. Thus it reminds the customer that credit is an earned privilege which requires care, thought, and effort to maintain. Thus established, it may serve as an effective collection appeal if payment becomes slow.

So forceful is this device in the opinion of one experienced credit manager that approval notices to credit applicants with prompt-pay records were often only one sentence:

> Because of reports from your references of your fine
> pay habits, we are happy to set up a regular monthly
> charge account for you.

Obviously, this should accomplish more than it does, even if no more than a little resale or sales promotion, as you'll see later.

Explanation of terms

Unless a firm wants to encourage delayed payments, the initial extension of credit should make unmistakably clear how you expect payments, implying the confident assumption that the customer will comply. Even a form can easily incorporate a simple statement like one of the following:

> On the first of each month you will receive an
> itemized statement of your purchases made through the

```
25th day of the preceding month; purchases made after
the 25th appear on the following month's bill. Your
payment is due by the 10th.
                        --
Under our system of cycle billing your statement of a
month's purchases will go to you on the 17th of each
month; we expect settlement within 10 days.
```

Clear, specific explanations of terms can not only prevent misunderstanding and delay but also serve as a stimulus to prompt pay.

How far to go with the explanation depends on the reader's credit knowledge and reputation. To those you think know and respect credit practices, you would tell only what the terms are; explaining that 2/10, n/30 means a deduction of 2 percent if paid in 10 days or pay the whole in 30 days would insult such a reader. To a reader who is new to credit business or barely passes your credit evaluation, however, you had better make the terms not only clear and emphatic but concrete (i.e., show the prompt-pay benefits as savings in money, what it will buy, and the continued credit privilege):

```
Under our regular credit terms of 2/10, n/30, you can
save $1.36 on this order alone if your check is in the
mail by July 10--which will almost pay for another
enamel display tray. Your check for the net of $68 by
July 30, however, will keep you in the preferred-
customer class.
```

Such specificness is not possible, of course, except in an individualized message. But the credit extension, whenever possible, should be individualized for the favorable effect on the customer.

Few credit approvals to consumers identify a limit (although one may go on the office record), whereas most business credit arrangements and consumer bank credit cards like Visa and MasterCard include limits as parts of the explanation of terms. To prevent the limit from appearing to be a penalty, with consequent negative reactions, a good writer phrases it in positive language:

```
Under our regular terms of 2/10, n/60, your No-Flame
will cost you only $117.60 if you send your check by
May 2; the full $120 is due on June 21. At any one
time you may carry as much as $250 worth of No-Flame
or other Bronson products on account.
```

To stop with the approval, the basis, and the terms would be foolish, however; a good credit writer can also help to further sales—through the goodwill elements of resale material on goods, resale on the house, or sales-promotion material on other allied goods. All should focus on repeat sales.

Stimulating sales

In credit approvals, sales-building passages should definitely be low pressure; if the service attitude does not dominate, the greedy overtones can repel the reader. But the writer of the following, you will note, is careful to tie in a service-to-you reference to all sales-building passages and thus make the customer feel welcome rather than pounced upon:

> Your company's fine record of promptly paying invoices, confirmed by the references you supplied, certainly qualifies you for an open account with Rutherford Chemicals. Now your company is only a telephone call away from one of the country's largest stocks of laboratory chemicals, and we promise "same day" shipment for almost every order.
>
> We will invoice your purchases to you when shipped and date the invoices two days after the date of shipment. Terms are 2/10, net 45, up to $4,000, and we are sure you will want to take advantage of the discount for prompt payment.
>
> Since we regularly stock every item in our catalog, you will experience almost invariably prompt shipment from Rutherford. In fact, over the last two years we have achieved a 98.5% rate of "same day" shipments, a point of pride among our people.
>
> A new service to our customers is our Small Order Department. We set this unit up specifically to handle your needs for small or sample quantities of many chemicals. Our Small Order Department allows you to order most chemicals in any quantity, from an ounce to a tank load, from one source. That's Rutherford convenience!

Making the customer feel welcome and appreciated

Credit-approval writers nearly all seem to know that making new credit customers feel welcome and appreciated helps to promote frequent and continued use of the account (increasing sales and profits). Indeed they so often begin by welcoming the customer to "our growing number of satisfied customers" that it is not only bad writing but is stereotyped. *The customer is more interested in finding out the decision on the application. So that decision should get the emphatic beginning position.*

Besides, do you really need to waste words on welcomes and thank-yous? If you approve the credit (implied by sending the goods immediately when the application accompanies an order), establish the basis, explain the terms positively, and then follow with resale and sales promotion material con-

CREDIT APPROVAL CHECKLIST

1. The direct opening should approve credit quickly.
   a. If you have no order, approve credit immediately in a cheerful, welcoming, ungrudging tone.
   b. When you are shipping goods, say so in the first line. Shipping the goods first also implies credit approval.
   c. Name the goods specifically (don't call them an "order"!); state the amount (of goods and dollars) or send an invoice.
   d. In general, you'd better identify the method of shipment.
   e. Choose words that get the goods to the reader and in use; don't stop with just getting them onto a freight car.
   f. A touch of resale (say a favorable adjective) is desirable early, but don't slow up your opening with much resale/goodwill.
   g. Use figures and symbols in orders and acknowledgments.
   h. Take care of all legal details: item prices, freight charges, total. You may assume an invoice or tabulate here.

2. The credit agreement/relation:
   a. For restraint, explain how the customer earned credit.
   b. Although you might identify terms incidentally in the opening, later (for people who might not understand or respect them properly) explain by
      (1) Attaching your interpretation of the terms to a purchase (present or future).
      (2) Concretizing the discount with specific savings figures (maybe a free unit of a purchase, a month's phone bill . . .).
      (3) Bringing in prompt-pay education, in a tone that implies your confidence that the reader will comply.
   c. With its negative potentialities, any credit-limit talk needs a you-viewpoint introduction and positive statement. You might want to label it temporary.
   d. But don't imply "If you don't like these terms, we'll change them."

3. Your resale or sales promotion material in closing the letter:
   a. Include reassuring comments about the reader's good choice.
   b. Mention your services and selling aids concretely.
   c. Consider selling the reader some seasonal or allied goods.
   d. Regardless of how you close, let it point to future orders.
   e. Be specific, not wooden and dull, as in "We have enjoyed serving you and look forward to supplying your future needs."

4. Your appreciation is best worked in incidentally, subordinately.

5. Transitions are easier with a logical order of points.

6. Watch the tone throughout.
   a. Avoid FBI implications about the credit investigation and condescending, mandatory, or selfish explanation of terms.
   b. Proportion affects your tone too; don't talk terms too much.

cretely implying the desire to be of service, your reader will not doubt whether you appreciate business. By implication you adequately establish such welcomes and thank-yous (see "Gratitude," Chapter 3).

The relevant checklist on credit approval summarizes our major suggestions about credit approvals, although, as always, you should apply them with discretion. We *know* they don't all apply in all cases.

SIMPLE CLAIMS AND ADJUSTMENT APPROVALS

[When things go wrong, see that you don't go with them.]

Claims offer you as a buyer the opportunity to get adjustments on unsatisfactory goods and services. If you are a seller and therefore receive claims, welcome them! They offer you an opportunity to discover and correct defects in your goods and services. And your adjustment letters are excellent opportunities for you to build or destroy goodwill. Whether you make the most of your opportunities in either claims or adjustments depends heavily on your attitude.

Any claim and adjustment situation necessarily involves negatives. Somebody is dissatisfied and unhappy. One of the major jobs in writing either claim or adjustment messages, therefore, is to keep these emotionally based negatives from making the situation worse. What you have learned about goodwill, resale, and handling negative material is especially important in adjustments.

In three kinds of situations you may have reason to write a persuasive claim: (1) you've tried a simple (direct) one and been turned down; (2) you know you're dealing with a tight-fisted firm; or (3) the claim is unusual or the facts leave at least some doubt about the justice of the claim. We treat such persuasive claims in Chapter 11.

Here we are talking about direct (A–plan) claims—situations where you have facts justifying the claim and you are supposedly dealing with an open-minded and fair person or firm.

Direct claims

You will probably write good direct claims if you remember these five often-forgotten points (which serve as a checklist for direct claims):

1. *If you think you have a just claim, go ahead.* Progressive firms like claims because they suggest ways of improvement. Many firms even advertise the request: "If you like our products, tell others; if you don't, tell us." Often they encourage claims by "double-your-money-back" guarantees and the like.

2. *Keep your shirt on! When things go wrong, the firm surely did not intend to mistreat you. Almost certainly the person handling your claim had nothing to do with the dissatisfaction. So restrain your anger or sarcasm!*

Very few manufacturers expect every item they manufacture to be perfect. Most know that ZD (zero-defect) production is an ideal rarely achieved even by the best quality controls. So nearly always they expect to replace or repair defective merchandise. This is more efficient than to insist on perfection in manufacturing—and consequently higher prices. The consumer who gets defective merchandise and takes the attitude that the seller tried to cheat, then, is usually wrong.

Furthermore, in most cases all that's necessary to get satisfaction is to make a simple claim and calmly give the justifying facts.

> Your last shipment to us (our order No. A–1753, your invoice No. 45602, dated May 6, 1983) was incorrect. Instead of the socket–head set screws with cups we ordered, you sent screws with flat points. We were able to hold this shipment of screws intact, having opened only one box.
>
> Will you please rush us 5,000 5–40 × ¼-inch socket–head set screws, black finish, with cup points. Our plant manager says we have enough of the proper screws on hand to last us through June 12; so we must have the replacement screws by then.
>
> How shall we ship the screws with flat points back to you? Do you want to cancel your invoice No. 45602 or let it cover the replacement order? We want to take advantage of your 2% cash discount.

To be nasty to the almost certainly innocent person who handles your claim is to be unfair and unreasonable, even foolish. Instead of creating a favorable mood that will help you get satisfaction, you turn this possible ally against you if you write in a nasty mood.

3. *Give the facts—calmly, specifically, thoroughly.* Usually a firm will grant an adjustment merely on the strength of a customer's adequate explanation of what is wrong and suggestions for a fair settlement. In that case you would be ridiculous to misjudge the situation and write a too-strong claim. Unless you have good reason to believe otherwise, assume that the firm will be cooperative. Little or no persuasion seems necessary; hence you use no appeal beyond a possible brief reference to the guarantee, reputation for fair dealing, and the like.

This kind of direct claim (A–plan) may start with the requested action, or it may start with the history of the case—date and conditions of purchase, conditions of use, development of troubles, and on to present condition. Beginning with the history of the case is a little less antagonizing and a little more persuasive.

The middle part is a carefully planned, complete, and specific explanation of the facts. A test of the adequacy of the explanation is to ask whether it is all you would want to know if you had to decide on the claim—and whether it is convincing. Since claims adjusters aren't stupid, they know that some people lie. Hence you may need to use other evidence to back up your word. The ending, then, is a request for action. It should be as specific as the conditions will permit.

4.   *When you know just what is wrong and what is necessary to set things right, you should make a definite claim; otherwise, explain and ask for an inspection.*

Sometimes you can be sure that the only fair adjustment is a refund of your money or a complete replacement of the product. On other occasions you can see that replacement of a part or proper adjustment of a machine will correct the trouble. You therefore ask definitely for what is necessary to make things right, as in the preceding claim.

Sometimes, however, the product just isn't right, but you don't know exactly what is wrong. Your claim then should be an explanation of how the product is failing to satisfy you and a request for the necessary action. You can make your own estimate and request that action, call in third parties to estimate (as on automobile insurance claims), or ask the firm to investigate and take the indicated action.

5.   *Sometimes a touch of humor can relieve the pressure in small claims.*

Somewhat like the nasty tone (point 2), another common error in writing claims is that many writers become deadly serious about small matters. A claim for replacement of a defective $3 item makes the writer look silly when written as if it were a matter of life and death. If the situation is really serious, of course, you would not want to treat it lightly. But to avoid the too-serious tone in small matters and make the reader an ally instead of a critic, you can often use humor effectively. You may inject only a touch or two, or the whole thing may be humorous.

Several dangers confront you, however, if you decide to be humorous:

1.   A failing attempt to be funny is worse than no attempt.
2.   Humor may make you write a longer letter than necessary.
3.   Humor making the reader the butt will nearly always arouse resentment.
4.   Humor which verges on the vulgar or sacrilegious may offend.

The following successful letter avoids at least the last two dangers:

> We all need air to live, I admit, but don't you think 89¢ a tube is a little high for atmosphere?
>
> In San Antonio, Texas, a few days ago, I bought a tube of Dento toothpaste. At least, that's what I thought I bought. But when I started to brush my teeth at home that night in Dallas, I found a little gob of toothpaste in the top of the tube, a little gob of toothpaste in the bottom, and air in between.
>
> I thought maybe you had a new type of toothpaste, so I tried it out. I'm sorry to have to tell you that air is pretty tasteless. And it doesn't do much of a job cleaning teeth, either.

I could go back to the drug store in San Antonio and demand another tube, but I don't see much profit in making a 540-mile round trip to replace an 89¢ tube of toothpaste—even when it's Dento.

Now, would you prefer to send me a round-trip airplane ticket to San Antonio so I can make a claim to the dealer, or a new tube—one with toothpaste in it?

I have instructed my attorneys not to bring suit until your Board of Directors has had a chance to meet and settle this important question of policy. Meanwhile, my breath is getting steadily worse—my wife and children won't kiss me, and my dog avoids me. I'm in an awful fix!

Adjustment approvals

Adjustment policies.   Invariably a claim represents loss of goodwill and of confidence in the goods or in the firm. The adjustment writer's key job is to minimize those losses by satisfying customers as far as possible at a reasonable cost to the company.

Some companies try to dodge the basic problem by almost literally adopting the policy that the customer is always right. They figure that the few unfair claims cost less in adjustment losses than the liberal policy pays in goodwill.

Other firms take the opposite view and make all sales final. Usually they depend on low prices rather than goodwill to attract a type of customer to whom price is the strongest possible appeal.

The great majority take the middle ground between those two extremes: *Treat each claim on its merits and lean a bit toward giving the customer the benefit of the doubt for the sake of unquestioned fairness and the resulting goodwill.*

Generally a customer will not leave a firm or product after only one disappointment if the firm applies this honest and reasonable policy with finesse. Usually a reasonable person will allow at least a second chance, unless the adjuster loses further goodwill by a poor attitude toward the claim or by bungling techniques in handling it.

Carrying out the recommended policy therefore requires

1. Careful analysis and classification of each claim according to the cause of dissatisfaction and consequently what adjustment is fair.
2. Retaining a reasonable attitude even with angry claimants.
3. Skill in the use of the tools and techniques of adjustment.

Analysis and classification of adjustments.   If the evidence in a claim (and from inspection when deemed necessary) shows clearly that the company or the product was at fault, you may replace the article free with a perfect one, repair it free, or take it back and refund the money.

The last is the least desirable for both buyer and seller. The purchaser bought the article to get the service it would render. If you take it back, you give the purchaser a problem—to make other arrangements or do without that service. If you replace or repair it, you give the service, regain goodwill, and make a satisfied customer who will perhaps buy from you again and pass on the good word about you and your products to other prospects. Indeed, about the only occasion when you would refund the money is when you see that a perfect specimen of the article will not do the job. And even then, if you have another (perhaps larger or of better quality) which you think will satisfy, you should try to give the service wanted and justify any higher price in terms of advantages.

If the dissatisfaction is clearly the buyer's fault, you will ordinarily refuse the claim. In rare cases you may decide that a compromise or even a full-reparation adjustment will be wise because of the amount of goodwill you regain at small cost. The weakness in this decision is that it implies your acceptance of responsibility and increases your difficulty in regaining confidence in your goods and service.

Whatever your action when the buyer is at fault, your major job is justifying your decision and (usually) educating the customer. By educating the buyer in the proper use and care of the product, you may establish the responsibility by implication, avoid irritating the claimant, and prevent future trouble.

If responsibility for the dissatisfaction is uncertain or divided between buyer and product, you will suggest a compromise or make a full adjustment. Again the educational function is usually important.

When you decide to approve the adjustment, our earlier discussion of favorable replies to inquiries and requests prepares you rather well to write full-reparation adjustments, which are in fact answers to requests (claims). They are essentially the same in organization and psychology, but with some basic differences. In answering other requests you have no legal or moral obligation to do anything against your will; in answering claims, you have a legal and ethical obligation to be fair.

Attitude of the adjuster. If a firm's adjuster thinks most claims are dishonest or from chronic gripers, this attitude will show and eventually reduce the number of claims—and probably the firm's sales too. People won't continue to trade where they are considered dishonest or unreasonable—as most are not. In an extensive survey, out of 5 million customers only 2,712 tried to take advantage of one firm in five years.

Claims are an invaluable clue to weaknesses in a company's products, methods, services, or personnel. But the weaknesses won't be corrected if the adjuster considers most claims dishonest.

On the other hand, if you start with the attitude that a claimant may be misinformed but is honest and reasonable, you will be right most of the time, and you will do much better. You will use claims as pointers to improve your firm's goods and operations, and your adjustment letters will thank customers for their help. (Even claims where the buyer seems completely at fault may point to a need for better instructions to users.) But more important, you create a pleasant climate in which people will buy more freely because they know they can get reasonable adjustments if anything goes wrong.

In addition to this sound attitude, you need a thick skin to be an adjuster. Many claimants are not calm. As a wise adjuster, therefore, you will ignore personal taunts. Remember the old saying, "You can't win an argument with a customer; even when you win you lose." So defend your firm, your products, and yourself insofar as you can by explanations; otherwise accept the claims made. Thus you can create a climate of goodwill and good business.

Adjustment tools and techniques. *Using resale.* Since the adjustment writer's main job is to regain goodwill and confidence, you will find resale a highly useful tool. Probably nowhere else is it more important. Indeed, the main job of an adjuster is essentially the same as the purpose of resale—to recover or strengthen goodwill and confidence in the integrity and efficiency of a firm and/or the quality of its goods. Naturally, then, resale is the main tool for doing that job.

Making positive explanations. Effective resale is impossible, however, unless you avoid the following special pitfalls which frequently trap the untrained adjuster:

1. Inadequate or inept explanation that leaves the customer thinking slip-shod methods of manufacturing or marketing caused the trouble. Explain how careful you really are.
2. Dwelling on the reader's dissatisfaction or likelihood of being a lost customer.
3. Passing the buck by attributing the difficulty to a new clerk or an act of God.
4. Trying to hide in the bigness of your firm. About the only way you can use bigness as an acceptable explanation is to sell it in terms of customer benefits along with its weaknesses.
5. Stressing your openhandedness. The customer does not want to be considered a beggar.
6. Suggesting future trouble. You only put undersirable ideas into the customer's head if you say, "If you have any more difficulty, let us know," or even "I don't believe you'll have any more difficulty." In fact, a big problem in adjustments is what to do about the inherent negatives in them.

Handling inherent negatives. As an adjustment writer, you need to be a master of the techniques for dealing with negatives. You'll do well to remember the definition of *negative* as anything unpleasant to the reader. Moreover, you should remember that *a good business communicator avoids negative material when possible and otherwise subordinates it*. You'll find that you can usually avoid most of the goodwill killers like the following, which creep into the work of untrained adjusters:

you claim	policy	damaged	delay
you say	amazed	broken	inconvenience
you state	fault	defective	regret
you (plus any ac-	surprised	unable	sorry
cusing verb)			

Such wording need not appear. Prune out the negative wording (and implications). Substitute positive phrasing.

Adjustment-approval messages.   Since an adjustment approval is good news (A–plan), you answer the big question in the first sentence as fast as you can. Not only should this sentence tell that you are approving the adjustment, but it should avoid any grudging tone and refrain from recalling the dissatisfaction any more than necessary.

The fact that you have approved the adjustment gives you a natural basis for some resale talk on the house. You should use it by interpreting the approval as evidence that you stand behind guarantees and treat the customer right, or something similar.

Somewhere, but not necessarily right after the good news and its interpretation, you should express appreciation for the claimant's report (because the information helps the firm to keep goods and services up to par). This "thank-you" does several important things quickly:

1.   It shows that you are fair-minded and do not take a distrusting or bitter attitude toward claims.
2.   It is basically resale in showing that you are interested in retaining (if not improving) your standards for goods and services.
3.   It makes the customer feel good because a claim seems welcome and appears to get careful consideration.

Of course, if you are taking any steps to prevent recurrence of claims such as you are answering, you should explain them (to rebuild confidence) and give the customer as much credit as the facts allow. Anybody likes to hear that "On the basis of helpful suggestions like yours, we have decided . . . ."

Your explanation of the situation will be important. If the product was obviously defective or the firm was at fault and no explanation will put either in a better light, you'd better accept the fact and frankly admit the error or defect rather than make excuses. If you explain specifically how your firm tries to see that everything goes well, most people will accept it as due precaution and will understand that mistakes do occasionally creep in, despite reasonable care—ZD production is an unattainable ideal.

If you have statistics to show how effective your system is in avoiding mistakes and defective goods, they may be effective in rebuilding the customer's confidence and goodwill. Be careful, though, not to present such data in a way that seems to say the reader must be odd to have trouble when nearly all your other customers don't.

Although you can't honestly or safely promise that a similar situation will

CHECKLIST FOR APPROVING ADJUSTMENTS

1. Make the beginning fast, informative, pleasant, and reassuring.
   a. Open with the full reparation—a specific statement of what you are doing.
   b. Avoid any grudging tone.
   c. Build up the favorable reaction with a few resale words.
   d. Too much resale on defective products before explanation may bring an "Oh yeah?"
2. Avoid emphasis on disappointing aspects and negative words.
3. Explain fully, honestly, and reassuringly any favorable facts.
   a. Include a goodwill-building sentence—either that you're glad to make the adjustment or that you welcome the report as a way of improving quality and service.
   b. Whichever you choose, be sure your facts relate logically to your wording of the adjustment you've made.
   c. Judicially, impartially—and preferably impersonally—establish the reason for the mishap in the minimum number of words. Often you can effectively imply the reason in your explanation of corrective measures taken or your ordinary care.
   d. Whether you name or imply the source of error, give concrete evidence of normally correct, safe shipments of high-quality goods, or—if applicable—explain changes you are making to prevent recurrence of the difficulty.
   e. Be quick to admit error; don't appear to be buck-passing.
   f. Avoid suggesting frequency of error.
4. Ask for any necessary cooperation from the customer. For example:
   a. Be tactful in asking the customer to sign necessary forms.
   b. What about the original article if you're replacing it? Make any customer action as easy as possible ("When the driver calls to pick up the original shipment, just have . . .").
5. Close pleasantly with a forward look.
   a. Don't ruin your good positive efforts with a backward look apologizing or otherwise recalling the disappointing aspects.
   b. Do leave the customer with a pleasant reminder of the pleasurable use of the perfect article now in hand, if applicable.
   c. You may end with resale talk, but sales promotional material on an allied or seasonal article may well suggest your additional thoughtfulness—and just may pick up an extra sale.

never happen again, you can end pleasantly. Having covered the good news, the explanation, the thanks, and any necessary action of the reader, you can end looking forward, not backward. (Apologies or other reminders of past dissatisfaction merely leave a bad taste in the mouth.) A light touch of resale—or even sales promotion material, if you have a related article you think would serve well—can provide you with a sincere, success-conscious look forward to future business. Customers so well treated will probably return.

The following letter sends the check in the first sentence then gives a clear explanation and strong resale (in answer to the claim near the end of Chapter 11):

> Here's your check as a refund on the XXX suit you purchased, for we support our salespeople in whatever they promise a customer.
>
> The person who told you that we would have no sale on XXX suits was, however, sincere. The XXX manufacturers have never before allowed their suits to be sold at reduced prices. We were notified one week before our summer clothing sale this year that they were permitting a reduction for the first time.
>
> We thank you for calling our attention to this situation, and we are glad to enclose our check for $21.87.
>
> When you again need clothing, see our salespeople. You can rely on what they tell you, with full confidence that we will back them up.

Sometimes you will need the customer's help on a few details such as filling out blanks for recovery of damages from a transportation company or returning defective articles. Be sure to cover such points in the one letter to avoid unnecessary correspondence. And in doing so, make the reader's action as easy as possible—as in this next-to-last paragraph:

> To simplify getting the insurance due from the Postal Service on the first shipment, we are sending a form completely filled out except for your signature. Will you please sign it and use the reply envelope to mail it back?

The related checklist for approving adjustments is comprehensive enough to cover most situations, but not all points are likely to apply to any one situation.

QUESTIONS AND EXERCISES

1. What are some reasons people order by mail rather than go to local suppliers?
2. You are answering an inquiry about an electric garage door opener. How would you describe this opener psychologically to a prospective buyer in the Northeast?
3. If you have to include some negative information about a product, where do you put it and how do you phrase it?
4. You are offering *The Wall Street Journal* at a special price. Where would be the most effective places to put this information in your letter?

5. You are soliciting subscriptions to a magazine, 12 issues a year for $100.
   a. What methods would you use to discuss the price?
   b. Where would you put the price?
6. In one sentence write a reference to an order card that is stamped, addressed, and enclosed.
7. Write a four-part action ending selling a modern camera to an executive.
8. Write a resale sentence on a product you are presently using.
9. In which of the letter-writing situations you have studied so far would you use resale material?
10. Write a statement that has adaptation to
    a. A college student selling that student a bargain-priced bicycle.
    b. A Japanese business executive who you hope will use your desktop computer.
    c. A 10-year-old stamp collector.
11. What don't you want to do when you have to explain to a customer that one of your new employees filled the customer's order with the wrong information so that the wrong goods were shipped?
12. Why is it important that you understand the culture of a country you are doing business with?
13. Can you give examples of some differences in culture in the United States?

CASES

(See p. xiii for some important explanations.)

Direct inquiry cases

5–1. Assume that you have a bright 12-year-old daughter and 14-year-old son who are mathematically inclined but who are not very turned-on by their teachers or schools. In *The Houston Post* you see an ad about a computer camp for boys and girls ages 10 to 18 under the direction of Michael Zeiss. According to the ad, a new camp will be in operation next summer in the Houston area. Since you live in Silsbee, TX, P.O. Box 548, 77756, your son and daughter would not have far to go to camp. But you have some questions to ask Zeiss (Computer Camps, Inc., Old Woodstock Road, Moodus, CT 06469): time spent on computers, time spent in outdoor activities, kinds of activities, homework, cost, kinds of computers (do students bring their own and if so would an Apple II+ do). Add any other likely questions.

5–2. As the representative for Diamonds International, 9000 Wright Rd., Cleveland, OH 44116, you have to travel a great deal throughout the Midwest selling diamonds to small jewelers. You were almost robbed once; so today when you read the ad in *Road* by Bennett's, Inc., 17502 Dartmouth Dr., Norristown, PA 19406, for Thief Alert, you took down some questions in preparation for writing an inquiry. The ad read—

Low Cost Pocket Pager & Theft Warning System by Coded Radio Signal. Calls you—only you—the moment a thief or vandal tries to enter your car, home, boat, or plane.

Guard your valuables 24 hours a day at low, low cost!

Your own, private, HF radio signal in your pocket; one full watt power, one-mile range, transmitter will fit any car or truck, one-year warranty, 10-day money-back guarantee, $160.95 retail.

There's no mention of installation. You have put in auto tape decks and would like to install the Thief Alert if the job is not too difficult. If it were too difficult, who would you get to finish the job? Does the receiver work effectively indoors? What type of warning sound does it make? Is the page signal different from the alarm tone? Will CB radio or lightning set off false alarms? What power sources operate the transmitter and receiver? Is the transmitter a sound-sensitive device, a motion detector, or is it switch activated?

5–3.   As director of sales for the southeastern region, Nuclear Medicine Division, General Selectric Company of Milwaukee, WI 53210, you interviewed a personable, attractive, intelligent, hard-working, overly ambitious and very headstrong 30-year-old, Malcolm A. McNally, for your opening in sales in the Miami, Florida, area. McNally earned a B.S. in chemistry and an M.B.A. from the University of Illinois, Champaign–Urbana, served in the military as a second lieutenant for two years, and represented the X-ray division of Bearle Radiographics in the Peoria, Illinois, area for four years. With Bearle he ranked third in the region in net gains the first year and consistently realized $350,000 in net sales gains annually. He sold to radiologists, hospital administrators, chief technologists, nuclear medicine departments throughout Illinois, Iowa, and Missouri; and he designed departments for nine major hospitals to incorporate Bearle equipment sold, and was appointed equipment coordinator for the district two years ago. While McNally earned his graduate degree, he worked as an assistant for a Professor Gayle Means, Marketing Department. While earning his undergraduate degree he worked part time and all summers.

In talking with McNally you learned that he quit work with Bearle (to make more money, he said) and he worked with his father-in-law in developing shopping centers around the St. Louis area. After a year of this type of work he is ready to get back into sales of X-rays, CAT scanners. Also he implied that he and the father-in-law didn't hit it off too well. The old man had old-fashioned ways, not progressive.

You asked for and got the name of his former boss at Bearle, Donald P. MacGillivray. You have some questions as to why McNally really quit Bearle (ambition, personality clash, family pull?). Although he seems to have many good qualities, you are concerned about his strong determination to get ahead, to make his own rules. Write a confidential letter to MacGillivray, Bearle Radiographics, Jefferson Rd., Peoria, IL 61611. (Related Case 5–13).

5–4. From your home address write a real estate firm in a place where you want to retire. Ask the firm about land you especially would like (around a golf course? fishing lake? shopping area? tennis courts?). Assume the kind of house that you think you might like to live in when you retire (one level? multilevel? frame? brick? air conditioned? garage?) and assume a price you think you can pay and still make money from your investment.

5–5. Clip (or copy) from the pages of any newspaper or magazine an ad featuring a product or service in which you are interested. Write an inquiry to the manufacturer or distributor asking for details not furnished by the ad. Price and local availability are possibilities. Servicing is another. Ask four significant questions, *at least one of which requires explanation on your part.* Attach the ad or copy to your letter.

5–6. *Write to:* Inclinator Company of America, 3015 S. 163d St., Racine, WI 53151, in response to an ad in *House Lovely,* last month, page 66.

Writer: John Morrison Giles, Rt. 2, Box 4, Lake Egypt, IL 62901, phone (618) 555-8925.

Product: Stair-Glide for outdoors to go to and from boat landing to home approximately 30 feet down and up steep incline.

Problems: Doctors just discovered that 70-year-old Giles has a mild heart condition (angina); so going up and down the steep grade from house to boat is out of the question. His wife, too, is finding the climb hard. So Giles wants to know if the Stair-Glide holds one or two people (the ad shows a picture that looks as if two could ride at once). Price, warranty, safety, appearance, 110 or 220 volt power, sales representative, rent or buy, tax deductible? Add any other questions that you think are reasonable.

5–7. You have the unhappy duty of making funeral arrangements for an elderly great aunt who now lives with you and must be buried next to her husband back in the family grave plot in Decatur, Illinois. Though the aunt is not dead yet, you think it wise to get some information from one of the funeral homes in Decatur, Memory Chapel, 800 W. Wood St., 65222. Write the manager, H. M. Dawson, and find out the different costs of caskets and charges for graveside versus church services. Since the aunt has few or no living friends, you'll have to count on the funeral home for pallbearers. Is there a charge for this? You checked with a local funeral home and were told that bodies had to be shipped in special sealed containers. Does Dawson agree with this advice? What other details involved in shipping a body cross-country and having it interred can you think of that need to be cleared up?

5–8. Write Fair Havens Home for Senior Citizens, 500 Owyhee, Paradise Valley, NV 89426, and ask for details about making arrangements for an 86-year-old relative of yours. Find out what the monthly charges are for basic, intermediate, and skilled care. Ask about facilities (private room, semiprivate). Ask what down payment is necessary and what the charges cover. Your relative insists on not living with you but wants to live near the old home-town, and that is why you considered this home. Your relative has circulatory problems and has to have a shot for pernicious anemia every 10 days to two weeks. You want your relative to have a comfortable place to live, but the cost of comfort is a real consideration. You and the relative have limited funds.

5–9.   While traveling through Amarillo, Texas, last summer, you and your friend stopped at the Patio Motel, I–40 at Ross 79102, for lunch. What really impressed you was the tasty pepper relish served at the salad bar. Once home you write the Patio Motel and ask what kind of relish that was and where you could buy it. Naturally you are interested in the price. Also find out what size jars it comes in.

5–10.   For eight additional direct inquiry cases, see Appendix E: I, A, C; II, A; III, C; IV, A; V, A; and VIII, A, D.

Favorable replies (no sales prospects)

5–11.   Before writing, read Case 11–1. You, John H. Bremer, are writing Steve Hanes, P.O. Box 4193, Northside Station, Winston-Salem, NC 27105, telling him that you look forward to making your presentation two weeks from now (name date), that you will need a slide projector and screen for your talk. You'll enclose a summary of your life that should help in the introduction. Your guest will be your son, David, a recent graduate of University of North Carolina, Chapel Hill. David is a budding insurance sales representative you would like to see in Rotary.

5–12.   After reading Case 11–18, as Professor Norio Aoyama write an acceptance letter to Dr. Mary B. Grunkemeyer, 71/1 Tivoligasse, 1120 Vienna 12, Austria. You will want to use an overhead projector to show transparencies of different tables picturing world trade from 1965 to the present. You plan to arrive in Singapore November 9 late afternoon. And you'll be ready to give your presentation 9:30–10 o'clock on the morning of November 11.

5–13.   After reading Case 5–3, as MacGillivray write Charles M. Perry, director of sales for the southeastern region, Nuclear Medicine Division, General Selectric Co., 9765 Executive Park, Atlanta, GA 30306, a confidential letter about Malcolm A. McNally, your employee for four years. McNally has drive and ambition, wants to make a good reputation in sales by the time he's 32. But he really has a dislike for doctors in general and distrusts many (an attitude that hurt some of his potential sales). McNally is headstrong, decisive, terribly hard working, and highly ambitious.

Part of his striving to make a lot of money, you felt, was from the pressures of his wife and two children. His wife is from a prominent, wealthy family in the St. Louis area and she wants to live in the style she was born to.

McNally is the type who wants to be boss, wants to tell the boss how to run things (wants to tell doctors how to run their shows, too). But, he can sell. He goes to all necessary meetings and does his homework, but he must be encouraged to turn in reports (for he thinks they are not important and are a waste of his time).

5–14. Avoiding many of the pitfalls of negativism, sexism, defensiveness, and overprotectiveness, write a first (memo) evaluation (a regular part of your job) about an employee following an informal evaluation interview. You are a supervisor for Nationwide Corporation. This subordinate is two years younger than you, is of a different sex, and has a college degree in the same line of work as yours. The knowledge this subordinate brings to the job and the hard-working attitude (doesn't mind long hours—even works on weekends) are this person's best qualities. But when it comes to managing people, this person acts like an overbearing military officer. The attitude seems to be—do it my way or else. Assume that leadership is important to this job. You are free to make up specific things that happened on the job to illustrate points (but be realistic!) that you bring out in the evaluation. This written evaluation will be read by the subordinate (who has the right to respond in writing or request a hearing) and by your superior.

5–15. Assume that you now have to write a second evaluation (see preceding case) for a different employee at Nationwide. This employee (same sex as you and same age) has less education than you have (no college degree and doesn't intend to get one). To compensate for the lack of education, this person keeps up with current material on the job and in the news. And in contrast with the employee in the preceding case, this one gets along famously with all other employees. No one seems to mind doing what this person asks. So the work relationship goes well except for one big problem—alcoholism. This person tries to hide a serious problem but usually comes to work smelling of vodka (no, it isn't odorless), is frequently useless in the afternoon after drinking lunch, and has a long record of absenteeism, especially on Mondays after weekend binges. You've had two conferences with the subordinate and also talked about this problem in a general way (there are other employees who have drinking problems). Write this memo that will be read by the subordinate as well as your supervisor. The subordinate has the right to respond in writing or to request a hearing before an impartial board.

5–16. Take the place of the subordinate in either of the two preceding cases and respond in writing to the evaluation of you. What can you say that will protect your position with Nationwide? Make it believable—and realistic. Your memo will be read by your immediate supervisor (who made the evaluation of you) and your supervisor's superiors.

5–17. As manager of the Patio Motel (Case 5–9), answer the inquiry from Jerry Garner, 56 Woodacres, Portland, OR 97202. The relish is bought by

Patio in 112-ounce or 7-pound cans at a cost of $36 a case, or $6 a can. The relish, made from red peppers, water, sugar, vinegar, onions, tomato paste, modified food starch, salt, spices, and flavoring, is made by LeGout Foods Division, 9680 Belmont Avenue, Franklin Park, IL 60131. You cannot sell the relish direct, but suggest Garner write the manufacturer.

5–18. For nine additional favorable replies (no sales prospects) cases, see Appendix E: I, B; II, G; III, B, D; VI, C; VIII, B, E, G, H.

Favorable replies (sales possibilities)

5–19. After reading Case 5–1, assume that you are Michael Zeiss, director of Computer Camps, Inc., and you will answer Mr. and Mrs. Harlan Zabinski's letter asking about your new camp that will open this summer. You plan to enroll 80 youngsters for each of four two-week sessions at the woodsy countryside location near Houston at a cost of $150 per week. Except for Sundays, each morning at breakfast the students sign up for at least two sessions of traditional camp activities such as hiking, boating, swimming, horseback riding (extra cost). But the chief focus of the camp is on computers, and there are three daily 90-minute sessions. Beginners study BASIC and introductory programming; more advanced students take courses in Pascal, assembly and machine language programming, graphics, peripherals, and related subjects. During free time campers play games on any of the 42 Atari, Apple, NEC, Hitachi, and Commodore computers. After several days of intensive instruction (including homework) the campers choose their own computer project. Students may bring their own computers, but the camp has enough for everyone. Generally about one fourth of the campers are familiar with computers before they arrive. Zeiss feels that in the future those who are not computer-literate will be at a terrible disadvantage. Training kids to work with computers is like training them to read—it's that critical. Besides answering the Zabinskis' questions, send along a colorful brochure picturing the camp (cabins for boys and separate cabins for girls, air-conditioned computer classrooms, swimming pool, horse stables, lake for boating and fishing, crafts cabin, nature trails). There are no tennis, handball, basketball, or volleyball courts.

5–20. Sit in for the director of sales, Bennett's, Inc. (Case 5–2), and answer the Diamonds International representative with the following information: $160.95 is cost (less than $10 a year). To lower or increase loudness of low-cost pocket pager and theft warning system to match surroundings, simply adjust volume control. Can distinctly hear intermittent beeping alarm and continuous page tone of Thief Alert over usual office and household noises or such outdoor sounds as low-flying jets or football games. To prevent false alarms, Bennett's engineers designed tone-activated squelch circuit for receiver and shielding circuit for transmitter, thereby virtually eliminating possibility of CB radio wave or lightning interference.

Thief Alert transmitter comes with complete, detailed installation instructions. Anyone having installed tape decks should be familiar with polarity and wiring and will find installation comparatively simple. Will need volt-ohmmeter to complete installation and test operation. If problem arises with installation of transmitter, US-Parts, 2600 Duncan Bl., Jersey City, NJ 07304, will help—or do any repairs under the one-year warranty.

Send a folder picturing the Thief Alert and drive for the order with an enclosed order blank.

5–21. Answer Case 5–4 with realistic information you can make up about land values, houses (prices, sizes, values), sports around the area, shopping, cultural events, demographic picture. Add logical details that you think appropriate. Address the letter to the person who would have written the inquiry in the case and write it on the letterhead of a real estate firm you know.

5–22. As director of Fair Havens Home for Senior Citizens (Case 5–8), answer the inquiry with the following information: Prices are subject to change, but at present in semiprivate room basic care runs $745 monthly ($26 daily), intermediate care $990 ($33 daily), skilled care $1,200 ($40 daily). Private rooms cost $100 per month in addition to the monthly care charge. Drugs, visits from doctors, beauty shop or barber shop service, cable TV, phone, cost of handicraft supplies not included. Charges are payable monthly in advance. No down payment needed. Each resident's condition is evaluated periodically and if the resident needs to be moved to another unit, then the resident will be moved when there's a vacancy. Basic care includes minimal assistance in activities of daily living (brushing teeth, combing hair, bathing, dressing, moving self). Intermediate care includes moderate help with the activities of daily living, assistance with general grooming, observation due to mild confusion. Skilled care includes moderate to total assistance with activities of daily living. Residents in the skilled care category must see their physician every 30 days, others every two months. Semiprivate room means sharing a room with someone else, and the two share a bath with one other room; so four people share one bath. Barber or beauty shop service costs $4. Residents may bring small TV and a chair.

5–23. *Write to:* Giles (Case 5–6). *From:* G. K. McConnel, Direct Sales Administrator, Inclinator Company.

Facts: One-year limited warranty; no rentals; purchase for $2,495; completely weatherproof with all-weather, heavy-duty motor (enclosed); aluminum track; maximum track length 35 ft.; load capacity 250 pounds; 115- or 230-volt, single-phase household current; holds one person. Looks like an outdoor green metal park bench (pictured on enclosure). Can add luggage rack for $29 that's handy to carry packages to the boat (lunches, Thermos, motor fuel). Automatic locking devices prevent chair from moving at start and finish of climb. The 24-volt control provides operation without fear of being shocked.

A broken cable instantaneous safety dog on the roller truck stops the chair. Brake stops chair in event of power failure. Control buttons installed in Stair-Glide as well as at boat landing and in home. Inexpensive to operate ($.02 a trip). Durable. Simplicity of design, long-lasting materials treated for outdoors (rust resistant). Over 80,000 users over 40 years. When Stair-Glide is installed for health reasons, the cost of equipment is deductible as medical expense on federal income tax return.

Enclosures: Assume a folder picturing Stair-Glide, with diagrams, detailed copy.

Action wanted: You are sending a copy of the inquiry and a copy of this letter to your representative, Russell G. Fry, Bagby Elevator and Electric Co., Inc., 4250 1st Ave. S., St. Louis, MO 63114, and asking Fry to call or write Giles. If for any reason Fry has difficulty getting Giles, suggest that Giles call (314) 555–8755 or write for an appointment.

Question: Should you tell Giles the price or leave that to Fry?

5–24. For H. M. Dawson, Memory Chapel, answer the inquiry (Case 5–7) with these facts: average range of funeral costs $1,300 to $3,000—depends on what type of casket is selected. Cemetery charges presently run $247. A burial box or a choice of five Wilbert burial vaults currently priced from $358 to $1,400. Flowers and clergy honorarium would also be added costs. Memory Chapel does not charge any more to conduct a service from a church as opposed to graveside service. It does not sell caskets as separate item but includes all items of service and facilities, such as care of the body, livery, professional staff, pallbearers as one price.

A prepaid funeral could be set up in a trust fund in advance of need, if desired. Suggest a visit to Memory Chapel to see what caskets are available for it is easier to discuss these matters personally so that the buyer can arrive at a definite overall cost. Cost of shipping a body varies according to the distance and type of shipping box purchased. Reply to David Wexler, Rt. 6, Box 1158, Parkersburg, WV 26101.

5–25. For an additional case, see Appendix E: I, D.

Orders (for goods and services)

5–26. As the vice president for personnel administration for a large, nationwide corporation, you have a memo to write.

The corporation rule has been that a husband and wife may not work together in the same department, though they may work in the same facility. Recently a husband and wife working at your Newark, New Jersey, warehouse got divorced. Subsequently the woman was assigned to work in the same department as her former husband. Later the man and woman decided to live together, though not to remarry. Since they would not cease living together, and no other positions were available at the facility for either, the man and woman were discharged. They raised a ruckus, the case went to arbitration, and the arbitrator ordered your company to take them back at their jobs—with back pay.

Write a memo to the personnel managers at all corporation facilities establishing as corporate personnel policy that any two people who are married or cohabit may not work in the same department. If the least senior of the couple will not take another job in the facility, at the same or a different salary, that person will be discharged. Recount the above happening in Newark as the reason for this altered policy.

5–27. Look around in your medicine chest and make a list of the kinds of drugs and drug supplies you would like to order from the Pharmacy Dept., American Association of Retired Persons (AARP), P.O. Box 1444, 3823 Broadway, Kansas City, MO 65151, and charge to your Visa card. Assume you are retired and a member.

5–28. Because of an increasing interest in intercultural business, for your company's library (make up the name and address) you are to order the following: Vern Terpstra, *The Cultural Environment of International Business*, South-Western Publishing Company, Chicago, 1978; Edward Hall, *Beyond Culture*, Anchor Books, Garden City, NY, 1977; Elise Boulding, *Women: The Fifth World*, Foreign Policy Association, New York, 1980; and Philip R. Harris and Robert T. Moran, *Managing Cultural Differences*, Gulf Publishing Company, Houston, Texas, 1979.

5–29. As the president of your school write a memo to Wilma Greason, Assistant to the Vice President for Student Affairs, Office of Student Affairs, asking for a report on the amount of personal property that has been stolen, the number of physical assaults, and an estimate of the amount of furnishings that have been vandalized in the last year. Also you want some positive suggestions of what the administration, the student government association, and administrators of university housing can do to improve the situation.

5–30. Jackson & Perkins Company, 1 Rose Ln., Medford, OR 97501, specializes in nationwide selling by mail of roses, trees, and other plants and flowers like amaryllis. You have J & P's brochure featuring the amaryllis and the roses but you have no order form. For the next holiday season (Christmas, Mother's Day, or the like) or special occasion (birthday, wedding, anniversary) you want to send gifts to two friends at addresses you provide in different cities (one appleblossom amaryllis #417, $8.95, to each friend). For yourself you want to order three rose bushes, #4973, French Lace, $22.95, and three crabapple trees (American Beauty, Pink Perfection, and Snowcloud) #W60, $57.95, and charge to your Visa account 3376–097–087–564. Shipments to New York and California residents require adding state and local tax. All customers must add $1.60 mailing and handling for each shipping address.

5–31. For an additional case, see Appendix E: VI, A.

Standard acknowledgment cases

5–32. As president of Blue Cross/Blue Shield of your state write a fill-in form letter that will go to new subscribers who transfer from another state's BC/BS system. You can assume that the contract and identification cards are enclosed. Remind the subscribers to read the contract and to keep one copy of the ID card with them at all times. They are to call your Customer Service Department (988–2200) if they have questions about their benefits or if they have claims. Add resale talk on BC and BS. Also, by filling in the blanks, tell the one person to whom you address each copy: (1) the effective date, (2) the end date of his/her transferred credit, and (3) your quarterly billing schedule.

5–33. As Wilma Greason (Case 5–29), assume that your records quickly provided the statistical data requested and that your head—refreshed by setting up the tables of (assumed) data you are listing—has developed the suggestions you really *are* itemizing in this memo acknowledgment.

5–34. When Stacy Sponseller lived in Paris, London, and Washington, D.C., she had no problem buying your cosmetics from exclusive shops in those cities, but now she lives in Brazil (2987 Avenida Rio Brinco, 37 c/704, Rio de Janeiro) and must order from your headquarters, Elizabeth Barden, P.O. Box 5461, Indianapolis, IN 45255. Acknowledge her order for

1 Revitalizing Tonic	5 oz.	$12
2 Night Renewal Cream	1 oz.	35
3 Hydrating Cleanser	4.4 oz.	15
1 Day Renewal Emulsion	2.6 oz.	35

and charge the cosmetics plus $5.09 shipping charges to her Elizabeth Barden credit card number 8 99229 6.

She has been a customer of yours for 30 years. From her order you can tell that she is on your Millenium program, which is designed for skin to look, feel, and function like young skin. Your research shows that cell renewal rate slows dramatically with age, but the Millenium cosmetics accelerate cell renewal rates at an average of over 25 percent. These four preparations she ordered perform together to provide outer and inner epidermal care.

Besides resale talk, can you add appropriate sales promotional talk on allied products (lipsticks, hand cream, body lotion for example)? Assume an enclosed folder featuring your cosmetics.

5–35. You are shipping Seattle Violin Shop's (17700 13th Ave., N.W., Seattle, WA 98177) requested 12 violin bridges and 6 cello bridges. The check for $78 covers cost plus shipping. Bridges are best aged hard maple, scientifically tapered for best sound, feet precontoured for easy fitting to top of instrument. Enclose your (Sperske Supplies, 90 E. Gay St., Dallastown, PA 17313) catalog of complete range of materials and tools for makers and repairers of stringed instruments. Promote your special prices this month on African ebony violin and viola pegs ($7.50 a set of four), pernambuco wood violin bow blanks (only $16 each for aged Brazilian pernambuco), and brass guitar fretting (reduced to $1.50 per 36-inch length). Point out all you carry is best quality, everything usually in stock, generally ship same day order is received, invite request for credit.

5–36. For three other possible standard acknowledgments, assume that all's well and write an appropriate response to your (or your teacher's) choice of Cases 5–27, 5–28, or 5–30.

Credit approvals

5–37. Grant a loan of $25,000 at current rates for an art painting to Thomas P. Otto, 4987 Hamburg Rd, La Crosse, WI 54601—from you, vice president of the private banking division of the First Wisconsin National Bank, Madison 53713. Otto has been an established customer of yours for the past 10 years and has borrowed money two times in the last five years for improvements on his dairy farm. The bank policy is to lend for art only to someone who doesn't have to worry about appreciation of the art work to cover the loan. You would not lend money just on speculation, but you are eager to assist collectors who are interested in loans for purchasing paintings, Chippendale pieces, Ming vases.

5–38. As credit manager, Karlin Fastening Tools, 3 Endich Ave., Reading, PA 19606, reply to Lange Leather Products, 305 Main St., San Manuel, AZ 85631. This small company has purchased an eyelet setter and stainless steel eyelets from you, cash with order. Now Lange sends you an order for 35,000 stainless steel eyelets ($12.45 per thousand) and two Model C eyelet setters ($79.95 each) and includes three business references. The references check out, but two of them have done credit business with Lange only once. Approve credit for the order on hand and explain your terms (2%/15, n/45), shipments UPS or freight collect, 18 percent annual interest charged on overdue accounts (1½ percent per month). Talk about your quick shipment: Lange's shipment is already on its way.

5–39. Since you are the credit manager for Delta Rubber Products, 8180 Holly Rd., Grand Blanc, MI 48439, grant credit and send $2,350 worth of vinyl sealing material for aluminum doors and windows to A-Ability Products, 424 Croton Ave., New Castle, PA 16101. Your sales representative says that until now A-Ability has bought sealing material from your biggest competitor. Explain your terms of 3%/10, n/60 and welcome this important new customer. Promise fast deliveries and technical assistance for free on any of your wide range of products.

5–40.   Jeff Shade, who was your sales representative for the south Texas territory of Miller Electric, 1615 Hillendahl Blvd, Houston, TX 77031, your small appliance distributorship, and now is the Houston director for the federal government's aid-to-small-business program, has written on behalf of Juan Wright, who has recently opened the Wright Appliance Company, 1300 Leicester, Galveston, TX 77550. Wright's location, you realize, is in the part of the city that was burned and looted during the riots several years ago. The neighborhood, which is on the edge of the ghetto, is predominantly chicano and has a high insurance risk. Wright, himself a chicano, has had some difficulty getting financial backing and credit from Galveston banks and businesses; and although there is a strong movement in the city to establish a chicano financial basis from which to finance chicano-owned businesses, Wright cannot afford to wait for chicano financial backing. The same afternoon you receive Wright's order for six table-model TV sets @ $71.70 and 12 small radios @ $11.97. Wright sent a $300 check and asked you to extend credit for 90 days for the $273.84 balance. He also included several credit references which you checked out and found satisfactory. Ship his merchandise UPS and extend credit (explain your terms—after the 90 days, 2/10, n/60, with limit of $500).

5–41.   As credit manager, Charles Knopf Publishers, 597 Fifth Avenue, New York, NY 10017, write a credit-granting letter to Ellen Weaver, The Book Mall, 642 Poplar Street, Denver, CO 80220, and send the books she ordered totaling $375.56. Your terms are 2/10, n/30. Even though Weaver has not had retail experience, she chose an excellent location for her store, has inherited money, has a husband with a good job, and is bright. Your sales representative, T. F. Pail, reports that she graduated with honors from Smith College 30 years ago. She got into the book business because she was bored with country club life and because she had always wanted a bookstore. In checking Weaver's accounts, you found she lived in a paid-for $100,000 home, had an excellent credit rating, and was well thought of as a leader in the community, as was her husband. By complimentary comment on the high intellectual level of her book selections, related to her personal background (including lack of business training or experience), try to hint that some Babbittry might be good business. In other words, as an analogy, a wise fisherman (though he loves steak) will use worms (not steak) for bait—because fish prefer worms. So push some lower-brow, more popular books.

Claims and complaints cases

5–42. You ordered $320.32 worth of furniture from Modern Furniture Manufacturing, 1417 N.E. 129th, North Miami, seven weeks ago. You put down $150 deposit and were promised delivery in three weeks. But the sales representative forgot to write down the color of Formica you wanted; so the store called about it. A few days later you went to the store to select the color and found the store burned down. Write a letter to Modern Furniture headquarters, 1033 S. Fancher, Mt. Pleasant, MI 48858, asking for your $150 deposit.

5–43. Effective Meetings Associates (2000 Altair Dr., Suite 300, Colorado Springs, CO 80906) set up your (Essex, Inc., 445 Del Sol Ln., Diamond Bar, CA 91766) national sales meeting in Highlands, Colorado, last week. At EMA's recommendation, you and your spouse (along with your sales representatives and their spouses) attended a play, *Tom Jones,* put on by the local Community Players of Highlands. The bawdy play was full of four-letter words and suggestive actions, and some of your people were upset. Since this night out was a reward for your company's increasing its sales 7 percent over last year, you feel that the choice of play was particularly in poor taste. Many of the actions and lines left nothing to anyone's imagination. As director of national sales for Essex, write Hilary W. Wells, president of Effective Meetings Associates.

5–44. Three weeks ago you taught "Accounting for Non-Accountant Executives" on a one-week cruise from Miami on the Norwegian Caribbean Line (M/S Southward). Eric Hansen, cabin steward, took good care of you and your cabin (436) on the Atlantic Deck. But as soon as the cruise was over and your luggage was delivered to you so that you could take it to your plane (and head for home), you noticed a caved-in area in the lid that cracked the lid of the case for your portable microcomputer (no damage to computer). When you packed the night before docking, there was no damage to the lid. Before you took the plane from Miami to your home, you reported the problem to the purser's office and you filed an Irregularity Report (as the instructions on page 43 of the Norwegian Caribbean Lines brochure said to do). The officer in the purser's quarters said that you would hear from NCL in a few days, but you have heard nothing. You cannot use this case any more, and you'll have to buy a new one to replace it (about $110). Address your claim to the Southward Purser, NCL, One Biscayne Tower, Miami, FL 33131.

5–45. Many things went wrong on your $2,000, 27-day trip to the Orient, India, and Nepal. Now that you are back home and have cooled down some, you still feel it your duty to write the headquarters (Mercival/Merci Tours, Inc., One Tandy Center Plaza, Fort Worth, TX 76102) and send a copy to your local travel agent, Jane Collins, All Seasons Travel. You feel that Mercival/Merci would want to know some of your problems. In Bangkok the hotel was not ready for you; so you had to sit in the lobby most of a day waiting for your room. Also the guide you had in Bangkok was surly—and spoke such poor English that you could hardly understand. In Hong Kong your hotel room leaked from the swimming pool that was above your room. The management would not change your room; so you had to suffer through four days and nights. One of the gifts you bought in Hong Kong (valued at $75) and had sent to the plane was misplaced; so you did not get it when you de-planed in LA. Earlier, Day 1, Tuesday, you left Los Angeles aboard KAL's jumbo jet for Tokyo but your carefully marked luggage did not come with you. You did not get your luggage until Day 4, the date you were to leave Tokyo for Kyoto. Once in Kyoto you had lunch at the Nara Hotel, but lunch was served so late that you were cheated of your time seeing the Great Buddha at the Todaiji Temple.

5–46. For two months you have been having trouble with your mother's bill at Fairmount Health Care Center in Jefferson City, Missouri. The bookkeeper, Warren Carl, blew his top when you asked questions about the bill. He said he did not have the time to fool with you but the bill should be $456. The bill that came for your mother's retirement home was for $910. Carl blamed the computer for the mistake and said that he would write headquarters again. The statement the previous month also had you incorrectly billed for $910. The parting remark foaming out of Carl's mouth was that he could not issue you a corrected bill. This is not the first time you have crossed with Warren Carl. You've talked with several other patrons about the retirement home and learned that they too have received incorrect bills. Because you want to get a correct bill and because you feel that the president of Fairmount Health Care Centers, 1609 N. 14th St., St. Louis, MO 63106, should know about Carl's behavior, you write a letter.

5–47. You and your spouse were set to enjoy a great vacation at your favorite resort. And then, because orders increased, your company (Cramin Paint Co.) asked you to postpone your vacation. You did so, but in the process had to cancel your reservations at the resort and lost your $60 deposit. Write a memo to the director of employee relations asking that Cramin reimburse you for the $60.

5–48. Today your long-overdue shipment from Spade China, 150 E. 39th St., New York, NY 10023, arrived in a smashed box. Of the six dozen Christmas cups, only two dozen were not badly broken. Two dinner plates and two salad plates were also broken. What makes the situation even worse is that you are having a special on this Christmas china and have already begun a promotion campaign to your regular customers (envelope stuffers in last month's bills). You plan to follow up with space advertising in the local paper closer to Christmas. Write a special delivery letter to Spade listing the broken pieces and asking for replacement for your jewelry store, Armstrong's, 19407 Audubon, Norristown, PA 19405.

5–49. The past year you've made one or two trips per month into O'Hare International Airport (Chicago) and have rented a car from Chicago Budget Rent-A-Car Corporation, with headquarters at 9575 W. Higgins Rd., Rosemont, IL 60018. Your plan has been to drive to Belvidere, Rockford, and sometimes Beloit, and then back to O'Hare the next day. The cost of the car rental has varied from $30 to $60 depending on make and model rented. But yersterday when you turned in your rented car (Contract 13835774) the charge was $110.04. You were overwhelmed by this charge, but the attendant on duty merely said the charge was $110.04. By letter ask Chicago Budget Rent-A-Car Corporation to check into the situation and issue an appropriate credit to your American Express Account 3675 359826 31009.

5–50. Because you are moving, you scheduled two ads to run a week beginning Sunday, June 8; and you paid $23.76 the Friday before, June 6. Sunday, one ad for the house ran under 86A, p. 11C, column 3, under the garage sales section, and the ad about your garage sale ran under 53, p. 6C, column 3, under House Sales. You were not able to call the paper Sunday (recorded answering service); so the ads ran the same way Monday (and more sales were lost). When you called early Monday, you were told that you would not be charged for ads run incorrectly. Later in the week you called to cancel the garage sale ad. Since you paid in advance for two ads for a week (and the check for $23.76 has cleared), you ask the classified department to figure and send the refund due. You will address Classified Department, *Kansas City Star*, Kansas City, MO 64132, from your present address.

5–51. For two more claims and complaints cases, see Appendix E: III, E; VI, B.

Adjustment approvals

5–52. As purser, Norwegian Caribbean Lines (Case 5–44), explain that you had a problem of shortage of help for the cruise three weeks ago and that every cabin was full of people. With so much luggage to handle (and fewer people to handle it), apparently something heavy fell on the microcomputer case. NCL is enclosing a check for $110 to cover the damage. Include some favorable comment about this seminar cruise to Cozumel, Grand Cayman Island, Ocho Rios, and an out island (a true tropical business vacation with excellent beaches, clear waters) and address the letter to yourself.

5–53. As adjustment manager for Spade (Case 5–48), write Frances Sanfillippo, Armstrong's, that you are replacing the Spade Christmas china. The UPS truck that carried the china from New York to Pennsylvania was in a serious wreck and the driver was killed. Ask Sanfillippo to sign some enclosed forms from UPS to recover on insurance and wish the store well on its sale. Add allied sales promotion on Wilton Armetale elegant 19-piece, 12-quart punch bowl set with 12 punch cups. Generally this beverage service set retails for $637, but Sanfillippo can buy this month for $300 wholesale.

5–54.   As president of six Fairmount Health Care Centers, answer the complaint letter of Mrs. Barbara S. Spinks, 987 Hickory Dr., Jefferson City, MO 65101 (Case 5–46). You are enclosing a corrected bill for $456 for the preceding month. Apparently the confusion stems from three months ago when Barbara's mother spent 26 days in the nursing-home part of Fairmount yet reserved the room in the retirement-home part of Fairmount. Since there were four other available rooms left vacant at this time, the manager, Ron Smith, decided not to charge Barbara for holding the room in the retirement part of the home. As for Warren Carl's behavior toward Barbara, you have no reason or explanation. Carl's family built the first Fairmount Health Care Center, and he was given a job as bookkeeper and receptionist because of his family connection. He has been at this job now 12 years.

5–55.   Mr. and Mrs. Song Jim Wha, 110 2nd Ave., Pelham, NY 10803, have a valid claim. Their "Miracle" pressure cooker shouldn't have blown up spraying kori kuk (whatever that is) all over their kitchen. Even if they had found a way to tie down the pressure cap (nearly impossible), the lead emergency pressure seal should have blown when the pressure reached 20 pounds, preventing the cooker top from cracking. You will have your local representative, W. H. Trane (who usually calls on wholesalers and retailers) call on the Whas to deliver a new pressure cooker, reimburse them for cleaning their kitchen, and pick up the remnants of the old cooker so you can see what went wrong. Besides thus standing behind your guarantee, is there anything else you can say to renew their faith in your company, Gran Prix Products, 3900 60th St., Kenosha, WI 53142?

5–56.   As claims manager for Sohn Laboratories, Townhall Rd., Belleville, IL 62221, draft a form letter to answer claims from retailers about your defective batch of insect repellant, "Bitex" in 6-oz. spray cans. Somehow cans of "Skunk Here" were mislabeled as "Bitex"—something of a surprise to the people who thought they were spraying an insect repellent on themselves! Hunters use Skunk Here to make themselves smell like skunks to cover the betraying human odor. It is pungent to say the least! Ask retailers to take one can of Bitex from each carton they have in stock and aim a quick spray at a piece of paper. If the can contains Skunk Here, they will immediately know. Ask them to return all such cartons to you, freight collect. If they send the enclosed postage-paid return card to you filled out with their names and addresses, you will immediately send them a carton of Bitex and replace the rest of the defective cartons when they arrive at your plant.

5–57. As sales director for Grandma Mary's fruitcakes (bakers of fine white and dark cakes, thousands of which are sold by mail), 7101 Corsica Drive, Germantown, TN 38138, answer the letter from one of your unhappy customers, Mary Battle, Apartment 707, 2200 South Ocean Blvd., Delray Beach, FL 33444. She reports that over a month ago she sent her order and check for one five-pound Grandma Mary's White Fruitcake, along with her card to be sent to her hostess of several days, Mrs. Ward Burtram, Sun Trap, West Pages, Scarrington, Bermuda. In Bermuda again last weekend, she called the Burtrams and discreetly found out that the gift had never been received. "Unless you have gone out of business—in which case you'd surely return my check for $18.95—will you please trace this or send at once and write a note to Mrs. Burtram confirming that I did order this gift very shortly after I was a guest in her home?" she ended. The facts are (*a*) you were caught short on the special raisins from Turkey and currants from California, without which Grandma Mary's White Fruitcakes would not be the distinctive culinary treats they are, and (*b*) someone slipped in not notifying the buyer or the recipient of the atypical delay in shipment. You've resumed baking and shipping, filling orders in the order received; the cake in question is en route and may already have arrived. Write the necessary letters (to one or both Mary Battle and Mrs. Burtram, as your teacher directs). (You should send Battle a carbon of your letter to the lady in Bermuda.) Certainly you'll want to try to convince both that a Grandma Mary's White Fruitcake is an appropriate gift any time and is well worth waiting for.

5–58. As general manager for Chicago Budget Rent-A-Car Corporation (Case 5–49) write a letter to Mr. Stephen C. Leslie, P.O. Box 5337, Winston-Salem, NC 27103, and explain that he was charged time and mileage rates rather than the corporate rate he was entitled to. Remind Leslie to present his corporate rate ID or sticker in the future so as to prevent any overcharge. His charge should have been $32 per day plus tax and fuel, or a total of $51.57. The American Express account has been credited for $58.47, but he must allow four to six weeks for the credit to appear on the statement.

5–59. For another adjustment approval case, see Appendix E: VI, D.

Special goodwill messages

6

In the preceding chapters we have made clear that all business communications should retain and even try to increase the reader's favorable attitude toward the writer, even when working primarily on something else.

Certain situations, however, call for messages that have no other immediate purpose than cementing friendly relations between writer and reader; and for years most successful people in business have responded to the call. Although such goodwill messages may not ask for any immediate action, indirectly they pave the way for continued business from old customers and new business from prospects.

Because readers know you do not have to send them, these unexpected special goodwill messages are particularly effective in overcoming the impression of indifference—indifference to business given, to the general public welfare, and to serving new customers. Since many of our non-American business friends (particularly the Oriental and Latinate) look upon business relations as more personal than we do, goodwill messages are particularly important in business relations with them—to avoid appearing indifferent.

Many goodwill messages used to go out as separate individualized mailings. Because of the high cost of mailing individual letters, however, goodwill messages today are often printed forms mailed with invoices and bills or in annual reports, newspapers, and magazines. Whether printed forms or individualized letters, however, the messages serve such a significant purpose that they are numerous—and someone has to compose them. This chapter will help you to write them and use them the way they ought to be.

In theory, goodwill messages sell only friendship. Some do no more than that—ostensibly. But we should admit to ourselves that a letter on a firm's letterhead, signed by a representative of the firm, is promotional, regardless of its personal nature. The cultivation of business is inherent in the circumstance itself. Though no business writer need be reluctant to establish the virtues of a firm's services and goods and to place them at the disposal of the reader, blatant promotion under the guise of a goodwill message will probably bring resentment. *The main thing to guard against is appearing to be offering only friendship in the first part and then shifting to an obvious, immediate sales pitch.*

Some of these "unnecessary" special goodwill messages are of such highly personal nature that to use an obvious form would be insulting, to include sales or even resale talk on either the firm or its merchandise would be ludicrous, and to write very much would likely result in gushiness. Notes giving deserved praise or extending sympathy certainly fall into this category. Those expressing appreciation, extending seasonal greetings, issuing invitations, accompanying favors (or services), or offering helpful information also do if they are strictly for purposes of goodwill; but most of these are forms including sales-building talk and thus are promotional.

GIVING DESERVED PRAISE

Although letters and notes praising people do not have to contain the word *congratulations*, you are recognizing a significant event or accomplishment in the life of your reader: a job promotion, election to an office, receiving an honor, winning a contest, graduation, marriage, birth of a child, or completion of a new plant, office, project, or report. All these and many more are instances when you can show not only customers but also friends and acquaintances that you are interested in what happens to them. Some of the better ones are just a few lines:

> When I saw that you've been named plant manager of Tri-States, I was delighted!
>
> It's a well-earned recognition.
>
> And it couldn't happen to a more deserving person!

Any good effects of the foregoing passages would disappear if the writer followed with such an idea as "Now that you're earning more, surely you'd like to consider more insurance" or ". . . buy more clothes."

> ——
>
> Thank you for doing so much to make our first annual management meeting a success. Your willingness to participate indicates exactly what kind of professional you are.
>
> ——
>
> I thought your talk on our booming international business went very well, and I have heard several comments from individuals indicating that your presentation has been of considerable value (and use) to them.
>
> ——
>
> We share your pride and happiness in the completion of the new Henderson plant.
>
> It is a criterion of business, as well as civic, accomplishment.
>
> Good wishes from all of us.

As we illustrate, timeliness and conciseness are important in these congratulations. The friendly thought behind the message, however, counts most.

A note like the following from any manager would certainly engender good feeling (and probably stimulate the reader to do even better work):

> Your analysis of production difficulties at the Saginaw plant was one of the clearest, most easily read reports I've ever been privileged to study.
>
> We're carrying out some of your recommendations immediately.
>
> Several of us look forward to discussing the report with you when you return to the home office.
>
> In the meantime, thanks for a job well done.

Many people in both their business and their private lives have discovered the gratifying responses of associates, customers, and personal friends to the receipt of a newspaper or magazine clipping of interest to the reader. A simple greeting (it may be no more than "Good morning") and a line or two like "This clipping made me think of you" or "I thought you might be interested in this clipping" are enough, followed by a note like:

> Let me add my commendation to those you've undoubtedly already received as a result of the enclosed clipping.

Still another variation on deservedly praising someone goes to a third person. The person who wrote the following letter made at least two friends:

> All of us who were at the recent NSGA show were impressed with the efficiency and professional work your people showed in erecting our exhibit. Our president has already complimented you on the unique design you came up with. I want to compliment you on presenting us a real "turn-key" exhibit—completely erected, with everything working, ready for the show.
>
> It was a welcome experience to go into our exhibit the first morning, find everything in its place, and be able to concentrate on talking to our customers. Please convey our appreciation to all of your people who helped so much to make the show a success for us.

Any time someone renders outstanding service is an appropriate occasion to relay your understanding and appreciation of its significance. Such a gesture not only impresses the reader with the writer's "humanness"; but it also can and often does earn preferential treatment on subsequent occasions.

> We appreciated the promptness with which your representative, Mr. John Wade, answered our call for help last Friday when one of our motors failed at a crucial time. But we appreciated even more his efficiency in getting it running again. He was even considerate and thoughtful enough not to leave a mess for us to clean up.

> Our thanks to you and to Mr Wade; we shall remember on
> other occasions.

Obviously, under such circumstances you could also write directly to the person whose performance you praise, as in the following instance:

> If an award were given by the U.S. Chamber Workshop,
> you'd certainly get the "E" for excellence, John.
>
> Your Thursday afternoon clinic met with more
> enthusiastic reactions than I've observed in a long
> time.
>
> It is a rewarding experience to work with people like
> you.

EXPRESSING APPRECIATION

You have observed that most congratulatory messages also involve an element of thanks. Likewise, most thank-you letters contain some commendatory passages. It's really just a question of where you want your emphasis to go.

Strictly goodwill thank-you messages—in response to a favor extended, for work on a project (member of a fund-raising team, for example), or for a contribution—often have their origins in civic, education, and religious surroundings rather than in business.

> For the 32,000 youths of Athens . . .
>
> Thanks a million!
>
> Your generous gift to the new "Y" building is another
> evidence of your concern for the boys and girls of our
> city and county.
>
> We appreciate your cooperation in this project. As
> citizens and parents, we'll all be happy about our
> "Y" for years to come.

Though such brief thank-you notes do not sell directly, the resale phrases help to convince the reader of the worth of the projects and thus encourage a repeat performance the next time a request comes along. When business firms write them, they are even more definitely promotional.

Any time is a good time to express appreciation to good customers for handling accounts satisfactorily. Even the notation on a current bill, "One of the pleasures of being in business is serving a good customer like you," has a heartening effect. But many firms wisely do more. Upon the first use of the account—or later in the first year—many send a thank-you note like the following:

> Thank you for using your newly opened account. Surely
> you found it a quick, convenient way to shop at
> Tilford's.

```
To make sure our merchandise and service are just the
way you want them, we'll always welcome any comments
you may have about improvements you would like us to
make.

We want to continue to serve you well, and we pledge
our efforts to keep your trust.
```

Because of the rush of business, such messages too often go out only around holiday and special-event times. In many such cases they don't do the effective job they might because too many other people and business firms are doing the same thing on those special occasions. By arriving unexpectedly and without apparent reason at some other time, something like the following note is probably a more effective pleasant reminder of the firm's appreciation:

```
Believe us——

——we appreciate your continued business.

And to hold your friendship and patronage, we
certainly intend to continue giving you the sort of
service and honest values you deserve. See us again
when we can serve.
```

When an account goes unused for some time and then an entry appears, many credit managers wisely send a message:

```
Although the adage "I miss you more than anything in
the world" is more appropriate for a lover, maybe it
will get the message to you that you are missed.

We genuinely appreciate you as our customer and are
eager to serve you in every possible way.
```

Messages thanking customers for paying promptly are simply a more specialized version of the ones we've been examining. They also help to discourage or reduce collection problems. Such a simple note as the following not only pleases the customer; it reinforces determination to maintain the good habit:

```
Your check this morning in prompt payment of your last
purchase made me think, "I wish all our accounts were
handled so efficiently."

It's a real pleasure to service an account like yours,
and we thank you sincerely for your cooperation.
```

You can also easily tie in the expression of appreciation with a concrete reminder of the benefits the customer gains from taking care of obligations as promised:

```
Thank you for the splendid manner in which you paid
your recent account.
```

> Your record of prompt payments firmly establishes your
> credit at Black's. You will find it handy in
> purchasing the many things this large, complete store
> can offer you.

If you keep your eyes and ears open, you'll find many other occasions for saying thank you to your customers. When a customer recommends you or your firm to another person, you'll certainly benefit in the long run by sending a cheerful, personalized note like the following:

> Thank you for telling Wexell Associates about us. On
> the strength of your recommendation one of the
> Associates came in to see us yesterday and we were
> able to contract to blister package many of Wexell's
> small parts.
>
> We appreciate your thinking of us, and we pledge to
> continue our efforts to supply you with the best
> packaging service we possibly can.

When a firm expresses appreciation to an individual, it expects no reply. And when an individual takes the time to pay a business firm a compliment or express appreciation for good service, no answer is *required*. But you establish yourself as courteous and polite if you do reply.

When a company receives suggestions for improved service, some of which will be outright complaints requiring adjustments, an acknowledgment *is* required, particularly if it has invited the suggestion.

> You are quite right, Mr. Von Bergen. The exhaust on
> your new Servaire portable air compressor should point
> away from the air intake, not toward it. That is how
> we originally designed the compressor. But apparently
> we did not make clear to our dealer how to install the
> pipe when assembling the unit for sale to you. We're
> glad you were able to reinstall it correctly.
>
> As a result of your experience, we are altering the
> exhaust flange mounting to make it impossible to
> install the exhaust improperly. Thank you for telling
> us about the problem. You have helped us to make an
> important modification that will result in improved
> and safer service for all our customers.

SENDING SEASONAL GREETINGS

A modified form of thank-you is the seasonal greeting. By far the most common times are around Christmas and New Year, although some retail stores send such messages shortly before Easter, Valentine's Day, or Thanksgiving, when they have less competition from other mailings. Since they must be mass mailings in most firms (to keep down costs), they are rarely personalized.

The "Y" thank-you was a printed form, thus conserving the funds of the organization. Business firms, too, must save time and money by using some modifications of form treatment for their many thank-yous and seasonal greetings. The undisguised form can be successful, however:

> Business firms, too, pause at this season to count their blessings.
>
> Good friends and customers like you are one of our greatest.
>
> So we want to tell you how much we appreciate your business at the same time we send heartiest wishes for
>
> A VERY MERRY CHRISTMAS AND A HAPPY, SUCCESSFUL, NEW YEAR!

CONVEYING SYMPATHY

Unlike seasonal greetings, congratulatory and thank-you messages are practically always individualized. Expressions of sympathy—the most personal of special goodwill messages—must be.

Most of us are accustomed to lending a helping hand and extending expressions of encouragement when friends and family suffer some adversity. The same sympathetic attitude should prevail when a business friend experiences misfortune.

Admittedly, condolences are some of the most difficult special goodwill messages to write because of the melancholy circumstances (which you can reduce by avoiding specifics). But certainly everyone appreciates them. When a report of someone's illness reaches you, a short, human, and essentially positive note like the following can gain goodwill.

> Sorry, Sam—
>
> —to hear that you're in the hospital again.
>
> But with rest and good care you'll be back at work soon.
>
> I've always valued you as a friend and appreciated you as a business associate; so for two reasons I hope all goes well with you.

Most of us sooner or later find ourselves having to write letters concerning the death of someone we've known. To the surviving partner of a business, for example, the following would be a comfort and goodwill builder by showing the writer's friendly interest and concern:

> We were genuinely distressed to learn of the death of Mrs. Guin, your partner and our good friend for many years.
>
> Although the firm of Guin and Beatty will feel the effects of her absence, the greater loss is to the

> community and the Guin family. The good judgment,
> vision, and integrity Mrs. Guin displayed as a
> business leader in your city undoubtedly carried over
> into her private life.
>
> In extending these words of sympathy, we also want to
> add a few of encouragement and confidence in the
> future; we feel sure that would have been Mrs. Guin's
> attitude.

Even though the writer of the preceding might not have met the widower, certainly Mr. Guin would not take offense at a message such as the following:

> For many years we enjoyed a business friendship with
> Mrs. Guin.
>
> We respected her as a good business associate who
> insisted on high standards in serving the public and
> was always just, fair, and cooperative in her
> relations with us. We admired the good judgment,
> vision, and integrity she showed as a business leader
> in your community.
>
> To you who saw these and other fine qualities in
> greater detail and frequency than we were privileged
> to, we offer our sympathy.

Such a letter will necessarily have an emotional impact. But that effect can be less if you will refrain from quoting Scripture or poetry. And sepulchral overtones will not be so powerful if you accept death as the inevitability it is and use the word itself rather than euphemisms like "passed away," "passed to his reward," and "departed." For greater comfort, emphasize the good characteristics and the outstanding contributions of the dead individual rather than the sorrow and anguish of the survivor. Accept the thought that good, worthwhile people continue to exert their influence in the hearts and minds of those who knew them.

Adversity also strikes in other forms—fires, floods, accidents and lawsuits, labor unrest, and work stoppage. When it does, the victim(s) will appreciate a message that says, "We're your friends; we understand the significance of this to you; we hope everything will work out well." If you really mean the offer and are in a position to extend it, you can add the equivalent of "Call on us if we can help."

> All of us were sorry to hear of the fire that
> destroyed your warehouse last night.
>
> It's a tough break.
>
> We're sure, however, that the same determination and
> ingenuity that helped you to build your business so
> successfully will also see you through this temporary
> setback.

Now, if you had some unused storage space and wanted to offer it, you might very well close with

```
We have a 30 × 40 room that we won't need for another
90 days; if that will help tide you over in any way,
give me a ring.
```

But to propose to rent the space would change the complexion of the message and destroy any goodwill built up.

EXTENDING WELCOMES AND INVITATIONS

One of the most popular forms of goodwill message greets newcomers to a community and offers to be of assistance, particularly during the orientation period. Almost always it is an invitation to come in and get acquainted; it also emphasizes the services of the inviting firm. One unusual and unexpected example is the following from a public library:

```
Welcome to Evansville!

We're glad to have you as new members of our
progressive city.

Your library card is ready for your use. We hope
you'll be down soon to pick it up and to become
acquainted with the staff and the services. For your
reading pleasure and research over 100,000 volumes are
available. Staff members will gladly assist you in
finding what you seek. All of the leading magazines
and newspapers are available in the lounge.

The children's room is also well supplied with both
fiction and nonfiction books on a wide variety of
topics of interest to youngsters 6 to 15.

If you enjoy music, you may want to check out some of
the thousand-odd albums and tapes, ranging from the
most recent popular music to the classics.

We shall be glad to give you maps of the city, to
supply directions--in short, to help you in any way we
can to know Evansville better.

The library is open from 9 a.m. until 10 p.m. every
weekday. We are glad to answer telephone inquiries
during that time.

Please come in soon.
```

Such a welcome—with no sales ax to grind—is the essence of goodwill in its spirit. The library has nothing to sell except service—free.

A bank or other firm with commercial/profit aspirations would have to be subtle to have its welcome accepted at face value—not such as the following:

> As a new resident of our friendly city, you are cordially invited to visit the Federal Bank. We should like to get to know you. Even though you may already have selected a bank, it would be a pleasure to welcome you to Blankville personally and to explain the many services the Federal offers its customers.
>
> The Federal has given prompt, courteous, and efficient banking services to the people of Blankville for over 75 years, and we would appreciate the opportunity of serving you.
>
> Among the conveniences in Federal's modern banking quarters are the four drive-in teller windows that enable you to bank without alighting from your car. And in the parking garage right in our own building you may have 30 minutes of free parking while taking care of your banking business.
>
> You may also bank around the clock at the Federal; a complete mail deposit service and a 24-hour depository are located in our parking garage.
>
> Won't you come in for a friendly visit soon?

That letter is an obvious attempt to get a new account, and the attempts to establish friendly feeling are thin and transparent, revealing the wolf in sheep's clothing it is. Better to discard the talk of "get to know you" and "friendly visit" and get right down to brass tacks with an opening like "Since you are a newcomer to Blankville and will need a conveniently located bank with complete facilities, may we tell you what we can offer you at the Federal?"

Someone connected with credit also can easily maintain a list of newcomers to the community and mail a welcoming form (which does not promise credit but only invites the application).

When you can verify credit reliability (usually an easy thing to do), you may elect to set up the account and so inform the reader:

> We know that stores, too, make a difference to a person establishing a home in a new community.
>
> To serve you in the best way possible is one of our aims.
>
> As an assurance of our desire to establish a permanent and happy business friendship, we have opened a convenient charge account in your name.
>
> The next time you are in the store, simply say "Charge it" to the person waiting on you.

On the other hand, the invitation to a special event extended in the following letter would probably be read with interest; it builds goodwill because it expresses a desire to render service; no sales promotion (except that inherent in the action itself) distracts:

> Will you come to our free seminar on industrial fire prevention?
>
> Between government regulation and the advent of new industrial chemicals and manufacturing processes, upgrading plant fire protection has become a necessity, not an option. That's why we have scheduled a free three-hour seminar on new fire prevention technology. We promise no sales pitches, just information. We'll even show you some of our competitors' products!
>
> You'll hear about and see the latest in extinguishers, wireless remote alarms, foam systems, smoke detectors, and much more. We won't promise to make you an expert, but after our seminar you'll have a far better idea of what is available in fire prevention to meet your company's needs.
>
> For your convenience we're scheduling two sessions, Tuesday, February 22, one from 8:30 to 11:30 in the morning, the other from 7:00 to 10:00 p.m. Use the enclosed reply card to tell us which session you want to attend and how many of your people will come. Since the hall we've rented at Frederick and Eighth Streets will hold only 160 people, we'll have to accept registrations on a first-come, first-served basis; so send in the card today.

The following to a new shareholder is typical of what many corporations do to cement goodwill (and possibly forestall some gripes when things don't go too well for the corporation):

> On behalf of the Board of Directors and employees of Pushman, I welcome you as a Pushman stockholder.
>
> Through your shares in Pushman, you participate in ownership of one of America's leading corporations . . . one with a bright and promising future.
>
> Your company has operations in virtually every part of the world, activities that reach into a broad range of products and services that help to make human life better.
>
> As your company progresses, you will receive regular reports. I've enclosed your company's latest annual report to give you an in-depth view of our achievements and status last year.
>
> Again, welcome to Pushman. We look forward to sharing with you.

Attempts to revive retail accounts are but modified versions of invitations. When an account remains unused for three months or six months, it may be a signal that the customer is drifting away because of the firm's indifference, or because of a real grievance. Form notes inviting the customer back, reselling your products or services, stressing "How can we serve you better?" and finally asking forthrightly, "May we continue to serve you?" can go out individually or in a series.

You can easily build your messages around special events, such as Christmas (although you may lose some effect by competition with many others):

```
A welcome warm as Santa's smile awaits you at Bowen's!

We're all decked out with our Christmas best; so you
can easily find the right gift for everyone on your
Christmas list.

Practical gifts, starry-eyed gifts . . . all
conveniently in one store . . . where you can just say
"Charge it" for ALL your Christmas giving.

                               Warmest holiday greetings!
```

Accompanying a new credit card, one letter solicited the renewal of the customer's business with:

```
Ordinarily we'd send you this enclosure with our
monthly statement. Since your account hasn't been used
recently, we're sending it along with some back-to-
school suggestions.

Whether you're thinking of complete outfits for your
child or a back-to-school gift for a favorite niece,
nephew, or friend, you'll find complete selections of
dependable, quality Bowen merchandise in every
department.

Your charge account is just as good as ever--whether
you come to the store, phone, or shop by mail.
```

Some writers studiously avoid asking whether anything is wrong (for reasons explained in the inquiry stage of collection procedures—Chapter 12). Others send a series of mailings before asking. A favorite form is the letter written on only one half of the page (usually the left side) with the caption "Here's Our Side of the Story." At the top of the right-side blank space appears another caption, "Won't You Tell Us Your Side of the Story?" (The message/reply duplicate memo form serves particularly well.)

TRANSMITTING PREMIUMS

Often as a goodwill reminder an alert executive finds some item to mail inexpensively along with a note stressing the desire to be of service, such as the following from a jewelry and optical shop:

The special pocket—size Rausch & Lomb Star Ban spray accompanying this note is for your use in keeping your handsome Everett glasses spotless.

Accept it with our compliments and the assurance that we want you to be completely happy with your recent selection from Everett's collection of fine frames for the discriminating woman.

In a somewhat humorous vein one firm mailed a pocket-size calorie counter to customers and prospects with this short note:

"Everything's expanding—especially my waistline," grumbled a friend recently.

Just in case you (or someone you know) may need to fight this perennial battle, we're sending you this handy calorie counter that you can use at home, at a banquet, or at a lunch counter.

Accept it with our compliments—and the hope that we'll be seeing you soon.

Small gadgets galore come into play in this manner. Like tricks in sales presentations, however, they work only if directly related to the product or service of the firm. A real estate agency might appropriately send a pocket-size map of the city to which a person has just moved, along with the following:

Welcome to Jacksonville.

To help you get places faster and to know your new city better, this map shows the principal thoroughfares and locations of the main landmarks and facilities.

Note that the Coleman Agency is in an accessible area with adequate parking facilities nearby.

We would welcome the opportunity to help you in any way we can.

OFFERING HELPFUL INFORMATION

Large companies sponsoring radio and TV programs, as well as research projects and publications, rapidly accumulate names and addresses of people who want to be kept informed. As part of their public relations programs, many of these companies occasionally send letters like the following:

Perhaps you will be interested in a program, "Life under the Sea," scheduled for Sunday, January 22, at 8 p.m. over NBS—TV.

"Life under the Sea" was directed by Emile Ravage, with the assistance of the marine biologist Albert

Gaudin. It is the third in a series of such
productions sponsored by the Rawlston System.

We hope these programs will help to broaden public
understanding of science and to encourage some young
people at least to consider scientific careers.

––

The exciting events in Detroit leading up to the
introduction of the new models last month made a story
too detailed to print completely in Tempo.

If you read the condensed version in the issue of two
weeks ago, you'll agree that the accompanying report-
analysis we're sending to selected educators and
business executives is a worthwhile supplement. If you
didn't . . . well, we think you'll want to now.

ANTICIPATING RESISTANCE

In business as in medicine, prevention is much better than a cure. In the
interest of forestalling complaints and minimizing dissatisfaction, many business executives therefore give advance notice when they foresee something
like an interruption of service, a curtailment of service, or a necessary price
increase. In almost all instances these notices (often only postcards) must be
obvious forms. They need to stress service—improved service, if possible; at
least, maintaining superior service or quality of goods—as an antidote for the
inherently negative material the message has to establish.

This message from a power company is typical (dates and times varied according to areas and so were stamped in). Notice, again, the effective psychology of good news first (justifying the bad), bad news embedded in the
middle, and a pleasant ending.

To provide better service for you and our other
customers in your area, we have installed new
equipment, which we plan to place in service

April 15, 19––
between 1 and 2 p.m.

To safeguard the workers who do this work, we shall
have to shut off power during this time. Service will
resume as promptly as possible. We appreciate your
cooperation in making this improved service possible.

A notification of a coming price increase is even more unwelcome. Admittedly, it is never easy to write. But with specific details justifying the increase, it may be successful in retaining the goodwill of some otherwise-lost
complaining or rumor-mongering customers. The following notice went to all
customers, riding free with their monthly bills:

It's been a tough year, hasn't it? Wages have gone up,
costs of materials and supplies have gone up, utility

bills have gone up, insurance has gone up,
transportation costs have gone up.

Of course this isn't news to you. Everybody's in the
same boat. Including us.

Our highly trained operators need more money, our
costs for machines and supplies are rising,
electricity is more expensive . . . everything is more
expensive.

To continue to give you the same prompt, efficient
service we have in the past, and to add new
technological advances as they become available, we
have to increase our charges. The rates on the
attached rate sheet will go into effect July 1.

Thus we can and do continue to guarantee, as always,
the same high-quality service you expect.

Such a notice as the preceding can be even more convincing (and hence effective) if you can give the specifics of your cost increases for the past few months or years.

IMPROVING SERVICES

To find out how to improve their services, hospital administrators (like other administrators) often use a goodwill message along with a special request asking the recipient to complete a questionnaire. It can sometimes ride free with the bill. Whether it brings helpful suggestions, complaints, unreasonable ideas, or no response, it will build goodwill by showing concern.

We tried to serve you well in our Emergency
Department. Since only you can evaluate our services,
however, we would appreciate your taking a few minutes
to fill out this questionnaire. Your comments will
help us improve our service and reward members of our
staff when deserved.

Your replies will be kept completely confidential.

—

Our main goal is to restore your health as soon as
possible so that you can happily return to your home
and community. We make every effort to make you
comfortable in an atmosphere of care and concern.

As communities grow, however, their demands on
hospitals for the delivery of health-care services
also grow. The ability to meet these demands
adequately depends largely on the continuing
excellence of facilities, equipment, and medical
staff. At XYZ Hospital we believe we have that

```
excellence and fully take responsibility for
maintaining it.

To help us, would you please complete the enclosed
Patient Questionnaire and return it in the addressed,
postage-paid envelope. Your comments or suggestions
will help us to help you better.
```

*   *   *   *   *

We could classify and illustrate hundreds of situations in which a special goodwill message would be appropriate and would cement a friendship for you and your firm. If you are alert to conditions, if you keep informed about what is happening to your clientele, if you honestly like people and enjoy pleasing them, however, you'll see plenty of opportunities. In this short treatment, therefore, we have tried to concentrate on the most common instances. We intend it only as a springboard for your thinking and practice rather than an extensive catalog.

In fact, opportunities for helpful goodwill messages are so numerous and varied that we cannot give you a checklist for them. We encourage you, however, to

1. Write all you can of these "letters you don't have to write but should." The subheads in this chapter provide you some starting points for thinking of appropriate situations.
2. Make them specific enough to fit and be meaningful even when forms (*not* as one big company began, "If you are one of the many motorists enjoying the benefits of an XX credit card . . ."). (The writer should have known.)
3. In these most personal of business messages, be especially careful to get names, addresses, and facts right.
4. Avoid gushing in tone or length.

Such special goodwill messages can do a big *extra* job for you, but remember that *all* your business communications should build goodwill through courteous, sincere tone and the service attitude (Chapter 3).

QUESTIONS

1. Can you think of any kind of goodwill message that should or should not have been written that is not mentioned in this chapter?
2. Can you remember any goodwill message that you have received?
3. A beauty shop sends billfold-size calendars to its customers at Christmas time. Was this a good idea? Why or why not?
4. What are two important general considerations in messages of congratulation?
5. Should you reply to a letter of appreciation from a customer?

6. In a letter of sympathy, is it a good idea to spare the reader's feelings by avoiding any direct references to death?

7. Match the appropriate premium (to accompany a goodwill letter) to each firm:
   - *a*. Retail fabric store   Personalized coffee mug
   - *b*. Travel agent   Small cloth tape measure
   - *c*. Office supply company   Paper model of Eiffel Tower

8. What would be the three major topics in a letter announcing a price increase, and in what order should they appear?

CASES

(See p. xiii for some important explanations.)

6-1. For your boss, a U.S. senator, write a letter for the word processor to go to one of the 15 leading persons in your state or a leading person in your district inviting that person to attend a Washington Progress Briefing two months from now on the third and fourth of the month. There is no charge (but you hope that this leader you are inviting will be impressed enough to give money to your campaign fund). Room costs and travel arrangements will be up to the individual, but you are reserving a block of rooms at the Hyatt Regency Capitol Hill ($80 single, $100 double). Upon receipt of a reply card, you will confirm room reservation.

You will provide all meals and transportation, which include a seated dinner the night of the third, breakast at the Heritage Foundation (with report on goals, programs, impact), and lunch at the Capitol Hill Club with talks on plans and strategy for the mid 80s. To make this case more interesting, you can get current figures as to how many conservatives versus liberals or how many Republicans versus Democrats are presently in the Senate and you can find some current topics that are hot issues.

6-2. As an independent insurance agent (you make up the name and address) write a form letter for the word processor that will tell your customers that you have adopted a new computerized accounting system which will provide better information about premium charges and payments. The insured will receive monthly statements showing the status of the account. From now on, a late charge of 1.5 percent per month (annual percentage rate of 18 percent) will be charged to customers whose accounts are past due. Besides thanking the insured for business, suggest that you are willing to discuss all fire and liability insurance and will give premium quotations before the next renewal.

6-3. From a weekly news magazine, select a current article that impressed you. Write a letter praising the article and send it to the letters editor of the magazine. Be very specific (answer *why* you were impressed).

6-4. After seeing a worthwhile program on television that impressed/depressed you, write a letter of appreciation/congratulations to the network responsible. Be specific in your remarks, giving specific comments about the performance.

6–5. *a.* Visit a church, Y, home for abused spouses, orphanage, home for unwed mothers (some worthwhile group), and write a letter to the organization commenting favorably on the work that is going on but making no other contribution (of money or other help).

    b. Assuming that you *do* want to make a contribution, write in longhand at the bottom of your letter for 5*a* the change you would now make and (by arrow) show where the additional wording would go in 5*a.*

6–6. Assume that you have had a commercial exterminating business for 30 years and are now going to retire. You have sold the business to a reliable person that you hope your long-established customers will continue to trade with. Write a letter to your customers (as part of your agreement with the new owner) telling them about the change and encouraging them to continue to do business with the same firm (same name, phone number, address).

6–7. For a month now you have been using ManageMem, a program for your microcomputer that lets you shift your computer's disk operating system into an auxiliary memory bank, thus freeing all your RAM (random-access memory) for use. ManageMem has performed flawlessly and as promised. This is unusual enough with software that you write to tell the company that sells it, Computer Data Service, Route 120, Amherst, NJ 03031, about your satisfaction.

6–8. You are to make up the name and address of someone who has given $100 to a worthy cause. You are to write an *appropriate* and *specific* thank-you letter to that person. For your letterhead use the name and address of any well-known charity.

6–9. As B. Mason Allen, Trust Department, First National Bank, 625 West Broadway, Sarasota, FL 33578, set up a form letter to be sent to well-to-do customers acquainting them with your monthly bulletin, *Taxes and Estates.* This bulletin briefly presents facts and ideas which deal with the conservation of property and the protection for beneficiaries through modern estate planning. You hope that your bulletin will raise questions and generate comments so that your staff can assist in reviewing the overall estate plan.

6–10. After reading claims Case 5–45 and after assuming that you are a vice president of Mercival/Merci Tours, Inc., One Tandy Center Plaza, Fort Worth, TX 76102, write a pleasant letter to Mr. and Mrs. Oscar H. Schroder, 416 N. Nicholson Ave., Monterey Park, CA 91754. The Schroder's trip was at the peak of the season, and the only explanation you have been able to get from the hotel in Bangkok was that every room was occupied with tourists. Five different tour groups use that famous hotel because it is considered the best and has the best location. You have not been able to find out who the guide was in Bangkok, but you have written to the tour arranger there, Tsugihiro Okuda, and told him about the Schroders' experience. You feel you'll hear from Okuda, a most reliable, intelligent manager.

The management of the hotel in Hong Kong could not change the room because there was not a free room to move the Schroders to. Now the leak has been fixed. Since you do not know where the $75 gift was bought in Hong Kong, you have no idea how to trace it but suggest that the Schroders write the shop and the airline explaining what was purchased.

The problem about the delay of the luggage in Tokyo is related to an accident at the airport (a small plane crashed and that caused confusion and delay). You have hired two new people to handle luggage during the peak periods in Tokyo.

To help soothe the Schroders' feelings of missing some time at the Great Buddha at the Todaiji Temple, send some pictures and folders bound in a handsome brochure.

6–11. For the signature of the chief executive officer of General Automotive (Appendix E: VII, A), draft a letter to go to all stockholders of the corporation informing them of the steps you are taking to assure that their company will survive this crisis. Since in the past two years General Automotive's stock has plummeted from 81 to 22, and you reduced the dividend from $2 per year per share to 40 cents, you may not have a particularly friendly audience. What you want to avoid is stockholders' selling their shares in disgust, further depressing the price per share and making borrowing even more difficult and costly.

6–12. As the president of a chain of nursing homes in Illinois, write a form letter from your headquarters (Fairview, 178th St. and S. Kedzie Ave., Hazel Crest, 60429) to your patient (or to the sponsor if the patient is unable to function). This letter is to welcome patients to your nursing home and to ask them to complete a questionnaire about your services. The patient or sponsor would receive this mailing a week after entering your nursing home.

6–13. For your telephone company write a goodwill message that will go along with next month's bill asking your subscribers to call the business office if they get any annoying calls. You have trained representatives who can investigate. If the customer is a victim of calls that are threats on life or property, then the customer should notify the police as well as the business office. Discourage customers from giving their names to nuisance callers, but encourage them to get numbers and names of the nuisance callers. If the nuisance caller makes obscene or suggestive remarks, then the customer should hang up.

6–14. Several months before the opening of a new mall, Northgate, Route 662, Douglassville, PA 19651, the chain of stores you are advertising manager for, Parisian, decided not to have a store there. But after a conference with a leading marketing consultant, Parisian's management changed its mind. Since it will take a year to get the large store built, management has decided to rent a little space for a classy store in one corner of the mall to promote cosmetics, accessories, and gift ideas—and has hired a manager. To get customers used to the idea that Parisian will be at Northgate Mall, you want to send a letter to a select mailing list inviting the consumers to bring in the letter you write and receive a generous size sample of Oscar de la Renta perfume. Other famous brands you carry—Estee Lauder, Clinique—will be on display too. Write an enthusiastic letter that will be processed to potential good customers inviting them to get the free perfume and meet the manager and the other friendly people at Parisian.

6–15. For additional cases see Appendix E: VIII, M.

Disappointing messages

7

*[Character requires the courage to say no firmly
but pleasantly when saying yes or saying no
unpleasantly would be easier.]*

Unless you recall clearly (from the first section of Chapter 4) our suggestions about handling disappointing messages, turn back and quickly review them. What we said there is important as a basis for this whole chapter, and especially in international communication. (People from other cultures generally expect even more gentle and gracious presentation of bad-news messages than we do in the United States.)

REFUSING REQUESTS

Most people are disappointed, irritated, or downright angry when told they can't have something, can't do something, or can't expect you to do something—unless you *first* give at least one good reason. If you make the psychological mistake of first saying no and then explaining, the emotional upset from your no will prevent the other person from listening reasonably.

In effective refusals, therefore, you have to explain some facts, circumstances, or unreasonableness of which the reader is apparently unaware. Hence the central theme for writing effective disappointing messages is "explain *before* refusing."

When you take something away from or deny someone something, therefore, you give a reason first. Then you give something else to compensate for the loss when you can, and you try to extend some gesture of friendliness.

Simply stated, the desirable pattern for refusals is therefore

—A buffer beginning (establishing compatibility; defined and illustrated below).

—A review of facts (reasons).

—The refusal itself, subordinated. ⎫ *or* A counterproposal which implies

—An off-the-subject ending. ⎬ the refusal.

Before studying this suggested structure, however, read the following refusal of a request for a charitable contribution:

```
While we are primarily manufacturers of extruded
```

plastic products, we are well aware that we are also
members of this community and share the
responsibilities for its well-being.

Each year we therefore actively support the United
Way. One of our chief officers usually serves on the
Board of Directors, as our Vice President of Finance
presently does. For the past five years Martin
Plastics has achieved its goals of employees
contributing a fair share and a substantial corporate
contribution to the United Way each year.

Since the United Way apportions its receipts among the
various charities at work in our community, we are
able to contribute to all at one time and in one fund
drive. We strongly feel that the United Way is the
fairest way of fulfilling our charitable obligations
and making the biggest possible contributions.

Next year, when the annual United Way drive is on, we
shall take comfort in knowing that your charity, Homes
for Homeless Pets, will again receive a portion of the
money collected to continue its valuable work for the
animals that depend so much on us--and in knowing that
we have done our part.

The buffer beginning

Since people don't normally ask for what they don't expect to get, a reader
opening your reply to a request almost certainly expects pleasant news. Probably that reader, in making the request, carefully figured out some seemingly
good reasons why you should do as asked—and may have had some strong
feelings about it. If you present a refusal immediately, you appear to ignore
those feelings and reasons—and are likely to arouse a negative reaction, causing a mind closed to anything else you say.

On the other hand, if you pitch right in with a presentation of your reasons,
you appear to be arguing—and dander, or at least suspicion, rises.

To prevent such mental impasses and emotional deadlocks, you need to
show your reader that you are a reasonable, calm person by indicating some
form of agreement or approval of the reader or the subject. Frequently you
can agree completely with some statement made in the request. At least you
can say something to establish compatibility, even if nothing more than that
you have given the proposal serious thought. This is your buffer.

The turndown of a request for your company's manual (p. 86) could easily
begin with

You are certainly right about the pressing need facing

>   most business firms for more effectively trained
>   business writers.

Or it could start this way:

>   Students attending Harwood College are fortunate to
>   have teachers who try so conscientiously to correlate
>   college training and business practice.

Both beginnings acknowledge receipt of the request, clearly imply careful consideration, establish compatibility, and set the stage for a review of the facts in the refusal—**later,** under better pychological circumstances.

Six warnings about writing buffers, however, deserve attention here.

1.   If you appear to be granting the request, you are building your reader up to an awful letdown! Such beginnings as these would mislead most readers:

>   I certainly would like to see Harwood students have
>   access to our manual.
>
>   --
>
>   You are right, Mr. Kolb, that abandoned pets deserve
>   help from each of us personally.

In fact, anything you say in the buffer that seems inconsistent with what you say later will produce more resentment than effectiveness.

2.   The *second* warning is against beginning irrelevantly or so far from the subject that the reader isn't even sure the letter is a reply. The buffer beginning must clearly identify the general subject. This beginning is irrelevant:

>   I well remember my first pet, a small white dog with
>   an irresistible sense of humor.

3.   The *third* warning is against recalling any disappointment too negatively—for example answering a claim with "We regret your dissatisfaction . . . ."

4.   As the *fourth* warning, you need to be careful about buffer length. You can easily go wrong by making the buffer too short to get in step with the reader and hence not really get off to a pleasant start or too long to suit an impatient and resultingly suspicious reader.

5.   As the *fifth* warning you need to phrase the buffer well so that it makes a smooth and natural transition to the next part (your explanation).

6.   Although many writers begin refusals with "I really wish we could . . . ," it is stereotyped, it sounds insincere, and it invites the belligerent response, "Then why don't you?" But the greatest disadvantage (and the *sixth* warning) is that it defeats the whole psychology and strategy of B–plan letters—it establishes the refusal unmistakably in the opening before showing any reason.

To sum up, we can say that a good buffer will be *relevant, pleasant, equivocal,* and *transitional*.

Reasons rather than apologies

If you will apply the positive thinking and positive phrasing we talked about under "Positive Statement" and "Success Consciousness" near the end of Chapter 4, you will resist the common impulse to apologize anywhere in a refusal *and especially in the beginning.* Apologies are no substitute for action or explanation. And they force you to phrase negatively the very ideas you should avoid—that you *will not, cannot, are unable to, do not have,* and similar negative expressions.

In most cases when you have to refuse, that refusal depends on good reasons. *Those reasons—not some apology or policy—form the bedrock of your explanation.*

When possible, you want to emphasize reasons which reflect benefits to the reader (individually or through a group), as the letter to Homes for Homeless Pets did. The following letter from a manufacturer refusing a dealer's request for samples also stresses reader benefits:

> Congratulations on your 25 years of service to your community!
>
> Through continued association with retailers, we know that their long-range success depends on sound managerial policies and services.
>
> We have tried to help in these successes by cutting costs whenever possible and passing these savings on to retailers in the form of lower prices. This aim led us to eliminate the high (and often unpredictable) manufacturing and shipping costs of special samples. You and hundreds of other druggists have benefited from these cost reductions over the years.
>
> Our favorable prices on quality products plus national advertising and help with point-of-sale promotions are the best ways we've found to increase your Walwhite sales.
>
> If you'll fill in and mail the enclosed card, Mr. Robert Abbott (your Walwhite representative) will be glad to arrange a special Walwhite exhibit that will attract many customers to your anniversary sale and well-deserved celebration.

You cannot, however, apply such reader-benefit interpretation in every case. To attempt to would sometimes result in artificial, insincere talk. Better than that is a thorough, logical explanation that is friendly and positive (without apology though basically selfish). The following letter refusing a request for permission to reprint some sales letters of a mail-order house is quite acceptable though (justifiably) self-protective:

You can count on a large, interested readership for your article about the importance of sales letters in business.

In our company, as you know, we depend upon such letters exclusively for sales. Of necessity, then, we have tested extensively to find the most effective procedures. Our highly paid writers are continually revising, sending expensive test mailings, and comparing the returns. The best letters represent a considerable investment.

In the past, rival companies have used some of our standard letters without consent. Because that use decreased the letters' effectiveness for us, we now copyright all our sales forms and confine them to company use. Should we release them for publication, we would have to incur the same expenses again.

Doing my best to help, therefore, I'm sending you some bulletins and a bibiliography which may help you with your article. Will you let me know the issue of the magazine your article appears in?

If you establish such good reasons, you have no cause to apologize for protecting your own self-interest.

The derived, positive refusal

Ideally, your explanation and reasons so thoroughly justify you in refusing that anyone would infer the turndown. Thus prepared, your reader is far more likely to accept your decisions calmly.

But you cannot always afford to depend exclusively on implication to establish the turndown unmistakably. The refusal must be clear; but even when you have to state it, it need not be brutally negative. In fact, it need not be negative at all.

If you will look back at the sample refusals in this section, you will see that the writers *established the idea of what they were not doing by a statement of what they were doing*.

Not	*But*
We don't contribute to individual charities.	. . . the United Way is the fairest way . . . of fulfilling our charitable obligations . . . .
We do not supply special samples to retailers.	We . . . help . . . by cutting costs . . . and passing these savings on

Not	*But*
	to retailers in the form of lower prices.
We cannot let you have samples of our sales letters.	We copyright all our sales forms and confine them to company use.

When you incorporate the limiting words *only, solely, exclusively* (even phrases like *confine to* and *concentrate on*), no doubt remains.

Saving some of your reasons until after establishing the refusal, or offering other ways of helping, enables you to **embed** the disappointing news and thus reduce the impact of the refusal. In any event, you certainly want to take leave of your reader on a more pleasant note than the refusal.

The pleasant, hopeful ending

In some cases when you must refuse you can do little but reassure the reader through a few additional words that you are not utterly callous—or indifferent. Good wishes for the success of the project, the suggestion of other sources, possibly the suggestion of being helpful in other ways, sending something other than what the reader has requested—all these are possibilities for ending your letter with a friendly gesture.

Sometimes you cannot comply with your reader's request but can suggest an alternative action, a counterproposal, or compromise proposal. In many instances it can both imply the refusal and furnish you with the positive ending you seek. The following letter is an example of this technique:

> Prudential's employees and clients will no doubt benefit materially from the reports manual you are planning, Mr. Lee—especially if it is the same caliber as the letters manual your staff prepared recently.
>
> I'm sure many college teachers would be glad to furnish you illustrative material. And I am no exception. In the past 15 years of working with business and college people to improve the quality of their reports, I've collected much HOW NOT TO and HOW TO teaching material.
>
> For most of this I have only my single file copy, which I use in teaching a report-writing course three times a week and which I carefully keep in my office.
>
> I'm sure my student assistant would be glad to photocopy it for you during off-duty hours at the regular rate of $4 an hour. Since the job involves no more than 50 or 60 pages, I feel reasonably sure that

CHECKLIST FOR REFUSING REQUESTS

1. Your buffer opening must pleasantly establish compatibility.
    a. One of the poorest starts is talk about how pleased or flattered you are. It's vain and selfish. Shift the emphasis to your reader.
    b. Beginning too far away from the subject results in incoherence.
    c. Don't appear to be on the verge of granting the request.
    d. Nor do you want to intimate the refusal at this point.

2. Your transition must follow coherently and logically from your buffer.
    a. To avoid sounding selfish, keep the emphasis on the reader.
    b. *Although, however, but,* and *yet* signal a turn for the worse. Avoid them as sentence beginnings.
    c. Avoid also the insincere "Although I should like to . . . ."
    d. Supply the bridging sentence showing why you are explaining.

3. Give at least one good reason before even implying the refusal.
    a. Emphasize unselfish reasons if you can.
    b. Don't hide behind "our policy." Reasons get more respect.
    c. For believability, you need specificness; but stick to the plausible.

4. The refusal itself should be
    a. A logical outcome of the reasons given. Ideally, the reader should deduce the refusal before you indicate it definitely.
    b. Presented positively—in terms of what you can do and do do.
    c. Preceded (and preferably followed) by justifying reasons.
    d. Unmistakable but implied or subordinated (as by a counterproposal).
    e. Written without negative words like *impossible, must refuse,* or *very sorry to tell you that we cannot.*
    f. Without apologies. Concentrate, instead, on what is hopeful.

5. Continue to convince your reader of your real interest and helpful attitude, without recalling the refusal, in the ending.
    a. Your ending must be positive and within the sphere of the reader's interest.
    b. Watch for bromides and rubber stamps in the end.
    c. Be wary of the expression "If I can help in other ways, please let me know." It can produce some sarcastic reactions.
    d. Follow through specifically with any wanted action.

```
securing the material this way would cost you only
about $10—15 (including cost of materials, copier
fees, and time).

I shall be glad to make the necessary arrangements if
you would like me to. I'm sure I can have the material
to you within four or five days after hearing from
you.
```

Please note again that this writer does not resort to negative phrasing or apologies. You too should resist the common tendency to resort to such expressions as "I regret my inability to do as you asked," "I'm sorry to have to refuse your request," or—much worse—"I hope you will understand our position," especially at the end. For these weaklings, substitute appropriate positive and gracious ideas such as those used in the examples given.

For writing goodwill-building refusals, check the accompanying reminder list of points.

REFUSING ADJUSTMENTS

A letter refusing an adjustment is obviously a bad-news (B–plan) letter requiring your psychology of saying no. For your buffer-paragraph beginning, look for something in the situation which you and the reader can agree on and which is pleasant. Even appreciation for the information you received could serve.

Although you may carefully introduce a sentence that serves as a transition and resale on the house, you need to get to your explanation or reasons fairly early. And you need to give the facts and reasons fully in a clear system of organization.

Several special techniques are important if your explanation is to rebuild goodwill while refusing to do what the reader asked. You already know better than to hide behind the word *policy* or to give no reason at all. But a flat-footed announcement of what a guarantee states is just as bad as unsupported talk about policy.

Since you are refusing, obviously you are not charging responsibility for the dissatisfaction to either the firm or the product or service. You must clear that point up with adequate explanation as a basis for refusing. Resale at this stage (before the explanation) in the area of the trouble is *not* the way, but only a head-on collision with what the reader thinks. You *have to* give the basic fact(s) on which your refusal depends. Doing so, of course, makes the reader guilty; but don't accuse directly.

In fact, if you arrange your reasons and explanations carefully, they will probably make the negative answer clear by implication without the necessity of stating it. If not this way, at least you subordinate the refusal by burying it (that is, putting it in the middle of a paragraph where it doesn't stand out unduly). If you still feel that you must state it, your best technique (for this special situation) is to fall back on the passive, impersonal presentation (something "was not done" instead of "you didn't")—rather than accuse. The reader will be able to see who is responsible if you explain well that your goods and your firm aren't.

After the refusal, which must be clear whether by implication or by direct statement, you may do well to add some more reasoning and explanation in support (thus embedding and further subordinating the refusal). Be sure you say enough to make your refusal clear and justified.

Your ending then becomes an attempt to get agreement or the reader's acceptance of your refusal as justified. That is, you write with as much success consciousness as seems reasonable about the future outlook. This does *not* mean that you write and ask for an answer as to whether your action is all right. If it isn't, you will learn without asking.

Often the best ending assumes that the preceding explanation and decision are satisfactory and talks about something else. Rather than looking backward (and reminding the reader of the unhappy situation now cleared up), it may *better look forward to the next likely relationship between writer and reader*. The following letter illustrates most of the points:

> Your customers certainly do have a right to demand that all Neenah monogrammed stationery be letter perfect. One of the reasons we specify that all orders be typed or printed is to accomplish this aim.
>
> For that same reason, on the rare occasions when a shipment is not exactly as ordered, we print and ship corrected letterheads without question and without charge. To be sure your Neenah customers get exactly what they want, however, we need your careful help. If you'll check your orders of the past two months, you'll see that we have replaced six. A similar check of the enclosed photocopies will show clearly that we followed the original directions exactly on this seventh request.
>
> A corrected shipment for Mr. Washburn reading "Freemont" instead of "Fairmont" and for Miss Wentworth reading "Montevallo University" rather than "Montevallo College" will nevertheless go out to you within two days after we receive your approval of our two-part plan: (1) We'll debit your account for the new shipment at the usual prices, subject to our usual terms; (2) for greater profit for both of us, we ask you to again instruct your sales personnel to type or print all orders and verify with each customer every letter and every number to appear in the final printing. You can then rely on our providing you exactly what you order.

The accompanying checklist reviews the highlights of refusing adjustments.

COMPROMISING ON ADJUSTMENTS

When you decide to try to compromise—usually because of divided responsibility, or uncertainty about responsibility or correction for the trouble—you may use either of *two* plans.

In the *first* you follow the refused-adjustment plan exactly down *to* the refusal. There you make your proposed compromise instead, explicitly. In effect, you are refusing the adjustment requested and are making a counter-proposal—a compromise. When you ask acceptance of it, your success in get-

REFUSED- AND COMPROMISE-
ADJUSTMENT CHECKLIST

1. Make your buffer relevant, pleasant, equivocal, and transitional.
   a. Begin closely enough to the situation to acknowledge.
   b. Reflect pleasant cooperation (try to agree on something).
   c. Don't imply that you're granting or refusing the request.
   d. Avoid recalling the dissatisfaction more than necessary.
   e. Watch buffer length: neither too breezy nor too long.
   f. Early resale in the trouble area bluntly contradicts.
   g. Should you show appreciation for the report?

2. Make your facts and reasons courteous, thorough, and convincing.
   a. An immediate plunge (beginning of the second paragraph) into "our guarantee" or "our policy" is abrupt.
   b. Don't accuse the reader or preach. Phrase your explanation impersonally—and let the reader decide who's guilty.
   c. Establish the explicit, adequate facts—the basis for refusal.
   d. Even intimating refusal before reasons is bad psychology.
   e. When possible, interpret reasons to show reader benefits.

3. Make the refusal logical, subordinate, and impersonal but clear.
   a. Preferably the reader sees the refusal coming.
   b. Give it little emphasis. Consider implying it.
   c. Keep it impersonal and positive—in terms of what you do.
   d. Be sure it is there, however; unclear is as bad as too strong.
   e. Follow the refusal with reasons, showing any reader benefits.
   f. Reader education or counterproposal may imply the refusal.
   g. What about the returned product (if applicable)? Resell it?

4. Make your ending pleasant, positive, and success-conscious.
   a. When you need reader action, ask for it positively.
   b. Otherwise an off-the-subject ending about services, seasonal goods, or some other topic of interest is appropriate.
   c. Don't suggest uncertainty of your ground. Watch *hope/trust*.
   d. Apologies are unnecessary reminders of trouble; your explanation has already made the best apology.

For the COMPROMISE ADJUSTMENT, use these for Items 3 and 4:

3. Make your counterproposal as logical, helpful relief.
   a. Be careful to make a smooth transition from the explanation (which implies refusal) to the counterproposal.
   b. Offer it ungrudgingly, without parading your generosity, but let the service element prevail.
   c. Don't belittle it ("the best we can do") or make it sound like a penalty ("a service charge will have to be made").

4. Use a modified action ending.
   a. Ask permission; you wouldn't go ahead without agreement.
   b. Tell what the reader is to do, but don't urge acceptance.
   c. For service attitude, talk prompt satisfaction.

ting a favorable reply will depend not only on (1) how well you have presented facts and reasons to justify the compromise but on (2) your success consciousness in presenting it and on (3) your phrasing it to encourage rather than discourage acceptance.

The following letter in answer to a strong request for removal of the heater, cancellation of remaining payments, and refund of the shipping and installation charges illustrates the points. You will notice that it offers to compromise to the extent of canceling the remaining payments, but it proposes another action instead.

```
You are right in expecting your Warmall to heat a
large area such as your entire office, for that is
what it was designed to do.

To do so, the Warmall requires careful installation.
It must be located so that the air currents can carry
its heat to all parts of the room. Our engineer
reports that it was installed in the proper position
but that later remodeling of your office has blocked
circulation of air with a half partition.

Your heater can be all you want it to be if relocated;
so removing it would be useless. That would mean
losing your down payment and what you have paid for
shipping and installation, although we would of course
cancel the remaining payments. Moreover, you must have
heat, and the Warmall will do the job.

We have absolute faith in our engineer's judgment, but
your satisfaction is more important. So we want to do
what is fair to us both.

At your convenience we can move the heater to the
position our engineer suggested; and, if it does not
heat to your satisfaction, we will remove it and not
charge you another cent.

Will you suggest the most convenient time for the
change that will make your whole office area warm and
comfortable? We can do the job so quickly and
efficiently that your business can continue as usual.
```

For a checklist following this plan of compromise adjustment letter, see the refused-adjustment checklist.

A *second* method of compromising—usually called the full-reparation beginning compromise—sometimes works better. You follow the plan of a letter *granting* an adjustment at the beginning, through the explanation. The facts, of course, will indicate divided or uncertain responsibility. Your resale talk will indicate that the repaired product (or a replacement up to par, in case the original was beyond repair) will give the service the customer wanted.

Since presumably the original desire for that service still exists, you ask the customer to make a choice—the refunded money or the product. And of course you word it to encourage choice of the product, because that way you have a customer satisfied with your product as well as your fair-minded practices.

Your main purpose is to restore goodwill and confidence. Again your success depends on three things: (1) a start which offers everything requested and thereby pleases the customer, (2) your explanation which shows the justice of a compromise, and (3) your fair-mindedness in allowing the choice. The danger—not a very serious one—is that some people might try to keep both the money and the product.

> Attached to this letter is a credit memorandum for $93.75, which we cheerfully send you for the five Bear Mountain hunting jackets you returned. It is an indication that you'll always be treated fairly at Bowen's.
>
> Under the assumption that these jackets would find a ready sale at a reduced retail price despite slight imperfections (a button mismatched, a crooked seam, or maybe a little nick in the fabric), we offered them "as is" and priced them at $18.75 instead of the regular $27.75. We felt that marking them "as is" indicated special circumstances.
>
> Generally we follow the accepted business custom of making all such reduced-price sales final for an entire lot. But as we evidently did not make the situation perfectly clear, we are leaving the decision up to you. If you feel that you're entitled to the adjustment, it's yours.
>
> Many of your customers, however, would probably be glad to get nationally advertised Bear Mountains at perhaps $46 instead of the standard $56. And even if you sell these five at, say, only $37.50, your percentage of profit will be about the same as if you sold perfect jackets at full price.
>
> As they are, these jackets are still ready to stand a lot of hard wear. They are made to suit hunters' needs, with ample pockets for shells and with comfortable tailoring. Selling them should be easy, especially at a discount.
>
> So if you'd like to reconsider and want to offer these jackets at a saving, just initial the face of this letter and send it to us with the credit memo. We'll absorb the shipping charges. The decision is yours, but we think you can make a good profit on them at the special price.

Applying the checklist for compromises with full-reparation beginning to this letter will show that it is pretty good and will review the principles for you.

CHECKLIST FOR COMPROMISE WITH FULL-REPARATION BEGINNING

1. The beginning giving everything asked for is basic—to dissolve reader emotions and get you a reasonable hearing.
   a. Make it immediately, specifically, and completely.
   b. Build up the wholesome effect by a friendly, adapted expression to emphasize your reliability and prevent a curt tone.
   c. Don't apologize; Item 1a does lots more.
   d. Carefully avoid unnecessary negative reminders.
   e. Beginning with the compromise would infuriate readers. Since they think they're entitled to what they asked, you have to show otherwise before compromising.

2. The explanation (facts and reasons) must show that the claimant is expecting too much.
   a. Don't be too slow about getting to at least some of the explanation.
   b. Interpret it with a reader viewpoint and positive statement.
   c. Do not directly accuse; show blame impersonally (perhaps by customer education on the use and care of the article).
   d. Establish the facts to show that the claimant is at least partly responsible or is overestimating the loss.

3. Show your service attitude and fair-mindedness in your proposal.
   a. As the foundation of your proposal, stress serving your reader.
   b. Recall the original desire for the service the reader wanted.
   c. Continuing the reader-benefit interpretation, state your proposal.
   d. Follow your suggestion with any other plausible sales points.
   e. Don't parade your generosity in the loss you take.
   f. Suggest—don't command or preach or high-pressure the claimant.

4. The modified action ending should give a choice but encourage the one you prefer.
   a. Tell what you want done: reject (return) the full reparation and accept your proposal.
   b. As in any action ending, make action easy.
   c. Do not bog down with apologies or emphasis on the full reparation.
   d. End with a short suggestion of reader satisfaction resulting from the proposal.

REQUESTS FOR CREDIT INFORMATION

Many applications for credit do not give all the data you must have. You therefore write for the needed information—in routine situations normally using forms.

The major problem is to avoid arousing the reader's indignation because you have not approved credit forthwith. Where the danger seems great, therefore, you write a special B–plan letter with careful explanation and tone not possible in a form.

To soften the effect of the delay in approving credit, begin with buffer material, stress the benefits of complying with the request, show that you treat all applicants alike, make action easy, and promise quick action. If character is not in question, be sure to say so. And to encourage response, use resale or sales promotion to embody your explanation.

The following letter is typical in stressing "All our customers fill out this application . . ."—an appropriate covering letter for the form.

> Your interest in the conveniences of an Allen Tilby charge account is most welcome, Mrs. Lee.
>
> So that we may assist you as quickly and as easily as possible, will you please fill out the enclosed routine credit application? All our customers fill out this form as a help to both them and us. The information is strictly for our confidential files, to be used in setting up the best credit arrangements we can make for you.
>
> You can be sure that we will give your request our immediate attention. Just use the stamped, addressed envelope enclosed for your convenience in returning the application.

A letter to a retailer employs the same strategy:

> Corone fishing gear is a good line to handle. Tackle dealers throughout the country report the favorable reaction of anglers. And our advertising in <u>Field and Stream</u> and <u>Sports Afield</u> continues to create demand for Corone dealers.
>
> We're just as eager as you are to have your Corone sales start; so will you supply the usual financial information that all our dealers furnish us, along with the names of other firms from which you buy on credit? Most of our applicants use the enclosed form, but if you prefer to use your own, please do.
>
> This confidential information will enable us to serve you efficiently——now and in the future.

Occasionally a poorly written request backfires, with a protest from the customer (sometimes quite vigorous). In such cases all you can do is write again, using a pacifying buffer, and then pointing out the value of credit and the importance (to your reader as well as yourself) of careful selection of credit customers. The letter reiterates the normalcy of the request and closes with a request for action. It is also a modification of the B—plan letter:

> We're glad you let us know unmistakably how you feel about sending financial information——and we're sure that as a fair-minded business manager you'll be willing to consider your supplier's side of the story. Only through complete frankness can we work together successfully in a credit relationship.

We have some pretty definite ideas too--learned from
selling about 2,000 successful dealers like you
several million dollars' worth of Corone fishing
equipment in the past 20 years. . . about 90 percent
of it on credit.

Because of our credit arrangements, Corone dealers can
do a large amount of business on a small investment.
In effect, we take the place of your bank, for the
goods we send you on credit are the same as cash. Like
your bank, we can make loans only when we have
evidence of ability and willingness to pay later. The
only way we can protect all our dealers against price
rises due to losses from bad debts is to check every
credit applicant and select carefully.

If you applied for a loan at your bank, you'd expect
to show your financial statements to your banker. We
are in the same position--except that we have no
mortgage to protect us, and we are not so well
informed as your banker about you and your local
market.

The confidential information we've asked for is
strictly for business purposes. It helps both of us.
Since the peak sales months are close at hand, I'm
enclosing another form and an addressed envelope so
that you can get this information back to us in time
for us to get your fast-selling Corone fishing gear
started to you by the first of next week.

Because most requests for credit information from customers are simply
modifications of direct requests, we run no checklist or cases.

CREDIT REFUSALS

In the light of poor standing on any or all of the four C tests of credit (refer
to Chapter 5), you will have to refuse some credit applicants. The most likely
reasons are unfavorable reports from references (character) or an unfavorable
financial position (capital). Sometimes you will need only to suggest some
modification of the arrangement the customer has requested. In the case of
an old customer it may be a refusal of a credit-limit revision or a suggestion
of curtailed buying. All these situations are inherently disappointing; they are
a reflection on the ability of the customer, who *may* interpret them as a reflection on honesty; and so they are fraught with negative possibilities.

As in any disappointing-news letter, you need to analyze the situation, search
out any hopeful elements (especially character), line up your reasons, and
write a B-plan letter.

The applicant may have receivables or payables out of line, or be too slow
in meeting obligations, or be undercapitalized. *Whatever the reason, you have*

to establish it, and in this function you have some educational work to do—without offense if at all possible.

You certainly do not want to close the door irrevocably on any debtor (except possibly deadbeats). A poor account now may be a good one a year later (and if your wise counseling has helped in the improvement, you have established yourself as a helpful friend and are thus more likely to receive the customer's business).

For that reason, most good credit refusals establish good feeling in a short buffer, show the reasons in an analysis of the circumstances, identify the deficiency, refuse in positive fashion, suggest how the customer can remedy the deficiency, and invite a later application. Unless you can make a counterproposal, point out its advantages, and then ask for action on that basis, *the best ending is an attempt to sell for cash*. After all, the reader wants your goods and possibly can't get them on credit elsewhere either.

In the following instance, involving an order for $352 worth of work coveralls, the retailer quickly responded with a financial statement and references in response to the request for them. Accounts receivable and payable were both too large; the trade association reported that strikes in the mines of the community affected all local trade. Since the references reported that the customer's payments were good enough during normal times, the credit writer sought to cultivate potential business (based on the references) while declining the account at present (based on the most impersonal and palatable spoiler—conditions):

> Your large order for Stalwart coveralls suggests the prospect of an early strike settlement in your area. We're glad to hear that.
>
> When the miners go back to work, the steady revival of business in and around Canyon City will no doubt help your collections so that you can reduce both your accounts receivable and accounts payable. In that way you can probably quickly restore your current ratio to the healthy 2:1 we require because we've found over the years that such a ratio places no burden on our customers. Such an improvement will enable us to consider your credit application favorably. Will you please send us subsequent statements?
>
> You'll probably need your Stalwart coveralls sooner than that, however; they're a popular brand because they wear well. Workers like the reinforced pockets and knees. They'll easily outsell other lines you might carry.
>
> You can stock this popular brand and thus satisfy present demand by paying cash and taking advantage of the liberal discount we can give you. On this order, for instance, the discount at our regular terms of 2/

> 10, n/90 would amount to $7.04--enough to pay interest
> for three months on a $250 bank loan.
>
> Or you might cut your order in about half and order
> more frequently. But with a $200 bank loan at 15
> percent and a stock turn of 12--which is a
> conservative estimate, Mr. Wolens--you'd make . . . .
>
> Since we can have your Stalwart coveralls to you in
> about five days, just attach your check to the memo
> I've enclosed and mail both of them back to me in the
> enclosed envelope to handle the order in this
> profitable way.

Usually you can specifically isolate the shortcoming(s) (in one or more of the four C's) in an industrial or wholesale situation (as underlined in the preceding letter) and use impersonal, positive phrasing to save the customer's pride, suggest the remedy, and leave the way open for future negotiations.

In consumer letters involving a retail customer, however, the usual reason for the refusal is the customer's failure to take care of obligations. This is a highly personal reflection, one which many credit people shy away from by feigning incomplete information and inviting the customer to come in and talk the matter over.

We do not agree with that dodging procedure. We think that a better method is the forthright credit refusal in the usual sequence of buffer, reasons, positive refusal, forward look, and counterproposal in the form of a bid for cash business.

> Thank you for requesting an account at Aiken's. We
> take it as a compliment to our way of doing business.
>
> For 50 years Aiken's has been bringing its customers
> quality merchandise at fair prices. This, as you
> realize, requires careful merchandising management.
> Not the least of our savings--the practice of paying
> cash for merchandise, thereby receiving discounts and
> eliminating interest charges, which we pass on to
> customers as lower prices--requires that we receive
> prompt payment from our credit customers.
>
> To assure that, we select our own credit customers
> carefully for both ability and willingness to pay.
> Though meeting all obligations promptly is often
> temporarily difficult, very likely you will soon
> qualify for a charge account at Aiken's by taking care
> of your other obligations.
>
> Meanwhile you will continue to receive the same
> courteous treatment that made you favor Aiken's in the
> first place. With our will-call, budget, or layaway
> plans at your disposal, you may own anything in

Aiken's within a short time by making convenient
payments of your own choice. Come in soon and let us
serve you in this way.

The following letter refusing credit to a young man just out of college and
with unsteady, low-income employment talks concretely and sensibly; it's a
good credit-education letter. Note how the writer stresses the idea that character is not the basis for refusal.

When you wrote last week asking for credit, as a
member of the Illinois Credit Union we automatically
asked the Union for your record. You can well be proud
of the report we received.

Such a complimentary report on your excellent
character indicates a promising future. The fact that
you have never defaulted or delayed in paying an
account means that you will be able to get credit
easily when your income becomes steady.

We could extend credit to you on the basis of your
personal record alone, for we know that you fully
intend to meet any obligations you undertake. If some
unforeseen expense should come up, however, with your
present fluctuating income you probably could not pay
your account. As a cooperating member of the Credit
Union, we would than be compelled to submit your name
as a poor credit risk. Such a report would limit your
chances of obtaining credit in the future--perhaps at
a time when you need it more than now.

For your own benefit you'll be better off to stick to
cash purchases now, but we shall look forward to the
time when you can comfortably and safely contract for
credit with us.

Meanwhile you can make your dollars reach further by
buying from Bowen's for cash, for we buy in quantity,
save on shipping costs, take advantage of discounts
and pass these savings on to you in the form of lower
prices. When you buy at Bowen's, you therefore make
the most effective use of your income by getting
quality merchandise at low prices.

Letters limiting the credit of an established customer are no different from
refusals to new customers; they just adapt the talking points.

Your $635 order for September delivery indicates a
bright outlook for fall sales. Apparently you are
selling lots of Carlton heaters. I'm glad to see that.

In trying to serve you well as always, we want to ask
whether this large order and the one you placed in

March mean that your business has outgrown the credit
arrangement you now have or that you may be
overstocking Carltons.

With this shipment your account would stand about $500
beyond the line of credit we agreed on when you first
started dealing with us five years ago.

If your ordering such a stock of Carlton heaters
indicates an extensive home-building program going on
in Fairview, your comments on local conditions and the
information requested on the enclosed form may serve
as a basis for extending your credit line to the point
where it will take care of your needs.

Or if you want to continue the present line of credit
and receive the additional shipment, we will extend to
July 10 the 5 percent discount on your $940 March
order. By sending us your check for $893, you will not
only put your account in shape for the present order;
you will also mark up greater profits on the sale of
your Carltons.

We're just as anxious as you are, Mr. Skinner, to send
you this latest shipment. Please take one of these
courses so that we may ship your new stock of Carltons
in time for the fall season.

As in any good refusal, these letters do not apologize or hark back to the
refusal in the end. To do so would indicate that you are not confident in your
decision. The accompanying credit refusal checklist incorporates the major
suggestions for handling its type of letter.

ACKNOWLEDGMENTS OF INCOMPLETE
OR INDEFINITE ORDERS

Any firm which sells by mail will receive some orders which can't be handled as the standard ("all's well") acknowledgments discussed in Chapter 5.
Some orders will be incomplete or vague, or for goods temporarily out of
stock, or from people to whom you cannot sell, or for something a little different from what you have, or for several items involving a combination of
these difficulties.

Keeping most of these problem orders on the books (and hence the profits
from them) is often the difference between success and failure. While a firm
may occasionally get into a situation where it can succeed in business without
trying, smart competitors soon learn about such a gravy train and jump aboard.
Those who don't know how to compete for problem-order business will lose
it—and the profits that go with it.

For that reason, we devote the remainder of this chapter to disappointing

CREDIT REFUSAL CHECKLIST

1. Your opening:
   a. Your best beginning talks about something pleasant: the market; timeliness; the reader . . . .
   b. Beware the selfish note of "We are glad to receive . . . ."
   c. To keep your reader from considering buying elsewhere, get to resale (product and/or house) early in the letter: consumer pleasure in use or dealer profit possibilities.
   d. References to the order, if there was one, should come in incidentally while you say something of more significance.
   e. Be careful not to mislead the reader.

2. Your explanation and refusal:
   a. Stick to the theme of a strong, healthy financial condition.
   b. Do not begin your explanation with writer-interest reasons.
   c. Give some justifying reasons before the refusal.
   d. Meet the issue squarely, making clear whether character is or is not the reason. Advantages in cash buying are not reasons for refusing credit.
   e. Avoid a negative, critical, nosey, or patronizing tone; state your reasons as helpfulness to the reader. Give just enough facts to show that you know without implication of FBI investigations.
   f. Be sure you've made clear that you will not now approve credit.
   g. Hiding behind "policy" evades the issue (and appears selfish).
   h. Phrase your reason in terms of your experience with others.
   i. Always leave the way open for credit extension later.
   j. But you can't make promises, except to reconsider.

3. Your counterproposal:
   a. Introduce a cash, reduced-shipment, or other plan as the solution.
   b. But first show why (help to the reader).
   c. If you propose cash with a discount, figure the savings.
   d. Possibly project the savings over a year's business.
   e. Can you suggest smaller orders? Local financing?
   f. Use the conditional mood in your explanation and proposal.

4. Your ending:
   a. Leave no details uncovered in your present proposal.
   b. In regular action-ending style, drive for acceptance.
   c. Success consciousness precludes the use of "Why not . . . ."
   d. You have to get approval before taking unasked action.
   e. Your last picture should show the reader's benefits.

5. Your tone:
   a. Throughout your letter retain an attitude of helpfulness.
   b. Sales promotion material on other goods is inappropriate.

(B–plan) acknowledgments of orders. And we do it in terms of letter writing—for good reasons.

In nearly all cases a well-done acknowledgment letter is the best way to keep the order on the books and the customer well served and satisfied. You could hardly expect to succeed with form letters because they cannot adapt adequately to highly varied circumstances and because their impersonality does not work well in handling negative situations. Telephone calls and face-to-face discussions, while having the advantage of speed, lack two important advantages of a good letter:

1. They do not give you the chance (without interruptions) to phrase the message so precisely, concisely, and persuasively as in a carefully done letter.
2. They do not provide a written agreement on the many details often important in the buyer-seller contract.

In acknowledging problem orders, you need a high level of know-how with various letter-writing principles and techniques. Since such orders are inherently negative (always involving delay and inconvenience, for example), you need to know how to keep the picture as bright as possible. You need resale to keep reader interest. Adaptation becomes important because of the varied and special circumstances. And since you often must ask the reader for a change of mind or for further action, you need all the principles of persuasion, including skill with action endings. None of these are likely to come out as well in form letters or conversations.

When you get an order that is incomplete (and therefore vague), you can either try to guess what the customer wants and thereby risk extra costs and customer dissatisfaction, or you can write for the needed information. Usually you write.

Since it is a *bad-news* letter, you will wisely use a buffer. Resale, thanks, and (if a new customer) a hearty welcome are all good buffer material for beginning the letter. A problem here is to avoid misleading the customer into believing that you are filling the order.

Very early—perhaps by starting to interweave some of it into the first part of the letter—you should stress the *resale* element. The more specific it is, the more emphatic it is. If you say the customer will like the product, make clear specifically why. Reassuring the customer that the product is good is resale that will help to overcome the drawbacks of additional trouble and delay. In this case it has a much more important role than in the standard acknowledgment. Although small bits of it may appear throughout the letter, at least some of it comes before the reader learns the bad news—to bolster the original desire in the moment of disappointment. It can be very short:

```
Modern, efficient offices everywhere are using
Castellan work stations like the ones you ordered, not
only for their wide color choice and modern styling
but because of their people-oriented design and their
durability.
```

When you have thus prepared the reader psychologically, *asking for* the needed information will reveal the bad news. Thus you save words, weaken the bad news by putting the reader's main attention on complying with your request, and avoid any goodwill-killing accusations. More specifically, your technique at this important crux of the letter is: *In one key sentence beginning with a reader-benefit reason for your request, ask for the information.* For example:

> So that we may be sure to send you exactly the work stations you need, will you please specify your color choice?

Now, if you add a touch of satisfaction-resale to motivate the requested action, do what you can to help the reader decide and answer (to overcome the extra trouble), and promise speed (to overcome as much as possible of the delay), you'll probably get the information you want, without irritation:

> Coming in harmonious shades of black, walnut, blue, and sand, Castellan work stations blend in well with any decor.
>
> Just use the handy return card, and you'll be enjoying your new work stations within two weeks after we receive the information.

When circumstances permit, even a better idea is to get the customer to return your letter with the necessary information marked on it. Beyond making response easy, you get the desirable effect of removing your reminder of shortcomings from the customer's sight. The letter above could also have ended this way:

> Just check the box at the bottom of this letter to tell us what color you want and return it in the stamped, addressed envelope. You'll be enjoying your new Castellan work stations within two weeks after we receive the information.

Notice that although it treats an inherently bad-news situation, this letter uses no negative expression ("delay," "inconvenience," "incomplete," "regret," "sorry"). Most of all, the acknowledgment does not irritate by accusing with such expressions as "you neglected," "you forgot," or "you failed."

The following letter illustrates good technique for an acknowledgment when you can fill part of the order but have to get omitted information about another part. If you want to consider it as a simple acknowledgment of an incomplete order, however, you can read it without the first paragraph and the phrase *the five file cabinets and* in the next-to-last paragraph.

> Soon after you get this letter you should receive the five black, locking, fire-resistant Chaw-Walker lateral file cabinets you ordered April 3. They are to go out on our delivery truck tomorrow.

The durable, easy-to-use VideoTel Model 2000 terminal you specified is our most popular one this year, perhaps because it adapts to such a wide range of computer systems. Readily available in two keyboard arrangements, it is suitable for virtually all kinds of work and various typists' tastes.

To be sure of getting the keyboard arrangement that will suit you best, please check your choices on the enclosed card and return it.

The VideoTel 2000W has a keyboard arranged primarily for word processing use. The 10 function keys are in a line directly above the top line of keys in the keyboard and the control keys are immediately to the right of the return key. The 2000S has the function keys in a pad to the left of the main keyboard and the control keys are above the keyboard, an arrangement best suited for statistical typing. The price is the same for the two models, and your check exactly covers the five file cabinets and the three terminals you ordered.

By returning the card with your choice of keyboard right away, you can have your three new VideoTel terminals Friday, ready for years of efficient, economic use. We'll send them out on the next delivery after we hear from you.

For requesting additional order information in business-building fashion, apply the suggestions in the checklist for acknowledging incomplete orders.

DELAYS AND BACK-ORDERING

Sometimes the problem in an acknowledgment is that you can't fill the order right away. In the absence of a specified time limit, try to keep the order on the books if you can fill it within a time that is really a service to the customer—that is, if you feel the customer would prefer to wait rather than cancel the order. After a buffer, tell when you can fill the order and (usually) assume that such an arrangement is acceptable. If the date is so far off that doubt arises (even within the 30-day maximum federal law allows for consumers), ask instead of assuming. In either case the wise business writer will acknowledge the order promptly.

Again your main problem is keeping the order. This time, though, the only drawback to overcome is delay. Your main element is resale—to convince the reader that the product is worth the wait. It may include both resale on your organization and resale on the goods. If the order is the customer's first, resale is even more important and more extensive.

Your plan and technique are the same as for the acknowledgment of an incomplete order, at least through the first paragraph and some resale talk.

CHECKLIST FOR ACKNOWLEDGING
INCOMPLETE ORDERS

1. If you are sending anything, say so and give necessary details.
   a. If not, begin with a short buffer which is basically resale.
   b. Quickly but subordinately identify the order specifically.
   c. Slow: "We have received . . . ," "Thank you for your . . . ."
   d. Selfish: "We're glad to have . . . ."
   e. Provide some resale on the problem article before the bad news, but don't imply that you are sending the article now.
   f. Make the resale specific, not "We're sure you'll like these shoes." Say why.
   g. Use only brief phrases for resale on goods sent, or for any new-customer aspects, until you've asked for the missing information.

2. Ask for the information naturally, positively, and specifically.
   a. The natural transition to the request follows from preceding resale talk.
   b. Preface the request with a reader-benefit phrase—like "So that you'll be sure to get just the X you want, please . . . ."
   c. To avoid puzzling, make the request fairly early—but not too quickly or abruptly.
   d. Avoid accusations and wasted words such as "You did not include" or "We need some additional information."
   e. Name the customer's options: color choices or different models, for example.
   f. Add explanations to help in the choice (or decision), to resell, and to show your interest in satisfying.
   g. Keep the you-viewpoint: "You may choose from . . . ," not "We have three shades."

3. Close with a drive for the specific action you want.
   a. If many words follow the first indication of what you want done, repeat specifically.
   b. Make replying easy (maybe a return card to check).
   c. If appropriate, have the reader mark your letter and return it.
   d. Refer to the enclosure subordinately; action deserves the emphasis.
   e. Stress your promptness—preferably a date of arrival if you get prompt response.
   f. But keep it logical; post-office speed is not always fast.
   g. Try to work in a last short reference to reader satisfaction.

If resale on the house and/or sales promotion material would be appropriate—as the first surely would be in a new-customer situation—use Items 3 and 4 of the checklist for standard acknowledgments in Chapter 5 as additional Items 4 and 5 here.

> Your order No. 5E361 (dated July 19) for 24 No. 536
> boron nitride standard ½-inch triangular inserts
> represents a wise purchase. This new material will let
> you operate at higher speeds and take deeper cuts than
> you ever have before. The resulting increase in
> productivity will mean increased profits for you.

The parting of the ways comes where the incomplete order acknowledgment asks for information and the back-order acknowledgment explains the situation. The explanation should picture the goods on their way (and imply receipt of them) in the first part of a sentence which ends with a clear indication that that does not mean now (usually by giving the shipping date):

> By going onto double shifts, we are confident we will
> have our new sintering machinery set up and operating
> in time to get these inserts, in the quality you
> expect, to you by the end of August.

As always, explaining in positive terms what you can do, have done, and will do is better than telling in negative terms what you can't do, haven't done, or won't do. As the writer of the preceding paragraph did, a good letter writer will avoid such unnecessary negatives as "out of stock," "cannot send," "temporarily depleted," "will be unable to," "do not have," and "can't send until."

Only a poor business manager gets caught short without a justifying reason. A good one will have a reason—and will explain it to customers to avoid the impression of inefficiency. Often it is basically strong resale material if properly interpreted. For example:

> By performing our own sintering operation, we can
> exert a higher standard of quality control and give
> you inserts that have uniform density throughout, with
> no weak spots, and with increased resistance to
> fracturing. We have given your order priority and are
> sure that by the end of August you will have your
> inserts.

More resale may follow the explanation to help make the reader want the product badly enough to wait. Because it has such an important job to do, it is probably more important in the back-order acknowledgment than in any other. It should be short, specific, and adapted to carry its full effect.

> We're sure you want only top-quality tooling that will
> perform to specifications—and that is what we insist
> on supplying you. You have a right to expect the
> best—we have an obligation to give it to you.

The ending of the back-order acknowledgment may go either of two ways:

1. You may ask outright whether you may fill the order when you have said you can. This plan is preferable if you seriously doubt that the customer will approve.

2. You may phrase it so that this letter will complete the contract unless the reader takes the initiative and writes back a cancellation. That is, you look forward with success consciousness to filling the order when you have said you can. Your assumption (that your plan is acceptable) will hold more frequently if you never suggest the thing you don't want your reader to do—cancel.

The following letter illustrates the handling of a back-order problem:

> The women's white tennis dresses you ordered April 7—
>
> 4 dozen—style No. 16J7 women's tennis dresses, 1 dozen each in sizes 8, 10, 12, and 14 @ $300 a dozen; terms 2/10, N/30
>
> —are leading the summer sportswear sales from Maine to Hawaii.
>
> We are increasing production on this model and have booked your tennis dresses for rush shipment by air express April 27.
>
> The unusual preseason popularity of this trimly cut tennis dress owes much to its shimmering polyester and cotton fabric. When we used up our stock of the genuine combed cotton material, rather than use a substitute we shut down production on this model. A large stock of Glachine cotton fabric is already en route here from Wancrest's famous North Carolina mills, however; thus we are able to promise your shipment by April 27.
>
> For this chance to prove once again Tropical's continuing fashion superiority, we thank you sincerely.

Much of the back-order acknowledgment technique is the same as that used in standard and incomplete-order acknowledgments. The checklist for back-order acknowledgments points out similarities and additional considerations.

ACKNOWLEDGMENTS DECLINING ORDERS

Only three likely reasons might make you decline an order:

1. The customer has asked for credit, and you are not willing to sell that way. In that case the problem is a credit problem (discussed earlier in this chapter).
2. You don't have the goods (or a suitable substitute), and you don't expect to get them in time to serve the customer. You then explain the situation, tell where to get the goods (if you know), maybe present resale on your

BACK-ORDER CHECKLIST

1. If you are sending anything, say so and give necessary details.
   a. If not, begin with a short buffer which is basically resale.
   b. Quickly but subordinately identify the order.
   c. Slow: "We have received . . . ," "Thank you for your . . . ."
   d. Selfish: "We're glad to have . . . ."
   e. Provide some resale on the problem article before bad news.
   f. Make the resale specific, not "We're sure you'll like . . . ." Why?
   g. Use only brief phrases for resale on goods sent, or for any new-customer aspects, until you've handled the key point.

2. Handle the bad news as positively as you can.
   a. Picture the goods moving toward or being used by the customer *before* indicating that you do not now have them.
   b. Avoid negatives: "out of stock," "can't send until . . . ."
   c. Do make clear when you can ship.
   d. Adapt to the one situation rather than a universal, like "In order to give you the very best service we can . . . ."
   e. Explain the reason for being caught short (if any)—preferably resale in effect—and clear up any money involved.
   f. To avoid cancellation of the order, some resale is important.

3. Resale on the house helps too, especially with new customers.
   a. For consumers: delivery, credit . . . .
   b. For dealers: sales representatives, manuals, displays, advertising aids.
   c. If you talk advertising, give publications or stations, amount of space or time, and schedules; show how it promotes sales.
   d. If you talk credit, invite application rather than promise.

4. Sales promotion material shows service attitude and builds sales.
   a. Keep it appropriate—usually on allied or seasonal goods.
   b. You-attitude and specificness are necessary to effectiveness.
   c. Emphasize service to the customer, not desire to sell more.
   d. In referring to enclosures, put the emphasis on reader action.

5. Look forward to future orders.
   a. If sales promotion is the basis, suggest specific action.
   b. If resale is the basis, talk of reader satisfaction.
   c. Guard against bromides and Greedy Gus wording as you close.

6. Word the back-order action phrase to stress the action you want.
   a. Ask only if you doubt that your plan is satisfactory.
   b. Be positive and success-conscious.
   c. Suggest acceptance; avoid the idea of cancellation.
   d. Also avoid reminders of the delay.

company and sales promotion material on any other goods which seem likely to be of interest, and end appropriately.

3. You don't market your products in the way proposed. Most of these problems arise because (*a*) the orderer is an unacceptable dealer or (*b*) you sell only through regular merchandising channels and the orderer (usually

a consumer or retailer) does not propose to go through those channels.

The following letter illustrates declining an order for the second reason:

> Your order for us to repair your Keller 5,000 hp.
> electric motor is evidence that you have been
> satisfied with our repair work——and, I assume, that we
> have been doing our job right.
>
> At present we are equipped to rebuild just about any
> electric motor up to 500 hp. This is the capacity of
> our armature lathes and rewinding machinery. As you
> know, working on motors the size of your Keller is
> highly specialized work requiring large machines.
>
> We suggest you try Charles Lindgren & Co., 4018
> Greenleaf St., Evanston, IL 60202. Lindgren
> specializes in repairing large electric motors and has
> the equipment to move your motor to the shop or to do
> the work in your plant. Because of its good name in
> the trade, we can confidently recommend Lindgren.
>
> Thanks, however, for offering us the job. For prompt,
> expert service on your motors up to 500 hp., you can
> still rely on us. We stock parts for and repair and
> rebuild most makes of motors, gear head motors,
> generators, alternators, electronic and mechanical
> variable speed drives and speed reducers, eddy current
> clutches, pumps, hoists, and welders.

Unacceptable dealer

A dealer may be unacceptable because (1) you sell only through exclusive dealerships and you already have a dealer in the territory or (2) because the orderer does not meet your requirements for a dealership. For example, the dealer may insist on consignment sales or unacceptable discounting.

The first part of the declining letter would be the same in each case and (except for the omission of resale) the same as the beginning of other bad-news acknowledgments we have discussed. In the first case your explanation (usually beginning in the second paragraph) would be how you operate and why you operate that way plus the simple fact of the existing dealership. In the second case it would be a simple explanation of your requirements, with justifying reasons. The ending for the one would be a purely goodwill ending of "keeping in mind" in case you should later want another dealer. The other would end with an offer to reconsider if a change or additional information shows the dealer meets your requirements.

Improper channels

Some buyers think that all manufacturers or producers should sell to anybody who has the money and omit jobbers, wholesalers, and retailers (who add so much to the cost of goods). Those who howl the loudest on this point also howl loudly when a producer from afar does not make the goods available in local outlets. Both methods of merchandising have advantages and disadvantages. We must grant, however, that a producer of or dealer in goods or services has the right to sell any legal way, must make a profit to stay in business, and deserves to profit only from serving customers.

Assuming that your firm has taken the customer-service attitude, you are in a good position to acknowledge the order of a person who does not (through ignorance or intent) choose to follow your merchandising plan—usually a consumer asking for goods from a wholesaler or producer instead of through the regular retail channel, or a retailer attempting to bypass your wholesaler.

Some of the customer-service reasons you can point out for selling only through local retail stores are the advantage of being able to get goods quickly from local stores; of being able to see, feel, and try them; of being able to get adjustments and service easier—indeed, all the disadvantages a seller-by-mail usually has to overcome are now in your favor.

For a retailer, point out that going through your distributor means the distributor holds the big inventory and thus the retailer avoids an unnecessary capital investment in stock as well as high shipping costs. The local distributor knows local conditions and can give valuable advice as well as extend credit where you might not be able to. And the distributor's representatives are immediately available with advertising and merchandising help. If you maintained a national sales force, the retailer would ultimately see that cost added to the cost of the items.

Your bad-news letter begins in the same way as those acknowledging incomplete and back orders: with a buffer, including resale to help keep the customer interested in the goods (on which you *do* make a profit, of course, wherever you are in the marketing channels). As before, you are careful not to mislead.

After this beginning, you explain how you merchandise your goods (not how you don't, except by implication) and why you operate this way. As far as possible, you explain the *why* in terms of benefit to the customer (you-viewpoint)—not the benefits to you. At least a part of the reader-benefit *why* should come before the part of the explanation which conveys the bad news (by implication) that you are not filling the order.

If your explanation is good, the reader will decide yours is the best way. If your resale talk has been good, the desire for the product will still be there although the purchase has to be elsewhere. You tell exactly how and where to get it, and you give a last touch of resale to encourage ordering the way you suggest.

If you have several equally convenient outlets, you name them all to give a choice and to be fair to all. This letter follows the directions:

```
Karsol shower curtains like the ones you saw
advertised will give you the wear you want for your
motel units.
```

So that you will be able to select personally the exact patterns you prefer (from eight different designs offered), we have set up a marketing plan of bringing Karsol shower curtains to you through local dealers only. This way you will save handling, shipping, and COD charges. You can get your curtains at the White House, located at 300 Main Street in Boulder, thus speeding your purchases and avoiding unnecessary delays.

We have recently sent a large shipment of Karsol shower curtains to the White House, and you will be able to see for yourself that although these waterproof curtains are of exceptional strength and durability, they are soft and pliable.

Stop by the White House and select your favorite pattern of Karsol shower curtains that will satisfy your customers.

If you are really a good business manager, you will notify the retailers, so that they can write or call the interested prospect who doesn't come in (especially if the order is for a big-ticket item).

The reminder checklist for rechanneling orders summarizes most of the guide points.

SELLING A SUBSTITUTE

Many times you will receive orders you can't fill exactly because you do not have the special brand, but you have a competing brand or something else that will render the service the customer obviously wants. You know that in most cases people buy a product not for the name on it but for the service they expect from it. If you think your brand will serve (and ordinarily you do, or you wouldn't be selling it), you remember your service attitude and try to satisfy the orderer's wants.

As a point of business ethics, you should not try to sell a substitute unless you sincerely believe you can truly serve by saving the customer time, trouble, or money in getting wanted products or by giving service at least comparable to what is available elsewhere in terms of cost.

Once you decide that you are ethically justified in selling the substitute, you need to remember several working principles:

1. Don't call it a substitute. Although many substitutes are superior to the things they replace, the word has undersirable connotations that work against you.
2. Don't belittle the competitor's product. Not only is doing so questionable ethics, it criticizes the judgment of the orderer who wanted to buy that product.

CHECKLIST FOR RECHANNELING ORDERS

1. Your buffer is a good place to work in resale.
    a. An exact reference to the merchandise ordered is a form of resale in that it attempts to etch the choice in the reader's mind. Other identifications (quantity, date of order, and the like) are wasted words here, since this is an outright refusal.
    b. But don't even intimate the refusal at this point.
    c. Nor do you want to imply that you are shipping the goods.
2. To avoid abruptness, continue the idea of reader benefit as you turn from the resale to your explanation.
3. Think—and write—positively in your explanation.
    a. As appropriate to your reader (a consumer or a dealer), focus on benefits (fresh stock, less inventory, savings on shipping costs, examination of all choices before purchasing, credit and adjustment services).
    b. Establish at least one good (preferably reader-benefit) reason for your merchandising plan before stating it (the statement of the plan is the refusal).
    c. State the plan in terms of what you do, not what you don't.
    d. Make it clear; otherwise, you may get a second, more insistent order.
    e. Follow the statement of the refusal with additional customer advantages.
    f. Is there any advantage in pointing out benefits other than those for the customer?
    g. When a price difference exists (as is usual), admit it but minimize it.
4. Your action ending should urge the reader to place the order with the appropriate outlet.
    a. Be as specific as you can (name and address if only one place and hence no playing favorites), and build up the image of service.
    b. Work in specific resale material as a safeguard against the possibility of brand switching when the reader places the order again.
5. If fitting, have the appropriate outlet contact the reader.

3. Don't refer to the ordered product specifically by name any more than you have to—perhaps not at all. You want the would-be buyer to forget it and think about yours. When you use the other name, you remind your reader of it—in effect, you advertise it. Conversely, stress your product, perhaps repeating the exact name several times.

Except for the fact that *the identification and resale are in general terms broad enough to encompass both the product ordered and the substitute,* your beginning of the substitute-selling acknowledgment is the same as other buffers for bad-news acknowledgments. If you phrase the beginning well, you'll have no trouble making a smooth transition to further talk about the substitute.

> Your repeat order of September 10 for 60 regular-duty
> batteries suggests that you find your battery business
> profitable. We're glad to hear it, but we think we can
> show you how you can do even better in the coming
> season.

You arrange to introduce at least one sales point favorable to the substitute
before revealing that you can't send what was ordered. You need to convey
the negative message fairly early, however, to keep the reader from wondering why all the talk about the substitute. Your best technique is the standard
one for subordinating negative messages: Tell what you *can* do in a way that
clearly implies what you can't.

> In our continuous effort to provide you the best
> automobile accessories and equipment at reasonable
> prices, we have found that the new Acme battery excels
> others of its price class in power, endurance at full
> load, and resistance to cracking. Because of those
> desirable qualities, we decided two months ago to
> stock the Acme line exclusively. Although Powell in
> Dayton still has the Motor King, we think your
> customers will be ahead in service and you'll make
> more profits with the Acme.

Once you are over that rough spot, clear sailing lies ahead. You continue
your sales talk, concentrating on why you carry the substitute and what it will
do for your reader, not on why you do not carry the ordered product. You
give a complete, specific description of the substitute's good points in terms
of reader benefits.

A good test of the adequacy of your sales talk is whether it is all *you* would
want to know if you were being asked to change your mind about the two
products.

> Because of its 115-ampere power and its endurance of
> 5.9 minutes at full load, your customers will like the
> fact that the Acme keeps a hard-to-start engine
> spinning vigorously and increases the chance of
> starting. They'll also like the tough new plastic case
> that performs its tough job better than any other
> material we know.

Sometimes your price will be higher than that of the product ordered. If
so, presumably you think your product is better. Your method of meeting the
price competition, then, is to sell the advantages and then point to them as
justifying the price.

> When you explain the advantages the Acme has over its
> competitors, you justify usually at least a $5 higher
> price in the customer's mind—and you usually produce
> a prompt purchase. The Acme battery will back you up,
> too, in the customer's long experience with it. It

> carries the usual 36-month pro rata replacement
> guarantee. And the fact that it wholesales to you at
> only $2 more means an extra $3 profit to you on each
> sale.

Sometimes you will have to admit (tacitly) that your product is inferior but adequate. Your technique then is to sell its adequacy and the fact that it is a good buy because of the price. If the customer had ordered a higher priced battery than you now sell, for example, you could replace the three preceding paragraphs with these:

> In our continuous effort to find the best automobile
> accessories and equipment at reasonable prices, we
> have found that the Motor King is a leading seller.
> Because of its low price, strong customer appeal, and
> complete range of sizes, we now offer only the Motor
> King for all cars. The fact that you could fit <u>any</u> car
> would give you a big advantage over competitors
> selling brands that come in only a few sizes.

> The $5 saving you can offer on the Motor King will
> have a strong appeal to many of your customers who are
> unwilling to pay higher prices for more than standard
> specifications for regular-duty batteries: 105
> amperes, 48 plates, 5.3 minutes' endurance at full
> load. The Motor King meets these specifications, and
> it carries the standard 36-month pro rata replacement
> guarantee.

> And while your customers would be saving, we estimate
> that you would be making more profits because of
> increased volume that would almost certainly come from
> a complete line at favorable prices.

Usually, however, quality and price are about the same; and you simply sell the product on its merits and as a service or convenience because it is available.

When your selling job is done, you are ready to try to get action. You can do either of two things:

1. You can ask the orderer whether you may fill the order with the substitute or ask for a new order specifying it.
2. You can send the product and give the orderer the option of returning it at your expense—that is, you pay transportation both ways. Thus no question of ethics arises.

The first way, you would have an ending something like

> May we help you increase your battery profits by
> filling your order with 60 of these new Acmes in the
> same sizes you ordered?

The second way will sell more goods if you word the offer carefully to avoid any high pressure. You should use it, however, only in an attempt to give the best service you can—for example when the customer indicated pressing need, transportation costs are small, and you are reasonably sure of acceptance. Indeed a recent Supreme Court decision may relieve the receiver of any responsibility for returning or paying for unordered goods.

If you do send the goods on option, you can greatly affect your chance of having them accepted by the wording of your offer. Note the difference between these two ways:

```
We believe you will find the Acmes satisfactory.
Therefore we are filling your order with them. If you
don't like them, just return them to us collect.
                        --
Because we are so thoroughly convinced that you will
like the Acmes, we are filling your order with them on
trial. When you see how they sell and satisfy your
customers, we believe you will want to keep the whole
shipment and order more.
```

The second puts the emphasis on the customer's accepting the merchandise, where it should be; the first, on returning the goods. The second way will sell more.

Whether your acknowledgment letter selling a substitute asks approval or explains that you are sending the goods on trial, you should merely ask or suggest the action and make it convenient. A last touch of resale may help, but you should not urge action—certainly not command it. This type of letter has the onus of suspicion on it from the outset. High pressure is out of place anywhere in it, especially in the end.

The checklist for selling substitutes summarizes the points you'll want to observe in writing successful letters of this type.

COMBINATIONS

In acknowledging orders, you will often find one for several items, some of which you can send and others of which you can't. To answer such an order, you have to combine the principles discussed for different types of acknowledgments. The writer of the following letter to a new customer had to do so because the firm could send one item immediately, had to delay another shipment, couldn't provide another item, and had to substitute for still another:

```
Your two dozen F78 × 14BW Firestone tires are already
on their way to you. They should arrive by Motor-Van
truck Thursday, ready for your weekend customers.

As evidence of our appreciation for your order, we
shall always try to serve your needs by keeping up
with the market and providing you with the best goods
available.
```

CHECKLIST FOR SUGGESTING A SUBSTITUTE

1. Your opening:
   a. For acknowledgment, rely mainly on implication: maybe the date of the order and a general reference to the class of goods.
   b. Make the reference broad enough to encompass A (product ordered) and B (substitute).
   c. But don't call either by specific name, model, or number yet.
   d. Let the buffer be resale in effect, but not specifically on A.
   e. Intimating at this point that you're going to ship anything could mean only A to the reader.
   f. Establish early the kinship—the similar nature—of A and B, with emphasis on points in B's favor.
   g. Show gratitude for the customer's coming to you with business.
   h. The routine "Thank you" or the selfish "We're glad to have" is usually not the best way.

2. Your transition:
   a. Introduction of B should follow naturally from what precedes.
   b. Before revealing that you can't send A, introduce B and at least one of its strong points.
   c. Calling B a substitute or "just as good" defeats your strategy.

3. Your statement of unavailability:
   a. Stress what you can do, not what you can't; saying that you can send only B makes adequately clear that you can't send A.
   b. Identify A by name no more than once—when you clear it out of stock.
   c. Present the bad news early enough to avoid puzzling.
   d. Make perfectly clear that you can't send A.
   e. Stress why you carry B rather than why you don't stock A.

4. Your sales message on B:
   a. Sell B on its own merits; it's a good product; no apologies needed, and no belittling of A.
   b. Seek out the sales points, and apply them specifically.
   c. Interpret these points in terms of reader benefits.

5. For overcoming price resistance, see Chapter 5.

6. For your action ending to keep the order and goodwill:
   a. Make responding easy, as always.
   b. Work in a last plug about satisfaction with the product.
   c. Avoid high pressure in this letter, especially in the end.
   d. If you send the substitute, make returning it a free option.
   e. But emphasize keeping, rather than returning.

The GR78 × 15WS tires are a case in point. In another effort to assure our customers of the advertised quality of all products we handle, we returned to the manufacturer the last shipment of those tires because they were slightly bruised in a shipping accident.

Since we are assured of a new shipment in two weeks, may we fill this part of your order then?

In trying to keep our operating costs and consequently our prices at a minimum, we have discontinued handling A78 × 13WS tires because of the small demand for them. Probably your best source for them is the Kimble Supply Company, 401 South State Street, Chicago IL 60632, which carries a large stock of obsolete auto parts and supplies.

When our buyer was at the NAP Show last year, he found a new automobile paint that seemed superior to other paints he knew. It is a General Motors product in all colors, with the standard General Motors guarantee. Our other customers have been so well satisfied with its quality and price (only $2.85 a quart and $9.85 a gallon) that we now stock it exclusively. As I feel sure that you, too, will be satisfied with this new product, I am filling your order with the understanding that you can return the paint at our expense unless it completely satisfies. I think you will like it.

Since I am awaiting the return of the enclosed card with your decision on the paint (sent with your F78 × 14BW tires) and the GR78 × 15WS tires to be sent in two weeks, I am holding your check to see how much the refund is to be.

For your convenience and information, I am sending a separate parcel of our latest catalog and a supply of order blanks. We shall be glad to handle your future orders for high-quality automobile supplies.

Note the organization of that letter. The first topic is the most favorable piece of information (usually the best start). The next two topics (delayed shipment and the "no-got" response) are decreasingly pleasant. (If the orderer had been vague or incomplete about another item, this letter should have treated it in second place because the fault was the orderer's—who couldn't well feel very negative toward a request for clarification.) A substitute-selling part would come last in any combination acknowledgement—not because it is especially unfavorable but because of its own structure. Its ending—somewhat like the ending of other sales letters, just will not fit coherently anywhere else in a letter.

Now note (as another illustration of selling a substitute) how the letter would read if the order had been for only the paint (where the letter writer made a substitution). Read only the second, fifth, and seventh paragraphs.

The checklists on preceding pages for standard, incomplete, back-order, rechanneling, and substituting acknowledgments apply to the combination cases near the end of the chapter.

QUESTIONS AND EXERCISES

1. Of the nine kinds of messages discussed in this chapter,
   a. For what kind(s) would "I really wish we could . . ." be a good beginning?
   b. For what kind(s) do you not need a buffer?
2. As a useful technique in bad-news letters and memos, what does "embedding" or "sandwiching" mean?
3. What are your main methods/techniques for subordinating/de-emphasizing unpleasant points you have to make?
4. Of the four C's of credit,
   a. Which is the most destructive of goodwill as a basis for refusing credit?
   b. Which is the least hurtful?
5. Suppose you have an order for five items, a–e, and
   a. You have to back-order,
   b. You don't sell but will refer to a source,
   c. You can send right away,
   d. You'll send a substitute, and
   e. You have to ask what size (or color). Put the a–e in the best sequence for the letter.
6. How can you improve these messages turning down a job applicant?
   a. If it disappoints you to learn that we have selected another candidate to fill the position for which you applied, we want you to know that this reflects no unfavorable assessment of you or your excellent qualifications.

      We hope you will apply again when another opening will possibly occur.
   b. We have reviewed your background and credentials with great interest, and we are particularly impressed by your scholastic honors and offices. The latter suggest leadership ability, which we always seek in our employees. However, at this time we have no opening. Perhaps at a later date something will open up.

CASES   (See p. xiii for some important explanations.)

Refusing requests

7–1.   Assume that you are Professor Norio Aoyama (Case 5–12) and you have to refuse the request of Dr. Mary B. Grunkemeyer. You are involved in a communication conference of the Japanese Business English Association in Tokyo at the time she wants you to speak (November 11 and 12). But suggest that Dr. Grunkemeyer invite Dr. Itaru Nagano, 88–1 Nakakibogaoka, Asahi-ku, Yokohama, 241 Japan, or Dr. Mikito Nakamura, 13–19 Satsukigaoka, Nishinomiya, 662 Japan. You know both educators personally and feel that either one would make a good presentation. Wish Dr. Grunkemeyer well on her important program.

7–2. As L. E. Sly, Jr., manager of General Selectric's Medical Systems Division, Post Office Box 987, Milwaukee, WI 53201, draw up a letter to turn down Sheldon Leonard, 3290 Claymount Circle, Joplin, Missouri 64801. Leonard applied for a job as X-ray sales representative. You have had an incredible number of applications and have tried to give the most careful consideration to each one. Naturally, you appreciate the applicant's interest in your company but have filled the job with one whose qualifications seem specifically suited to your needs.

7–3. As director of grants for the Bureau of Technological Development, Department of Commerce, Washington, DC 20202, write a letter to Professor Jerry B. White (your school) turning him down for a Summer Research Grant because your bureau does not have available funds. Government spending has been cut drastically, leaving you with a restricted budget. White's research on dialysis is a worthwhile subject. Perhaps if the government alters its policies or there is a change of administration there will be more funding.

7–4. As an IRS employee write Mr. and Mrs. Muennink the letter referred to in Appendix E, III, B. Use good form and style (not IRS form, tone, and style), refuse now and forever to refund the $850.31 (with explanation of why, even if you have to ask a tax-accounting teacher), and promise careful consideration of the other items when Mrs. Muennink refunds the money to the state retirement system.

7–5. For additional cases, see Appendix E: II, C, D; IV, B; V, B, D, G.

Refusing adjustments

7–6. As Purser, NCL, One Biscayne Tower, Miami, FL 33131 (Case 5–44), write a refused adjustment letter to P. Shepherd Walden, accountant in the firm of Timm, Walden, and Vines, 539 Thornton Way, Ashland, OR 97520. (For this case, assume that Walden did not notice or report any damage till he got home.) According to Eric Hansen, cabin steward, who was responsible for getting the luggage from cabin 436, and according to a newly hired worker who sent the luggage to the Cloud Nine flight (Pan Am 23 to San Francisco, connecting to United 987 to Medford, Oregon), the portable case for the microcomputer was not damaged (the lid was not caved in). Suggest that Walden file claims with the airlines.

7–7. Your company, Al Kahhal, P.O. Box 2476 Horria, 166 Hegaz St., Heliopolis, Cairo, Egypt, makes and sells handwoven carpets in silk and wool to several areas of the world. One of your customers, Fahed Al Katami, House of Carpets, 1711 Massachusetts Ave., N.W., Washington, DC 20036, complained in his letter that in the first shipment of carpets he received from you that some of the patterns in the rugs were not uniform (colors varied and so did the patterns). He wants you to replace two Ghionde (4' × 6') and two

Ladik (8' × 12') rugs. You must refuse because in all handmade carpets there are discrepancies in pattern and in color. The dyes are made from leaves, roots, barks, and certain insects and shellfish. Each designer creates patterns and colors for the dyers to follow. Each tuft of pile is knotted in place and all knots are kept about the same size. The workers weave two weft threads through the warp and hammer the weft and row of knots with a blunt comb. Because the rugs are handmade, they are not as perfectly made as rugs made on machines, but their imperfectness adds to their beauty and value. They are also valuable because of the closeness of weave and scarcity.

7–8.   Six months ago while the Charles Shellabargers were in their Florida home (9793 Midnight Pass Rd., Siesta Key, Sarasota), they had you replace a self-framed thermopane glass window next to a glass door (cost $109.55). Although you could not tell exactly, you felt that something had hit the glass (bird, rock, air rifle shot). Three days ago you got a letter from Shellabarger from his summer home, 1105 Country Club Dr., Warsaw, IN 46580, telling you that the neighbor who regularly checks on his home in Florida found that the very same glass was cracked again and bulging out. Shellabarger asked you to examine the glass and replace it at your cost. A neighbor, Mrs. Gordon Lloyd, would let you in to examine the glass. When you looked at the glass, you figured that this time pressure made the glass crack. You do not feel the fault was in the glass nor do you feel your installers were at fault. You can replace the glass for $109.55, using a different type of insulation so that the new glass will have more room for expansion when the temperature is high. Your company is Pittsline Glass, Buttonwood Dr., Sarasota 33580.

7–9.   Barbara Hoskinson, Rt. 9870, Box 29, Knoxville, TN 37916, returned her Easy Food Processor after two months (under one-year warranty). Slicer/shredder won't run, food pusher is so out of shape that it will not fit into the food hopper. She had taken machine to a local repair shop where estimate of parts and labor to repair it was $32.50. Easy Food Processor retails for $85.95. She requests that you fix it free and replace the pusher.

As adjustment manager, Customer Service Dept., Hudson Corp., Syracuse, NY 13214, write a refusal. Motor has been immersed in water and will have to be replaced. Food pusher has been subjected to intense heat (probably in a dishwasher). The 20-page booklet that accompanied Easy Food Processor clearly said motor base was not to be immersed in water but was to be wiped clean (page 2). On same page in large print is the instruction *Do not put pusher in automatic dishwasher.* Processor will have to have a new motor; food pusher will have to be replaced. You'll need her authorization and money order or cashier's check for $28.95 (including return shipping charges) to repair and return in a week after you hear from her.

7–10.   As Hilary Wells (Case 5–43), answer R. C. Wegner, Director of National Sales for Essex, Inc. You have to agree that the classic play is bawdy and the actions most revealing. Perhaps the play was not in the best taste as a reward for people who had increased business over last year—but that was the first time Highlands Community Players had performed it, and you had never seen it before. On the positive side stress how professional the acting was, how authentic the stage sets were, the lighting also well done. Anthony Hull, who played Tom Jones, got rave reviews through the local paper, TV, and radio. Answering requested refund, you talked to the Community Players manager and could not get a refund; so you can't make any adjustment in your fee to Essex.

Compromise adjustments

7–11. You operate Rent-an-Oldie, Inc., 1120 Utica Ave., Tulsa, OK 74115. Your company rents old but good cars at daily, weekly, and monthly rates, keeping them running as cheaply as possible. Rent-an-Oldie offers adequate transportation for about half the usual rates. Last week you rented a car to Gerald Piechowski, 141 Grand Oak, San Antonio, TX 78232. Before Piechowski got to his business conference, the air conditioning stopped working and a radiator hose broke. He missed an important sale that cost him a $500 commission. He blames you and your car for the lost sale and threatens to haul you into court. One of the clauses in your lease agreement covers you against this kind of lawsuit, but he's pretty powerful and can be quite vindictive. Write him a compromise adjustment in which you calm him down, point out tactfully the clause in the lease agreement which he signed, and offer to reimburse him the $30 cab fare it cost him.

7–12. Norman Estes, president of Fairmount Health Care Centers, 1609 N. 14th St., St. Louis, MO 63106, claims that the insect spray your service representative (Missouri Pest Control, 606 W. Main St., Jefferson City, MO 65101) spreads around the nursing home at Jefferson City (under a year's contract) has had no effect on the roaches. They line up like Napoleon's army to eat the stuff when they see the sprayer coming with it. Write a letter in which you subtly stress the necessity of keeping the premises clean and promise him that your service representative will be out by the end of the week (no charge) to use a new pesticide bomb, Quick-Kill, which kills roaches quickly by attacking their nervous systems. Together (Fairmount doing its part, you yours) you'll annihilate those bugs.

7–13. After reading the background information for Case 7–8 under refusing adjustments, assume that you are going to compromise with Shellabarger and will install the glass for $60.95 instead of $109.55. You suspect that the glass you put in six months ago was put it too tightly and had no way of expanding during the recent very hot spell.

7–14. For background information, read Case 5–44. As Melvin Johnson, purser, Norwegian Caribbean Lines (M/S Southward) write Sherwood H. Smith,

Jr., 2500 Bitter Creek Road, Raleigh, NC 27602, and explain that Eric Hansen, cabin steward, carefully took all of the luggage from cabin 436 of the Atlantic Deck and turned it over to the baggage handler at the dock. Hansen says that the computer case was not damaged when he handled it. The baggage handler to whom he delivered it has quit work and cannot be found. NCL wants to do the fair thing, but it feels that the case had good handling while in its care. To keep Smith's goodwill, however, NCL will pay half of the replacement cost ($25).

7–15. E. J. Bravata, Binghamton Realty, 3400 S. 1350 W., Ogden, UT 84403 (good customer for 10 years) wrote you—"I'm returning the four file cabinets you shipped me in response to my order of two weeks ago. I specified No. 2R76 four-drawer steel files at $60, and you sent No. 2R78 at $80. Please refund the $20.87 shipping charges that I paid and send me a credit memo for $320. I'm returning the four, shipping charges collect. As far as I'm concerned you can forget the whole thing."

Several months ago you sent out a correction slip for your current catalog indicating that you no longer carry the No. 2R76. Since you notified everyone to whom you had mailed a catalog, you assumed that Bravata realized you'd fill his order with No. 2R78 (as your correction slip indicated). Possibly it didn't reach him; maybe some of the office help threw it away. Whatever the reason, you certainly want to sell him this superior file with its improvements; heavier steel, baked-on enamel instead of sprayed, polished aluminum drawer pulls (instead of chrome-plated), plus automatic stops that prevent drawers from rebounding or being accidentally removed. Before you can hope to convince Bravata, however, you'll need to refund the $20.87, assure him that you'll send him a credit memo for $320 as soon as you receive the file cabinets, and explain why you did not follow his original instructions. But most of all you want to sell him No. 2R78. You'll be willing to ship the four cabinets charges prepaid if he'll reconsider.

7–16. You own and operate Essex Interiors, 149 Beauregard, Mobile, AL 36611. While Mr. and Mrs. Leonard Calhoun were in England, flood waters and mud damaged the carpet and draperies of their fine home, 10 Holly Bluff, Gulfport, MS 39501. On their return to the states they selected new carpet and drapery material, which you installed before they left again (for New Zealand for another six weeks). Today you get a letter from Mr. Calhoun (Box 1560, Dunedin, New Zealand) telling you that they both were very unhappy about the draperies because they did not realize that (in their selection of #937) there would be so much pattern. The small sample you sent did not show much pattern. They ask you to re-check the sample to be sure that the draperies were made from the sample they selected and to make new draperies (at no cost to them) from material that has no design. Although they are pleased with the new carpet, it has too much self pattern to go with the patterned draperies.

In checking you find in your notes that #937 was what they selected for the draperies and you had told them at the time that the draperies would be very colorful, "busy" looking. Mrs. C. had responded that she led a busy life and wanted a busy-looking home. You followed the Calhouns' selection. To calm down the appearance, however, you can put a black-out interlining in the draperies for an additional cost of $200. To help them visualize what the draperies would look like, you're sending a minature 2' × 6" drapery for their examination. You can have the present draperies interlined in time for their return from New Zealand.

7–17.   Appendix E: VI, D.

Credit refusals and modifications

7–18.   As credit manager of Weatherford Office Supply Co., 626 Broadway, Cincinnati, OH 45202, you have to acknowledge the order for three Viscount III word processors for Hector Mfg. Co., 900 Victory Dr., Portsmouth, OH 45662. A credit check shows that Hector's 10-year-old business is related to the building trade and recently there has been little building because of the high interest rates. The company owes $50,000, about half of it overdue, and it has been laying off workers. At this time you feel that Hector is too big a risk to take on a debt of $15,000 for the word processors.

7–19.   As credit manager of Bloomingdale's Department Store, Sunrise Shopping Plaza, Fort Lauderdale, FL 33311, you have these notes on a long letter from Mr. Timothy Nicol (RR 5, Box 89), a free-lance writer: Father of three small children (ages nine, four, and one), has trouble making ends meet. Wife has steady job but doesn't make much. Have to let bills slide occasionally. Revolving charge account with you . . . past three months paid only minimum $10 charge, total bill close to $300 credit limit. Wants credit limit raised to $400 so he can charge a new food processor. Says he needs to save time so he will be free to write.

7–20.   Although in X state liquor is available only through state stores generally, a well-known family (Clara and Claude Baker) have started an independent liquor store in the Northgate Shopping Mall in Y city and asked your wholesale liquor house to sell them $80,000 worth of liquor and wine on credit. A check on their credit shows that the Bakers declared bankruptcy five years ago as a result of some wrong speculation in land development in Phoenix, Arizona. They own their home, have two grown sons who will help them in this new liquor business. They have some run-down apartments worth about $50,000, but they still owe $30,000 on them. Since the Bakers started their independent liquor store, there has been much talk against it in the papers, mostly from preachers and politicians. One powerful city and state politician says he's going to propose a bill in the state legislature that will prohibit private liquor businesses. After all, the state makes a great deal of money from the state stores. Refuse credit to the Bakers now, but offer to review the situation when/if the laws are in favor of private liquor establishments. You are free to make up the name and address of the wholesaler and the Bakers' address.

7–21. As credit sales manager of the Thompson Company, Kansas City, MO 64105, you have to acknowledge the order of Hector van Dalsem, who (according to the financial statements he sent with his application for credit and for his first order for work pants amounting to $300—he buys for $3 and sells for $6) is the sole owner of the Van Dalsem Dry Goods Company, Eureka Springs, AR 72632. References he gave spoke well of his personal integrity and indicated that he is a reasonably good payer. Two sources said he pays within the terms; three said he was 15–45 days slow; one said "slow but sure." You are reluctant to extend credit to a man in a predominantly agricultural area who, at a time when farm income is high, has allowed his current ratio (quick assets to liabilities) to fall closer to 1:1 than to the desirable 2:1. Now is a poor time for Van Dalsem to be taking on new obligations without straightening out his present ones. You suspect maladjusted inventories and lackadaisical collections. As much as you'd like to fill this order, you have to refuse. It's wiser for him to cut his order in half and pay cash (he'll still get the customary 2 percent discount). Since rush orders can be handled within four days, he can keep adequate stocks on hand. Perhaps later on when he has reduced his current liabilities and strengthened his cash position, your regular credit privileges of 2/10, n/30 can be made available. Offer a compromise solution as attractively as you can, and strive to convince him that Thompson pants are the best buy he can make.

Incomplete- and back-order acknowledgments

7–22. As president of Ever-Ready Mfg. Co., 132 West Broadway, San Diego, CA 92101, you find that your company is short of coiled sheet steel because of recent strikes. You need the steel to produce your fire extinguishers and so you are looking into foreign sources from which to buy it. In the meantime write a form letter to customers in the United States telling them that their orders are back ordered.

7–23. As head of the women's coat department for Rack's Department Store, 9843 Capitol Heights, Washington, DC 20010, answer a letter from a lieutenant colonel's wife, Mrs. Kelly B. Kruger, 1120 Tivoligasse, Vienna, Austria, Europe. She wants you to (charge to her Rack's account) send her a light gray wool coat that has no fur or buttons but has a tie for the closing. She tried one on when she was in Washington a month ago and regrets that she did not buy it then. She needs the coat right away because it is cold in Austria and she has not been able to find a coat that pleased her in all of Europe. You can't just pack up a coat because you have no idea of her size (6, 8, 10, 12, 14, 16, or 18). Also there are several shades of gray wool that these $200 coats come in. To be sure there's no mistake, you'll ask her to select the kind of material from some swatches you'll enclose in your letter of inquiry. Separately you're sending the Krugers a Rack's Christmas catalog.

7–24. Mrs. Kruger (preceding case) airmailed back an answer to you at Rack's and said she wanted a size 12 coat in color selection #657 (a dark gray). By the time you got her letter, however, that particular all-wool coat was sold out; but you could back order it for shipment to her three weeks from now. You could, however, send her a size 10 but the seams would have to be let out and the sleeves and hem lengthened. The alteration people assure you that the coat will not show where it is let out. Ask for her decision to (1) send the smaller coat or (2) wait for the size 12 coat.

7–25. After reading the two preceding cases, assume that Mrs. Kruger ordered several Christmas gifts from your catalog (make up the kinds of gifts). Assume that one of the gifts you have to back order because of its popularity; for another gift there's one missing piece of information (color, size, where one gift is to be sent, etc.). You are on your own to add the necessary resale also.

7–26. A. H. Al Zamil & Sons, P.O. Box 285, Manama, Bahrain, ordered 100 rolls of bronze solar screening 48″ wide and 100 rolls of white 36″ wide from your firm, Howard Owen Wire Products, Inc., Industrial Park, Taylorville, NY 14268. You can send the bronze, but you have to back order the white because the special chemicals used for the white are in short supply. You (export marketing manager) should be able to send the white in 10 days.

7–27. As an employee in the College/University Department of Mid-Western Publishing Company, 5101 Madison Road, Cincinnati, OH 44227, write a personal letter to Mr. Jeffrey Larsen, Larsen's Business College, 1st Floor, Victoria House, 79 Moorabool Steet, Geelong. Vic. 3220, Australia, telling Larsen that two books *Secretarial Procedures and Administration,* seventh edition, and *Let's Talk Business,* copyright 19— are due from the printer in April; *Let's Talk Business* will be available in May. Larsen's name has been placed on the follow-up list; so he should receive a copy of each of these publications as soon as they are available. Show your appreciation for his ordering these examination copies.

7–28. Computique, 2362 University Ave., St. Paul, MN 55114, has sent you, sales manager, Lemon Computers, an order for six Mark V1 computers (complete with keyboard, computer processor unit, CRT screen, and sample programs). Unfortunately, you cannot ship the computers until you find out how many Computique wants with cassette tape drives and how many with disk drives. Write and find out.

7–29.   For Computique (preceding case) write to P. R. Anderson, 495 E. State St., Iola, WI 54945. You are shipping the 16K Static RAM Board, the YA5-1016A UART, and the two 18-slot Iso-bus kits. You are out of assembled and tested Parallel/Serial Interfaces, and will ship one just as soon as you receive some more from your supplier. Interfaces are very popular, and manufacturer has a hard time keeping up with the demand, but you think the quality is well worth waiting for. Hope to be able to send one to Anderson in three weeks.

7–30.   For an additional case, see Appendix E: VIII, E.

Declining orders

7–31.   You are working in the Customer Service Department of the Child-Craft Toy Mfg. Co., 4300 Willow Ave., Pittston, PA 18644, and must handle the following letter from Mr. Won Bok, 151-11 Sanglim-Dong, Chung-Ku, Seoul, Korea: "Please to use the enclosing check for my U.S. $50 to be buying some of your excellent games or toys for a 10-years-of-old boy who is my son who is confined at bed by undergoing many surgery on the knee which he is injuring."

Write to Mr. Bok, tactfully referring him to the nearest retail outlet of Child-Craft toys, Balboa's, 350 Powell, San Francisco, CA 94104 (which has a catalog from which he may select suitable toys and games), and return the $50 check. Although Mr. Bok will be disappointed at not receiving the toys and games direct, be courteous and thoughtful, keep his goodwill, and produce a sale for your dealer.

7–32.   Three months ago, David L. Temkin, representing himself as a retailer, DLT/Micro, ordered your cheapest computer, a Mark V, with no accessories, on credit. You refused credit, and Temkin then sent a check to cover the order. You sent the computer. Now Temkin has sent you an order, with check, for one of your inexpensive Model 303 printers—designed to plug into a Mark V. His order is handwritten on lined paper and the check is a personal one. Phone calls to him during business hours are unanswered. Obviously he is trying to purchase equipment for himself direct from you, bypassing your retailer outlets. Return order and check—nicely. His nearest dealer is Compustore in the Keystone Mall, San Bernadino, CA 92401. You are the sales manager, Lemon Computers.

7–33.   Digidata, 101 Gatlin Ave., Orlando, FL 32806, would like to become a dealer for Lemon Computers. Presently handles BYK Computers, Cherry II Computers, and Pactprint Printers. Store is in good location, business almost a year old, financial record good. But you already have an exclusive dealer in Orlando (Home Computers). All your dealers have exclusive territories to assure them maximum profits. But the way the computer business changes, who knows? You'll keep Digidata in mind.

7–34. As head of sales for Mueller Copiers and Duplicators, 49 Industrial Park, Providence, RI 02914, decline the order from Wilbur's Stationers, 2716 Bridge Ave., Dayton, OH 45408, for three Model 2000 copiers @ $1,115.78. You have given an exclusive copier franchise for Montgomery and Greene counties to Dayton Office Products and Supply Co., 11 W. Monument Ave., for 12 years. (Since that has only two years to go, try to *hint mildly* of Wilbur's chances. You have thought of the need for another dealer in the Dayton area— different section, where Wilbur's is located.) All your dealers must have factory-trained service technicians on call to keep the Mueller copiers running dependably, efficiently, and economically. Perhaps Wilbur's could work out an arrangement with Dayton Office Products and Supply Co. to be a subdistributor. You have an office supply company in Kansas City, Kansas, that is the subdistributor for an exclusive franchise held by a business in adjoining Kansas City, Missouri.

7–35. On your desk in the office of the sales manager of the National Cereal Company, 99 Beachfield Drive, Battle Creek, MI 49014, appears an order for two cases of N&N (Natural and New, one of your popular new cereals), to be shipped direct to Jackie Simpson, Quick Food Shop, Five-Points, Hamburg, MN 55339. His check for the correct amount at your jobbers' prices is pinned to one of your current mimeographed jobbers' lists. You don't know how he got the list, and you don't propose to mention it in the letter. You cannot sell to him direct or at jobbers' prices, list or no list. Your exclusive distributor for his district is the Roberts Wholesale Grocery Company, St. Paul, MN 55143. Certainly you want Simpson to handle your popular new breakfast cereal; so you will return the check and ask him to place the order with Roberts. In the light of the ultimate advantages to retailers, make a presentation that emphasizes Simpson's advantages rather than your own or your jobber's.

7–36. Masanobu Hoshikawa, 3–43, Nakanoshima 4, Kita-ku, Osaka 530, Japan, orders six Model 1500 copiers from your company, Mueller Copiers and Duplicators (see preceding Case 7–34). As sales director for Mueller, write Hoshikawa suggesting he purchase the copiers from your new authorized distributor, Mitsunobu Miyahira, 98–3 Chung-Lee, Osaka. This distributor has factory-trained service technicians who will keep the Mueller copiers running dependably, efficiently, and economically. Add any other resale points about copiers that will help the situation.

7–37. Howard Owen Wire Products, Incorporated, Industrial Park, Taylorville, NY 14268, manufactures solar screens of fiber glass. They stop 70–75 percent of sun's heat before it reaches window glass.

A school superintendent, Charles P. Sprayberry, 2491 Sycamore Lane, Ocala, FL 37620, wants to order enough wire to cover three windows measuring 12′ × 6′. You must divert him to the nearest dealer, Blodgetts and Moore, 32218

Bengalin Avenue, Jacksonville, FL 32211. B & M can measure the windows and fit them accurately. Although easy to remove, solar screens are intended for all-year continuous use.

Substitute-selling acknowledgments

7–38. As owner of the House of Lights, 41 Frye Road, Lawrence, MA 01844, suggest a substitute of Chinese silk instead of pure Indian silk for the lamp shade for Mrs. Aileen Shelby, University Circle, Morgantown, WV 26506. You have found the Chinese silk more durable and richer in tones. The 19-inch diameter shade will cost $32 ($12 more), but the quality of material is worth the extra expense. You cannot get the pure Indian silk anymore and do not know why. Enclose samples of the Chinese silk and suggest ordering.

7–39. To: B & K Electronics, 1811 Woodbury Ave., Portsmouth, NH 03805. From: Computique, 1546 John's Plaza, Brooklyn, NY 11213. Penske no longer makes its K-3200 Floppy Disk Drive ($510 each) and you cannot send B & K the 12 ordered. You now carry the Koster KDF-200 ($540 each). Features 40-track drive instead of Penske's 37-track drive, stores 138K bytes on each side instead of 110K bytes on one side; comes with system to de-glitch and up-grade computer's drive to 40-track operation; you have one-, two-, and three-drive systems in stock. Ask whether you can substitute the KDF-200; use resale on your company to keep this order and the customer.

7–40. At Northern Hardware Wholesalers, 987 East River Road, Boston, MA 02119, you have an order from Roe Hardware, 6708 North Charles, Baltimore, MD 21231, for two dozen Flamet fire extinguishers, auto size. About 13 months ago you shipped Roe four dozen Flamet extinguishers in the larger sizes. Four months ago you acquired the Massachusetts distribution of the nationally advertised Stamp-Fire extinguishers and have sold out your entire supply of Flamets in the size ordered. The Stamp-Fire is a more effective and dependable instrument than the Flamet—fights all fires (flammable liquid, cloth, wood, paper, and electrical equipment); the clean, odorless carbon dioxide gas smothers fires and won't conduct electricity; approved by the Underwriters' Laboratories, Inc., and the Coast Guard. The 1-quart size has clamps for installing it on the automobile steering post (no holes or screws). This model is $6 a dozen higher than the Flamet, but sells better—vigorous national advertising. Ask permission before substituting the Stamp-Fire. If Roe still prefers Flamet, try Young's Hardware Company in Silver Spring, MD, the nearest distributor you know of.

7–41. As the Olde Book Finder, 806 Desale St., Vienna, VA 22180, write to Edmund George, 3405 Magnolia St., Texarkana, TX 75503. From your fall list George ordered the copy of Rober P. Elmer's *Archery*, published in 1926 (good condition, $110). By the time his order (with check) arrived, you had sold and shipped the 1926 *Archery*. However, you have just acquired a copy of Robert P. Elmer's *Target Archery*, published in 1946 (very fine condition, with dust jacket, $65). You are holding this later edition for George and are holding the check pending his decision. You will either refund the difference or, if George prefers, you will send both *Target Archery* and a copy in very good condition of James Duff's *Bows and Arrows* in the 1927 first edition (a $55 value) for $110.

7–42. Mr. Salem Soikhahi, Aluminum Distribution Service (ADS), P.O. Box 1633, Damman, CA 94619, used to order from you (Howard Owen Wire Products, Inc., Industrial Park, Taylorville, NY 14268) when he operated out of Saudi Arabia. His firm wants to repeat an order he made five years ago for some plain black screen wire of 200 rolls in sizes 102, 122, 192, and 183. Since his order five years ago, you have improved your screen wire and you make only aluminum, fiberglass, or sun screen. Recommend sun screen because it stops 70–75 percent of the sun's heat from reaching glass and therefore lowers energy costs. Costs $100 (more than old black screen wire) for 100 foot roll in 48″ width. Good for restaurants, hospitals, office buildings, schools, store fronts, trailers, motels, apartments, greenhouses, patio covers, buses. Won't burn. Unaffected by most acids or organic solvents, salt, air, water, or sunlight. Enclose a brochure promoting sun screen and drive for the order of this substitute.

7–43. As Jean Stoeberl, in charge of the shutter department, Mastercraft Industries, Inc., 120 West Allen Street, Rice Lake, WI 54868, answer the request of Mr. Stephen C. Lovemen, P.O. Box 5337, Winston-Salem, NC 27103. You do not manufacture exterior shutters (the kind Loveman asked about). You manufacture interior, movable louvered shutters and use interior glues and finishes. You would be happy to work with Loveman in supplying this type of shutter. You do not know who makes the type of panels Loveman wants.

Combinations

7–44. As manager of men's furnishings, Hudsons Department Enterprises, 130 Elizabeth Street, Detroit, MI 48236 acknowledge the order from David Ransome, P.O. Box 634, Dubai, United Arab Emirates. Ransome's international company has him working overseas for three years and he needs some supplies. His faithful Schick electric razor of 30 years won't shave closely anymore, he writes. He tried to sharpen the three heads, but that didn't help much. He wants a new Schick for worldwide use and doesn't care how much it costs. For his wife and daughter he orders a hair dryer but doesn't say if he wants tabletop, bonnet-style, or turbo-flow blow dryer. He must have the dryer for worldwide use and doesn't care about price.

To help the Ransomes make up their minds about the three styles of dryers, you'll send pictures with details. All are designed for worldwide use. The 1400-watt turbo flow with mica heat shield stands on folding handle and costs $16.99 while the bonnet-style dryer costs $24.99 and the tabletop, $34.99.

No longer can you get Schick razors, but you recommend the Rasormatic, engineered for quiet, comfortable shaving—three floating steel heads with 36 steel blades. Pop-up trimmer trims mustache and sideburns. Six-foot cord. Select electric, $39.95 (UL listed) or rechargeable model (UL listed) $49.95. Replacement cutters for either razor cost $17.99. Make ordering easy. Suggest Ransome Telex order if in a hurry.

7–45.   As the customer service representative for Chef's Bazaar, 616 Chestnut St., So. Charleston, WV 25309, acknowledge the order from C. R. Hirsch, 5776 Grant Ave., Cleveland, OH 44105, for a Combo Starter Set of Phalcalon cookware and check for $342. Pots made of cast and machined aluminum, anodized with a finish 30 percent harder than stainless steel. Cast iron handles tin plated and riveted to pots with ¼-inch diameter rivets. Used by world's leading chefs since 1966 because of superior cooking performance, ease of cleaning, durability. Pots' surface will not crack, chip, rust or peel; once seasoned virtually stick-free. You are shipping set today except for the 5-quart saucepan and the 8-inch omelet pan. You have these items on order and when they come in you will send them on to Hirsch. Unfortunately, Hirsch ordered from your advertisement in an old magazine; the price of the Combo Starter Set has gone up to $362. Get Hirsch to send you a check for the difference.

7–46.   As a supplier of Creative Toys, P.O. Box 306, Route 147, Herndon, PA 17830, write one of your long-standing customers, Geraldine R. Hoover, 7830 East Broadway, Tuscon, AZ 85710, telling her that the Consumer Product Safety Commission has recalled the McCrory gyms because they are dangerous to children. Children can get caught between the platform and top ladder rung and be strangled. These gyms sold for $100 retail (generally 100 percent markup). For $25 more (per gym) Hoover can buy safe Tarzon gyms with 2-inch diameter tubular steel frames, molded plastic gym rings, steel trapeze bar with nylon ropes, ⅝-inch diameter hemp climbing rope, chinning bar, hand-over-hand bars, 6-foot long parallel bars. Suggest Hoover order the Tarzon in replacement for the dozen McCrory gyms.

Because of the popularity of the battery-run, tabletop model of Pac-Man arcade games, you have to back order them for 30 days. When you can, you'll send the 5 dozen ordered. You have a good supply of other computer games such as Speak & Spell, Easy Math, and Star Wars. Send along a new catalog and suggest Hoover keep the computer games on her shelves for they are much in demand and will be more in demand for Christmas buying.

7–47.   To: The Bait Shop, 5001 N. Dawn Dr., Peoria, IL 61614. From: Sporting Goods Liquidators, 1800 Pike Rd., Longmont, CO 80501. Bait Shop's order of May 17: 12 #1430 Coho Silver King lures @ $.89; 6 #4009 Safe-T-

Snip folding pocket scissors @ $1.19; 12 #2850 Sun-Sensitive sun glasses @ $5.98; 12 #2780 Deadly Dick lures, 6 red and 6 yellow, @ $.89; 6 #260 light action manual fly reels @ $8.37. You cannot ship the Coho Silver King lures until you find out what color or colors The Bait Shop wants; they come in silver and blue. You cannot send the folding pocket scissors since you no longer carry them; perhaps The Bait Shop can find another supplier. You have stopped carrying Sun-Sensitive sun glasses and now carry the superior Sun-Sensor sun glasses. These new glasses darken more quickly when exposed to sunlight, the lenses are optical quality, and the frames are heavy duty plastic; the price for Sun-Sensor glasses is $8.97 a pair. (Will you send the Sun-Sensors or wait for a decision from The Bait Shop?) The 12 Deadly Dick lures are being shipped today as ordered. You are temporarily out of stock on the popular light action manual fly reels but expect to have more in two to three weeks; will ship then. Bait Shop has credit privileges with your company.

7–48. (a) For Case 5–27 assume that you have to substitute one item and are out of another item. (b) For Case 5–30 assume you have to back order one item and add another item that needs clarification.

General bad news

7–49. Write the letter to Mrs. Muennink as directed in Appendix E, III, A. Explain fully.

7–50. Because of the depressed housing market, Central Foundry (a large maker of sewer pipe), where you are working as vice president, will have to close temporarily. As tactfully as you can, write a memo to 200 employees telling them that they will be laid off for an unlimited time. Meanwhile they are free to find other work. They will get their last paychecks in the mail. If they have any questions, they are to come by your office. You are writing the most recently hired people because they are the ones being laid off.

7–51. An audit reveals that you overpaid R. K. Faust $268.44 for two pay periods, those ending September 15 and September 30. The personnel department asked Faust to repay, but Faust refused, claiming that because those paychecks also included a good deal of reimbusement for expenses, the overpayment was not recognized as such. To repay the overpayment would constitute an unusual hardship, and this would put Faust in the position of suffering for the company's mistake.

Now the case is in your hands as the director of administrative affairs. You have learned that Faust is a valued, if somewhat eccentric, member of the optical department's research team, which does not want to lose him. Using your best diplomatic approach, write a confidential memo to Faust, pointing out that the company is completely within its rights to demand repayment.

Suggest that, as a compromise, repayment could spread over several months if Faust prefers but that failure to repay will result in dismissal.

7–52.   As a consultant in administration, you have received a point system one of your clients (Bonanza Air Lines, 5266 W. Pierson Rd., Flushing, MI 48433) plans to establish to determine discipline for excessive absences. You are to make comments and suggestions. Here is the plan:

Employees who have 10 points against their record during any three-month period will be warned that failure to improve their attendance record will result in disciplinary action. Points are to be awarded as follows:

For each unexcused and unreported absence . . . . 3 points
For each reported but unexcused absence . . . . 1 point
For each unexcused lateness . . . . 1 point

Bonanza defines a reported absence as one in which the worker reports the absence before the time scheduled to begin work.

You hate to throw cold water all over this plan, especially as the personnel manager who designed it, S. J. Abrams, is very enthusiastic about it—and tends to sulk when told something isn't great. While the plan will take some of the uncertainty out of when an employee will be disciplined, it is still not a clear guide as to when discipline will occur and what the penalty will be. Even if Bonanza gives points for a first warning, second warning, and so on, suppose an employee does not receive notice of points assessed. And if an employee calls at night, the message may not get through to the proper supervisor, since Bonanza operates with a skeleton staff at night. Further, what arrangements will insure that messages received during one shift will be passed on to the next shift? Another problem is telling employees promptly that they have reached the 10-point warning level; the system won't do much good if an employee may have accumulated 20 points before receiving the warning.

Write a letter to Abrams detailing, in an organized and considerate fashion, your comments on the proposed plan. Add any other realistic comments you can come up with.

7–53.   You have been with Rollins, Incorporated, for 10 years, are well thought of and admired, and command a six-figure income. Rollins, a $10 million company is family-owned and only about 30 years old. When you came to Rollins you inherited a fun-loving, party-going, likeable, friendly, compatible, conscientious, and tactful male secretary, Howard Binnion. Obviously Binnion liked to drink, was moody, would fly off the handle for no reason, and was most unpredictable. Howard has been absent from work one to two days per week.

You have been in Mexico buying another business for Rollins and when you returned you found the office a mess. Other employees are upset over Binnion and so are your superiors. You call Binnion in for a conference and he admits to heavy drinking (trying to drown the problems of a rocky marriage and to forgive his wife for having an affair and forgiving himself for having an arrangement with a woman 20 years younger than himself). He promised to straighten up, get the work done, and not miss work.

Two months later you had to return to Mexico to see about the company you bought and were gone two weeks. When you returned you found the same sad story—Binnion had been absent four days while you were gone. Two days he came to work so under the influence of alcohol that he was inefficient, belligerent, demanding, and insulting to one of the fine secretaries. You have two alternatives: Fire Binnion or transfer him to a less sensitive position in another department. If you transfer him, he'll make less money and have less authority. Also, his attendance problem might affect the work in this other department.

    a.   Write a memo to Binnion transferring him to the order department.

    b.   Write a memo dismissing Binnion.

7–54.   Before you can write this assignment, you'll have to look at the example of a Telex message 19c in Appendix C. Assume that you are the vice president of the Peerless Manufacturing Company, P.O. Box 993, Gardendale, AL 35701. Your company manufactures fire extinguishers and one of your buyers is Comercio Y Industria Brasileiro Ltda., Avenida Rio Branco, 295-11 Rio de Janeiro, Brazil. This company has reordered 1,000 fire extinguishers, Model 967, 6 KG's; and you contracted for delivery two weeks from now. Then last night vandals broke into your Gardendale plant, used axes to damage machinery, broke windows causing water to damage some dry chemicals, so there will be a one-week delay.

7–55.   For additional cases, see Appendix E: II, H; VII, A, C, D, E, F, H; VIII, H, L.

Persuasive messages: Sales

8

Although this chapter deals mainly with advertising and selling by mail in the United States, we are aware that the value of world trade currently is over $1.3 trillion per year and has been growing at a nominal rate of almost 20 percent a year.

If you are working in international business, you'll have to be aware of the cultural differences, differences in size and age compositions of population, language, income levels, extent of urbanization, currencies, climate, resources, trade and investment regulations, tax laws, channels of distribution, and structure of consumption. For more discussion on international business, see Appendix C.

Whether you are doing business overseas or in the United States, if the potential users or sellers of a product or service realize their needs and desires, marketing it is a matter of making it available when and where wanted at an acceptable price, and filling the orders. Often, however, ultimate users and even resellers are not conscious of their needs or desires until somebody points them out. In those cases, marketing also involves sales promotion—pointing out needs and desires, and how the product will satisfy them—by personal selling, advertising, and mail. This chapter deals with advertising and selling by mail.

Direct marketing to business (one company writing a sales letter to another) often does not attempt to complete a sale but rather to pave the way for a sales representative to call and tell the whole story, and then get the order. Or such direct marketing may attempt to generate sales leads or to maintain customer loyalty.

We estimate that the average industrial sales call (a representative physically visiting a prospect) cost $172.59 in 1982. This includes the representative's traveling and talking time plus transportation, food, and lodging expenses. As the costs of sales calls rise, less expensive ways of reaching customers (such as advertising and direct marketing) assume greater importance.

While some sales letters sent to businesses could be called junk mail, a study by IBM several years ago proved that 75 percent of business people found the direct marketing they received helpful. (Though 21 percent said they didn't find it helpful, when asked what medium they preferred, they said send the direct marketing anyway!)

245

Direct marketing to consumers usually attempts to complete a sale by having the prospect return an order, though sales letters for certain products or services may ask for an appointment for a sales representative (insurance, yachts, and the like).

For two reasons, in this chapter we will deal mainly with direct marketing letters that ask for the order. First, if you can write a letter that asks for the order, you will surely be able to write one that doesn't. Confidently and positively asking for the order is the part of the sales process most people find hardest. Second, since asking directly for the order is a characteristic of consumer direct marketing efforts, you will find that the examples and problems in this chapter are about products and services with which you are likely to have had personal experience.

GENERAL SALES STRATEGY

Whether you sell by mail or in person, your procedures are essentially the same. You seek to gain attentive interest, convince your prospect that your proposal is worthwhile, and confidently ask for the action you want.

In some cases you already have favorable attention, as when you answer an inquiry about your product or service. In those cases your job is to marshal your sales points and adapt them to your reader in a message that satisfactorily answers questions, convinces, and asks for action. You've already learned to do this in your study of invited sales (Chapter 5).

But in prospecting—or "cold turkey" selling, as many professionals call it—you have the preliminary job of getting attention and then arousing interest so that your reader will be eager to see what you have to say.

The surest way to get your reader to read, and ultimately to buy, is to *stress some reader benefit coming from what you have to sell*. To construct this benefit theme, you must know a good deal about your product or service, its uses, and the kinds of people who can benefit from having it (your prospects). From analyzing your product and your prospects comes the selection of the appeal to emphasize. And from a knowledge of marketing methods and people's buying habits comes the decision of what you want your prospect to do after reading your message.

Analyzing the product or service

Experienced, successful sales executives know that a thorough knowledge of the product or service is essential to successful selling. You will have a hard time convincing someone to purchase something unless you know it well. So you begin your sales effort by thoroughly analyzing what you want to sell.

Begin with some questions. Why was this product created? What was it designed to do? Was it to satisfy a need which existed and was recognized? Or was the product perhaps created for a need which does not yet exist or which is unrecognized? In either case, you must ascertain how the product meets the need.

Get to the designers and engineers, if applicable. What was their reasoning behind the overall design? What problems did they meet, and how did they overcome them? What are the product's outstanding features? Get all the information you can. The more you have, the better (and more easily) you'll do your job.

Now you can answer the most important question in marketing any product or service: *What will it do for people?* How will it make their lives better or their jobs easier, add to their security, increase their status, or otherwise satisfy a need or desire? This question is the same whether you're selling to consumers or businesses.

Although you need to know a great deal about the physical characteristics of a product (overall size, shape, color, length, breadth, height, composition, design, operation, for example), physical description of the product will not sell it. *The psychological description—interpretation of physical features in terms of reader benefits—is the effective part of selling.*

A pocket-size recorder, for example, has buttons, wires, battery, mike, and a motor. So what? It enables a business executive to record ideas, in or out of the office. But it also allows the executive to:

—Release the high-priced dictation time of a secretary for other duties.

—Dictate when and where desired—as time permits and as ideas occur.

—Arrange work for the office staff in the executive's absence.

—Have a record which does not get "cold," which anyone can transcribe with greater accuracy than is possible from shorthand notes.

—Have a record to play back without needing an interpreter.

Insulation is not just pellets or batts of certain sizes and materials. To a true marketer, it keeps houses warmer in winter, cooler in summer—and conserves energy, reducing heating costs in cold months and cooling costs in warm months. It also deadens outside noises. Since it is fire resistant, it reduces chances of fire and also decreases fire damage if and when fire breaks out. Thus, insulation adds to the resale value of a house.

Even a child's tricycle (made of steel and chrome, with first-grade rubber tires) does more than provide pleasure for its youthful owner. It teaches muscular coordination, helps to develop visual perception and judgment, and develops leg muscles. It also releases parents from a certain amount of time spent in direct supervision.

Such analysis identifies the promises you can make your reader, the benefits you can point out. Such psychological description helps the reader see your offer in terms of benefits to be received. That's what turns a prospect into a customer. (See pp. 36, 119, and 123 (4) for further explanation and illustration.)

Psychological description is interpretation, which deserves primary emphasis. Physical description is specific detail, evidence incorporated *subordinately* to bear out the promises established in psychological-description phrases and passages. Though physical description is necessary for conviction, in the final sales presentation it is subservient to psychological description—the interpretation of the thing to be sold in terms of pleasure, increased efficiency, increased profit, or whatever benefits you can most specifically promise your prospect.

Finding the prospects

True prospects are people who (1) need your product or service, (2) can pay for it, and (3) do not have it. In selling by mail, determining who these people are and their addresses involves making a mailing list. Of course you can easily get names and addresses; but are all those people *prospects?*

Some people who appear to be prospects will already be enjoying the benefits of your product or service—or one like it. But unless you know for certain, you need to find out. And the inexpensive way to find out is to try to sell them.

If you are selling a product everybody needs, all you have to verify is your prospects' ability to pay. But few products are useful to everybody (and when they are, direct mail is not the best way to sell them; direct mail is a selected-class medium rather than a mass medium like TV, radio, or newspapers).

In determing need, you have to start with logical analysis. For instance, you wouldn't try to sell bikinis to Eskimos or snowblowers in Puerto Rico. Nor would you try to sell a central heating unit to apartment dwellers or baby carriages in a retirement community.

You would seek to sell a microfiche reader to some business owner or manager, aluminum cookware to homemakers and restaurant owners, insulation to homeowners or building suppliers.

Sex, age (and a close corollary, physical condition), family and dwelling status, vocation, geographical location, and financial situation are some of the more significant considerations in assuming that someone is a logical prospect for your product. In some cases you will need to go further than a logical analysis and make a marketing survey.

Logical analysis, and a marketing survey if necessary, will give you a list of characteristics that describe the most likely prospects for your product or service. If enough people share these characteristics to make it practical to approach them by sales letter, you have a direct-mail market.

Most sales letters have to go out in large numbers to secure the volume necessary for profit. But even when they go out by the thousands, you send them to a *selected* mailing list. As one direct marketing specialist put it, sales letters and direct mail are "not *mass* media but *class* media."

Assured of a direct-mail market, you next need a *good* mailing list. That means names and addresses that are *accurate* (no waste on incorrect or obsolete addresses), *pure* (all true prospects), and *homogeneous* (having the desired characteristics in common—the more the better for adapting your letter).

To get such a list, you can make your own, buy one, rent one, or—if you've already made one yourself—trade for one, sometimes even with a competitor. Making your own list may be the best way *if* you know how and can afford the time and money for necessary tools.

The obvious place to start compiling a list of prospects is your list of customers—people who have already bought from you. If your marketing plan includes advertisements, especially in trade magazines, inserting coupons in them offering free literature on the product or service will bring in names and inquiries of interested people.

Several directories (Dow's, Poor's, and others) classify names of companies by type of business and areas of operation. The Yellow Pages are a fertile source of prospects, especially if you are restricting your effort to a limited geographical area. Another alternative is to hire a clipping service to send you clippings of items (with names) printed in consumer and/or trade publications that deal with the type of people or companies you are seeking.

Like many other activities, however, *making* and *maintaining* a good mailing list requires not only more time and money but more *know-how* and facilities than most people can and will devote to the job. (Some of the best direct marketing books devote whole chapters of 20–30 pages to mailing lists.) Therefore, unless you are going to study the subject to learn the procedures and techniques, and spend the money for the tools of the trade, you will do better to buy or rent your list from one of the many firms that specialize in them.

Hundreds of companies make, sell, and rent lists (so many that the Department of Commerce publishes a directory of them). You can purchase virtually any list you want from such list houses. Most of them have catalogs of the lists they offer, giving the selection criteria, the size, and the cost of each list. If they do not have the list you want, they will build it to your specifications, if you are willing to pay the price.

As a rule, the price is according to the difficulty in compiling the list, usually from 2 to 20 cents per name for an existing list. A major factor is the number of common characteristics you specify. That same factor, however, affects directly the desirabilty and *purity* of the list. This last is important; it refers to the percentage of names that are not likely prospects.

You can buy a big list of auto owners very cheaply (probably no more than 2 cents a name because of specifying only the one characteristic). But for promoting purchases of new Cadillacs, the list would have very low purity. Many of those people would have relatively new cars, and others would have too-low incomes. To purify your list considerably, you could add as specifications that presently owned cars be at least four years old and that annual incomes be at least $35,000. Your list would now be much smaller, and the total cost might be just as much because of the much higher cost per name; but you would save lots of money you might have wasted on people who weren't prospects. Furthermore, you might sell more cars, especially if you made good use of the new information to *adapt* your letters by references to the financial status of the readers and the age of their cars. These facts point up an ever-present question in selling by mail: How far should you go in purifying the mailing list?

Another big problem is the list's *accuracy*, the percentage of correct names and addresses. About 19 percent of the people in America change their addresses each year. People who use old lists and are not aware of this situation are unpleasantly surprised at the number of undeliverable letters.

Mailing-list houses usually do not charge for incorrect addresses if you report them. This is how they qualify their lists (delete the inaccurate names and addresses). As a rule of thumb, any list that has not been qualified within the past year is suspect, and you can expect a good part of it to be useless. First-class mailings, or third-class with return instructions to the Postal Service, are how you qualify a list.

Whether you buy, rent, trade for, or compile your list, however, for sales effectiveness it must contain the correct names and addresses of people or companies with enough desirable characteristics in common to make them a group of likely prospects. Only then can you adapt your talking points and your references in persuasive fashion, as discussed in Chapter 4.

Choosing the appeal

From the analysis of your product will come your sales points. You know your product or service, and you know things about it that might convince people to buy. Obviously you can't put all of them in detail into one letter, or you'll have a cluttered message. Your next step is to select for emphasis the *central selling point*—the one big theme around which to build your letter. It is the answer to this question: *What one feature of the product or service is most likely to induce the prospect(s) to buy?* Your other sales points you can interweave, relegate to an enclosure, or leave for a subsequent mailing. In selling completely by mail, one incidental point that you may need to make clear (by explicit statement or implication) is *why* the reader should buy by mail instead of locally.

People buy for many reasons: to make or save money, to build or protect their reputation or status, to preserve health, to save time or effort, to protect themselves or their families or companies, for example. If you want to, you can find buying reasons listed in multitude in countless books on psychology, salesmanship, sociology, advertising, and marketing.[1] Pride, love, beauty, acquisitiveness, self-indulgence, self-preservation, curiosity, and sometimes fear play their parts in inducing interest and stimulating the final action—making the purchase.

People are both rational and emotional. They need a rational reason to support an emotional desire for something. Arguing the relative importance of rational and emotional appeals in selling, however, is comparable to a vigorous debate over which came first, the chicken or the egg. In writing good sales letters, if you remind your reader of a need your product will meet and

---

[1]Abraham Maslow's writings provide the best classifications.

supply evidence to back up your promise, if you stress what you think is the most important reason why the particular group of readers will buy, you won't need to worry about whether you are employing rational or emotional techniques. You'll be using both. And that's as it should be.

You may, however, need to vary the division of emphasis according to the kind of thing you're selling. Goods that are durable, tangible, expensive, and essential call for major emphasis on rational appeals. Conversely, things that are ephemeral (quickly used and gone), intangible, inexpensive, and nonessential (luxuries) call for more emphasis on emotional appeals.

Certainly effective adaptation is necessary. Your choice of theme for your message will derive from one or more of the significant considerations of the prospect's sex, vocation, location, age, source and amount of income, and social, professional, educational, or corporate status. One of the most obvious differences that affect your choice of theme is that between manufacturers and dealers on one side and consumers on the other.

Consumers buy for the various benefits the product or service will render. Manufacturers buy for the ultimate profit they will make by using your product or service to improve their manufacturing or other activities. Dealers and other resellers buy for the profit they will make on reselling. That depends on the number they can sell and the markup, less any expense and trouble necessary in backing up guarantees with replacements, repairs, and service calls. The logic of selling to resellers lends itself to a formula statement as $P = VM - C$ (profit equals volume of sales times the markup, minus operating costs).

You can't always be certain, either, about your choice of theme. Testing two or more different letters on a part of your list in a preliminary mailing (about which we'll say more later) may help you to arrive at a choice, but sometimes even testing does not solve your problem.

For example, in selling steel desks and chairs to fraternity houses, two writers came up with two different themes. One played up comfort and subordinated appearance; the other stressed appearance over durability and comfort.

Both these letters are well-knit presentations of their selected themes. Each establishes the same information about the product. But we suspect that the first version would sell more chairs to house committees, because on most campuses comfortable study conditions are more important than appearance, and for a longer time than rushing conditions. You would have to test to be sure. You don't have to test, however, to recognize the effectiveness of both the psychological description and dramatization in both letters. (If you didn't see them, look them up in the Index.)

First version	*Second version*
How many hours of each day do you spend at your desk?	Wouldn't you be proud to show your rushees uniform desks and chairs?

First version (continued)	*Second version (continued)*
Three? Four? Maybe more?	Fine—looking study equipment will create an initial favorable impression. And they will realize, as you do, that following rush week comes work.
From experience you know how important it is that your desk be roomy and your chair comfortable. You can be assured of the comfort and convenience you need with Carroll steel desks and chairs. Especially designed as study units for college men, they are also sturdy and good looking.	In Carroll steel desks and chairs you'll have study equipment that will stay good looking and provide years of comfortable use. The chemically treated top resists burns and scratches and eliminates stains from liquids. Welded steel construction assures you that your Carroll desk and chair will retain their attractive straight lines. A choice of battle gray, olive green, or mahogany provides a blend with your present furnishings.
Since the desk is 31 inches high, you can cross your knees beneath the top. Or if you want to sit with your feet on the desk, you can do so without marring the surface or breaking the welded steel chair.	
Whether you choose the steel top at $140.75 or the laminated plastic top at $135.75, you don't need to worry about nicks and scratches. Either top, 28 inches wide by 42 inches long, gives you ample room for all the books and papers you have in use. Shelves at one end and a large drawer keep your other books and supplies at hand.	Either the steel top at $140.75 or the laminated plastic top at $135.75 will retain its attractive appearance over the years.
And you can have Carroll desks and chairs in battle gray, olive green, or mahogany.	The ample work space of the desk—28 inches wide, 42 inches long, 31 inches high, with shelves at one end and a generous drawer—and the swivel chair of body—comfort design mean comfort for study as well as for long bull sessions.
After you've had a chance to read over the enclosed leaflet (which explains the attractive quantity discounts available), you'll see why	After you've had a chance to read over the enclosed leaflet (which explains

First version (concluded)

```
dormitories at Michigan,
Iowa, and Dartmouth
recently chose Carroll
study equipment.
```

Second version (concluded)

```
the attractive quantity
discounts available to
you), you'll see why
dormitories at Michigan,
Iowa, and Dartmouth
recently chose Carroll
study equipment.
```

A letter addressed to the appropriate purchasing agent for the dormitories would wisely have stressed still a different possible theme—holding down maintenance and replacement costs.

Identifying the specific goal

You may know before you begin your prewriting analysis exactly what you want your reader to do. But you'll want to *be sure that the action you request your reader to take is logical* in the light of purchasing conditions, which are governed by the nature of the product, the circumstances of the customer, and authorized, organized marketing channels. You should *identify it specifically before you begin to write*.

Any possible version of the letter about fraternity desks and chairs should have some type of action ending, identifying payment and shipping conditions if an order by letter is appropriate or—more likely in this case—inviting the reader to come to a display room or to authorize the visit of a representative. Whatever you decide is the appropriate reader action, you've already learned how to ask for it (back in Chapter 5).

WRITING THE PROSPECTING SALES LETTER

After thorough study of your product and prospect, selection of theme, and decision on your specific goal, you develop your theme in a C–plan letter following some adaptation of the line of thought that underlies *every* selling situation: Attention, Interest, Conviction, and Action. (If you want to substitute Desire for Conviction in letters appealing largely to emotion, go ahead; it won't alter your basic procedure. If you want to call it Promise, Picture, Prove, and Push, you won't go wrong because of your label.)

But don't think of a presentation in terms of four or five or even three parts. In a good letter, smoothly written for coherence and unity of impression, you can't separate the parts cleanly. Although we analyze the writing of a sales letter in terms of getting attentive interest, establishing belief and trust, overcoming price resistance, and confidently asking for action, the final version of it should be a presentation that is smooth because of its coherence and persuasive because of its singleness of purpose (giving it unity) and progression of thought.

If there is a key to selling, we think it is this: *Help your prospects imagine themselves successfully using your product or service*. Your readers must clearly picture mentally how your product or service will contribute some benefits wanted—status, well-being, self-satisfaction, and so forth.

You help your readers imagine themselves successfully using your product or service through psychological description in dramatized copy. (If you don't remember how to dramatize, look back at Chapter 5.) To help them justify acting to get the benefits you have made desirable, you interweave (or follow up with) physical description and other evidence that they can get the wanted benefits.

The sales messages in this chapter all exhibit this fundamental sequence of the persuasion process, which we will examine in detail.

Getting attentive interest

If you believe in your product and what it can do for your reader, you'll have no big problem starting a sales letter effectively. All you need to do is *hold up the promise of the big benefit your product can contribute to the reader*. If it's a genuine benefit and your message is to a real prospect, you'll get attention.

Yet because of the clamor for attention which many advertisers talk and write about, many advertisements and letters put on a show with the bizarre, the irrelevant, and the irritating to make the reader stop and listen. They seem to say: "We know you won't listen otherwise; so we're standing on our heads to attract your attention. Of couse, standing on our heads won't tell you a thing about our product or what it can do for you, but it'll make you sit up and take notice."

To that, all we can say is: "Sure! The freak at the circus commands attention. And if sheer attention is all you want, walk naked down a busy street. You'll get attention. But is it appropriate? Is it in good taste? Will it really help to induce the reader to buy?"

Relevancy is essential. Without it, your trick or gadget will be only a distraction and a detriment rather than an assist to your sales effort. Tricks are legion, and they create talk, even notoriety, about you. But *unless they lead naturally, plausibly, and shortly to what your product can do for your reader, they're not worth the effort and expense*.

The American public is educated and sophisticated. It is quick to criticize or, worse yet, to laugh at poor advertising. It hasn't bought the Brooklyn Bridge for a couple of generations. The farmer's children have been to town— even if only via TV. Smug patter about the 14-year old mentality is beguiling—and dangerous. Even 14-year-olds recognize the difference between showing off and real selling.

You'll read much and hear much about tricks, stunts, and gadgets for sales letters. Good-luck pennies, four-leaf clovers, keys that open the door to everything from business success to a happy home life with your dog, rubber bands (which most of the time only stretch the reader's patience), cartoons, faked checks in window envelopes, simulated handwritten messages, names of readers written at the top of the page in red, blue, gold ("the symbol of things precious, and your name means much to us!"), Chinese writing, the early bird with the worm in its mouth, alarm clocks—all these and many others may distract from your sales message rather than assist it unless they enable you to *cut through quickly to the benefit your product can render.*

You may dream up a trick or gadget occasionally that naturally, plausibly, and quickly illustrates or introduces the benefit your product can render. If it can meet the tests of relevance, plausibility, good taste, and speed, you may want to use it. A fire-sale letter typed in red may have salutary appeal. A check form made out to the reader, immediately followed by the lead, "What would it mean to you to get a *real* check like this *every month?*" may plausibly preface sales talk about an annuity or health insurance.

We do not mean to imply that all tricks, gadgets, and humorous letters are undesirable. Certainly you'll find occasions for the whimsical, the gracefully turned phrase, the chuckling at humanity's idiosyncrasies, and the outright humorous. But before you use what you think is a bright, clever, or punny approach, recall the old story of the woman who asked her husband if he had seen a certain clever ad. "What was it about?" her husband asked. "I don't remember," the lady replied, "but it was right next to that homely X, X, and Y ad."

If you can phrase an opening which is deft, novel, and catchy, use it—provided it paves the way quickly and naturally to the introduction of what your product can do for your reader. If you can't, forget about it.

The benefit-contribution-product beginning is always applicable and always good. Associate the benefit with your reader, then bring in the product as the provider of the benefit, and you have a good opening.

A business-reporting service used the following successful opening in a letter to contractors:[2]

```
A lot of money spent
now and later
on new construction

in your area--

--is going to wind up in somebody's pocket . . . and
it might as well be yours instead of your
competitor's!
```

Selling word processing equipment to office managers, the following opening (below a clipped-on photograph of a girl powdering her nose while surrounded by three of the machines referred to) pinpoints a real problem and its solution:

---

[2]Many large-volume sales forms, having no inside address and salutation, use this facsimile or faked layout to look like the usual letter and reduce readers' missing those parts.

> What happens when a girl "powders her nose" in the
> offices of the Northeastern Mutual Life Insurance
> Company?
>
> When her machine stops, production ceases. And office
> costs go up.

A variation of theme for the same product went this way:

> "I've had five years' experience with the Mutual Life
> Insurance Company, can type 300 words a minute, am
> willing to work each day indefinitely, do not get
> tired, and demand no salary."
>
> Would you hire this typist? We did. And it typed this
> letter in two minutes.
>
> Of course, it isn't human. It's a machine—the Robo—
> Typist—which types any letter you want from recorded
> data at better than 300 words a minute.

Note that in all these quoted openings *the lead is simply a reminder of a need which the product comes in shortly to satisfy*. They do not command, preach, cajole, beg, or exhort. They do not challenge. They do not scream in superlatives (finest, amazing) with exclamation points! They do not begin with talk of the product itself ("Now you too can have XYZ dog biscuits!") or the company ("53 years of doing business . . ."). Here's an example of an opening that does just about everything wrong:

> Recently I was appointed Director of Sales—Midwest
> Region for the Hardly Used Tool Company and I will now
> have the pleasure of working with you in handling your
> used tool requirements with our company.

Good openings positively, specifically, and vividly, but believably, say or imply, "As help in handling this specific problem, I suggest . . . ." They get attentive interest through psychological description of the product in use benefiting the reader. Thus they cause the reader to want more information, especially on how the product can fulfill the promise.

Establishing belief and trust

Having made the promise, a letter must quickly supply explanations and evidence to back it up. If the opening is successful, it has established tentative approval or agreeableness rather than serious doubt. The next part of your sales letter—which ordinarily consumes the greatest amount of space—tells how your product does meet the need and *gives specific information that will make your reader believe you*. You thus maintain and continue the agreement you establish in the start of the letter.

Explanations and descriptions of the product or service *in use* are how you handle this part. Word pictures of how it works and how it is made, performance tests, testimonials of users, statistics of users, facts and figures on sales, guarantees, free-trial offers, offers of demonstrations, and samples are some of your most common devices. Note how the following classic sales letter supplies evidence to support its opening claim.[3]

```
The Carriage Return Lever
On a Manual Typewriter
Is Costing You Money . . .

. . . and it's money you don't have to spend any more.

Human Efficiency, Inc., has completed a series of
exacting tests showing that you can save as much as
one hour each day for each typist you employ when you
install Speedo Carriage Returns on your manual
typewriters.

Watch one of your typists. Every time she returns the
carriage to the next line, her left hand makes three
movements. When the bell signals the end of a line,
her hand moves from the keys to the lever, throws the
lever, and then returns to the keys. It looks fast and
easy, doesn't it? It is--an expert typist can do it in
just one second.

Just one second, but one second becomes one minute
when your typist types 60 lines. And that one minute
multiplies to one hour every 3,600 lines. From your
experience as an office manager, you know that 3,600
lines aren't very many for an efficient stenographer
to type, especially the short lines required for
orders and invoices.

Using a Speedo, your typist performs one step--not
three--to return the carriage to the next line. When
the bell signals the end of the line, she presses a
foot pedal; the carriage automatically spaces
correctly and returns to the left margin. One tenth of
a second--not one second--has elapsed.

And because her hands do not have to leave the
keyboard, accuracy increases when you install Speedos.
Human Efficiency tested 150 typists using Speedos for
```

---

[3]We have three comments before you read the letter: (1) Though the product sold is obsolete because of electric typewriters, the letter is an excellent one to illustrate the point of convincing the reader by detailed logic and facts about the product *in use*. (2) Yes, this letter is long—as most effective sales letters are. But don't confuse length with a lack of conciseness. If you're worried about length, remember that the firm which has tested more of its sales letters than any other, Time, Inc., never writes one-page sales letters any more—they always pulled less under test. Remember, too, the statement of one of the nation's most renowned consultants, Howard Dana Shaw, that in general a long letter will outpull a short one if it tells, in an interesting way, something of value to the reader. (3) And yes, this letter is sexist—as so many letters were years ago when it was written. But it is still a classic sales letter.

two weeks in 20 different large plants. They showed a 16 percent reduction in errors—and, naturally, a similar 16 percent reduction in time spent erasing errors.

Part of the explanation for the increase in output and decrease of errors is a reduction in fatigue. Throwing a carriage just once doesn't amount to much, but when your typist repeats hundreds of times she uses up as much energy as if scrubbing the floor. The Speedo not only reduces the strain by two thirds but shifts it to the leg and foot, which can bear it far better than the arm. Tests of 45 typists employed by the Kenoya Wholesale Grocery Company of Columbus, Ohio, showed that after two weeks they increased by 9 percent the amount of copy produced daily.

Clamped to the carriage-return lever, the Speedo connects to the foot pedal by a thin wire. The adjustment is simple; you can put one on any standard typewriter in less than five minutes.

Turn to pages 1 and 2 of the enclosed folder and read the complete report of the tests. On page 3 you'll find comments of typists who've used the Speedo and the comments of their office managers. Read how the typists all agree that they had no difficulty learning to use the Speedo efficiently.

Page 4 gives you data on prices and shipping. Note that the Speedo with all its advantages—plus an unconditional 90-day guarantee—is yours for only $4.50 because we sell Speedo only by mail to help keep the cost down. And by ordering a dozen for $46 you save 70 cents on each one.

Fill out the enclosed order blank and send it to us in the return envelope provided. We'll immediately ship your Speedos by whatever method you direct, either prepaid or c.o.d. Within 10 days at the most you'll be able to see the increased output and accuracy of your typists.

Surely you remember that sincerity is essential to the reader's belief and trust, that you-viewpoint description is vital, that psychological description in terms of the reader's use and benefits is far superior to mere physical description of the product, that specific words in positive language are necessary to effective sales techniques, and that enclosures (properly introduced) can often supplement letters effectively. If not, turn back and review the persuasion principles in Chapter 4 and the analysis of the invited sales letter in Chapter 5. All we're suggesting is that you apply the same principles.

PROSPECTING SALES CHECKLIST

1. Get started effectively and economically.
    a. Suggest or hint at a specific reader benefit in the first sentence.
    b. Show a need before naming the product as serving it; but usually use positive selling, not predicament-to-remedy pushovers.
    c. Concentrate on a well-chosen central selling point at first.
    d. Quickly get to the distinctive thing about your product (not just anybody's). Avoid unnatural or delaying gimmicks.
    e. Don't begin with an obvious statement or foolish question.
    f. Suggest, remind, but don't preach: "You will want . . . ."
    g. Don't claim too much for your product. Be reasonable.

2. Back up your opening promise with a persuasive description.
    a. Subordinate and interpret physical features in terms of benefits.
    b. You-viewpoint is not automatic from use of you ("you will find" and "you will note"); but as the subject or object of action verbs, *you* helps.
    c. Guard against stark product descriptions (beginnings like "Our goods . . . ," "We make . . . ," or "XYZ is made . . .").
    d. Specificness in description is necessary for conviction.
    e. Even in form letters, refer to some action or condition that applies and avoid references which brand them as forms.
    f. The history of the product or firm will bore most readers.
    g. Eliminate challenging superlatives.
    h. Guard against the trite "truly" and "really" and the indefinite "that" ("that important conference").

3. Be sure to cover all important points with proper emphasis.
    a. Develop the most appropriate central selling point adequately.
    b. Stress your central theme for singleness of impression.
    c. Give enough detail to sell your reader on reading an enclosure when you have one, and even more when you do not.
    d. Provide adequate conviction through selected methods.
    e. Introduce any enclosure only after most of your sales points, stressing what the reader is to do with it or get from it.

4. Remember the price; it is an integral part of any sales message.
    a. Unless using a recognized-bargain appeal, minimize price.
    b. Keep price out of the ending, at least the last sentence.
    c. If you choose not to talk price now, offer to sometime and reassure the reader that it is not out of line.

5. Forthrightly ask for appropriate action (and tell why buy by mail).
    a. Name the specific action you want your reader to take.
    b. Be confident. Avoid "If you'd like . . . ," "Why not . . . ?"
    c. Avoid high-pressure bromides: "Why wait?" "Don't delay!"
    d. Refer *subordinately* to ordering aids (blanks or envelopes).
    e. End with a reminder of what the product will contribute.

6. Check for any unintentional promises of safety or warranty.

Overcoming price resistance

You've already studied effective ways of handling dollar talk too (back in the discussion of the invited sales letter in Chapter 5). The principles are the same in prospecting sales.

Asking confidently and specifically for action

If we discussed again what we've already told you and illustrated for you repeatedly about action endings (indicate confidently what you want your reader to do and how to do it, make it easy and make it sound easy, and supply a stimulus to prompt action in a quick reference to the contribution the product can make to the life of the reader), we'd be using your time unnecessarily. Furthermore, the summary prospecting sales checklist itemizes the points specifically.

ADAPTING TO CLASSES

All good sales letters follow the basic procedures advocated in the preceding pages. Only in their talking points and in their interpretation and references do they differ as they go to farmers instead of bankers, to lawyers instead of engineers, to consumers as opposed to dealers or manufacturers. Though sales letters are not a major medium in intercultural/international business, even there the same basic principles apply. Of course you do have to recognize differences in language and in social, family, religious, and business beliefs and practices (as we've explained at appropriate places in this book). If you know and give attention to those differences, however, and are a person of feeling and imagination, unselfish enough to forget yourself in analyzing another person's (or group of persons') circumstances, you won't have much trouble writing successfully adapted letter copy.

The major adaptation in sales letters depends on whether you're selling to a consumer (user) or to a reseller (who buys to resell at a profit). As an illustration of how tone and talking points differ, study the following two letters. The first is to a homeowner, the second to a dealer. In both cases the product is a special kind of lawn mower which eliminates hand clipping.

```
Lawn-mowing Time

Extra Time for
Summer Rest and Fun!

You can cut your lawn-mowing time in half with an
easy-operating Multimower because you can eliminate
the hand clipping and trimming and the raking. The
Multimower gathers all the grass it cuts.

So with just one run over the lawn with your
Multimower, your lawn is in shape. And it's just a
light workout. You can cut your grass flush against
```

fences, trees, and flower beds. The interlocking rotary cutters enable you to mow tall grass and tough weeds with no more effort than it takes to cut short grass. And you're less tired when you get through because you handle only the minimum weight when you use this 58-pound mower. It's light enough for almost any member of the household to use.

Even though the Multimower is light, you have a precision mower of sturdy construction and strength-tested materials. The drive shaft runs on free-rolling, factory-lubricated, sealed ball bearings which keep dirt and water from rusting these parts. And the cutters are self-sharpening. So add gas and your Multimower is ready to go.

If the weather keeps you from mowing your lawn on schedule and grass gets a little too high, simply adjust the handle knob to the cutting height you want and drive your Multimower easily across your lawn, cutting a clean, even 21-inch swath.

Many of the 8,000 enthusiastic Multimower owners have been using theirs for over two years. Some of their statements, along with illustrations and the details of our 90-day structural guarantee, you can read on the two inside pages. You'll see, too, that we pay shipping charges to your door. Multimower is available only by mail at the economical price of $139.95. The time you save on the first summer's Multimowing is probably worth more than that.

Use the handy order mailer to send us your check or money order. Within a week after you mail it, you'll be able to cut, trim, and gather up the grass on your lawn in only one easy, timesaving Multimowing.

The letter to a dealer stresses the same points, to show *why to expect high-volume sales to customers;* but it does so more rapidly and concisely, in order to concentrate on sales aids, price spreads, promptness and regularity of supply, and service as parts of the profit-making picture. Remember the formula $P = VM - C$. And since V (volume of sales) is usually the main variable, give it the major attention it deserves by pointing out how the features of the product will appeal to buyers.

Still the approach is the same as in any sales letter: It seeks the answer to the ever-present question, "What will it do for me?" To a dealer the answer is always "profits," but profits depend on salability (the features of the product that cause people to buy), on serviceability, and on markup. Since salability— features attracting buyers—is usually the main point, the psychological description becomes *interpretation of those features in terms of consumer appeal*. A dealer is also interested in your promptness and regularity in filling orders, in guarantee and service arrangements, and (if you provide any) advertising or other selling aids to help sell more—as in the following letter:

> When you show a customer a Multimower——a lawn mower completely new in design and principle, which cuts, trims, and "rakes" a lawn in one operation, you have a quick sale, a satisfied customer, and a $46.65 profit.
>
> Your customers will like the Multimower because it gives them more time to spend in enjoyable summer recreation. It cuts right up to walls, fences, trees, and flower beds and thus eliminates the need for hand trimming in spots not reached by ordinary mowers. Its easily adjustable cutting—height regulator and self—sharpening cutters that slice down the toughest kinds of grass, dandelions, and weeds will assure them of having a trim, neat lawn in half the time they've formerly spent.
>
> Both men and women like the Multimower because its light weight——only 58 pounds——means easy handling. The quiet operation of the interlocking cutters has won approval of 8,000 Multimower users. They like it, too, because it is permanently lubricated and self—sharpening. With a minimum of care it's always ready for use. So normally you just put in the gas and it's ready to go.
>
> No doubt many of your customers have been reading about the Multimower in the full—page, four—color monthly ads that started running in <u>Homeowners</u> and <u>Vacation</u> magazines in March and will continue through July. A reprint, along with testimonials and conditions of our guarantee, appears on the next page. Note the favorable guarantee and servicing arrangements.
>
> In these days of high prices, the $139.95 retail cost of the Multimower will be popular with your customers. Our price to you is only $93.30.
>
> By filling out and returning the enclosed order blank along with your remittance today, you'll be sure to have Multimowers on hand when your customers begin asking for them.

In looking for differences that adapt the two versions of the Multimower letter to users and dealers, did you notice that the main differences are in the psychological description while the physical description is essentially the same—and subordinated? If not, perhaps you should read the instructions again.

The helpful dealer sales checklist summarizes significant points to keep in mind for selling to dealers.

DEALER SALES CHECKLIST

1. A dealer sales letter opening has to move fast.
   a. Devote at least the beginning to the reader and benefits to come—not yourself or even the product per se.
   b. Picture the act of selling and the product's consumer appeal.
   c. Stress a distinctive point; avoid obvious, slow, general copy.
   d. Avoid exaggeration and questionable superlatives.

2. Though you might mention profits, the first point to develop is salability (volume). Without consumer appeal the product stays on the shelves and makes no profit regardless of price spread.
   a. To stress consumer demand, explain the product's points in terms of customers' reactions, demands, and approval—hence high-volume sales.
   b. Talk about the dealer's selling—not using—the product.
   c. Adaptation here means talking of sales demonstrations, wrapping up a purchase and handing it across the counter, ringing up a sale, answering customers' questions, and the like.

3. Show how the manufacturer helps to push the sale, if applicable.
   a. Refer to whatever dealer aids you have (advertising, displays, mats, cuts) with emphasis on how they build local demand.
   b. Give working ideas of size (quarter page, half page), extent (time it will run), and coverage (specific medium—magazine, newspaper, radio, and/or TV station—and type of audience).
   c. Interpret any advertising as promoting inquiries and sales.

4. Continue pointing to appeal and profitable selling in the price talk.
   a. Price is most appropriately handled late, most naturally as you ask for an order and talk payment details.
   b. Include a specific mention of price spread, percentage, or both.
   c. Terms and manner of payment have to be cleared up.

5. You will almost always have some enclosures to handle.
   a. Don't divert attention to the enclosure until near enough the end that the reader will complete the letter.
   b. Make the reference to an enclosure carry a sales point too.
   c. Don't depend too heavily on an enclosure to do the selling.

6. Make the action ending brief and businesslike too.
   a. Probably better avoid commands to the seasoned buyer.
   b. Exaggerated superlatives are out of place here too.
   c. Of course, you name the specific action you want.
   d. And you make that action easy.
   e. Use a whip-back suggesting prompt handling and profitable selling.

7. Check for any unintentional promises of safety or warranty.

LEGAL CONSIDERATIONS

Whether writing to a user or a reseller, a sales writer must keep in mind legal responsibility for what the message says. Recent court decisions have firmly placed product liability squarely on the manufacturers and designers of products. And they may still bear the responsibility even if an injured user admits reading and understanding the instructions supplied with the product. Clearly the ancient doctrine of *caveat emptor*, "let the buyer beware," is changing to *caveat venditor*, "let the seller beware."

As an example, suppose the Multimower letters above said

```
The unique spring-loaded on-off switch, cuttings-
deflecting exhaust, and rugged blade shield make the
Multimower safe to use.
```

If worded that way and the spring in the switch broke and hurt a user, or if the mower accidentally got on someone's feet, severely injuring them, that sentence would make Multimower's position in court indefensible. The letter would have made an absolute claim for safety, and the company would be legally responsible for making that claim good.

Better would have been to qualify the statements: ". . . safe to use with normal safety precautions," or "In normal use, and observing proper safety precautions . . . ."

Warranties and guarantees are an area in which writers of sales letters are even more likely to get into trouble unwittingly by (1) implying a warranty where no warranty exists or (2) extending an existing warranty infinitely. As an example, the third paragraph of the first Multimower letter originally ended:

```
So your Multimower is always ready for you to use. All
you need to do is put in the gas.
```

First, the writer implied a warranty unintentionally, saying that *all* that is needed is gas, and the mower will operate. Second, that word *always* extended the warranty or guarantee infinitely. The writer unintentionally made a legally binding promise that the Multimower will perform until time and the universe end, provided only that the user puts in gas!

Here's how those sentences could read to avoid the problem:

```
A minimum of easy maintenance will help keep your
Multimower ready for use. Virtually all you need to do
is put in the gas and start it.
```

Words to watch out for when you are writing sales messages are *always, never, whenever, all, perfectly, trouble-free, simply,* and others like them. They signal that you may need to reword what you said, or qualify it.

TESTS AND TESTING

Testing a mailing to predetermine the returns (or the pull or the pulling power) of a letter is serious business among high-volume mailers. Testing means simply mailing the letter to a portion of the names on your list to see whether you can get a profitable percentage of people to take the action you want. You can see why a business executive would be wise to test a mailing before risking the money to send 10,000 letters, especially if the mailing pieces are expensive.

Suppose your mailing pieces cost 50 cents each (not unusual in a mass mailing) and you make $5 on each sale. Obviously, you have to make sales to 10 percent of the list to break even. Now suppose you have a 90 percent accuracy factor (that is, the percentage of correct addresses). Each 100 letters have to bring ten orders from every 90 people who get them. Further suppose the purity (how many names on the list are likely prospects instead of deadwood) is 70 percent. This means that your 100 letters have to bring ten orders from every 63 good prospects (70 percent of 90). This requires about 16 percent pulling power from your letter (10/63).

Most sales letters don't do so·well. But you could make the situation profitable by increasing any or all of the accuracy, the purity, or the pulling power—or by decreasing costs of the mailing or increasing the profit on each sale.

Other significant reasons for testing are to find out which of two or more messages has the greater pull or which of two times (day or week or month the mailing piece arrives) is more profitable.

You can test one color against another; but if you also vary size, copy, or time, your test doesn't mean a thing. You can test one lead against another; but if the rest of the copy and the time of arrival are not the same, you still have no basis for saying that one lead is better than the other. *You can test only one factor at a time!*

Many published test results concern format and timing. If you talk with enough people in the field or read long enough, you'll be reassured—often vehemently!—that every color you've ever seen is the best color for a mailing. You'll find one person swearing by third-class mail and another at it. You'll find out, however, what all experienced persons with judgment discover: Because people and circumstances constantly change, so do the results of testing; what a test suggests this week may not be true next week and probably will not be next year. The only way to be safe is to test in each new situation and then follow through as fast as you can.

Even so, you usually expect only 5–10 percent pulling power. But especially effective copy, carefully selected mailing lists, or unusual offers often increase these percentages.

Even such apparently insignificant things as the time of arrival are important. Experience has shown that sales letters should not arrive in an office at the beginning or ending of a week or month or at the homes of laborers or farmers in the middle of the week. Around Christmas time and April 15 (income tax time) are especially bad times of the year to mail to consumers, and the fall and winter months are better than spring and summer. Of course, seasonal appropriateness of the goods and geographical locations can easily affect this. Even temporary local conditions may.

By keeping careful records on the tests and on the whole mailing, through the years users develop a considerable quantity of experience data that may help guide them in future work.

WRITING SALES SERIES

The sales letters we have been discussing are lone efforts to produce or promote sales. Because single sales letters frequently cannot do all the work a series can, probably just as many sales letters go in series as singly. Usually they are obviously processed (form) letters, sent out in large numbers by third-class mail. For further economy they often use some simulated address block instead of an inside address and salutation (like some of our examples). By careful phrasing, however, a skillful writer can *make the one reader of each copy forget the form and feel that it is a well-adapted message that certainly fits personally*. Where the mailing list is small, individualized letters and first-class mail are the rule.

Whether a letter is a single sales letter or one in a series makes little difference in the techniques or preliminary planning, but in one of the two types of series (wear-out and campaign) the letter's organization is more complicated.

The wear-out series

Probably the most widely used of sales series is the wear-out. In it each mailing is a complete sales presentation on a relatively inexpensive product (usually not over $50). The product almost has to be inexpensive, because one letter cannot hope to succeed in persuading most people to buy expensive items by mail from a complete stranger.

After the market analysis, preparation or purchase of a mailing list, and preliminary planning comes the writing of the letter. Probably you and several other executives, and perhaps a letter consultant,will spend hours preparing the letter, or several versions of it. These first few copies may cost several hundreds of dollars in time and consultant's fees.

Then you test your list, and perhaps several versions of the letter. If one letter seems to have a high enough pulling power to make it profitable, you run off hundreds or thousands of copies and mail them out at a carefully selected time. Now that the big investment divides among so many, the cost per letter is not so big.

After an interval, usually of one to three weeks, you remove the names of purchasers (unless the product has frequent recurring demand) and send another letter (or sometimes the same one) to the remaining names on the list. Sometimes the third or fourth mailing brings better results than the first, even with the same letter, because of the buildup of impact. You continue to repeat the mailings until returns no longer yield sufficient profit to continue. Those left on the list are the "hard cases" that apparently won't buy no matter what. The list is worn out; hence the name.

The campaign series

What has been said about the cost of the first copy, the general preliminary planning, the testing, and the usual interval between mailings of the wear-out series also applies to the campaign series. But there the similarity stops.

The theory of the campaign series is that people and businesses buy some (usually inexpensive) items quickly, without much thought; but before buying certain other types of items (usually more expensive), most people and firms ponder for a month or more and talk over the situation. To send one letter which first introduced such an item and, after only two minutes of reading time (as in the wear-out series), asked for the decision on an order card would be to pour money down the proverbial rathole. Instead of the wear-out, you would use the campaign series for such a situation.

Your preliminary planning is as different as the price involved. You decide approximately how long most people on the mailing list would want to think over your offer before making up their minds. Then you decide how frequently they should be reminded to keep them thinking about your product or service. On that basis you decide the length of the series—in time and number of mailings.

The essence of planning the series of letters (whether two or a dozen) is to make the whole series cover the parts of a complete sales presentation and knit them together. In any case the first letter will try hard to get attention and start working at interesting the prospect. Further letters will strive to develop interest in buying until the last makes the strongest drive for action. As people respond, you remove their names from the list.

The last letter is not the only one, however, to which a reader can easily respond. Sellers by mail know that they will not usually get any action from more than half of their prospects. But they also know that in almost any large group some people will be sold on the first contact. Consequently, they usually provide order forms with almost every mailing.

If you have ever let your subscription to a magazine lapse, you have probably received campaign series letters. To help illustrate further the differences between a campaign series and the single-letter sales presentations discussed earlier, however, we have included the skeleton of a typical campaign below.

*   *   *   *

The following direct-mail campaign directed to accounting firms, tax services, and law firms emphasizes the economy of making dry photocopies instantly with an Adeco Auto-Copier (costing about $3,000). The letters could go to only one city or over the entire country. A sales representative within a city could readily assemble a mailing list from the Yellow Pages, or buy the list. Certainly a nationwide mailing list would be more inexpensively purchased than assembled.

The mailings are planned for intervals of about three weeks. For economy they use a simulated address block (first few words of the copy set up like an inside address and salutation), are printed, and go third class. Each mailing includes a reply card which reads something like this:

```
Yes, I would like to know more about how the Adeco
Auto-Copier will help me. Please call me and arrange
an appointment.
```

The card provides blanks for indicating name of individual, position, company, and address.

The first mailing includes a 12-page, two-color booklet containing illustrations, savings estimates and comparisons, and information about the company and its organization.

```
You can save
Up to 80 percent on
Copying jobs . . .

. . . by letting your typists make photocopies with
the Adeco Plain Paper Auto-Copier.

In less than 15 seconds an unskilled operator can turn
out a legally acceptable, error-proof copy of an
original--one that would take your typist at least 10
minutes to copy. If your office produces only 15
copies a day, the Auto-Copier can save you about $15
each working day. When you need to turn out large
numbers of copies, the Auto-Copier makes them for you
as fast as 200 an hour, at proportionate savings.

Your Auto-Copier takes a picture without using a
camera. So in turning out copies of complicated tax
forms, accounting forms, government records, and
deeds, it assures you of error-proof copies.

The Auto-Copier is a fully automatic, continuous
copier. In just two simple steps you can turn out
copies made from any original up to 11 by 17 inches
whether printed on one or two sides. Copies are ready
for your instant use.

Just put the Auto-Copier on any convenient desk or
table, plug it in, and you're ready to start. You can
copy any confidential material right in the privacy of
your own office in just a few seconds. Read the
description in the enclosed folder of the Auto-
Copier's easy, simple operation.
```

The Auto—Copier will actually enable you to have one
unskilled clerk do the copying work of six expert
typists. Just return the enclosed card so that your
Adeco representative can show you how to let the Auto—
Copier cut the high cost of duplicating records.

Auto—Copies of tax forms are fully acceptable and
approved by the Internal Revenue Service.

The second letter accompanies a four-page, two-color folder headlined "Make photocopies of tax returns instantly!" In the upper left corner of the letter appears the picture of an office worker operating an Auto-Copier. To the right of the illustration is a SOLID CAP headline stressing the near-instantaneous copying. The five-paragraph letter then talks speed and IRS acceptance, reduced number of typists and costs, absolute accuracy without proofreading, and summary (as a demonstration can show).

Letter No. 3, accompanied by a one-page folder, offers a week's free trial (with the postcard altered in wording accordingly). It recaps previous points (in different wording), adds convenience (of light weight, small space, and easy plug-in), and pushes for a free-trial demonstration.

The fourth letter pictures an office worker turning out copies on the Auto-Copier while looking directly at the reader and saying:

I've typed thousands
of tax returns.

And I _know_ the Adeco Plain Paper Auto—Copier can save
you money because it can reduce your tax copying work
up to 80 percent.

For two years I have typed tax forms in the offices of
C. C. Putnam, CPA, 166 Stallings Building, Atlanta
30218.

Turning out an original copy of a complicated tax form
is a job in itself, but typing 10 or 12 clear, correct
copies is next to impossible.

Now just a minute! I'm not a poor typist. I can type
60 words a minute with no errors on a 10—minute test.
That is certainly as good as the average typist. But I
still have trouble aligning forms, making corrections,
and typing perfect copies.

With the Auto—Copier I simply type the original and
run off as many copies as I need. I can now turn out
in one day reports that used to take several days.
Each detail on the original reproduces accurately and
legibly——and the only copy I have to proofread is the
form itself!

Our clients like Auto—Copied forms, and the government
accepts them without question.

> In addition to tax form copies, I use the Auto-Copier
> for letters, bank records, claims, graphs, or
> invoices. No more costly retyping or hand copying!
>
> My employer and I agree that the Auto-Copier is the
> answer to our copying needs. Your Adeco representative
> would like to show you how the Auto-Copier can solve
> your copying problems too. Check the enclosed card
> today for a demonstration in your office.

The letter carries the signature of the speaker and the title as secretary to Mr. Putnam.

The fifth mailing reestablishes the main talking points and stresses much harder the advantages of having the sales representative come in and demonstrate

> Can your typists turn out
> 200 perfect copies an hour?
> With the Plain Paper Auto-Copier they can!
>
> The Auto-Copier will enable one unskilled clerk to do
> the copying work of six expert typists.
>
> In addition, you are assured of perfect accuracy--each
> detail of the original is accurately reproduced
> without any possibility of error. And there's no need
> for tedious, time-consuming proofreading and checking
> either.
>
> In turning out copies of complicated tax forms, legal
> reports and records, and accounting data on the Auto-
> Copier, your typist can run off up to 20 clear copies
> in no more than five minutes. Since no errors appear,
> Auto-Copier eliminates erasing time and messiness.
>
> You can put your Auto-Copier on any convenient desk or
> table, since it measures 20 by 11 inches. You simply
> plug it in, and it's ready to use. No special
> installation is necessary. Anyone can run it.
>
> Copies are ready for instant use. You need no
> developing, washing, drying, or printing space because
> the Auto-Copier does everything in one simple
> operation.
>
> Your Auto-Copier representative would like to talk
> with you about your particular copying needs and show
> you how other companies are using Auto-Copier to help
> cut copying costs. Just sign and mail the enclosed
> card for a demonstration in your office.

Mailing No. 6 (the last) is the booklet sent with the first letter. Attached to the booklet is a memo in simulated handwriting:

> If you didn't get a chance to read the first copy of
> the booklet I sent you recently, here's another.

It will explain how the Plain Paper Auto—Copier can help you cut the high cost of duplicating records.

For a demonstration in your office at a time you specify, just fill in and return the enclosed reply card.

QUESTIONS

1. What are some advantages of selling by mail rather than through sales representatives? What are some disadvantages?
2. Name some products that would be better sold by direct mail rather than mass advertising (television, radio, newspaper). Why better?
3. What appeals would you use to sell:
    a. A subscription to *The Wall Street Journal?*
    b. A special showing to wealthy customers of fine paintings at an exclusive gallery?
    c. A new, expensive health spa?
    d. New clothes for overweight people (through a special order house)?
4. Describe a bicycle in terms of psychological description.
5. Describe a bicycle using physical description.
6. Just as physical description involves color, shape, design, size, materials, and (sometimes) mechanical operation, give a similar three- or four-word explanation of psychological description.
7. What are some different ways you would test a sales letter you wrote from *The Wall Street Journal* to a mailing list of recent graduates from a school of business?
8. If you were going to use a sales letter campaign to sell a word processing machine, where and/or how would you get a list?
9. Write an action ending to your letter selling a word processing machine to a list of office managers of small companies in the Midwest.
10. What are the main differences between the wear-out and the campaign series?
11. a. If your mailing costs are 40 cents per addressee, your product and shipping costs come to $13, and your selling price is $16, to what percent of your mailing list would you have to succeed in selling to break even?
    b. For that percentage of successes, what would you consider the most likely figures on (1) mailing-list purity, (2) mailing-list accuracy, and (3) pulling power?
    c. Would you use a wear-out or campaign series? Why?

CASES

(See p. xiii for some important explanations.)

8–1. Masco Corporation, 300 East County Line Road, Cumberland, Indiana 46229: *Mailing list:* Subscribers to *Sports Illustrated. Product:* Inflatable boat called Eaze-fish made of tough rubber-coated nylon. Lab tests show better weather and ozone resistance and 40 percent greater strength than neoprene-coated boats. Takes up to 3–5 HP motor. Wooden transom motor-mount supports motor that attaches with nylon ropes. Plastic oarlocks, nylon side grab ropes, plastic grommets. Charcoal gray, blue floor. Two separate chambers—each will support boat's rated weight capacity. Two varnished marine plywood, removable seats. Measures 11¼ feet, weighs 66 pounds, costs $290. Certified by Boating Industry Association. Repair kit included. Can stow in closet, transport in car's trunk, set up and launch at beach, riverbank, or dock. Unparalleled stability and load-carrying capability. Safe and seaworthy (avoid possible legal problems). One person can set up boat in 10 minutes. *Action:* Ask reader to fill out a card for more information.

8–2.   Sell the Eaze-fish (preceding case) to resort owners in Michigan, Wisconsin, Minnesota to use on other lakes than the ones they're on. Saves hauling heavy boats to other lakes in spring and bringing them back in fall. Avoids theft/damage of boats left at other lakes. Reduction of 10 percent for more than three boats.

8–3.   Try selling the Eaze-fish (preceding cases) to the best marine supply store in your area. To dealers the cost would be $180.

8–4.   Western Relocation Programs, 500 W. 12th Ave., Vancouver, BC V5Z 1M2, Canada, has a new service that helps companies with their problem of making employees happy with changes in location. Western charges the companies (like Eastern Electric) $1,000 per family for its service. And its service includes helping a family find a new home and obtain financing, line up job interviews for spouses, find baby sitters and day care centers for children, change drivers' licenses, secure reliable medical services, find churches, and so on. Assume that you are the president of Western and you are writing a form letter that sells your service to 300 of the companies listed in Fortune's 500. Along with the letter (that will be done on a word processor) you'll enclose a folder that has testimonials from some of the 10,000 people you have helped in Canada and the United States.

8–5.   With a mailing list of owners of small industrial plants in Wichita Falls, Texas, write a sales letter inviting these potential customers to authorize a salesperson to demonstrate how awnings made from Astrip Fabrics can improve their buildings' appearance and efficiency. Points to cover: custom design; wide variety of colors; solids, stripes, geometrical patterns; lowers indoor temperature 15 degrees on sunny days; helps to prevent fading of rugs and draperies; covers up architectural flaws and enhances building's good features; increases worker productivity (how?). Write the letter for the director of sales, Astrip Fabrics, Yolanda Dr., Wichita Falls, TX 76307, phone 817/555-3690. No guarantee.

8–6. *Variation:* Oral assignment related to preceding case. Assume that you are the director of sales and you get a phone inquiry from Dr. Henrietta Jackson of Texas Semiconductor Products, Inc. Her building is pink brick, 8 16-light casement windows on each of three sides, none on fourth (loading docks). One glass double entrance door in front. At her management meeting next week she wants you to make a 5–10 minute presentation. Do it.

8–7. *Variation:* Design an attractive one-sheet folder (printed black and one other color on white or colored paper)—with copy—that can be enclosed with a sales letter. (See Case 5.)

8–8. Your advertising agency has the account for Lincoln Steaks International, 4522 S. 96th St., Lincoln, NE 68522. After a two-week campaign in mid-October in *The Wall Street Journal* promoting Lincoln's 5-oz. filet mignons (box no. 484 of 8 1″ steaks for $46.25 and no. 535 special of 16 steaks for $73.75), you now are following up with a sales letter to *The Wall Street Journal* subscribers who are presidents or vice presidents of firms or are of equivalent rank in other organizations. All meat ordered is guaranteed. For any reason if customers are not satisfied, Lincoln will replace or refund money. The meat is cut from the center of choicest beef tenderloin, trimmed so no waste but so there's a little fat on each filet to keep it tender and moist during cooking and so it arrives at table juicy and full of flavor. Can deliver them in insta-frozen pack for freezer. Central idea for this mailing is the Christmas gift box. Suggest filet mignons as Christmas presents or, even better, the filet mignon gift plan with four boxes of 6 steaks, each 6 oz., 1½″ thick, that will arrive by December 25, March 30, June 30, and September 30, for a total of $174 plus $3 handling charge for all four shipments. The box of steaks arrives with a delicately seasoned butter sauce and accompanied by easy cooking and serving instructions. Assume enclosure of a business reply envelope, order blank, and a folder picturing the steaks on a serving platter and in the box with the butter sauce. The letter and folder carry the address of Lincoln plus the toll-free number 800/228-9055.

8–9. Two weeks after your sales letter to subscribers to *The Wall Street Journal* (preceding case), you send a second to the same list with the theme of saving $10 by just mentioning *The Wall Street Journal* on an introductory shipment of 6 superb 6-oz. filet mignons for only $29.95 (plus $2 shipping), or save $20 on 12 filets for $59.90 (plus $2 shipping). Steaks are packed frozen in reusable picnic container with Lincoln Steaks cookbook and catalog attached. Can charge order to any of the five major credit cards, send check, or money order. Make ordering easy. Suggest buying for Christmas.

8–10. With the theme "Try a Little Tenderness," follow up the two preceding cases. Suggestions of candlelight, wine, Lincoln steaks made from luscious corn-fed beef can appear in your copy. Experts select and prepare each filet from the choicest tenderloins. Cutting and aging is customer's assurance of the utmost in enjoyment. Suggest phoning or mailing order in. With the steaks comes a free cookbook and a 24-page catalog. Repeat price offer of previous letter.

8–11. As president of Your City Federal Savings & Loan, write a form letter to the people who have come to your establishment in the past to buy tax-saving investment instruments. You are inviting these people to a free seminar, two weeks from tonight (7:30–8:30) at the main hotel/motel in your city. The seminar will cover new and old regulations affecting tax-saving and tax-sheltered retirement programs (Keogh, S.E.P., and I.R.A. retirement plans and how they work), how to select the best program as an individual or for employees (and employer), how to eliminate cost of setting up and administering a personal or company pension plan. These new tax-saving accounts can save $600 to $4,500 or more on income taxes (for people in 30 percent-up income tax brackets). Retirement and tax experts will answer questions. Make reservations by calling (your telephone number).

8–12. *Product:* Stair-Glide (see Cases 5–6 and 5–23).

Writer: You, direct sales administrator, Inclinator Company of America, 3015 S. 163d St., New Berlin, WI 53151, Telephone 414/555-1100.

Mailing list: Homeowners who live on lakes and rivers in Michigan and Wisconsin.

Assignment: Write a cold-turkey sales letter to be generated on a word processor.

Central selling point: Ease and convenience of going from house to boat dock. Ease of going up stairs to and from the house. Many people—arthritics, paralytics, cardiac and postoperative patients, victims of emphysema, senior citizens—find it impossible to climb stairs or steep slopes. With Stair-Glide a person rides up and down in a normal sitting position, facing forward with feet firmly supported by a footrest.

Enclosure: Assume a four-page folder picturing outdoor Stair-Glides for one rider as well as for wheelchair victims who have to go up and down stairs to get in and out of houses. Assume a business reply card also.

Action: Pave the way for a sales representative. Ask reader to fill out the enclosed business reply card.

8–13. *(a)* As Mary Simpson-Warner, promotion manager, American Geographic Society, Columbus, WA 98416, sell your new book, *Nature, USA* ($11.95, 8¼″ × 12″, 350 pages of vivid, authoritative text) to members of the society. Its 320 full-color illustrations—90 percent never before published—include 25 double-spread panoramas and 22 maps; most show major roads to each area, main trails, and key points of interest. Readers can examine the book at no obligation. Assume that the mailing includes brilliant full-color photographs showing many of the country's most beautiful or breathtaking scenes displayed on an 18- by 22-inch full-color broadside, your letter, and a business-reply card. Somewhere in your letter use the quotation from John Muir: "Nature's peace will flow into you as the sunshine into the trees."

(*b*) As Kenneth Pickard, vice president marketing, Richard D. Irwin, sell your text (this book) to each of the top 5 to 10 executives in each of the *Fortune 500*—names available in directories.

(*c*) As Kenneth Pickard (*b* above) offer the text at a special reduced price, say 20 percent discount, to companies to use as a gift to prime customers or incentive rewards to employees deserving recognition (say leaders in sales).

8–14.   For the signature of the president, Superior Power & Light Company, 1200 College Ave., Elmira, NY 14901, write a form letter to go to all nonparticipating shareholders (and enclose a brochure) telling them about your Automatic Dividend Reinvestment Plan. Under the plan (and under a recent federal law), shareholders can defer federal income taxes on dividends reinvested in the common stock up to $750 per year ($1,500 on joint returns). So far the plan has more than 20,000 shareholders enrolled. Participants can automatically (without brokerage or other fees) invest dividends from Superior common, preferred and preference stock in additional shares of common stock at 97 percent of current market value. To join, stockholders fill out enrollment card and return it in provided envelope. Company then reviews enrollment application and sends a prospectus for the plan, which describes provisions in detail. After shareholder gets prospectus and notice of confirmation, shareholder can participate in the plan—beginning the next dividend-declaration date.

8–15.   *Company:* Kenya Tourist Bureau, 60 E. 56th St., New York, NY 10021.
Mailing list: Corporate executves with salaries in the $60,000-up range.
Product: Big game safaris. Two hours north of Nairobi the Mt. Kenya Safari Club continues to cater to crowned heads of state with style, luxury, and Old World furnishings. Luxury lodging takes the discomfort out of roughing it. Beds opened in evening, mosquito nets draped and tucked, morning kahawa (coffee) or chi (tea) brought to bedsides. Less than an hour's flight from Arusha, Seronera Lodge offers view of Serengeti Plain, site of annual animal migrations. Mala Mala Game Reserve on edge of Kruger National Park offers luxury housing for up to 12 guests per cottage. *Price:* Average $200 a day per person, American plan. Number of major air carriers flying into Nairobi (Kenya), Arusha (Tanzania), and Johannesburg (South Africa) has increased.

8–16.   *Company:* Craftmakers, 3510 Northeast 41 Street, Seattle, WA 98105.
Mailing list: Motor inns (Holiday Inns, Quality Courts, Ramada Inns) in United States.

Product: Bugwacker, electronic insect killer with 150-foot (1½ acre) lure radius. Bait tray, reflector for more luring power. Self-cleaning grid. Photocell turns unit on at dusk, off at daylight; can be overridden for continuous operation. Uses two 40-watt bulbs. Measures 13 × 13 × 30 inches high and weighs 22 pounds. Operates continuously for pennies a day but does not use any chemicals to harm environment. Outer grid helps protect fingers. Ideal for around swimming pool and entrance area of motor inns. Full one-year warranty. If within one year from date of purchase, Bugwacker fails due to defect in material or workmanship, Craftmaker will repair or replace it, free of charge. Replacement bulbs just $8. Regularly sells for $199.95, but have special price of $175.95 this month.

Action: Enclose brochure with order card and drive for the sale.

8–17. Craftmakers (see preceding case) has a mailing list of hardware stores, furniture stores (that sell patio furnishings), and electric stores in the western part of the United States. Write a letter to these dealers offering Bugwackers. Dealers generally get a 60 percent markup.

8–18. Staying in Style—leasing a villa for a stay abroad has advantages over a hotel suite: space, privacy, more personal atmosphere. Variety Leisure, 1515 Walnut St., Philadelphia, PA 19102, lists premier properties worldwide—more than 1,700 villas, apartments, homes. Sample listing: Villa Nirvana, in exclusive Las Brisas section of Acapulco, overlooking bay. Formal living and dining rooms decorated in Louis XVI style, with floors of marble or onyx. Sundecks, gardens, pools, various levels of terraces lead down cliffside to beach below. Write personal promotional letter (with enclosed brochure picturing villas at Acapulco) to mailing list of wealthy people like Henry Ford II, Hugh Hefner, Henry Kissinger, Richard Burton, Shirley MacLaine, and Princess Maria Beatriz de Saboya (all of whom have stayed with you).

8–19. *Company:* Intergolf, Ltd., York House, Avonmore Place, Avonmore Road, London P14 8RH, phone 01-602-3114.

List: Golfers and travelers with income of $40,000 or over.

Price: $1,800 a year.

Product: A service called Intergolf. People who travel a lot and love golf can be members of Intergolf and play at the world's best golf courses, including Doral in Miami, Wentworth in London, Fujioka in Japan, and Royal Durban in South Africa. Only restriction is that they can't play more than 10 times a year at any one club. Add any logical ideas. Assume an enclosure picturing some of the golf clubs.

Action: Make replying (signing up) easy.

8–20. Using the letterhead of the alumni association of your school with your school address and phone number, write a letter to graduates of 10–50 years ago who are in the $30,000-up income bracket asking them to buy a Perrigo

Westminster Chime Clock (15″ height, 12″ width, 6″ in depth) featuring Main Hall (or whatever landmark would be important for your school). This offer will never be repeated. Design: hand sculpted, high relief, by famous international artist, Caesar Wenig. Minted in solid brass. Cabinet: selected maple hardwood, hand rubbed, lustrous finish. Hands: antiqued brass. Dial: roman numerals, finely detailed. Brass plate: engraved with owner's personalized inscription and placed near base of clock. Operation: does not require winding because it is powered on two standard C batteries for one year. Chimes: melodically marks quarter hours or can be quiet with silencer switch. Cost and arrangement: $195. Make checks to Official College Westminster Chime Clock or charge to American Express, MasterCard, or Visa. Envelope enclosed. Picture of clock enclosed. *Emphasis:* treasured family possession for generations to come. *Possible mailing time:* send letter early September to get orders for Christmas delivery.

8–21.   Using the information in the preceding case, write a sales letter on the Perrigo clock to go to a list of manufacturing company CEOs. Offer the clock as a suitable Christmas gift for favored customers. Design (executed by Wenig) can be any logotype, picture, or design customer chooses within reason (minimum order: 10 clocks). Payment by company check must accompany order. When should this letter be mailed?

Evaluating yourself and potential employers

9

Unless you are extremely fortunate (or unambitious), sometime in your life you will write letters to get work: a summer job; an internship; a job launching a career when you graduate; a change of jobs for more money, for a better location, for work that has greater appeal to you . . . .

And even if you never write such letters, the experience of job analyzing is essential preparation for interviewing—an inevitable part of the job-seeking procedure.

When you seek work, you are selling (as discussed in the preceding chapter); and as in any sales situation, you are simply marketing a product (in this case your services). You market that product to prospects (business firms or other organizations which can use your services).

In some cases those firms make their needs known—through advertisements, word of mouth, placement agencies, or recruiting personnel. In these circumstances we call the application *invited*. In other cases firms do not make their needs known, so it's a case of *prospecting*. You'll find, then, that job-getting letters will be directly comparable to either the invited sales letter (Chapter 5) or the prospecting sales letter (Chapter 8). Both must convince someone of your ability and willingness to do something; the big difference between the two is in the approach.

If you are content to accept what life doles out to you, you will probably never write anything but invited application letters. But the *prospecting application* is the logical first choice for learning because you will write better applications of any type as a result of thorough analysis and writing of this kind. Moreover, in the job market the prospecting letter has these advantages over the invited:

—You have a greater choice of jobs and locations, including jobs not advertised.
—You don't have as much competition as for an advertised job, sometimes no competition, as when you create a job for yourself where none existed before.
—Often it is the only way for you to get the exact kind of work you want.
—You can pave the way for a better job a few years later after having gained some experience.

Of course you need to *know what kind of work you want to do* before you ask someone to let you do it. You may now know exactly what you want to do—that's fine! You may even know exactly the organization where you will seek employment and may be thoroughly familiar with its products, operations, and policies. But if you don't know for sure, the following few pages will help you arrive at those important decisions.

And even if you *think* you know, you will profit from reading—and maybe revising your present plans (and maybe avoiding a serious mistake). Life holds many changes, occupational as well as personal. In fact, the average American changes jobs every four years. One's goals at 30 often contrast sharply with those one had at 20. Many a job plum turns out to be a lemon. Columbia University even has a booming program for retooling college graduates who find, after a few years, they don't like the career for which they first prepared.

Some of the reasons people give for changing jobs are that they want

—More prestige (bigger title), opportunity to advance, independence.

—A bigger salary, new career, geographical location.

—More creative, challenging, mental/physical, or routine work.

—More/less excitement, pressure, travel, dealing with people, vacation time.

—Control over budgets, subordinates, work schedule.

—Better fringe benefits, hours, office, or other working conditions.

—To own part of a business or follow a spouse.

—Less time to get to/from work.

For you, probably the most significant reason will be your ambition to get ahead: to assume more responsibility in work that is more challenging and interesting and thus merits more respect, prestige, and pay.

The starting point in your thinking and planning, in any case, is yourself.

ANALYZING YOURSELF

If you are going to sell your services, you will do so on the basis of *what you can do* and *the kind of person you are*. Today we talk in terms of skills. What is your strongest skill, second strongest skill, third, fourth, . . . ? Your skills are marketable products and deserve careful analysis. The *education* you have, the *experience* you've had (which is not so important in many instances as college students assume it to be), and your *personal attitudes and attributes* are your qualifications which enable you to get along with and do something for someone by using the skills you've developed.

Attitudes and attributes

Early in your career, especially, attitudes and attributes may be the most important of the three. If you don't like a particular kind of work, you probably won't be successful in it. *Of all the surveys of why people lose jobs, none has ever cited less than 80 percent attributable to personal maladjustments rather than inability to do the work.*

Because your attitudes play such an important role in determining whether you will get the job you want, perhaps a good start in analyzing yourself is to consider reasons why some interviewed people are not hired. Professor Frank S. Endicott, long-time Director of Placement at Northwestern University, has given us the most frequent reasons (listed in order) from his survey of 153 companies. Because the list grows out of job interviewing, we have put it under "The interviewee" in Chapter 17.

No one but you can decide whether you will like a particular kind of job. Your like or dislike will be the result of such general considerations as whether you like to lead or to follow, whether you are an extrovert or an introvert, whether you prefer to work with products and things or with people and ideas, whether you are content to be indoors all your working hours or must get out and move around, whether you are responsible enough to schedule your own time or need regular hours under tight supervision, and whether you want to work primarily for money or for prestige. (Social, professional, or self-respect or greater security can partially compensate for less money to some people.) Certain kinds of work call for much traveling, entertaining after work hours, frequent contact with strangers, staying "dressed up" and "on call" physically and mentally; other kinds are just the opposite.

After you have had several years of work experience, you will know better under what conditions you work best and what kind of work you prefer. If you have yet to establish such preferences, the accompanying checklist on your abilities, skills, and interests may help you clarify your thinking about yourself (and at the same time give you some advice). The more checks you can *honestly* put in 1c–f, the more desirable you are as an employee—almost anywhere.

Education

For most readers of this book, education is already a matter of record or soon will be. In some college or university you are laying a foundation of courses pointing to job performance in some selected field. While graduation is a certification of meeting certain time and proficiency standards, the individual courses and projects have taught you to do something and have shown you how to reason with judgment so that you can develop on the job. Unless you intend to forfeit much of the value of your education (in which you have a considerable investment), you will want to find work which makes good use of it.

Experience

Experience, likewise, is already partially a matter of record; you've held certain jobs or you haven't. Most employers look with greater favor on the

CHECKLIST ON YOUR ABILITIES, SKILLS, AND INTERESTS

1. Read the statements below and think before checking the one(s) which most accurately fit you.

   a. I prefer a job requiring: ___ physical work; ___ brain work; ___ both.

   b. I would like to work: ___ indoors; ___ outdoors; ___ both.

   c. I like to: ___ work with things, tools, or equipment; ___ work with people; ___ work with ideas: ___ work where I can think my own thoughts; ___ work alone; ___ work as part of a team; ___ express my ideas; ___ help others; ___ see the results of my work; ___ take on new duties; ___ keep everything in good order; ___ look for other jobs that need doing when my own work is finished; ___ learn new things; ___ fill requests fast and accurately; ___ stay with a job until it is well done; ___ keep a good appearance; ___ do better than others performing the same work.

   d. I have: ___ the ability to make friends easily; ___ a good sense of humor; ___ a strong sense of responsibility; ___ a cheerful outlook.

   e. I am: ___ energetic; ___ a fast learner; ___ good with words; ___ good with figures; ___ good with my hands; ___ accurate with details; ___ easy to get along with; ___ careful to follow directions; ___ dependable and prompt; ___ neat in work habits; ___ cooperative with others; ___ not a clock-watcher; ___ willing to do extra work; ___ self-disciplined; ___ imaginative.

   f. I want to: ___ obtain more training after work hours; ___ move ahead on the job; ___ make my own opportunities; ___ do an outstanding job for my employers; ___ contribute to the support of my family.

2. Write down about five courses in school (or other learning) you liked best and/or disliked most.

3. List any nonacademic activities you particularly liked and any accomplishments that made you feel proud.

4. Jot down any kinds of tasks you have done well or really liked in the past—at home, school, military service, or elsewhere.

5. Write down, as best you remember, good things people have said about you.

person who has already demonstrated some good work habits and exhibited enough drive to work and earn than they do on the person who has held no jobs. But if you've never earned a dime, don't think your position is bleak or unique. Many employers prefer a less experienced person with vision, judgment, and a sense of responsibility to some experienced plodder or failure with none. And as you know, many employers prefer to give employees their own brand of experience in training programs. When you are young, then, you sell hard your education (learned skills), basic abilities and personality, creativity and talent, and long-range potential.

Regardless of your status, when you show that you understand and meet the requirements for the job, you have an effective replacement for experience. Furthermore, if you discard the kind of thinking that brands your education as theoretical or academic, you will realize that it is as down to earth as it can be—whether you have stressed cost accounting or a study of people and their environment.

Since you may still need to come to a specific vocational decision—because your learning may apply equally well in many different lines of work and because you probably don't know as much about job possibilities as you could (most folks don't)—you'll do well to do some research.

To get some idea, you may want to read a description of job opportunities, requirements, and rewards in the kind of work you are considering. Publications like *Occupational Briefs* and other job-outlook pamphlets published by Science Research Associates (155 N. Wacker Drive, Chicago 60606), and the publication *Occupational Outlook Handbook*, put out by the Bureau of Labor Statistics assisted by the Veterans' Administration, will help you. If you check in *Readers' Guide, Applied Science & Technology Index,* and *Business Periodicals Index,* or *Public Affairs Information Service,* you may find other leads.

You may want to consult some guidance agency for tests and counseling. Most colleges and universities have facilities for testing vocational aptitudes and interests, and they are usually free. So do U.S. Employement Service offices and Veterans' Administration offices. And in practically any major city you can find a private agency which, for a fee, will help you in this way. Reading and talking with other people—professors, friends, parents—can help you, but only you can make the choice.

Having chosen the particular kind of work you want to do, you should make an organized search for those who can use your services.

SURVEYING WORK OPPORTUNITIES

If you are dead sure that you have chosen the right kind of work to satisfy your personal interests and financial needs, that the firm of your choice will hire you, and that both of you will be happy ever after, this discussion is not for you. You have a closed mind and are not receptive to suggestions. Though you may be right, most job seekers are better off to avoid, up to the point of signing a contract, unduly limiting their choices of either kind of work or employer. Only by remaining somewhat open-minded can you reasonably take the next two steps in a wise job search—surveying work opportunities and analyzing companies of interest.

As a timesaving and eye-opening means of checking your previous self-analysis and relating the findings to appropriate work opportunities, we suggest a comparatively new but rapidly spreading job-search procedure—the information interview. It is not an interview for a job but an interview about you, your career plans, and your job-search plans. The purpose is to check your own thinking and get information and advice from a practicing professional on the kind of job to fit you, where to look for it, and how to get it.

The procedure is in several steps. First, read in Chapter 17 about interviewing. Then make an appointment to talk with a recruiter or other personnel representative of a convenient business firm—a person who knows the job market well, whether a possible employer for you or not. (To avoid seeming sneaky, you'll want to make clear that you're not asking for a job—though information interviews often do lead to job offers.)

While awaiting the appointment time, (1) phrase your career goals precisely and concisely, (2) write up the brief autobiographical sketch explained later, and (3) think of the 2–5 places you consider the most favorable places you might find a job.

When you go in for the appointment, you'll want to explain (1) your purpose (to tap the recruiter's knowledge and advice on suitable career plans and job prospects for you) and then (2) (concisely, from memory) the essence of your autobiographical sketch. That should start an interesting and informative interchange between the two of you. An experienced recruiter could hardly avoid diagnosing your personality (almost as a doctor diagnoses symptoms) and similarly prescribing the suitable kind of work (the medicine) and where to get it (the job).

Though you should not mention the idea or count on it, the recruiter may (as doctors sometimes do) hand out the medicine right there—in the form of a job offer or a favorable referral to a friend. Professor Kerr[1] found that people who have information interviews impress recruiters very favorably by their extra initiative and interest, their implied respect, and their demonstrated assertiveness. Such interviews are among the very best means of initial contact with potential employers—partly because they tap the hidden job market (the high percentage of available jobs not advertised or even recognized until a well-qualified worker shows up). Furthermore, through information interviews you can quickly develop a geometrically growing network of informed friends in strategic positions who will be keeping you in mind.

Meanwhile, of course, you will be pursuing your job search by other means.

The annual Market Data and Directory issue of *Industrial Marketing* and Standard and Poor's industry surveys analyze major industries, with comments on their current positions in the economy. (S&P also identifies outstanding firms in each field.) The *Dictionary of Occupational Titles* (U.S. Employment Service) and the *Occupational Outlook Handbook* help you to keep informed on vocational needs. (Our condensation in Chapter 14 of the *Handbook* article, with projections to 1990, is a good starting point.) The special reports on individual fields which *Fortune* and *The Wall Street Journal* run

---

[1]Daryl L. Kerr, "Effectiveness of Information Interviews: A New Approach to Job-Seeking Strategy," *Proceedings* (ABCA Southeast Regional Meeting, Atlanta, 1982), pp. 123–41.

from time to time are helpful also. And study of trade journals devoted to the field(s) in which you are interested can help you decide on a given kind of work.

Once you make that decision, you seek names of specific organizations which could use your services. You can find names of companies in *Career, The Annual Guide to Business Opportunities* (published by Career Publications, Incorporated, Cincinnati and New York), *The College Placement Annual,* Standard and Poor's manuals, Moody's manuals, and the Dow directories. *Career Employment Opportunities Directory* (Ready Reference Press, Santa Monica, CA, 1980) comes in four volumes: (1) Liberal arts and social sciences, (2) Business administration, (3) Engineering and computer science, and (4) science. Trade directories are also useful. If you are concerned with staying in a given location, the city directory—or even the classified section of the phone book—will be helpful.

If willing to spend a little time, you can assemble a good list of prospects from reading business newspapers and magazines. When significant changes occur within a company—for example, a new plant, an addition to an already existing structure, a new product launched, a new research program instituted, a new or different advertising or distribution plan—some newspaper or magazine reports that information. Widely known and readily available sources of such information are *The Wall Street Journal* and the business section of a good newspaper in the region of your interest. *U.S. News & World Report* and *Business Week* (in their blue and yellow pages) give you outstanding developments; *Marketing Communications* summarizes what is happening in marketing.

Of special value are the thousands of trade magazines. No matter what field you are interested in, you can find a magazine directed to people in that field. The monthly *Business Publications* edition of Standard Rate & Data Service (SRDS) lists trade magazines by the fields they serve. If your library does not subscribe to SRDS, advertising agencies do, and a local one will probably give you an old copy or let you look at a current issue. Most trade magazines have student subscription rates (often free) and will also usually send a copy or two at no charge, or supply copies of specific articles. From such reading you can assemble a list of companies, the nature of each business, the location, and often the names of key personnel.

Many large companies distribute literature describing employment opportunities with the company and qualifications for them; all you have to do is write for some.

If you're interested in a corporation, frequently you can get a copy of its annual report from a business library in your locality. If not, you can write the company for it. The report will also often identify key personnel, one of whom may be the person you should direct your letter to.

Certainly other people can also help you. Teachers in the field of your interest and business people doing the same thing you want to do can make many good suggestions about qualifications, working conditions, opportunities, and business firms. Before taking their time, however, you should do some investigating on your own.

ANALYZING COMPANIES

The more you can find out about an organization, the better you can decide whether you'll be happy there and the better you can write specifically about how your preparation fits its needs. And remember, that's what you have to do in a successful application—*show that you can render service which fits somebody's need.*

For that matter, even if you are fortunate enough to have interviews arranged for you, you'll want to find out all you can about the company. Look into its history, financial and organizational structure, home office and other geographical locations; relative size in the industry (number of plants and/or other operations; array of product lines and services); growth picture (sales for the past five years; potential for new markets, products, or services; competition; growth in per-share earnings and stock prices); and the corporation as an employer (ages of top managers, typical career paths in your field, nature of developmental training, average time in nonmanagement assignments, relocation policies, pay scales and—often more important—fringe benefits like medical and life insurance, stock-purchasing plans, tax shelters, and retirement benefits).

Probably the best source of such information—and the easiest for you to obtain—is the annual report. Most annual reports summarize the year's overall activities in terms of products, employment, sales, stockholders, management conditions affecting the industry and the company (including governmental activities), and a wide range of other topics. Careful reading of the last five years' annual reports will make you well informed on almost any company—and able to write or talk more impressively about working there. Or you might learn even more from reading a company's Form 10-K.

Standard and Poor's manuals and Moody's manuals summarize history, operations (including products or services, number of employees, and number of plants), and financial structure. These are usually available at stockbrokers' offices as well as libraries.

If you can't find the needed information in such sources, you may be lucky enough to find it in some magazine. *The Wall Street Journal* is a basic source (see its index); and *Fortune,* for example, has published many extensive articles about specific companies. Indexes—*Readers' Guide, Applied Science and Technology, Business Periodicals, Public Affairs Information Service*—may show you where you can find such an article.

We have mentioned trade magazines as a basic way of learning about the field you are interested in. Another source you should investigate is associations in that field. Such trade associations abound, and they are the medium for exchanging information about new developments, who's who and where, and who has job openings or is looking for a new position. If you have pretty definitely settled on the field you want to work in, you can do some invaluable spade work by joining the appropriate trade association, especially if you are still in school. Most associations welcome student members (often at reduced dues); and many run matchmaker services to get employers and prospective employees together. You can find the one you want in *National Trade and Professional Associations of the U.S. and Canada.*

If you want to get a head start on your competition, tell the officers of the association you want to get involved actively, perhaps by working on some committee. Associations need *active* members, and you are pretty sure to be welcomed with open arms. Such association work is generally not too demanding and will have the immediate benefit of giving you information useful in pursuing your major. But most important, people working with companies will get to know you. They can provide entrée to job opportunities you might otherwise not learn about—and may serve as references.

From whatever source you can find, learn as much as you can about what the company does, how it markets its products or services, the trends at work for and against it, its financial position, its employment record, what kind of employees it needs and what it requires of them—plus anything else you can.

FITTING YOUR QUALIFICATIONS TO JOB REQUIREMENTS

Actually what you are doing when you analyze yourself in terms of a job is running two columns of answers. What do they want? What do I have?

The answers to both questions lie in three categories: personal attitudes and attributes, education, and experience—but not ordinarily in that order of presentation! In fact, as explained in greater detail in the section "Compiling the Résumé," you will put yourself in a *more favorable light if you follow an order emphasizing your most favorable important qualification in the light of job requirements. But remember that desirable attitudes and personal traits and habits are basic equipment in any employee (and for writing a good application). Without them no amount of education and/or experience will enable you to advance in a job.*

One way to maximize the benefits of your personal traits, education, and experience in preparing your résumé (and preparing for an interview) is to write for yourself an autobiographical sketch, starting with your earliest years. Tell about where you grew up, your parents, your interests, hobbies, and how they changed over the years; about your hopes, goals, satisfactions, your feelings regarding remembered events and situations, and about "special" people you remember and how and why you remember them. Account for your early work experience, school experience, and (if any) military experience. Write down your reasons for your college choice and curriculum interest. Try to formulate your career and personal goals. Try to recall dates and organize your autobiographical sketch for clear continuity.

Most of this material will not, and should not, appear in your résumé. You will distill the essence of the content into a one- or two-page summary which is effectively a summary of you, now! Preparing that summary can stand you in good stead if an interviewer asks you, a week or so later, what many of them do ask—"Tell me a little about yourself" or "Tell me your life story in two minutes." You will know how to stress attitudes and interests, education, experience, and goals.

The right work attitude

A company, other organization, or individual puts you on a payroll because you give evidence of being able and willing to perform some useful *service*. That means work. The simplest, easiest, and most effective way to think, talk, and write about work is in terms of doing something for someone.

The only way you'll convince someone that you can do something is first to realize that you're going to have to be able and willing to produce; that hard work is honorable; that recognition in the form of more pay, more benefits, and flexible hours comes only after demonstrated ability; that you have to be as concerned with *giving* as you are with *getting,* and that you have to give more than you get, especially at first; that you know you can learn more than you already know, and are willing to in order to grow on the job; and that glibness does not cover incompetence or poor work habits—not for very long, at any rate.

The only way you can earn the right to stay on a payroll is to give an honest day's work and to give it ungrudgingly. That means punctuality, reliability, honesty, willingness, cheerfulness, adaptability, leadership, and cooperativeness.

Without a desirable outlook toward work and working conditions, competence can be a secondary consideration. Before you can ever demonstrate competence, you have to gain the approval of other people. You can be good, but if you don't get along well with people, your superior abilities won't be recognized. Even if recognized, they won't be rewarded.

You can be very good, but if you indicate that you think you are, you're going to be marked down as vain and pompous. One of the most frequent criticisms of college graduates is that they have overinflated ideas of their abilities and worth. Of course, if you don't respect your own abilities, no one else is likely to either. The key is to recognize you can do something because you've prepared yourself to do it, that you have the right mental attitude for doing it under normal business conditions, that you believe you can do it, and that you want to.

Confidence in yourself is essential, but so are reasonable humility and modesty. You can achieve a successful balance if you imply both in a specific interpretation of how your education, experience, *and disposition* equip you to perform job duties.

Specific adaptation of personal qualities

The work-for-you attitude in an adaptation implying confidence in yourself is basic in any application. The value of some other attitudes or personal qualities depends on the particular circumstance. Affability, for instance, is highly desirable for work in which a person deals primarily with people (saleswork, for example); it is not so significant in the makeup of a statistician or a corporation accountant. Accuracy is more to the point for them, as it is for architects and engineers. Punctuality, while desirable in all things and people, is more necessary for public accountants than for personnel workers; for them, patience is more important. While a salesperson needs to be cheerful, a sales analyst must be endowed with perseverance (although each needs a measure of both). Certainly in any position involving responsibility, the candidate for the job would want to select details from personal experience which would bear out the necessary virtues of honesty as well as accuracy.

While all virtues are desirable—and employers expect truth, honor, trustworthiness, and cheerfulness in most employees—a virtue in one circumstance may be an undesirable characteristic in another. Talkativeness, for example, is desirable for an interviewer seeking consumer reactions; the same talkativeness would be most undesirable in a credit investigator (who also does a considerable amount of interviewing). Both would need to inspire confidence.

Indeed, finding the right balance between self-confidence/aggressiveness and humility to sit well with the reader and the job (and reflecting it in style and content) is one of the hardest things about writing good applications. Most employers want neither a conceited, cocksure, overbold and uninhibited, pushy extrovert nor the opposite extreme. They do not want new employees to take over their own jobs in a few weeks, but they know that the meek do not exhibit the leadership needed in future managers either.

In analyzing any job, estimate what you think are the two or three most important personal characteristics and plan to incorporate evidence which will imply your possession of them. The reader will then likely assume the others. You can't successfully establish all the desirable ones. Besides, you have to show that your education and experience are adequate in selling yourself to a potential employer.

Enhancing your college preparation

With the desirable work-for-you attitude, you'll think in terms of job performance. If your reading has not given you a good idea of the duties you would be expected to perform on a particular job, you'll profitably spend some time talking with someone who has done the work and can tell you. You cannot hope to anticipate everything you might be called upon to do on a given job (nor would you want to talk about everything in your application); but if you anticipate some of the *major* job requirements and write about your studies in a way that shows you meet these requirements, you'll have enough material for conviction.

Although recruiting ads often stipulate a level of academic attainment, your academic status (units of credit) or a diploma is not what enables you to perform a useful service. *What you learned in earning them does*. To satisfy the arbitrary advertised requirement, you'll need to establish quickly your graduation (or whatever the requirement is). But the *primary emphasis in your presentation needs to go on those phases of your education which most directly and specifically equip you for the work under consideration*.

Similarly, in planning your application (but not in writing it), you should list, as specifically as you can, job duties you can be reasonably sure you'll have to perform and, in a parallel column, the background that gives evidence of your ability to do them.

An applicant for work in a public accounting firm knows that the job requires analyzing financial data, preparing working papers, assembling financial statements, and presenting a report with interpretive comments. The direct evidence of having learned to do these things is experience in having done them in advanced accounting courses and/or work experience. The applicant must also communicate findings intelligibly and easily to clients, and (as evidence of ability to do so) should cite training in report writing (and letter writing) as well as in speech. If the applicant assumes that pleasant relations with clients are a desirable point to stress, citing study of psychology and sociology might be useful.

A secretarial job-seeker appears more valuable by talking in terms of relieving a busy employer of much routine correspondence as a result of having studied business writing. Since the job would involve handling callers both face to face and on the telephone, the applicant should cite courses in speech and in office procedures too.

If you are interested in sales as a career, your specific work in direct selling (both oral and written), market analysis and research, advertising principles and practice, and report writing needs emphasis (along with any other specifically desirable preparation that you know about).

In all instances, applicants need to be selective, concentrating on that study which most nearly reflects the most advanced stage of preparation. For example, a person who cites evidence of training in market analysis and research will certainly have studied marketing principles. Similarly, the successful completion of an auditing course implies a background of beginning and intermediate principles of accounting. Careful selection of the most applicable courses precludes the necessity for listing prerequisite courses and thus enables you to place desirable emphasis on the most significant.

Making the most of experience

Any job you've ever held that required you to perform some task, be responsible for successful completion of a project, oversee and account for activities of other people, or handle money is an activity you can cite with pride to a prospective employer. You may not have been paid for it; that doesn't matter a lot. The college student who directs a campus unit of the United Way drive gets a workout in organization, delegation of authority, persuasion, systemization, persistence, punctuality, responsibility, honesty, and accuracy that is good work experience. It is experience which is more valuable than that of the student who operates a supermarket cash register four hours a day—and nothing else, though that indicates experience in responsibility for money and customer relations. Especially if both students are aiming at managerial work or some kind of contact work, the one who has earned no pay but has had more experience working with people and assuming authority and responsibility is more desirable.

You may not have held the job for any length of time—maybe for only a summer or over the holidays or briefly part time while in school. But didn't you learn something that increased your ability to render service?

You may have held a job that does not appear to be related to the work you hope to do. The checker at the supermarket, for example, may have punched a way through college because that was the only way to pay for an education in marketing. But didn't that person demonstrate vision, perseverance, accuracy, the ability to work under pressure, the willingness to be cheerful and polite to customers, and—if observant—get a good workout in interpreting consumer demand?

Even the person of limited experience can interpret it in relation to job requirements, giving the most significant part the emphasis of position. The most directly related phase of experience is the one most nearly preparing you to do something. For example, if the supermarket checker had also been a fraternity or sorority house treasurer (involving handling and accounting for money), an application for accounting work would want to emphasize the treasurer's duties over the checker's job; but, an application to do selling would make the checker's job more significant.

If you are fortunate enough to have a wide range of experience, your problem is simply one of picking and choosing and presenting (in an order of descending importance to the job sought). Chronology (a time sequence) rarely should be your governing choice at graduation. Later when you have experience, you might wisely elect to present it in reverse chronological order, emphasizing progress to your present state of preparation. Such order-of-time presentation suggests a well-defined goal and success in attaining it.

Whatever experience you elect to present, you want to show as directly and specifically as possible that as a result of this experience you come equipped with the skills to do the job or at least to learn how quickly. The surest way to present this information about yourself in the *most favorable light is to describe past-experience job duties related to the job you're seeking*. You will strengthen your application if you interpret the experience to show what it taught you about important principles, techniques, and attitudes applicable to the hoped-for job. Evaluating work experience is the same as evaluating education; it's matching up as far as possible the answers to "What skills do I have?" with the requirements under "What do they want?"

You will rarely, if ever, meet all job requirements; and you will always have some points that are stronger than others. Outright lack of a specific point of preparation or below-average standard are negative points to be handled in the same manner that any good writer handles them: embedded position and corollary positive language.

Determining a favorable order of presentation

After you have listed the necessary and desirable qualifications for the job and your own specific qualifications (personal qualities, education, and experience), you will then need to decide on an order of presentation that is most favorable to you.

Most people get their jobs in the first place because of competence, not personal charm or good looks. While undersirable personal attributes and attitudes can keep you from getting the job of your choice (sometimes from getting *a* job!) and may result in your losing the job even if you fool someone and get it, good personality will not ordinarily get you the job unless you *first show ability to do the work*. Competence stems from good education or worthwhile experience, or a combination of the two that produces the needed skills.

If your strongest point is thorough preparation, that is what you want to start with; if it is experience, begin with that. And within each of these categories, arrange your qualifications so that the best comes first (as any good seller does).

Without telling your reader what they are (surely your reader knows them!), be sure to give evidence that you meet all important job requirements. And write your evidence *not* in the order it occurs to you, or even in an order of what you estimate is of greatest significance in the evaluation, but in *an order that stresses your strong points*.

For this comprehensive presentation, a résumé (often called a data sheet or personal record sheet or—recently—a qualification brief) is the preferred form.

COMPILING THE RÉSUMÉ

Timing and purpose

We emphatically recommend that you prepare your résumé *before* you write your letter. Making the necessary self-analysis and job analysis helps you recognize your assets and see yourself realistically in relation to requirements and duties in the job you want. Thus it can bring you back into alignment if you have swung too far up (overconfident) or too far down (in the dumps). Perhaps more important, organizing your data usually shows you what to stress in your letter, the problems of which we will discuss more fully in the next chapter.

The purpose of a résumé is *to help sell you to a prospective employer*. So remember that, because a company's job-application form isn't trying to sell you, you should avoid filling out one (if you can graciously) and write your own *selling* résumé. (Even if you do have to fill out a company form, you can put down the necessary personal details and then write "see attached résumé" for the rest.) You will find that a well-prepared résumé can help you gain appointments for interviews and serve as a useful tool during interviews. If several people are to talk with you at the job location, send a copy for each to whoever arranges your schedule. You might even give copies to friends and relatives to hand to their associates where jobs might be available.

Caution: Though we encourage you to make your résumé a selling presentation, we caution you equally against overselling. Put your best foot forward; but don't put any false foot in. Even stretching the truth just a little can snap back and slap you down.

Don't think for a moment you can get by with lying. Many employers are now using the services of the National Credential Verification Services (Mega Maloney, chief investigator). NCVS reports have blocked all chances of many falsifying applicants for good jobs. In one situation, NCVS found (and reported) falsification of facts in 86 percent (113 out of 131) of the résumés college graduates submitted in applying for a good job. The recruiters would then not even talk to any of the 113.

Your résumé can accompany either a prospecting or an invited application letter—and often serves to start off an interview favorably. It tells your complete story—the little details as well as the big points—thus *enabling your letter to be shorter and to concentrate on showing how the high spots of your personal qualities, education, and experience equip you to do good work.*

As one authority said, a résumé gives your life's history in two minutes, indicates your organizing and language ability, and leaves your letter free to sell. It is a tabulation of your qualifications, giving pertinent, specific details concerning your education and experience, and sometimes supplying the names, addresses, and telephone numbers of references who can (and will on request) verify what you say about yourself.

Divisions and phrasings

Since the résumé must carry a wealth of detail and condense the material into a small space, it uses the space-saving devices of tabulation and noun phrases (rather than sentences and conventional paragraphs). The best form is the one that enables you to make the most favorable presentation of your qualifications, attractively displayed and concisely stated.

To facilitate rapid reading, you should use headings, differentiate type for the various classes of information, and observe uniform indentions for rows and columns of information. Parallel construction in phrasing requires special care. (If you stick to noun phrases, you'll eliminate this problem.)

Impersonal style, without opinions and comments, is usually best for this concise, basically factual presentation (but be careful not to fall into unnatural, stuffy, pompous phrasing).

Though *no one* form and set of divisions is right and all others wrong, usually the desirable tabulation form will be in three to five parts.

First, you need a selling, identifying, and informative heading. Specifically, for selling quality, conciseness, and easy finding of necessary information, we suggest something like this heading (which is simple and inexpensive with word processing equipment):

(your name)'S QUALIFICATIONS FOR (kind of) WORK WITH
(company name)

Such an informative heading stresses *work,* the *kind of work,* and your *qualifications* for doing the work. Those things—not your name—are your only chances of interesting a prospective employer. Because it is more emphatic, more service-minded, and more concise, we think such a heading is better than your name followed by your "objectives" (discussed later). An exception might be if you have more to say than you can in a heading.

Write the heading in solid capitals, centered or at the left margin, about an inch from the top (or wherever necessary for the best uncrowded placement on the page). If the line is too long, break it near evenly and double-space the parts. If you're going to use the same résumé for several applications, of course you'll have to omit the company name (and *lose some favorable effect of individualizing and specific adaptation* unless you use word processing equipment to put it in later). If you feel like using a favorable adjective—like *effective, successful* or *helpful*—before the kind of work, go ahead. It can do a lot of selling for one word.

To get the necessary information of your address and telephone number (with ZIP and area codes) in for easy finding but without undue emphasis, we suggest putting it parenthetically, single-spaced and centered, under the heading or at the left margin. If some of an extended series of letters or calls might come when you are at different places (home versus school or office, for example), you might well give both, one to the left and one to the right, labeled and with dates if known.

Second, if you can express your career plans and goals clearly and concisely, consider whether to state your objective in the résumé. Only a few years ago some applicants started using the then-new idea of putting their Job Objective and/or Career Objective as the heading of the second part (right after the title). Some personnel workers liked it for showing the applicant's serious thinking and goal orientation pointing to an upward course. Though it is not obsolete, it is already obsolescent because many people now feel that it is too confining or restrictive on both employers and applicants, and frequently makes applicants appear immature. Among our illustrations at the end of the chapter we have nevertheless shown some with various forms of the objective in case it appeals to you.

One successful applicant, who knew the receiving company well, used simply "Objective" as the heading with a statement that fit specifically but also applied broadly:

> To work in a marketing line or staff job. To handle projects and assignments concerned with the various aspects of marketing and offering cross training into other major functional areas. To gain additional business knowledge, experience, and judgment necessary for advancement.

If you use one, your statement of job or career objectives should be specific enough to show that you know where you want to go. Too broad a statement like "I want to use my talents and abilities in the best manner to advance myself and my employer" will present a damaging appearance of self-interest, immaturity, or naiveté. For optimum effectiveness (if you can do it briefly enough), you might make your statement a summary or abstract of your qualities, experience, and accomplishments in terms of their benefit to the potential employer. By implying the jobs/titles you qualify for, it could help an organization immediately to match you to a job assignment it may have.

Third, for most college students ready to go on the job market, their *education* is usually the topic deserving treatment next. Then any significant experience can follow. For applicants with extensive related experience that would weigh heavier than their education, the reverse would be true.

In presenting your *education,* give the section a heading, perhaps with a favorable adjective like *professional* or *thorough*. (You waste an opportunity to sell yourself by labeling it just "Education.") Then give a clear total picture (beyond high school, or including it if something there was particularly pertinent to the job), with emphasis on the most relevant parts. Quickly establish the main area(s) of study, your status in the program—any degree(s) received or to be received (with dates)—and the institution(s). To highlight your specific preparation for a particular job, you might then list (with descriptive titles or following explanations) several especially pertinent courses—particularly if they were electives.

Don't, however, try to snow the reader with a long list of courses required for your degree. You will only be insulting and look stupid, for most business employers know pretty well what's required for degrees they're interested in. They also understand the concept of prerequisites; so don't list any beginning or principles (prerequisite) courses along with more advanced ones in the same area. Worth more would be a list of several less directly specialized courses that are useful and/or broadening. For instance a few good courses in statistics and business communication (letters, memos, reports—the topics of this text) would be helpful in almost any salaried business job—and any prospective employer knows that.

Whether you should indicate your grade average depends somewhat on the nature of the work but more on whether your record is favorable or unfavorable. Work as a clerk or at something where physical action is more important than mental effort may not require good grades (or usually pay much money); but good grades will count for any kind of management, professional, or technical work. Contrary to much student excuse-making and/or ego-stroking, solid statistical evidence shows that grades have a high positive correlation with success in all fields except two—politics and athletics. Business employers know that and act accordingly.

So if your grades are low, forget them and hope the interviewer does. If they're favorable, say so—in a clear way. Perhaps best is the A, B, C . . . system, because everybody understands it. Point averages, on the contrary, are often confusing. What most college people call a GPA (grade-point average), others call a QPA (quality-point average). More confusing is that some schools use a five-point system, others a four, and others a three. As a consequence, reporting a QPA of 2.78 (pretty good from a three-point school) will cause a reader from a five-point GPA school to wonder (after figuring out the meaning of Q) how you graduated with that D+ average!

Fourth, if you put education as the third part (after the title and job or career objective), will come *experience* (if any). (In some very rare cases experience may combine with education. For instance, a successful applicant to a college-textbook publisher for a job as book representative (getting professors to adopt company books) wisely used a double heading, "Education and Teaching Experience." The reason was that the only relevant experience (too little to deserve separate-section listing) was two years of part-time teaching of beginning courses while getting the MA.

Usually, however, experience appears as the second (or first if the more important) part of qualifications. Again, the single word should carry justifiable qualifiers. We've seen these in successful applications: "Work Experience Requiring Accuracy" (an accounting applicant); "Experience Working with People" (a public-relations applicant, who stressed extensive leadership roles in campus activities); and "Business Experience Requiring Accuracy and Judgment" (the mature marketing applicant whose objective you read earlier).

Then follows the *work experience*—usually in reverse chronological order, to stress the most recent, most advanced, and usually most relevant. Items to cover in each job listed are beginning and ending (inclusive) dates, job title, duties performed, and name and place of employer and name of immediate superior—with emphasis on what you actually did (thus implying *skills,* the important element).

In this section particularly, remember that the less experience you have to list, the more important even seemingly irrelevant work experience is if it taught you anything (good work habits, dealing with people, . . .). Even small jobs like part-time work while in school can carry impact on the important points of leadership and honesty, for example, if you had responsibility for directing other people or handling money. Similarly, though mere membership in a campus organization amounts to little, election to and significant accomplishment in officer roles in campus activities show two desirable qualities: general approval by others and leadership.

Together the dates given for your education and experience should cover your life since high school. If not, an alert interviewer may wonder what you're hiding—and may ask, as one did, whether you spent some time in jail.

In describing your experience, you want to show potential employers progress in your accomplishments. Using reverse chronological order will put your last (and supposedly highest status) job at the beginning of the section. In setting down your experience, remember that while you can't change your record, you can (truthfully) change how you describe it.

When talking about any experience you have had, the key ideas to get across are *responsibility* and *accomplishment*. Evidence that you have been responsible also implies honesty, maturity, punctuality, and a host of other virtues. When you (alone or as a former officer in an organization) talk about achievements, you will be wise to use these ideas often as you write up your experience.

Writing in noun phrases rather than in sentences will have the desirable effects of shortening your résumé while simultaneously making it clearer, more concise, and more effective:

```
Tobias & Olendorf, Inc., 520 N. Michigan Ave.,
Chicago, IL 60611 (312/555-7575), 12/78-5/82.
Responsible for media research and internal traffic
functions; later promoted to copy contact on major
accounts. Prepared marketing plans, developed
marketing research procedures, oversaw production and
directed preparation of print, radio, and television
advertising; supervised media scheduling; conceived,
presented, and implemented improved reader/viewer
response techniques.
```

Note the heavy use of action verbs that imply creative, managerial, and customer-relations work—*prepared, developed, oversaw, directed, supervised, conceived, presented*, and *implemented*. These are the kinds of words you should strive to use (but realistically) in talking about your experience. Not only will you present yourself in a good light, but consciously using such vocabulary will keep you thinking in terms of management, professionalism, creativity, and, most important, *doing*. To help you, here is a partial list of such words:

administered	applied	assigned	commanded
advanced	approved	awarded	conceived
analyzed	arranged	began	conducted

controlled	extended	negotiated	reshaped
coordinated	governed	opened	resolved
corrected	guided	operated	restored
created	handled	ordered	revised
decided	headed	organized	scheduled
delegated	implemented	originated	served
determined	improved	oversaw	settled
designed	inaugurated	planned	shaped
developed	increased	prepared	solved
directed	initiated	presented	stabilized
discovered	installed	produced	started
employed	introduced	progressed	steered
enlarged	invented	published	straightened (out)
established	judged	ran	superintended
evaluated	launched	raised	supervised
executed	led	recruited	systematized
expanded	managed	regulated	trained

The rest of your résumé (after education and experience) requires less skill but even more discretion.

Traditonally résumés used to include a section on "Personal Details," usually with photo attached. Since federal regulations now make it illegal to consider such information in making employment decisions (unless demonstrably related to the job), employers now generally prefer not to have the facts—for fear of later accusations that the information counted (illegally) in the decision. You'll see that we, therefore, do not include a personal details section or anything about race, religion, sex, marital status, age, or physical measurements in our illustrations.

Yet you should realize that if a particular personal feature will clearly affect performance in the wanted job, you should (wisely and safely) put it in your application; and an employer can wisely and safely count it in the employment decision. For example, if you were a statuesque black male with a well-trained, deep voice, in applying for the lead in *Showboat* you should tell all those personal facts. A pretty and agile young woman applying for a place with the Dallas Cowgirls would even wisely present a photograph.

Again traditionally, the ending of a résumé used to be a list of about three *references* (people able and willing, on request, to write or talk evaluatively about you to interested employers). Though we give you one illustration of that practice, most people now omit the list and add only "References gladly furnished upon request" (with or without the heading "References").

Merely offering to provide references may be wise in a solicited application. The prospective employer may have so many applicants to evaluate that getting information from all the references (if listed on all the résumés) would be too big a job. Even in the early stages of negotiating, where you have no idea whether the prospective employer is interested, however, you should have your references ready for presentation. Unless you've presented them before, any interviewer will likely request references if getting interested in you. Your references will not likely receive inquiries, however, until your prospective employer is considerably interested—and true friends won't mind the bother of helping you.

The thinking of an employer considering a recent university graduate usually goes about like this: (1) I hope to get a good employee who will stay on the job a long time. (2) Adding the recruiting and training costs to the employee's salary and fringe benefits for 40 years (more or less), I expect to spend well over $1 million. (3) Wise decision making calls for me to get all the information I reasonably can to select a good employee worth the money. (4) That means getting information not only from the applicant but from other people (references).

Whether you will list them on your résumé or have them available for a follow-up session, here are some helpful pointers on references:

1. Select three or four people who (at least collectively) know well your personality, your education, and your job performance (if any).

2. The more accomplished or prominent they are (as shown by their titles), the better; but don't make the mistake of listing a corporation or university president who barely knows you instead of a low-level supervisor under whom you worked three years (or a professor or dean who knows you only from a one-term, once-a-week, big-lecture group you attended instead of an assistant professor who taught you the three most-advanced courses in your major).

3. Avoid any reference who is biased. That rules out (except for very unusual circumstances) relatives, lovers, associates from social or church organizations, and law enforcement officers.

Employers used to want a character reference and often got a church official or the local chief of police. Now they have pretty much dropped the idea of a special character reference because police chiefs (unless a personal friend) usually indicate only whether the applicant has a police record or not. And as one personnel manager said (and seven others on the panel agreed), "At my company we don't write ministers because those people won't tell the truth. They report only the good or only the bad they see in people—and we want the truth, the good *and* the bad." The panelists also agreed that the best references are former or present employers and teachers—who also do a better job of describing the character traits that are important. Try to get one who will write a specific, analytical letter like that on p. 113.

4. When you've settled on your best references, get their permission. That is not only the courteous thing to do (because you *are* asking a favor); but it gives you a chance to help them, the employer, and yourself by telling them the main criteria for the job (points to cover in their responses).

5. List your references with names, titles, and addresses and telephone numbers (with ZIP and area codes and with indication that you have their permission). Unless other information in the résumé (such as a reference's title and address) at least implies the relationship with you (say former employer or teacher), make the relationship clear. No listed reference should cause an interviewer to wonder (as one did, and asked, "Who is this Joe

Doakes—your father-in-law, who would take care of you to help his darling daughter?").

6. Then, to help your references do the best job for you, send each one a copy of your résumé.

Appearance

Having finished with the content, organization, and style of your résumé, you still have to decide on its general and specific appearance before you put it in final form. Until you get an interview, it is your representative. Make sure it has a quality appearance—like you.

Naturally you will consider the quality of paper and type, the margins and line balance for good layout, and the form and spacing of the section and subsection headings.

The big question is whether to use a word processing machine, to type each copy individually, or to type one and print many copies. The individual copy is the most effective for several reasons. Employers are about as proud and subject to jealousy as people courting. They all want to assume—even when knowing better—that you are particularly interested in them. Furthermore, you can put the employer's name in your heading and thus gain the favorable effects of individualizing and better adapting—things you can't do with a broadcast message.

A change of company name in the heading, and perhaps other minor changes, will adapt the résumé to any number of other applications for the same kind of job. Even when the kind of work changes, you can quickly reevaluate your qualifications and reorganize and rephrase in the light of circumstances—things you would not likely do if you had a pile of the same (generalized, or worse, misfitting) résumé copies.

As a practical matter, however, you may have to run off multiple copies— because you don't have time or money to type or have typed all the copies you need: Do not use carbons, photocopies, or mimeographed or dittoed copies. Instead, to be sure your résumé represents you fairly, get the *best* reproduction you can afford—to look as near as possible like the original neatly typed copy.

Modern word processing equipment allows you to provide each prospect with what is in effect an individually prepared résumé. You can have your résumé recorded on equipment which will then type it out repeatedly, at high speed, stopping at designated points so that an operator can add, for example, the name of the company that copy of the résumé will go to.

In addition, some of the machines allow you to justify (even up) the right-hand margin if you wish. You will find companies with word processing and composing equipment in the Yellow Pages under "Cold Type Composition."

If you elect to have your résumé printed, do *not* type in the company name or anything else. You can never satisfactorily match a typewriter (even electric with a one-time carbon ribbon) to printed material, and such an attempt is more damaging when it misfires than any poor effects from a printed résumé.

Illustrations

The following five illustrations vary considerably in content and form. Study them thoughtfully. Notice how the varied illustrations all still follow closely the suggestions for form and content.

The first illustration (Figure 9–1) gives a great deal of information in a readable, compact layout but lacks the desirable informative head. The second illustration (Figure 9–2) is perhaps the most typical for college undergraduates. By careful selection, concise phrasing, and good layout, Charlene Hutton neatly put on one page, in specifically individualized wording, just about everything employers want in a résumé. Charlene knew she was to have an interview with a Deloitte, Haskins & Sells representative; so she took the time and trouble to tailor-make her résumé and included references.

Because Dwain Lamon (Figure 9–3) had no particularly pertinent course work outside the standard major, he led with his objective and skills experience. In contrast to Lamon, Mary Span (Figure 9–4) had a great deal to report. Rose Henderson used side heads and stressed what she did on her jobs. (See Figure 9–5.)

Most résumés summarize education and work experience and say little about abilities and skills. A covering letter can and should explain about your abilitites, skills, personal attitudes and attributes, and what you can do for the prospective employer.

Though the varied forms in the five résumés illustrated here show the majority of current practices, many personnel people and university placement officers will accept a somewhat different form (with a different name, "qualification brief"). It is particularly effective for stressing the skills and abilitites learned from the considerable working experience that mature workers are likely to have but also adapts readily to a just-graduating college student with more education than experience.

Especially if you do not send a covering letter, then, you might consider sending (instead of a résumé) a qualification brief that emphasizes your qualities, accomplishments, and abilitites. We have therefore given you two illustrations. (Though the résumé checklist does not exactly fit a qualification brief, particularly in regard to form, its basic principles on service attitude and basic content are good guidelines.)

The sixth and seventh applicants we chose as illustrations were special situations—a little older, more educated, and more experienced. Both were shooting for (and got) bigger game. Both had jobs and wanted better ones. Both companies Stockman wrote were pleased with his individualized qualification brief. He received two job offers and increased his salary by 25 percent. Yes, his presentations took time, but they brought the results he wanted. By implying both administrative and secretarial skills demonstrated through progressive experience based on solid education, Joanna Knol moved from a hectic academic life with seven bosses to a quieter life in industry, one boss, and a 30 percent increase in salary. (See Figures 9–6 and 9–7.)

Figure 9–1

RITCH T. SORMUNSEN

Address: 3028 Robinhood Road, Winston-Salem, North Carolina 27104
Phone: (919) 555-8765

Career Objective

To obtain permanent work in real estate development or new business development. Special interests include resort development, new business ventures, or tax shelters.

Varied Educational Background

Wake Forest University School of Law, Winston-Salem, NC
Juris Doctor Degree, May, 1982, in corporate, tax, and general business law
Top 20% of class, Treasurer of Law School 1980-82,
Chairman of Library, Curriculum, and Executive Committees
Recipient of 1981 Outstanding Service Award, member Phi Delta Phi

University of North Carolina, Chapel Hill, NC
MBA, May, 1979, in tax, portfolio management, and new-enterprise development
Top 15% of class, Participant in managing Reynolds Securities Investment Fund,
Grader for Dr. Robert Levine, member of Alumni/Bottom
Line Committee, Nominating Committee (for class officers)

B. S. in Accounting, May, 1977 (qualified to sit for C. P. A. exam)
Top 10% of class, Dean's list (four years), Beta Gamma Sigma,
Search Committee (for new dean)

Work Experiences

January, 1982-June, 1982
Legal clerk, Koons & Smithwick.
Assisted senior partner in all
  facets of communication practice
  FCC license applications;
  license renewals; radio/TV
  consulting.

Summer, 1981
Legal/Tax intern
R. J. Reynolds Industries
Prepared foreign subsidiaries'
  tax returns.
Did research and drafted memos
  on international tax law.
Prepared Revenue Rulings and
  taxpayer protest statements.

June, 1980-February, 1981
Intern, R. J. Reynolds Industries.
Prepared cash management and foreign
  exchange exposure reports for
  International Treasurer on foreign
  operating companies.

Summer, 1979
Assistant Manager, Forsyth Country Club.
Managed all club operations
  Had complete responsibility while
  manager in Europe three weeks.

Summer, 1977
Intern, R. J. Reynolds Industries.
Implemented Watnick Investment
  Manager Analysis System:
    Prepared Investment Manager Analysis

Public Service

Class Agent in Winston-Salem for U. N. C. General Alumni Association.
  Organizer of concession operations for Winston-Salem Arts Council.

(References furnished upon request.)

Figure 9–2

CHARLENE HUTTON'S QUALIFICATIONS FOR

MANAGEMENT ACCOUNTING WORK WITH DELOITTE, HASKINS & SELLS

(P. O. Box 5423, University City, State ZIP, Phone 315/555-0876)

Thorough College Training

B. S. in Business Administration, major in accounting and minor in economics in the School of Commerce at State University. Expected graduation, June 2, 1983.

"A-" average in accounting courses and also the following courses important in all areas of business.

Report Writing	Business Statistics
Business Law	Marketing
Computer Science	Business Letters and Memos

Work Experience

(Paid 100% of college expenses)

1981 to present--Work with Mosley and Coons, CPA, as an assistant in preparing tax statements.

1979-1981--Four years with Red Mill Restaurant. Responsible for kitchen and food preparation, maintained inventory, ordered products.

1978-1979--Worked at Kroger's Supermarket as a stocker.

Activities/Honors/Awards

College: Alpha Lambda Delta, first-year honorary
          Beta Gamma Sigma, business academic honorary
          Beta Alpha Psi, accounting honorary
          Blood Drive, TB Detection Drive, Homecoming Committee

References (by permission)

Dr. Paul B. Gunter   Ms. June Bain, CPA
Professor of Accounting   Mosley and Coons
State University   Central City, State ZIP
University City, State ZIP   Phone: (315) 765-0654
Phone: (315) 555-0987

                    Mr. Harry Healey
                    Red Mill Restaurant
                    700 University Avenue
                    University City, State ZIP
                    Phone: (315) 932-4447

Figure 9–3

DWAIN P. LAMON

46 Northwood Lake, Main City, State ZIP -- (325) 555-9843

Employment Goal

Writing/Editing--Aiming for employment where a strong sense of responsibility, strong technical skills, and willingness to learn and grow are valued characteristics.

Skills, Experience, and Accomplishments

Writing/Editing--Staff writer for independent weekly newspaper, writer for college newspaper, editor of high school yearbook.

Reviews--Reviewer of concerts, movies, television (reviews for newspaper, class assignments).

Public Relations--Publicity Chairman for fraternity; active in 1984 Presidential campaign.

Copywriting--Advertising copywriter for weekly newspaper, college newspaper.

Advertising Sales--Sold advertising space for weekly newspaper, college newspaper.

Education

B.A., West State University, 1983.

Major: Journalism and English   B average

Activities and Honors

College: Communications Achievement Award, Men in Communications, Inc.; Alpha Omega Fraternity; Student Government Association.

High School: Valedictorian; Society of Outstanding American High School Students; Student Council Vice President; History Award (1979); French Award (1979); Beta Club; Youth Legislature.

Employment History

Summer, 1982: Staff writer and advertising space salesman for Decatur Herald, Decatur, Illinois.

Summer, 1981: Clerk for the U. S. Government Printing Office, Washington, D.C., under the Summer Intern Project.

Summer, 1980: Bookkeeper/Receptionist for WSOY Radio Station, Decatur, Illinois.

Summer, 1979: Traveled in France (lived with a French family for five weeks).

References

Will be furnished upon request.

Figure 9–4

MARY SPAN'S QUALIFICATIONS

FOR LAW SCHOOL ADMISSION

Educational Experience

Bachelor of Science, the University of X, College of Commerce and Business Administration, major in accounting. Expected graduation: May, 1983. Grade Point
Average: 2.70 (3.0 scale).

Graduate, Springfield High School, Springfield, State, May, 1979. Graduated first
in class with an emphasis on college preparatory courses.

Work Experience

Part-time work while attending college:
Since May 15, 1981--Student assistant in the Accounting Office, The University
of X, working from 15 to 20 hours per week.

1980-1981--Research assistant, Research Center, Office of Development, The
University of X; worked 20 hours per week.

Summer employment:
1982--Clerk, Inventory Control, Robert Zbozny Window Components (Robert Zbozny
Corporation), Houston, Texas.

1981--Appraiser's assistant, John Korinek and Associates, for the County Tax
Assessor, Springfield, State.

1980--Disc Jockey, WWBW Radio, Springfield, State.

1979--Manager, Tennis Pro Shop, Springfield Country Club, Springfield, State.

College Activities

Student Development Council, 1979-83
Publicity Director, 1980-81
Treasurer, 1979-80
Founding member, 1979

The College of Commerce and Business Administration

Academic Honors Committee, Leader, 1982-83
Honors Proposal, Co-author, 1982
Student Advising Report, Author, 1982

Accounting Society, 1982-83

Student Executive Council, 1980-82

Peer Advisor, 1980

Insurance Society, 1981-82

Figure 9–4 *(concluded)*

```
MARY SPAN'S QUALIFICATIONS, page 2

                    Student Government Association

                    Student Senate, Off-Campus Senator, 1981-82
                        Rules Committee, Leader, 1981-82
                        Parliamentarian, 1980-81
                        Off-Campus Task Force Leader, 1981

                    Off-Campus Association Advisory Board, 1979-83
                        Housing Supervisor, 1980
                        Landlord Relations Committee, Leader, 1979-80

                              College Honors

Beta Alpha Psi, accounting honorary
Beta Gamma Sigma, business academic honorary
Dean's List, 1979-82
1982 Dean's Service Award, College of Commerce Mortar Board
Selected to Who's Who Among American Colleges and Universities

                    Permanent Address and Telephone

10 Park Place                                  453/555-9876
City, State ZIP

References will be furnished upon request.
```

Figure 9–5

```
                        Qualifications of

                      ROSE J. HENDERSON

            To Work Effectively in Health Care Management

3316 Stonebrook Lane                    Phone:   (813) 555-9999
Tampa, Florida 33618

Educational History:
      Will receive B. S. degree in Business, University of X, major in
        Health Care Management, May, 1983.

      Minor emphasis in economics, finance, and accounting.

School Honors and Activities
      Dean's list (1981-83)
      Student adviser (1982-83)      President, Health Care Management
                                          Society

Employment History:
      Summers 1981 and 1982
      Baptist Medical Centers        Assisted Manager
      9876 5th Avenue South          Did reconciliation of records
      City, State ZIP                   and treatments
                                     Sat in on meetings

      From 1979-1982
      Temporary work for holi-
        days and semester breaks     Sold merchandise
      Blank Department Store         Handled cash
      Northpoint Mall                Helped change store windows
      City, State ZIP

      From 1977-1979 (Summers)
      Smally Incorporated            Demonstrated S. C. M. copy machines
      1980 30th Street               Sold machines
      City, State ZIP                Accompanied service representative


Availability: August, 1983.  Able to relocate.

References available upon request.
```

Figure 9–6

DONALD STOCKMAN'S QUALIFICATIONS FOR

REPRESENTING BEARLES RADIOGRAPHICS

2277 Greenleaf Street   (205) 555-3456
City, State ZIP

Work Accomplishments

Medical--

- Represented X-ray Division of E. I. duPont, Nashville, Tennessee, July, 1978–January, 1982.
- Assumed territory with 72% penetration and $1.4 million in sales. Ranked 4th in region in net gains the first year.
- Consistently realized $250,000 in net gains annually. Final penetration of 92% reflected over $25 million in sales.
- Served and sold to radiologists, hospital administrators, chief technologists, nuclear medicine departments throughout Southern Kentucky, Middle Tennessee, and Northern Alabama. Principal products included medical imaging, film processing, and film handling equipment.
- Designed departments for seven major hospitals to incorporate duPont equipment sold.
- Appointed as Equipment Coordinator for district in 1981.
- Authored three technical presentations for customer and field training.
- Originated an extremity exposure technique that formed the basis for Dr. Ray Drew's article on arthritic studies.
- Introduced three technical representatives and two service representatives into the field.
- Serviced Kodak and duPont equipment routinely.

Industrial--

- Represented Betz Laboratories from January, 1982, to present.
- Sold water treatment to engineers in paper, tire, ammonia, and chemical plants.
- Improved customer relations at Reichhold Chemical, General Tire, Southern Natural Gas, and Gulf States Paper by thorough investigation of existing treatment programs.
- Formulated water treatment guidelines for these plants as well as Demopolis, Union Camp, Hunt Oil, B. F. Goodrich, and Car-Ren.
- Drafted successful proposals at all listed accounts.

Military--

- Commissioned second lieutenant, 1976; discharged as first lieutenant, 1978.
- Served as platoon leader over 44 men and six E-6 sergeants. Duties included those of supply officer, pay officer, motor pool officer, dispatcher. Became Brigade Legal Officer advising all Fort Lee company commanders.

Figure 9–6 *(concluded)*

```
DONALD STOCKMAN'S QUALIFICATIONS FOR REPRESENTING
BEARLES RADIOGRAPHICS. PAGE 2

University--
              · Worked under Dr. Wendell Hewitt as graduate assistant.
              · Organized class presentations, lectured, graded class work.

Additional--
              · Worked four summers without absenteeism on shift work as summer
                laborer at Gulf States Paper Corporation, City.
              · Worked part time after high school as a sales representative in
                retail store for two years.
              · Mastered Dale Carnegie course while working for duPont.

                        Professional College Education

Master of Business Administration, 1977, University of X with 2.5 average (3.0
scale).
     Some courses that instilled practical sales skills: business communication,
     financial analysis, statistics, accounting, economics, management, marketing,
     report writing.

B. S. Chemistry/Mathematics, 1975, University of X.

Electronics (by correspondence), completed May, 1982, Bell & Howell School,
Chicago, Illinois.  The course objective: learn modern electronic principles for
field repair.

                               References

Will be furnished upon request.
```

Figure 9–7

JOANNA J. KNOL
606 Cook Street, Barrington, Illinois 60643   (321) 555-8989

Objective: Administrative Assistant to an executive looking for a dependable
person to take over detail, improve procedures, and increase office
productivity.

Directed   Worked 1975-1983 as chief secretary, College of Communication Arts,
Seven   Michigan State University. Coordinated office work in dean's and
Secretaries: six department heads' offices.

Graduated   B. S., Journalism, University of Illinois, 1975. Honors student.
with   President of Theta Sigma Phi, on staff of Daily Illini, editor of
Honors: sorority newspaper, The Iota Lyre.

Assisted   As an undergraduate (1971-75) worked two years in Journalism
College   Department. Administered and graded examinations, kept records,
Professor: handled correspondence, and did office work. Professor's comment:
            ". . . the hardest worker I've ever had and the best . . . . Your
            ability to take over gave me more time to do research and writing."

Worked in   Did layouts and wrote copy for Kilgore Advertising Agency, Chicago,
Advertising: summer, 1974.

            Helped in advertising department, Marshall Field, summers 1973 and
            1972. Helped with composition and production of sales copy for ads
            and for Christmas catalog. Designed envelope stuffer promoting
            special fashion show for the "back-to-college" market.

Made extra Managed church nursery for Saint Mark's Episcopal Church every
Money while Sunday, 1971. Entertained, fed, and cleaned 10-25 children ages 2
in High   months to 5 years.
School:
            Took care of many children on regular baby-sitting assignments.
            Cooked, washed dishes, directed homework, bathed, and fed varied
            children from varied families 1969-1971.

            Worked as waitress after school and Saturdays, 1970, at Barrington
            Motel.

RÉSUMÉ CHECKLIST

1. Give your résumé an informative heading worded for the appropriate degree of selling.
    a. Identify your name and (preferably) the type of work you desire and the company you are addressing.
    b. Be sure you apply for work, not a job title.
2. If you use a job objective, state it clearly and concisely.
    a. Service-mindedness appeals more than selfish interests.
    b. Excess specificness may narrow your chances.
3. For appropriate emphasis, ease of reading, and space saving:
    a. Give your address(es)—and phone(s) if likely to be used—in minimum space where easy to find but not emphasized.
    b. Balance material across the page in tabulated form.
    c. Use difference in type and placement to affect emphasis and show awareness of organization principles.
    d. Centered heads carry emphasis and help balance the page.
    e. Capitalize the main words in centered heads and underline the heads unless in solid caps.
    f. If you have to carry over an item, indent the second line.
    g. Remember to identify and number pages after the first.
4. Lead with whatever best prepared you for the particular job, but account for the chronology of your life since high school. (Gaps of more than three months may arouse suspicion.) When older and extensively experienced, such complete coverage is less necessary.
5. Education details should point up specific preparation.
    a. Show the status of your education: degree, field, school, date.
    b. Highlight courses which distinctively qualify you for the job. Listing everything takes away emphasis from the significant and suggests inability to discriminate.
    c. In listing courses, give them titles or descriptions which show their real content or briefly give specific details of what you did.
    d. Give grade averages in an understandable form (letters, quartiles, or percentages; GPA systems vary too much).
    e. Avoid belittling expressions like "theoretical education."
6. Experience: for jobs listed,
    a. Give job title, duties, firm or organization name, full address, specific dates, *responsibilities*, and immediate superior's name.
    b. If experience is part time, identify it as such.
    c. Consider reverse chronology or other arrangement to emphasize the most relevant and important.
    d. Use noun phrases and employ action verbs that imply duties and responsibilities.
7. List or offer to supply references. When you list references (to conclude your résumé or supply later on request):
    a. Give the names, titles, full addresses, and telephone numbers of references for all important jobs and fields of study listed.
    b. Unless obvious, make clear why you list each reference.

8. Remember these points about style:
   a. A résumé is ordinarily a tabulation; avoid paragraphs and complete sentences.
   b. Noun phrases are the best choice of grammatical pattern.
   c. Items in any list should be in parallel form (Para. in Appendix F).
   d. Keep opinions out of résumés; just give the specific facts. Use impersonal presentation, avoiding first- and second-person pronouns.

QUESTIONS AND EXERCISES

1. Is your intended career pointed toward one of the predicted-as-booming areas to 1990?
2. What significant points could you add to the checklist on abilities, skills, and interests? What points would you delete?
3. What kind of information do you need to gather about a company before applying for work there?
4. Give at least five reasons why you might change jobs or not change despite higher pay.
5. List at least three companies or other organizations you've thought you might like to work for and score them on the bases we suggest in "Analyzing Companies."
6. Which of the seven illustrations at the end of the chapter appeals to you most for your possible future use? Why? Be specific.
7. If a person has never worked on a regular job for pay, what might that person put in place of work experience on the résumé?
8. What are some uses of résumés besides as supplements to application letters?
9. What techniques can you use to make résumés easy to read?
10. What three people (specific name and/or position and relation to you) would be good references for you when you finish your intended schooling and why would you select them?
11. How should a student who graduates with a C average handle that fact in the application letter and/or résumé?
12. Before you write your application letter and résumé, but after reading Chapter 9, write a memo to your instructor answering the following questions:
    a. What are your career plans?
    b. What training, attributes, or attitudes does one need to obtain a job and succeed in your chosen field?
    c. What will you be required to do on the job? (Give a job description.)
    d. What is the demand for people in your field this year? What is the

outlook for availability of jobs in your field five years from now? Ten years from now?

e. What company or organization would you like to work for? Why?

f. What do you need to know about this company before applying for a job? Where would you get this information?

g. Give the pertinent information about the company you have chosen.

Since you will be using library materials, refer to Chapter 14 for ways to tell how you got your information.

13. Suppose your career has so far consisted of three jobs progressing regularly in responsibilities, prestige, and salary; but, because of a severe recession, your fourth and most recent was two years as a clerk doing general office work at your employer's lowest salary level. How would you describe your work experience on your résumé?

14. To help you find out about the kind of work you want to do and to find out what a particular company does, ask for an information interview and visit a company in your hometown area or area of your school. Often this type of interview leads to summer employment, an internship, or promise of a job upon graduation. Before you ask for the information interview, read about the company and have good, appropriate, and meaningful questions about the work and the company. (Keep in mind that this is not an employment interview.)

Letters about employment

10

WRITING THE PROSPECTING APPLICATION

In selling as in fishing, you almost have to have a feeling of success consciousness and optimism—the ability to think positively. You can hardly force yourself to really try to catch fish or make sales unless you feel that you have an attractive bait or an appealing product or service. Other people (and seemingly even fish) quickly sense how you feel about yourself and respond accordingly. And since application letters are sales letters in every way—sales letters selling your services—you have to have self-confidence and positive thinking.

Sometimes getting a job may be harder than doing the job you get. Even organizations which advertise for employees sometimes neglect common courtesy and don't always give a warm welcome to applicants. In applying, you may have trouble getting through a wall of protective secretaries to make an appointment. Promised "will calls" or your unanswered letters may keep you dangling for days or even weeks—or, as one job seeker put it, may "make an applicant feel like a supplicant."

Though such treatment is not usual, if it happens to you it will test your patience—and your spirit of self-confidence—unless you're prepared.

That was one of the reasons we urged you in the preceding chapter to prepare a good résumé *before* writing your application letter. Especially if you're down because you are earning less than A's in courses or encountering questions about whether you'll graduate—or your present job is going sour (or worse, you've been fired)—*realistically assessing your strong points through preparing a good résumé can be a big step toward retaining and increasing your self-confidence and optimism*. With a well-prepared résumé you will have done a good job of lining up your qualifications, of realizing what you can do, and of deciding on those qualifications that most nearly equip you for efficient performance. You are then in much better shape to write an application letter—a sales letter selling your services.

At times you may want to send a prospecting letter without a résumé. That's your decision. We don't think it's the better decision; most personnel people prefer to receive one. Even if you elect not to use one, you'll write a better letter for having prepared a résumé. And having prepared it, you're throwing good money away if you don't let it work for you.

The purpose of this chapter is to help you write your application letter by giving suggestions and analyzed illustrations. You'll be foolish, however, if you slavishly follow the points and ape the style of our or other people's illustrations. The good model application letter doesn't exist—and never will for applicants of average intelligence and above. So be smart and write your own. *A good application letter must be an accurate reflection of the writer's personality as well as aptitudes and skills.*

If you're smart about sending your prospecting application to a company, you'll also do some research to find out the name of the person it should go to. Except in applying for a very low-level job, sending a prospecting application to a personnel department or to a title is generally useless. If you want to work in the purchasing department, address your letter personally to the vice president of purchasing or director of purchasing. You can get that person's name from trade directories (see Chapter 9) or by telephoning the company and asking for the name.

Securing favorable attention

As in sales letters, the infallible way to secure interest in your application letter is to stress your central selling point in writing about serving the reader. Your central selling point may be an ability based on education, experience, or personal qualities—or a combination of them.

A 19-year-old secretary with two years of college summarized important qualifications for a job in an exporting firm in the following well-chosen lead:

```
As a secretary in your export division I could
transcribe your dictation accurately in attractive
letters and memos at 50 words per minute—whether it
is in English or Spanish.
```

Another student just graduating from college got favorable attention with this:

```
Because I have had an unusual five-year educational
opportunity combining the study of engineering and
management, I feel sure of my ability to do efficient
work in your industrial engineering department and to
steadily increase in usefulness.
```

```
I could conduct a time-and-motion study with a
technical knowledge of the machines concerned or work
on the problems of piece wage rates without losing
sight of the highly explosive personnel situation
involved.
```

To state the central point, a more mature and better educated writer with more experience began as follows to a textbook publishing company:

> With my college background of undergraduate and
> graduate work, my teaching experience, and a
> temperament which helps me to adapt easily to college
> people and circumstances, I believe I could do a good
> job as a field representative for you.

Those openings have nothing tricky about them. They just talk work—and the education, experience, and/or personal qualities that point to doing a good job.

You may be able to capitalize on a trick in some situations—provided it shows knowledge of qualifications and job requirements. The young advertising candidate who mailed a coconut shell to agencies with the lead "They say advertising is a hard nut to crack" got results from the message enclosed in the shell. The statistical worker who drew a line graph showing the Federal Reserve Board Index of Industrial Production and in the opening lines commented on the significance of its recent movements certainly had a head start on other candidates for the job.

If you can think of a trick or gimmick which is *pertinent, in good taste,* and *not sterotyped* (such as the balance sheet from an accounting candidate), it may help you. But it is by no means a must and can do you more harm than good unless you handle it carefully and thoughtfully. Generally personnel people don't like gimmicks.

You *do* need to concentrate on rapidly and naturally establishing your qualifications with the attitude that you want to put them to work for the reader in some specific job. Having held out such a promise, you need to back it up.

Supplying evidence of performance ability

Your evidence in your application letter is simply a job of *interpreting* your qualifications—the highlights of your opening and résumé. For persuasiveness, you phrase it in terms of skills that point to "doing something for you."

The secretarial applicant to the exporting firm continued in the following vein:

> In secretarial courses during my study at Temple
> College, I've consistently demonstrated my ability to
> handle material at that speed. And as a matter of
> practice in my course in conversational Spanish I take
> down what my teacher and my classmates say. I have no
> difficulty transcribing these notes later.
>
> I learned a good deal about your markets and your
> clientele while doing research for a report I
> submitted this semester in marketing, "Some Recent
> Developments in International Markets." In the process
> I became familiar with such publications as The
> American Importer, Exporting, and The Foreign Commerce
> Yearbook.

The A I made in Business Communication suggests my tact, language facility, and persuasion. On the telephone, in person, or in letters and memos, therefore, I could communicate pleasantly and effectively with your employees and customers.

Various courses (listed on the enclosed résumé) have given me skill in operating office machines of different kinds and in filing and record keeping. Putting these skills to use as a part-time assistant secretary in the Marketing Department here at school the past two years has enhanced those skills and given me the confidence to serve you well.

An applicant for an apprenticeship in an architectural firm wrote a short letter, but it's packed with statements of accomplishments as evidence of desirable skills.

At this point in my career, I have two main qualifications to offer you: my job experience and my bachelor's degree in architecture from the University of Nebraska.

My practical experience covers six years of part-time work with the same architectural firm, Mosely Architects. I started with Mr. Carl Mosely when I was a senior in high school, handling the firm's printing in the afternoons. My duties as well as responsibilities grew in proportion with my experience and education, to include many aspects of drafting, together with design.

Projects I worked on ranged from $40,000 houses to $5,000,000 office buildings, with banks, churches, and small condominiums completing the spectrum. While working on these jobs I had the opportunity to associate directly with mechanical, electrical, and structural engineers, in addition to the six members of the firm itself.

Of course I could not have developed and advanced that way without furthering my education. I graduated in the upper 5 percent of my class from the five-year program in architecture at Nebraska. While in school I competed in four major design competitions and received an award for each entry—one first prize, one second, and two thirds. Please refer to the enclosed résumé for additional information on my education and extracurricular activities.

I would like to show you my portfolio of school and job work and would be grateful if we could set up a time at your convenience. Please call me at 555-6360

so that we can talk about my working as an efficient
apprentice for your firm.

The frequent problem of *overcoming deficiencies* is a difficult function of
the letter, not the résumé. In almost any application situation you'll have one
or more. If you feel that a deficiency is so important as to merit identification
and possibly discussion, embed it in your letter and endow it with as much
positiveness as possible.

The applicant wanting to be a publisher's representative faced a two-strike
situation and knew it. The following fifth paragraph of the letter met the issue
head on and capitalized on it:

> The fact that I have studied busness at Oklahoma
> rather than liberal arts at an Ivy League school may
> actually make me a better representative, Mr. Dayton—
> especially if I'm assigned to the Southwest, where I
> already know the territory. I could serve happily as
> your representative in any district, however; I've
> traveled over most of the U.S. (and in Europe and the
> Far East while in the Navy) and can adapt readily to
> the fine people and country one finds everywhere.

Probably the finest example we've ever seen of turning an apparent handicap into a virtue is that of a young applicant who at first didn't know where
to turn when confronted with the necessity of getting a job. Thoughtful analysis of accomplishments in college and how to use them in business led to the
following letter (to a large Chicago mail-order firm). The third paragraph is
the epitome of positive thinking.

> Isn't one of the significant qualifications of a
> correspondent in your company the ability to interpret
> a letter situation in terms of the reader?
>
> Because I believe that I could express an
> understanding of a situation clearly and imaginatively
> to your customers (a degree in English from the
> University of Iowa, an A in Business Communication,
> and the editorship of my sorority paper suggest that I
> can), will you allow me to become a trial employee in
> your correspondence division?
>
> Learning your particular business policies and
> procedures in writing letters would come quickly, I
> believe; I am used to following assignments exactly,
> and I have no previous working experience to unlearn.
>
> I have a good background in writing. And the varied
> extracurricular activities listed on the enclosed
> résumé are my best evidence for telling you that I've
> successfully passed a four-year test of getting along
> with people.

```
Will you call me at 876-2401 and name a time when I
may come in and talk with you?
```

It worked! And the same kind of positive approach to any handicap you may have—physical or otherwise—is probably your best way to treat it.

Talking the special language can help convince your reader of your performance ability. In all the examples in this analysis, you've probably noticed that each incorporated specific and special references to conditions or products or activities peculiar to the given job. Such references certainly further the impression that you are aware of job requirements and conditions.

The secretarial applicant for work in the export field referred to transcription in Spanish, recent developments in international markets, and communicating effectively with employees and customers. The would-be publisher's representative (in parts not quoted) referred to books, teachers, college circumstances, and textbook adoptions (the end and aim of that particular job). The industrial management applicant referred easily and sensibly to time studies, piece wage rates, explosive personnel situations, and (later) to tractors and cotton pickers, two products of the company. The would-be architect apprentice referred to drafting, design, and various kinds of buildings.

From your research you can readily establish such references. If significant enough information, they may be good choices of talking points for your beginning, especially if they show knowledge of the company and its working conditions and requirements, along with a desire to serve:

```
Lions International's growing membership no doubt
makes planning the annual conventions an increasingly
complex job. My major in business administration and
my minor in hotel/restaurant management lead me to
believe that as a member of your convention planning
department I could quickly be effective in helping
choose hotels and other facilities at convention
sites.

              --

The regular Saturday night reports your retail dealers
submit show consumer trends which I want to help you
translate into continued Whirlpool leadership--as an
analyst in your sales department.
```

The applicant who wrote the following for an accounting job showed obvious research on and adaptation to Texaco:

```
I believe that I can perform the duties expected of
accountants in your expanding financial department.
The combination of a challenging undergraduate program
at the University of X and much work experience will
enable me to work effectively and be productive
immediately.

Upon completion of your required orientation program,
I assure you that I could work in a way which would
```

benefit Texaco and contribute towards achieving the
company's goals. My advanced studies in cost
accounting will equip me to analyze and communicate
financial information which may benefit top
management.

Your increasing involvement in overseas projects is an
area in which I am deeply interested. Through my
studies in international finance, I have learned many
things which may be incorporated into the plans of
your company.

My work experience has enabled me to apply my
education to actual working conditions while gaining
insight into the total field of accounting. As a
summer intern for Deloitte, Haskins & Sells, I was
able to participate in audits and deal with numerous
problems in costing procedures. I learned the value of
hard work and developed an acute desire to excel.

As a conscientious person, I always strive to do my
best for my employer. I am eager to learn, easy to
train, and ambitious to be a productive part of your
organization. I believe that I have a great deal to
offer Texaco, and I know that Texaco has a lot to
offer me.

At a time convenient for you, I would be most grateful
for an opportunity to meet and discuss with you ways I
could possibly best serve Texaco.

Just as each of these candidates continued to talk the terminology peculiar
to the job, you want to show such knowledge of company activities, working
conditions, and job requirements. But if you state it in independent clauses
(obvious or flat facts which the reader already knows), you'll sound wooden
and dull. Suppose, for example, that the accounting applicant had told Texaco
the following points flatly, as stated here: Your financial department is expanding. I have taken advanced courses in cost accounting. You are increasingly involved in overseas projects. I have studied international finance. I
have also been a summer intern with Deloitte, Haskins & Sells.

The desirability of *emphasizing qualifications instead of analysis* will be
clearer to you through comparing the following original letter (its flat statements underlined) with the revision.

Original	*Revised*
It takes a secretary who is versatile, accurate, reliable and dependable for a firm like the Brown Insurance Company. I re- alize the importance of your having such a secre-	My year's work as secre- tary, four years' thor- ough college training in commercial studies, and lifetime residence in Tuscumbia should enable me to serve you well as a

tary, and I believe I have the necessary qualifications.

Having graduated from the University of Alabama with commercial studies as my major, I am familiar with such machines as the adding machine, mimeograph, and calculator. Since my graduation I have been employed as a secretary with the Reynolds Metal Company. <u>This has given me an opportunity to combine my knowledge with experience</u>. <u>Insurance takes a lot of time and patience</u>. <u>A large amount of bookkeeping is required because every penny has to be accounted for</u>. My one year of accounting at the University will enable me to keep your books neatly and correctly; and if it is necessary for me to work overtime, I am in good physical health to do so.

<u>The Brown Insurance Company has many customers in different parts of the country</u>; <u>so a large amount of business letters and transactions are carried on</u>. As your secretary, I could take dictation at 100 words a minute and transcribe your letters accurately and neatly at 45 words a minute.

Even though accuracy and speed are important, <u>per-</u>

secretary and further the friendly relations between you and your clients.

Whether you want to send a memo to a sales representative, a note to a client, or a letter to the home office, I could have it on your desk for signing within a short time. While earning my degree at Alabama, I developed a dictation rate of 100 words per minute and a transciption rate of 45, which I demonstrated daily during my year's work as secretary with the Reynolds Metal Company.

To help with the varied kinds of record keeping in a large insurance agency, I can use the knowledge and skills from a year's course in accounting and my study of filing systems, office practices, and office machines—all applied during my year of work. You can trust me to compute premiums accurately, send notices on schedule, and devise and turn out special forms when necessary.

I realize that in an insurance agency everyone from the janitor to the bookkeeper affects the feeling of the public and that all must exercise friendliness and tact in any contact with a client. I anticipate the

Original (concluded)	*Revised (concluded)*
sonality is an important characteristic too. Because of the many kinds of people who are connected with this type of business, it is important to have a secretary who not only can file, take dictation, and type, but who can be a receptionist as well. Since I have lived in Tuscumbia all my life, I will know most of your clients as individuals and can serve them in a friendly manner.	unexpected, and I meet it calmly; so I am prepared to handle a number of duties and to adjust to the demands of a busy, varied work schedule (including overtime work when it's necessary). I would expect to maintain cordial relations with all your clients and prospects quite naturally and easily because most of them are the neighbors and friends I've lived around all my life.
I have enclosed a data sheet for your convenience.	Ms. Bills and the other references I've listed on the enclosed résumé will be glad to confirm my statements that I can work efficiently and cheerfully for you. After you've heard from them, please call me at 374–4726 and name a time that I may come in and talk with you.
Will you please call me at 374–4726 and tell me when I can talk to you?	

The original, you notice, is almost painful in its flat, obvious statements. It also uses so much space stating requirements of the job that it fails to establish qualities of the applicant. Note how the revision eliminates the flatness and preachiness through subordination, implication, or incidental reference.

Although the revision is a little longer, it accomplishes a good deal more: It establishes qualifications in a good lead; it talks the special language of the reader; it establishes more qualifications. It also has a much better work-for-you interpretation. But the major improvement of the revision over the original is that it eliminates the preachy, flat statements (particularly at the beginnings of paragraphs) that made a smart applicant sound dull.

Asking for appropriate action

Whatever action you want your reader to take, identify it as specifically as possible and ask confidently for it. Ordinarily it is to invite you in for an interview. As a self-respecting human being who has something to offer, you do not need to beg or grovel; but you do need to remember—and to show you realize—that the reader is under no obligation to see you, that giving you time is doing you a favor, that the time and place of the interview are to be at the reader's convenience, and that you should be grateful for the interview.

The full-fledged action ending of the sales letter, however, requires slight modification for the application letter. You cannot with good grace exert as much pressure. For this reason most employment counselors and employers do not advocate using any reply device (an employer is happy to pay the postage to reply to a potentially good employee, and writing and mailing a letter are routine actions). But your application action ending should still *suggest a specific action*, try to *minimize the burdensome aspects* of that action through careful phrasing, *establish gratitude*, and *supply a stimulus* to action with a reminder of the contribution you can make to the firm.

You've already seen several action endings in this chapter. But to drive home the point, let's look at some others.

A Red Cross applicant definitely planned a trip to Washington for job-hunting purposes; so the letter logically and naturally ended with:

> When I'm in Washington during the first two weeks in August, I should be grateful for the opportunity to come to your office and discuss further how I may serve in filling your present need for Red Cross club directors. Will you name a convenient time?

The industrial-management applicant ended in this simple fashion:

> Please suggest a time when you can conveniently allow me to discuss my qualifications for work in your industrial engineering department.

And the secretarial applicant confidently asked the exporter-reader:

> Won't you please call me at 615-5946 and tell me a time when I may come to your office and show you how well my preparation enables me to serve your firm?

The publisher's-representative applicant was in a slightly atypical situation. Lack of both the money and the time right then prevented asking directly for an interview in New York. Here is the solution:

> After you've had a chance to verify some of the things I've said about myself in this letter and in the résumé, will you write me frankly about the possibilities of my working for you?

> Possibly I could talk with one of your regional representatives in this area as a preliminary step. Or I can plan to go to New York some time this summer to talk with you further about my successfully representing your firm.

As it turned out, the applicant flew to New York at the expense of companies on two occasions within two weeks after sending the letters, but that was the result of further correspondence—and it's certainly not anything to ask for or count on!

One other item you should consider is whether to include an *availability date* in your prospecting application. If you are presently working for someone, you would want to give proper notice, and you can tell a prospective employer this in your résumé: "Available to come to work for you one month after giving my present employer notice." The other common reason for not being immediately available is pending graduation: "Available to come to work for you immediately after graduation on June 10." Otherwise we do not recommend you mention availability. To say "Available immediately" implies that you are presently out of work, something you would not want to mention.

If you mention availability in your résumé, you should also mention it in your letter as a point in good communication (clearing up all questions between you and the reader). Even if you feel that a stated graduation time implies an availability date, by skillful and brief wording you can reemphasize your knowledge of the company and add mild urgency to your letter with it. For example, suppose the publisher's-representative applicant had changed only the last sentence to:

```
Or I can plan to go to New York this summer--in time
to get in on this year's training program--to talk
with you further about my successfully representing
your firm.
```

* * * *

Such letters as suggested in the preceding pages won't work miracles. They won't make a poor applicant a good one. They won't ordinarily secure a job; usually they can only open the door for an interview and further negotiations, but that is their purpose. To make yours do all it can, you may want to review the checklist of suggestions on pp. 326–27.

WRITING THE INVITED APPLICATION

Often a firm makes its personnel needs known by running an ad, by listing with an agency (commercial, where you'll pay a fee, or governmental like the U.S. Employment Service offices and state-government equivalents), or simply by word of mouth. As you probably know, most large companies also list their needs for college-graduate personnel with college placement bureaus and have recruiting personnel (talent scouts) who regularly visit campuses.

Situations where the prospective employer actually goes out searching for new employees give you one drawback (you'll have more competition because more people will know about the job) and two advantages in writing a letter: (1) you don't need to generate interest at the beginning (you already have it!);

PROSPECTING APPLICATION CHECKLIST

1. The prospecting application must generate interest from the start.
    a. Establish early your central selling point of education or experience or both, in terms of doing something for the reader; later, develop them in the order mentioned. (You may also cite your research on the company or the field, or tell a human-interest story; but they postpone the real message.)
    b. Avoid the preaching or didactic, flat statement.
    c. Avoid implying that your up-to-date techniques are better, or telling the reader how to run the business.
    d. Make clear early that you are seeking specialized work, not just any job.
    e. Be realistic; talk work and doing, not "forming an association with" or *position, opening, vacancy,* or *opportunity* (all of which are self- rather than service-centered).
    f. You need verve and vigor, not sterotypes like "Please consider my application . . . ," "I should like to apply for . . . ."
    g. Don't let your biography drown out what you can do now.
    h. Don't give the reader an opportunity to shut you off with a negative response.
    i. Mere graduation (rather than the learning back of it) is a poor lead anywhere, especially at the beginning.
    j. Eliminate selfish-sounding statements or overtones of them.
2. Interpretation and tone are important from the start.
    a. Maintain a consistent, acceptable tone, neither apologizing for what you don't have nor bragging about what you do.
    b. For conviction, back up your assertions of ability with specific points of education or experience as evidence.
    c. Generalizing and editorializing are out of place: "invaluable," "more than qualified," even "excellent."
    d. Avoid needlessly deprecating your good qualifications.
    e. Project your education or experience right to the job.
    f. Use enough "I's" for naturalness, but avoid monotony.
    g. Show the research and thought which have gone into the project. Address the letter to the appropriate individual if at all possible; talk about company operations and trends in the industry; even a deft, tactful reference to a competitor can be a point in your favor.
3. Your education and experience are your conviction elements.
    a. Talk about your experience, schooling, or personal characteristics in terms of accomplishing something. For example, you may register for, take, attend, study, receive credit for, pass, learn, or master a course.
    b. The emphasis should go on a phase of work connected with the job you're applying for.
    c. Refer to education as work preparation (in lowercase letters) rather than exact course titles (in capitals and lowercase).
    d. You need highlights rather than details in the letter.
    e. But even highlights need to be specific for conviction.

PROSPECTING APPLICATION CHECKLIST
(concluded)

     f.   Your résumé supplies thorough, detailed coverage. Refer to it incidentally, in a sentence establishing some other significant idea, just before asking the reader to take action.

     g.   A one-page letter may be desirable, but telling all of your story in the most effective way for you is more important.

4.   Reflect your personality in both content and style.

     a.   Refer to the more significant personal characteristics affecting job performance, preferably with evidence that you have them.

     b.   Incorporate phrases which reveal your attitude toward work and your understanding of working conditions.

5.   Ask for appropriate action in the close.

     a.   Name the action you want; make it specific and plausible.

     b.   Don't beg and don't command; just ask. And avoid the aloof, condescending implications of "You may call me at . . . ." Usually you ask for an appointment to talk about the job.

     c.   Eliminate references to application, interview, position. Use action references to work and the steps in job getting.

     d.   Clearly imply or state that you will be grateful. But "Thank you for . . ." in present tense sounds presumptuous.

     e.   Show success consciousness without presumptuousness.

     f.   A little sales whip-back at the end (perhaps tied to an availability date, if appropriate) will help strengthen the impression of what you can contribute.

FOR WRITING INVITED APPLICATIONS

6.   When writing an application in response to an ad or at the suggestion of an agency or friend:

     a.   Don't send *just* a résumé, even when asked.

     b.   Primary emphasis should be on putting your preparation to work for the reader. But since your reference to the source is an automatic way of securing attention, you should identify it early and *emphasize it if it carries an implied recommendation.*

     c.   Avoid stating what the reader would infer ("I read your ad").

     d.   Don't ask questions or phrase assumptions which are clear pushovers: "If you are seeking X, Y, and Z, then I'm the right person." "Are you looking for an employee with X, Y, Z? I have X, Y, and Z."

     e.   Postpone salary talk until the interview if you can. If the phrase "State salary required" is included in the description, your reply of "negotiable at interview," "your going rate" or "your usual wage scale" is acceptable to any firm you'd want to work for.

and (2) the ad, agency, or talent scout will give you the job requirements or as a bare minimum identify the job category and principal duties.

Organizing appropriately

Even when you hear of the job through other people, they will usually tell you what you'll be expected to do. So matching up your qualifications with the job requirements is easier in the invited situation than with prospecting applications, because your source will usually identify requirements in some order indicating the relative importance to the employer.

If you are equally strong on all points of preparation, you have no problem. You simply take up the points in the order listed. But such a happy condition you'll rarely find. Most often your best talking point is not the most significant requirement, and usually you'll be deficient in some way. The solution is to employ the same strategy you did in writing the invited sales letter: Tie in your strongest point of preparation with something the reader wants done; take up those points wherein you are weakest in the middle position of the letter and attempt to correlate them with some positive point.

Your analysis of job requirements and compilation of a résumé are exactly the same procedures as in a prospecting situation. Adaptation is simply easier. And once past the opening, supplying evidence and asking for appropriate action are the same. Since the beginnings in the prospecting and the invited applications do differ somewhat, however, we need to consider why and to make some suggestions that will help you write good ones.

Whether you learn of the job through an ad, through an agency, or via a third person, your beginning is pretty much the same. The first requirement is that it *mention your main qualifications;* the second, that it *identify the job;* the third, that it *show a service attitude;* and the fourth, that it *refer to the source of the information (subordinately* unless it is significant).

The reason for telling how you learned of the job is simply that the reference to the ad, or the bureau, or the person who told you about the job is an automatic attention getter which favorably reinforces the reader's willingness or even eagerness to read your letter. One good sentence can accomplish all four functions and point the trend of the letter.

The opening of the following letter puts emphasis on service through work, clearly identifies the specific kind of work sought, and desirably subordinates the reference to the source. Note that after the opening the letter reads much the same as a prospecting application (indeed, if you omit the lead in the faked address block and the first two lines, it could be a prospecting letter). Note also the adaptation of talking points—the stress on experience rather than on formal education.

```
Five years' experience
Plus technical training in
Insurance and sales

Would aid me as
```

The aggressive sales representative you advertised for in today's Express.

As a pipeliner in Louisiana I made friends with the kind of prospects to whom I'd be selling your policies. I had a chance to study people, their hopes and fears and desires for protection and security, while doing casework for the Welfare Society in San Antonio. And while working as a waiter both in high school and in college, I learned how to work for and with the public.

The most significant thing I learned was to keep right on smiling even though dog-tired at the end of my 6-12 p.m. shift after having been to school most of the day. And I certainly learned the meaning of perseverance when I had to go home after midnight and get on the books for the next day's assignments.

The same perseverance that earned me B's in Insurance and Income Protection, Liability Insurance, and Personal Sales Principles will help me find leads, follow them up, persuade, and close a sale. I know an insurance representative makes money personally and for the company only by sticking to a schedule of calls. But I'm equally aware of the value of patience and the necessity for repeat calls.

As you see on the enclosed résumé, I was elected a Favorite at Schreiner Institute; and at the University of Texas I was tapped for Silver Spurs, a service-honorary organization. Making these many friends has resulted in my knowing people from all sections of the state.

I would be grateful for your telling me a convenient time and place when I may talk with you further about my qualifications for being the hardworking sales representative you want.

Frequently your source—especially if an ad—gives you an effective entering cue and provides you with useful reference phrases throughout the letter. From the key phrases you can almost reconstruct the ad answered in the following letter:

Because of my college education in accounting and my work experience, I believe I can be the quick-to-learn junior accountant for whom you advertised in the May Journal of Accountancy.

Having successfully completed down-to-earth studies in tax accounting and auditing while earning my degree, I should be able to catch on to your treatment of these problems quickly.

And while working as assistant ledger clerk for the Grantland Davis firm in St. Louis one semester, I developed a great respect for accuracy as well as an appreciation of the necessity for the conscientious, painstaking labor so essential in public accounting. There, too, I saw clearly the necessity for working with confidential information without divulging it.

My natural aptitude for analysis and synthesis, strengthened by special study of the analysis of financial statements and reinforced with a broad background of economics, law, and statistics, should enable me to handle the recurring tasks of compiling comparative statements of earnings and net worth. And my training in writing reports will help me to tell the story to my supervisors as well as to clients.

Realizing that the public accountant must gain the confidence of clients through long periods of accurate, trustworthy service, I welcome the offer of a long-range advancement program mentioned in your ad. I'm not afraid of hard work; and I enjoy the good health essential in the long, irregular working hours of rush business seasons.

Will you study the diversified list of courses and the description of my internship listed on the attached résumé? Note also, please, the wide range of activities I took part in while maintaining an A average. Then I would be most grateful if you will write or call me so that we can talk further about my qualifications for beginning a career of immediate usefulness to you.

I can start to work any time after graduation on June 4.

A variation of source doesn't affect your procedure—except that you *emphasize a source that would be influential in your getting the job; otherwise, subordinate the source*. If you learn of the work through an agency or a third person, the procedure is still the same. Here are some openings bearing out our statement:

I'd like the chance to prove that my education and personal characteristics closely parallel the description of the desirable management trainee that you gave to Dr. Morley, head of our placement bureau, when you visited the campus last week.

——

When I talked with Ms. Sarah Lomer this morning, she assured me that I am qualified by experience and

```
professional training for the duties of a field
auditor with your firm.
```

We need to give *two warnings*, however. The *first* is to guard carefully against stupid questions, questions made perfectly clear from the ad or the situation. One applicant to a legal firm began with:

```
Are you looking for a college-trained secretary who
can do the work in your law office efficiently and
accurately and who is eager to learn law work? If so,
I think I can meet your exacting requirements for a
legal secretary.
```

The ad had made the answer perfectly clear! And an efficient candidate only looked silly.

The *second* warning is against showing signs of selfish glee over having discovered a job possibility of your choice. When you read or hear about a job, you may rightly think, "That's just what I want!"—but don't write this or any variation of it. Start writing in terms of doing something for the reader: what you can give instead of what you hope to get.

Beating the competition

Perhaps a *third* warning is in order—against assuming that you don't have much of a selling job to do because the reader is on the asking end. Nothing could be further from the truth. The competition you're up against for an advertised job is keen even in times of prosperity. And because many others will apply, you'll have to write a superior letter to be chosen as one of the final few for interviewing.

In fact, the reader may face such a heap of letters that yours may not even get read. For that reason you may want to do something to assure a reading:

1. When competion is keen, you may want to get the first edition of the newspaper and have your material in such shape that you can have a complete, well-written letter and résumé in the employer's hands hours or even days ahead of other candidates. Your letter (if it is good) becomes better in the eyes of the employer as poorer ones come in through the mail. Remember, too, that the first application that comes in relieves the fear of every such advertiser—that maybe no one will answer the ad.

2. As an alternative strategy, you can wait 10 to 16 days after an advertisment appears before sending in your application, for two reasons: (*a*) Companies are usually slow and careful about filling a job. If your application is superior to those that arrived earlier, you will stand out. (*b*) Roughly 82 percent of the answers to a job advertisement will come in during the first week; why have yours arrive with so many others? (For maximum effect, mail so yours arrives on Tuesday or Wednesday.)

3. A favorite device, if you are in the same town, is to deliver the letter yourself, with the request that it be turned over to the appropriate person.

4. If you insert your letter and résumé in an envelope large enough to accommodate 8½-by 11-inch pages without folding and add a piece of cardboard to keep the pages smooth, the contrast between your application and all the others that have been folded will call attention to yours.

But none of these devices will make much difference if you do not write from the viewpoint of contributing to the firm through effective, efficient work.

Handling special problems

While an advertisement or other source of information usually gives you some advantages in writing invited instead of prospecting applications, ads often give you one or more of three special problems.

1. When the ad asks you to "state salary expected," "give salary history," or "give salary on last job," take the advice of eight personnel directors on a panel: Don't do it. You hurt your chances if you shoot too high or too low. Instead, say something like "Your usual salary range," "Negotiable in the interview," or the like. A company should want to hire you for what you can do for it, not because it can get you cheap.

2. Ads often say "Send résumé." Again, don't do *only* that. These ad writers want to save time by screening only factual résumés; and they are not interested in selling you on the job, but *you* are interested in selling yourself. An interpretive letter is a much better selling instrument than a résumé alone. (Does anyone buy a new car after just receiving a window sticker in the mail? Selling a car usually takes a sales talk followed by a demonstration, or in job-hunting parlance, a letter and résumé followed by an interview.) So send your letter *and* your résumé—or a qualification brief.

3. What we said about availability date also applies in an invited application letter, but to a lesser degree. When a company advertises for help, it needs someone right away. You can assume that you must be available immediately (or very soon) and should give the earliest date you can start work (which can eliminate any of your competition who cannot start that soon).

As you already realize, most of the items we suggested to you in the prospecting application checklist apply equally when you write an invited letter. Study them again, and review the additional items at the end of that checklist which are peculiar to the invited situation.

CONTINUING THE CAMPAIGN

Regardless of the results from your application, you have some follow-up work to do.

If you get an invitation to an interview, you know how to handle it (before reading up on interviewing in Chapter 17). Accept promptly, pleasantly, and directly (if that's your decision) as suggested in Chapter 5. Just remember to continue your job campaign by indicating continuing interest in serving. If you decide to turn down the invitation, Chapter 7 has shown you how; but remember, also, the adage about never burning your bridges behind you.

If within a reasonable time you do not hear from the person or firm you've applied to, you'd probably better send a follow-up letter indicating continuing interest.

Follow-up letters

A good salesperson doesn't make one call and drop the matter if that doesn't close the sale. Neither does a sales-minded job applicant. Election to an office or an honorary society, an extensive trip that has opened your eyes to bigger and better possibilities of the job, a research paper that has taught you something significant to the job, and certainly another job offer are all avenues of approach for reselling yourself and indicating continuing interest.

Even if you receive the usual noncommittal letter saying that the firm is glad to have your application and is filing it in case any opening occurs, you need not hesitate to send another letter two, three, or six months after the first one. It should not be another complete application (yours will still be on file); it is just a reminder that you are still interested. One acceptable one is this:

> I know that many organizations throw away applications over six months old.
>
> Because that much time has elapsed since I sent you mine (dated April 15), I want to assure you that I'm still interested in working for you, in having you keep my record in your active file, and in hearing from you when you need someone with my qualifications.

Only a lackadaisical applicant would end the letter there, however. Just a few more words could bring the information up to date and perhaps stimulate more interest in the application, like this:

> Since graduation I have been doing statistical correlations at the Bureau of Business Research here at the University. I've picked up a few techniques I didn't learn in class, and I've certainly increased my speed on the computer keyboard and calculator.
>
> I still want that job as sales analyst with your firm, however.

Thank-you letters

Following an interview, whether the results seem favorable or unfavorable, your note of appreciation is not only a business courtesy; it helps to single you out from other applicants and to show your reader that you have a good sense of human relations.

Even when you and the interviewer have agreed that the job is not for you, you can profitably invest about two minutes writing something like this:

> I surely appreciate the time you spent with me last Friday discussing employment opportunities at Monitor and Wagner.
>
> The suggestions you made will help me find my right place in the business world.
>
> After I get that experience you suggested, I may be knocking at your door again.

When you are interested in the job discussed and feel that you have a good chance, you're plain foolish not to write a letter expressing appreciation and showing that you learned something from the interview.

> Your description of the community relations program of Livania has opened new vistas to me, Ms. Lee.
>
> The functions of the public relations department in your company as you described them made me much more aware of the significance and appeal of this work.
>
> As soon as I returned to the campus, I read Mr. Fields's book that you suggested and the pamphlets describing U.S. Steel's program.
>
> Many thanks for your suggestions and for the time you took with me.
>
> I shall be looking forward to hearing the decision about my application as soon as you can make it.

Job-acceptance letters

When an employer offers you a job and you decide it's the one for you, say so enthusiastically in a direct A–plan letter that keeps you in a favorable light—perhaps by restating your interest in serving well. Just remember, also, to seal the contract by brief accepting references to (not flat repetition of) the terms—or by filling out and returning supplied contract forms, as in the following:

> I certainly do want to work with Franklin & Franklin— and I didn't need a week to think it over, Mr. Bell, although I appreciate your giving me that much time to decide.
>
> I've filled out the forms you gave me and enclosed them with this letter. Anything else?
>
> Unless you tell me differently, I'll take off two weeks after graduation. But, as you asked, I'll call you on Friday, June 11, to get report-to-work instructions for Monday, June 14.

Job-refusal letters

Sometime in your life you'll have to tell somebody that you don't want to accept an offer. You may feel that it's routine, that it doesn't mean anything one way or the other to a busy person who interviews many applicants and has many other people available. Remember, though, that a human being with pride and ego is going to read your letter. So make yourself think, "I don't want that job *now*," for you may want to reopen negotiations at some future point.

To wind up negotiations pleasantly and leave the way open for yourself, write a B–plan letter (as discussed in Chapter 7) with a pleasant buffer of some favorable comment about the company or the work, some plausible and inoffensive reason, the presentation of the refusal as positively and subordinately as you can phrase it (possibly with the statement of where you are going to work), and an ending expressing good feeling and appreciation or both. The following letter is a good example:

> Meeting you and talking with you about working for Bowen's was one of the more interesting job contacts I have had.
>
> As you will remember from our discussion, I am still primarily interested in product research. Since I feel that my abilities will be utilized best in that way, I am going to work for (a company) that has offered me such employment.
>
> I shall certainly continue to watch your company's progress with interest, and I shall look forward to reading or hearing about the results of your new prepackaging program.

Letters of resignation

The way you quit a job is just as important as the way you get a job. It can have powerful repercussions on you later. So leave with style and grace by following a few simple, basic rules.

—When possible offer to allow additional time for the company you are leaving to replace you (although two weeks' notice is standard procedure except for higher level jobs).

—Explain your decision orally to your immediate supervisor and then write a letter explaining your reasons for leaving and saying something pleasant about your work with the company or with the superior or both.

—Be cooperative and work hard right up to the last minute.

—Train a person who will succeed you (if asked to do so).

—Keep all confidences to yourself.

—Don't brag to fellow workers about your new job (maybe not even mention you are going to leave if your employer suggests).

—Clear up all financial debts and return all company property.

—On your new job, talk positively (or not at all) about the company you left.

Resignation letters, like job-refusal letters, are modified B–plan letters. You want to stay in the good graces of the individuals who have assisted you in your career. The suggestion "Be kind, courteous, and considerate to the people you pass on the way up the ladder of success; you will likely meet them on your way back down" is good advice to keep in mind when you leave a job.

When you have worked for a firm, you have benefited in some way (besides your pay). Regardless of how you feel at the time, remember that you can say something complimentary about how things are run, about what you have learned as a result of your experience, or about the people with whom you have associated. By all means, say it!

In many circumstances your resignation can be oral. And in many circumstances it may be better that way. But when you need to write a letter, consider adaptations of the following:

> In the past 18 months, I've certainly learned a great
> deal about . . . from my work as . . . at . . ., and I
> shall always be grateful to you and the other people
> who have helped me to do the job and to prepare for a
> more challenging one.
>
> You will perhaps recall that when I had my interviews
> with you before starting to work, I stressed my
> interest in working toward a job as . . . . Since I
> now have such an opportunity . . . , I am sumbmitting
> my resignation. Apparently it will be some time before
> such an opportunity is available for me here.
>
> Would terminating my employment here in two weeks be
> satisfactory? I can make arrangements to work a little
> longer if doing so would help you.

Often when another offer comes your way, you'll feel free to discuss the opportunity with your current employer before making a final decision. Such a conference has many advantages for both employee and employer. Often a counteroffer results, to the mutual satisfaction of both, and the job change doesn't take place. If, despite a counteroffer, you still decide to make the change, you can resign in good grace with a letter somewhat like this:

> Your recent offer is one I appreciate very much, and
> it made me give serious thought to continuing at
> . . . .
>
> I have appreciated the cooperation, the friendliness,
> and helpfulness of everyone with whom I've been
> associated here.
>
> After considerably more evaluation, however, I believe

> I can make a greater contribution and be a more
> successful business manager by accepting the position
> offered me by . . . .
>
> I hope that I can leave with your approval by
> (specific date). I feel sure that all my current
> projects will be complete by that time.
>
> You'll hear from me from time to time——if for no other
> reason than that I'll be interested in how the new
> credit union works out.
>
> But I'll always want to know how things are going for
> . . . and the many friends I've made here.

When appropriate, a possible talking point is the suggestion of a successor to you; often this is a big help. A constructive suggestion, phrased positively, implies your continuing interest in the organization.

Letters of resignation written by college students who resign after having agreed to work for someone but before actually reporting for work are quite different—something we take up with reluctance. Many personnel people regard them as breaches of contract. Certainly a practice of sliding out from under such agreements will soon give you a black eye employmentwise.

We urge you to give serious thought before definitely accepting a job offer. Don't make the mistake of grabbing the first job offered you, only to have something infinitely more to your liking come along later. We further urge you never to let yourself get caught in the position of being committed to two employers at the same time. If you have agreed to go to work for a firm and then you have a later offer which you want to accept, do not accept it until you are released from the first contract. To the second potential employer, reply in some vein like this:

> I certainly would like to accept your offer to come
> with your firm. As attractive as your proposal is,
> however, I must delay accepting it until I can secure
> a release from the Jenkins firm in Blankville. After
> my interview with you, I accepted this position, which
> at the time appeared to be the most promising
> available.
>
> Can you allow me enough time to write the Jenkins
> personnel manager, explaining my reasons and
> requesting a release? (I can give him the names of two
> friends who might be suitable replacements.)
>
> This problem shouldn't take longer than a week to
> settle. I appreciate your offer, regardless of how
> things work out.

If necessary, phone the second potential employer, explain frankly, and get approval to wait.

TWO USEFUL MODIFICATIONS
OF APPLICATIONS

The following two letter possibilites for helping you get the job of your choice are *not here with the implication that they will take the place of the complete sales presentation* we have suggested to you. Only because they may help you some time do we even remind you of them.

The job-anticipating letter

Most personnel people are willing to give advice. Most of them are also pleased with a show of interest in their companies and evidence of long-range planning on the part of a student. With that in mind several of our students have had successful results from letters like the following, sent in the junior year of college:

> A course in the operation of business machines under Mrs. Lora Osmus in the Statistics Department at school gave me skill in their operation and showed me the tremendous possibilities of . . . equipment for business use.

> After comparing . . . and ABL equipment that was on exhibit on Commerce Day and talking with . . . representative in charge of your display, I am coming to you directly and frankly for some help.

> Since I have completed almost all the courses required for the B.S. in commerce, I am free to elect practically all courses I shall study next year before June graduation. On the attached sheet I've listed the courses I've completed and those I'm contemplating. Will you please rank the ones you consider most beneficial for a prospective . . . representative?

> Naturally, I will regard your suggestions as off–the–cuff assistance that implies no commitment. I'm just trying to equip myself as well as I can to meet the competition for the first available job with your company after I graduate.

> I shall be most grateful for your comments.

The telescoped application inquiry

We realize that good applications take time. They're worth the time, however.

But we also know that sometime, somewhere, you may need to send some inquiries in a hurry and simply cannot write a complete one. You may, in such a situation, be able to make profitable use of the services of your college placement bureau in a letter, as one student did. The applicant was too busy writing a thesis and sitting for graduate examinations to prepare a thorough application. So six firms received the following request and reply card:

> With completion of an M.S. degree in accounting at the University of North Carolina and two years of retail merchandise accounting experience, I believe I could make you a good accountant with a minimum of training—and be able to advance more rapidly than the majority of accountants you could hire.
>
> I am not just an accountant: A well-rounded background of finance, transportation, economics, and other related subjects will enable me, in time, to do managerial work as well.
>
> May I have the Placement Bureau here at the University send you a transcript of my college record together with a detailed record of my experience, faculty rating statements, and names and addresses of former employers?
>
> I shall be happy to furnish any additional information you may want and to be available for an interview at your convenience later if you will check and return the enclosed card.

All six firms replied, but only one resulted in an interview.

This kind of quick note may be a stopgap measure sometime. But this person's experience simply reconfirms the fact that you must tell a complete story if you expect to get a show of effective interest.

* * * * *

Although letters exchanging information about applicants are a part of the employment routine, applicants themselves do not write them. For that reason, and because you studied them in Chapter 5, we see no point in taking them up again here. They are A–plan letters, characterized by directness and conciseness.

Likewise, we do not think you need to study or write the kinds of letters an interviewer or employer writes offering an applicant a position (clearly an A–plan good-news letter) or turning down an applicant (a B–plan disappointing news letter). With but simple changes of talking points and references, they follow the principles of their basic plans (Chapters 5 and 7).

QUESTIONS AND EXERCISES

1. What is your central selling point for an application letter you're most likely to write?
2. Think of the nearest thing you have to a handicap. How would you han-

dle it in your prospecting application or invited application letter?

3. Suppose you never had a paying job but have worked as a hospital volunteer. What might you tell in your application letter about such experience?

4. How is the ending of a sales letter different from the ending of a prospecting application letter? How are they similar?

5. How does the beginning of the prospecting application letter differ from the opening of the invited application letter?

6. How should you follow up—
   a. An interview?
   b. An interview and visit on invitation at a company where you want to work?
   c. A statement from an interviewer that you would hear from the company three weeks ago.

7. You applied for an accounting job you really want at a local firm and had a promising preliminary interview. In the meantime a bank that you also applied to offered you a job and wants your response in writing right away. How would you phrase a letter of delay to the bank?

8. Visit a plant or company and get an application form, fill it out, and analyze it from the applicant's point of view.

9. If you were an employee responsible for revising the form in Question 8, what about it would you keep? What change? Why, specifically?

10. Visit your campus career placement office, talk with some of the employees there and gather some of the forms they give out. Write a memo to your teacher describing your experience, with emphasis on answering the same questions as in Question 9.

CASES   (See p. xiii for some important explanations.)

Preliminaries to preparing résumés, applications, and interviews

10–1.   Write out 10 points which you would try to bring out about yourself in an interview for a desired job.

10–2.   Write out 10 questions which you feel you should (or could) ask a corporation's campus recruiter who might interview you.

10–3.   After reading Chapters 9 and 10 and the first section and the "Interviews" section of Chapter 17, make an appointment with a personnel director or other hiring decision maker of a firm. Interview that person to determine what the firm feels is vital to include in an unsolicited application letter and résumé. Find out the best methods for securing a job there. Then report your findings to the class in a written or oral presentation (as your instructor directs).

Prospecting application

10–4. Assume that you are in your last term of school and near graduation. You want to find work which you like, for which you have been preparing, and in which you could support yourself now and support (or help support) a family later as you win promotions.

Newspapers, trade magazines, and placement bureaus list no job of your choice. So you decide to do as any good seller does: analyze the product (yourself); then appraise the market (companies which could use a person who can do what you are prepared to do); then advertise (send the companies an application letter and résumé). Such a procedure sometimes creates a job where none existed before; sometimes it establishes a basis for negotiations for the "big job" two, three, or five years after graduation. And very frequently it puts you on the list for the good job which is not filled through advertising or from within the company.

To analyze the high points of your preparation, you will need to consider the courses you have had and make plausible assumptions (don't go daydreaming and woolgathering; stick to probabilities) about the courses you will have completed on graduation. *This means you'll have to study your college catalog*. It also means that you will have to make a temporary decision about the kind of work you want to do. If you haven't the faintest idea of what you'd like to do, follow the suggestions in Chapter 9.

Distinguish between those courses that actually qualify you to do the type of work you are seeking and those that give you background education. If you've had experience directly related to the job you want as a career, that's fine; but any work you've done means qualifications (military experience— active duty—is in almost the same category as on-the-job experience). With these training and work sections mapped out, complete a tentative résumé with appropriate references.

Then study the market, as suggested under "Analyzing Companies." In actual practice you might compile a list of companies and send them an application. For this assignment, after some preliminary digging around, select one company and plan a letter-résumé combination addressed to that company. Adapt it as specifically as possible to the one company. You may or may not be able to find out the name of the specific individual to address it to. If not, address it to the personnel department or to the head of the particular department in which you are interested.

You will benefit from this exercise in application letter writing only if you approach it earnestly and seriously. *It should be a job utilizing your education*. It should be a job geared to what you could reasonably assume will be your level of performance at graduation. Few just-out-of-college folks can expect to be sales managers, chief buyers, senior accountants, copy chiefs, and the like; you'll have to begin at a subordinate level and work up; you'll want to *show in your letter that you realize this fact*. On the other hand, don't waste your time and your instructor's applying for something that you could readily do if you had never gone to college.

You will sometimes hear advice to confine your presentation to a one-page letter and a one-page résumé; but don't be afraid to go to two pages for either. As in sales letters, some highly successful ones run to two and sometimes even three pages. What is important is that you make your presentation fully, and in the way that is most favorable for you. Take as much space as necessary to present the facts about yourself in the best light, remembering that employers don't like to buy pigs in pokes but don't like padding either.

10–5. You've decided that you want to earn some money, see some new places, and have some fun this coming summer. So you're going to address an application for summer employment to a summer camp or an inn at a resort (possibly one of the national parks). You'll have to indicate a willingness to do housekeeping duties (including kitchen and dining room work), although if you have enough maturity and the right kind of experience you may be able to get some kind of clerical or even more specialized assignment. Since college students chosen for such jobs are really hosts and hostesses to the guests, stress poise, dignity, and cheerfulness, as well as any talents for entertaining or instructing (maybe in your hobby).

10–6. Modify the preceding problem to this extent: You want to be a counselor at a summer camp for children of any age group at least eight years younger than you. Choose a camp with which you are familiar, or find out about one. Address the letter and résumé to the camp director (by name if you can get it). Note here the importance of understanding and getting along with youngsters, the ability to direct activities, and the emphasis on leadership, athletic, and teaching abilities. Apply to a camp which is not in your home town or your college town; it should be a residence camp, not a day camp.

10–7. Look over your local situation for part-time job possibilities, perhaps on your college campus or in the college community (close enough for you to arrange a schedule of classes that would permit you to work in the afternoons). Word the application so the reader will understand about how many hours a week you can work. Prepare a résumé and letter that summarize and interpret your background up to the time of writing.

10–8. With plausible assumptions and appropriate modifications, write a job-anticipating letter to the company of your choice. Assume that you have one more year of college before graduating.

Invited applications

10–9. A good starting point in job getting is the want-ad columns of newspapers (local or large city) and magazines (especially trade magazines). Study the ones of your choice and find an ad that describes a job you would like to have, requiring qualifications you could reasonably assume at the time of your graduation (or some other assumed time as affected by your intentions). It should be a job utilizing your college education. And it should clearly call for letter—not telephone—answers. Clip the ad neatly to your letter; or if you find the ad of your choice in a library copy, make an exact copy, with exact reference: name of publication, date of the issue, and page on which you found the ad.

Draw on imagination, experience, and whatever information you can find out to bring the situation as close to reality as you can. Read the ad thoughtfully for what it says, and search mentally for those qualifications it only implies. Then evaluate your own education and experience in the light of the specific job. You can readily distinguish between courses that actually qualify you to do the job you're considering and those that are only background. You can certainly classify your work experience in an order of applicability to the given job. Further, analyze significant personal factors. And finally, decide upon references. You will need to send along a résumé (and refer to it in your letter) unless you have contrary instructions.

10–10.   When you went past your department bulletin board yesterday, you noticed that the . . . Corporation was advertising for a _____ (put in a job for which your experience and training can qualify you). Your adviser thinks you can fill the job. Write a letter to . . . at . . . in which you present your qualifications and ask for an interview during a short span of days you plan to be in that area.

10–11.   Your college adviser (use the name) just mentioned to you that a good friend (provide the name), the personnel director of . . . at . . . , has asked that good prospects be steered to that company's on-campus interviews coming up next month. Because you like the company's positive views toward intercultural business (expansion into 10 countries abroad) and protecting the environment, you have thought of writing a prospecting job letter. Now, however, you can write an invited job letter. Your adviser told you that . . . needed people with your qualifications. Write an invited job application letter that shows your qualifications for going to work there and asks for an appointment during the interview period. Assume that your résumé goes with the letter.

10–12.   This morning you had a walk-in interview with the representative of a firm you'd like to work for. After half an hour of talk which appeared to be mutually satisfactory and during which time you found out a lot about the company, the representative handed you one of the company employment forms for applying, shook your hand, and ushered you out of the room, saying, "Fill this out and return it to me with a letter of application." *Assuming* the form is filled in neatly and completely, draft your earnest but enthusiastic letter of application. Be careful to talk work rather than employee benefits. Assume specific names for the representative and the company.

10–13. From the head of the department in which you are majoring, this morning you learn that a firm you hold in high regard is seeking a person with substantially your qualifications for a particular job you want—*a job calling for an unusual combination of qualifications that you have*. Fill in with the necessary specific details and write the letter you would send, assuming that your résumé presentation will accompany it.

10–14. The director of your college placement bureau (use name) has just told you about the training program of a large corporation. The personnel director indicated in a letter that the company seeks college graduates to train for managerial positions throughout the organization. During a year trainees work in every division under close supervision and attend a series of classes. Assume a specific company, indicate your particular field of interest, but reflect a receptive attitude toward the various phases of the training program, showing your realization of its benefits regardless of the specific work you'll eventually perform, and send an application letter and résumé.

Follow-ups

10–15. In response to your application you receive an invitation to come in for an interview at a time and place convenient for you. Write the acceptance confirming the circumstances.

10–16. Assume that in response to your prospecting application you receive an invitation to come in for an interview at a time which would be convenient if you had the money for traveling to the distant point. Write the letter which reaffirms your interest. Admit your lack of funds and ask if you might see a representative of the firm at a place which is more accessible to you.

10–17. Assume that you have had an interview as a result of your letter and résumé. You know the company representative interviewed several other candidates for the job. In a thank-you letter, confirm your interest in employment by the company and add other details to show that you picked up something from the interview. The representative promised to get in touch with you in a week or 10 days.

10–18. Not having heard from the application letter you sent several weeks ago, write a letter reemphasizing your desire to work for the firm. Clearly refer to the original application by date and type of work discussed. Include any additional data you think will help sell you. This letter, however, should not be a rehash of what you have already written. It should identify the action you want the reader to take.

10–19.   You have just been informed that you were not chosen for the job you have worked so hard to get—and still want. Remember, however, that you were considered; that someone spent a good deal of time with you; and that, employmentwise, nothing is ever final. Write the letter expressing appreciation for the courtesies extended you, revealing how you have profited from the contact, and showing your determination to reach your intended goal. Above all, the letter should reflect a friendly feeling toward the company and the representative addressed.

10–20.   Assume you have an intolerable situation where you are employed. Your boss lies, covers up, misleads, is basically dishonest. Although physically attractive, a money-maker for the firm, this person is most difficult to work for, and you cannot take the situation any longer. Write a letter of resignation and assume you have another job to go to. You assume names of company and people.

10–21.   Although you were offered a job in response to your application, you have decided that you do not want to accept it because it is not in the field of your primary interest and for other plausible reasons—not salary. Write the tactful letter that expresses appreciation for the time spent with you and the interest shown in you and that leaves the way open for you to resume negotiations later if you care to. Comment favorably on some aspect of the company.

Persuasive messages: Requests

11

SPECIAL REQUESTS

The special requests we discuss here are more difficult than the direct inquiries we discussed in Chapter 5. There the receivers usually had a built-in motivation to reply because of their desire to sell the goods and services inquired about or to help the people (friends) inquired about as possible employees or credit customers.

In this chapter we explain how to get favorable responses from people who initially have no built-in reasons to respond that way. This situation requires more ability with psychology and language. That ability, however, is one of the most important you can develop—for both your business and nonbusiness use. It is a major reason some people are leaders, managers, and administrators while others (often with equal or better general abilities) are their followers and employees.

Each person comes into the world with certain abilities—and some with the proverbial silver spoons in their mouths. The important question is not what you were born with but what you do with it. As a worthwhile person you should use at least some of your time and abilities to make the world better instead of just taking what you can get from it. Since you can do little alone, the extent to which you can contribute—in business, education, government, science, or a profession—will depend more on your ability to create ideas and persuade other people to help you implement them than on any silver spoon or almost any other asset you may have.

In enlisting the help of others, you need to realize that no one ever has enough money or time to give either of them spontaneously and unquestioningly. No one is willing to reveal certain kinds of information without knowing its intended use and deciding that the purpose is good. To put the question directly in these cases is to get an immediate turndown. So the special request has to be persuasive. Like the simple inquiry, the effective special request is specific and concise, but it is not direct.

Favor-seeking messages are, as already explained briefly in Chapter 4, C–plan messages. The secret to their successfully persuasive copy is to

1. Secure interested motivation first by offering, suggesting, or implying a benefit—the you-attitude as explained in Chapter 4 and under **YA** in Appendix F—or at least talking about something of interest;

2. Justify the request by interweaving necessary information with explanations and reminders of the benefit(s);

3. Try to foresee and preclude or minimize objections; and

4. After giving the necessary information and persuasion, confidently ask for the desired action.

Before we go further in telling you how to phrase persuasive requests, however, a point of caution deserves your attention: *You should not be making such requests unless you cannot get what you want by your own efforts*.

Securing Interest

If you are going to strike the appropriately persuasive theme, you need to analyze the situation to select the most pertinent and forceful *motive* as the beginning.

Money being what it must be in business thinking, the strongest appeal is one that holds out the prospect of sales, of saving money, or of promoting goodwill with an audience wherein sales may ultimately materialize. Such potential-dollar themes offer the most concrete form of benefit and are responsible for this opening to an advertising manager of a manufacturing company:

> What would it be worth to Field's to add some 8,000 potential customers to its prospect list?

and this opening to the circulation manager of a magazine:

> Who will be your subscribers 10 years from now?

If you can apply such reader-benefit themes appropriately and remain within the realm of good taste (avoiding the suggestion of bribery), you undoubtedly have the strongest appeal you can make.

In many instances, however, such dollar-minded talk would arouse indignation or would not apply. But you need not despair of finding a point which will stress the reader's benefits or interests rather than your own. The letter illustrating C–plan strategy in Chapter 4 and beginning

> How often have you received--even from well-educated people--letters that are not worth your attention?

clearly proposes a benefit by talking in terms of making the reader's job easier. Many times the reason a busy person fills out a time-consuming questionnaire is the hope for improved efficiency.

Indirect benefits may serve too. When you can show how your project will promote the welfare of a group in which your reader holds a membership or other interest, you can make a strong appeal. On this basis you might persuade a public accountant to speak to a college accounting club, an alumnus of a professional fraternity to take on a responsible office in the organization, or a correspondence supervisor to address a group of teachers or students of business writing.

The following letter written to the founder of the successful *Direct Marketing/Mail* magazine got results (the founder came to Gainesville and talked to two groups of students):

What can I do with students who consistently turn in sales letters with the same old overused and misapplied tricks as the dominant message?

Year after year I lecture to my students in Business Communications on how to write a good sales letter. I put my book (Communicating Through Letters and Reports) in front of them, give them outside readings for additional help, and still a few repeatedly miss major points.

Don't you agree that all of them would benefit and more thoroughly understand the techniques of writing sales letters if they could hear an explanation from a specialist with a flair for speaking to groups and winning their attention?

Next Monday (February 26) at 1:20 p.m. and 7 p.m. I have scheduled the first of two 50-minute lectures on sales letters to the two groups. I can always count on the attendance of at least 200 students in each group; and with the announcement of a guest speaker who is a specialist in this area of communications, I'm certain their enthusiasm would soar.

Since they received their assignment last week, they will have been exposed to the material in my book by the Monday lectures, and I will be able to notify them in their discussion classes of your arrival. Of course, I'm looking forward to having you as my overnight guest, and my wife is a splendid cook. She's been looking forward to meeting you for years.

The students on the campus this year are an eager, active group. They respond particularly well to visiting speakers. Won't you call or write me within the week to let me know I can expect you on Monday? I would appreciate having my students hear from an expert before they become tomorrow's sales letter writers.

Although many such special requests appeal to friendship, interest in a particular field, or altruism,[1] in most business situations you will do better if you select and emphasize direct-benefit talking points—such as the three one-sentence beginnings at the start of this section imply.

The basic appeals we have mentioned for persuasive messages are universals—i.e., reader benefits which apply equally in international communication. Adaptations of the basic appeals, however, do depend somewhat on special interests of the receiving people, who evaluate various kinds of benefits differently. Since those differences are reflections of their social, familial, religious, and political beliefs and practices, successful adaptation depends on an understanding of those aspects of different cultures. For an insight into those differences, therefore, refer to Appendix C.

As you look back at the beginnings quoted so far in this section, you will note that in addition to highlighting benefits (or at least supposed interest), these openings are questions. You will note, too, that the questions are rhetorical (asked not to get their answers, as in inquiries, but to promote thinking and encourage reading on).

We do not mean to imply that all persuasive requests must begin with a question. But a question beginning commands greater attention than a declarative statement, is never as challenging as some statements are, can be subtly flattering, and more readily *leads to thinking about your suggestion*. In phrasing such questions, however, you will be on safer ground if you eliminate the possibility of either a yes or no answer because such an answer stops thought about the mentioned or implied benefit. To promote thinking about the circumstances that will lead up to the request, each of the preceding openings employs the strategy.

Neither do we mean to imply that to secure interest you must studiously avoid *all* yes or no questions. If the answer leaves an intriguing wonder about how to get the mentioned benefit, you've achieved your purpose of leading into interested contemplation of your message. The following opening addressed to a national retailer contemplating entering the Texas market, for example, is certainly a good one:

> Wouldn't you consider the respect and attention of some 200 key Texas retailers a valuable opportunity to test the true business conditions in that state?

[1]Though letters seeking funds for worthy causes are special-request letters and thus within the scope of this analysis, we do not take them up here because they are too highly specialized and often have civic, religious, and fraternal manifestations. When faced with such problems, you can be sure that the fundamental principles we present here will apply; but for more detailed techniques and tricks of the trade, check some books like the old standby, Margaret Fellows and Stella Koenig's *Tested Methods of Raising Money for Churches, Colleges, and Health and Welfare Agencies* (New York: Harper & Row 1959). Belinda Hulin-Salkin's "Strategies of Charities" (*Advertising Age*, January 19, 1981, p. 829) updates with some new guidelines and techniques using computers for personalizing mass mailings.

The mental response to such a question is positive and pursuing; and as long as you can be fairly sure of a positive reaction, you are probably on safe ground.

The danger lies in getting an irritated answer—whether that answer is a yes or a no or any of the variants of "So what?" The student who invited the head of an accounting firm to speak to a college group and began with

    Do you believe in preparing for the future?

apparently gave little thought to the probable snort that would result from such a question. To eliminate the irritating aspects (and get closer to the subject) a supervisor changed the opening to read:

    What, in your opinion, are the desirable personal
    characteristics of a successful public accountant?

True, that beginning implies no benefit; but it is certainly a subject of practical interest. Of possibly greater benefit implications is this one:

    What does it cost you when you have to dismiss a well-
    grounded junior accountant because of poor personal
    characteristics?

Careful study of the preceding beginnings will show three other advantages that come from question beginnings implying reader benefits: (1) they are more likely to keep the reader in the picture, (2) they keep you from beginning with uninteresting explanations or details of curcumstances, and (3) they make the transition to the explanation easier.

Justifying the request

Having secured interest with a beginning which holds some promise of benefit or at least talks of interesting things, you usually need to devote the greater part of your letter to explaining what your project is and what good comes of it—particularly the *good* (benefit) coming to the person you're trying to persuade. Thus and only thus can you keep that person involved—and you can't persuade without that involvement.

In almost any request, details concerning who, what, when, where, why, how (sometimes how much) need clarification; but they do *not* deserve first place. Even in this second section (where they belong) you need to *subordinate* them to reminders of benefits coming from granting the request. In inviting a speaker, for instance, you need to tell the nature and size of the audience, the time and place, the facilities available, the amount of time allotted, and the topic (if you are assigning one). Sometimes knowing about other speakers who will precede and follow would be helpful. But even after a benefit-oriented beginning such details should come in *subordinately* as much as possible.

A common mistake is ignoring the reader and the benefit beginning just to write about the project. The following, for example, would be laughable if it weren't so pitiful. Written by a Texan too immature to have outgrown chauvinism and too lazy to have studied this book, it sounds like a candidate campaigning for a county judgeship:

> The Texas Business Conference will be held the 28—30th of next month at the Lakeway Inn just outside Austin where we again expect 200—300 business executives to convene for our twenty—fifth annual meeting.
>
> We boosters of the great Lone Star state are interested in her future. We have observed her vast resources being utilized more and more through the years and have seen her taking her place in the vast industrial economy of our country . . . .

What should the Texan have said in view of the following known facts?

—The purpose of the letter was to get a big-name speaker for the retailers' group of 50 to 100.

—In *Time* the week before, an article about one of New York's biggest retailers explained that Mr. Hoving (our fictional name) was considering branches in the Southwest.

After following some advice to study a previous edition of this book, the same Texan wrote this:

> What was your final decision regarding the installation of an employee bonus system in your stores, as mentioned in last week's <u>Time</u>?
>
> Leading Texas retailers are eager to hear how you solved this problem and others like it, and the reasons behind the solutions. They'd look forward with interest to sharing ideas with you. And you'd get a very accurate reflection of Texas retail conditions if you'd talk to the group from 2:00 to 3:00 on the 29th and then lead a half—hour's informal discussion when the 50—100 members meet for the 25th annual Texas Business Conference at the Lakeway Inn just outside Austin on the 28th to 30th this month.
>
> Your ideas on sales promotion, ways to meet the competition of discount houses, and personnel— management problems in department stores would be eagerly received, shared——maybe even contested if you care to invite a vigorous discussion——by these men and women. And they'd certainly bring you more than usual appreciation because our members are fully aware that our prominent speakers appear at their own expense—— that the pay they receive is the self-satisfaction of

having their ideas accepted and the benefits of
sharing experiences and viewpoints.

To help us get the desirable publicity for your
appearance, will you write us by the 10th that you'll
be with us? We anticipate your "Yes" with gratitude
and enthusiasm--and we're certain that you could pick
up some useful ideas and information about a section
of the country that is expanding rapidly.

By casting the proper bait—a package of just about all the principles explained in this chapter and epitomized in the checklist—the Texan caught the
particularly wanted big fish. The well-chosen appeal, taken from the *Time*
story, is the chance to learn more about Texas business waters before coming
in. Of particular note is the skillful way of telling Hoving he gets no fee. By
such know-how—including the legitimate use of several passives in the third
paragraph to put the emphasis on Hoving and his ideas rather than on *we*—
the Texan talked a busy man into preparing a speech and leaving his business
to fly from New York to Austin and back at his own expense to give it (something $1,000 would not usually do).

Conversely, nobody would be enthusiastic over a beginning like this:

As a master's candidate at Harvard University, I am
planning a thesis on industrial robots. Professor A.
R. Hopper of our industrial engineering department has
suggested that I write to you to find out the results
of your experience.

Notice in the following copy how the student seeking this information not
only changed the opening to an interest-arousing question but also *subordinated* the necessary but uninteresting details of the original opening:

Just what economies are you experiencing from your
installation of industrial robots?

Are they as great as my limited experience and study
have led me to believe?

Have industrial robots been adopted by an increasing
number of manufacturers in recent years?

Regardless of your experience in using robots, your
comments in answering these questions could contribute
materially in making a worthwhile, authentic, down-to-
earth thesis of the one I am preparing as partial
requirement for an M.S. degree. Too, the finished
thesis may well be of practical interest to all users
and potential users of robots.

Perhaps you have some printed material which you can
simply enclose in the stamped, addressed envelope I've

included. If not, will you take a few minutes to tell
me your experiences with robots, the cost of
converting to robots (with particular emphasis on
personnel considerations), current uses of or ideas
about industrial robots, and/or possible sources?

Although I don't have to, I'd like to be able to quote
you; but I'll handle the material with whatever degree
of confidence and anonymity you specify. And no part
of this correspondence will ever be used for any
purposes other than research, I assure you.

Since I have to assemble material and start writing by
June 1, I'd be most grateful if you'd let me hear from
you before that date.

If you would like to read the finished thesis for a
new idea or two that you might be able to put to work,
I'll be glad to lend you my personal copy shortly
after August 25.

Why—besides the interest-arousing question beginning and the skillfully
subordinated facts justifying the request—did seven copies of that letter bring
five detailed replies? Did you notice (second, fourth, and last paragraphs) the
prospect and reminders of the reader's possible benefits—the last a usual one
(where fitting) of offering to share ideas? Did you notice (fifth paragraph) how
clear and specific the writer made the requested action and how easy it seems?
And did you notice (sixth paragraph) the reassurance against any fears as to
how the information might be used? And how (next-to-last paragraph) the
writer avoided seeming to push the reader around by justifying the request
for action by a necessary end date? Any one of these points may make the
difference between your getting nothing and getting what you want in a persuasive favor-seeking situation.

Minimizing obstacles

Even though your interest-arousing first sentence and justifying explanation may have supplied good reasons which highlight the reader's advantage
or interest, in most circumstances some fly is in the ointment: a negative
factor you have to overcome. It may be a sum of money you are asking for.
Then you break it down into several payments. It may be that you can offer
no fee or a smaller fee than a program speaker is accustomed to receiving;
then you cite other (perhaps intangible) rewards. It may sound like a lot of
trouble or work (say, a questionnaire). Then word it to sound as quick and
easy as possible. It may be that you're asking for secret information. If so,
give assurance that you will do all you can to protect the reader's interest.
Regardless of the case or the circumstance, you can usually find some positive
corollary to the drawback.

As added inducement, you want to make the job sound as easy as possible and as pleasurable as possible. Phrasing can do a lot here. At least you should reduce the mechanical aspects of complying with your request to the minimum of detail, time, and money. That is why most questionnaires are fill-in or checkoff forms and why a return-addressed reply device requiring no postage ordinarily accompanies such requests.

Positively anticipating acceptance

After establishing the reader's benefit or contribution, making clear exactly what you want and why (along with reminders of the benefit), and minimizing obstacles, you should confidently ask for the response you want. Hesitant, apologetic expressions belittle the request itself and have the disadvantage of suggesting excuses as reasons for refusal. Such expressions as the following hinder rather than help:

```
I realize you are very busy, but . . . .
I'm sorry to trouble you for such an apparently
insignificant matter; however . . . .
I hesitate to bother you with such a request . . . .
If you consider this a worthwhile project, . . . .
```

Eliminate such thinking (maybe by rereading the discussion on "Success Consciousness" in Chapter 4) and forthrightly name the specific action you want. Although you may have referred to it earlier, be sure to ask for it or at least refer to it near the end.

PERSUASIVE CLAIMS AND POLICY COMPLAINTS

Sometimes you will believe that you need to be rather persuasive to get results on a claim. Your reason may be that you know the other person to be reluctant to grant claims, that your case is subject to some question and you need to make as good a case as you can within the facts, or (most frequently) that you have already tried a direct claim (as explained in Chapter 5) and have been turned down.

Whatever the cause, you use C–plan organization and psychology (similar to the special request) when you need to be persuasive, and you can appeal to any desire that might motivate. Some of the main appeals (more or less in ascending order of force and objectionable tone) are to the desire for (1) customer satisfaction, goodwill, and favorable publicity; (2) a continued reputation for fair dealing; and (3) legal meeting of a guarantee.

Again your message divides rather distinctly into three parts, but their contents are somewhat different from those of the direct claim:

1. You begin by stating and getting agreement on a principle which is the basis of your claim. (In logic, it is the major premise.)

SPECIAL-REQUEST CHECKLIST

1. Your opening should stress something of reader interest.
   a. When you can, develop a benefit theme.
   b. A subject line (unsound in any C–plan letter) or unmotivated request is likely to defeat your purpose.
   c. Though a rhetorical question is usually best, one with an obvious yes or no answer stops rather than starts consideration.
   d. Are you promising too much (like total attendance of a group) or so bluntly as to be suspect?
   e. Don't appear to suggest a bribe or depend on obvious flattery.
   f. Explanations do not arouse interest; put them in the middle.

2. Keep the addressee(s) involved as you shift to your explanation.
   a. Give necessary details to prove that your project deserves consideration and to enable informed action on your request.
   b. But subordinate these details to reminders of benefit(s).
   c. Adapt your message; when you can, personalize it.
   d. If it is long, consider using name(s) in the second half or referring specifically to the city, work, or . . . .
   e. Don't phrase the exact request until after most of the benefits.
   f. Make participation sound easy—maybe even fun!

3. Any potentially negative element requires careful treatment.
   a. Elimination of a negative element is unethical and wasteful.
   b. Minimize it by positive statement, embedded position, and minimum space.
   c. Maintain a tone of confidence; avoid apologies; but, to avoid presumptuousness, also use the conditional mood in talking about requested action: *not* "you will be scheduled to speak . . ." but "you would (or could) . . . ."
   d. Don't supply excuses for nonacceptance.
   e. Give assurance that you will handle confidential or other restricted material in whatever limited way specified.

4. Introduce any enclosure skillfully:
   a. Not too early—until you have finished the key message.
   b. With emphasis on what to do with or get from it.

5. After justifying it, ask confidently for the desired action.
   a. Good action endings indicate specifically what to do, how to do it, helps and/or suggestions for ease of action, and reason for prompt action. Make specific and clear the action wanted.
   b. Justify, and establish specifically but subordinately, any time limits.
   c. Establish appreciation cordially in first-person future conditional. Offer to reciprocate if appropriate. Don't "thank in advance."
   d. When you include a return envelope, subordinate it.
   e. Inject a last punch line on the available benefit(s).

2. You explain all the facts in detail, as in any claim. (The term in logic is the minor premise.) This part may be several paragraphs long. In it you show clearly the other's responsibility.

3. You apply the facts or minor premise to the principle or major premise so as to draw a conclusion, as the logician would call it. The conclusion will point clearly to a certain action. You then request that action.

Here are two examples of how the system works. The first was an initial claim. It was successful, in spite of the fact that a glance may suggest that the writer had no justified claim. A closer look, however, will make the justification clear. The situation was quite different from a person's just buying something and finding a few days later that the seller has reduced the price. The key difference is the sales clerk's assurance to the claimant—you save no money by waiting. The appeal is therefore to the desire for customer confidence.

> Going to a lot of trouble and expense in selecting and training your sales personnel doesn't do much good, does it, Mr. Barnes, unless your customers trust them? That's why I'm writing to you.
>
> On July 5 I was in your store looking at an XXXX suit priced at $257.75. I decided to leave and wait for a late-summer sale, but your salesclerk assured me that you would have no sale on XXXX suits, that the manufacturer had never allowed its suits to be sold at reduced prices and would not do so this year. So, since I wanted the suit, I bought it.
>
> Now I notice that you have reduced the price to $235.88. My plan, you see, would have saved me $21.87. Because your sales clerk induced me to buy through assurance that I could not get the suit cheaper by waiting, I believe you will agree that I'm entitled to a refund of $21.87.
>
> I am sure that you want me to trust your salespeople. You can renew my faith by standing behind what they say.

The following illustration is a persuasive claim written after a first claim brought a proposal to compromise. It got the money, the full amount without compromise, by appealing to fair-minded analysis of the facts (and hence the injustice of compromise in the case).

> ### Claim No. 070–6289
>
> Do you think a sales representative for the XXXX Casualty Company would sell me a policy if I offered to pay half the premium requested? I don't. That would be a compromise on the value of the policy.
>
> Compromises in the adjustments on policies likewise are for cases involving doubt about responsibility or

about the amount of damage done. In my claim no more doubt arises about either than about the value of the policy.

Analysis of the facts will show that Mr. Hall ran up behind me so fast that he could not control his car and hit the left rear part of the side of my car. Clearly he was responsible. Three reputable repair shop estimates of the repair job make sure of my having a fair appraisal of the damages. The lowest of the three is $286. So no doubt exists about the damage.

Therefore I am returning the Release and Settlement form you sent and asking that you send another based on one of the estimates I formerly sent in. That is the only fair settlement.

Since your job is to keep your loss ratio down as low as possible while being fair about the obligations the company assumes in insuring clients, the solution is to settle on the basis of one of the estimates submitted.

I look forward to receiving that settlement.

Whereas claims ask restitution for mistakes, damage, or unsatisfactory products, *policy complaints* request correction of poor service or unsatisfactory policies and practices. A policy complaint may be like a direct claim or a persuasive one, but it is more likely to be persuasive, as in the following example:

Am I right in thinking that Racine Motors wants its policy on direct—sale commissions and cooperative selling campaigns to promote long—range goodwill and increased sales in this territory?

Because I think so but find the present practice is not working out that way, I think you will want to review your policies in view of my experience.

Recently one of our sales representatives called on a prospect in our territory and found "the prospect" already enjoying the reliability and efficiency of a 20—hp Racine motor, which we normally stock. Further investigation revealed that you sold the motor directly at a price below our selling price. Yet we have received no dealer's commission on this sale. This is one of several occasions brought to my attention in the past year which prompt me to ask you for a clarification of our agreement.

Admittedly with the helpful assistance of your missionary sales personnel, we have been able to sell a substantial group of the industrial users in this area on the economy and dependability of the Racine electric motor. We want to keep and expand this patronage, but that will be difficult if we are working at cross-purposes with you.

For our mutual good we and you should quote uniform prices, and we should get our dealer's commission on any direct sales. You would gain by being relieved of the marketing functions and by having a ready-made market for your motor, and we would gain by getting our just profits and keeping the goodwill of our customers. That, I thought, was the intent of the exclusive-dealership contract you signed with me.

We have been contemplating an expansion of our stock to include your 60-hp motor, which would play an important part in our sales program. Please give us a definite working policy so we will know where we stand.

PERSUASIVE REQUESTS FOR CREDIT

You can apply for credit in direct, brief style (as explained in Chapter 5) when you are reasonably sure you can meet the firm's credit tests. When you know you are going to have to ask for special concessions, however, a persuasive application patterned after the special request may be in order. The presentation establishes interest by stressing potential profitable business, stresses your capacity for management, establishes a sensible plan for meeting the obligation, and confidently asks for action.

In the following example the applicant asks for 150 days' credit, knowing that 30 days is the usual time allowed by the Long-Shearer Company. *Although the letter is unusually long, detailed, and persuasive for a credit application, it is for an unusual situation.*

Lots of auto-accessories dollars are floating around in booming Lubbock. Yet the chains sell only a standard line.

An alert independent retailer offering a complete line of parts and accessories could certainly count on the reputation of Long-Shearer accessories to give a rapid turnover and a good share of this increasing market.

Hence I am optimistic about the store I plan to open on June 24. Right on Main Street, near several garages and body shops, the 50-foot-front store is out of the high-rent district, yet accessible enough to get me my share of the walking trade.

The market survey I made last week indicates that

conservatively I can expect 300 people in my store every day. And the managers of all the garages and body shops in the area of my store have promised me they'll buy from me.

They got to know me while I worked in my father's Ford service shop during and after high school. We became better friends in the year and a half I spent in the parts department after serving in the Navy and before returning to the University of Texas to complete my degree in marketing. I made friends with them—and I learned a lot about the business. I also made friends of most of the young business leaders in town through membership in Rotary and serving a term as president of the Jaycees.

I'm willing to put every bit of the $20,000 insurance money my father left me into the new store. I have no illusions of getting rich quickly and am fully prepared to plow profits back into the store so that it will get started on the right foot. You can see from the following allocation of the $20,000 that the store will be financially sound.

With $2,000 for store equipment, $3,600 for rent and operating expenses, and $3,600 plus a small personal fund for six months' personal expenses, I'll have about $10,000 left to buy an initial inventory. For the sort of stock I'll need to have an edge on my competitors, however, I should have an initial inventory of $20,000. I would therefore like to finance a $10,000 Long-Shearer accessories stock by paying $5,000 now, $2,500 in 120 days, and the other $2,500 30 days after that.

I plan to finance a $10,000 parts stock from the Auto-Life Company in the same manner. With Long-Shearer accessories selling as well as they do, plus living close to my budget, I'm confident that these estimates allow an adequate margin of safety.

An accessories stockturn of 3 and a markup of 50 percent should give me a gross profit on accessories of $10,000 in 120 days. Since I've budgeted my own money for operating expenses for six months, almost all of the $10,000 should be left to pay for the credit stock and to reorder another $10,000 of accessories stock. Look over the enclosed order and see if you don't agree that the accessories I've ordered will sell quickly.

You'll notice that the enclosed list of references is a diversified group of Lubbock business executives,

ranging from the president of the Lubbock National
Bank to the manager of the largest auto repair shop,
the Fix-um Garage. Any one of them, as well as the
Lubbock Retail Credit Bureau, will be glad to tell you
about me.

I shall be grateful for your help in starting my new
store. With business progressing as it is in Lubbock,
and with fast-moving Long-Shearer accessories to sell,
I feel certain that the new store will be a success.

QUESTIONS AND EXERCISES

1. Do you think the basic principles in this chapter would fit the typical proposal of marriage? Why or why not?
2. What appeals would you use to
   a. Raise money for a hospice program in your city?
   b. Urge your representatives and senators to stop the government from using the area around your city for a radioactive waste dump?
   c. Get your school to give you a scholarship?
   d. Get parents to support public schools in your area?
3. Can you think of anybody in an important leadership job or other position—who did not get there by inheritance or parental pull—who is sadly lacking in the persuasive techniques discussed in this chapter? If so, how did the person get there?
4. In what ways is a special request message more difficult than a direct request?
5. Briefly describe a situation wherein *you* managed to get wanted results by using any or all of the techniques discussed here (or, wherein somebody else used them on you).
6. How do you handle the negative material in the following special request situations?
   a. An important questionnaire will take time to complete.
   b. A request for $100 for a worthy cause.
   c. A speaker's fee less than the speaker generally gets.
7. Of the four parts of a special request (listed as subheads at the beginning of the chapter), which looks to you like the hardest part? Why?
8. What is wrong with the following openings for special requests?
   a. Although we know you are a busy person, we want you to take just a few minutes to answer the questions . . . .
   b. Since you are the greatest authority on . . . , we want you to speak to . . . .
   c. We are having an international meeting, January 3, Hotel Hilton, Tokyo, Japan, and would like for you to be our keynote speaker.
   d. The enclosed brochure tells you about the new home for abused spouses.

    e.   Do you wish you could make a million this year?

9.   What do you think of the idea of end-dating requests?

10.   Reread the illustrated credit application letter and list some points to show why it is a good letter.

11.   How are special request messages like sales?

CASES

(See p. xiii for some important explanations.)

11–1.   You leased one of your villas in Maadi, Cairo, Egypt, to an actress (Janice Dolecheck) and her live-in friends, Austin Jurovics and LaRue Hytche. During two months of living in style, these people tore your villa apart by damaging the furniture and walls. In all the many years you have leased your villa, you never have had such a bad experience. You called Ms. Dolecheck in France where she was making a movie, but you got no satisfaction about a fair settlement for the $5,000 damage. Write a letter to her at Studio B, International Artists, Lac Bouchette, Lyons, France, describing the damage (you make up the realistic details) and asking for a settlement.

11–2.   *Letterhead:* University of Puerto Rico, Rio Piedras, PR 00601. *Mailing list:* 10,000 students from the university directory. *Date:* January 10, 19—. *Information:* As a member of the student government you have been concerned about the recent rumblings from the legislature about tuition increases. And these noises come close upon a large increase last year. Fellow students have been complaining about dorm facilities, lack of parking, poor advising, and class scheduling.

One legislator, Senator Anasco, has introduced a bill whereby students will be charged for half the cost of their education. What you and your concerned students committee (called SART—Students Against Rising Tuition) have in mind is to set up some kind of campus organization (a student union) to look after the rights (and some suggest the wrongs too) of students and perhaps, after you have gained support and influence, to ask the administration to give you representation on university committees. It seems logical to you that students ought to have some say in formulating the policies that will affect them for four years, and even longer if they go on to graduate school.

Your immediate problem, however, is organization. How do you overcome traditional student apathy about student government? Write a form letter that can go to students inviting them to come to an organization meeting January 22, at 5 p.m. in Centro Comercio on the main campus. Dean Jesús Garrachales has given your organization permission and encouragement to start such an organization.

11–3.   As the letter-writing consultant for a local community improvement association, write the copy for a form letter to local merchants for donations of money, clothing, candy, toys, canned goods, or other products to go in Christmas baskets to be distributed to needy families. The major emphasis is to be on money, but invite other contributions too. Except for the money (which they are to mail in), you will offer to pick up contributions at the merchants' convenience (they are to tell you time and place within M–F, 8–5). You have arranged with the local newspaper to list contributors without specifying what the donation was, in a story about the results of your drive.

11–4a. For a bulletin you are writing on various machinery, procedures, and techniques in the processing of forest products, you have devised a two-page questionnaire to go to a sizable mailing list of small mills. The bulletin, which your state university extension service will publish, is to cover your three years of research on the best methods of processing different forest products for different purposes. You are a professor of forest products in the state university—half-time teaching and half-time research through the extension division.

In return for each filled-out questionnaire, you will send respondents a marked copy of the bulletin—plus a brief statement of recommended changes for improving their operations.

Your research is complete and written up except for a section on current practices and problems. You and the bulletin editor have therefore scheduled your bulletin to go to press in two months—two weeks to get the questionnaires back, four weeks for analysis of the data, and two weeks for writing and editing. You will present the data from mills statistically—no names attached—and you will later get specific approval before writing about any individual mill's problems your questionnaire asks for.

b. While trying to work out a good questionnaire (preceding case), you decided that a questionnaire really couldn't get the information you need. So instead of sending one, you worked out a series of one-day visits to a sound sample of 15 mills on your list.

You still need to write a persuasive-request letter, however, to go to each of the sample mills to get approval of your coming and snooping and asking a lot of questions. You'll use essentially the same letter (changing names, addresses, and dates for the visits). You will want the mill to provide a well-informed company officer to go along with you through the plant and answer questions.

Of course you'll still send a copy of the completed bulletin; but worth more, you think, will be your willingness to answer questions as well as ask them and to make suggestions on the spot for improving operations. In effect you are offering your services as a consultant for one day free—the kind of thing for which you usually charge $250 plus costs.

11–5a. As a graduate student in the School of Law Enforcement and Administration, (your) State University, you are writing a thesis on the use of photography in law enforcement. A part of your research method is a questionnaire which you will send to a large number of law-enforcement agencies.

Write the covering letter you will send to induce Paul Herzog, a lawyer who is secretary to the Vermont Chiefs of Police Association, to fill out the three-page questionnaire. Data from returned questionnaires will be largely statistical (no specific names attached); but for any quotes you want to use, you will write to get specific permission. The questionnaire takes only 10 minutes (it's largely a checkoff form), a return envelope is enclosed, and you're sure Herzog has information that will be helpful and appreciated. You suspect he will be interested in your findings, an abstract of which the *Police Magazine* has already said it wants to publish. Your schedule means that you'll have to start tabulating and interpreting results in two weeks to meet both university and *Police Magazine* deadlines.

Herzog's recent speech before a national convention of law-enforcement officers, reprinted in the current *Police Magazine*, shows his concern for the bad reputations some law-enforcement agencies have developed and his interest in improving methods of investigation and data collection for courtroom use.

b. Instead of 5a, induce Herzog to speak at the forthcoming convention of your state's chiefs of police. You set the time and place.

11–6. Write a policy complaint to (any insurance company) on your Homeowner's Policy 382163 following the company's payment of $69.50 (fair) as coverage of other damages and losses you recently reported concerning a break-in at your home, but refusing payment for the reported $15.50 you paid a bonded locksmith for resetting your door locks and cutting new keys.

Significant facts: (1) As you first reported, the burglars took one set of your keys; so your four $29.50 locks became useless (until you saved the company money through the locksmith). (2) The adjuster says the policy doesn't cover the locks (which were not taken).

11–7. You know that your insurance company (offices in another city) wants to make its own descriptions and appraisals of gems before insuring. That's the answer you got to your former letter. But you want to avoid the folderol and expense by writing another letter to ask an exception to the policy for a diamond you've just bought your wife and had set in a small heart-shaped pendant necklace. You see no use in the policy in your case—and in many similar cases, where it simply causes extra trouble and expense, runs rates up, and hence deters business. Any fool buying an expensive gem would have it on record, described and appraised by a competent person (a member of the American Gem Society). That's what you did—by two registered members. Their appraisals and descriptions were exactly the same, as shown on the signed, certified, and recorded sales ticket, photocopy of which you're attaching this time: $6,875; class 1 in each of the criteria of color (blue-white), clarity, and cut; weight 0.64.

11–8. At the local power company where you are manager, your meter readers have been having trouble with biting dogs. About 10 readers sustain dog bite injuries each month, and that doesn't count the near misses. Set up a form memo that is to go along with monthly statements asking your customers to please be sure that their animals can't harm meter readers. Unless these readers have safe access to the customer's electric meter, you have to estimate the electrical usage for the month. This practice is as inconvenient to the customer as to you. You do not want to continue the present system (good readers are hard to replace, and three have quit in the last three months because of dogs). Still some people have ignored your two former little barks about this situation. See if you can, without really drawing any blood (or even fire in their eyes), convince these people that you too could become a "biter." That is, show some teeth in this bark, but don't bite—at least not yet. Be persuasive but not mean or nasty.

11–9. For Ernest Satoff, Rt. 2, Box 210, New Braunfels, TX 78130, write a persuasive letter for credit to the John Lear Farm Implement Company, Old Indianola Road NW, Topeka, Kansas 66619. He, 30, inherited 800 acres of good farm land with an old house, a good shop, an implement shed, and some old and small farm equipment from his father two years ago. Satoff knows farming, is hard working, ambitious, but lacks the capital to buy $80,000 worth of needed new equipment. He's been to see Felix Mostellar, dealer in Lear equipment, San Antonio (Case 12–15), and the two have agreed on the needed equipment; but Mostellar said that he was not in a position to sell Satoff the equipment on credit. Satoff can get reliable helpers (including relatives around New Braunfels), but he badly needs the new equipment for the scale of farming he will now undertake. He can pay $20,000 down and wants to pay the rest in similar $20,000-a-year payments. He has a good credit and farming reputation in the area, as references will verify: First National Bank of New Braunfels; Felix Mostellar, New Castle Drive, San Antonio, TX 78202; and Wilson's Seed and Feed of 4860 NW New Braunfels Road, San Antonio, TX 78311.

11–10. For an interesting variety of 11 more cases, see Appendix E: II, B, F; IV, A, C; V, C, E, F; VI, E; VII, G; VIII, I, J.

Persuasive messages: Collections

12

The only sure way for a business firm to prevent collection problems is to sell strictly for cash. Even with the most careful selection of credit customers, a credit manager will make an occasional mistake and will allow a credit sale to somebody who will not pay promptly.

Unfortunately, however, strict cash selling is also an almost sure way to keep sales and profits unnecessarily low. For that reason the old battle among sales personnel who wanted to sell to everybody, credit departments which preferred to approve sales only to gilt-edged credit risks, and collectors who insisted on prompt pay regardless of consequences has ended in compromise.

Today the thinking sales representative accepts the fact that you make no profit if you can't collect, does not try to sell without a reasonably good chance of collection, and helps the credit department find out about the chances. The credit manager accepts the fact that every sale turned down for credit reasons is a lost chance for more profit and approves sales to some marginal credit risks. Collectors remember that they *not only must collect the money but must retain the goodwill of customers* or see them drift away as fast as the sales department can bring them in.

Indeed, modern credit theory stresses selling not only to good risks but also to marginal risks as a means of increasing sales and profits. If a business firm follows this theory, as most do these days, it will have collection problems—but they will be expected and manageable, as we explain here.

Even the smallest organization today can afford a computerized information processing system (data processing plus word processing). And even an unsophisticated computerized accounting system can automatically pick out past-due accounts and type programmed collection letters to them—if a human tells it to. That is what we talk about in this chapter, what *human beings* must do in the collection process: make the decisions about number of collection efforts, types, timing, and especially their wording.

A debtor doesn't care whether a collection letter is printed by a 300-line-per-minute computer-driven printer, typed with two fingers on an old manual typewriter, or even handwritten with a quill pen. But what a human being decides the letter should say will determine whether the debt is paid now and whether the customer remains a customer.

DEFECTS OF OLD-STYLE COLLECTION PROCEDURES

In the early days of credit sales, only the best risks could get credit. When one of them did not pay promptly, the seller was surprised, disappointed in a trusted customer, and irked by the interruption to the bookkeeping routine. All these emotions usually showed up in the efforts to collect—especially in the letters, then and still the main collection means, despite some use of telephone calls and professional collection agencies. Combined with stock letter-writing phrases, these emotions led to letters characterized by curt, exasperated, injured, accusing, or self-righteous tone and ineffective appeals to sympathy, fear of getting one's nose broken, or fear of a legal suit.

Indeed, you still see such letters from people who learned all they know about letter writing years ago only by reading and imitating the poor letters of others.

Besides the old faults, all too frequently collectors send obvious form letters to collect long-overdue accounts where a form hardly has a chance, or write many short letters when a good one only a paragraph or two longer would do the job. They then defend themselves by claiming that they don't have time or money to spend on individualized letters or long letters, or by saying (without testing to find out) that debtors won't read long letters. (But tests have shown repeatedly that longer letters nearly always pull better than shorter ones, and individual-sounding letters always pull better than obvious forms in collecting accounts that are very long overdue. The apparent reason is that in the longer letters you can present enough evidence and reasoning to be persuasive, and individualized letters convince the debtor that you will not overlook the debt.)

The approach of using several poor letters delays collections and leaves the business to be financed through borrowing instead of through current collections. Thus it loses one of the main values of promptness, an improved cash flow.

The loss, however, is a small consideration in comparison with the main shortcoming of poor collection correspondence—its disposition to drive away customers that the sales department has brought in only at great expense for advertising and sales promotion. Here is a typical example:

> We are trying to avoid getting impatient over your delay in settling your account amounting to $18. The amount is considerably past due, and your failure to answer our letters (all of which we believe have been polite) has been very annoying as well as discourteous.
>
> It is therefore our intention to seek other means of collection of this account as we do not intend to let you beat it if at all possible to prevent. Just

> remember, the time to settle a debt is before it gets into court.
>
> It will be to your benefit to communicate with this office at once.

Notice that the only reason given for payment is the implied threat to sue (for $18?). Such letters increase the difficulty of collecting because they make the reader hate to pay someone so thoroughly disliked, resolve never to do business with the writer again, and tell all their friends about their mistreatment.

After seeing the losses and other ill effects of their own inept collection procedures, such as the preceding letter, many business firms began to turn long-overdue accounts over to outside collection specialists. That, however, was in many cases jumping from the frying pan into the fire. Often the specialist charged 30 to 70 percent of the debt for collecting it. But worse—as they prospered and grew into some 5,000 professional collection agencies in the United States—many of them developed more and more distasteful, goodwill-killing methods that made debtors hate them and the firms that used them.

Gradually state laws have clamped down on the most unfair or annoying practices. For lack of uniformity, complete coverage, and enforcement in state laws, the federal government passed two significant acts (effective in 1975 and 1978) that make unfair and annoying agency procedures illegal. Collection agencies can no longer use abusive or obscene language, threats of violence, extortion, harassment, "shame" lists, debt-revealing inquiries to friends or employers, pretense (of being an attorney, police officer, or government official), or other misrepresentation (like the threat or even implication of suing without clearly intending to do it).

Thus the laws encourage essentially what we have been teaching for 45 years in hundreds of university classes and in all seven previous editions of this book—learn effective but gracious collection procedures that avoid the following unnecessary losses from poor practices:

1. A series of costly collection letters when one good one would do the job.
2. Delayed collection of money needed for operating expenses.
3. Additional purchases which may be added to the account before it is closed (and thus will increase the loss if the account is uncollectible).
4. Loss of sales (customers with overdue accounts commonly trade elsewhere rather than face the embarrassment of buying where they owe money).
5. The declining chance of ever collecting (33 percent of accounts are uncollectible when 6 months past due, 55 percent are uncollectible after one year, and 77 percent are uncollectible after two years).
6. Permanent loss of many disgusted customers.
7. The unfavorable attitudes these customers pass on to other customers and prospects.

ATTITUDES AND OBJECTIVES OF
MODERN COLLECTION WRITERS

Modern collection methods can usually prevent these undesirable consequences. The trained collector takes the attitude that the debtor should pay because of a promise to do so by a certain date—which has come. So a collector need never apologize about asking for money due.

In asking, however, a good collector realizes that *people and organizations pay because of benefits to themselves rather than sympathy or any other reason*. The collector therefore not only associates the obligation with the goods through resale talk but, in persuading the debtor, points out the benefits of paying now.

The modern collector's thinking is quite analytical:

—I'm not the bookkeeper irked by broken routine. *Avoid a tone of exasperation and self-righteousness.*

—A delinquency is no surprise. Most people who do not pay promptly are still honest, and some are in temporary financial difficulty (needing only a little more time). *Avoid a curt tone. Be understanding and cooperative but firm.*

—Feel no hurt or disappointment as if let down by a trusted friend. *Avoid an injured, pouting tone.*

—Some delinquents withhold payment because they are dissatisfied with the goods or charges. *The job is one of adjustment, not collection.* (Federal law requires that sellers to consumers cannot even try to collect on customer-disputed goods or billings of $51–up for purchases within the state or 100 miles of home. The law applies equally to a holder in due course— that is, somebody like a credit-card company who has bought the original seller's rights in the accounts.)

—Some will have to be persuaded to pay. *Use the you-attitude.*

—A few, but only a few, are basically dishonest and will have to be forced to pay or marked off as losses. *Forcing payment does not include even threats of physical violence, extortion, or rumor-mongering (all of which are illegal). Civil court suit, the only legitimate forcing method, is so destructive of goodwill that you should not even mention it until you say (and mean, according to present law) it is the next step.*

Most important of all, the modern collector (unlike some predecessors) recognizes the true nature of the job and expects letters to do *two jobs:*

1. They must collect the money, promptly if possible.
2. They must also retain the goodwill of the customer if at all possible.

By adding the second job, the collector hopes to retain the customer, prevent unfavorable word-of-mouth publicity inevitably carried by a disgruntled former customer, and make each letter more likely to succeed in its first job— that of collecting. In many cases the second job is more important than the first. Certainly to collect $9.50 but lose the goodwill of a customer who has been buying hundreds of dollars' worth of goods a year is stupid.

If the collector has to sacrifice anything, promptness goes first despite the inherent losses (previously listed).

For effectiveness in both collection and goodwill, the modern collector co-operates with the sales department and may even inject some sales promotion material into *early* collection letters to a good risk when it might be of interest to the customer. It not only promotes future sales, but it shows confidence in the debtor and willingness to sell more on credit. Thus it is a subtle appeal to pride which helps to save the reader's face and goodwill. If used at the end of the letter, it relieves the sting and solves one of the correspondent's touchiest problems—how to provide a pleasant ending for a letter in which some element is displeasing.

Even when resale is not the basic collection appeal (as we discuss later), the collector can use a few phrases of resale talk to keep customers convinced of the wise decision in buying *those goods* from *that firm*—and to make the obligation to pay concrete by attaching it to the goods. The following letter includes both resale and sales promotion talk:

> You probably remember your first feelings of pleasure and pride when you saw the rich, dark wood and the gracefully proportioned design of the Ambassador office furniture arranged in your office. That furniture is the finest we have ever sold, and we were well pleased—as we thought you were—when you selected it for your office.
>
> At the time, we were glad to arrange convenient credit terms so that you could have your furniture while paying for it. Now if you will look over your bills, you will notice that those for October, November, and December have not been marked paid. The sooner you take care of them, the more pride you will retain in your furniture because each time you use it or even see it you will subconsciously remember that you are up to date on your payments.
>
> If you come to our store to make your payments, be sure to see Ambassador's new matching line of receptionist's and secretary's furniture: desks, chairs, cabinets, credenzas—everything to furnish a modern, efficient office. And of course we still carry the most complete inventory of office supplies in the area, available to you usually the same day you call.

This letter pretty well exemplifies the attitudes and objectives of modern industrial and retail collection writers: Ask for the money without apology because it is due, persuade by showing the reader benefits, use calm understanding and patience, collect but retain goodwill, and cooperate with the sales department.

CHARACTERISTICS OF THE COLLECTION SERIES

Collection procedures for businesses and for consumers differ mainly in that (1) business collections tend to progress more quickly unless they involve very large amounts, and (2) in business collections more personal contact occurs (personal calls by sales representatives and their immediate superiors, usually). Except for the more businesslike flavor of the messages, no other significant differences exist.

In trying to collect and retain goodwill, the efficient collector classifies delinquent accounts and prescribes the best treatment for each. The method is like a process of repeated siftings or screenings. Classification determines which and how many screenings each debtor will get. The procedure is a series of mailings, each of which eliminates some names from the delinquent list as they pay and aids in reclassifying and prescribing for those remaining.

To do its two jobs best, the collection series should have the following characteristics:

1. *Promptness.* Credit and collection people know that the sooner they start trying to collect after an account becomes due, the better the chance. The U.S. Department of Commerce has found that a dollar in current accounts is worth only 67 cents after six months (67 percent chance of collecting), 45 cents after a year, 23 cents at two years.

2. *Regularity.* Systematic handling of collections increases office efficiency and has a desirable effect on debtors. They see quickly that they are not going to slip through the holes in a haphazard procedure.

3. *Increasing forcefulness.* To retain the goodwill of the customer as well as collect the money, the collector starts with as weak a letter as is likely to work. Like the doctor who uses stronger and stronger medicine or resorts to surgery only as the need develops, the good collector applies more and more forceful methods and goes to court only after weaker methods fail.

4. *Adaptation.* Not all credit and collection people classify their customers into neat categories of good, medium, and poor risks as some books suggest; but all competent ones vary their procedures according to the quality of the risk (as well as according to the general bases of adaptation already discussed). Usually the poorer the risk, the more frequent the mailings and the more forceful the messages. Whereas three months might pass before anything stronger than a few statements go to a good risk, much less time might run a poor one through the whole sifting process and to court.

5. *Flexibility.* The collection procedure has to be flexible to take care of unusual circumstances. A collector would look silly to continue sending letters every 15 days to a debtor who had answered an early one with the message of being financially two months behind because of a fire but able to pay the bill by a certain date.

STANDARD COLLECTION PROCEDURES

Collection plans and procedures vary so much that only a specialized book could discuss all variations. Also, various collection theorists and practitioners use different terms to mean essentially the same things. The befuddling complexity is more apparent than real, however. Many of the differences are only minor ones of mechanics rather than significant ones of substance. Most well-planned series apply essentially the logic and psychology explained in the next few pages to a screening process somewhat like the six-screen one shown in Table 12–1.

Of course, you would send only one mailing at each of the notification, inquiry, or ultimatum stages. The nature of the letters makes repeating them illogical. The number and frequency of mailings in the other stages vary from firm to firm, and often within firms according to class of customer and other circumstances, such as the type of business (retail or industrial) and type of sale (open account, installment).

In general, the better the credit risk, the greater the number of mailings and the longer the intervals between them. A typical retail series might be two to four reminders, two or three appeals, and one urgency letter at 10- to

TABLE 12–1

Stage	Assumption	Nature	Gist
Notification	Will pay promptly	Usual statement	Amount due, due date, terms
Reminder	Will pay; overlooked	Statement, perhaps with rubber stamp, penned note, or sticker; or form letter or brief reference in other letter	Same as above, perhaps with indication that this is not first notice
Inquiry	Something unusual; needs special consideration	One letter	Asks for payment or explanation and offers consideration and helpfulness
Appeal	Needs to be persuaded	One or more letters	Selected appropriate and increasingly forceful appeals, well developed
Urgency	May be scared into paying	Letter, sometimes from high executive or special collector	Grave tone of something getting out of hand; may review case; still a chance to come through clean
Ultimatum	Must be squeezed	Letter	Pay by set date or we'll report to credit bureau (or sue, now illegal to threaten and not do); may review case to retain goodwill by showing reasonableness

30-day intervals (which usually become shorter near the end). A series to a business or other organization would probably involve personal contacts (at first by telephone, later in person) after the reminders and just before or after the urgency letter. Especially in cases of large debts, collectors will seek to establish negotiations, and lawyers will enter the picture sooner.

The assumption, nature, and gist clearly call for modified A–plan messages in the first two collection stages (where no persuasion seems necessary) and for C–plan letters in the last three. The inquiry stage is middle ground, where one might well use either. B–plan letters would be appropriate in collections only if the debtor had asked for an unapproved concession, such as an unearned discount (discussed later).

Notification (usually a form telling amount, date due, and terms)

On or about the due date, you have no reason to assume anything except prompt payment if the customer knows how much is due, what for, the due date, and the terms. Most people will pay in response to form notices—the first sifting—which give these facts. A personal letter at this stage would insult most people by implying distrust and concern over the account. Instead of a costly letter, then, the notification is almost always a statement (bill) sent on or about the due date. Such forms have the advantage of avoiding insults and saving lots of money (especially with modern office equipment) on the large mailings while reducing the mailing list for the later, more expensive stages.

Reminder (usually forms giving basic information and adding a push)

If the notice brings no response, the collector gives the customer the benefit of the doubt, assumes oversight, and sends one or more reminders—the number and frequency depending on the circumstances (Item 4 below). The collector knows that most of the remaining delinquents will respond at this stage and further reduce the list. Therefore avoiding offense while giving the necessary information (amount, what for, due date, and terms) is an important concern.

Reminders are usually forms, in order to save both money and the customer's face, but they may be of four types:

1.   The form may be an exact copy of the original notice, or a copy plus a penned note, rubber stamp such as "Second Notice" or "Please Remit," or colorful gummed sticker. Effective examples are "Don't delay further; this is long overdue," "Your prompt remittance is requested," "*Now* is the time to take care of this," "Prompt payment ensures good credit," "Prompt payments are appreciated," "Don't delay—pay today," "Remember, you agreed to pay in 30 days," and "Have you overlooked this?"

Less effective wordings (with the apparent reasons for ineffectiveness in parentheses) are "We trusted you in good faith; we hope we were not mistaken" (undesirable implications and tone, stressing *we*); "We are counting on you; don't fail us" (selfish view); "If there is any reason for nonpayment, write us frankly" (suggests finding something wrong; lacks success consciousness); "If this checks up clear, clear it up with a check" (same criticism as preceding; the word play is questionable).

2. The second type of reminder form is a brief gadget letter:

```
We enclose a small piece of string, just long enough
to tie around your finger to remind you that you
should send your check today for $48.50 in payment of
. . . .
```

```
              --
```

```
The little alarm clock pictured in this letterhead,
like any alarm clock, reminds you that it's time to do
something you planned to do. This is a friendly
reminder that you intended to send your check today
for $28.65 . . . .
```

3. An incidental reminder (underscored in the following example) may appear in a personalized letter mainly about something else:

```
With school starting soon, no doubt you have been
planning to order some more fast-selling Queen candies
to have plenty on your shelves before the fall rush
begins.

By this time you have surely realized the advantage of
handling Queen products in your new store. You will
want to take advantage of our special Back-to-School
offer too. It includes many delicious assorted candies
popular with children.

When you mail your payment of $126 due July 30,
covering our last shipment under our invoice No. 134,
dated June 30, won't you include your next order, so
we can assure you an early delivery of factory-fresh
candies? Notice the variety shown in the latest
catalog, a copy of which I'm enclosing for your
convenience in making your selections.
```

If we let XXXXXX represent collection talk and _____ represent resale or sales promotion talk, the reminder letter may look like either of the following (usually the first, as in the preceding letter):

	This	or	*This*
	_____		
	_____		XXXXXXXXX
	XXXXXXXXX		_____
	_____		

Up through the reminder stage in the collection procedure the assumption is that little or no persuasion is necessary. Thus forms or incidental reminders can do the job more cheaply and avoid the sting that personalized, full-length collection messages would carry. You may have noticed that even the incidental reminder in the Queen candies letter is in dependent-clause structure to avoid too much sting.

4. An individual-sounding letter solely about collection is the fourth type of reminder form. For greater force in the last reminder, or to poor risks, or about large amounts, the collector may decide to write a letter that talks collection all the way and seems to be individualized. Since most delinquents have so much in common, it still may be a relatively inexpensive fill-in form if the writer watches the tone and content carefully, typing each copy (perhaps made of form paragraphs) or using word processing equipment.

The following letter for a wholesale concern, for example, adapts easily to a large number of customers. With only one fill-in (for the underscored part, conveniently placed at the end of a paragraph) besides the inside address and salutation, it will serve for a large mailing list. It has a touch of pride appeal along with the reminder to reduce the sting of the apparently individualized message.

> As owner of a successful business, you know what a good credit reputation means. You have one.
>
> That's why we immediately extended you 30–day credit on your recent order. We know that the reports of your good credit reputation are correct. And we likewise know that you'll send us payment as soon as this letter recalls the fact that you owe $85 due November 15 for . . . .

Beyond the reminder stage, however, *obvious* form letters can hardly do the job. In the inquiry stage and beyond, the very nature of the collector's working assumptions calls for individualized messages.

For the later stages of the collection procedure the collector fortunately has ample information on the credit application form and in the credit records to adapt an individually dictated letter. And earlier mailings usually have reduced the list of delinquents so that giving some personal attention to each letter late in the collection procedure is both possible and productive.

Inquiry (giving the debtor a chance to pay or explain; offering help)

When the collector has sent enough reminders to decide that oversight is not the cause of delay, another assumption comes into play. With a new customer or a poor risk it may be that persuasion or force is necessary—and thus may lead to skipping a stage or two in the usual procedure.

With an old customer who has paid regularly, however, reason says that unusual circumstances must be the cause. The collector still has confidence in the customer (based on past favorable experience), still wants to retain goodwill, and is always willing to be considerate of a person temporarily in a financial tight spot.

The logical plan, then, is to write *one* letter in a spirit of friendly understanding and helpfulness, asking for the money *or* an explanation. Because the money is the real goal (not the explanation of what's wrong, or possible ways to help), it deserves the major emphasis. Care not to offend this formerly good customer apparently in a temporary jam, however, is important. So is care not to suggest that something is wrong with the goods or the billing (for reasons explained later). The only persuasion is in frankness, the offer of help, and a considerate attitude. Most people react favorably to requests presented in such a spirit.

The letters below illustrate the technique for the inquiry stage. The first (using form paragraphs) goes out over the sales representative's signature.

In the three years I have been calling on you and we have supplied you with truck and trailer parts, Mr. Kingman, we have sincerely appreciated your business. We have also appreciated the way in which you have consistently kept your dealership's account paid up.

To a good customer and a friend, then, can I offer some help? We're sure you want to settle your account; and since some unforeseen circumstances appear to have come up, your agreement to one of these plans will give you an easy way to pay your account and maintain your good credit rating:

1. If you can, please send a check today for the full $823.40 to bring your account up to date and clear the outstanding April and May balances.

2. As an alternative, send a partial payment now for half the full amount and agree to pay the remainder in two equal installments within 30 and 60 days. If this is acceptable, just sign your name next to this paragraph and return it right away with your first check. Your signature will indicate agreement to this contractual arrangement.

3. Third, we can put you on a revolving credit plan, like many of our smaller and less well-rated customers. You may continue to keep your open account, subject to a limit of $1,000 on your open balance. The finance charge will be 1½ percent per month of your previous balance after deducting current payments, credits, and past-due insurance premiums. This finance charge becomes part of your outstanding balance. The annual interest rate is 18 percent.

4. If for some reason you cannot accept any of these three plans, tell me what the trouble is, what we can do to help you, and how you propose to settle your account.

Please answer as quickly as possible so I can report
your decision to my management.

--

I wish I could sit down and talk with you for a few
minutes about the circumstances that leave January and
February charges to you on the books.

But because of the distance, I can only study our past
experience with you, and various kinds of credit
information. Your past record of prompt payment leaves
me unconcerned about ultimate collection, but it also
leaves me wondering what's wrong now.

Please either make immediate payment of the $157.47
balance due or drop me a note today telling just how
you intend to handle the account. You'll find me
cooperative in accepting any reasonable proposal for
your taking care of it--or better, the $157.47.

You may have noticed that these letters avoid *two common collection-letter errors* that have their first chance to come up in the inquiry stage:

1. The *first* is that in writing inquiry-stage letters, collectors sometimes ask *questions about the customer's possible dissatisfaction with the goods or charges or both*. The apparent purpose of the questions is to secure some kind of answer—to keep the debtor thinking about the obligation and renew acceptance of it.

But aren't such questions pyschologically unsound? If anything was wrong with the goods or the billing, would not the debtor have made a claim? Isn't the collector practically suggesting that the debtor, by claiming something is wrong, can gracefully postpone payment and perhaps even produce an unjustified adjustment? Certainly such a suggestion works in the opposite direction from both resale talk and success consciousness.

2. The *second* common error is *backtracking*—that is, going back to the assumption of an earlier stage in the collection procedure (see Table 12–1). Apparently in an effort to save the delinquent's face, a timid collector sometimes grabs back at "oversight" (the assumption of the reminder stage) after starting a letter in the inquiry stage. If oversight is still apparently the reason for the delay, the collection series should not advance to the inquiry stage.

The same kind of nerveless collector sometimes shows the same tendencies in two other places in the collection procedure. After an inquiry-stage offer of special consideration gets no response, it sometimes incongruously comes up again in letters of the next stage.

Not many collectors will send an ultimatum and then back down on it—the worst kind of backtracking. Those who do now violate federal law as well as spoil customers and lose their respect, just as many parents do with their children by issuing ultimatums and not carrying them out.

Appeals (basically reader benefits, made increasingly forceful)

The delinquent who does not respond to a friendly inquiry evidently is taking the wrong attitude toward the indebtedness. The collector's new task is to persuade the debtor to pay.

Basic considerations. The appeal stage is the collection letter writer's main work. Four important points are guidelines:

1. For persuasiveness, write individualized messages. The earlier brief notices, reminders, and inquiries will have collected most of the accounts (the easy ones) as inexpensively as possible in terms of time and goodwill. The remaining few will be harder to collect. Usually they will require individualized (or at least individual-sounding) letters rather than forms, because of the need to be persuasive. By using information in the credit records, the collector can write individualized messages that are specific and therefore persuasive to a degree impossible in a form.

2. Develop only one or two points. Scattering shots like those of a shotgun over several undeveloped appeals weakens the message too much to reach the remaining hard-to-collect-from delinquents. Something like a rifle bullet, with all the powder behind one fully developed central theme, will be more forceful. This procedure usually means longer letters because they must be specific and say enough to make the point emphatic, but they pay off in results.

3. Retain goodwill as far as possible. Because they are individualized, pointed, full-length collection messages, appeal stage letters necessarily carry some sting. Like doctors and patients, however, collectors and debtors have to accept the fact that the needle carrying strong medicine for advanced stages of a disease often has a sting. Still, the wise collector, like the humane doctor, will minimize the sting as much as possible without weakening the medicine.

You want to be firm without being harsh. By skillfully stimulating the customer's desire to pay, you'll make both happy.

4. Select a reader-benefit appeal. Successful collection, like successful selling or any other kind of persuasion, involves showing that the debtor will get something wanted or avoid something not wanted—in other words, using the you-attitude.

Appeals to sympathy (variously called the "poor me" appeal or the appeal to cooperation) do not meet the requirement. They are fundamentally selfish.

Though a cleverly and humorously overdrawn picture of the writer's family in need might bring the money (indeed did in one well-known case), it is more likely to bring a wisecrack answer. For instance, one man built a letter around a picture of his hungry-looking wife and 11 children, with the note below: "This is why I *must* have my money." The answer was a picture of a beautiful blonde with the note "This is why I *can't* pay."

Basically, people want

1. To get the service the product supposedly gives.

2. To have self-respect and the approval of others (they have to live with both themselves and others).

3. To avoid loss of what they have and add to those things (money, property, and the credit privilege, for example).

So a collector can be persuasive by reminding debtors of their obligations to pay for what they got and by showing how they benefit in self-respect or in economic self-interest.

The true collector is therefore really a seller of those ideas—by a careful analysis of the customer, selection of the appeal most likely to succeed with the particular individual in the specific situation, and selling the idea of paying by showing the benefits. The resale, pride, and fair-play appeals show the reader how to retain a clear conscience, keep self-respect, and preserve good credit.

The resale appeal. Touches of resale belong in every collection letter to keep the debtor satisfied with the purchase and to show what came in exchange for the promise to pay, but resale may also be the theme of a whole appeal letter. Essentially it goes back and almost repeats the points a good presentation would make in selling the product. By the time the collector is through reselling, the debtor will see the good value received. That can motivate payment as the way to a clear conscience.

Although inept phrasing may make any appeal ineffective or kill goodwill, the danger is not great in the resale appeal. Really effective use of it, however, requires imagination enough to paint a vivid, interesting *picture of the product in use*—and willingness to make it complete, detailed, and long enough to be persuasive. The following letter illustrates the type:

Now that Asbex and Asbar have had time to prove their profit-making ability to you, can you say that we were right? We said that they would be a good selling team for you.

When you followed up your original Asbex order of April 15 with the April 27 order for 20 gallons each of Asbex and Asbar, you showed that you thought the fire-retarding twins would move quickly together. With your good reputation for prompt payment as our guide, we were glad to have such a desirable outlet as your store for this pair of fast sellers. Although your payment of $130 for the first shipment, invoice BT-41198, is now 10 days overdue, you can keep your record intact by sending us a check in the next mail. If you make the check for $390, you can also pay for the second shipment, invoice BT-41390, on its net date.

From all reports on the way business is in Ardmore, you'll be sending us repeat orders before long. We'll

be looking forward to serving you now that you have
learned that Asbex and Asbar fill a recurring need of
your customers.

The following letter from a building and loan collector who made the loan originally and knew the family quite well is even more personal in its resale appeal. The reference to passing pleasures in the second paragraph is a subtle way of telling Barnes, without preaching, that the collector knows where the money went—into expensive parties designed to keep up with the Joneses.

When you and Mrs. Barnes moved into your new home two
years ago, I was very proud that I had something to do
with it. If anything contributes to the pleasure of
life, it is a good place to live—and especially if
that place belongs to the occupant. I feel that much
more than mere sentiment is behind the words "There's
no place like home."

Indeed, so much of comfort, security, and pride comes
with home ownership that anyone should forego passing
pleasures that eat up income, take the savings, and
invest in a home—just as you decided to do.

The importance to you of keeping up your payments on
your loan deserves your serious attention. Perhaps by
now you are used to your home, and you take it as a
matter of course. But take a walk around the lawn.
Note the landscaping; note the beautiful architectural
lines of the building. Then go inside and think for a
minute how comfortable you, Mary, Jim, and Jane are
there.

Think where you would be without it. And suppose you
were going to build today. Instead of the $48,000 you
paid, you would now have to pay about $70,000 because
of increased prices. Really, you cannot afford to stop
enjoying those comforts.

So will you please come in and take care of your
March, April, and May payments as soon as possible?

Pride appeal.   Often resale talk joins a subtle appeal to pride, or the appeal to pride may be more or less independent of resale on the goods. In either case the writer uses practical psychology to know when to encourage pride by sincere compliments, when to needle it, and when to challenge it. A bungled approach may get a surprising answer, as did the collector who asked (some years ago; illegal now) what the neighbors would think if the seller repossessed the debtor's new car. The answer was that the neighbors all agreed it would be a low-down, dirty trick. The collector had erred in challenging instead of encouraging pride.

One collector succeeded by quoting from a highly favorable credit report on the debtor, asking if the description fit, and encouraging prompt action to retain the good reputation. Others have given percentages of customers who pay at different stages in the collection procedure and said that of course the debtor does not want to be in the minority groups at the bottom of the list. The essence of success with the pride appeal is to *encourage the debtor toward prideful actions* and to avoid the use of accusations and implications of shame as far as possible.

The following example shows the method. Note that it ends with sales promotion.

> Your choice of 18 Dustex coveralls for a total of $449.10 shows your concern not only for maintaining a dust—free environment in your plant but also for your employees' health and comfort.
>
> We feel sure that you have the same concern for maintaining your preferred credit rating. Drop your check for $449.10 in the mail today, and your account, due on March 17, will be paid in full.
>
> To help keep your "clean room" and the employees in it working at top efficiency, look at the matching Dustex hoods, gloves, and shoe covers on page 18 of the enclosed catalog. They will help keep your people cool and comfortable while preventing contamination of your clean room environment.

Another example (to a university senior) incorporates a reference that is as effective and legitimate in collecting as a left hook is in fighting:

> Twenty—seven other Lansing residents bought Monora television sets the same week you got yours.
>
> That was just a little over three months ago. Yet 23 of them have already taken care of their payments as agreed. We made a note of their prompt payments on their records. And they walked out pleased with themselves, their sets, and us.
>
> When you stop to think about it, the good credit rating you establish by promptly paying as agreed is more than a matter of personal pride. It adds to the value and desirability of your account with any store in Lansing. It's a personal recommendation too, for employers often check the credit record of an applicant for a job.
>
> Take the two minutes now to send us your check. Or bring your payment to the store tomorrow.

Fair-play appeal. By using slightly different wording, you can turn the basic pride appeal into an appeal to fair play. The wording may recall the debtor's sense of respect for a contract, feeling of duty to do as promised, or conscience that commands doing the right thing. It develops the feeling that the debtor should carry out the buyer's part of the bargain, since the creditor has been fair in carrying out the seller's. Integrity or honesty may be as good a name for the appeal. Some people call it a request for cooperation.

Whatever the name, a well-developed, positive presentation (without accusations), showing that the reader should pay to be fair, is an effective appeal. It goes back to the fundamental idea that the debtor promised to pay by a certain time for certain goods or services. Having received the benefits, the debtor knows the fair thing is to pay for them. Almost everybody wants to be thought of as fair in dealing with others. Here are two examples of the appeal:

> On the basis of your urgent need for drive rivets, and because you supplied us with references, we were happy to fill your order February 6 for eight gross of our "Stellar" ½-inch diameter drive rivets.
>
> When we filled your order, we explained that our terms on open accounts call for payment within 30 days. Our suppliers have faith that we will pay them on time, and we have faith that our customers will pay us on time, enabling us to do so.
>
> You know that your account is now past due more than 60 days.
>
> When we shipped you the drive rivets, we had faith that you would do the fair thing and pay for them promptly. Won't you renew our faith?
>
> Make out a check today for the amount past due—— $921.60——and mail it in the enclosed stamped addressed envelope. That's the fair thing to do, isn't it, Mr. Spiegel?
>
> ——
>
> How would you feel next payday if you received no paycheck?
>
> I'm sure you would feel that you had given good service and that your employer should pay for it.
>
> When we ask you for the $84.95 for the coat you bought on November 18, we are only asking for what is due us.
>
> At the time we placed your name on our credit list, we made clear that accounts are due on the 10th of the month following purchase. Perhaps more important, you accepted the terms in accepting that becoming coat.
>
> In fairness to us and to yourself, won't you please come in today and give us our paycheck according to our agreement?

Appeals to economic self-interest.   Even those who have no sense of obligation to pay for value received (as developed in the resale appeal), or of pride, or of fair play in treating decent people fairly will likely pay if their own economic self-interest is clear. You may therefore write forceful collection appeals to a debtor's desire to retain the valuable credit privilege. In fact this is the main appeal in commercial and industrial credit collection.

> Why is a prompt-pay rating like money in the bank?
>
> Both are able to command goods and services immediately when you want them.
>
> On the basis of your ability to pay and your reputation for meeting payments promptly, we extended credit immediately when you asked for it. Now we ask that you send your check for $898.76 to cover your August shipment of small jewelry, sold to you on credit just as if you had drawn on your bank account for it.
>
> Then look through the enclosed booklet. Notice the color pictures of things you'd like to have in stock for Toledo's Christmas shoppers. The heavy hollow silver plate described on page 3 is a line for moderate budgets. It's durable as well as handsome, since it's triple-plated silver on copper.
>
> Should you care to order on our regular terms, enclose a check covering your balance of $898.76 and order the new stock; use your credit as if it were another check drawn on money in the bank.

Though the following letter speaks of fair play, it is an appeal not to fair play, as explained before, but to the debtor's economic self-interest in enjoying the benefits of the credit privilege:

> Are you playing fair—
>
> —playing fair with yourself, I mean?
>
> You want to continue to get what you need promptly by merely mailing orders to your suppliers. Rightfully you can expect the best service along with good-quality products when you arrange a businesslike transaction. You will agree that your company would not be fair to itself if its actions caused it to lose this privilege.
>
> The Reliable Paint and Varnish Company has continued to honor this privilege because in the past you have always settled your account satisfactorily. At present, however, you owe us $4,723, now three months overdue, on invoice 362773 covering a shipment of 575 gallons of Reliable Dual-Coat Zinc Primer.

```
To treat yourself fairly and to preserve your
company's good, businesslike reputation, you will want
to get your account balanced promptly. Please use the
enclosed envelope to send your check today and put
your account in good condition again.
```

Urgency

When the regular collector is getting nowhere with appeals like those in the preceding letters, the next step may be stonger letters, perhaps from a higher executive taking over the final few.

When the treasurer, president, company lawyer, credit bureau, or collection agency signs letters, the psychology gives a reader the feeling that things are getting pretty serious. Although urgency-stage letters are not actually the end of the collection procedure, they should seem close.

Actually the letter sent over the signature of the higher executive is usually a forceful development of one of the appeals already discussed. It may go a bit further on the economic interests of the debtor and talk about the cost of facing suit (since the debtor would have to pay the bill and court costs), but usually not—especially since it has become illegal for professional collectors to threaten lawsuit unless really intended. Any executive knows, too, that mentioning a court suit drives customers away—and hence will postpone it as long a possible. Even now the firm is still interested in goodwill. It knows that a chance of retaining the customer remains—if not as a credit customer, as a cash customer who may still speak of the firm favorably. So the executive more frequently plays the role of helper who allows a last chance and still does not turn the screws all the way down by setting an end date. The following letter, signed by the company treasurer, illustrates:

```
When you began your business, a good reputation in
Ardmore made it possible for you to get loans, and
your hard work and prompt payments--good reputation
again--got you credit on your purchases.

This reputation is more important to you now than ever
before, for with unsettled world conditions causing
wide fluctuations in the securities market, credit
agencies are becoming more and more strict in their
policies--and businesses are learning to be more
insistent on their terms.

We have not received your check for the $260 for our
invoices 69507, covering our shipment of 10 gallons of
Asbex on April 10, and 76305, covering the shipment on
April 20 of 10 gallons of Asbex and 20 gallons of
Asbar. Some arrangement for this settlement is
necessary right away. We are willing to accept your
90-day note at 12 percent for this amount so that you
```

can retain your credit rating without lowering your
cash balance.

We would of course prefer to have your check; but for
the benefit of your business, your customers, and your
creditors, please settle your account some way with us
today.

Ultimatum

If the serious mood, the strong appeal, and the bigheartedness of the executive's offer of still another chance do not get the money, the collector will give the screw its last turn—now assuming that the only way is to squeeze the money out of the debtor. Apparently as long as any slack remains, this debtor will move around in it. The collector therefore says calmly and reluctantly but firmly that on a definite date, usually 5 to 10 days later, the account will go to a lawyer to institute suit—unless payment comes before that time. (The tendency of some collection agencies to use this approach as an insincere threat is one of the abuses the 1978 law stopped.)

Though the language of the ultimatum should be firm (and sincere), it should not be harsh. To minimize resentment, the collector commonly reviews the case at this point. Carefully worded, this letter may collect and still retain goodwill because of the fair-play appeal in the whole review. Usually it will at least collect.

It is more likely both to collect and to retain goodwill, however, if the writer is careful about these points:

1. Show your reasonableness in the past (without becoming self-righteous), your reluctance to take the present action, and the justice and necessity of it.
2. Word the ultimatum clearly, precisely, and calmly—not as a form of vengeance, penalty, or threat but as a progress report (including the usual future plans).
3. Stress the positive side (pay and keep all the advantages of your credit) instead of the negative (if you don't pay, you'll get a bad credit record—and lose in court).

As you read the letter below, notice how the writer did all of those things.

When we sent your first credit shipment, $95 worth of
Christmas supplies under invoice CA–872 on December 4,
we took the step all stationery wholesalers take when
approving credit: We verified your good credit
reputation with the National Stationery Manufacturers
Guild, of which we are a member.

The Guild's certification meant that you invariably
pay your bills. When we received a second order on
January 26, we were happy to serve you again by

shipping $42 worth of Valentine cutouts and art
supplies, under invoice CB-345. Since then we have
tried to be both reasonable and considerate in
inducing you to pay by our usual collection
procedures. Now we shall be compelled by the terms of
our membership agreement with the Guild to submit your
name as "nonpay" unless we receive your check for
$137 by April 15.

I ask you to consider carefully the privileges and
conveniences you can retain for yourself by making
that payment--the privileges and conveniences you get
from your hard-earned and well-thought-of credit
rating. You can continue buying from your old
suppliers (including us). Credit requests to new
supply houses will be approved on the basis of the
Guild's favorable reports. You will save the extra
costs of a court suit to collect, in which you would
pay not only the $137 but the court costs.

All the advantages of an unmarred credit standing
among suppliers are yours now, insofar as we know; and
we want to help you keep them so that you can continue
to stock your shelves on credit. Mail us your check
for $137 by the 15th and retain those advantages.

If an ultimatum like that does not bring the money by the date set, the
only remaining letter to write is a courtesy letter, not a collection letter, telling the customer of the action taken. Then the case is out of the collection
writer's hands and in the hands of a lawyer.

The trouble with that arrangement is that your public relations went with
the case—into the hands of the lawyer—and most lawyers don't seem to understand public relations. Therefore you should go as far as you can with your
own good collection letters.

BEGINNINGS AND ENDINGS

For most writers the beginnings and endings of letters, including collection
letters, are trouble spots. Beginnings are more difficult than endings because
the background, point of contact, and theme vary more than the desired action; therefore the beginnings require more imagination and care if they are
to be adapted and effective instead of dully standardized.

This much, however, we can say: You have to capture the reader's attention and interest and hold it through the letter. Identification of the account
(the amount due, what for, and when due) should be clear in every case, *but
these facts do not make good beginnings for persuasive letters* (those after the
notification and reminder stages); the reader has already shown lack of interest in them.

Neither are references to former collection efforts good as beginnings. Such references may sound like whining or may suggest that the debtor can *again* ignore the request with impunity. Since collection letters are bascially sales letters—selling the debtor on the benefits of paying—the collector will do well to reapply the principle of reader-benefit beginnings discussed in Chapters 8 and 11.

Just as the sales writer drives for an order at the end, the good collection writer strives to bring in a check or an explanation that will name a payment date. So the standard action ending—telling what to do, making clear how to do it, making action easy, and providing a stimulus to prompt action—is always proper except in the early stages of the series, where it would be too forceful. There, resale or sales promotion talk rather than the request for payment usually ends the letter to imply faith, appeal to pride, perhaps promote sales, and remove the sting.

Although the collector always writes with success consciousness, expecting each letter to bring results, all except the one serving notice that the account has gone to an attorney should leave the way open for more severe action.

Whenever feasible, the collection writer should make response easy for the debtor. An addressed and stamped envelope does this, provides a strong stimulus to prompt action, and pays off. (An extensive research project found an increase of 12.29 percent in responses.) Even the casual "Don't bother to write a letter; just slip your check into the enclosed envelope . . ." will show the debtor your friendly attitude and will frequently produce the check.

HUMOR IN COLLECTIONS

Generally, past-due accounts are not laughing matters for either the debtor or the collector. But small amounts early in the collection procedure are not deadly serious matters either (though some inept people make themselves look silly by writing as if they were). In the early stages, where little or no persuasion seems necessary or even desirable, the main job is to gain attention and remind the debtor. Under these circumstances a humorous touch may be just the thing. Its sprightliness will supply the attention and memory value needed. The light mood will take the sting out and make the collector seem like a friendly human being instead of an ogre.

A widely known and highly successful collection letter, the famous "Elmer" letter by Miles Kimball, pictures both kinds of collector. The writer, a friendly human, warns the debtor against the ogre Elmer, treasurer of the company, who sometimes gets out of hand and writes letters that destroy a reader's will to live. The whole thing is a detailed and ridiculous account of the kind of ogre Elmer is and the disastrous effects of the letters, plus a brief warning to pay now before Elmer writes.

Shorter humorous letters are more usual. One merely asks for the name of the best lawyer in the debtor's town, in case the collector has to sue. One collector simply mailed small, live turtles to slow payers. *Time* has long used two humorous letters for people who don't pay promptly for their subscriptions. One, on the back of the current front cover of *Time*, begins "I'm sorry—sorry I can't send you any more than the cover of this week's *Time*." It then goes into a brief resale appeal. The other begins with the assertion of how much is due, pokes fun at the usual collection letter that breaks into tears in the first paragraph and yells for the law in the second, shows how large numbers of small accounts add up, and ends with the pun that "procrastination is the thief of *Time*." Another journal begins a subscription collection with

> "CHECKING, JUST CHECKING,"
>
> said the telephone line worker when the lady jumped out of the bathtub to answer. I'm just checking to find out whether you want to continue to receive . . . .

The rest of the letter is the usual resale appeal with a standard action ending.

Another device is that called the one-sided or half-and-half letter. The writer presents what is essentially an inquiry-stage collection letter in a narrow column on the left half of the page and asks the reader to use the right half to attach a check or explain.

Though humorous touches (usually inexpensive forms) may be effective in collecting small amounts early in the series, they are too flippant for large amounts or late-stage collections. The exception is that they might serve just before an ultimatum to jolt the debtor. But we must not forget that

1. The credit obligation is a serious responsibility, and we can't expect the debtor to take it seriously if we are undignified about it.
2. A written joke is more likely to offend than an oral one.
3. Gadgeteering and humor in letters of all kinds are overrated because we hear more of the occasional successes than of the numerous failures.

COLLECTING UNEARNED DISCOUNTS

A special problem which does not fit into the regular collection procedure is that of collecting unearned discounts (that is, discounts taken when sending payment *after* the end of the discount period). The fact that the amount is usually small—always small in comparison with the volume of business the collector risks in trying to collect—complicates the problem. Moreover, some large purchasers know the collector would think twice before losing their $200 or $200,000 orders to collect an improper $4 or $4,000 discount.

Fortunately the collector usually has some advantages too:

1. When the occasion arises, the debtor is almost certainly an experienced person who will understand a reasoned business analysis. For instance, if the collector cannot get the money in early and has to pay interest on money borrowed for financing, the debtor will understand that the end result will be a revised system with no possibility of discount.

2. The sizable purchaser has almost certainly investigated various sources of supply and might be as reluctant to change suppliers as the collector would be to lose a customer.

3. The fair-play appeal can include playing fair with all the collector's other customers. That is, you cannot well allow one to take the unearned discount while requiring others to pay according to terms.

Armed thus, the collector is ready for the taker of unearned discounts. First, assuming a little misunderstanding of the terms is a reasonable start. Then make the terms clear, and overlook the improper deduction *the first time*.

When no doubt exists, the collector can certainly assume (reasonably enough) that the unjustified deduction comes from failure to check the dates—an unintentional chiseling—and that the additional money will be forthcoming after a little reminder. One writer used an analogy for the reminder by telling the story of the boy who presented nine apples as his mother's offering for the church's harvest festival. When the pastor proposed to call to thank the mother, the boy asked that the thanks be for 10 apples.

If neither misunderstanding of the terms nor failure to check dates is the reason, the collector has a real letter-writing job. Although well armed—with justice, legal advantages, and some psychology on their side—some collectors fear to go ahead. The almost inevitable result is chaos in the collection department, or at least in the discount system. Word gets around.

The bold do better. Their appeals are Item 1 above (the economic justification of discounting practices) and Item 3 (the broadened fair-play appeal). Often a good letter combines both as in the following illustrations:

> From your letter of May 25 we understand why you feel entitled to the 2 percent discount from our invoice X–10 of April 30. If some of our creditors allowed us discounts after the end of the discount period, we too might expect others to do the same.
>
> The discount you get from us when you pay within a definite, agreed-on period is simply our passing on to you the savings our creditors allow us for using the money we collect promptly and paying our bills within 10 days after making purchases. It's certainly true that your discount of $9.14 is small; but large or small, we would have allowed it if we had had your payment in time to use in making a similar saving in paying our own bills. If our creditors gave us a longer time, we'd gladly give you a longer time.
>
> Since they don't, the only solutions besides following the terms are (1) stopping all discounts, (2) taking the loss on all our sales, or (3) being unfair to our many other customers by making exceptions and showing favoritism. I don't think you want us to do any of those things, do you, Mr. Griggs?

> When you mail us your check for the full invoice
> amount of $457.14, we know that you will do so in the
> spirit of good business practice and fairness.
>
> Thank you for your order. You will find that our
> merchandise and attractive prices will always assure
> you of a more-than-average profit.

The letter above did both its jobs of collecting the money and retaining the customer. Certainly the writer was not the distrusting merchant who told a new employee that if somebody wanted to pay a bill and somebody else yelled "Fire," the proper procedure was to take the money first and then put out the fire.

The problem of unearned discounts sometimes becomes particularly difficult because you have allowed one exception, explained the terms carefully, refused to allow a second exception, and received a reply including statements like these:

> . . . I thought that an organization such as yours
> would be above such hair-splitting tactics . . . and I
> resent your hiding behind a mere technicality to
> collect an additional $3.69 . . . oversight . . . . If
> you wish . . . a new check will be mailed, but . . .
> it will be your last from us.

Here's how one collection writer handled this hot potato—successfully:

> I appreciate your letter of December 5 because it
> gives me an opportunity to explain our request that
> you mail us a check for $184.50 in place of the
> returned one for $180.81.
>
> Our sincere desire to be entirely fair to you and all
> our other customers prompted the request. For years we
> have allowed a discount of 2 percent to all who pay
> their bills within 10 days of the invoice date. Such
> prompt payment enables us to make a similar saving by
> paying our own bills promptly. Thus we pass on to you
> and our other customers the savings prompt payments
> allow us to make.
>
> But if our customers wait longer than the 10 days to
> pay us, we make no saving to pass on. Of course, an
> allowance of $3.69 is a small matter; but if we
> allowed it in one case, we would have to allow similar
> discounts to all our customers or be unfair to some.
>
> I feel sure that you want us to treat all customers
> alike, just as you do in your own business. Certainly
> I do not think you would like it if you found that we
> were more lenient with somebody else than with you.
> Our request for the additional $3.69 is necessary if
> we are to treat all alike.

COLLECTION LETTER CHECKLIST

1. Follow a reasonable philosophy and adapted procedure.
    a. Associate the specific goods with the obligation to pay for them, and show that you expect payment because it is due.
    b. Always identify how much is due and how long overdue.
    c. Except in the first two stages and the ultimatum, the points in *b* and *a* are not good beginnings.
    d. Stick to your sequence of assumptions for different collection stages; backtracking shows weakness and loses reader respect.
    e. Try to get the money and keep the customer's goodwill.
2. Fit the tone carefully to the circumstances.
    a. Avoid seeming to tell the reader how to operate.
    b. Nasty, curt, injured, pouting, exasperated, or harsh tone doesn't help; it turns the reader against you instead.
    c. Scolding or holier-than-thou attitude brings resentment too.
    d. To avoid credit platitudes, relate credit principles and regulations to the particular case.
    e. Show confidence that the debtor will pay, by
        (1) Avoiding references to past correspondence (except in late-stage reviews).
        (2) Stressing positive benefits of payment.
    f. Be sure any humor avoids irritation or distraction.
    g. Avoid (1) accusations, (2) apologies, and—except in the reminder and inquiry stages—(3) excuses invented for the reader, including any hint of fault in the goods or billing.
    h. To increase the force, use more collection talk (and less sales promotion—good only in early letters to good customers).
    i. To decrease stringency and apparent concern, reverse *h;* watch proportions.
3. For persuasiveness (after the first two collection stages):
    a. You have to stress what the reader gains by doing as you ask.
    b. Remember the effectiveness of a developed central theme.
    c. Select an appeal appropriate to the circumstance and reader.
    d. Remember that any kind of antagonizing works against you.
    e. Individualize your message for stronger effect, even in forms.
4. Guard against the legal dangers.
    a. Reporting the delinquent to anybody except those requesting information because of an interest to protect is dangerous.
    b. Don't threaten physical violence, blackmail, or extortion.
    c. Be careful about your facts, and show no malice.
    d. Be sure that only the debtor will read (seal the envelope).
5. Adapt your drive for action to the stage of the collection.
    a. A full-fledged action ending is too strong and stinging early.
    b. But in the later stages, anything short of it is too weak.

> Thank you again for writing me and giving me this chance to explain. May we have your check——in fairness to all?

This—a letter refusing to allow an unearned discount or some other concession when forcefully requested—is the only likely kind of situation for B–plan collection letters. But it is not the usual B situation. Here you're not just refusing to do something for the other person (give a discount). You're refusing to *let* that person *not* do something (send you the extra money). That is, you have to say both "I won't do what you ask" and "Now you do what I ask." It's a combination of the two most difficult kinds of letters—the B–plan and C–plan—and hence an appropriate culmination of your study of letters and end of our treatment of them.

*   *   *   *   *

Because collection letters vary so much, they have few universal truths suitable for a specific checklist such as we have provided for some other kinds. The broader suggestions we have provided, however, will be helpful as a partial checklist.

QUESTIONS

1. How would you rank (most important first) the possible results from poor collection practices?
2. Do the two jobs of a collection letter always rank in the same order of importance? Why?
3. Of the five characteristics of a collection series, which three do you think are most important? Why?
4. Of the six stages a collection series may go through,
   a. In which three would you never send more than one mailing? Why?
   b. In which one are you most likely to get into trouble?
   c. In which one are you most likely to send more than one message?
5. What is the assumption a collector makes at the inquiry stage?
6. An incidental reminder of the debt, included in a personalized letter mainly about something else, is characteristic of what stage in the collection process?
7. Asking in a collection letter whether the debtor is dissatisfied with the goods or services is one common error. What is the other? At what stage(s) is it most likely?
8. Of the four basic appeals to persuade a debtor to pay,
   a. Which is least likely to offend?
   b. Which is most likely to offend?
9. Which of the four basic appeals is most used in commercial and industrial credit collection?
10. Which of the four basic appeals would you use to collect an unearned discount?

11. When can you legally threaten lawsuit?

12. In the late stages of a collection series, how would you end the letters?

13. What reader benefits might encourage

    a. A recent college graduate to pay back a student loan?

    b. An owner of a new restaurant who owes $4,000, 60 days past due, has a good location, works hard (but manager says business is off)?

    c. A homeowner to pay mortgage payment for last month and month before?

14. What are some reasons a slow payer might give you for not paying?

15. How does a collection series to a retailer from a wholesaler differ from that of a retailer to a consumer? How are they similar?

16. Suggest any better wordings you can for the assumptions a collector makes at the various stages in a collection series.

CASES

(See p. xiii for some important explanations.)

12–1. Recently your (Agee Business Forms, 5265 W. Pierson Rd., Flushing, MI 48433) sales department signed up a new customer, Mannion & Fitzsimmons Fuses, 910 E. 2d St., Winona, MN 55987 (general manager: Marjorie Youngquist). With an initial order came a financial statement, credit report, and references. Your usual check showed that Mannion & Fitzsimmons was on occasion late in paying but did eventually pay bills. You (Agee's credit manager) granted this new customer an open account with a $5,000 limit. Your normal practice is to offer no cash discount, payment due 30 days after date of invoice.

Mannion & Fitzsimmons ordered $4,756 worth of continuous letterheads and envelopes (like the usual letterheads and envelopes, but attached to each other at top and bottom and fan-folded, like computer printout paper, for continuous feeding through a computer printer). When your invoice was first past due, you sent a copy of it as a statement. Two weeks later you sent a reminder (copy of invoice prominently rubber-stamped "Past Due"). Now another two weeks have gone by. Write this new customer a letter.

12–2. Since reminders have not worked, send an appeal letter to Mannion & Fitzsimmons Fuses.

12–3. Mannion and Fitzsimmons Fuses ignored your appeal and the bill is now 12 weeks past due. You will have to take stronger steps with this new customer who placed only one order. Unfortunately your sales representative in Minnesota is ill and can't personally investigate the reasons for not paying your invoice. Prepare an urgency letter for the signature of Agee's executive vice president.

12–4. For several years Midwest Striping Co. (5216 S. Westnedge Ave., Kalamazoo, MI 49008) has had a contract to repaint the stripes on Coronal

Supermarket parking lots (67 big supermarkets in Michigan, Ohio, and Indiana). Recently Coronal notified Midwest to repaint the parking lot at the Elkhart Indiana, store. Midwest did, and as Midwest's office manager (and credit manager, personnel manager, advertising manager—it's a small company) you sent the usual invoice to Coronal's headquarters (4215 Fallcreek Pkwy., Indianapolis, IN 46202).

Coronal didn't pay for the Elkhart job. You sent the customary end-of-the-month statement and Coronal paid all the items except for the Elkhart store. You had better send a reminder (addressed, as usual, to the purchasing manager). Since Coronal has always paid promptly, make this reminder a letter. While extolling the virtues of the new longer-lasting vinyl-based paint you now use, see if you can get Coronal to bring its account up to date.

12–5. Your reminder to Coronal Supermarkets (Case 12–4) brought no results. Write an inquiry letter to Coronal over your signature (as office manager of Midwest Striping) to find out what is wrong or get the money (the contracted price of $.007 per square foot plus $.15 per mile). At 210′ × 480′, the Elkhart parking lot is 100,800 sq. ft. ($705.60). Mileage round trip was 154 ($23.10). Coronal should either pay the $728.70 or tell you why not.

12–6. Although Coronal Supermarkets has been a good customer and is still authorizing Midwest Striping to repaint various parking lots, you have received no payment for one job you did, the Elkhart, Indiana, store. Strangely Coronal has paid all your invoices promptly except those for Elkhart. And Cronal has ignored your inquiry letter.

Bearing in mind that Coronal is a good customer, write an appeal letter to the purchasing manager, basing your appeal on resale (work done quickly and with least disruption of store traffic, four years of smooth relations, quality materials and workmanship, your guarantee to make any faults good, customer confidence built by your professional striping jobs on its parking lots, increased safety, and whatever else you can think of that will help).

12–7. Coronal didn't reply to your appeal, but otherwise its relations with Midwest Striping are smooth and normal. Write another appeal, but this time base it on fair play.

12–8. Since Coronal Supermarkets has not acknowledged your two appeal letters, you will have to go to the urgency stage. Keep it calm because meanwhile Coronal has been giving your company (Midwest Striping) work and paying everything (except the Elkhart bill) promptly. Your boss, the owner of Midwest Striping, will sign the letter. Drive for either the money, part of the money, or at least an explanation.

12–9. *From:* Inter-Galactic Corporation, Coomaraswamy Road, San Francisco, CA 94107. *To:* John Shellabarger, Office Machines, 9200 Evergreen,

Chicago, IL 60627. Shellabarger purchased three Model I word processing machines for $15,000 on terms 2/10,n/60, but he has not paid anything. You sent the usual discount-reminder note, then the usual due-date statement, and another statement with a penned friendly reminder on the bottom 15 days later. You also wrote an excellent appeal-stage letter when the account was 110 days old (50 overdue) and an urgency-stage letter when the account was 130 days old (70 days overdue).

Still Shellabarger ignores your letters; so today when the account is 110 days overdue, you write him the ultimatum. He has 10 days to pay or you will turn his name over to the Manufacturer's Guild (but don't let it sound spiteful). Stress the positive side (pay and keep all the advantages of credit). Show your reasonableness (not your holier-than-thou-ness) in the past, your reluctance to take the present action, and the justice and necessity of it. Word the ultimatum clearly, precisely, and calmly. When his name is listed with the Manufacturer's Guild, he will have a difficult time getting new sources of credit—and his old ones may dry up unless he waters them regularly.

12–10. Maier Laboratories (3005 Elm St., Dallas, TX 75226), manufacturer of "essential oils and aromatic chemicals," recently filled an order for $812.36 worth of fragrances and essential oils from Strauss Perfumes, 2465 Stirling Rd., Ft. Lauderdale, FL 33312, a small blender of custom perfumes. Maier has sold to Strauss Perfumes before, and Strauss paid the invoices fairly promptly. The invoice for $812.36 is now four weeks past due. You, Maier's credit manager, sent two reminders, but without result. Now send an inquiry letter. You know the perfume industry is in a down cycle, but you have to have your money.

12–11. Your inquiry to Strauss Perfumes brought no answer and no money. Now, three weeks later, write an appeal based on economic self-interest. If Strauss doesn't settle the invoice for $812.36, you will have to report it to PCH (Perfumers' Clearing House). That could cut Stauss off from all credit, forcing payment in advance for all future purchases.

12–12. Two weeks have passed and Strauss Perfumes has not responded to your appeal; so you will have to use stronger medicine. Prepare an ultimatum letter for the president of Maier Laboratories to sign. If you do not have payment or hear from Strauss in 10 working days, you will inform PCH of its delinquency and turn the invoice over to your collection agency.

12–13. You customarily allow your customers to deduct 2 percent when paying your invoices if they pay within 10 days of the invoice date. But Sebastian Brothers, 5518 W. McNeeley, Ellettsville, IN 47429, paid its last invoice 34 days after the invoice date and still took the 2 percent discount, something it has done before. As the credit manager of Cowan & Hoffmann, 60 Spring Glen Dr., Granby, CT 19607, write Alonzo Sebastian, president, a letter calling a halt to this taking of unearned discounts and ask for a check for the $38.88 discount Sebastian Brothers took on your invoice No. 4115 for $1,943.76 for piano string pegs and hammers, dated May 13 and paid on June 16, check no. 5822.

12–14. Your letter to Alonzo Sebastian brought a sharp reply, excoriating you for "chasing after a paltry $38.88" and refusing to refund the discount. Don't take no for an answer. You can't let this go on. Your company can't give up 2 percent of its gross profit for nothing. Using all your persuasive tools, write Sebastian again for a check for the unearned discount. Would you tell him you are not going to allow him any discount at all on future invoices?

12–15. As credit collection manager of John Lear Farm Implement Company, Old Indianola Road NW, Topeka, Kansas 66619, you must write Felix Mostellar, dealer in Lear equipment, New Castle Drive, San Antonio, TX 78202, a dependable customer for the past five years, who still owes $3,500 for equipment purchased four months ago on terms 2/10, n/60. You have sent a regular due-date statement and a reminder letter from your form series on the 21st day of delinquency. Mostellar ignored them. Though you suspected the reason—in southwest Texas the drought has hurt the crops and thereby hurt the farmers—in view of your past experience with Mostellar, you skipped the inquiry and appeal stages and were about ready to write an urgency letter when you did hear from Mostellar—a high-spirited, joshing, joking letter blaming the weather, no crops, and the laborers who won't work. He tells you that he can't collect from the farmers who owe him. You admire his good spirits in view of the hard times, you are sympathetic, and you feel like entering into his jovial mood (probably a case of "whistling-in-the-dark psychology")—but you can't afford to lose the $3,500, or even to forgo payment much longer. Write Mostellar the best you can. You are not hard-hearted enough for an ultimatum. You might want to read the text section on "Humor in Collections" and see if you want to use the old collector's joke with him—that you love him but since you aren't his mother he can't expect you to carry him a whole nine months.

Reports—written and oral

part 3

Why study report writing?

As we said about memo and letter writing, two basic facts about report writing are that (1) regardless of the work you do (except work for yourself or for wages), your ability to prepare good reports will be an important consideration in whether you get a good job and how fast you move up on the job; and (2) most people who have not studied how to prepare and present reports do it poorly.

The basic language of *good* reports differs little from the standard English appropriate in any good functional communication. Though report forms deserve some attention, you can learn them easily. So if you have done well in a good course covering letters and memos (as presented in the preceding chapters of this book), you have a running start on a course in report writing. (If not, you certainly need to study Chapters 1, 2, and the first big section of 4 prior to studying reports.)

Good reports, however, require more preliminary preparation effort, more objective style, and use of certain supplementary communication techniques rarely learned except in reports courses. If you think about the meaning of *communicating through reports,* you'll realize that preparation *before* writing involves most of the work: making a plan, getting the facts or evidence (research), organizing for meaning and coherence, analyzing this material to arrive at an interpretation and solution to the problem, and *then* writing up your analysis as clearly, concisely, and objectively as you can.

You'll realize, too, that improving your ability to do all these things is an important part of a liberal education and especially the kind of education needed to cope with today's information-oriented world. Because reports serve so many important purposes in almost all fields, an educated person needs to know how to prepare them well to perform effectively. Study and practice in preparing and presenting reports *will* help you, therefore, when you're a job candidate and when you're on almost any work assignment.

History, functions, and present need of reports

In early history nobody needed reports. Almost everybody operated a complete one-person business or directed a small group of people under an on-the-spot-manager, who had all the facts needed for making managerial decisions. When a shipowner operated a small ship, for example, observation provided all the information needed and thus served the one general function of most reports—*to help the receiver make a decision by providing needed facts and/or ideas*.

Later, as society became more complex, some individuals gained power as tribal chiefs, masters, or employers—and found reports essential. When one of these managers sent somebody to scout an enemy tribe or do some work, part of the job was a report indicating difficulties encountered and suggestions on such things as materials, personnel, necessary time, and plans for overcoming the difficulties. For example, when a successful shipowner built a second ship and put a hired captain on it to develop trade along a different route, the owner needed reports to make wise decisions about future operations. Thus the ship's log came into being as one early form of written report.

Specific ways reports serve. The impossibility of a manager's being in two places at the same time made reports necessary. Overcoming the problem of *distance*, then, is the first specific function reports may serve in achieving their general purpose.

When organizations grew to where the manager could not find time to oversee all operations (sometimes even under the same roof) and some of the processes became so technical that the manager did not have the knowledge to evaluate all of them, reports became more and more widely necessary to solve two more specific problems: *time* and *technology*.

With the increasing complexity of society, *records* became more important too; and as their fourth specific function, written reports provided permanent records. Thus they became important in preparing tax returns, in preventing later repetition of the same work, and (through extra copies) in informing interested secondary readers.

As managers became responsible for more and more varied activities, the wiser ones realized that they could not do all the necessary thinking about new products, processes, and procedures. They therefore invited employees with initiative to submit ideas in reports. Hence reports began to serve management in a fifth way as vehicles for *creative ideas*.

As managers became responsible for numerous employees, some of whom they rarely saw, they often found that submitted reports were the best indicators they had of how well an employee was doing an assigned job. Thus reports began to serve in a sixth way—as a basis for *evaluating the employees* who presented them.

You see readily that reports have become essential tools of modern management if you bring these trends up to the present world of large and complex organizations, where

—Top management may be thousands of miles from some operations.

—Management cannot possibly find time to oversee all the activities (even in one location).

—Some of the processes are so technical that no one can be competent to decide wisely about all of them without guidance through reports from specialists.

—Numerous records are necessary to keep various involved people informed.

—Competition pushes a manager to use all the creative brainpower of all employees in developing new ideas, through reports and other means.

—Personnel managers may never see employees they have to evaluate for raises, promotions, and (sometimes) the opposite.

Questions reports answer.   In helping managers in those six ways, reports help with decision making by answering one or more of three key questions:

1.   Is the project under consideration feasible?   In thinking about any proposed action that is not obviously possible, the decision maker's only logical first question is whether it *can* be done. Can you imagine spending time or money considering other questions about any project until you have a favorable answer to the necessarily first question of *whether it can be done?* Michigan could not, in thinking about building the Mackinac Straits Bridge; nor could the U.S. government in thinking about trying a landing on the moon.

2.   Should we take a certain proposed action?   With feasibility established, decision makers trying to decide on a proposed new product, plant, or other project will want—in answer to a second question—a report showing whether expected benefits will result in higher profits, better quality or quantity, or less time, material, or effort expended. That is the cost-benefits question. Particularly in reports for public institutions, at least some of the benefits are likely to be in terms of better service, safety, goodwill (including international relations), law enforcement, ecology, health, or education.

3.   Which is the best (or better) way (or solution)?   Only with the feasibility and benefits established can one logically consider this third question. Then the study and report may consider a choice between or among proposed ways, or it may have to propose and evaluate different ways to lead to a choice. Often the answer is a choice between the present way and a proposed new way or between repairing the old and buying the new . . . . It may be a choice between or among products to buy for a given purpose (office or farm equipment, line of trucks), financing procedures (buy or lease), or location to seek a job or establish a plant.

Any board of directors, president, governor, manager, superintendent, or department head in any organization—public or private—wants satisfactory answers to all three questions before approving substantial expenditures, changes in operations, or new regulations. Many times those questions lead to the assignment of reports. For this reason management today expects all employees (except possibly day laborers) to be able to prepare and present reports.

If you need more evidence that learning to present better reports will be a worthwhile activity for you, consider how your study of reports can help you as a student, as a job candidate, and later as an employee.

Help when you're a student and job candidate

Learning the things necessary for a good report can help you to earn better grades. Increased familiarity with sources of information—not just published sources and how to find them in libraries, but also methods of securing original data—enables you to do research more efficiently for papers required in other courses. (Reports are certainly not like term papers in objective or in some phases of treatment, but the information-gathering research behind them is similar.)

Documenting—that is, backing up what you say with factual evidence, citing publications you use as authorities or sources of information, and explaining your research methods to assure soundness—is also similar in reports and term papers. Certainly you'll profit from the carry-over of organization principles and improved language ability. For these reasons students who have studied and applied reporting principles usually earn better grades on term papers in advanced undergraduate courses and hence better grades in the courses.

If you go on to graduate school, you will find that your study of reports has been your most useful preparation. When you have to write the many long research papers and a thesis, you will already know how to collect, organize, and interpret data and to write up your findings in good style—using techniques and readability devices learned only in studying reports. Indeed, you will probably join the many graduate students we have heard make comments to the effect that "Thanks to my reports course, I know how to go about writing course papers and my thesis."

When you apply for a job, you'll find that employers put a premium on the services of people who can produce good letters and reports. Because reports play such a prominent role in most businesses, prospective employers often give preference to applicants who have learned how to prepare and present them. They prefer to hire people who can already do so rather than to spend vast sums of money on company-sponsored reports courses (as hundreds of companies do) for people who have not had such preparation.

Directors of college placement services report that an increasing number of talent scouts (recruiters) ask, as one of the first questions, what grade a prospective employee earned in reports. (Note that they assume students have taken the course.) These recruiters apparently regard the performance of the student in a college reports course as an indication of abilities that are important to their organizations.

Help when you're on the job

If you are surprised by the interest *prospective* employers have in your ability to produce good reports, you may be even more surprised by their interest as employers. The reports a trainee on a new job usually has to submit may not only help to determine assignment to a division of the company but they also often determine whether to promote or drop the employee at the end of the training period.

Even after you become a full-fledged employee, typically your superiors will study your submitted reports not only for information and ideas but for evidence of your ability to communicate clearly, quickly, and easily. To an immediate superior, you will often report orally; but your immediate superior is not usually the one who makes the final decisions about salary increases and promotions. Since those who do may never have met you, they often consider equally important your immediate superior's evaluation and your *written* reports. Employers often regard reports as the best (and sometimes they are the only) indication of how well an employee is doing the job.

Your study of reports, as you see, can help your grades in school, your chances at a desirable job, and your effectiveness and status in your career. Indeed, a recent study of how top executives got there showed that many of them mentioned their reports as important to their various promotions. The board chairman of the world's largest corporation (AT&T) gave major credit to his reports. You can hardly find a better set of rungs for the ladder to success than a series of good reports.

(A more specialized ladder—though not exactly a report, a first cousin—is the proposal. You therefore might want to take a look at Appendix D.)

Reports: Definition, classification, and short preparations

13

[Wanting to know is the first big step toward wisdom.]

DEFINITION AND CLASSIFICATION OF REPORTS

In our preceding discussion of the general and specific functions reports serve, you have seen several implications of their nature. Yet the word *report* is such a broad concept that most attempts at one-sentence definition are either incomplete, too general to be useful, or not quite true. We therefore give you an *extended definition*.

Definition. An extended (or expanded) definition starts with a four-part *standard definition*—that is, one sentence involving

1. The term to be defined,
2. A copulative verb (usually *is*),
3. The genus or general class to which the term belongs, and
4. The differentiae (the specifics that distinguish the term from others in the same general class).

Then the extended definition explains more fully with such things as analyses, etymology, characteristics, and different species or classes; history, uses, and importance; and construction and/or method of operation and example or illustrations.

To make clear what we mean by *report*, we now define the term by all those methods except the three already used (history, uses, and importance) or the three to be used later (construction, method of operation, and examples).

The best *standard definition* we know for *report* is this: ***A report is a presentation of facts and/or ideas to people who need them in decision making.***

Analysis of that definition involves several points: A presentation may be oral or written (as reports may be). "Facts and/or ideas" covers the possibilities of just facts without interpretation, facts *and* interpretation, or just interpretations of already known facts—and that statement fits.

Perhaps the most discriminating part of the definition, however, is the last part. As we use the term here, a report *does* go to somebody who faces a problem of making some kind of decision; and the purpose of the report message is to help in making a wise decision. That, you recognize, rules out such things as term papers and write-ups about books read—things often referred to in academic circles as reports.

Etymology can help in defining *report*. One meaning of *re* as a prefix is "back," as in *recall*. The *port* is from *portare* ("to carry"). Hence the Mountain States Telephone executive who explained a problem and assigned a report-writing job quite properly said "Find the answer, Jim, and bring it back."

Still, the best way to get a clear idea of the meaning of the word *report*—as of many others—is to consider the *usual characteristics* of reports, along with the special characteristics of different classes. Here, therefore, we give you those *characteristics*.

Usually, but not always:

1. A report is a management tool designed to help an executive make decisions. Thus it is *functional* communication for the *benefit of the receiver*. The important person involved is the receiver, who wants some useful information which is not already available—quite a different situation from a professor's receiving a term paper from a student.

2. A report is an assigned job. Usually the assigner will make clear the kind of report wanted; if not, the reporter should find out by asking.

3. A report goes up the chain of command. A few reports go between people of equal rank, as between department heads, and some (usually better called directives) go downward from executives (but most reports executives prepare go to still higher authorities—boards of directors, legislatures, or the people who elected them).

4. A report is for one person or a group (usually small) unified by a common purpose or problem, and usually having a leader who authorizes (orders) the report and thus becomes the primary addressee. A primary reader, however, may then send a written report on up the chain of command to just a few higher executives or reproduce it and send copies to the whole group. Corporation annual reports, aiming primarily at groups unified as stockholders or employees, have unusually large readership for a report.

5. A report gets more than normal attention to organization. Of course, all good communications are organized; but because reports are usually expositions of complex facts and ideas for practical purposes and for busy receivers, reporters work harder at organization than most other communicators. (Still the most common serious criticism of reports is their poor organization.)

6. A report makes more than normal use of certain techniques and devices for communicating clearly, quickly, and easily. (Though these techniques and devices can be very useful in almost any kind of communication, good courses on reports seem to be about the only places they get adequate attention, as in Chapter 14.)

7. A report should be accurate, reliable, and objective. No executive wants to base decisions on a reporter's errors, assumptions, preconceptions, wishful thinking, or any kind of illogic. Therefore a good reporter strives to be as objective as possible—though nobody can be strictly objective because selec-

tion of facts to include and evaluation of them will vary according to who (what kind of person, as a product of background) is doing the selecting and evaluating. (See Appendix A.) And where the receiver might otherwise question the validity, the reporter explains sources and methods of collecting data to show the soundness of the facts presented.

8.   Good reports—like good buildings, pieces of furniture, or anything else—vary in design according to their functions and conditions of use. People who deal with them have naturally given names to the different designs and then tried to classify them—and there they have run into trouble. A strictly logical classification of reports is impossible because the various "namers" have shifted bases for their various names. To remove some of the confusion, however, we give you the following explanation and *classification* as the best we know for *(a)* clarification and *(b)* use of names most widely accepted (though we can't say universally).

Classification.   From the reporter's standpoint the most important *classification* is **on the basis of content**—whether the report includes only facts (an *informational* report) or whether it goes further into interpretation (conclusions and/or recommendations) and becomes an *analytical* report. A reporter can go wrong, and probably be embarrassed, either way. If the person who authorizes a report does not indicate which kind (informational or analytical), the reporter should ask.

Two kinds of confusion often attend that important two-part classification. Since an analytical report has more in it than one giving the bare facts on a subject, it is naturally longer. Hence some people refer to any *long* report as analytical and (at least by implication) think of *short* reports as *informational*. They may be wrong in all directions; long or short, a report may be analytical or informational.

Similarly, since long reports are more likely to be somewhat formal than are shorter ones, we often see an analytical report on a sizable subject referred to as a *formal* report and shorter ones as *informal*. In fact, no necessary relation exists between the length of a report and its formality. The only legitimate basis for calling any report formal or informal is the degree of formality in its style; and that should be a reflection of the relationship between reporter and receiver(s).

We see no use for **classification on the basis of subject matter** that produces such names as engineering reports, business reports, or technical reports. Regardless of the subject matter, the principles don't change, though the subject matter and sometimes the formats do. Furthermore, nobody ever completes such a classification (perhaps because doing so would serve no purpose and would require some detailed identification system such as the Library of Congress or Dewey Decimal systems used in libraries).

Other minor **classifications on various bases** are all more clear-cut than the immediately preceding. Perhaps the neatest is that on the basis of the issuing schedule. *Periodic reports* (coming out regularly—*daily, weekly, monthly,* *quarterly*, or *annually*) are the counterparts of *special reports* (prepared when a special occasion arises). Similarly the names of two other two-part classifications make their bases clear: *private/public* and *internal/external reports*.

Somewhat similarly, the names *letter* and *memo* (or *memorandum*) *report* mean that the reports are written in those forms (of any length, though usually short; informational or anlytical; and about any kind of subject matter).

At that point, however, form as a basis of naming and classifying reports stops—unless you want to consider the *credit report* as a special form. In actual practice it usually is, because the sameness of subject matter and purpose have led to a nearly standard form. But variations are enough that you cannot use the name to mean necessarily a certain form.

Two other often-used names of reports (which we treat later) clearly indicate their bases of classification and refer to true independents. *Progress reports* explain what has been done on a project and usually try to predict the future (both in relation to any preset schedule). *Justification reports* (usually short and sometimes called *initiation reports* because the reporters usually initiate them) propose certain specific actions and provide evidence to show the wisdom of those actions. As such, the justification report is much like a well-prepared suggestion that might be dropped in a firm's suggestion box.

The term *research report* may mean merely that preparation required some research (as most reports do). Most authorities, however, restrict the name to mean a report of research done to push back the forefronts of knowledge (often called pure or theoretical research) and perhaps without any immediate, practical applications in mind. To avoid being misled, you have to know who is talking. (When we use the term, it carries the second meaning.)

Since we deal largely with analytical reports (on the principle that anybody who can prepare them can leave out the interpretation and make informational reports), the primary basis of classification in our treatment is length. We call them *short reports, short analytical reports* (usually 6 to 10 pages), and *complete analytical reports* (or long reports, usually 10 or more pages).

Admittedly our naming is imperfect (as is any other we've seen), but we think ours is more functional. By *complete* we mean not only "with interpretations" but also including all the standard parts; hence such reports are usually long. The short analytical report has interpretations, but it may omit certain standard parts or combine them as explained in Chapter 15.

For the reporter, much more important than knowing the names and classifications of reports (except possibly the distinction between *informational* and *analytical*) is close attention to the characteristics reports should have: They should be full of useful information that is *accurate, reliable, and objective; presented in functional rather than literary style; adapted to the receiver(s); carefully organized; and clearly, quickly, and easily understandable*. That relates directly to the preparation of reports—our main concern in the rest of this and the next three chapters.

BASICS OF REPORT PREPARATION

Preparing an analytical report (short or long) is a five-step process. Because the steps become more complex as the report length increases, here we give you adequate explanation for only short reports. Additional explanation on each step comes where needed—in Chapter 14.

1. First the reporter *plans the attack* by getting a sharp concept of the problem, breaking it down into its essential elements, and raising questions to be answered about those elements.

2. Then the reporter *collects appropriate facts,* using the most suitable methods and checking for reliability. Often reflective thinking, records in the files, observation or inspection, or a few interviews or consultations will do. If necessary an experiment, a survey, or library research can come into play (as explained in Chapter 14).

3. Then comes *organizing the facts* according to the most suitable of *A–, B–, or C–plan* (Chapter 4), *chronological order,* or *order of importance or location.*

4. While *interpreting the facts* into logical conclusions and workable recommendations (omitted in informational reports), a good reporter attempts to be objective by avoiding all possible prejudices, preconceptions, wishful thinking, and fallacies (explained in Chapter 14).

5. Finally, the reporter *puts the report into words, symbols, and graphics,* using all suitable techniques and devices so that it makes clear what the problem is, shows that the information is reliable by explaining the sound research methods, and presents the facts and what they mean. To make understanding the message clear, quick, and easy, a good reporter:

a. Uses commonly understood words (uneducated, technical, and educated people all understand them and all appreciate the ease of comprehending everyday English).

b. Chooses specific, concrete, humanized wording rather than generalizations and abstractions by showing how the facts affect people (preferably the receiver).

c. Keeps sentences so direct and short (average about 17 words) that they need little punctuation except periods at ends (or the oral equivalents).

d. Keeps paragraphs direct and short (questioning those of more than eight lines because short ones seem easier, are easier, and need fewer transitions).

e. Uses headings, topic sentences, and summarizing sentences to show the reader the organization (that is, where the line of thought is going and where it has been).

f. Itemizes (as here) to call attention to important points and to force concise and precise phrasing.

g. Uses all kinds of nonverbal means of communication (charts, graphs, tables, pictograms, maps) to assist words in presenting ideas clearly, quickly, and easily—thus making the report both clearer and more interesting, and thus meeting the two requirements for effective communication—that the message be *interesting enough to get attention and clear when attended (read or heard)*.

PREPARING SHORT REPORTS

The best form for a report depends on the situation—mainly who its recipient is (and the relation to the reporter), its purpose, and its length. The remainder of this chapter explains and illustrates various kinds of short reports written in the most important forms. To save your time and our space, we use cross-references instead of repeating relevant parts of the other reports chapters. Thus we concentrate here on written short reports.

As with all reports, classification of short ones can be on various bases. Although we recognize that strictly informational, periodic reports are the most numerous kind, we do not devote our main attention to them because they are mostly printed forms to be filled in with figures and perhaps a little other writing. We therefore treat the commonly used kinds which do raise real report-writing problems.

To avoid making up new names for short reports, we list and discuss them by their common names. The primary basis of classification here is therefore form (with the exceptions explained where they apply). Yet our primary emphasis is not on learning the forms themselves but on the uses of different forms and information, organization, interpretation, and style in the reports.

As you study these topics, please realize that we do not present the illustrations as perfect reports, and certainly not as models for you to follow slavishly or copy parrotlike. At best, they show acceptable content, form, and general style for their particular situations as starters to your thinking on these points for your situation.

Since you have presumably studied letter and memo writing in the preceding chapters of this book (the best background you could have for studying short reports), you already know the two main forms (letter and memo) and most of the desirable characteristics of style. You also know the basic organizational sequences—the A–, B–, and C–plans you learned for welcome messages, bad news or disappointing messages, and persuasive messages (Chapter 4).

You will, however, have to make seemingly minor (though sometimes difficult) modifications.

1.   Start the changes by substituting *convincing* for *persuasive*. Ideally a report is strictly objective and logical in presenting valid arguments and supporting facts to convince your reader of your conclusions and recommendations. Though no person can be strictly objective the way a traffic light or a computer is, as a report writer you must try by using only validated facts and sound logic. Those things stem from our mental processes (not our emo-

tions)—and affect the reader similarly. The word *conviction* fits the situation, whereas *persuasion* often depends at least partly on emotional appeals and language—forbidden here. No report reader wants to base business decisions on whims, prejudices, illogicalities, or emotions (writer's or reader's).

    2.   Always use a subject line (as the title) in letter as well as memo reports.

    3.   Make full use of itemization, tables, charts, graphs, and attachments when they will help the reader get the message more quickly, clearly, or easily. (Because the amount of quantified data is usually greater in long reports than in short ones, our treatment of graphic presentation is near the end of Chapter 14.)

LETTER REPORTS

Many short reports of one to four pages are in regular business letter form (with a subject line as the report title). Usually they go between organizations rather than between departments of the same organization, where memorandum form is more likely.

Since the letter report is likely to be longer than the usual letter, however, and since it *is* a report, it may, while otherwise using the regular letter form explained in Chapter 1, take on the following special features of reports:

1. More than usually careful organization.
2. Objectivity (absence of emotional suasion, viewing both sides of the situation, enough interweaving or implying of methods and sources to assure soundness).
3. Use of appropriate subject lines, subheads, and itemizations where helpful.
4. Use of tables and graphic devices (usually as attachments) where helpful and economical.

Depending on whether the message will likely meet with reader approval, disappointment, or resistance, the letter report should follow the A–, B–, or (rarely) C–plan, as explained in Chapter 4 and illustrated thoroughly in Chapters 5, 7, and 8, repectively. More specifically, any of the organizational plans under "Organizing the findings" in Chapter 14 may apply to a letter report.

Although a letter report, like any other, needs to convince the reader that its facts are reliable, it rarely needs a separate section or even a separate paragraph explaining authorization, purpose, or methods and sources used in collecting data. Most likely the writer got the assignment because the assigner, usually a superior, knew that person had the information immediately available, was already a recognized expert on the subject, or knew just how to study the problem. For the simple problems appropriate to letter reports, the methods and sources are frequently so obvious as to need no explanation anyway.

If any explanations are necessary, usually the best way to give them is in incidental phrases interwoven right along with the information: "Inspection of . . . reveals . . ."; "Legal precedent in cases like . . . is clearly . . ."; "Microscopic examination shows . . ."; or ". . . , according to such authorities as . . . ."

Indeed, letter reports are like other reports except for the form which gives them their name, the limits of length and hence of topics for which they are suitable, and their usually more familiar style. A letter in impersonal style would be almost a joke. We do not think any kind of report should necessarily be in impersonal style, and even those people who do will almost certainly approve a natural style in letter reports.

Two common types of letter reports are those about job and credit applicants (personnel and credit reports), discussed in Chapter 5. You should study both the explanations and the illustrations there. Notice that both the illustrations use subject lines effectively. Note, too, that both begin immediately with important information (A–plan) because they face no problem of reader disappointment or resistance.

Personnel and credit reports, however, do have the legal problem of avoiding libel suit by referring to the request for information, trying to be fair to both parties, and asking confidential use of the information. Notice how the two illustrations handle that problem.

These two kinds of reports should be informational, in that they should rely on facts and subordinate or entirely eliminate unsupported opinions—and certainly recommendations. But letter reports may be either informational or analytical. In some cases they are more nearly directives than reports, but directives are more likely to be in memo form.

Because the following message is somewhat bad news and the reader may be reluctant to take the suggested action, the report uses the more convincing inductive rather than the faster-moving deductive plan. You will note, too, that it uses no subject line. To do so would defeat the psychological purpose of the inductive plan of getting in the arguments before giving the conclusion. As you always should when you have a step-by-step procedure or a series of pointed, emphatic principles, qualities, conclusions, or recommendations to convey, this report uses itemization effectively at the end.

Dear Mr. Rogers:

In our audit of your company's books on January 16, we discovered that for years the total net profit has been added to surplus. This procedure is usually correct.

For the past three years you have had a bond agreement, however, which specifies that a sinking-fund reserve of 3 percent of the par value of the bonds must be set up annually out of surplus. That

agreement is legally binding. Moreover, state law
requires you to set up the reserve in this situation.
Only the remaining profit, of course, can be added to
surplus.

Laws of this type protect investors and brokers who
desire a true picture of the financial condition of
companies.

The laws also give you protection. Setting up a
separate reserve prevents directors' unlawful
declaration of dividends. In other words, the proper
presentation of surplus figures is an aid to better
management.

We therefore recommend that you

   1. Take immediate steps to set up the reserve.

   2. Transfer to it now, from surplus, 3 percent of
       the par value of the bonds for each of the past
       three years.

   3. Regularly each year for the duration of the bond
       agreement transfer the required amount from
       surplus to the reserve.

Both the shortness and the nature of the material made divisional headings
unnecessary in the preceding illustration.

Conversely, both length and content make headings almost mandatory for
effective presentation in letter reports of two pages or more, as in the following. It is a reply to a school superintendent's request that recent graduates
report on their college expenses for passing on to high school seniors. (You'll
notice that the way of life pictured is not common on college campuses today,
but that does not keep the report from showing the helpfulness of carefully
classifying information under suitable headings.)

Dear Mr. Loudenslager:

Please give John my congratulations on his good record
in school last semester. Apparently he will be ready
for college next year; so I hope the information you
requested will help him as well as your other seniors.

I've based the cost figures I'm giving on one semester
here for a male student. Although I have not kept
detailed records, my figures are more realistic than
the somewhat outdated ones in the catalog you have.

Being neither plush nor poor, I have spent according
to the Typical column, but I have classmates whose
expenses more nearly match both the Liberal and the
Conservative figures.

Estimated Expenses Table

	Conservative	Typical	Liberal
Course fees	$000	$000	$000
Room and board	000	000	000
Books and supplies	00	00	00
Physical education	00	00	00
R.O.T.C.	00	00	00
Clothing	00	00	00
Laundry and dry cleaning ...	00	00	00
Transportation	00	00	00
Incidentals	00	00	000

FIXED EXPENSES

Course fees.——Although the regular course fee is $000, certain courses and curricula like music, law, medicine, and veterinary medicine do require extra fees. Insofar as I know, these extra fees have not changed from the catalog you have.

Physical Education.——All students must take two years credit in gym. The $00 fee is for locker rental and wear and tear on equipment.

R.O.T.C.——All able-bodied students may take two years' credit in military science. When the equipment is returned after completion of the course, the fee will be refunded.

VARIABLE EXPENSES

Living Expense

College residence halls.——Adequate dormitories are available on the campus. The dining rooms serve meals seven days a week. Room and board is $000 a semester. The resident supplies linen, toweling, and pillow.

Fraternities.——Room and board in a fraternity may vary from a low of $000 to a high of $000. The average is about $000.

Cooperatives.——A student who desires to may join a co-op, in which a group may defray part of the cost of living by each helping with the work. Room and board in a co-op usually runs to about $000 a semester.

Individual rooms.——Rooms in approved homes cost about $00—$00 a semester, two students to a room. Food in local restaurants costs about $000—$000.

Apartments.——Rent for an apartment will run from $00 for the most modest to $000, depending upon closeness to school, quality and comfort, and whether the student shares it or occupies it alone. Utilities are usually extra and are not included here.

<u>Working for meals</u>.--Students who want to do so can nearly always find jobs working for their meals in dormitory dining rooms or in local restaurants.

<u>Clothing</u>.--Some students who attend college buy nearly entirely new wardrobes. Others may get along quite well for some time with what they have. So clothing expense is highly variable, as my figures in the table show. For most students, college clothing costs should be only a little more than for high school clothing.

<u>Laundry and dry cleaning</u>.--Facilities are available for a student to do laundry in the dormitories. Several laundromats are also convenient to the area. Dry-cleaning prices are the same as at home.

<u>Transportation</u>

<u>At school</u>.--The majority of the activities are on the campus or within walking distance. Bus fare to town is 30 cents a round trip. Taxis are also available. The student who expects to have a car will find that a jalopy is not the thing here and that keeping a respectable car can hardly cost less than $000 a semester. Depreciation alone could cost that much on some cars without anything for insurance, upkeep, and gasoline.

<u>To and from school</u>.--Most students will find it inconvenient as well as expensive to go home more than twice a semester. The round-trip bus fare, the cheapest way, is $00.00.

<u>Incidentals</u>

<u>Necessities</u>.--Students need a small amount of money to spend while out with a group for coffee, cokes, shows, and the like. Also, the ever-present needs of haircuts, shoestrings, razor blades, toothpaste, etc. require a few dollars. Normally one may expect to spend $000 a semester on such things.

<u>Dating</u>.--Taking a date out for an evening can cost a lot of money, or it can be fairly inexpensive. Some of the larger dances can cost up to $00 for the evening. The item is highly flexible.

If anyone in your senior class has any specific questions about this school, I'll try to answer as best I can. One thing you can safely tell all who are thinking about coming here: They had better learn to write correctly and to handle simple math or they will be in trouble.

CHECKLIST FOR MEMOS

1. Form:
   a. Use a neatly arranged heading, including at least the company name (if needed for identification) and a dateline.
   b. Begin To, From, and Subject at the left; preferably, double-space between them; and use colons right after each or align all the colons with the one after Subject. In either case, align the beginnings of what you fill in after the colons.
   c. Use courtesy titles (Mr., Ms., Mrs., Miss) with the names of others (but not yours) if you would in talking with them; do not use official or professional titles unless some readers might not know them or you need to show authority.
   d. For emphasis, underscore or capitalize subject lines. End-of-line periods are unnecessary, even undesirable.
   e. Single-space within paragraphs and double-space between.
   f. Use itemizations, headings, tables, and graphics where helpful.
   g. For pages after the first, put at least the addressee's name, the date, and the page number on the first line and triple-space below it.
   h. Use no salutation, complimentary close, or typed name of writer at the end; sign only nonroutine memos requiring authentication, unless your organization's practice is otherwise.
   i. When used, file and other references may go under a flush-right date or to the right of the To-From-Subject block. (Copy distribution lists more commonly appear at the end instead.)

2. Organization and coverage:
   a. Bring in your main point (whether it is a request, conclusion, recommendation, or something else) in the first sentence unless your reader might resist; if so, lead up to it with whatever facts, reasons, or explanations are necessary to convince—especially any reader benefits you can point out.
   b. Be sure to make clear that your information is valid and pertinent by showing what the problem is and how you got your information to solve it (unless obvious); but see 3b.
   c. Effective dates (for directives)—and when necessary, other time limits, places, and people concerned—are important points.
   d. Consider whether you should mention alternatives to your recommendation.
   e. Should you explain more specifically how to carry out your proposal?
   f. Be sure you have covered all points your reader will need or want covered—especially all steps in your logic.
   g. Check your sequence for coherence, logic, and psychological effect (A–, B–, or C–plan).

3. Style:
   a. Make the subject line indicate the content accurately.
   b. Emphasize the important and avoid undue emphasis on the unimportant. What you found out and the likely effect are more important than how you found out or from whom; so for 2b, usually you should

CHECKLIST FOR MEMOS (concluded)

just imply or interweave in incidental phrases the necessary but unknown parts of purpose and method of the report. Usually the reader will already know the purpose; and if not, stating the facts will usually imply it and your method of getting information: "Sixty-two percent of your employees favor a company snack bar" indicates both the problem and the survey method.

c. Be sure your terminology, sentence length and structure, and paragraph length and structure make for quick, clear, easy reading. Short words, sentences, and paragraphs usually help; itemizations and tabulations may help further.

d. Display really significant data, conclusions, and recommendations by such means as increasing white space around them, decreasing line length, itemizing, and tabulating.

e. For coherence (and often for conciseness), precede displayed items with an appropriate introductory statement.

f. Don't develop a fever (with numerous strong adjectives and adverbs, for example); remain logical and objective.

4. Tone:

a. Soften commands for acceptable tone; sharp imperatives rankle even in directives. "You will . . ." and "You must . . ." are too commanding for most situations. Four directives from which you can usually select one appropriate one are (in descending order of sharpness): "Please . . . ," "Will you . . . ," "I ask that you . . . ," and "I would appreciate your . . . ." "If you will . . ." is usually too weak.

b. Phrase recommendations for acceptable tone (depending on the reader-writer relationship and the firmness of your conviction): "You must . . . ," "I recommend . . . ," "I suggest . . . ," "The only way . . . ," "The best solution is . . . ," and "Probably the wise decision is . . . ."

c. Direct accusations (stated in independent clauses) are always objectionable.

d. Positive is better than negative phrasing.

e. Item 2a is an important factor in tone.

f. Consider whether to write impersonally or (usually better) naturally ("Employees will receive their checks . . ." or "You will receive your checks . . .").

Except for Item 1 (on form), the checklist for memos applies equally to memo and letter reports.

MEMORANDUMS

Just as letter reports are more likely for communicating between organizations, memo reports are more appropriate within an organization. There they flow in quantity—especially with the increasing use of word processing and photocopying equipment and the goals of speed, efficiency, and economy that often have made unnecessary even the formerly used specially printed memo forms. The headings used in the illustrations of memos in Chapter 1 show the main variations in form, and Item 1 of the checklist for memo reports gives further details.

Except for the differences in form and use, memo reports generally follow the instructions already given for letter reports. They are, however, inclined to (1) be ephemeral and hence less formal (often being handwritten without carbons), (2) make even greater use of itemization (almost characteristically), and (3) become directives going down the chain of command.

One of the most common and effective techniques is itemization. Numbering each paragraph almost forces a writer into careful organization, precise statement, and conciseness.

The two simple memos in Chapter 1 showing slightly different forms illustrate—the one, to "All Occupants," is wholly typed; the other, to "Andrea," is handwritten on a printed form.

Notice these details in the two memos: One is on an ephemeral topic to one reader; so efficiency pointed to a quick, handwritten memo. The other went to many people; so it was photocopied in sufficient number. Since some of its readers would not have known who "R. F. Noonan" was, he gave his official title. The other writer would have wasted time even with a full signature. The careful phrasing of subject lines in both indicates the contents concisely, and the underscoring makes them stand out. Itemization seemed helpful in one but would have served no purpose in the other, and the writers used it accordingly. Neither needs the kind of authenticating signature a bank requires on your check. Where that is necessary, the usual practice is for the writer to initial by the name in the "From" line.

Those two memos, however, are mere interoffice memos exchanging simple information. The following memo likewise shows a usual layout and typical A–plan but a typical memo-report problem:

```
Date    : 2/10/83
To      : Mr. J. G. DeWolfe
From    : R. R. Fortune
Subject: REDUCING ABSENTEEISM CAUSED BY RESPIRATORY
         DISEASES

1.  Conclusion.--Our recent high rate of absenteeism
    seems to be a result of too low humidity.
    Absentees reported colds or other respiratory
    diseases as the causes in 73 percent of the cases.

2.  Humidity in relation to respiratory diseases.--
    According to the U.S. Public Health Service, the
    higher the humidity in buildings the lower the
    rate of respiratory diseases. You can see this
    relationship in Figure 1 on the attached pages.
```

The explanation is that a high humidity prevents excessive cooling from evaporation of skin moisture.

3. <u>Desirable humidity–temperature relationships</u>.-- Although our 68 degrees is considered the best temperature, it isn't warm enough for most people unless the humidity is about 40. Ours is 20. As Figure 2 of the USPHS study shows, a humidity above 50 makes most people feel clammy and below 30 causes them to feel a dryness in their noses and throats.

4. <u>Recommended corrective steps</u>.-- To reduce absenteeism, improve the health of our personnel, and enhance employee relations, I suggest the following:

   a. Raise the humidity to 40 by making a pan with the necessary evaporation surface for each radiator (to be concealed from view by the radiator covers).

   b. Assign the janitors the job of keeping water in the pans.

   c. Purchase one temperature–humidity guide for each office. Besides providing a constant check on room conditions, these meters will remind the employees that you have done something about their comfort and health.

   Prices range from $2 to $200. The cheapest ones are likely to be inaccurate; but the Wechsler at $8.50 carries the recommendation of <u>Consumer Reports</u>. It looks like a small clock with two red hands pointing to temperature and humidity scales. Hardware, department, mail–order, and speciality stores carry it in varied colors to fit the decor of any office.

JUSTIFICATION REPORTS

Another kind of short report often using memo form has its own special name. Of course, any analytical report could be called a justification report because it draws conclusions (and makes recommendations if wanted) and presents facts to justify them. But as used in report writing, the justification report is a special kind.

Almost invariably it is an initiating report in which the writer makes an original proposal, rather than a requested study, although it may well be the requested full write-up of a suggestion that you have dropped in a suggestion box.

It is deductive (A–plan) presentation that gives the recommendation immediately, followed by concise statements of the most important considerations and conclusions, before giving detailed explanations and supporting facts. Thus it *quickly* gives all a busy reader needs to know (*if the reader trusts the writer*). Probably this point is the main reason for the increasing popularity of the justification report among executives. But if the reader wants to read the whole explanation, the plan is still good. The reader can follow the details better by having already read the conclusions and recommendations.

You will provide good organization and coverage for your justification reports if you set up the five standard headings and do the following in this order:

1. State the purpose in one sentence. The first part, in phrase or dependent-clause structure, should mention a benefit. The second part should be the recommendation in an independent clause.
2. State the cost and saving (or advantages) in no more than two sentences. Don't delay the fast movement by explaining here.
3. In a third part called "Procedure" or "Method of Installation" or whatever is most appropriate, cover concisely such things as necessary space, personnel, training, special materials, time, restrictions (rules, regulations), and interruptions of work. Usually one to three sentences will do.
4. Itemize the conclusions, state them pointedly, and keep them to the minimum number that will cover all aspects. One of them has to be on cost and saving. They are not always all benefits; some may point the other way. One frequently overlooked is the goodwill of all people concerned.
5. In a discussion section (sometimes called "Discussion of Conclusions" or "Explanation of Advantages"), give all the details supporting the statements already made—itemized to match the itemized conclusions. Interweave into your explanations enough of your methods to answer the reader's question: "How do you know?" This point applies particularly to your method of figuring cost and saving.

The following typical example illustrates both plan and technique:

HOW MECHANICAL PENCILS WOULD SAVE MONEY
FOR MORGAN COMPANY

Purpose.--To save the Morgan Company more than $200 in pencil expense each year, I recommend that we purchase mechanical pencils instead of wooden ones for employee use.

Cost and Savings.--A year's supply of mechanical pencils and refills would cost $457 as compared with more than $685 for wooden pencils--a yearly saving of well over $200.

Procedure.--A dependable automatic pencil manufacturer--Ray & Company, Rome, Georgia--would supply the yearly need of about 750 pencils with the

Morgan name on them at the quantity–discounted price of 40 cents each. The stockroom clerk could distribute them.

Conclusions.––The Morgan Company would gain four benefits by using mechanical pencils.

1. We would save at least $225 a year.

2. The stockroom clerk would have fewer pencils to store and issue––750 compared with over 13,000.

3. Employees would be more careful about misplacing them.

4. Mechanical pencils stay sharp and thus provide uniform, neat writing without loss of time and patience at the pencil sharpener.

Discussion of Conclusions.––

1. During the past three years pencils have cost us about $1.80 a year per employee, as shown by the following calculations:

	19––	19––	19––	Average
Pencil costs	$ 765	$ 554	$ 731	$ 684
Employees	450	298	395	381
Cost per employee	1.70	1.86	1.85	1.80

Converting to mechanical pencils would require, for each employee, an estimated two pencils (at 40 cents each) and 40 cents worth of lead and eraser refills, for a total annual cost of $1.20 per employee.

Cost comparison shows a saving of $228.60 with mechanical pencils:

Cost of wooden pencils, 381 employees,
@ $1.80 .... $685.80
Cost of mechanical pencils, 381 employees,
@ $1.20 .... 457.60
 Saving................................... $228.60

2. In the past three years, the clerk in the stockroom has had to allot space for about 1,104 dozen, or 13,248, pencils and has also had to take the time (considerable in the aggregate) to distribute each one. Having only 762 pencils to store and issue would release space and time for other things.

3. Since mechanical pencils are more valuable and more conspicuous (especially with the Morgan name on them) than wooden ones, I believe employees would be more careful about carrying them home and not bringing them back. Those

> misplaced might be worth at least a part of
> their cost as advertising.
>
> 4. The mechanical pencil needs no sharpening and
> writes with the same neat uniformity throughout
> its use, instead of becoming progressively
> blunter and less neat. Moreover, mechanical
> pencils would avoid interruptions to thinking
> and work when employees take their wooden ones
> to the pencil sharpener (which often annoys by
> breaking the lead or needing to be emptied).

You might well notice several specifics about the preceding report.

The writer who *initiated this idea*—usual for this kind of report—moves fast in presenting the basic idea and facts.

The boss, if trusting the reporter, may approve after reading less than the first half; but simply reading further provides details if wanted.

The clear, concise, and prominent (by underlining) but easily typed heads serve as guideposts to the reader.

The matched pair of itemizations helps the reader relate pointed conclusions with supporting facts and explanations.

Deserved emphasis justifies the inevitable repetition of cost and saving—the reason you make such proposals, though neither has to be in dollars and cents.

Perhaps most important of all, notice how the writer *concisely but subordinately interweaves* only enough methodology to answer the reader's question: "How do you know?" But the writer wasted no words about tracking down former pencil costs. The answer is obvious.

Although the form of justification reports is commonly memo, it may be letter or some other such as that illustrated. In letter or memo form the title would serve as the subject line. Of course, the five division heads may be centered heads or sideheads above the text if you prefer. If you use memo form, Item 1 of the checklist for memos will apply. Then you can use Items 1–5 of the text discussion as the subheads under Item 2 of that checklist and have a good checklist for justification reports.

PROGRESS REPORTS

As the name suggests, a progress report tells how you are getting along on a project. It may be a single, special report but often is one in a series of required periodic reports. (In a series the last one is the *completion* report.) As a periodic report, a progress report is usually strictly informational. A special progress report is likely to be analytical because of the special problem that called for it.

The general purpose of a progress report is to keep top management informed so that it can act wisely. An owner may want to consider whether to continue as planned, change the plan or methods, or drop the project. A contractor may need to consider such questions as when to order certain materials, whether to increase workers and equipment assigned to a job, and whether to bid on another job.

Basic contents of a progress report are the answers to three questions:

1. Whether the project is on schedule.
2. If the project is not on schedule, why not and what corrective measures were taken or recommended?
3. What will be done next and what the plans and prospects are for completion on schedule.

Although neither those nor the following are necessarily the subdivision headings, a progress report may cover any or all of the purpose and nature of the project (usually the reader already knows), what has been done, present status, what is now being done, plans and outlook for the future, and unexpected developments. The last may be of major importance if the report is designed to get a decision on a problem that has arisen. In series, each progress report briefly summarizes former work reported but stresses developments since the preceding report. Progress reports on research projects may or may not include tentative findings and conclusions—depending on the writer's confidence in them and the immediate need for them.

No single plan is always best for a progress report. What is best depends upon the whole situation, especially the content, deserved relative emphasis of parts, and the attitudes and wishes of the reader.

Preferably all the progress reports in a series should follow the same plan. It may be topical by division of the subject (supervision, equipment, materials, and labor; or steps, phases, or divisions of the job); or it may be chronological (by days, weeks, or months; or past, present, and future). One simple plan calls for

1. The transitional elements of background and summary of work already done.
2. The body giving the details of recent progress.
3. The prophetic or future prospects, in relation to scheduled completion date.

A more specific but somewhat flexible plan is

1. Quick introduction (purpose and nature of the project, unless known; summary of work to date; status, including any significant results).
2. More detailed summary of earlier progress reported, if any.
3. New progress (work done, methods and personnel, obstacles and what you've done about them) in relation to schedule.
4. Realistic forecast (plans in relation to schedule, and recommendations or requests, if any).

More important than *what* plan, in most cases, is that you have *a* plan—a unifying thread to hang your beads on.

Like the plan, the form of progress reports may vary with the circumstances. Short ones usually are in memo or letter form, longer ones in some adaptation of complete report form.

Since the form, plan, and content of progress reports vary so much and we cannot well illustrate all the possibilities, we think we can help most by illustrating some common weaknesses in progress reports: (1) having nothing to say but trying to pretend that you do, (2) using pompous jargon to cover up, and (3) being nonspecific. The following humorous illustration properly lampoons the main weaknesses.[1]

STANDARD PROGRESS REPORT
FOR THOSE WITH NO PROGRESS TO REPORT

During the report period which ends (fill in appropriate date) considerable progress has been made in the preliminary work directed toward the establishment of the initial activities. (Meaning: We are getting ready to start, but we haven't done anything yet.) The background information has been surveyed and the functional structure of the component parts of the cognizant organization has been clarified. (We looked at the assignment and decided that George should do it.)

Considerable difficulty has been encountered in the selection of optimum materials and experimental methods, but this problem is being attacked vigorously and we expect that the development phase will proceed at a satisfactory rate. (George is looking through the handbook.) In order to prevent unnecessary duplication of previous efforts in the same field, it was necessary to establish a survey team which has conducted a rather extensive tour through various facilities in the immediate vicinity of manufacture. (George and Harry had a nice time in New York last week.)

The Steering Committee held its regular meeting and considered rather important policy matters pertaining to the overall organizational levels of the line and staff responsibilities that devolve on the personnel associated with the specific assignments resulting from the broad functional specifications. (Untranslatable—sorry.) It is believed that the rate of progress will continue to accelerate as necessary

---

[1] So widely reprinted in the literature of report writing as to be in the public domain—like many jokes.

personnel are recruited to fill vacant billets. (We'll
get some work done as soon as we find someone who
knows something.)

The following progress reporters did much better, as a writer usually does
when having something to say to somebody for some purpose. Especially if
all goes well, as in the first item, the report is easy to write. (All these writers
used memo form; we'll begin with the subject line.)

SUBJECT: <u>Monthly Progress Report No. 2 on Orangeville</u>
<u>Expressway</u>

<u>Present status</u>

1. Work on the 10.8-mile section of expressway
    running south to Brownville is on schedule. The
    final surface is 80 percent complete. We have had
    no delays during the past month and have regained
    the two days formerly lost and reported.

2. The 18.4-mile section of expressway running north
    to Malden remains approximately two weeks behind
    schedule. We have cleared the right of way to
    Malden, and the roadbed is completed along the
    first 8.6 miles north of Orangeville.

3. We completed the overpass for U.S. 1 on December
    14, ahead of schedule by 18 days.

<u>Expected progress</u>

1. During January we expect to complete the southern
    link to Brownville except for the drainage
    preparation and the approaches. Work on them will
    most likely have to fit in between rains normally
    expected at this time of year in this area,
    especially in the valley of Hogtown Creek. Present
    progress and normal weather expectations suggest
    that this link will be ready for traffic just
    before the completion deadline of March 3.

2. During this month we will extend the roadbed along
    the north section to Malden. The first layer of
    tar will go on a 5-mile strip, beginning at
    Orangeville and extending north. Additional
    workers being hired should insure completion of
    this section before the deadline of June 24.

Sometimes progress reporters must explain their difficulties to defend
themselves and to justify requests, as in the following:

SUBJECT: <u>Special Report on Interlocking Plant</u>
<u>Installation</u>

Because of a shortage of track cable, I am asking your
permission to advance cutover day to at least January

18. The installation is now about 88 percent complete, as shown by the broken line on the attached graph [omitted here to save space] comparing the predicted work schedule and the actual schedule.

If the track cable ordered December 1 arrives within the next few days as promised two weeks ago, and if we have good weather, the future work schedule should appear as the dotted projection line. This points to 100 percent completion on January 18.

Since progress reports often deal with technical work, you need not be surprised if you fail to understand some things in some of them. If you have trouble with the following, for example, remember that the technical writer did not write for you but for another technical person, who understood perfectly. (The situation accounts for the stiff, formal style.) This report also illustrates a not unusual organization around topics rather than time, while the time sequence and relation to schedule are still clear.

SUBJECT: Progress on Prototype Power Supply for Collins (Job 280)

At the end of three weeks on the two-month schedule for developing a prototype power supply for Collins Radio, the project is two days ahead of the preliminary time estimate. The circuit has been designed and tested for dependability. It is now undergoing final inspection.

1. Results of circuit dependability test.--The test circuit operated within the desired limits of ± 2 percent of the desired voltages and currents. Measured by a thermocouple in the 3' × 3' × 3" base mounting plate of aluminum, the temperature readings (with attendant voltages) ran as follows:

Hour	Transmit Voltage @ 200 Ma.	Receive Voltage @ 100 Ma.	Bias Voltage @ 65 Ma.	Temperature (Degrees Centigrade)

[No use to waste space in this book on the recorded results.]

2. Printed circuit board.--The basic sketch work for the printed board is finished. The component placement and hookup connections were frozen yesterday. Now the enlarged negative is being drawn. It should be ready for the developer on January 13, five days ahead of the final acceptance date.

3. Chassis design.--The chassis drawings went to Alsfab on January 9. The prototype chassis, with

```
finishes of black anodize on the base and gray
enamel on the cover, will be ready on January 14.
The dimensions are 6" × 4" × 3" or 2 inches smaller
than the maximum Collins allowed.
```

    4. <u>Remaining work</u>.——The printed board has to be
```
etched and built. It will be tested in the small
chassis, and the complete unit has to be tested
for all conditions, including vibration, moisture,
and temperature. Unless now-unseen troubles
develop, the present rate of progress should
continue, and the prototype should be ready for
shipment by February 7.
```

CREDIT REPORTS

A typical credit report, illustrated as a letter report in Chapter 5, illustrates those written by individual references about a credit applicant. But various trade associations, credit bureaus, and special credit-reporting agencies have to write so many credit reports that each develops special forms for convenience and the economy of standardization. So no form is standard except within a particular reporting agency.

Because the purpose of a credit report is always the same and known to the reader, and because the methods and scope are always the same, the credit report omits the introduction. Because the credit report is an informational rather than analytical report, it also omits conclusions and recommendations (though the extent of decrease in a Dun & Bradstreet rating can mean anything from "Look out" to "Don't dare" or an increase anything from "Looking better" to "Shoot the works"). And because it is a short-form report, it omits other parts of a complete report—all except the text and perhaps a synopsis.

But because the credit report must protect the writer against libel suit, it includes the necessary legal defenses (in addition to assumed truth in the facts presented) by specifying confidential use for the purpose mentioned in the request for it. Because the four C's of credit—capital, character, capacity, conditions (explained in Chapter 5)—are the bases for credit decisions, the report invariably covers these topics (but not under these headings). The information includes anything which might have a significant bearing on the credit worth of the subject (individual or firm) and omits anything else.

The old report in Figure 13–1 is just one of the many kinds, but it illustrates most of the points. When you notice how the note in fine print at the bottom provides legal protection against libel suit, you will understand that Dun & Bradstreet (the granddaddy of credit-reporting agencies) had to get permission from Simpson to release this report for educational purposes—and why D&B sent an old report.

Figure 13–1 Credit report

Dun & Bradstreet Report

RATING CHANGE

NAME & ADDRESS			RATING

| 52 51 | SIMPSON HARDWARE CO
SIMPSON, WILLIAM J., OWNER | CD 26 FEB 2 19-- N
HARDWARE & PAINTS | 1948 | E 2 .
Formerly E 2½ |

495 N MAIN ST.
SPRINGFIELD OHIO

TRADE	DISC-PPT
SALES	$89,446
WORTH	$27,908
EMPLS	1 + 1 P.T.

SUMMARY AN ESTABLISHED BUSINESS CONDUCTING A STEADY AND PROFITABLE VOLUME. FINANCIAL CONDITION IS WELL BALANCED.

TRADE

HC	OWE	P DUE	TERMS	Jan 19 19--		SOLD
1551	356		2-10-30	Disc		1948 to date
900	600		2-10	Disc		yrs
400			2-10-30	Disc		1950 to 11-1-6-
1600	300		30	Ppt		Active acct
733	112			Ppt		yrs

FINANCE

Statement Dec 31 19--			
Cash on hand & bank	$ 4,604	Accts Pay	$ 3,064
Accts Rec	1,315	Accruals	621
Mdse	19,158		
Total Current	25,077	Total Current	3,685
Fixt & Equip	4,008		
Auto	2,113		
Ppd & Def	395	NET WORTH	27,908
Total Assets	31,593	Total	31,593

Net Sales January 1, 19-- to December 31, 19--, $89,446; gross profit $19,551; monthly rent $175; lease expires 19--. Fire insurance on fixtures $4,000; on merchandise $20,000.
Signed Jan 30, 19-- SIMPSON HARDWARE CO. by W.J. Simpson, Owner

When Simpson took over the business in 1948, sales were about $45,000 a year. By working long hours and advertising in the Suburban News he built up volume a little every year. Also there has been an increase in residential building on his side of town. Profits have increased as sales have expanded. Cash withdrawals from the business have been conservative. Merchandise turns satisfactorily and Simpson has been able to improve his financial condition a little each year. Carries good balances at his bank and has not borrowed since 195-.

OPERATION Retails shelf hardware and tools (65%), S & W Paints (20%) and housewares, cutlery, garden implements, glass, lawn mowers, seeds and sporting equipment (15%). About 90% of sales is for cash; 30 day credit is extended to contractors and householders. Two clerks, one part-time, are employed. LOCATION: Rents a store 25 × 60 in a residential shopping area on the outskirts of town. Premises are well maintained.

HISTORY Style was registered by Simpson July 17, 1948. Used for buying and advertising. Owner purchased this established business July 1, 1948 from Ralph T. Meyers. Capital was $18,000 of which $10,000 was a loan since repaid.
William J. Simpson, born 190-, is married, a native of Ohio. After graduating from Miami University in 1930, taught school until 1936. 1937-1945 employed by the Wilson Wholesale Hardware Co., Columbus, Ohio, latterly in the accounting department. 1946-48 was a salesman for Davis & Crocker, wholesale builders supplies, Springfield.
2-2 (201 49)

ANNUAL REPORTS

In accounting to their various publics for their management of funds entrusted to them, corporations and governmental units summarize each year's activities in their annual reports.[2] The mail is thus heavy with these annually February–May.

In the middle of the 19th century, when annual reporting really started, stockholders were the only public considered. Since they were usually wealthy and educated—or advised by investment specialists—early annual reports were little more than financial statements in the formal accounting terms of the day. And the usual attitude of management was to tell as few people as possible as little as possible.

Today all that is changed. Stockholders have increased greatly (now estimated at about a 10th of the U.S. population, many of whom are not acquainted with accounting terminology). Labor has increased its power and become intensely interested in corporate affairs. The changed thinking of the times considers corporations essentially public institutions affecting the public welfare. Management has seen that its publics include stockholders, the financial community, employees, customers, government officials, and the general public. It has realized that many of these people are not educated in accounting and that many of them are interested in more than strictly financial data. They want to know about wages, fringe benefits to workers, products, and research and development of new products, and overall policies—for example, company ecological policy.

Annual-report writers today, therefore, try to write so that everyone can understand; and they try to cover topics of interest to all publics. With the realization that people are inclined to distrust and take a dim view of things they don't know about, management has shifted to the attitude of telling as many people as possible as much as possible (limited only by security regulations and information that might hurt the competitive position of the company).

Indeed, today the annual report is a major part of the public relations programs of most corporations, a means by which they hope to tell their story to all their publics to justify their existence and their way of doing things. They know that any business firm exists, in the long run, only with the approval and patronage of a public whose goodwill it has. Most corporations therefore make their reports available to anybody who asks, and some go to consider-

---

[2]Although most annual reports are not short, they are largely factual reporting (informational) rather than problem-solving analytical studies with conclusions and recommendations discussed in the following chapters. They are periodic reports and are something of a special type and form. Certainly they are the most voluminous of reports (many companies distributing more than a million copies annually), and the writings about them are probably the most numerous (we could easily give you a 10-page bibliography). Yet we do not think they deserve extensive treatment here in view of the purposes of this book. Still, you deserve some introduction to them, and it belongs in this chapter more appropriately than elsewhere.

able expense to make their reports appealing, readable, informative—and available to anybody for the asking.

Some have gone so far in telling their stories that the reports seem more like propaganda or advertising brochures than objective reports—and have sometimes thereby lost faith and face. But the usual annual report today is highly informative about the organization it represents. The facts presented are quite reliable. If you read annual reports knowing that they are likely slanted (by not telling everything rather than by misrepresentation), you will be adequately cautious—and well informed.

Usually today's annual reports contain a letter from the highest official as well as financial statements and the auditor's statement of opinion (sometimes called the "certificate"). Often the letter from the president or top executive is only a short introduction to a review of outstanding influences, developments, and trends affecting company operations. Frequently it is both an introduction and a synopsis. And in some cases it is the entire report, running to 10, 12, or more pages.

Either way, most annual-report writers adapt all the devices already mentioned here—readable style, liberal use of meaningful headings, graphic illustrations—to make reading easy and interesting and the reports effective representatives for their organizations. Though we authors have done considerable consulting for various companies on their annual reports, we do not go further (in this book) with instructions on how to write the reports—writing them is largely the work of specialized journalists with the necessary full authority to squeeze any kind of wanted company information out of any office or anybody in the firm. Without that authority you could not write an annual report if you knew how.

You can find a tremendous volume of material about annual reports in a good library. And as we mentioned in the chapters on application letters, you can get examples by writing to almost any corporation. The annual report of a company is a source of information which anybody should read before investing in a company's stock or applying for a job with that firm.

QUESTIONS AND EXERCISES

1. Justify or disapprove each word in the text statement of the general function of reports.
2. For our time and place, arrange in order of importance the six specific ways reports serve.
3. Give any other changes (additions or deletions) you think we should make in the six specific ways reports serve.
4. For our time and place, arrange (in order of logic and/or importance) the three questions reports answer.
5. Give any other changes (additions or deletions) you think we should make in the three questions reports answer.

6. Assume (unless you truly believe) that study of report writing will not help you in the ways we've said and justify your viewpoint.
7. Apply Question 1 to our standard definition of a report.
8. Play the devil's advocate further by attacking one or more of our eight listed characteristics of reports.
9. Now apply Question 8 tactics to our treatment of names and classes of reports.
10. Of the seven things we say a good report writer does for clear, quick, easy reading,
    a. With which do you expect to have the most trouble?
    b. Which do you consider most important and which least important?
11. Of the five steps we list in preparing an analytical report, which do you expect to cause you the most trouble?

CASES

(See p. xiii for some important explanations.)

13–1. This year Henry Mosshart (67) retired from 25 years of selling with Electroflux vacuum cleaners and took a lump sum of $40,000 rather than monthly retirement checks. Henry and his wife, Alice (61) ask you (a relative) to draw up a portfolio of recommended investments for them. They live in a modest, paid-for home (609 Pecos Street, Austin, TX 78704), drive two cars, contribute heavily to the Baptist church, and are generous with their three children and five grandchildren (to whom they hope to leave some money when they die). The Mossharts want investments that pay well, are safe, and will help them live well and leave a nice estate. They do not want to invest in real estate because they are not good at that type of thing. They have no other income except Henry's social security ($504). At age 62, Alice can draw social security that will be $252 a month. Besides library research on different stocks, bonds, money market funds, tax shelters, you might talk with different investment brokers and with people who understand the market.

13–2. As the president of Colonial Insurance Company, 2299 Queen Ridge, Kansas City, Missouri 64106, you are to write a letter report to your policy-holders telling them about the rising costs of health care.

This year total hospital costs were up an average of 18.6 percent per patient admission. Since health-care costs are tied to inflation, a recession with continuing inflation won't break the rise in medical costs. Reduction in the inflation rate must last four or five years before there's much effect on health-care costs.

National average of hospital-day costs this year amounts to $285 as compared to $244 for last year.

By the year 2010, Americans over 65 will represent 51 percent of the population, as opposed to 49 percent who will be working. People over 65 go to the doctor roughly four times as often as those below that age. They occupy nursing homes at 30 times the rate of other age groups.

These increasing health-care costs will have effects that policyholders need to be aware of and to plan for: (*a*) needed modifications in health-care insurance coverage; (*b*) increased insurance premiums (yours and others); and (*c*) increased importance of carrying health-care insurance. Tell your readers that your policy advisers are up to date on the necessary information to answer questions and suggest wise changes in policies as they approach renewal dates. Preliminary discussions can be by convenient toll-free calls (1-800-291-4585), but final agreements for rewriting policy terms must be in writing (for legal reasons).

13–3. Your boss, Victoria Grenier, asks you to find out if your bank should lease or buy plants for the office, and to write a memo with your information and recommendation.

You called Jim Leider of Tropical Plant Rentals and learned that a typical office rental and maintenance agreement involves 20 to 30 plants and a fee of $200 or $250 a month. Once-a-week maintenance is part of the deal, and ailing plants are replaced if office employees have kept hands off. Five-foot palms and 6- to 7-foot Ficus trees at about $25 each are most popular; but rubber trees, split-leaf delphinium, and jade plants are equally in demand. But you also learned that you could buy these same plants (30) for $400 (no maintenance and no replacements).

Your modern bank has little natural light, has employees who are too busy to feed and water plants. Because of the poor cleaning service, there's lots of dust around—dust for the plants. Make up an order that is reasonable and suitable; then recommend either buying or leasing.

13–4. Because of a rate hike effective January 10, churches and charities must pay 2.1 cents more for each piece of third-class mail sent out. For the March of Dimes, this means an added expense of $2.1 million during this year. As Clyde E. Shorey, Jr., the charity's vice president for public affairs, write a memo to all your centers telling them that these added mailing costs will mean reduced money for research and the prevention of birth defects. Ask for suggestions as to how costs can be kept down.

13–5. As chairperson of the Future Committee in your church, you have the duty of writing a progress report to all church members. A survey has shown no need for a second church in the community. You will therefore remodel the present church. For the capital fund drive you have hired Osborne and McElroy, Inc. Mary McKay, architect, rendered a preliminary drawing for a new young people's center that will join the east side of the present church. Other things to report on are that 300 elementary-age children attended Church Week, June 10–17; 500 attended Camp Crory (a church-sponsored camp in the mountains) June–August; 15 teachers are signed up to teach Sunday school September–June, grades 1–12 and preschool, while 5 teachers will teach adult learners in classes such as Paul, death, marriage, comparative religion, women in the New Testament; women of the church made $10,976.34 on a recent bazaar; free nursery service will be provided for the morning services on Sundays; the new 60-foot × 80-foot paved parking area is completed; coffee will be served in the library between the 10 and 11 o'clock services on Sundays; an anonymous gift of property worth $70,000 just received; new church project—home for battered spouses.

13–6. As a vice president for Americo, Inc., a large chemical firm, 500 Brandywine Blvd., Wilmington, Delaware 19810, you have to find some ways to fight inflation by holding down costs. One way you are going to justify in a report to the president of Americo is to cut down on the expenses of meetings of home office executives with the executives at your regional offices. You estimate that it will cost $3,000 and take 60 work-hours, for example, to send three officers to the San Francisco office for a four-hour meeting. A television conference takes a few hours and costs $440. A conference room at the Delaware and at the San Francisco plant can be set up for the video conference and as many as six executives can be in on the conference at each plant. Before the conference you recommend that each group have an agenda and background information on the problem to be discussed. If the people involved in the conference are not well acquainted, you recommend that pictures and general information be distributed before the video conference.

13–7. As a long-time concerned (and recently victimized) citizen, write a letter to the chief administrative officer (mayor?) or group (city council?) of your city about the increasing rate of uncleared crimes. (*Cleared* means that the suspected criminal has been arrested and charged.)

What you want to say comes out of four facts:

1. The following set of figures from a nationwide study made by a Chicago professor of sociology last month.
2. The fact that (incidentally) your back door was bashed in two weeks ago when you were out of town and your $500 TV set was taken (no arrest yet).
3. Your city taxes are going up nearly every year (11 percent last year).
4. The city police department got a 7 percent increase at the beginning of this year (mostly for police officers' pay increases, according to the local paper).

| Type of crime | Cleared | | National average last year |
	This year	Last year	
Murder	87.5%	100.0%	75%
Rape	51.5	20.0	51
Robbery	52.0	62.0	27
Assault	9.0	57.0	62
Burglary	12.9	9.0	16
Larceny	9.8	14.6	20
Motor vehicle theft	19.4	10.0	15
Total	12.5	17.8	21

Though you may feel indignant, write reasonably instead of emotionally, as Lincoln suggested by his quip that a drop of honey catches more flies than a gallon of vinegar.

13–8. As a management trainee in the Iowa regional office of Nationwide Insurance Company, you have observed how crowded the working conditions are; so you have investigated possible solutions. Last year your office increased its policies in force by 12.1 percent from the year before in homeowners insurance and 29 percent in commercial fire policies; and you expect to do even better next year. With the growth of business, the demand for underwriters, claims representatives, and file clerks has increased; but the area partitioned off for the file section has not. File clerks find it hard to keep records in order without adequate room to do so.

The present building, built in 1954, has a foundation designed to support only one floor; therefore you cannot build upward. You do not have sufficient land to expand outwardly. Nationwide policy is to buy a minimum of 25 acres for new regional offices. Locating and developing this land, however, would not give immediate relief for the problem.

Your reading on the problem seems to suggest microfilm as the solution. You've found seven pertinent articles—four of which are specific success stories for microfilms: three in *The Office* (87:40–41, April, 1982, about a bank; 86:114–18, September, 1981, about Michigan Blue Cross; 86:44–45, September, 1982, about Flying Tiger Line); and one in *Infosystems* (24:80, December 1982, about Datsun). In another article ("Taking the Mystery Out of Microfilm," *The Office,* 87:69, January, 1982), Richard J. Connors says that microfilm can save over 90 percent of the space needed for paper files. Connors also says, "Microfilm virtually eliminates misfiles (1–5 percent in most paper systems); so files can be found quickly and accurately." Two other articles generally support Connors and add these points:

1. Microfilm reduces record retrieval because thousands of files can be stored in a single file cabinet available at the touch of a button, resulting in a cost saving by reducing the work hours searching for a document ("Pro and Con on Micrographics and the Office," *Administrative Management,* 38:116, November 1981).
2. You can file 25 inches of paper on microfilm for what it usually costs (about $6) to file one inch of paper in a paper system. Also, microfilm images last longer than paper files ("Taming the Paperwork Explosion," *Management World,* 5:3, July, 1981).

Since your automobile section occupies the largest amount of space in the building, you estimate that by converting the approximately 500,000 auto policies to microfilm you can gain about 4,000 square feet of office for the file section—about what you seem to need for the next several years.

According to Bob Hall, your service superintendent, who carefully observed a similar microfilm conversion for the Missouri-Kansas office, you would need 50 persons to work in your conversion efforts (to minimize disruption of operations). He suggests that you hire college and high school students. If you hire 14 employees to be trained as lead workers (as Hall suggests) and 36 students two weeks later, their combined pay will be $62,382.40 (14 × 58 days @ $3.07/hr. × 8 hrs. and 36 × 48 days at the same rate).

Using figures Hall gave you from the Missouri-Kansas conversion, you and the purchasing department figure (proportionate to the sizes of the jobs) that you will need to spend about (figures rounded) $147,000 for new microfilm files, cameras, readers, jackets, film, processing equipment, and miscellaneous equipment and supplies; $9,500 for rental of temporary (conversion-period) equipment; and the $62,500 for temporary employees, for a total of about $219,000. Not all of that, however, can be justly charged to the conversion. For $147,000 spent on new equipment, you have left at least 9 of its 10 years of useful life (worth $132,000 and making the cost only $15,000 for the one full year of depreciation on its extra-heavy use during conversion). Furthermore, Loren Devore of corporation headquarters has agreed to allow you $70,000 for the used equipment you listed as salvage when/if you convert to microfilm; and the accounting department figures you will get a $7,000 investment tax credit on the figured equipment purchases.

Since the benefits are clearly worth more than the remaining $10,000 cost, write a justification report to T. M. Covington, Deputy regional vice president, recommending the conversion.

13–9. The department store where you work as a buyer is going to open a department devoted to cleaning supplies (for cars, walls, countertops, floors, windows, woodwork, carpets, furniture, mirrors, fabrics, flowers, bathtubs, toilets, shower curtains, cookware, large and small appliances, jewelry and precious metals, base metals, barbecue grills, brick, garbage cans, . . .). Your job is to write a report to the store manager, H. C. Glisson, recommending products for the new department. Before you can write the report you might read about products in *Consumer Reports* that the editors have had tested and/or read *The Fastest, Cheapest, Best Way to Clean Everything* by the editors of *Consumer Guide,* Simon and Schuster, New York, 1982. You might also do your own observation and research, such as listing products available in other retail outlets (like supermarkets) that you therefore may not want to carry. Since Glisson's budget and space for the new department are limited, you have to limit your selection to 50 items. Your other limitation is to not investigate the tools of the trade such as brooms, brushes, mops, gloves, scouring pads . . . .

13–10. Should Mr. and Mrs. Shumaker, South Garden Road, Knoxville, TN 37919, pay $60 a year to United American for its home-banking privilege? Both the Shumakers work 9–6, five days a week, and have joint income of about $35,000. They average sending 8–10 checks a month through the mail.

The computer they would need to buy for home banking costs $400. At an appropriate time each month to pay all bills before overdue (say the 10th), one of the Shumakers would sit down in front of the television set, phone the bank, plug the receiver into the personal computer, use the computer's keyboard to summon an electronic checkbook to the TV screen, and in 10 minutes or less instruct the bank to pay all the monthly bills (without licking any stamps or addressing envelopes).

Because the Shumakers are so busy, they have asked you (a college friend majoring in business) to do the research and write them a letter report from your school address.

13–11. Assume that you have a scholarship from the Wadsworth Foundation based primarily on industry and seriousness of intent rather than high scholarship. Wadsworth does expect satisfactory work and above all diligent effort. As part of your responsibility to the foundation, you must write a report once a year on your progress during the past year. Using the facts of your own record, write in letter form a progress report to Faye Cunningham, director of scholarships.

13–12. As president of an elementary school PTA (Parents–Teachers Association) you have been asked to write a report to parents telling them how they can intelligently guide their children concerning television.

If a child looks at TV one hour a day from the age of 2 to 17, that viewer watches 4,500 hours and is considered a light viewer. A heavy viewer spends three hours a day (or more), amounting to 15,000 hours. But each viewer spends an average of 13,000 hours in the classroom. The light viewer sees over 112,000 commercials from ages 2–17, while the heavy viewer sees over a million TV ads.

Research has found differences between children who are light viewers and those who are heavy viewers. Heavy viewers put in less effort on school work, have poorer reading skills, play less well with friends, and have fewer hobbies and activites than light viewers.

Parents can keep a time chart of a child's activities (including TV viewing, homework, play). They can discuss with the child what to eliminate and what to put in its place. Parents can set weekly viewing limits and make 'em stick. They can assign points to programs and give the child a point total to spend weekly. What parents consider undesirable programs can cost the child more in points than desirable programs. Parents can rule out TV before breakfast or on school nights—and make lists of alternative activities like riding a bicycle, reading a book, working on a hobby. Before watching TV, the child must select and do something from this list. Parents set the example; so they must control their own TV habits. Parents can watch at least one episode of the programs the child watches—and discuss violence and explain how violence is faked on TV—how TV uses stunt people, camera zooms, dream sequences, and animations to create fantasy.

About ads: Teach the child facts from nutrition (read package labels). Explain the purpose of advertising and explain disclaimers in a child's words.

13–13.   As a new employee in the advertising department, International Airlines, 2300 North Street, N.W., Washington, DC 20037, write a memo with graphics to George Garn, head of advertising. International has been running 30-second TV ads at prime time (between 5:30 and 6:30 P.M.) during the popular news presentations on CBS, ABC, and NBC. Ads up to now have featured mainly businessmen rushing to catch a plane; but already 18 percent of business passengers are women. Your concern is that more women should be featured in the ads in view of their increasing role in employment and in airplane travel.

Women are increasing in the work force at a rate of almost 2 million every year. More than half the country's 84 million women, including a majority of mothers with school-age children, now work or seek jobs. The management-consulting firm of Sandler & Heidrick, Inc., says the number of women corporate officers in the 1,300 largest companies rose to 416 last year—a one-year increase of 28 percent. According to the U.S. Department of Labor and Commerce 6 percent of the nation's working women are managers and administrators, 1 percent farm workers, 35 percent clerical workers, 7 percent sales workers, 6 percent schoolteachers, 21 percent service workers, 15 percent blue-collar workers, and 10 percent other professionals. Among the approximately 38 million women in nonfarm jobs, 87.3 percent are white and 12.7 percent black. Marital status shows 19.0 percent single, 56.4 percent married, and 24.6 percent divorced, separated, or widowed. In addition, millions of other women work at home or in volunteer tasks each year. Mothers working at or seeking jobs represent 53 percent; 47 percent are not in the labor force.

Women also are going to professional schools in record numbers. The Labor Department says that they will comprise 18 percent of all professionals in seven years. About 10,000 are studying engineering—10 times as many as nine years ago. Total earnings of working women seven years ago were $127.4 billion; today they are $254.3 billion (up 100 percent). Working women earning $25,000 or more seven years ago numbered 25,000 and today 217,000 (up 768 percent). Life insurance coverage in force for women ran $200 billion seven years ago and today $380 billion (up 90 percent). Individual women holding American Express Cards six years ago numbered 0.7 million; today there are 1.9 million (up 171 percent).

13–14.   You are a young paralegal assistant working for a young, beginning lawyer. Up to now you have been going around the corner to Kinko's Duplicating Service to make copies at 5 cents a sheet (legal or regular size).

Today, a letter from Copox, 1350 Jefferson Road, Rochester, NY 14623, offers its reconditioned Copox 490, for $1,195 or $41.31 a month with down payment of $119.50. If you and the lawyer take Copox up on its 15-day-trial offer, you get (1) free copier stand (31″ high × 18″ wide × 30″ wide with large roomy shelves to store paper, dry imager, developer, and office supplies) that regularly sells for $165; (2) starter supply kit, worth $28; (3) free delivery and installation worth $64.

The brochure says

"These machines have merely been outgrown by their previous users. We select only the finest copiers from this supply. Copiers have received the meticulous care of skilled Copox technicians throughout their history. We take these "cream of the crop" copiers, carefully clean and disassemble them, and then rebuild them "from the ground up." Defective and worn-out parts are replaced, working surfaces lubricated and adjusted. Once this is done, we run a complete operational check."

The brochure adds that the machine makes 11 copies per minute, each copy costs less than 1.5 cents for paper and supplies.

Should the lawyer invest in this Copox? The lawyer wants you to write a memo report with recommendations. Last month you finalized 10 wills and in the course made copies of 50 pages. As a guesstimate you assume that you use about 20,000 sheets of copy paper every two months. The lawyer pays you $60 a day.

13–15. As the very successful owner-manager of a large wedding-planning service, you are confronted with a report that makes you wish you had taken your report-writing course more seriously a few years ago. You remember one thing, however, that you *know* you have to be careful about this time—the point of objectivity in report writing. So you'll get the latest edition of your textbook and bone up on that point and others. (You used the sixth edition—and sold it, to your regret several times before this.)

The problem: In talking with the prospective clients involved in a forthcoming wedding, you've already heard so much disagreement that they have asked you for a full report (six copies, one each for the bride and groom and each of their parents) with recommendations in line with what they've all said in talking with you.

That will be difficult—but profitable if you can convince them all. The bride's clear attitude (in line with her whole life) is basically "shoot the works." The groom said (seriously) he wished they could just elope—but tried to make a joke of it to appease the bride in shock. Her mother has taken almost the groom's line; but her wealthy father has merely asked you to keep it reasonable but delightfully stylish and conventional. The groom's mother rules out any alcoholic drinks (will not attend if any are on the premises), whereas her husband urges engaging the ballroom of the country club (with a good bar close down the hall) and a boisterously risqué orchestra. Consider recommending or not recommending (with prices) reception (food and drink, catering, restaurant, country club, home)? Invitations, announcements, flowers (real or permanent), music, photographer, minister, gifts for attendants, clothing for attendants, bride, and groom? Wedding rings? Honeymoon?

13–16.   As city manager in a sizable city with an excellent three-year-old city hall, you want to write a justification report to the five city commissioners recommending two daily 20-minute breaks for employees and an arrangement for an employee snack bar in available space in the hall. Adapting the selected space will cost $1,700, according to a careful estimate made by the contractor who built city hall.

Though breaks have never been approved, your talks with the 9 department heads and every 10th name on alphabetical lists of employees reveal that about 67 percent of the 200 employees take one or more anyway (15–40 minutes), conscientious workers resent the liberties taken by others (and many of the guilty feel guilty), and department heads have quit trying to prevent the unapproved breaks.

The city attorney tells you that your proposals are legal, within the power of the city commissioners to authorize. The proposed breaks are in line with allowed coffee-break time of at least half the business and industrial firms of the city and with the nationwide practices of three fourths of such firms (as reported in a recent survey by the National Office Management Association, *Coffee Breaks in U.S. Business and Industry,* Philadelphia, 1982, p. 17). Three usual restrictions—which you would want to attach—are that no more than half the employees of a department may be out at any time, breaks longer than 20 minutes will result in deduction of an hour's pay (though with good cause and special permission of the immediate superior, an employee may occasionally combine two breaks for the day), and break time is not to compensate for tardiness or early departure.

The doctoral dissertation—*Efficiency and the Coffee Break,* Harvard Press, Boston, 1981, p. 268—of E. E. Jennings, now professor of personnel management at Harvard, reports that breaks up to 20 minutes increase office-worker efficiency 4 percent in the morning and 6 percent in the afternoon.

From three highly respected restaurant owners who would like the concession, the best offer you could get was from a local man: A five-year lease renewable by mutual agreement, he to pay the city $100 a month plus 2 percent of gross profit. The hall is three blocks from any presently existing restaurant.

13–17.   As Martin Bellinger, personnel director of Four–N Company, write a memo report to R. H. Hamilton, executive officer, on the progress in the equal employment opportunity program in your company, using today's date. Your study included male and female of Caucasians, blacks, Orientals, American Indians, and Spanish, for three years ago and now, during which time total employment grew 14 percent. You are reporting on just the blacks and whites because the other groups made up such a small percentage.

Percentage of male, female, and black employees in each job category for three years ago and now

Job category	Male 3 years ago	Male Now	Female 3 years ago	Female Now	Black 3 years ago	Black Now
Officials and managers	99.0%	97.2%	1.0%	2.8%	0.3%	0.9%
Professionals	96.9	92.1	3.1	7.9	0.9	2.0
Technicians	88.1	85.7	11.9	14.3	2.4	4.1
Sales workers	99.7	96.0	0.3	4.0	2.2	3.5
Office and clerical	28.0	19.3	72.0	80.7	2.6	4.1
Craftsmen	98.6	97.2	1.4	2.8	3.2	3.6
Operatives	60.5	58.7	39.5	41.3	6.2	6.9
Laborers	78.1	70.3	21.9	29.7	10.9	12.0
Service workers	77.2	84.6	22.8	15.4	5.4	6.4
All categories	75.4	72.7	24.6	27.3	3.6	4.5

The key word here is *progress*. As a principle and an agreement with EEOC (Equal Employment Opportunity Commission), the 4–N Company is committed to evolutionary (but not revolutionary) employment practices that lead to a work force which reflects the statistical picture of the competent people in the population of the area.

13–18. Assume that you are Donald R. Samdahl, toolroom foreman, and you want to prepare a justification report for your boss Harvey Mappin, Operations Manager, Robinson Machine Company, New Brunswick, NJ 08901. For three years the Robinson Company has been sending tools for numbering to the Revere Electric Company, Patterson, New Jersey, for a cost of $477.50 annually, or 16 cents per tool. Robinson has more than 6,000 items in the toolroom, and purchasing department records indicate that annual replacements and additions average 2,980 items. Also, there's added cost of bookkeeping and transportation. And you're getting tired of all the lip (or worse) you have to take from mechanics when they want a tool and it's gone to Patterson for numbering.

An electric pencil with necessary attachments costs $63.85 and is made by the Heinz Products Company. Instruction on its use will be given to the employees of Robinson in an hour's time with no interruption of toolroom operation. Your men spend most of their time on tool maintenance, except during the rush at the first of a shift, and they would have plenty of time to number new tools as they are received. Much of tool maintenance is performed as a time filler.

13–19. Moving across the United States is big business to your Bowe Chemical Company, since you pay for the moves of new employees and employees whom you transfer. There's no way to guarantee a perfect move; but from the

Interstate Commerce Commission (ICC), which requires every moving company to hand it and each potential customer a copy of its performance report for the previous year, you have made a chart of 21 moving companies. From these figures select a company (identified by number—left-hand column) that would be the best carrier for moving your employees' household goods. Your short report in memo form goes from you, the treasurer, to the president, Donald Shellabarger, explaining your choice and your reasons.

Moving company	Underestimated (percent)	Shipment (percent)			
		Picked up late	Delivered late	With damage claim of $50 or more	Average time to settle claim (days)
1	24%	5%	19%	23%	42
2	25	16	21	24	54
3	24	5	23	17	40
4	26	4	24	13	46
5	23	6	12	16	18
6	21	21	30	17	24
7	8	5	12	16	52
8	21	2	16	19	37
9	20	8	14	13	46
10	16	18	21	15	45
11	16	11	26	12	20
12	25	1	20	12	26
13	11	7	30	16	63
14	25	1	27	20	44
15	21	1	14	26	28
16	27	13	15	16	50
17	30	2	12	17	67
18	23	1	16	11	32
19	19	10	18	11	43
20	25	16	15	13	31
21	17	3	23	13	46
Average for all 21 carriers	21%	7%	19%	16%	41 days

13–20. As a sociologist-demographer consultant to *Ebony* magazine, you have the job of helping the editors and writers keep informed on the progress of the 24 million blacks the magazine strongly desires to appeal to by careful adaptation. To help *Ebony* serve in this changing society, you collected the following facts from the U.S. Census Bureau's four-year study, "Social and Economic Status of the Black Population," published last July. Basically the study compares significant figures four years ago (labeled "then") and now. Write a memo using these facts and explain the interesting and significant trends. Though the editors might see the effects these trends should have on the content and style in *Ebony*, you want to go as far as you can in pointing them out—as recommendations. (Interpret the given data but stress trends rather than the constantly changing raw figures as follows.)

Median family income	Blacks	Whites	Blacks' income as percentage of whites' income
Then	$6,279	$10,236	61.3%
Now	7,808	13,356	58.5

Unemployment	Then	Now	Increase
Blacks	8.2%	9.9%	21%
Whites	4.5	5.0	11

Education	Then	Now
Proportion of blacks in college (age 18–24)	15.0%	18.0%
Proportion of blacks with 4 years of college (age 25–34)	6.1	8.1

Migration	Moving in	Moving out	Net migration
West	172,000	49,000	+123,000
South	276,000	241,000	+ 35,000
Northeast	88,000	143,000	− 55,000
North Central	96,000	199,000	−103,000

Black demography	Then	Now	Change
Suburbs	3,433,000	4,101,000	Up 19.5%
Central cities	12,909,000	13,777,000	Up 6.7
Small towns, rural areas	5,714,000	5,748,000	Up 0.6

13–21. Using the data in Case 13–13, assume that you are working in the advertising department of American Express. You feel that your job is to get backing for a campaign promoting American Express cards to women. Before you begin work on the campaign (direct mail, ads in women's magazines, TV spots), you write a memo with graphs to Hugh Mayer, vice president—marketing.

13–22. As supervisor of refrigeration and air conditioning at the biggest hospital in your area, you have a crew of three service and repair mechanics and three mechanic's helpers. Because of the amount of work, the turnaround time (report, work-order, repair) on repair and nonroutine service jobs is sometimes a month; and your department has been taking a considerable amount of heat (flak) from everybody else. Although the hospital has grown from 250 to 350 beds over the past five years, your crew has remained the same. Furthermore, 60 percent of your equipment is 10 or more years old; and, according to your experience and an article in the *Refrigeration and Air Conditioning Journal* last month (pp. 15–19), frequency and seriousness of repair on such equipment rise rapidly in the last 5 years of its 15-year normal-expectancy life. The article also says that regularity of maintenance affects the average life more than the amount of running does. Your replacement costs for the past four years seem to be in line with the article: (in round numbers) $17,500; $26,250; $35,000; $43,750.

You and all your crew feel that you need a fourth work team of a mechanic and a helper to take some of the pressure off your work force. You also all agree that the best mechanic you know you can get is one of your helpers, Aubrey Ilkerson (just over three years on the job; knows the equipment; has been servicing it under supervision, as the other helpers have, for two and one years). If you upgrade Ilkerson to mechanic, you will need to add two more helpers; so the added costs will be $20,800/yr. (increase of $4,160 for Ilkerson going from $4/hr. to $6/hr. for 52 weeks of 40 hrs. and two new helpers at $4/hr.).

You want to prepare a justification report to convince your boss (Eugene Scott, the plant manager) to authorize your plan. You want to have your program in effect by late spring, before the warm weather increases your work load. You are sure you can reduce the turnaround times on both service and repair—and thus increase patient and employee comfort (and, you hope, reduce the flak you and your crew swallowed last summer); but you also feel strongly (because of experience and the *Journal* article) that you can arrest if not reverse the steadily increasing replacement costs by more regular maintenance service, more prompt repair, and (in some cases) repairing instead of replacing.

13–23. Check with your campus police and other sources to find out how much personal property has been stolen from your campus in the last year. Also find out the number of physical assaults and get an estimate of the amount of furnishings that have been vandalized in the last year. As assistant to the vice president for student affairs, Office of Student Affairs, write a memo report for the president of your university. Make some positive suggestions as to what can be done to improve the security on your campus. Possible ideas: registration of valuables and engraving of an identification number on each item, bicycle registration, escort service, car check or survey, well-lighted walkways. Perhaps you could begin "Campus Watch," a week set aside to encourage preventive measures. What films could you show? How can you make the students aware of crime?

13–24. For an additional progress report, see Appendix E, II, E.

Preparing major analytical reports

14

[To think you know something that isn't so is worse than not to know.]

Having seen from the preceding discussion what a major analytical report *is*—along with main report uses, characteristics, and classes—you should be ready to learn *how to prepare one*. You should realize, too, that a good course in business reports is a course in research procedure, a course in the organization of ideas, a course in logic, a course in English composition, a course in supplementary communication devices, a course in organizational behavior and communication, and a course in human relations—all in a current and *practical* setting.

Since we are concerned here with major analytical reports, you need to realize that they (being comparatively long ones) involve much learning that shorter ones do not. We are aware that today's efficiency-minded organizations make much more frequent use of the short reports fully discussed and illustrated in the preceding chapter than of longer analytical reports explained and illustrated here and in the next two chapters. You need to be aware, however, that only those employees who can prepare these longer and more demanding reports are likely to get on the fast track of the promotion line in almost any business firm. The starting point is a sense for planning.

Preparing a major analytical report, whatever its length, is a five-step process: (1) planning the attack on the problem, (2) collecting the facts, (3) organizing the facts, (4) interpreting the facts, and (5) presenting the report in appropriate form and style. Since any or all of these five steps may be necessary in varying degrees in the preparation of a particular report in any form, we present the steps in this chapter before explaining and illustrating different forms in the next two chapters.

PLANNING THE ATTACK

Whether a report is oral or written, planning the attack is a job to be done at the desk—the headwork before the legwork. It involves six procedures, in the following sequence:

1. Get a clear view of what the central problem is. (If you can't see the target you're shooting at, you're not likely to hit it.)

This procedure requires reflective thinking. It may also require a conference with the person who needs the report. As a check, you can try writing a *concise* and *interesting* title that *clearly indicates the content and scope*. If you can also put in one sentence a precise statement of the purpose, clearly indicating what problem you are trying to help solve, you have the necessary clear view.

2. Consider conditions that influence the report—the attitude, degree of interest, knowledge, and temperament of the reader or audience; the use to be made of the report; and its importance.

The reader's or listener's temperament and knowledge of the subject have considerable influence on how much background and detailed explanation you need to give, and whether you can use technical terms. Your reputation as an authority and the reader's or audience's attitude will influence how persuasive you need to be (whether you use the convincing inductive plan or the faster, more interesting, but possibly less convincing deductive plan). Any known biases and special interests may influence what you should stress and whether you must use impersonal style. Your relationship to the primary receivers will indicate how formal or informal the style should be.

In considering use, remember that reports commonly go in the files for future reference after they have served their immediate purpose. Therefore they need to be clear to various people years later. Also, the person who asked for a written report may have to send it on up the chain of command for approval before anything can happen. So it needs to be intelligible to possible readers other than the one who asked for it.

Limitations on time, money, or availability of data may affect how thorough you can be and whether you can use costly plates and charts.

3. Divide the central problem (the *text* of your report) into its elements, the main divisions in an outline of the topic. The idea of dividing to conquer applies in report organization as well as in military strategy.

Whatever you do at this stage toward outlining will probably be only tentative and skeletal. You'll probably change it later, after you have the facts. At this point you merely need a starting guide to what kinds of facts to collect. So don't worry too much now about form and accuracy; specific instruction on the finished outline comes later in this chapter.

Of course, not all problems divide alike, but the dividing process is a job of finding the natural divisions of the whole. Since an introduction will be part I in your final outline, for now you can skip it and begin listing your criteria or other major divisions as II, III, IV, . . . or (as we explain later) 2.0, 3.0, 4.0, ...

If the problem is one of deciding between/among two or more things, the *criteria* are usually the best major division headings. For example, if you are trying to decide which of several jobs to take, on what bases (criteria) do you decide? Maybe

II. Kind of work		2.0 Kind of work
III. Location		3.0 Location
IV. Beginning pay	or	4.0 Beginning pay
V. Chances for advancement		5.0 Chances for advancement
VI. Working conditions		6.0 Working conditions

Some topics common to many business problems are history (if affecting the present and/or future), disadvantages of present system, advantages of proposed system, costs and means of financing, taxes and tax effects, personnel required, effects on goodwill, transportation, method of installation, utilities available and their costs, materials required, time involved, safety, increases or decreases in quality, market, competition, convenience, and availability of land.

4. Raise specific questions about each element. These questions further divide the problem, lead to subheads in your outline, and point more directly toward collecting data for answers. For instance on the job-choice problem under III (location) you might want to put subheads about moving, housing, climate, educational and recreational facilities, and perhaps others. Under IV (pay) you would surely think of beginning pay, chances for advancement, and retirement and other fringe benefits.

Put down all you can think of in this planning stage. But, so long as you have three to five major divisions between the introduction and the conclusions, don't worry too much about completeness. As you do your research, you'll think about (and add or combine) other major and/or subdivision topics for completeness in the final outline.

If cost is one of the elements in a problem, for example, you want to ask what the costs are for operating one way and what they would be under a revised system. You would then want to question further about how to find the costs in each instance. And you might do well to break the questions down further into first costs, operating costs, and depreciation; costs for personnel, for upkeep and for power; and the like. Specific questions on goodwill might include those about customers, stockholders, workers, and the general public.

5. Take stock of what you already know. You may pose a hypothesis, but don't let it close your mind to other possible solutions. Don't assume that you know the answer until all the facts are in. *You certainly don't want to start out to prove a preconceived notion* (a blinder on the truth and hence a danger in hypotheses).

Get a clear concept of the assumptions you are willing to make, and separate those that you can hold without further checking from those that you must check and perhaps validate by supporting evidence (or drop because of controverting evidence).

Jot down answers known for the questions raised. Clearly indicate information gaps you need to fill, and jot down what you think tentatively are the best sources and methods for getting the missing data—experts, books and articles, and maybe the person who faces the problem you're helping to solve. You might even have to devise some kind of experiment. Or perhaps you need to plan a survey and must decide on the kind and size of sample, kind of survey, and the like.

6. Make a working schedule. Assign estimated time blocks for each of the remaining steps in producing the report: collecting remaining data—and organizing it, interpreting it, and wording the final report. If you plan a survey,

remember that mail requires time and that people don't always respond to questionnaires immediately. For any except the most routine kind of reports, be sure to allow some time for revising early drafts to put the final report in clear, interesting, and inconspicuous style and form.

The first item on the working schedule is the next step in report preparation—collecting the facts.

COLLECTING THE FACTS

[*The ladder to success must rest on something solid.*]

For collecting complete and reliable facts, you may use any or all of the four basic methods of securing information: (1) library research (reading), (2) observation, (3) experimentation, and (4) surveys. The first provides secondary (secondhand) data, and the others provide primary (firsthand or new) facts. In most cases you should use at least two of the methods in such a way as to get at the essential facts and assure their reliability.

Library research

While we know that many (even most) reports in business and industry are short ones dealing with day-to-day operations and not making much use of library research, we also know that high-level managements making major decisions nearly always do depend partly on major reports. For them, library research is almost invariably a part.

Indeed study of published books, articles, theses, brochures, speeches and other reports is the most universally useful method and is *usually the best first step*. When you face any problem of consequence, somebody else has probably faced the same or a closely related problem and written something worthwhile and relevant to your problem. And when pertinent data are already written, getting the facts by reading is nearly always easier and quicker than the laborious process of getting primary data by any of the other research methods.

Besides being the quick and easy way to collect facts, reading may also give a bird's-eye view of the whole problem, acquaint you with terminology and methods you may not have thought of, refer to other good sources, show formerly overlooked natural divisions and aspects of the problem, and in general help you to revise your tentative outline and plan of attack.

Reading about almost any topic, however, can be so extensive as to bog you down. Fortunately, you have good reasons to avoid that pitfall in doing research for a report. A report is a practical communication concerned with *currently* and *foreseeably pertinent* data. *It is not* a compendium, an encyclopedia, or a definitive treatment. Hence you can and should be *selective* in your reading for a report—ignoring the long ago and far away that is outdated or otherwise irrelevant. A good start is to weed out bibliographic materials by looking at their dates.

In what we give you here, to be helpful in your bibliographical research, we are selective on the basis of dates and on other bases. Instead of giving you even a large sample of the mind-boggling and space-wasting quantity of constantly obsolescing business-oriented publications in a good library, we give you the essence of library-research procedures or approaches and the main *keys* (guides) to finding what you need. With them—plus a little effort and help when needed from reference librarians (and sometimes a little bit o' luck)—you can find what you need for your report.

Today most libraries have computer bibliography search help with major retrieval systems such as DIALOG, ORBIT, and BRS. You are able to get fast, current, comprehensive, and precise bibliographic citations and numerical data, sometimes at no cost. The more complex the subject, the more likely the cost will increase. After you and the librarian arrive at appropriate data base(s), the librarian enters the terms that describe your topic. The computer responds immediately with a printed bibliography (often with abstracts).

Another helpful device is the cumulative business index on computer output microfilm. You can sit in front of this machine and find current sources of information under either subject or author.

Besides these machines, libraries nearly always have at least three broad categories of materials—reference books, books in the stacks, and periodicals. Some main ones of regular reference books are:

Encyclopedias *(Americana, Columbia, Encyclopaedia of the Social Sciences, Encyclopedia of Science and Technology,* and the definitive *Encyclopaedia Britannica).* (For any rapidly changing topic, check the publication date.)

Collections of generally useful, up-to-date statistical and other information, surprising in variety and amount *(The World Almanac* and *Facts on File).*

Census reports (U.S. government censuses of agriculture, business, government housing, manufacturing, population, minerals, and other breakdowns. Remember that the U.S. census is decennial; so the information you read in 1985 is really 1980 data.)

Yearbooks of various countries, trades, and professions (commerce, shipping, agriculture, engineering, and others).

Atlases (especially those by Rand McNally, the *Britannica, National Geographic*, and Hammond).

Dictionaries *(American College Dictionary, Standard College Dictionary, Webster's Collegiate Dictionary, Webster's New International Dictionary* [unabridged], and [for etymology particularly] the *Oxford English Dictionary).*

Directories (such as Thomas' for American manufacturers and Ayer's for newspapers and magazines).

Who's who in various fields (including the *Directory of American Scholars, American Men of Science, World Who's Who in Commerce and Industry,* and Poor's *Register of Corporations, Directors and Executives*).

Statistical source books *(Statistical Yearbook, Statistical Abstract of the United States, Survey of Current Business, County and City Data Book).*

These are just a few main examples of the numerous reference books usually in a library. Constance Winchell's *Guide to Reference Books* (recent editions revised by Eugene P. Sheehy) tells about them and many more. Other helpful guides are Herbert W. Johnson's *How to Use the Business Library*, Robert W. Murphy's *How and Where to Look It Up*, Gale Research Company's *Encyclopedia of Business Information Services*, and Rae E. Rip's *United States Government Publications*.

The standard key to books in the stacks is the card catalog, arranged alphabetically by author, subject, and title. But because libraries available to most researchers will not have all the books published on their subjects; because it takes months for books to be published, bought by libraries, and cataloged for distribution; and because not all topics appear in full-book treatment, for reports often the best up-to-date printed sources are periodicals (pertinent articles found through appropriate periodical indexes).

Fortunately, one or more of the numerous periodical indexes, both general and specific for almost any field, covers most periodicals. Table 14–1 describes the main current indexes; but if you do not find one for your specific field, look around and/or ask the reference librarian. And if the abbreviations or the system of indexing is not immediately clear to you, the preface always explains.

Whatever library key you use, you need to develop resourcefulness. Often when you look under one topic (say "Business Letter Writing" or "Report Writing"), you will find little or nothing. Don't give up. You have to match wits with the indexer and try to think of other possible wordings for the topic. "Business Letter Writing" might be under "Business English" or "Commercial Correspondence" and "Report Writing" under "Technical Writing" or something else.

When your resourcefulness brings you to a book or article that seems to be useful, scan it to see what portion (if any) of it is grist for your mill. A look at the table of contents may tell you whether it will be helpful.

If it seems pertinent, check its *reliability*. Remember that no decision maker wants to base decisions on unsound data, yours or anybody else's. Consider whether (1) the material is outdated, (2) the textual evidence and the reputation of the publisher and of the author reveal any possible slant or prejudice, and (3) the author is a recognized authority in the field. Reading a review in a related journal can help in judging the worth of a book. A sound reporter will not be duped by the usual undue worship of the printed word; just realize that something's being in print does not make it true.

Table 14–1 Main current indexes

Title	Coverage	Publication facts (most frequent issue and cumulation)
Accountants' Index	International; technical books and magazines	Quarterly, annually
Applied Science and Technology Index	Scientific, engineering and technical American and international magazines	Monthly except July; annually
Biological and Agricultural Index	International; books and magazines	Monthly except August; annually
Business Periodicals Index	Business, industrial, and trade magazines	Monthly except August; quarterly, annually
Chemical Abstracts	International; all phases of chemistry	Biweekly; semiannually
Education Index	Professional literature	Monthly except July and August; annually
Engineering Index	Domestic and international literature on engineering	Monthly; annually
Index Medicus	International; medicine and related fields	Monthly; annually
New York Times Index	The news in the paper	Semimonthly; quarterly, annually
Predicasts, U.S.	U.S. business activity	Weekly; quarterly, annually
Predicasts, International	International business activity	Weekly; quarterly, annually
Public Affairs Information Service (PAIS)	Periodicals and government documents and pamphlets of general, technical, and economic interest	Semimonthly; quarterly, annually
Readers' Guide to Periodical Literature	General American magazines	Semimonthly; annually and/or biennially
Social Science and Humanities Index	Emphasis on history, international relations, political science, and economics	March, June, September, December; annually
Wall Street Journal Index	Corporate and general business news	Monthly; annually
Work Related Abstracts	Labor activities and problems	Monthly; annually

If the material meets the tests for reliability and relevance (including its date), take notes—*a separate card or sheet of paper for each important note*. If you put more than one note to the card, you will have trouble in arranging the cards later because the different notes on a card will not all fit at the same place in your report, and hence some multinote cards will belong in two or more places in your arrangement. To save time later in arranging notes, put a notation at the head of each note card (that is, one which indicates where the information fits in your plan). It may well be the heading in your outline or the divisional symbol from your outline, say Section 3.3.

Of course, if you take a needed note on some topic not in your tentative outline, you make a slugged card for it and add the topic to your outline. Using cards for your notes gives several advantages:

1. They encourage taking concise rather than wordy notes. (Most notes should be mere jottings. But don't let them get you into trouble.)
2. You can handle them better than sheets of paper—and move them around better for adding to, subtracting from, or reorganizing your original (tentative) outline.

When in doubt, take fuller rather than scantier notes than you think you need; it's easier to omit later than to come back for more.

Some notes you may want to take as verbatim quotations, but usually not. Good researchers do not use many direct quotations—only (1) to gain the impact of the author's authority, (2) to be fair by stating exactly before criticizing, or (3) to take advantage of the conciseness, exactness, or aptness of phrasing. If you do quote, be sure to quote exactly and not change the original meaning by lifting a small part from a context in which it means something different.

In most cases you can save words and express the idea better for your purposes if you paraphrase. When you paraphrase, however, be sure not to change the original meaning.

In some cases you can save time later by writing your notes as a review of the article or book—that is, from your own point of view, giving the essential content of the article along with your comment on it—because that seems to be the form it will take in the final report. In other cases you will condense, digest, or abstract the article.

Whether you quote, paraphrase, review, or abstract the article or book, list in your bibliography *all* printed sources used directly in the preparation of the report; so you need to take the necessary bibliographic information while you have the book or magazine in hand. Although bibliography form is not standardized, the usual information is author's name (surname first, for alphabetizing), title of book or article and magazine, publisher and place of publication for books, edition if not the first for books, volume and inclusive page numbers for magazine articles, and the date. (The exact form comes later.) For use in citations in the text, record the specific pages used for each note.

What we have suggested here are sound, basic library research procedures. If you follow them, you will make your library research effective, efficient, economical—and painless.

Observation

The second method of collecting data—observation—includes not only its usual meanings but also investigation of company records of finances, production, sales, and the like. As such, it is the main method accountants and engineers use for audit, inspection, and progress reports.

The job of collecting data by observation usually involves no particular problem of getting at the facts. The important part is more likely to be *knowing what facts to consider*. This problem requires keeping in mind what your purpose is, so as to notice everything relevant and to relate each pertinent fact to the whole situation.

A skilled police officer's investigation of a murder scene or of an automobile accident site exemplifies the technique. Camera, measuring tape, and note pad are standard equipment for outside observation, just as the accountant's special paper, sharp pencil, and calculator are for inside inspection of the records. Still, the most important pieces of equipment are sharp eyes to see the situation, judgment to evaluate it, and (most important) imagination to see the relevance of a particular observed fact to the whole problem.

Observation has the advantage of being convincing, just as the testimony of an eyewitness convinces a jury more than circumstantial evidence. But it has the disadvantage of not getting at motives. That is, it may answer *what* but not find out *why*. For instance, an observer stationed in the aisle of a supermarket may tabulate which brand of detergent each shopper chooses, but that will tell nothing about why each shopper made that choice. And an observer who is not careful may put too much stress on a few isolated cases or may ignore factors (weather, place, time of year, month, week, or day) influencing what was visible for recording.

Experimentation

For the most part, experimentation is useful in the physical sciences rather than in business and the social sciences. And of course, the methods used vary almost infinitely according to the particular experiment to be done. Regardless of field or problem, however, an experimenter should be as zealous as a reporter about the reliability of results. The basic requirements for reliability in experimentation are three:

1. Accurate equipment (if used). If a laboratory balance is inaccurate, or if a tachometer or thermometer misrepresents the facts, the results of an experiment using them will be unreliable.

2. Skilled techniques. A technician who doesn't know how to set a microscope won't be able to see an amoeba and, if unable to pipette both accurately and fast, will be no good at Kahn tests. Skilled techniques also include proper selection of specimens for study.

3. Sufficient controls or repetition of results. If an experimenter takes two specimens just alike and treats them exactly alike except in one way (perhaps inoculates one, keeping the other for a control), different results (say one gets a disease and the other does not) make a strong start toward convincing us. If repeating the experiment produces exactly the same thing every time (100 percent), only a few repetitions are thoroughly convincing. For every drop from 100 percent, however, the experimenter has to multiply the number of tests many times to produce similar faith in them.

Testing only one variable at a time is basic. If soil, seed, and temperature all change in two runs of an agricultural experiment, you cannot attribute different results to any one of them. If you clean your tank and refill with different gasoline, repair your carburetor, and adjust your ignition system all at the same time and your car runs better, you won't know what caused your troubles before.

Experts in certain phases of business can use experimentation that closely parallels laboratory methods if they are careful about their *equipment, techniques,* and *controls.* For example, marketing specialists can test the comparative effects of different advertising campaigns and media, sales promotion devices, prices, and packaging. Their problems of equipment and technique may be more psychological than mechanical and manual, and their controls can be difficult to set up to make sure that only one element changes; but experts can manage all three to assure reasonable reliability. (See "Tests and Testing," late in Chapter 8, on testing sales campaigns.)

Surveys

Often the quality to be tested is not subject to exact laboratory-type examination—the sales appeal of a new car, for example. The only place to get an answer to that is from people. In fact, the survey for fact and opinion is a major method of collecting data for business and social science reports. It is particularly useful in discovering *why* people do certain things and in *forecasting* what will happen (both frequently important jobs of reports).

Regardless of which of the three kinds of surveys you use—mail questionnaire, personal interview, or telephone interview—research by survey involves certain basic problems, principles, and techniques.

Determining what people you will survey is the first problem. In some cases you may decide that the opinions of a few experts will be worth more than the answers of thousands of the general public, as they will be if the problem is technical or professional (say medical or legal). In that case, Chapter 11 and the "Interviews" section of Chapter 17 will help you more than the discussion of sampling here. If the whole group involved (called *the universe* by statisticians) is small, you may decide to ask all of them. But in most cases you take a sample.

How large a sample you need for sound results then becomes your next problem. The answer will depend on the degree of accuracy required and on the variety of possible answers. For instance, if plus or minus 10 percent is close enough, your sample can be much smaller than if you have to be accurate within a range of 1 percent. And if you have to forecast election returns only in terms of Democratic, Republican, and other votes, your sample can be much smaller than if you have to forecast the purchases of the 50 or more makes and body styles of cars. As an even simpler illustration, you can certainly better predict the fall of a coin (only two choices) than of a pair of dice, with 11 possible readings.

Although a full treatment of sampling theory would require a complete book, statisticians have provided us with some *simple devices for determining adequate sample size*. The simplest is the split-sample test. You break your sample arbitrarily (that is, to avoid any known differences) into two or more parts. You then compare the results from the various parts. If the results from the partial samples are acceptably close together, the results from the total sample will be acceptably reliable.

More precise checks on the adequacy of sample size require only a little mathematics and procedures explained in any beginning book on statistics. We do not present them here because judgment, a study of statistics, and our observation of professional pollsters' accuracy based on surprisingly *small* samples show two things: (1) most people think a sample must be larger than it (statistically) needs to be and (2) most people give too little attention to the other equally important requirement for a sound sample—stratification.

Even your adequate *sample must be stratified* (sometimes imprecisely called *representative*) or your results can go wild. That is, *each segment of the universe must appear in the sample with the same percentage as in the universe*. According to sampling theory, this will be the result if you take a large enough *random* sample (one in which each item in the universe has an equal chance of getting into the sample). In practice, however, you often have trouble making sure you really have a random sample. Unsuspected selective factors may work to produce an unstratified (and hence unsound) sample.

To avoid such a possibility, you can (as professionals usually do) use stratified sampling if you have data showing the proportions of different segments in your universe. Fortunately, you usually do. Just as a college registrar's office knows the number of students in different classes, majors, age groups, grade-point groups, and the like, the statistical source books provide breakdowns of people in nearly every imaginable way. Whatever group you may want to sample, you probably can find the proportions of the different segments making up the universe. The U.S. Census Bureau breaks its population figures down in almost every imaginable way. Remember, though, that the bureau's real head count is every 10 years (those ending in 0—1970, 1980, 1990, . . .). Figures between those years are only estimates—but good ones. If 50 percent of your universe are farmers and 70 percent telephone subscribers, half your sample must be farmers and 70 percent telephone subscribers.

Adequate size and stratification together make a sound sample.

A sound sample can still produce unsound results, however, unless your techniques of getting answers from it are also sound. If you start out by surveying a minimum sound sample but get answers from only half of it, the sample of actual answers is unsound because it is too small. If you survey more than enough and get a large enough sample of answers, but 100 percent of one stratification group answers and only half of another group answers, your returns are not stratified and hence are not reliable. Of course, the best solution is to get 100 percent returns from all groups—an ideal rarely accomplished.

How can you induce people to answer survey questions? Sometimes a respondent is already so much interested, because the benefit is obvious, that you need not point it out. You can therefore begin directly with the request for help, as in the direct inquiry letters discussed in Chapter 5. At other times you have a selling job to do, as in persuasive requests (Chapter 11). Whether you are using a mail questionnaire, a personal interview, or a telephone interview makes little difference in the approach. Neither does the amount of information you want make much difference—whether you want to ask just one or dozens of questions. But to misjudge the situation and make a direct inquiry when you need a persuasive request may result in decreased returns and hence an unreliable sample.

Fundamentally, your persuasive method is the same as in persuading people to do anything, as in sales and collection letters: *Show them a benefit to themselves*. It may be a gift or reward, direct payment of a fee, or less obvious and less material benefits such as appeals to pride and prestige (but not obvious flattery), appeals to their desire for better service or more efficiency in their kind of work, or the possibility of their getting answers to some questions or solutions to problems they encounter in their own work.

The last two are frequently the best (because they avoid suggesting a bribe or being too mercenary, as the first two might), and they are more immediate and tangible than the others. For instance, personnel officers who read lots of poor application letters are likely to answer a textbook writer's or a teacher's questions about preferences in application letters—because of the possibility that they may as a result get more good applications and thereby make their work easier. A frequent method of inducing answers is the offer of a copy or digest of the survey results.

A big point to remember in making persuasive requests is to show a benefit *before* making the request. Then if you explain who is making the survey and why; make answering as easy, quick, and impersonal as possible; assure respondents that you will honor restrictions they put on use of the information; and tell pointedly just what you want them to do, enough people will usually do it to make your results reliable. Skilled approaches, both oral and written, often bring percentages of answers that surprise the untrained who have tried their hands and failed.

Chapter 11 explains in detail how to induce reluctant people to respond as you wish. If you feel more adept at talking on the phone than at writing a persuasive letter, you might consider calling people in your selected sample and asking them to cooperate in answering questions you plan to send. If you do, the principles in Chapter 11 apply to the oral persuasion too. It has been very successful in several situations that we know.

The approach you use will be a major factor in determining your success in getting returns by personal interview, telephone interview, or mail questionnaire; but *the questions you ask and how you ask them will affect both the percentage of returns and the worth of the answers*. For that reason, writers of questionnaires and people planning interviews need to keep in mind the following main principles professionals use:

1. Ask as few questions as you can to get the necessary information. Don't ask other people for information you should have dug up for yourself, possibly in the library. And don't ask a question when you can figure the answer from the answers to others. To avoid unnecessary questions—which reduce returns—write down all you can think of, group them, and then knock out the duplicates. (One kind of duplication is permissible: double-check questions which get at the same information from different approaches as a check on the validity of answers.)

2. Ask only what you might reasonably expect to be answered. Requests for percentages and averages are either too much work or over the heads of many people. Questions requiring long memory may frustrate and bring erroneous results. And most people don't even know *why* they do many things.

3. Make your questions as easy to answer as possible (perhaps by providing for places to check); but provide for all likely answers (at least the "no opinion" answer and perhaps the blank to be filled as the respondent wants to because no one of your suggested answers is suitable).

4. Make your questions perfectly clear. To do so, you may sometimes have to explain a bit of necessary background. If you ask "Why do you use X peanut butter?" you may get "It is cheapest," "A friend recommended it," and "I like its smooth texture and easy spreading" from three respondents. If you really want to know how the customer first learned of X, you should phrase the question in such a way as to get answers parallel to the second. If you are interested in the qualities that users like (as in the third answer), you should ask that specific question. Questions about *how* cause as many different interpretations as those asking *why* and require the same kind of careful wording. Also, doubled-barreled questions ("Did you see X, and did you like it?") frustrate the reader who wants to answer one part one way and the other part another way.

5. Carefully avoid leading questions—questions which suggest a certain answer, such as one to agree with the questioner's obvious view.

6. Insofar as possible, phrase questions to avoid the "prestige" answer—the respondent's answering according to what apparently would make the best impression.

7. Avoid unnecessary personal prying. When your question is necessary to your basic purpose, make it as inoffensive as possible (for instance, by asking which named *income* or *age* or *educational group* the respondent falls in, if that rather than the exact figure will serve your purpose).

8. Arrange questions in an order to encourage response—easier or impersonal ones at first, related ones together in a natural sequence to stimulate interest and aid memory.

9. Insofar as possible, ask for answers that will be easy to tabulate and evaluate statistically; but when they are important, don't sacrifice shades of meaning or intensity of feeling in the answer for easy handling. Often the most helpful answers a survey brings are those to open-end questions; but if you ask many of them, you will reduce your returns. Such questions require time and thought to answer as well as to analyze.

Often *scaled* answer forms can bring responses desirably showing intensities of feelings that are still easy to tabulate and evaluate statistically. For example, a form asking for students' evaluations of professors might use a labeled continuum, thus: "On (a certain aspect of teaching), how would you rate Professor X?"

Excellent	Very good	Good	Average	Poor	Bad	Terrible
+3	+2	+1	0	−1	−2	−3

After you have decided on the questions you want answered, your next problem is deciding *which type of survey* (mail questionnaire, personal interview, or telephone interview) will best serve your purposes. No one type is always best. The main *bases for your decision* are:

1. *The kind and amount of information requested from each respondent.* People are more willing to *tell* you personal information—and more of it—than they are to put personal facts in writing or to do very much writing. So if the requested information is personal or extensive, the personal interview would probably be the best form. The comparative anonymity of the interviewer and reluctance to talk long over the telephone with strangers are against the telephone method for such a situation. On the other hand, factual information (especially statistics, percentages, and averages) which the respondent may not know at the moment would come best in writing because the respondent can take a little time to dig up the information for a mail questionnaire.

2. *Costs.* Two facts about the sample to be surveyed affect the choice of method on the basis of cost—its size and dispersal. Within one telephone exchange, if your group is not large, the telephone is the cheapest method; but if it involves long-distance charges, they become prohibitive unless the group is small. The mail questionnaire has the advantage of wide geographical coverage at no additional cost; and the bigger the group, the greater the advantage, because duplicating and (even two-way) mailing of copies of a good set of questions costs little. The personal interview is almost always the most costly (mainly in interviewer's time) unless the group is both small and close together.

You need to consider cost per return, however; and since the mail questionnaire unusually brings in the lowest percentage of returns, its advantages may not be so great as at first thought unless a good covering letter and set of questions mailed at an opportune time induce a high percentage of answers.

3. *Speed in getting results*. If you have to have the answers today, you can get some of them by telephone (and by personal interview if your sample is not too large and the people are close together); but you can't get them by mail. Mail answers will flood you in about four days and dribble in for a week or more after that, unless you made clear that you need the information by a certain time (a point which needs careful justifying through end dating to avoid the bad manners of rushing a person to do you a favor).

4. *Validity of results*. Each of the three kinds of survey has advantages and disadvantages in terms of validity. Personal and telephone interviews, both being oral, have more traits in common than either has with mail questioning. Either the personal or the telephone interview can better clear up any confusion about questions and thereby get appropriate answers. In addition, the personal interviewer may pick up supplementary information (such as the general look of economic conditions around the home and incidental remarks of the talker) that will provide a check on answers given—an impossibility by mail.

On the other hand, in personal and telephone interviews people may give you offhand answers to get rid of you because the time of the call is inconvenient; and they may answer according to what they think is your view (playing the prestige-answer game). Moreover, high-pressure personal selling, obscene phone calls, and other abuses have made many people wary of personal and telephone calls, thus making oral surveys increasingly difficult and complicating the job of keeping samples stratified (and thus valid). Also certain segments of the population have fewer telephones than others and thereby skew a telephone sample—just as certain kinds of doors (maybe apartment dwellers'), being especially hard to get into, skew samples for personal interviewers.

Perhaps the biggest advantage of mail questionnaires is that people can choose the most convenient time to answer and are therefore more likely to answer thoughtfully. That includes taking time to check records for information not on the tip of the tongue. Moreover, everybody has a mailing address where a mail questionnaire can get in; so in view of costs and time, the mail questionnaire is less likely to be limited to a too-small group or one that is geographically or economically limited. But those who choose not to answer may be a special group (say the less educated who don't like to write) and may thereby unstratify your carefully planned sample.

5. *Qualifications of the staff*. Some people who can talk well and thus get information may not be able to write a good questionnaire and covering letter; and, of course, the opposite may be true. Even some good talkers have poor telephone voices that discourage that method. And others have appearances that discourage personal interviews.

If you select an adequate and stratified sample, induce people to answer by showing a benefit, ask good questions, and use the type of survey most suitable for your situation, surveys can get you a great variety of valuable information for your reports.

ORGANIZING THE FINDINGS

However you collect and record the necessary facts for your report, you have to organize them for interpretation (in an analytical report) and for presentation. Good organization is the marshaling of statements and supporting details, the orderly procession of paragraphs, the disposition of parts so that each finds its proper place.

Fundamentally, organization is the process of grouping things according to likeness and then putting the groups into an appropriate sequence. For example, if you explain in your letter or report how something is made, you should treat that part fully before going on to explain how it operates. Either of these topics may be just one paragraph, or it may be several. But you do want to group together all the details about how it is made before proceeding. Thus you achieve unity of that topic.

Having grouped according to likenesses, you have several choices of sequence for a whole letter, memo, or paragraph. Common paragraph sequences are (1) general to specific, (2) cause to effect, (3) order of importance, (4) nearest to farthest (space relations), and (5) order of happening (time relations). All of these may be reversed.

Your problem of organizing is probably easier than you suspect, however, because conventional practice (or someone who set up a standard plan of reports where you work) will have done most of the job for you. If you have no set plans to follow where you work, Chapters 15 and 16 explain and illustrate overall organization that is almost standard for any major analytical report.

Your only problem—and the only one we are talking about here, therefore—is the final organization of the *text* of major analytical reports. The introduction is the first major division (1.0) of your final plan, and the conclusions and recommendations (together or separately) are usually the last one or two. The text includes the several (usually 3–5) major divisions between the introduction and the conclusions.

For a graphic, overview of what we're saying, look at the first section of Chapter 15. We're saying that you now must revise your earlier tentative outline for a final one whose skeleton is like ours, but you must put flesh (the meat of your report) on your skeleton.

Because the text is the essence of the report, *you do not have a section heading for it*. (If you did, it would be the same as the title of the whole report.) The divisions of the text, then, usually constitute sections 2.0., 3.0., 4.0., and so on—where you present all your facts, explanations, and reasons leading to your conclusions and recommendations. According to the instructions in an earlier section ("Planning the attack," items 3, 4, and 5), you should already have set up the organization of your text as a tentative and probably incomplete plan to guide you in collecting data. If you didn't read and follow those instructions, you need to do so now.

That preliminary plan is the starting point for doing the present job—making a final outline as a guide to interpreting and presenting the facts.

Basically, organizing (outlining) is the process of putting related things into groups according to common characteristics *and your purpose* (playing poker instead of bridge, for example), and then putting the groups into a desirable sequence. In the process you may find that you need to revise your tentative outline because the information classified according to your first plan is not logically or psychologically arranged for good presentation. For instance you will want to *make sure that things the reader or audience needs to compare are close together*.

Certainly you need to check your tentative plan before going further. You may now be able to see enough interpretations of your data to make a sentence outline, as you couldn't earlier, because sentences require you to *say something about* the topics. If you can, it will be easier to follow while wording the report, it will force more careful thinking, and it will give the essence of your report (not just the list of topics discussed but the key statements about those topics). Because of its helpfulness in phrasing the report, you may want to make a full-sentence outline (like a lawyer's brief or a précis) for close-knit, logical wording, and then change it to one of the less cumbersome forms (later discussed) for final presentation.

Whether you use full sentences or noun-phrase topics, close adherence to the following principles is necessary for a good final plan (outline):

1. Stick to the *one basis of classification* implied in your title and purpose as you break down any topic (such as your text) into its parts. For example, on the basis of credit hours earned, college students are freshmen, sophomores, juniors, seniors, or graduates. You can't logically classify them as juniors, Protestants, and Democrats. Such a procedure shifts bases in helter-skelter fashion from credit hours earned to religion to politics. You would have overlapping topics, whereas the divisions of an outline should be mutually exclusive.

If your title is "Reasons for (or "Why) . . . ," the major divisions of your text can't logically be anything but the list of reasons. If the title is something like "Factors Influencing . . ." or "Ways to . . . ," each major division of the *text* will have to be one of those factors or ways. The title "Market Factors Indicating Why a Rexwall Drugstore in Savannah Would Sell More Than One in Charleston" commits you to show for each subject—Charleston and Savannah—market factor evidence supporting your thesis. (This does not forbid giving the introduction, conclusions, and recommendations similar major-division status. They are not parts of the text you're organizing.)

Your proper basis for dividing the text will depend on the nature of the problem. It may be the parts of a whole, the factors to be considered, time periods, space areas, and many others. Cost-benefit and before-after analyses sound good but are too simplistic, and they defeat juxtaposition too much, for good report writing about more than simple problems. Organizing on the basis of how or where you got the information is never desirable—except possibly in a simple comparison study to evaluate the method or source. Even then, however, you have a better way.

In outlines of comparison leading to a choice, use the criteria (bases on which the choice depends) rather than the subjects (the things between or among which you must choose) as the major divisions. Your criteria are the things on which your choice will stand or fall, and hence they deserve the emphasis. In evaluating a Ford and a Chevrolet, for example, you should use both names frequently in your organization scheme, but neither would be a major heading as such. Your major headings would be the tests you decide to apply: costs (initial and operating—and possibly trade-in value), performance, comfort, safety, and appearance. Under each head you would have to analyze each subject (Ford and Chevrolet).

2.   Follow one good system to show the relationship of all the parts. The increasingly used system in business and industry is the decimal (sometimes called scientific) system, which has become popular because it immediately tells exactly where a reader is in a report and (because it developed in the physical sciences) it is thought to lend an air of scientific authority. The older Roman system of outline symbols still appears in business use, and is still popular in many areas of education.

	Decimal			Roman		
1.0.				I.		
	1.1.				A.	
	1.2.				B.	
	1.3.				C.	
2.0.				II.		
	2.1.				A.	
		2.1.1.				1.
		2.1.2.				2.
	2.2.				B.	
3.0.	(etc.)			III.	(etc.)	

You can use the decimal system without indentation—but the time and space you save yourself costs readers in speed and ease of reading; so they prefer indentation. Many writers and readers also prefer to use only the first decimal point.

3.   Cover all categories—that is, all the divisions at any level must add up to the whole indicated by your heading over those divisions. All the roman-numeral divisions together must add up to everything covered by the title, and all the capital letters under Section II must total the II data (and the same if you use decimal notation). If you classify students according to political affiliation, you would most certainly have Republicans as well as Democrats, in addition to others. If you classify according to religion, you would

have to include non-Protestants along with Protestants (or word the title to show the limited coverage).

4.   Use no single subdivisions. If you start to divide section 2.1 by putting a subhead 2.1.1, you must logically have at least a subhead 2.1.2; you can't divide anything into one part.

5.   Use parallel grammatical structure for parallel things. All the roman-numeral divisions are parallel things; all the capital-letter divisions under one of them are parallel, but not necessarily parallel with those under another roman-numeral division. They may all be complete sentences, all nouns or noun phrases (probably the best), or all adjectives.

6.   Consider the psychological effects (reading ease) of the number of parts in any classification. Three to seven is the optimum range. Of course, the nature of the topic may dictate how many you have. For instance, according to credit hours earned, the classes in a university are just five—from freshmen to graduates—no more and no less. In breaking down some topics, however, you have some choice in the number, depending on how broadly you name the parts. Having too few suggests that you didn't need the breakdown or that you have not completed it; having too many puts a strain on the reader or listener to remember them. In some cases you may be wise to shift to a slightly different basis of classification that will lead to a more suitable number of divisions. In other cases you can group some of the less important classes together (perhaps as "Others" or "Miscellaneous"); but this practice may appear sloppy to critical observers.

7.   Organize for approximate balance. That is, try not to let some of your divisions cover huge blocks of your subject and others almost nothing. Of course, the nature of your subject may force you to some imbalance. You probably need to reorganize on a different basis, however, if you have five major divisions and any one is more than half of the whole report. If you are writing about American politics, for example, the Democratic and Republican parties will each be bigger parts than all the rest, which you might group together for approximate balance.

8.   Put the parts of each breakdown into the sequence most appropriate for your purposes and the situation. The *overall sequence or plan of a report* is usually one of the following:

a.   *Direct (sometimes called deductive), giving the big, broad point first and then following with supporting details*. This plan arouses more interest than some other plans because it gets to the important things quickly, saves the time of the busy person who wants only the big idea, and provides a bird's-eye view that helps in understanding the rest more intelligently. It is therefore desirable if the report's conclusion is likely to be welcomed or if the reporter is an authority whose unsupported word would be readily accepted, at least tentatively. But it is psychologically unsound where it risks the danger of objections at first and continued resistance all the way through.

b.   *Inductive (sometimes called scientific), giving a succession of facts and ideas leading up to the big conclusions and recommendations at the end*. The inductive plan is slow and sometimes puzzling until the conclusion tells where all the detailed facts lead; but it is necessary in some cases for its strong logical conviction, especially when you expect opposition to the conclusions and recommendations that are coming.

c. Narrative (usually chronological accounts of activities). If no good reason argues against it—but usually one does—the chronological sequence is both the easiest to organize and the easiest to follow. The main objections are that it doesn't allow you to stress important things (it may have to begin with minor details, and the biggest things may be buried in the middle) and it doesn't allow you to bring together related things that have to be seen together for clear significance. The somewhat similar spatial arrangement (from top to bottom, front to back, left to right, or by geographical area) is usually the obvious choice if it is appropriate for the material.

d. Weighted (that is, according to importance). The weighted plan's basic advantage is that it enables you to control emphasis by putting the most important points in the emphatic positions, first and last.

For certain kinds of material and conditions, arrangement according to difficulty or from cause to effect (or the reverse) may be the wise choice. Similarly, some kinds of things almost have to appear in a definite order for the necessary logical sequence (the way proving a geometry proposition does).

Whatever the plan of organization, in the final presentation you will need to use meaningful headings and subheads, topic sentences or paragraphs, standard transitional words and sentences, and summarizing sentences to indicate organization, to show the coherence of parts in the organization, and to tell the hurried or half-attentive reader or listener the essence of the sections. The summarizing sentences, however, grow naturally out of your interpretation of the facts.

INTERPRETING THE FACTS

If the report is just informational, you are ready to put it in final form when you have organized the facts; but if it is to be analytical, you have to study the facts and interpret them into conclusions and/or recommendations for the boss, as required.

Interpretation is probably the hardest part of report preparation to teach—or to learn. Realization of six points, however, can help:

1. Without substantial, verifiable facts, you have nothing worthwhile to interpret. The solution is to go back to the data-collecting step and get the facts.

2. A fact alone is not worth much. Significance comes only from *relating* two or more facts. *Seeing* formerly unknown relationships requires *imaginative intelligence* and *careful analysis of two or more different sets of facts at the same time.* Whether the analysis is simply logical reasoning or mathematical (usually statistical) figuring, a necessary ingredient is *imagination.*

For example, consider how George J. Van Dorp, water commissioner of

Toledo, developed his method of determining the public interest in TV programs. As a fan of the "I Love Lucy" program, Van Dorp noticed that pressure in the water mains ran consistently high during the program. When commercials interrupted the show, the water pressure dropped appreciably—for about the length of the ads—then went up again when the players returned to the screen.

Many people seeing the changes in water pressure *and* the beginning, interrupted, and ending times of "I Love Lucy" would never have *seen* a relationship between the two sets of clear facts. Van Dorp had the *imaginative intelligence* to *see* the relationships—to interpret facts.

3.   Since the report user wants a sound rather than a prejudiced or illogical basis for decisions, your first consideration (beyond the ability to see relationships) in making the interpretation is *objectivity*. Nowhere else in report work is objectivity more important—or harder to achieve. Since you are a human being, your whole background and personality influence your thinking; you therefore must strive to be as objective and logical as possible and to avoid the temptation to stretch the truth a bit for dramatic effect. The following two basic kinds of unobjective attitudes require attention if your report is to be unbiased:

a.   *Preconception*. A reporter who jumps to conclusions and closes out other possibilities before collecting and evaluating the facts will, under the influence of that preconception, overlook or undervalue some facts and overstress others. Such is the danger of working from hypotheses—unless you check results by pursuing a directly opposite hypothesis.

b.   *Wishful thinking*. If you have a strong desire that the investigation turn out a certain way (because of a money interest or any other kind), you will find it hard not to manipulate facts (like the referee who has bet on the game) to make them lead to the desired result. Such attitudes can also lead to unintentionally slanted wording, since they will unconsciously affect your choice of phrasing.

4.   In addition to these dangerous attitudes to shun if you are to be a sound reporter, you must avoid the pitfalls to logical thinking (called *fallacies*). Although some of them—like circular argument and shifting the meanings of terms—are not likely to trap an honest reporter, avoiding these pitfalls requires constant alertness (especially if you've never studied logic):

a.   Avoid using sources (both books and people) which may be unreliable because of basic prejudice, because they are uninformed, or because they are out of date. Further, your sources may have misquoted or misinterpreted *their* sources—a common occurrence. Although you should have checked these things in collecting your data, you might well examine them again in the interpreting process.

b.   Avoid making hasty generalizations—that is, drawing conclusions on the basis of too little evidence (maybe too small a sample, too short a trial, too little experience, or just too few facts). The temptation to make hasty generalizations will weaken if you remember that sometimes you can draw no logical conclusion from the available facts. Certainly you need to remember that lack of evidence to establish one hypothesis does not prove its opposite.

c. Avoid using false analogies. True analogies (comparisons of things that are similar in many ways) are effective devices for explaining unknown things. You simply teach the unknown by comparing it to a similar known. But, even at their best, they are weak as logical proof. Because no two things are identical, the truth may escape through one of the holes of difference. And false analogies (applying principles valid in one case to another case where they don't belong) are tools of the dishonest and traps to the careless thinker. Essentially the same error results from a person's putting a thing in the wrong class (say a persuasive request situation misclassified as a direct inquiry) and applying the principles of the wrong class to it.

d. Avoid stating faulty cause-and-effect relationships, such as

1) Assigning something to one cause when it is the result of several. Comparisons which attribute the differences to one cause need careful controls to be valid. Otherwise, some unseen (or intentionally ignored) cause may deserve much of the credit for the difference.

2) Attributing something to an incapable cause (for instance, one that came later).

3) Calling something a cause when it is merely a concurrent effect— a symptom, a concomitant.

e. Avoid begging the question—just assuming, rather than giving evidence to support, a point that is necessary to the conclusions drawn.

f. Avoid using emotional suasion (usually characterized by strong and numerous adjectives and adverbs, or any kind of emotionally supercharged language like that of a defense attorney pleading with a jury) to win your point, instead of depending on logical conviction through marshaling facts.

g. Avoid failing to distinguish, and make clear, what is substantiated fact, what is opinion, and what is merely assumption.

5. Another important *consideration* in making your interpretation is discovering the really significant things to point out. If you avoid basic prejudice prompted by preconception or wishful thinking, avoid the pitfalls of various fallacies, and know what to look for, you should be able to interpret the facts and draw sound conclusions.

When you do, you should be sure they grow out of the facts, state them pointedly, and itemize them if they run to more than three or four. You can then turn them into practical recommendations that are general or concrete and specific, according to instructions you get with the report assignment. Itemization will usually help to make the recommendations desirably pointed too.

Some bosses want answers to all of what to do, how to do it, who is to do it, when and where; others feel that the reporter with so specific a solution to the problem infringes upon their prerogatives of making decisions. But all expect you to show the significance of your facts to the problem. In addition to an organization and presentation of facts that lead to the conclusions, you have a duty to point out lesser interpretations along the way. Avoiding doing so is not, as some people (bureaucrats) think, the safe way. It is failing to do the job properly.

Causes, symptoms, effects, and cures are always important—in report problems as in medicine. So (in terms of graphic statistical data) are high points, low points, averages, trends, and abrupt changes (especially if you can explain their causes). Without going into disturbingly technical statistics, you can probably hold interest with such measures of central tendencies as the mean (call it average), median (midpoint), and mode (most frequent item). Sometimes you might well use indicators of dispersion, such as standard deviation, range, and the -*iles* (percentiles, deciles, quartiles).

Appropriate comparisons can give significance to otherwise nearly meaningless isolated facts. For instance, the figure $7,123,191 given as profit for the year has little meaning alone. If you say it's 7 percent above last year's profit, you add a revealing comparison; and if you add that it's the highest ever, you add another. If your volume of production is 2 million units, that means less than if you add that you're now fourth in the industry as compared with tenth two years earlier.

Breaking down big figures into little ones also helps to make them meaningful. For instance, you may express capital investment in terms of so much per employee, per share of stock, per stockholder, or per unit of production. The national debt becomes more meaningful if you give it per citizen; the annual budget makes more sense as a per-day or per-citizen cost; library circulation means more in terms of number of books per student. Often a simple ratio helps, such as "Two fifths (40 percent) of the national budget is for defense." A pie chart showing the percentage going to each category in the whole budget would be especially meaningful.

6.   Whatever the analysis reveals, you need to state it precisely. Guard carefully against stating assumptions and opinions as facts. And select graduations in wording to indicate the degree of solidity of your conclusions. The facts and analyses will sometimes (but rarely) prove a point conclusively. They are more likely to lead to the conclusion that . . . , or indicate, or suggest, or hint, or point to the possibility, or lead one to wonder—and so on down the scale. Usually you can do better than stick your neck out (by claiming to prove things you don't) or draw your neck in too far (with the timorous last three of these expressions).

* * * * *

But phrasing the ideas well is a problem for the fifth and last step in preparing a report—writing it or speaking it.

We want you to understand clearly that everything we have said so far is applicable to both written and spoken reports. Whether you type up a report and package it in a folder or deliver it in the form of a speech, the steps in preparing it are the same. You must plan your attack, collect the facts you need, organize your findings, interpret the data if appropriate, and finally put your report in the proper style. Only in this last step do written and oral reports begin to differ materially.

So don't think you should put an oral report in fully written form and read it. As we point out in Chapter 17, reading a speech is usually the worst kind of oral presentation. As you develop your outline and assemble notecards, you will be generating the notes from which you should speak. In fact, your speech notes should be all of your divisions and subdivisions, with enough information on each so that you will remember all you want to say. Since your report notes are in essence your speech notes, the next section of this chapter deals mainly with written reports.

USING EFFECTIVE REPORT STYLE

Your final phrasing of the report will not be difficult if you have done well the preceding four steps of preparation. But if your methods of planning the report and collecting, organizing, and interpreting data have been faulty, you're trapped. Our suggestions for a good report style will help only if you have something worthwhile to say and a pretty good idea of the sequence of points.

You will notice that our suggestions relate more to the *effectiveness* than to the *correctness* of your style, for two reasons:

1. Correct spelling, grammar, punctuation, sentence structure do not assure effectiveness—we assume that you have pretty well learned these aspects of your language before studying reports. And if you haven't, a more basic study of composition—or a careful review of Appendix F or some other good handbook—may be advisable.

2. Effective presentation presupposes reasonable correctness of language as well as information but also requires that you help your reader or audience to get your message clearly, quickly, and easily. How to do this is our next concern.

Basics of report style

Because almost everything we say about letter and memo style in Chapter 2 and about communication in Appendix A applies equally to report style— and the few exceptions are obvious—we recommend that you read that material carefully before going on to the special points about report style.

As you have already seen (Item 6, first section of Chapter 13), effective reports use various techniques and devices for communicating clearly, quickly, and easily: commonly understood words, short sentences so direct that they require little punctuation, short paragraphs so direct that they require few transitional words, itemizations, graphics, and headings.

Even though you have read those other parts of the book, several points of basic style and some of the special techniques deserve a bit fuller treatment for preparing reports.

Adaptation requires that you consider not only your primary reader but likely secondary ones. Even though some may know the background of the problem and the technical terms of the field, others may not. The good report writer must therefore provide explanations necessary for the least informed of important readers. This duty includes restricting your vocabulary to words they will understand readily. If you feel that you must use specialized terms, you had better explain them. Usually a parenthetical explanation right after the first use of a technical term is the best way. But if your report includes many such terms, it should provide a glossary in the introduction or in an appendix—to keep it from being "all Greek" to nontechnical readers.

Coherence becomes a greater problem as the length and variety of points in a report increase. Hence as a report writer you need to observe carefully the use of transitional words, previewing topic sentences and paragraphs, and summarizing sentences and paragraphs in the illustrations in the next two chapters. **Coh** in Appendix F and items S5–7 in the checklist for major analytical reports (see Chapter 15) should also prove helpful.

A particularly effective means to coherence in report writing is the use of informative and interesting "clipped-sentence" headings. J. H. Menning (a coauthor of the first five editions of this book) named them "talking heads"—and seems to have established (so far) generally but not universally respected proprietary rights to the name, the use, and even instruction on them.

Here is how one writer helped keep readers on the track with good talking heads, topic statements, summary paragraphs, and transitional ideas. (For economy of space, we have quoted only some of the *transitional* parts from various places in the 27-page report. The bracketed parts are our commentary.)

II. NASHVILLE'S LARGER MARKET AREA

Since women often will travel long distances to buy clothes, the secondary area surrounding the metropolitan area is important in determining the location of a Four Cousins retail store. [After this topic lead-in, several paragraphs followed identifying for both Nashville and Knoxville principal communities and number of people in them.]

Even though 370,000 more possible customers live within the market area of Nashville, most of the sales will come from the people within the immediate metropolitan area. [Summarizes II and makes transition to III.]

III. BETTER POPULATION FACTORS IN NASHVILLE

The total population and its rate of growth, number of women, and number of employed women show more clearly the potential buyers of women's clothing. [This topic statement preceded A, B, and C headings of subsections giving the facts about and the interpretation of the topics as announced.]

Even though Knoxville has a larger population and
about the same growth rate, Nashville has more women
and a significantly larger number of employed women.
Thus it furnishes the kind of customer Four Cousins
sells to. [Indicates what A, B, and C add up to.]

Potential customers are buyers, however, only when
they have sufficient buying power. [Clearly
foreshadows a topic coming up and why.]

IV. MORE BUYING POWER IN NASHVILLE

Effective buying income (total and per capita),
income groups, home ownership, and automobile
ownership give estimates of ability to buy. [The
information as presented then follows in four
sections.]

[This summary statement comes at the end of the
section.] The Nashville shopper has more dollars to
spend, even though home- and auto-ownership figures
imply more favorable financial positions in Knoxville
families. Higher expenditures for homes and cars in
Knoxville explain, in part, why Nashville merchants
sell more.

V. GREATER RETAIL SALES AND LESS
COMPETITION IN NASHVILLE

[The writer continues the use of these coherence
devices throughout the report.]

(Though illustrated here only as major heads, such talking heads are equally effective at any or all heading levels.)

Parallelism is a special pitfall to the unwary report writer because reports so frequently involve series, outlines, and lists. Each is in effect the partition of a whole, the sum of the parts equaling the whole. Hence the law of logic and mathematics—that you sum up, or add, only like things—applies. Thus the breakdown of anything must name all the parts in similar (parallel) grammatical form—usually all nouns or noun phrases, adjectives, or complete sentences. (See Item 5 in the earlier section, "Organizing the findings," for parallelism in outlines and **Para** in Appendix F for a more comprehensive treatment.)

Timing of the verbs (tense) in reports also often trips a careless report writer. One simple rule answers most questions of tense: *Use the present tense wherever you can do so logically*. It applies to things that existed in the past, still exist, and apparently will continue to exist for a while (the universal present tense). Otherwise, use the tense indicated by the logic of the situation. Thus in talking about your research activity, you say that you *did* certain things, like conducted a survey (past tense in terms of the time of writing). But in reporting your findings, you say "70 percent answer favorably, and 30 percent are opposed." The universal present tense implies that the findings are still true. Surely you would not want to imply doubt on that point by using *answered*. (See **Ten** in Appendix F for further applications of the universal present tense.)

Ten common faults listed in American University Professor William Dow Boutwell's study of government reports (and printed in the *Congressional Record*, Vol. 88, Part IX, p. A1468)[1] occur frequently in business and industry reports too:

1. Sentences are too long. Voted unanimously as one of the worst faults in nearly all writings analyzed. Average sentence length in poor government writing varies from 65 to 80 words per sentence. In exceptionally good government writing . . . average length is from 15 to 18 words per sentence.

2. Too much hedging; too many modifications and conditional clauses and phrases. The master writer will say, "A third of a nation ill-clothed, ill-housed, ill-fed." The amateur will write: "On the whole it may be said that on the basis of available evidence the majority of our population is probably not receiving the proper type of nutriment . . . ." Psychologists say that "conditional clauses cause suspension of judgment as to the outcome of the sentence, and therefore increase reading difficulty."

3. Weak, ineffective verbs. *Point out, indicate,* or *reveal* are the week reeds upon which many a government sentence leans. Writers overuse parts of the verb *to be*. Hundred-word sentences with *was* or *is* as the principal verb are not uncommon.

4. Too many sentences begin the same way, especially with *The*.

5. An attempt to be impersonal, which forces use of passive and indirect phrases. Example: "To determine whether retail sales have been out of line with expectations based on the past relationship of retail volume to income, estimates of retail sales in the first half of each year . . . have been charted against income payments for the same periods, and a line of estimate fitted to the resulting scatter." The good writer would say: "Our statisticians have charted estimates of retail sales, etc., etc."

6. Overabundance of abstract nouns. Such nouns as *condition, data, situation, development, problem, factor, position, basis, case* dominate the writing of too many government documents. How bright and real writing becomes when picture-bearing nouns take the place of vague ones may be seen from this sentence: "During the lean years when salaries and wages were low and irregular, the people who drifted into the credit-union offices came around because they had dropped behind in their personal and family finances and had to get a loan."

7. Too many prepositioned phrases. In a study of reading difficulty, investigators (Drs. Leary and Gray of Chicago University) found that prepositional phrases ("of the data," "under the circumstances," etc.) add to reading difficulty. Yet, samples of government writing show that many officials use at least one prepositional phrase to every four words. Samples from good writing contain only one prepositional phrase to every 11 words.

8. Overabundance of expletives. "It is" and "there are" and their variants ruin the opening of many good paragraphs.

---

[1] An AP Newsfeature, "Gobbledygook; Language of Government," by Richard E. Myer, September 5, 1971, stresses many of the same points; and books like Don Miller's *The Book of Jargon* (Macmillan, N.Y., 1981) and Jason Brown's *Jargonaphasia* (Academic Press, N.Y., 1981) are still doing the same thing.

9. Use of governmentish or federalese. "Shop words" serve a proper purpose for "shop" audiences. But many government writers make the mistake of talking to the public in technical, office terms . . . .

10. Tendency to make ideas the heroes of sentences. People think in terms of people and things for the most part. The government official writes in terms of ideas and phenomena only. Hence, when a writer means "Employers refuse to hire older workers in defense industries," he writes instead: "Refusal of employment of older workers continues." In other words, the writer has substituted "refusal," an idea or phenomenon, for "employers"—living people.

Headings and subheads

Because written reports are sometimes long and because readers may want to recheck certain parts, they use headings and subheads, in addition to topic and summarizing sentences, to show their organization and coherence. As you'll see in Chapter 17, a good oral reporter will use the oral equivalents for the same purposes. Also, for the same purposes, we have used headings in this book. If you have not thought about them already, for illustration flip back through some parts of the book with which you are well acquainted and see if they don't serve these purposes.

Skill in using heads and subheads can be a valuable technique in your presentations, not only of reports but of anything else that is very long—even long letters.

The only reasonable test of how far to go in putting in subheads is this: Will they help the reader get your message? If so, put them in; if not, leave them out.

Despite the fact that headings and subheads are often great helps, no single system of setting them up is in universal use. More important than what system you use is that you *use some system consistently* and that the reader understand it. Most readers understand and agree on the following principles:

1. A good heading is a title for its section. As such, it should indicate clearly the content below it, should have reader interest, and should be as brief as possible without sacrificing either of the other two requirements.

Trying to keep titles too short, however, frequently leads to sacrifice of exactness and/or helpfulness. Usually a short heading is too broad (includes more than the discussion below it covers), and it tells nothing about the topic. Note the difference, in examples from annual reports, between "Profits" and "Profits Up 8 Percent from Last Year," and between "Position in the Industry" and "Position in Industry Changes from Eighth to Fourth." Particularly in reports where some readers might only skim, you can help them by *making your headings tell the big point about the topic instead of just naming the topic*. You've already seen some good examples of such helpful *informative* headings, as opposed to merely *topical* ones, in the quoted illustration a few pages back. The headlines in any newspaper or informative magazine article provide others.

2. The form and position of the head must make its relative importance (status in the outline) clear at a glance. That is, headings for all divisions of

equal rank (say the roman-numeral heads in an outline) must be in the same form and position on the page, but different from their superiors (of which they are parts) and from their inferiors (their subdivisions). Putting heads of different levels in the same form and position is confusing; it misrepresents the outline.

3.   Centered heads are superior to sideheads in the same form (compare second- and third-degree heads in the following illustration); heads in capitals are superior to those in caps and lowercase; and heads above the text are superior to those starting on the same line with the text (compare third- and fourth-degree heads in the illustration).

4.   You should not depend on headings as antecedents for pronouns or as transitions. The one word *This* referring to an immediately preceding head is the most frequent offender. Transitions between paragraphs and between bigger subdivisions should be perfectly clear even without the headings.

5.   In capital-and-lowercase heads capitalize the first word and all others except articles (*a, an*, and *the*), conjunctions (for example, *and, but, for*, and *because*), and prepositions (such as *to, in, of, on*, and *with*).

The following not only illustrates *one good system* but further explains the principles. Note that *above* second- and third-degree heads the spacing is more than the double spacing of the discussion.

FIRST–DEGREE HEADINGS

    The title of your whole report, book, or article is

the first–degree heading. Since you have only one

title, no other head should appear in the same form.

As illustrated here, the title uses the most superior

form and position (as explained in Items 2 and 3

above). If you need more than this five–level

breakdown for your report, you can type the first

heading in spaced CAPITALS and move each level of

heading up one notch.

<u>Second–Degree Headings</u>

    If you use solid capitals centered on the page for

the first–degree heading (title), a good choice for

the second–degree headings (the major divisions in the

outline) is centered caps and lowercase. Preferably, in typewriter face they and any other uncapitalized head should carry underscoring to make them stand out. If you do not need the five-level breakdown illustrated here, you could start with this form.

Third-degree headings

To distinguish third-degree headings from their superiors, you may put them at the left margin above the text, underscore them to make them stand out, and write them in initial-cap form (as here) or in cap and lowercase (which would require capitalizing the D in Degree and the H in Headings).

Fourth-degree headings.--For a fourth level, you may place headings at the paragraph indention on the same line with the text and write them as caps and lowercase or as straight lowercase except for capitalizing the first word. These headings definitely need underscoring and separation from the first sentence, preferably by a period and dash, as here. Some people drop the dash or the period.

Fifth-degree headings can be integral parts (preferably beginnings) of the first sentences of the first paragraphs about topics. Underscoring (italic type when printed) will make them stand out

sufficiently without further distinctions in form.

Objectivity in presentation

Clearly a report user expects a writer to be as nearly objective as is humanly possible in collecting the facts, in organizing and interpreting them, and finally in presenting them.

That does not mean, however, that you must use impersonal style (which some people erroneously call *objective* style). You can be just as objective when saying "I think such and such is true" as when saying "Such and such seems to be true" or even "Such and such is true." The second and third versions mean only that the writer/speaker thinks something is true. The only sound objection to the first version is that it wastes two words, not that it is *natural* style.

The only real justification for recommending impersonal style in reports, as many books do (meaning no use of the first or second person—i.e., pronouns referring to the sender or receiver of the message), is that methods and results are usually the important things and therefore they, rather than the person who did the research, deserve emphasis as subjects and objects of active verbs.

But, since most things happen because people make them happen, the most natural and the clearest, easiest, most interesting way to tell about them is to tell who does what. A report about research done by its writer therefore naturally includes *I*'s; and, if it keeps the reader(s) or audience in mind properly, it also naturally includes *you*'s. To omit them is unnatural and usually dull, because it goes out of the way to avoid the natural subjects of active verbs or uses too many inactive ones and leaves out the most basic element of an interesting, humanized style—*people doing things*.

Because they are professionally trained, constantly practicing, and usually writing about people doing things (although in the third person, a part of impersonal style), newspaper reporters often write well. An equally trained and practiced business report writer (a rarity) *can,* by great care, write well in impersonal style. But most business report writers find it unnatural and difficult. Unless they exercise great care, it usually leads them into awkward, wordy, and weak passive-voice constructions; it gives away the third leg (frequent personal references) to Rudolf Flesch's three-legged stool of easy readability, so that the stool falls; and it *does not* gain objectivity.

Strangely, the strongest promoters of impersonal style are people who pride themselves on being scientific. They usually also insist that their style should avoid any kind of exaggeration about the true state of things. But they then argue that impersonal style gives the reader more confidence in their statements. When one of them draws a conclusion, therefore, it comes out as "It was concluded that . . . ," as if (falsely) some omniscient oracle had drawn the conclusion, when the true meaning is "I conclude that . . . ."

Actually, more destructive to objectivity than the use of a natural style is the use of too many or too strong adjectives and adverbs, or any kind of feverish, high-pressure, hot-under-the collar wording. Such a heightened style—using emotional connotations, fancy figures of speech, and other techniques of oratory—has its place where the author feels deeply and wants the reader to feel deeply about the subject; but it leads to distrust and is inappropriate in reports anyway, where both parties supposedly think hard rather than emotionalize.

Simply put, then, our advice on natural versus impersonal style is this: Find out whether your primary reader thinks reports have to be in impersonal style. If so, accept the burdensome restrictions and do the best you can by

1. Avoiding "It is" and "There are," especially as sentence beginnings (**Exp** in Appendix F).
2. Putting most of your verbs in the active voice (**Pas** in Appendix F).
3. Picturing people, other than yourself or the reader/listener(s), of course, taking the action of as many as possible of your verbs.

But any time your primary reader/listener(s) will let you, *phrase your report naturally but calmly and reasonably*. Where the natural way to express an idea involves an *I* or a *you*, use it. Don't let anybody talk you into referring to yourself as the writer—or the speaker.

Except for the fact that letter style allows more use of emotional suasion than report style does, the discussion of style in Chapter 2 applies to reports as well as letters.

In addition, reports also make more extensive use than letters of certain other techniques of presenting ideas clearly, quickly, and easily: using headings and subheads, presenting quantitative data skillfully, and using graphic and visual aids to effective communication.

Presentation of quantitative data

Most reports make considerable use of quantitative data. Consequently, you need to know how to present figures for clear, quick, and easy comprehension. Most people will want the figures on measurable topics you discuss; and unless they have made clear that they want only the facts, they probably will want your interpretations showing what the figures mean (conclusions) and what you think should be done about them (recommendations). Even if those people have the ability to make the interpretations themselves, they likely will want you to make them—for possible ideas they might not see and for economy of their time.

The following brief suggestions will help you present quantitative information the way most people want it:

1. Make sure your figures are reliable by checking your sources and derivations of them. And when you present an average, make clear whether it is the mean, the median, or the mode.

2.   Write isolated quantities in one of the standard ways explained under **Fig** in Appendix F.

3.   Present key figures as simply as possible. Usually some ratio, rank, difference, or correlation is more important than the raw data. Instead of a gross of $2,501,460.70 and expenses of $2,124,101.40, the simple figures $2½ and $2⅛ million tell the story better. The ratio 1:7 or about 15 percent for the net certainly reads easier than $377,359.30 and is probably the more important figure. Moreover, except in bookkeeping and highly technical research, such rounded and simplified figures are precise enough for most purposes. Indeed, rounded figures in most cases are as accurate as the unrounded ones which are their bases. The means of arriving at most large figures are not accurate enough to make the last few digits anything but a bogus precision and a hindrance to readability.

4.   Another way of increasing readability is to break big figures down into so much per . . . (whatever is an appropriate divider). If the divider is the number of persons involved (employees, students, or citizens, for example), you also gain interest by humanizing the presentation.

5.   Insofar as possible, avoid cluttering your paragraphs with great masses of figures. Tables are better if you have many figures—say more than six, as in a table of two lines and three columns (or vice versa). Ordinarily, however, extensive tables are not necessary to clear understanding of the text but are in a report to show that you really have the facts. In that case put tables in an appendix and refer to them specifically in the introduction or text.

6.   Put necessary statistical information as close as possible to the place in the text where it is most pertinent. Readers will likely refuse to flip pages back and forth to find a table, or at least will resent having to do so; and their concentration (and comprehension) will suffer.

7.   Small tables (usually called spot tables), perhaps using key figures based on extensive data in an appendix, are not only easy to read but can appear close to the relevant discussion on a page. Use them freely.

8.   Help your reader by pointing out (in terms of line graphs) highs, lows, averages, trends, ranges, and exceptions or extremes. They are not always readily apparent, especially to the many people who are not accustomed to analyzing statistical data; but they are usually important, especially if you can also explain their causes and/or effects.

Graphic aids as supplements to words

Just as tables are useful for presenting large amounts of related quantitative data clearly, concisely, and precisely, various graphics can present small amounts (often the key figures from tables) even better. Their strengths are in presenting information for clear, quick, easy, interesting, and memorable reading (though usually not with precision).

For these reasons, various studies have found that graphic aids (and visual aids in oral communication) help readers/listeners to understand and remember. Though the impact varies with kinds of people and kinds of material (quantitative data versus ideas, for example), the rounded figures go about like this:

	After 3 hours	After 3 days
Read or hear	70%	10%
See	72	20
Both	85	65

Since reports so frequently treat quantitative data, designs, organizational plans, and the like, you often almost have to use charts, graphs, pictograms, drawings, and maps as well as tables to present your information well, especially in oral reports.

But in most cases these devices *only assist, not replace, words*. And since interpretation of graphics is not one of the three R's everybody learns, most graphics help to explain and/or support the text *only if the text helps them by telling how to look at them and what they mean*. Good communication therefore often involves care and skill in *interplaying* words and graphic aids.

If you haven't already done so, you could and should learn much about using graphics effectively by observing them in current use as you read other books, newspapers, and especially news magazines like *U.S. News & World Report* and *Newsweek*. Still we think our explanations and illustrations of the commonly used types will help. We give explanations and enough related text to show how to interweave the graphics as assistants to words.

As you study our explanations and illustrations, look not only at the graphics; but notice what kinds of information call for them, whether the graphics really help, and how the authors *interrelate them and words* so that each aids the other. Besides that key point of interplaying graphics as aids, keep in mind the five other most important points about using them:

1.   A graphic device should not call attention to itself until *after* an introduction to it (some discussion of the point and reference to the graph); in most cases it would otherwise only confuse and break continuity of thought.

2.   The existence of the graphic aid, or where it is, is not the important thing and does not deserve the emphasis when you refer to it. So refer to it *subordinately* and use the main clause of your sentence to make the significant point. "Twice as many men as women like X, as Table 2 shows," is one good way.

3.   Insofar as possible, place graphic aids close to (usually between) comments on the point. In written reports, that means (preferably) right before the reader's eyes. Unless the device is staring the reader in the face when you mention it, tell precisely where it is—*subordinately* (for example, "As Fig. 1 on the next page shows, X goes up as Y goes down").

4.   Carefully label each graphic device (unless obvious) as a whole (title and easy-reference number) and by parts, and provide a key (legend) if nec-

essary. (Some people insist that at least major tables should carry titles and Roman capital numbers below the display—though lesser ones may use Arabic numbers.) Variations in color, shading, cross-hatching, and kind of line (solid versus broken, for example) are common means for distinguishing the different kinds of data in lines, columns, bars, and the like.

Where precision of quantified data is important, help the reader with grid lines (such as on graph paper) and by labeling significant points with the exact figures. *And remember that percentages or other ratios are often more important than the raw figures from which they come.*

Avoiding two kinds of possible distortion deserves particular caution.

a. *Be sure to start at 0 as the base.* If, for example, you use 0 as the base of the quantity scale and the first year presented has a volume of 50 and the second 60, the second year will look like what it is (10 points or a 20 percent increase, from 50 to 60). If you start at base 40, however, the second year appears to have doubled the first (20 above the base 40 and thus twice as high on the scale as the 50 of the preceding year, which was only 10 above the base).

Because you must begin on base 0, you have a problem if all your quantities going on a scale (usually the vertical or Y scale) are high. To avoid both leaving large open spaces at the bottom and distorting by ignoring the 0-base logic, you may begin at 0 and make a scale break as fair warning to a reader (see page 482).

b. *(a)* If you handle the preceding situation *(a)* properly in a line graph on a vertical scale of 0–70 that is 3½ and a horizontal scale of 24 months that is 4 inches, the line will appear to rise at about the proper incline—10 points or one-half inch in 2 inches (12 months). If you shorten the base to 2 inches, however, the incline will be twice as steep (one-half inch in 1 inch) and will give the distorted impression of a much faster rise.

Readers generally view a graph line rising at anywhere between 0 and a 30° angle as a normal slope (much as you feel walking on a roof of that slope). Similarly, a slope of 30° to 45° (on a graph or on a roof) seems a little threatening; and a steeper slope on either seems treacherous. You therefore must *select both the vertical and horizontal scales to produce a slope that looks and feels right for the situation.*

5.   Interpret your graphics (usually right after them) unless doing so would be insulting because the meaning is so obvious.

To begin seeing what illustrations of graphics we have provided, start flipping the pages of the book from the front. You'll notice that they illustrate (more or less in order) special layouts like the title page, tables of contents, boxed checklists, outlines of chapters, photolike reproductions (of letter, envelope, and memo layouts), parallel-column presentations, symbolic drawings (of A–, B–, and C–plans), résumés, regular tables—and literally dozens of other special arrangements on the page that help you to *see* the information.

You'll also notice that the best procedure in using graphics begins by (1) introducing the topic and the key point, (2) subordinately referring the reader

A good illustration of how to show a broken scale

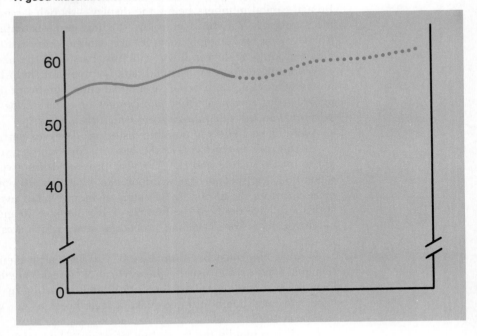

Another illustration of a broken scale

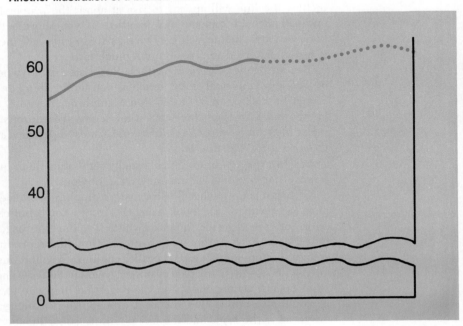

to the graphic aid at the point where it will be helpful, (3) using the best type of graphic for the purpose, and (4) further commenting on (interpreting) the graphic device.

If you've made the observations we've suggested, you've seen how useful graphics can be and have also learned the basic principles you need to know to use graphics skillfully. You've noticed that even in a book emphasizing the psychological, linguistic, and business procedural aspects of effective business communication, we have made extensive use of many forms of graphic presentation. In most other aspects of business, which are more easily quantifiable, graphics of a few specific types can play an even bigger role.

For purposes of illustrating our specific explanations of the most commonly used graphics, besides three others we have chosen five from an article in the most recent *Occupational Outlook Handbook* (U.S. Department of Labor, 1982–83) and have paraphrased enough of the text to interplay our further instructions about graphics with the best available information on job prospects from now until 1990.

Bar charts are among the easiest graphics to make and to interpret. In their simplest form, you set up a row of bars (usually on a horizontal base of time periods; but it may be on a vertical base and represent time or any other function). The varying lengths of side-by-side bars show changes in the other variable (as in Chart 1).

The *Handbook* writer probably chose wisely not to provide more grid lines (because the data were not precise) and (to avoid distraction from the main point) not to segment the bars (by different shading) into percentages of males and females in each bar. We don't think, however, that the writer was wise to change the standard graphic-language code for distinguishing known data (solid lines for line graphs or for boxing-in bars) from projections (all lines broken). The shaded versus white distinction used in Chart 1 is not familiar to most Americans reading charts.

You recognize that drawing a line connecting the exposed corners of the bars in Chart 1 would produce another simple and widely used kind of graphic—a *line graph* or *line chart*. In this case it should be a *faired* (smoothly curved) line—a truer representation of the given facts—because the data change more or less smoothly (instead of in jumps at intervals, which would call for stepped straight-line connections between the jumps).

You should recognize, too, that like the simple bar chart, the simple line graph can present projections (broken lines such as - -, — —, or . . . .) and several concurrently changing kinds of data on the same base. If they might otherwise become confused, you would distinguish the different functions by lines of different color or form; and you should limit their number to the range of easy comprehension/comparison.

A frequent two-line business chart pictures one line labeled *costs* and the other labeled *income*—where they cross being the break-even point (or the owner's nightmare, the going-broke point).

An important side development since 1970 has been a significant geograph-

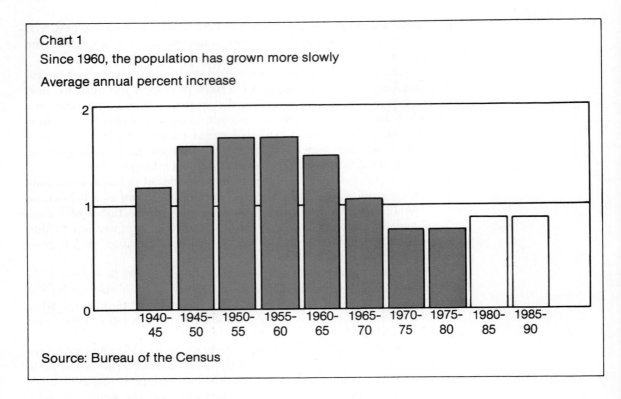

Chart 1

Since 1960, the population has grown more slowly

Average annual percent increase

Source: Bureau of the Census

ical shifting in the population—a population increase of only 0.2 to 0.4 percent in the Northeast, North Central, and Midwest regions while the South and West zoomed 20 to 40 percent.

For graphic presentation of such data in relation to geography, *maps* of various kinds are the obvious choices. You've no doubt seen, for example, isothermal maps with lines marking out labeled and differently colored or shaded sections of the U.S. map indicating the proper time in each area to plant your garden (or specific parts of it, like beans, okra, tomatoes). You've also probably seen average annual rainfall for different regions pictured on maps labeled in inches and shaded heavier and heavier in keeping with the rain—and similar maps with lighter and lighter coloring in keeping with the rarefied atmosphere as the mountainous elevations rise.

For its Chart 2 (not shown here) the *Handbook* uses a vari-shaded U.S. map to show regional population growth rates 1970–80 as (1) faster than national average, (2) average, or (3) slower than average. Group 1 includes the whole South and West (of the Rockies) plus Maine, New Hampshire, Vermont, and Delaware. Only Tennessee and West Virginia fall under 2. The rest—nearly all of the Northeast and all of the Midwest—is in Group 3.

While giving a generally true picture, the *Handbook*'s following the state lines in this situation exemplifies one of the common distortions of fact in graphic presentations. The data used came from censuses of the states; but anybody knows that the straight lines separating many states are not precise dividers of population-growth areas. The distortion here is the opposite of that of using faired-line graphs to represent a college's enrollment. Since enrollment obviously does not increase smoothly throughout any period but by steps at registration times, a stepped-line graph would be more accurate—as faired lines on the map would better represent population-growth areas.

Despite its breaking the code for graphic distinction between known and speculative (forecast) data, still Chart 1 shows clearly the baby boom that increased U.S. population so fast during 1945–1965, the small population increase in the 70s, and the projected (predicted) slow rise of about 0.9 percent a year for the 80s. Interpreting that chart by putting its bare facts with others (not presented yet, but some well known) would suggest several likely consequences:

1. That more women might come into the work force in the 70s as fewer births let them and as the boom babies became old enough to operate without constant maternal care;
2. That the work force would start booming about 1965 (causing strong competitition for jobs) as the boom babies began reaching their 20s;
3. That growth in the labor force will slow down in the 80s; and
4. That the 1990s will offer more jobs than the available new workers (born in the low-birth-rate 70s) can fill—hence little competition for jobs and high pay.

Instead of skating ahead on the insecure ice of such interpretations, however, the *Handbook* writers take up other developments in chronological order—and so shall we. (But we'll skip Chart 3 because it's another row of bars predicting slow labor-force growth in the 1980s as expected from Chart 1.)

Though the *Handbook* does not show it, given statistics do provide data (as Chart 1 had given bases for speculative interpretation) for another use of a faired two-line graph—of men as a decreasing and women an increasing percentage of people coming into the labor force. That's what you would have if you removed the walls and left only their upper-front edges from Chart 4. (We modified the chart design slightly—to make a faired two-row bar chart—for ease of reading.)

In addition to population and labor-force trends, other factors affecting the job outlook are changes in the kinds and amounts of goods and services the public wants—and hence in the kinds and numbers of workers needed to produce them. Employment has increased faster in service-producing industries (to about 67 percent) than in the goods-producing industries (farming, mining, manufacturing, and construction), as Chart 7 shows (but we omit because it is an oddball—a properly faired two-line chart, but with the lines topping confusingly superimposed rows of bars.)

To show the percentages of different kinds of workers employed in each

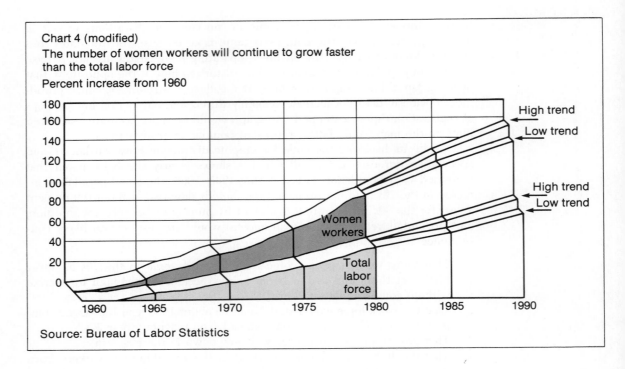

Chart 4 (modified)
The number of women workers will continue to grow faster
than the total labor force
Percent increase from 1960

Source: Bureau of Labor Statistics

category, the *Handbook* wisely uses the standard (and best) graphic form for breaking down wholes—the *pie chart*.

Pie charts are specialists in showing the parts of a whole—preferably with different colors or shading to distinguish the parts, labels to identify them, the raw figures for precision, and (usually the most important figures) their percentages for quick, easy comparison. Even they, however, can broaden their service by showing more than one breakdown. Chart 6, for example, would be better as one pie with different cross-hatching to distinguish the two broad categories.

Since pie charts are stationary rather than moving partitioners (i.e., pictures breaking a whole into its parts at a given time), they cannot well present projections. The authors of the *Occupational Outlook Handbook* article we're paraphrasing therefore should have turned to two better ways of presenting such information—a *line graph* (two lines, projected, for the emphatic picture) and words for precision and details—to trace the expected trends of all the subgroups.

Instead, getting more specific on its general theme, the *Handbook* presents (and pictures graphically) four more points. Its difficult-to-read bilateral bar Chart 8 shows 1980–90 changes in employment in nine industries. Bars beginning at the 1980 employment level (in millions) and ending at the predicted 1990 level show agriculture a negative quantity at both ends of the

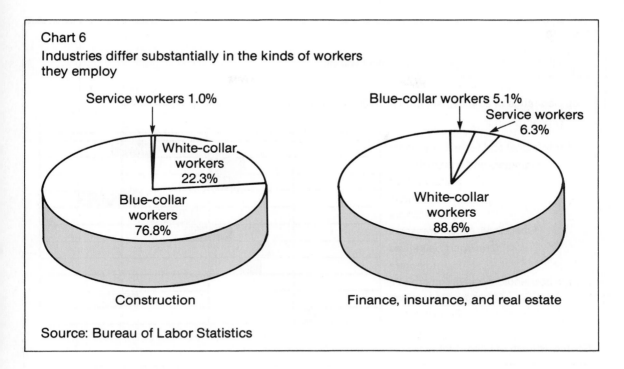

Chart 6

Industries differ substantially in the kinds of workers they employ

Service workers 1.0%

White-collar workers 22.3%

Blue-collar workers 76.8%

Construction

Blue-collar workers 5.1%

Service workers 6.3%

White-collar workers 88.6%

Finance, insurance, and real estate

Source: Bureau of Labor Statistics

short bar; mining a slight gainer from about 0.3 to 0.4; construction, 0.9 to 1.3; manufacturing, one of three big gainers, 2.4 to 3.5; transportation, communications, and public utilities, 0.5 to 0.7; trade, 4.5 to 6.2; finance, insurance, and real estate, 1.2 to 1.7; services, 5.0 to 7.2; and government, 0.4 to 0.6.

Chart 9 (a no-name, easy-to-read, but difficult-to-describe chart based on five-year time blocks 1960–80 and scaled in millions) shows farm workers slightly decreasing, service workers more numerous and slightly increasing, a larger number of blue-collar workers increasing irregularly, and white-collar workers (the largest group) increasing the fastest.

Chart 10, like Chart 7 a bilateral beginning/ending bar chart, forecasts (for 1980–90) changes in employment (in millions) by occupational groups. As you see, farm workers remain on the negative side and the big gainers (clerical workers) go up from about 3.5 to 5.2. Other sizable gains of about 1 million each will be among professional and technical workers, craft workers, operatives (not counting transport), and other service workers. Managers, sales workers, laborers, and transport operatives all gain slightly (in that order) but remain below 2 million.

Perhaps the most intriguing of the *Handbook*'s charts is the last—partly because you rarely see mention of its significant data and partly because its facts are so hard to factor into the job-outlook equation. When you see figures

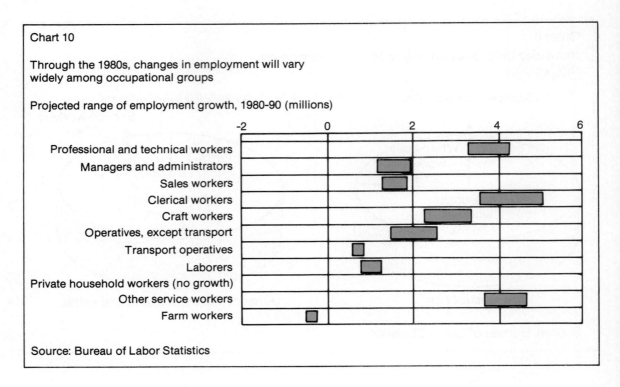

Chart 10

Through the 1980s, changes in employment will vary
widely among occupational groups

Projected range of employment growth, 1980-90 (millions)

Source: Bureau of Labor Statistics

on job separations, you know that nearly all of the jobs are then openings for
somebody else; but when you see transfers, you don't know where they went.
Commendably, however, the *Handbook*'s Chart 11 uses *segmented* bars to
distinguish the two and lists them by occupation.

Though the preceding explanations and illustrations give you a good look
into graphics, we still think the following suggestions on the uses of different
graphics may be helpful as a kind of summary/reminder. We'll also interweave
two kinds not formerly illustrated.

1. A table is usually the starting point for quantified graphics of other
kinds. We don't illustrate tables here because you've already seen many in
use. If you want to see more, however, flip through our two longest illustrations of reports in Chapters 15 and 16.

2. Use line graphs (perhaps marking the tops of columns in a bar chart)
to represent trends according to time. Usually the perpendicular axis should
represent volume of the subject treated and the base (or horizontal axis) should
represent time. Two or more different kinds or colors of lines can show relative quantities as well as the absolute quantities of several subjects at any
given time.

3. Use segmented bars or pie charts (preferably moving clockwise from
12:00) to represent the proportions in the breakdown of a whole. Usually the
color or shading of sections distinguishes the parts (which should not be con-

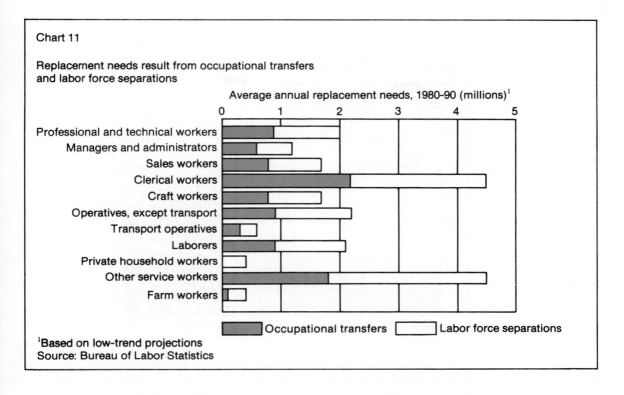

Chart 11

Replacement needs result from occupational transfers
and labor force separations

Average annual replacement needs, 1980-90 (millions)[1]

Occupational transfers   Labor force separations

[1]Based on low-trend projections
Source: Bureau of Labor Statistics

fusingly numerous). They should carry labels of both the raw figures for precision and (usually the more important point) the ratio or percentage of the
whole for easy comparison.

4.   A kind of hybrid showing the partitioning characteristics of multiline
graphs, segmented-bar charts, and pies is the belt chart in Figure 14–1 (also
called the cumulative line chart and the component-part line chart). Intended
to give only an impressionistic (rather than precise) picture of six and a half
decades, it gives a pretty good idea without any precise figures. (We got it
from an earlier edition of the *Handbook* and omitted the date and source to
concentrate on the design and use.)

5.   Use maps for geographical distribution of almost anything; organization
charts of rectangles arranged and connected to show lines of authority and
communication; flow charts showing movement and stages in processing;
blueprints giving precise sizes and relationships; and photographs picturing
accurate size, texture, and color. All are useful graphic devices in their places,
which are sometimes in engineering, architectural, and other professional/
technical work instead of in business. In any case, you need to keep them
simple enough for easy reading and concentrated on the point under discussion.

Figure 14–1

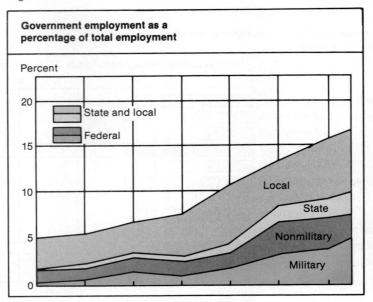

Government employment as a
percentage of total employment

Percent

State and local

Federal

Local

State

Nonmilitary

Military

20

15

10

5

0

6.   Use symbolic pictograms (such as little people representing workers or bags of money representing profits) to add interest, especially for nontechnical presentations, when you have the time and money and are preparing a report in enough copies to justify the cost.

But *keep all the little characters the same size* (although each may represent any quantity) and vary the *number* of them to represent different total quantities (usually lines of them making bar charts). Otherwise, you mislead because the volume in the pictogram involves a third dimension (depth perspective) not shown in the pictogram. Of two cylindrical tanks representing oil production, for example, one actually twice as big as the other looks only slightly bigger because of the unseen third dimension. (If you remember from your geometry that the volume of a cylinder is $\pi r^2 h$, you'll see why.)

Though it may appear to be a contradiction to the *number/not size* rule for showing quantity in pictograms, the map in Figure 14–2 (using side-by-side piles of sales contracts as bar charts, with percentage figures) for the two years covered, is particularly effective for showing shifts in regional sales. One of the reasons is that the one chart involves multimedia—map, bar chart, and just a hint of pictograms—and the piles of sales contracts are bars in a bar chart showing the quantities.

As a weekly news magazine wanting to report current quantified data interestingly, *U.S. News & World Report* makes frequent use of pictograms, purely for their interest value, while the figures appear in other forms. For instance,

Figure 14–2

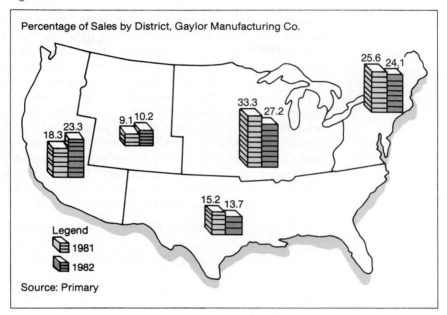

Percentage of Sales by District, Gaylor Manufacturing Co.

Legend
1981
1982

Source: Primary

in a thorough article on inflation it used eight pairs of bars to present (in black) the current costs of eight cost-of-living items and (in red) the costs five years later (assuming continuation of the rate of inflation). Along with the cost figures at the top of each bar was (above each pair) a clever little symbolic drawing: a hospital bed for a day in the hospital, a pack of cigarettes, an ivy-covered tower, an apron (maid service), and so on.

7.   If you have to provide multiple copies of your report, consider whether your graphics are reproducible. What may be fine for offset printing may not work in some kinds of photocopy processes. Computer-generated graphics, increasingly common, often pose problems. A computer printout or a photo-graph of a visual display may be of such poor quality that you would lose important details in reproduction, necessitating expensive and time-consum-ing tracing or redrawing.

8.   Graphics and other visual aids (usually flip charts or slides) for oral presentations pose problems peculiar to speaking situations, and we deal with these in Chapter 17.

By way of summary, we believe that careful study of the illustrations, warn-ings, and instructions on graphics we have given here will enhance your abil-ity to use these effective devices to become a better report writer. At the same time you will have had an up-to-date insight into the current job picture and some valid bases for projective thinking about career planning to 1990.

Documentation

Since a report is usually the basis for an executive decision which may be costly if it is wrong, business executives rightfully expect reports to answer at least two important questions: What are the facts? How do you know? In an analytical report, two more questions arise: What do you make of (conclude from) these facts? Then what do you recommend that I do?

The second question means that the report must provide evidence that the information is trustworthy. Usually you do that by explaining your sources and methods of research as a basis for judgment about the report's soundness. The only exceptions are in the reports of unquestionable authorities (whose word would be taken at face value) and in cases where the methods and sources are already known or the presentation of the facts clearly implies them.

In short reports usually you can best explain the sources and methods in incidental phrases along with the presentation of data, as in the following:

```
Four suppliers of long standing report him as prompt
pay and . . . .

Standard quantitative analysis reveals 17 percent
carbon . . . .

Analysis of the balance sheet reveals . . . .
```

Notice how the illustrative reports in Chapter 13 (the short ones) interweave the references to methodology of research and to published sources—right within the text of the report.

In the complete analytical report the introduction explains methods and mentions printed sources (which the bibliography, footnotes, and/or other citations in the text explain more specifically).

At least, any report writer except the recognized authority precludes what one reader expressed as "the distrust I have of those people who write as if they had a private line to God."

Since you often use some published materials in collecting data for major reports, citing those sources is an important part of assuring your reader about the soundness of the facts. By paraphrasing a recognized authority (or quoting directly when justified—rarely, as explained earlier in this chapter under "Library research"), you add support for and impact to your statements. When you use another author's special ideas, facts, or wording, however, to avoid plagiarism you have a moral (and in some circumstances a legal) obligation to give credit where it is due. You do *not need to cite* your source for information (as distinct from the exact wording) that is "in the public domain"—information that is (1) common knowledge, (2) obvious, or (3) readily available in many sources of the kind (like dictionaries and encyclopedias). Otherwise, you cite your sources by one of the somewhat varied but established systems.

Unfortunately, *bibliography* forms are not standardized. For the past 50 years the trend in documentation forms has been toward simplicity and efficiency, especially in business, industry, and the sciences. This statement does *not*, however, mean less documentation, but more efficient forms. Some people in the humanities, on the other hand, have tended to hold on to the older forms, especially their punctuation. Others have adopted the library practice of capitalizing only the first word and proper nouns (specific names of people, products, and places) in titles. *So unless you are sure that both you and your reader(s) understand and prefer other generally accepted forms used in your field (in the main professional journals, for example), we recommend that you use the following content and form.*

Readers generally expect a bibliographical entry to give the author's name, the title (of both an article and the journal), and (for books) the edition (if not the first), the publisher and place of publication, and the volume (if more than one); the volume number (if on the magazine) and all page numbers for magazine articles; and the date of publication for anything (noting n.d. for "no date" when you can't find it).

Preferably the pieces of information are in that order. Some people omit the publisher of a book or put it in parentheses with the place of publication and a colon preceding. The same people (usually in the humanities) use roman numerals for magazine volume numbers and follow immediately with the date in parentheses. In some specialized fields even the date or title may come first.

Usually the several entries in a bibliography appear in alphabetical order by author's name, which is inverted for the purpose. In some specialized fields, however, you will find other arrangements; and in extensive bibliographies (unusual in reports) you often find books and articles alphabetized separately, with headings for each group.

Unless you choose to follow the well-established form of your special field, we suggest that you be up to date and enter books as

```
Wilkinson, C. W., J. H. Menning, and C. R. Anderson
    (eds.), Writing for Business, Third Edition, Richard
    D. Irwin, Inc., Homewood, Illinois, 1970.
```

In the humanities, however, most authors would enter this book as

```
. . . , Third edition. Homewood, Ill.: Richard D.
    Irwin, Inc., 1970.
```

Even in this simple entry, you have three somewhat unusual items:

1. Three people worked on the book, but the name of only the first needs to be inverted for alphabetizing.
2. Since the "authors" were editors rather than writers of the book, you see eds. right after their names.
3. Because the book is not the first edition, the entry tells which it is. Some writers would add, at the end, 369 pp., $9.95—two pieces of information usual in reviews of new books but not in bibliographies.

The recommended form for magazine articles is

```
Gallagher, William J., "Technical Writing: In Defense
   of Obscurity," Management Review, 55:34-36, May,
   1982.
```

Or (often in the humanities):

```
Arnold, C. K., "How to Summarize a Report,"
   Supervisory Management, VII (July, 1979), 15-17.
```

If you want to be more helpful to the reader, you may annotate your bibliography with brief notes indicating the content and your evaluation of the book or article:

```
Darlington, Terry, "Do a Report on It," Business,
   94:74, 93, May, 1981.
   Good treatment of report functions and short,
   simple, direct approach for report writing.
   Especially good on five-point plan for organizing.
```

You need to note two points here:

1. Enclose titles of parts like magazine articles and book chapters in quotes; but underscore titles of whole publications (italics in printed copy) with the first word and all others except articles *(a, an, the)*, prepositions, and conjunctions capitalized.
2. Listings of magazines do not include the publisher and place but do include the volume number (if available) and all page numbers, hyphenated for inclusive pages and separated by commas for jumps in paging.

If no author's or editor's name appears on a book or article, the entry usually appears in the alphabetical list by first word of the title (not counting *a, an,* and *the*). Sometimes, however, a writer chooses to alphabetize by publisher instead—especially pamphlets, booklets, reports, and the like put out by corporations and governmental agencies. Thus you will see entries like

```
"Are Your Memos on Target?" Supervisory Management,
   9:39-40, August, 1982.

Texaco, Inc., Annual Report of 1982.

U.S. Department of Agriculture Bulletin 1620,
   Characteristics of New Varieties of Peaches, U.S.
   Government Printing Office, 1979.
```

(Note, in the first illustration, that when a comma and a stronger mark—question mark or exclamation point—need to come at the same place, you simply omit the comma.)

At those points in the report text where you make use of printed sources, you also tell the reader about them by specific references or citations. One way of doing so is *footnoting*, which is decreasing in use (especially in business and technical writing) because footnotes heckle readers. A better method for most situations, now coming into wider and wider use, is to interweave the minimum essentials of a citation subordinately right into the text, like this:

> Wilkinson says ("The History and Present Need of
> Reports," The ABCA Bulletin, 19:14, April, 1982)
> that reports . . . .

Still, footnote citations (indicated by raised numbers in the text and matching numbers before the notes) may be necessary in some cases to keep long, interwoven citations from making the reading difficult. Remember, however, that footnotes at the bottom of the page (or worse, grouped at the end) are more interruptive to a reader than parenthetical citations.

The first footnote or interwoven citation, plus whatever bibliographical information may appear in the text, is a complete reproduction of the bibliographical entry with two minor changes: The author's name is in the normal order (given name or initials first), and the page reference is the specific page or pages used for that particular part of the report. Accordingly, first footnote references to a magazine and a book would be as follows:

> [1]H. R. Jolliffe, "Semantics and Its Implications for
> Teachers of Business Communication," Journal of
> Business Communication, 1:17, March, 1979.

> [2]J. H. Menning, C. W. Wilkinson, and Peter B. Clarke,
> Communicating through Letters and Reports, Sixth
> Edition, Richard D. Irwin, Inc., Homewood, Illinois,
> 1976, p. 469.

Later references to the same works can be shortened forms with the specific page number(s) and just enough information for the reader to identify the source. Usually the author's surname, the title, and the page(s) will do, whether interwoven in the text, put in footnotes, or divided between the two. Thus later references could be as shown below:

> Jollife ("Semantics and Its Implications," p. 18)
> makes the point that . . . .

> Menning, Wilkinson, and Clarke (Communicating . . . ,
> p. 29) discuss letters in three broad
> categories: . . . .

The short-form citations of sources, enclosed in parentheses here, could be footnotes if the writer prefers.

The old practice of using Latin abbreviations (such as *op. cit.*, *ibid.*, and *loc. cit.*, to mention only a few), which have long confused many people, is disappearing along with footnotes. Except in scholarly writing for other scholars, the practice is to use English words and a few standard abbreviations like p. for page and pp. for pages—preceding page numbers which do not follow volume numbers.

The newest and probably the best bibliographical citation system—coming into wider use, especially in science and industry, probably because of its efficiency—involves these steps:

1. Numbering the listings in the bibliography after you've arranged them in the usual way.
2. Using these numbers and the specific page number(s), usually separated by colons and enclosed in parentheses, at the points in the report requiring documentation—usually just before the periods at the ends of sentences, like this (4:39).
3. Explaining the system at its first use, by footnote or parenthetical note something like "(4:39, meaning p. 39 of Item 4 in the Bibliography)."

(Look through the illustrative report in Chapter 15 for further illustration of this method of citing published sources.)

Letters, speeches, and interviews used as sources of information do not belong in a bibliography. The method for citing them is by footnoting or by interweaving in the text the information about the giver and the receiver of the information, the form, the date, and any other pertinent facts.

Although we've given the main points about documentation, several large books and many smaller ones, plus numerous pamphlets, deal extensively with this subject. As further illustration of bibliography forms, and as sources of more detailed information about them, footnotes, and other details of form, we list the major publications:

A Manual of Style (Twelfth Edition), University of Chicago Press, Chicago, 1969.

The MLA Style Sheet (Second Edition), Modern Language Association of America, Washington, D.C., 1970 (revised as *MLA Handbook*, 1977).

U.S. Government Printing Office Style Manual (Revised Edition), U.S. Government Printing Office, Washington, D.C., 1973.

Turabian, Kate L., *A Manual for Writers of Term Papers, Theses, and Dissertations* (Fourth Edition), University of Chicago Press, Chicago, 1973.

* * * * *

Beyond that, the preparation of a report depends on the particular form to be used; and the form you choose should be the one best adapted to the situation, as explained along with the illustrations in Chapters 13, 15, and 16. (The cases for major reports of different kinds are all at the ends of Chapters 15 and 16.)

QUESTIONS AND EXERCISES

1. If you want to get the best buy for your money in a new TV set, in what magazine in your library would you probably find the needed information?
2. For information on a current topic would you start looking in the card catalog or in one of the indexes?

3. You have many indexes to choose from to find information, but which one would you be most likely to use for the following topics?
   a. A story about a liquor company's buying an oil company.
   b. News story for doctors about a breakthrough for cancer cure.
   c. From London, a story about ACCA exams.
   d. L. H. Mueller, Salzburg, Austria, wrote up his experiment of grafting a dogwood and redbud.
   e. A new experiment in the Los Angeles schools about protecting teachers from student abuse.
   f. News releases from the present administration of the U.S. government on budget cuts.
4. As the chief of graphic arts in the U.S. Surgeon General's office, you have the job of devising the graphics to go in a thorough report to the nation on the effects of cigarette smoking. The writer of the report has fed you the following research data and asked you:
   a. How many and what kinds of graphics do you think would be helpful?
   b. In what sequence would you use them?
   c. To please draw up graphics (as many as your teacher assigns) that you think will help in the report.

   Cigarettes will be the major cause of 129,000 of 430,000 U.S. deaths from cancer this year. Deaths from lung cancer alone have risen from 18,313 in 1950 to 111,000 a year. That increase is in spite of the fact that since the 1964 report of cancer research 30 million people have given up cigarette smoking (95 percent without help from organized programs). But even after a person quits, the ex-smoker's chances of cancer remain above those of nonsmokers for 15 years. Only 10 percent of cancer victims survive five years after diagnosis.

   Children of a smoker (either parent) are twice as likely to smoke, but (conversely) going to college doubles the chances of quitting.

   The high point of smoking was (for men) in 1955 (53 percent); for women, 1966 (33 percent); today's men 37 percent, and women, 29 percent.

   Besides its major contribution to lung cancer, cigarette smoking is the number-one cause of emphysema and a major cause of heart disease. Pregnant women who smoke also increase their risks of spontaneous abortions or children with birth defects.
5. Arrange the following entries (a–e) for a bibliography in the preferred up-to-date form suggested in your text:
   a. The entry for this textbook,
   b. *Communications for the Executive* by Robert Duggin, 1983, Harper & Row Publishers, New York,
   c. "Are You Preparing Your Students for the Job Interview?" by Mona J. Casady and James Marcum, *ABCA Bulletin,* vol. 40, September, 1983, pp. 15–18,

      d. *Administrative Management,* vol. 22, March 1982, pp. 40–43, "The Mailroom Goes Electronic," and

      e. "Computer Graphics: Looking Sharp for the Eighties," from *The Wall Street Journal,* page 7, May, 1983, vol. 64.

6. Write the following statements in first-degree heading (one statement), second-degree heading (one statement), third-degree heading (two statements and two headings), fourth-degree (two statements and two headings) and fifth-degree heading (two statements and two headings): The Super Suds Company should change from radio to TV advertising; TV gives better coverage; Nelson survey shows high TV rating, Belle survey gives TV high rating; a 1983 study in Southwest, a 1983 study in Northeast; random sample shows . . . ; possible error of 3 percent suggests . . . .

7. Which type of graph is best for:

    a. Showing Americans how their tax dollar is spent for government costs.

    b. Showing population growth during the past 25 years.

    c. Showing the growth of men and women in the labor force.

    d. Showing an uninterested audience (subscribers to a news magazine) figures on inflation in the Northeast, Midwest, Southeast, and Far West of the United States.

8. What methods of research would you use to solve the following problems:

    a. Reasons why the sales of one of your branch stores are down for the last two years.

    b. To find out what university teachers of business communication consider important areas to cover in their classes.

    c. To help you decide which city would be the best for starting a dental practice.

9. Make up two questions that would

    a. Likely lead to prestige answers.

    b. Encourage answering in a certain way.

    c. Pry unduly into personal affairs.

    d. Require unduly long memory.

10. Which type of questionnaire would be best to use

    a. If you have unlimited time and money and need the information in order to write a paper and need to document your information?

    b. You work at a state adoption agency and you need personal information as to how well adopting families have adjusted for the past two years?

    c. To investigate smoking habits of a selected group of students on your campus (for use in a paper for a marketing class)?

11. Which heading talks?

    a. City Y's Attitudes toward Industry.

    b. City Y's Attitude toward Gulf States Saw Mill.

    c. Population Growth Greater in San Diego.

    d. Population Growth in Austin.

12. Make suggestions to improve the following partial outline:

   1.0. City Y's Favorable Attitude toward Gulf States Saw Mill

     1.1. Attitudes mixed toward labor policy

   2.0. Labor Supply Limited

     2.1. Not enough skilled labor

     2.2. Wage problems

       2.2.1. Union threatens strike

       2.2.2. Rates for longevity unequal

       2.2.3. Why rates are unfair

13. Your boss at First Federal Savings and Loan wants to know whether giving gifts to new customers and previous customers (who have come back) pays off. After a great deal of research investigating the last five give-away campaigns, you have the information and will write the report. Which sequence or plan would you use, and why?

14. Which plan would be best if you want to control emphasis in your business report?

15. Can you poke holes in the following statements and give the reasons for your answers?

   a. Students at Y University make poor grades because they drink too much.

   b. All students at the highly thought of Y University support the football team.

16. Which is the best/better way of handling figures? Why?

   a. (1) Y company increased its profit over last year's by 10 percent (almost $9 million).

     (2) Y company increased its profit by $8,996,496.46.

     (3) Y company increased its profit.

   b. (1) The Department of Defense spent X dollars in 198—.

     (2) The 198— cost of defense in the United States comes to X dollars per year or X dollars per day per person.

17. To be sure you understand the roman and decimal systems of outline symbols, illustrate each system through five levels below the title, which is the first level.

18. Assume that you are writing a report on whether to live in a dormitory or an apartment. Draw up a tentative outline.

19. Using the citation system recommended by your textbook, how would you cite a reference to page 90 of the sixth bibliographical entry?

20. In a report you want to cite an interview with Professor E. J. Filbey, head of the accounting department at Y University. What are two ways you can cite this interview?

Analysis and illustration of major analytical reports

15

AN OVERVIEW OF REPORT FORMAT

In petty details the makeup of major analytical reports varies only a little less than the organizations sponsoring the reports. Hence we cannot give you a report form that is acceptable universally in all details.

Yet in the larger aspects of report parts and their interrelations, agreement far exceeds disagreement. In this chapter we explain and illustrate major report makeup with emphasis on the generally acceptable main points. Since you will also want some guidance on details, however, we will suggest *a* good way to handle them; but, as we do, we ask you to remember three things:

1. What we present on details of form is *not the only way*.
2. Since we are talking here about major analytical reports, which are generally five or more pages long and are written, we refer to report *writers* and *readers*. (We'll explain and illustrate the shorter reports in this chapter, the longer ones in Chapter 16, and oral reports in Chapter 17.)
3. We do not present the illustrations as perfect reports, and certainly not as wording for you to follow slavishly or copy parrotlike. At best, they show acceptable content, form, and general style for their particular situations as starters to your thinking—not as solutions to all your problems.

Layout and pagination

Most major analytical reports include three broad categories of several parts each. The parts marked with asterisks in the following list normally do not appear as separate parts except in long, formal reports; but the others are almost universal—and in the order listed.

Preliminaries
- Cover*
- Title fly*
- Title page
- Letter of authorization*
- Letter of acceptance*
- Letter of transmittal
- Table of contents*
- Table of illustrations*
- Synopsis* (but maybe in transmittal)

Body
- Introduction
  - I. (or 1.0) Introduction
  - II. (or 2.0) Text is minimum of
  - III. (or 3.0) two major divisions
- Text
  - IV. (or 4.0) with needed
  - V. (or 5.0) subheads and sub-
  - VI. (or 6.0) subheads
- Conclusions — VII. Conclusions and
- Recommendations — VIII. recommendations, together or separately as last one or two major divisions

Supplements
- Appendix(es)*
- Bibliography*
- Index*

The following specifics will help in layout and pagination:

1. Generally each of the listed parts except text, conclusions, and recommendations begins a new page; otherwise, only the filling of one page calls for a new one. If used, the table of illustrations may go on the same page with the contents if space allows without crowding. Each appendix begins on a new page.

2. Counting the preliminary pages begins with the title fly, if used (but the numbers, in lowercase roman numerals, do not appear until the pages beginning *after* the title page). Pages in the body and supplements take arabic numerals. The first page number of any part beginning a new page goes at the center bottom of the page; others appear (preferably) at least two spaces above the end of the first line. No page numbers need adornments such as parentheses, hyphens, periods, and underscores.

3. For bound reports, the "bite" of the binding requires typing with an extra wide margin where the binding will be so that the binding will not hide any writing and margins will be proper when the report is open.

Optional and minor parts

Now, before we present the parts that require full discussion and illustration, let's clear out the no-problem parts and the optional parts marked with asterisks in the preceding list.

The *cover*, much like the cover of a book but generally useful only for reports of 20 pages or more, is there to hold the report together and protect it. But unless it is transparent or has a cutout revealing the identifying title page, it needs to carry at least the title (perhaps in shortened form) and the author's name. (It may carry the rest of the title-page information too.)

The *title fly* is a full page carrying only the title. Whatever its use in printed books, it is only excess paper in typewritten reports. If used, it counts as the first of the preliminary pages (lowercase roman numerals), although the page number does not usually appear on it.

When the person who authorizes a report makes the assignment by a *letter (or memo) of authorization,* a copy of it should appear in the report. This situation is most likely when the assignment is a big one, especially if it is a public affairs problem or the report writer is an outsider working on a consulting basis. By showing what the assigned job was, the letter enables any reader to judge the adequacy of the report. To make sure of getting a useful report, the writer of the authorization needs to state the problem precisely and make clear the purpose, scope, and limits on time, money, and the like. Asking specific questions and, if known, suggesting sources, methods, or approaches may help further, and also save money.

A *letter of acceptance*—rarely included—is the answer to a letter of authorization. Together they constitute the working agreement or contract.

A *table of illustrations* will help only if some of the tables and graphics might be useful to a reader independently of the discussion around them. In table-of-contents form it lists separately the tables, charts, and figures in sequence by their identifying numbers and titles—and gives the pages on which they appear.

An *index* would serve little purpose in most reports both because they are not long enough to need one and because readers do not use them as reference books. Ordinarily the table of contents adequately helps a reader to find a certain point. If, however, you find that you must prepare an index, take some good advice from people who have tried indexing: (1) Hire a professional indexer to do the job or (2) study at least one of the several helpful books on the subject before you start. Indexes done by nonprofessionals are mostly rather poor, including those in most textbooks—because they are usually too scant and too full of errors.

STANDARD SHORT PRELIMINARIES

Title page

The title page is usually the first of the preliminary pages (counted as lowercase roman numbers down to the introduction), but the page number does not need to appear on it. Four other blocks of information usually do: the title itself, the name and title of the writer, and the place and date. In many instances the name of the organization where both writer and reader work is desirable information. When needed, a brief abstract, a list of people or departments to receive copies, project or serial-number identifications, and classifications for secrecy ("Confidential," etc.) may appear also.

Phrasing the title well is usually the main problem. (Unfortunately the writing of functional titles—as opposed to literary-style titles for stories, poetry, plays, and movies—is something schools do not generally teach.) First, a good report title, like any other title or heading in functional writing, should be *precise* in indicating clearly the content and scope. Frequently, however, first-attempt report titles are too broad, too narrow, or tangential—suggesting more or less than intended or a related rather than the real topic.

A good report title narrows the topic and then zeroes in on the real problem. Secondarily, a good report title should be *interesting*—at least to the intended reader. (You cannot reasonably expect to interest everybody in most report topics.) As a third desirable quality, a good report title should be *concise*—have no wasted words like "A Report on . . . ," "A Study of . . . ," or "A Survey of . . . ."

An example will make clearer some frequent false steps and final solutions to the problem of writing *precise, interesting,* and *concise* report titles. A student proposed a report on "A Study of the Compensation of Executives." Discussion with the professor quickly led to omitting the first four words, and then changing to "Executive Compensation" for a further 33 percent reduction in words. That adequately solved the problem of conciseness.

Further discussion soon revealed, however, that the student never intended to write about all executives but only high-level ones in corporations. The problem of precision had come up—in the usual way, pointing to a need for narrowing the topic to the intended coverage. But that wasn't even the worst part of imprecision in this case. Despite the emphasis on compensation, the student wasn't even interested in the executives' basic salaries, having already seen evidence that up to $600,000 annually didn't keep executives from leaving jobs. The student revealed that the real topic of interest was evaluation of several new means some corporations were beginning to use to keep their top executives. Traditional means—high salaries, stock options, bonuses, and retirement programs (the things most people would envision from the word *compensation*)—were only tangential to the main topic.

The student felt pride in accomplishment with "New Methods Corporations Use to Retain High-Level Executives"—but almost gave up when the professor said it wouldn't do. The assigned report was to be an *analytical* report, and this title suggested a mere presentation of undigested facts.

Assuming assignment by Pow Chemical Company to study the problem and write a report on what the corporation might do to reduce executive turnover, the student (with only a little more help) arrived at a different title: "Pow's Possible Benefits from Applying Some New Means Used by Corporations to Retain High-Level Executives." That title narrowed the topic and then zeroed in on the real problem. It said precisely what the report was to be about (no more, no less) and implied an analytical rather than informational report. (You might note that it doesn't even—and doesn't need to—contain the key word of the original, *compensation*.) The first three words could not help *interesting* Pow officials, the intended readers. But is it concise—not short, or brief, at 16 words—but concise? Are all the words *possible, applying, some,* and *used by corporations* worth their space? What do you think?

Since an analytical report is about a specific problem of an individual or group, its title should indicate that specificness, often to the extent of naming the person or group as well as the problem. You can't answer such a general question as "Should Spot Radio Advertising Be Used?" The answer would be sometimes yes and sometimes no. For that reason, one student phrased a title as "Why the P. L. Lyon Company Should Discontinue Spot Radio Advertising."

That title, however, was a *final* title, written *after* the writer had done the research and made the analysis. Knowing what the decision was, and knowing that the key point would be readily acceptable, the reporter reasonably chose to tell the reader directly—as in an A–plan letter. To have phrased it that way *before* doing the research, however, would have been to act on a preconception that could have prevented the writer from facing facts fairly.

With the title well done, you should have no more trouble with the title page. In looking at the illustration later in this chapter, note how the writer grouped information into four parts and used balanced layout (each line centered) for good appearance.

Letter of transmittal

Following the title page—unless the report is an extensive and formal one, including such things as a copyright notice, title fly, letter of authorization, and letter of acceptance—page ii (counted, but not necessarily physically numbered) is a letter of transmittal. (In a formal public-affairs report with large numbers of indefinite readers, a typical preface often replaces the personalized letter of transmittal.)

Written after completing the report, in regular letter form and in a style appropriate to the circumstances (Chapters 1 and 2), the letter of transmittal must do at least two things: transmit the report and refer to the authorization (if any). In informal situations one sentence can do both: "Here's the report on fish poisoning you asked me to write when we were talking on May 10." Usually it needs to be a little more formal than that, but it needs no bromidic "As per your request, . . ." and rarely such formality as "In accordance with . . . ." Certainly it needs to subordinate the reference to the authorization to avoid a flat and insulting sound—seeming to tell about the request for the report as if the reader were too dumb or forgetful to remember. In the rare cases where no authorization happened, instead of the reference to it the writer tells enough background to arouse interest.

Despite the importance of conciseness and the possibility of doing in the first sentence all it *has* to do, a letter of transmittal will say more, if for no reason than to avoid a curt tone. Some appropriate additional things it might talk about (but not all in any one letter) are

—A highlight particularly significant in affecting the findings, or a reference to special sections likely to be particularly interesting to the reader.

—A summary of conclusions and recommendations (or even an interwoven synopsis if the reader is likely to be sympathetic and unless a synopsis two or three pages later says the same thing). Even then, the letter can give very briefly the general decision but not supporting data.

—Side issues or facts irrelevant to the report but supposedly interesting or valuable to the reader.

—Limitations of information, time, and/or money if they are true and not a part of the introduction, where they naturally belong—and provided that they do not sound like lazy excuses.

—Acknowledgments of unusual help from others whom you have not cited later as sources.

The letter may appropriately—almost always should—end with some expression indicating your attitude toward the significance of the report and/ or appreciation for having the opportunity to work on it, because—

—If you are in the business of making such studies, you surely appreciate business.

—If you're within the company, you certainly should appreciate the opportunity to demonstrate your ability and to learn more about the company.

—An important report assignment is a chance to make a good impression (and be marked for promotion). The value of that chance and a good report could easily suffer, however, if you do not express your appreciation for the chance.

Table of contents

The next part, usually page iii (with the number centered at the bottom, as always on a page with extra space at the top because of a part heading), is the table of contents (or simply contents)—often omitted in short analytical reports because a good set of internal headings does the job. It sets out the major, if not all, headings of the report and their beginning page numbers. Thus it quickly shows the organization and serves as a handy guide for the reader, especially the busy reader who may want to check only some parts. In the absence of an index, for long reports it needs to be adequately detailed for the purpose.

To list in the table of contents the table itself and those parts that come before it would look a little odd; the reader would already have seen them. You therefore list only those divisions (with subdivisions down the scale as far as you think helpful) following the table. Remember, however, that the *preliminary parts down to the introduction are* not *parts of the outline and do not get outline symbols,* such as I and A (or 1.0 and 1.1) but only their names and page numbers (small roman numerals). If a separate synopsis comes immediately after the table of contents, for example, you list it flush left without an outline symbol, as the first thing on the list.

Then comes the real outline of the report—the headings and subheads. In most reports you may well give all of them, reproduced in exactly the same wording as elsewhere (but not in different styles of type). Preferably you should put the outline symbols before them—in the decimal system or in capital roman numerals for the major divisions (including the introduction, conclusions, and recommendations) and capital letters for their subdivisions. *(Remember that roman numerals, like arabics, line up on the right.)* If any heading is too long for one line, break it at least seven spaces before the page-number column and indent the carry-over. After each heading is a leader line of *spaced* periods (with a space or two before and after) leading to the page-number column. For proper appearance (vertical alignment), make *all* those periods while your typewriter carriage is on either even or odd numbers on the scale.

Supplementary parts such as appendixes and a bibliography continue the arabic page numbers of the body copy, but they do not carry outline numerals to the left in the table of contents because they are not logical parts of the discussion being outlined.

The table of contents may be single- or double-spaced, or single-spaced within parts and double-spaced between, whichever makes the best appearance on the page; but double-space at least between the parts and major divisions.

Synopsis and/or abstract

Written after you complete the report proper, the synopsis is a condensed version of the whole report (preliminaries, introduction, presentation of facts and the interpretations of them, and conclusions and recommendations). It is the report in a nutshell—usually reduced somewhere between 10:1 and 20:1. In most cases you reduce the introduction even more and the conclusions and recommendations less because they deserve the main emphasis as the report's reason for being.

Since a synopsis stresses results, in terms of the psychology of communication you might feel that you should not use one in a report which needs to be strongly convincing because of the reader's likely resistance. In such a situation the condensed presentation of findings might not be adequate to do the necessary convincing before the reader sees the unwelcome or inadequately justified conclusions. (You would be using A–plan organization for a C–plan situation—as explained in Chapter 4.)

The increasing recognition of readers' benefits from having synopses in long reports and the way readers read such reports, however, override the preceding psychological objection. Neither psychologically nor practically can you hold an impatient reader away from the conclusions long enough to read a long report anyway, the way you can on a short one or a letter. (You may, however, still achieve at least some of the benefits of psychological planning—by organizing your synopsis according to the appropriate B– or C–plan letter.)

So—as in a report which may properly follow the deductive A–plan because the results are probably welcome to the reader—even in a long report which needs to convince, the synopsis serves several important purposes:

1. It saves time in many cases by giving all a busy reader wants.
2. Even for the reader who goes on through the whole report, the synopsis gives a brief view which helps in reading the rest more easily and more intelligently because already knowing the final results makes clearer how each fact or explanation fits.
3. Often the synopsis also serves as the basis for a condensed oral presentation to a group of important readers such as a board of directors (as explained in Chapter 17).
4. Sometimes a number of readers who do not get the whole report but need to know the essence of it get what they need from reproduced and distributed copies of the synopsis.

Particularly for the first and last uses, many excutives now insist that major reports coming to their desks have *one-page* synopses up front—an increasing trend. You should therefore try to keep synopses down to one page, even if you have to single-space within paragraphs (but of course double-space between).

For an example of a good synopsis, read the detailed one below. It specifically and concisely synopsizes a report of six major divisions (besides the introduction and the conclusions and recommendations) running to 27 pages. Desirably, it focuses on a quick presentation of results (the conclusions and implied recommendation) in the first paragraph, while also making clear the purpose, the readers and authorizer, and the writers. Then it summarizes, in a paragraph for each, the six data-filled sections in the same order and proportionate space given the topics in the full report.

For readers not used to standard kinds of market-research data for choosing favorable locations, we give you the *topics* of those six sections (not the informative headings actually used): Population and Buying Units; Buying Income; Retail Sales; Drugstore Sales; Overall Business Factors and Stability; and Business Activity.

<u>Synopsis</u>

Savannah people are likely to buy more at a Rexwall
Drug Store than Charleston residents are, according to
this market evaluation prepared for the Chairman of
the Board, Rexwall, Inc., by Factseekers, Inc.

Though metropolitan Charleston merchants serve 11,000
more customers from the shopping area, Savannah

retailers can expect some trade from almost twice as
many out-of-town buyers (340,000 versus 184,000).
Savannah's 1,000 more family units more than
compensate for the fact that the Charleston family
averages 3.62 people while the smaller Savannah family
averages 3.4.

Savannah individuals average $85 more buying income,
but the larger Charleston families average $35 more
per family for a total of half a million more annual
buying income. With less first-mortgage money to do
it, 2,800 more people in Savannah have built homes in
the past four years; but 17,000 more Charlestonians
own autobmobiles.

The higher income of the individual Savannah buyer and
the larger number of customers from around Savannah
explain why $2.5 million more passed through the hands
of Savannah retailers last year. Individually,
Savannah residents spent $75 more; the small Savannah
family, however, spent only $55 more.

Though five years ago Charleston druggists outsold
those in Savannah by an average of $3,000, last year
the 61 Savannah drugstore managers and owners
collected about $5 million—$170,000 more than 62
Charleston druggists—for an average of $4,000 more
per drugstore in Savannah.

Overall business factors also point to Savannah as the
choice. Savannah's estimated business volume of $989
million is almost twice that of Charleston. Since a
significant part of this difference is attributable to
the 10 million more tons of cargo handled by the
Savannah docks, Savannah consumers and retailers will
feel the pinch of recessions and strikes more than
Charlestonians. The extra $36 million added by
Charleston manufacturing, however, is almost as
uncertain in the stability of that city as the effects
of shipping are on the economy of Savannah.
Charlestonians benefit from $35 million more of the
relatively stable wholesale business; but $32 million
more agricultural income from farms averaging $4,000
more in value helps to bolster the Savannah economy.

Certainly Savannah's business activity has been
consistently better than Charleston's in the past four
years. Though the trend continues up in both cities,
construction has averaged $12 million more annually in
Savannah. Bankers in Savannah have consistently
received about 10 percent more deposits than their
Charleston counterparts have—for $150 million more in
commercial accounts and $12 million more in savings.

> In both cities postmasters have collected about 8 percent more each successive year, but Savannah citizens have steadily paid for $200,000 more postage than Charlestonians have.

Since a synopsis derives exclusively from the report itself—which has adequate illustration and documentation—it needs neither graphics nor citations. But you do need to give the main supporting facts. Otherwise the synopsis becomes a nutshell with no meat. This is one reason we use the term *synopsis* rather than *abstract*.

Abstracts are of two kinds—topical, giving *only the points discussed* (shells without meat); and informative, giving the findings about each topic, with emphasis on conclusions and any recommendations made. A synopsis is like an *informative* abstract, emphasizing results, but is usually fuller and more helpful.

CONTENT AND FORM OF MAJOR PARTS

Introduction

The introduction to a major analytical report serves primarily to answer the second of a report reader's two inevitable questions: How do you know? Rarely does it answer any part of the first question: What are the facts? If that question needs a brief and early answer (before the text gives all the facts), the synopsis does the job. Unless a synopsis or informative abstract is a part of the introduction, therefore—as in some forms of reports—the introduction is no place to put your data.

Since the introduction begins the *body* of the report—which also includes the text (the facts and analyses), conclusions, and recommendations if the reader wants them—the title of the whole report appears at the top of the page. Remember to set up that title exactly as on the title page, to reign as superior over all other headings—in content and in form. (Number the page 1, centered at the bottom as always on a page with extra space at the top because of a heading there.)

The first real problem in writing an introduction (often best done after the other parts) is selecting a heading for it. The stock term *Introduction*, which fits all but none well, is neither a precise nor an interesting preview of the contents. The illustrative reports we're using here and in the next chapter, you'll notice, do better. You can too after reading further below about the content of introductions. One of the best we've ever seen was "The WHY and HOW of This Report," but you don't need to use its wording. In fact you should not copy anybody's word patterns in a title or anywhere else, especially if they are unusual. You should look at illustrations for ideas and principles of communication—then express your thoughts in your own way. Regardless of what it says, the heading of the introduction, as the first major division of your outline (usually I or 1.0), should be in the same grammatical and type form you intend to use for all the other major-division headings. (See *parallel structure* and *headings* in Chapter 14.)

In explaining how you know your forthcoming facts are reliable, you need to state your *purpose, methods,* and *scope* so that the reader can judge whether the research would produce information that is sound and adequate for the purpose. Clear and explicit statement of the purpose is essential. No reader can judge a report without knowing what the writer set out to accomplish. Similarly, unless the research seems basically sound (in methodology and scope) for the purpose, the reader naturally discredits the whole report. The introduction, then, is an important part of the conviction in the report and therefore deserves careful attention from both writer and reader.

The section headed Purpose may take several paragraphs for full explanation, especially if it includes history or background of the problem; or it may be short. Long or short, it should contain some *one* sentence which is a pointed, concise statement of the problem you set out to solve. That sentence should come early, too. So, although any necessary background of history is the natural start, to avoid delay if it becomes very long you should state the key purpose sentence early and use the flashback method to follow quickly with clarifying background. As another alternative, you may relegate any very long background story to an appendix and refer the reader to it—especially if it is nonessential for most readers.

Methods and scope come under separate headings or (because they are often nearly inseparable) under a combined heading. Your reader does want to know, however, what you intended to cover (scope) and how you got and analyzed your information (method—that big question again, How do you know?). In a study involving a choice or evaluation, for example, the introduction needs to explain the *criteria* or *standards* used, as a part of method and scope or as a separate part. In fact, since the criteria in such a report should become the major subdivisions, explanation and justification of them should be an important duty of the introduction.

How thoroughly you need to explain your methods depends on two major points: (1) how new and questionable your methods and findings are and (2) your reputation as a researcher. On both bases nobody questions the audit report of a reputable auditing firm that says no more on methods than the following: ". . . in accordance with generally accepted auditing standards, and accordingly included such tests of the accounting records and such other auditing procedures as we considered necessary in the circumstances." Most report writers, however, cannot depend so completely on either such standardized procedures or their reputations to convince their readers that they used sound research methods.

A frequent question is how much methodology to put in the introduction and how much (if any) to relegate to an appendix or to interweave along with the presentation of findings. No simple answer fits all cases and relieves you of thinking. A general answer is that you explain your methods at the best place(s) to show that your facts have a solid basis in valid research. Your reader will want at least a general idea from the introduction.

If specific details of research procedure, special materials and apparatus, or technique are too difficult for your reader(s) to remember and associate with the later resultant findings, you had better omit the specifics from the introduction and interweave them with the presentation of findings. (A specific question with its answers from a questionnaire is a good example.)

Like long and unnecessary background, certain details of methodology may sometimes go in an appendix, but only if (1) they would interrupt or unduly slow up the fast movement of the report proper and (2) most readers of the particular report would not want or need them. (Detailed explanations of unusual statistical procedures are good examples.)

Besides the standard parts (purpose, method, and scope), an introduction may take up one or more (rarely all) of several other possible topics. Unless the letter of transmittal has already done so, the introduction should forewarn the reader of any unavoidable *limitations* that make the report less than might be expected—limitations of time, money, or availability of data, for example. The explanation may be a part of method and scope if it is not so extensive as to need its own heading. But in no case should you use it as an excuse for your own shortcomings.

Sometimes a report uses technical words or certain terms applied in a sense unfamiliar to some likely readers. If so, you may explain them in the introduction or, preferably, in brief parenthetical statements immediately following the first use of each special term. If the list is extensive, the *glossary* may be an appendix.

The important point is for the introduction to answer the big question—How do you know?—*before* the reader asks it. Then you are ready to present the assuredly reliable facts.

Before asking the reader to go on this mental journey, however, consider whether you can help by giving a final reminder of the route: a concise statement of your *basic* plan. Such a statement should not be long or detailed in its itemization of *all* your headings. It *does,* however, need to remind the reader of the major steps in your organization and logic—usually naming, in order, the topics from II (or 2.0) to the conclusions in your table of contents.

Usually one effective sentence can chart the way through to the end, like this: "As bases for determining the more favorable market conditions, this report examines—in this order—population characteristics, buying power, retail sales and drugstore sales and the attendant competition, stability of the economy, and the current business outlook." If you compare this statement of plan to the separate synopsis presented earlier, you will see that they both reflect the careful organization of the same report.

Text

Even the lazy writer who gets by with *Introduction* as the inadequate heading for that part cannot get by with *Text* as a heading covering the report's biggest part, which presents the findings and analyses of them. The stock term, fitting all reports and therefore useful in talking about them, fits no one report specifically enough for a heading.

But more important, the text section of the report is fundamentally the report; so if you try to phrase a suitable title for the section, it will be the same as the title of the whole report. Then the basic elements of your report—the factors or criteria which serve as the basis for the final decision—would become third-degree headings with seemingly too little significance.

That is the first of the two major problems confronting the writer in presenting the text: (1) showing the reader the organization carefully worked out as the third step in report preparation and (2) phrasing well the findings of the second step (collection of data) and the interpretations made in the fourth step. Satisfactory solutions to both are necessary if you are to give your reader the reliable information wanted.

Your main methods for showing the overall organization, the relations between parts, and the relation of each part to the whole are headings and subheads, topic sentences, and summary and anticipating statements. (You will find ample illustrations of all in the illustrative reports in this and the next Chapter.)

The headings and subheadings grow directly out of your attack on the problem, where you broke it down into its elements and further subdivided it by raising questions about each. Now that you are presenting the facts that provide the answers, you need only phrase these elements and questions into headings and subheads. Remember that good headings, like functional titles, are indicative, interesting, concise, and (in some cases preferably) informative to the extent of telling the most important findings about the respective parts. (Notice the heads in the illustrative reports.)

Just as a well-phrased heading may tell the main point about the section over which it stands, a topic sentence can give the essence of a paragraph and clearly foreshadow what the paragraph says. The topic sentence puts the big point across fast, arouses the reader's interest in seeing the supporting details that follow, and makes reading easier because of the preview. Although the resulting deductive paragraph plan is not the only one possible, it is the most useful for most kinds of writing, including report writing.

Reversing the plan produces a paragraph which presents a series of facts and arguments leading to a summarizing and maybe a concluding sentence at the end.

Both plans may apply to larger sections as well as to paragraphs. In fact, both a paragraph's topic sentence and the first part of a larger section may reflect, summarize, or provide a transition from a preceding part, as well as give the essence and preview of what is to follow. And endings of both paragraphs and larger parts commonly summarize them, show the significance of the just-completed part to the whole problem at hand, and foreshadow what is to follow in the next section (as do the endings of the illustrated introductions). Although the summaries may imply the advisability of a certain action, they should not go further and steal the thunder of the recommendation section by actually suggesting what action to take.

Little more need be said about how to put the findings of fact and the interpretation into words. You have already learned in Chapters 2 and 14 to use commonly understood words, short and direct sentences and paragraphs, itemizations, summarizing and transitional phrases and sentences, headings and subheads, and graphic aids to words. You know, too, that you need to support your statements of questionable fact with explanations, additional specific and concrete details as evidence, citations of sources, and any meaningful statistics.

But remember that graphic presentations are not complete in themselves, that they only help words to present facts. They cannot interpret. The reader who wants an analytical report will consider your job only half done if you present a mass of undigested data and leave the interpreting undone. But if you put graphics and comments about them close together so that the reader can see both at once, each supplements the other.

References to the carefully chosen, most suitable graphics (about which you learned in Chapter 14) should be *subordinate* to the interpretation of the facts shown. The mere fact that the graph is there, or even the facts shown in the table or graph, are less important than the *significance* of those facts to the whole problem or the particular point being made at the time. So the emphasis should be on the interpretation. (Note the references to charts throughout the text of the illustrative reports.)

Here's a flat example which is short only because it forces the reader to dig in its Figures 1 and 2 for the information:

> The greatest majority of the students interviewed showed their preference for buying at home in place of buying in the larger cities of Birmingham or Tuscaloosa. The overall percentage for the entire body of male students represented by the sample was 78. The freshmen showed an even greater tendency for home buying by their percentage of 84.
>
> Figure 1, below, gives a picture of the place of purchase of the entire group without regard to the nature of the group. Figure 2 divides the group according to the students' rank.

This rewrite is more informative, emphatic, and readable:

> When University of Alabama men are ready for a new suit, they buy at home 78 percent of the time. Although 4 out of 100 will buy in Tuscaloosa and 7 in Birmingham, as shown in Figure 1, these 11 atypical cases do not warrant extensive advertising.
>
> The Alabama man, although never weaned from hometown buying in the majority of cases, does slowly shift his

```
clothes-buying sources from home to Birmingham to
Tuscaloosa. The gain of only 13 out of every 100
purchasers over a four-year span, however (Figure 2),
only confirms the suspicion that Bold Look advertising
dollars in Tuscaloosa would be wasted.
```

Although basically an interpretation may point out trends, high and low points, and significant differences brought out by comparisons and analyses of facts and figures presented, you need not waste words by talking about "a comparison of" or "an analysis of" or "a study of." If you state the significances, you imply the comparison, the analysis, or the study. And the comparisons become more quickly clear and significant if you put them in terms of percentages or ratios instead of, or in addition to, giving the raw figures.

To avoid monotony of both sentence pattern and length, especially in a series of similar comparisons, consider different types of sentence beginnings. Nearly always you can do better than use the expletives "It is . . ." and "There are . . . ," which waste words, delay the idea, and lead you to weak and awkward passive constructions.

And unless the logic of the situation clearly dictates otherwise, you'll do best to use the present tense throughout the text. When a reader reads it, your report analyzes, presents, takes up, examines, establishes, and finally concludes (all present tense). Of course, you'll have to use some past and future tenses; but in general, use them for matters of historical record and things not yet done. You have to assume that your most recent information is still applicable; hence, even though last year's sales figures are a historical record of what people bought, you are justified in saying, "People buy . . . ," meaning that they did buy, they are buying, and they will buy.

With your well-organized, clearly presented, and sharply summarized facts and analyses at the ends of sections, you will have led the reader to your statement of conclusions and (if wanted) recommendations.

Conclusions and recommendations

When you put your conclusions and recommendations into words, they should not be surprising—and they won't be if you have done an adequate job in the preceding part. There you should have presented all the evidence and analysis necessary to support your conclusions. *No new facts or analyses should appear in the conclusions or recommendations.*

Whether you separate conclusions and recommendations into two parts makes little difference. Some people prefer separation because, they say, the conclusions are strictly objective, logical results of what the report has said, whereas the recommendations are the individual writer's personal suggestions of what to do about the problem. Whichever point of view and plan you use, the important thing is to be as objective as possible in stating both conclusions and recommendations.

As evidence of that objectivity in your conclusions, and as a means of saving the reader the trouble of looking back into the text to see that you do have the data, you may well lift basic figures or statements from the earlier presentation and interweave them into the conclusion sentences. The writer of the previously illustrated synopsis knew that the reader could not possibly retain the 200 or more facts and figures given as evidence in 27 pages of analysis. In reminding the reader of the significant evidence affecting the decision in the conclusion, shown below, that writer wisely attached a specific figure to every fact. Note, too, the specific wording of that ending section—as well as the selectivity and brevity.

```
             VII. THE PREFERRED CITY: SAVANNAH
Although a Charleston druggist enjoys the advantages
of
  --a population with a half million dollars more
    buying income annually and families with $34 more
    to spend
  --11,000 additional potential customers
a Savannah drugstore would likely sell more because of
these advantages:
  --$170,000 additional drugstore sales and $4,000
    greater sales per drugstore
  --$2.5 million more retail sales and $162 more per
    person spent in retail stores
  --1,000 more families and per capita income $87
    higher
  --four-year trend increases of 8 to 10 percent in
    construction (12 million more), bank deposits
    ($150 million more), and postal receipts ($200,000
    more).
```

Both conclusions and recommendations need to be as pointed and positive as the facts and the writer's judgment will allow. (Usually itemization will help you to make them so and help the reader to see them as such.) If you toss the problem back to the reader with indefinite conclusions or alternative suggestions, you leave the feeling that the salary or fee paid you for doing the report has been wasted.

Still, the reader retains the right of final decision; so even when asked for your recommendations, present them as definite suggestions but certainly not as commands. The example just cited—phrased specifically in terms of the objective of the report, to select the city which will likely be the more profitable scene of operations—avoids indecision on the one hand and its equally undesirable opposite, imperative command.

STANDARD SUPPLEMENTS

Appendix

Although neither of the reports reproduced as illustrations in this and the next chapter needed an appendix, many reports do. The key to the decision is this: Use an appendix for material which the reader does not *need* to see to understand the text but which some readers may *want* to see to be sure your textual statements are clear and valid. Frequent uses are for survey questionnaires; for extensive formulas and statistical calculations; for extensive history, or detailed experimental methodology too long for the introduction; and for large maps, diagrams, or tables of figures that may be the basic data of the whole report but do not belong at any particular place in the text. Often the best way is to put a big table in the appendix and use appropriate figures from it as spot tables at key places in the text.

Bibliography

As we said before, on almost any big problem somebody has published something relevant. If that applies to your problem, finding and reading what others have written is almost certainly the quickest and easiest way to get at least some of the information you need. When you do that, you must tell what your sources are, not only to avoid the accusation of plagiarism but to show that you didn't just dream up the facts and to get the backing of the other writer for what you say—and perhaps to provide your reader with places to get fuller information.

Your footnotes and/or internal citations in the text give the specific references. But at the end you list—in alphabetical order of authors' surnames (or titles of unsigned sources)—books, magazines, and other printed sources. If you need to cite letters, lectures, speeches, interviews, or other oral communications, usually you cite them by references within the sentences or in footnotes. If you want to list them solely (or again) at the end, however, *do not* put them under the *misfitting head "Bibliography."* Instead, you may use something like "Sources Used" or "References."

For illustration, we present the following bibliography from a 20-page report on a problem in intercultural business communication. After arranging the items alphabetically, this author also provided item numbers for concise, specific citations in the text (as explained at the end of Chapter 14). The spacing is the preferred form of single within items (except when preparing copy for a printer) and double between them.

PUBLICATIONS CONSULTED

1. Condon, John C., and Faithi S. Yousef, <u>An
    Introduction to Intercultural Communication</u>,

Bobbs–Merrill Educational Publishing,
Indianapolis, 1975.

2. Graham, John L., "A Hidden Cause of America's
   Trade Deficit with Japan," <u>The Columbia Journal of
   World Business</u>, 16:5–13, Fall, 1981.

3. Mason, R. Hal, Robert R. Miller, and Dale R.
   Weigel, <u>International Business</u>, Second Edition,
   John Wiley & Sons, New York, 1981.

4. Morris, Desmond, <u>Manwatching: A Field Guide to
   Human Behavior</u>, Jonathan Cope, London, 1978.

5. Terpstra, Vern, <u>The Cultural Environment of
   International Business</u>, South–Western Publishing
   Co., Cincinnati, 1978.

ILLUSTRATION OF SHORT ANALYTICAL REPORTS

As you have seen, some of the short reports in forms already discussed (Chapter 13) have been informational while others have been analytical—that is with interpretations of the data into conclusions and (if appropriate) recommendations. Yet the name "short analytical report" often has a special meaning in report-writing circles—a meaning indicating a certain form rather than any very definite limits of length. In that sense—the sense used in this chapter—a short analytical report is somewhat different from a complete analytical report because the writer has (1) omitted certain parts, (2) combined parts where possible, or (3) written less in the remaining parts simply because their topics required no more. Even so, it is still likely to be longer (maybe up to 10 pages) than what we generally mean by short report (usually five pages or less).

Since the principles and parts of a short analytical report all have parallels in the complete analytical reports discussed in the preceding two chapters and illustrated in Chapter 16, we see no need to explain them again and illustrate them extensively here. *For your study of short analytical reports, therefore, we ask you to keep in mind the following points as you reconsider the preceding two chapters* and read the illustration.

1. The short analytical report usually omits all the preliminaries except the title page, letter of transmittal, and (possibly) the synopsis.
2. It often also combines the letter of transmittal and synopsis, omits the table of contents and depends on headings throughout the report, omits the bibliography and provides the full references as footnotes or interwoven citations, and interweaves the essential parts of possible appendix material right into the text.

3. It may (but rarely does) also put the title-page information at the top of the first page and move right into the next part on that page; combine the essentials of authorization, transmittal, and synopsis as a summary right after the title-page information; and omit the introduction as a separate part and interweave its essentials into the text. It could thus have only three sections—the title-page information, the summary, and the text. This is about as far as it can go. Any report would have these elements, although they might be arranged differently and presented in different forms.

The following report (slightly revised for our purposes) is a good short analytical report—though you may see improvements we could make—but notice particularly:

1. The exactness of the title, including the general answer (appropriate in the final title but not in a tentative one, where it would show preconceptions). The appropriate tentative title should change only the first word—to "Would."
2. The telescoping (omitting certain standard parts of longer reports like those discussed early in this chapter and combining others). In this case you see the letter and synopsis combined and omission of the table of contents but provision of its information in a well-displayed system of heads and subheads.
3. The use of tables and charts where they help to highlight important quantities (the original contained others, omitted here because we do not think they were worth their space and costs in this book).
4. The smooth continuity and coherence of the whole report, helped by numerous beginning topic sentences and paragraphs and ending summary-transition sentences and paragraphs.

Now for the feel of report continuity, read straight through the following report. It illustrates adequate handling of the standard parts of a short analytical report. Notice particularly its careful organization, phrasing of informative headings, and use of topic and summary statements needed at the beginnings and endings of sections.

Then, as further help before you prepare such a report, we suggest that you test this one against the checklist that follows it, as you will certainly want to check your own before final typing.

Although the checklist is primarily for complete analytical reports, many of the items apply to shorter ones. Those which may not apply to short analytical reports have an asterisk at the end. For greatest usefulness the sections appear in the order of presentation in the final report. Remember, however, that this is only a checklist. If you need fuller explanation of a point, find it in the appropriate chapter or in Appendix F. (The index may help.)

HOW A CORRESPONDENCE-IMPROVEMENT PROGRAM

WOULD SAVE MONEY AND BUILD GOODWILL

FOR BURNS, INC.

Prepared for

Mr. C. D. James, President

By Patricia Jean Barksdale

Assistant, Research Department

January 28, 1983

Letterhead

January 28, 1983   RESEARCH DEPARTMENT

Mr. C. D. James, President
Burns, Inc.
2619 Powell Street
San Francisco, California 81001

Dear Mr. James:

Here is the report you requested on October 20 evaluating the possibilities for improvement and, if needed, the best methods Burns could
employ to improve its correspondence.

The report shows that Burns could both save money and improve goodwill
by instituting a correspondence-improvement program.

To achieve the quality we want in our correspondence, Burns should
employ an instructor to conduct classes, issue a correspondence manual,
and hire a permanent supervisor to maintain quality correspondence.

In the month given me to prepare this report, I have learned some
interesting and useful facts which I believe will help you in establishing a correspondence-improvement program. Please call on me if I
can help further.

Sincerely yours,

Patricia Jean Barksdale

(Ms.) Patricia Jean Barksdale
Assistant

HOW A CORRESPONDENCE-IMPROVEMENT PROGRAM

WOULD SAVE MONEY AND BUILD GOODWILL

FOR BURNS, INC.

Purposes, Methods, and Plan

Purposes

This report has two purposes:

1. to determine whether Burns needs to improve its correspondence and
(if so)

2. to propose and explain the needed actions.

Methods

Information to serve the first purpose comes from analyzing 1,000
outgoing letters and making a careful estimate of Burns correspondence
costs and quality. To stratify the sample, the office manager provided
copies of letters from each department and from each dictator in proportion
to their usual letter-output percentages.

Three methods provided the information for making the recommendations:
a) a reading of the current literature on correspondence-improvement
programs; b) a questionnaire survey of companies experienced with such
programs; and c) interviews with two experienced correspondence consultants.

Basic plan

For clear explanation in logical sequence, the report considers: a) the
costs of Burns letters; b) the quality of Burns correspondence; c) the
effectiveness of correspondence-improvement plans; and d) the usual procedures and costs of the most effective plans. Analyses of the facts about
these topics provide solid bases for the conclusions and recommendations.

1

2

<u>The High Costs of Correspondence</u>

The average cost of business letters today is $7.11 (according to the
latest report of the Dartnell Corporation, which annually studies and
reports such figures). On the basis of this figure, Burns spends a
million and a half dollars yearly on correspondence:

Average number of letters annually 212,500

Average letter cost $7.11

Yearly correspondence expense $1,510,875

The high total expenditures for correspondence seem to offer a vast area
for possible savings, and analysis of outgoing Burns letters points to one
quick and easy start.

Among the 1,000 letters studied, 8% were essentially duplicates of the
same message going to three or more persons. In many cases apparently a
good form could do the job and save most of the waste. But let us figure
on a surer, though more costly, way. Only a little training should teach
Burns dictators to use the efficient secretaries and office equipment to
save an estimated $103,000 annually.

Saving of 8% of annual costs ($1,510,875) $120,870.00

Less (estimated) attributable training costs 10,000.00

Less (estimated) duplicating, stationery, and

   stamping costs (at $0.447) on 17,000

   letters (8% of 212,500) 7,600.00

                                                           $103,270.00

In addition to the ready dollar saving of over $100,000 a year on
correspondence, however, Burns also needs to consider the intangible yet
highly significant goodwill and other effects of its correspondence.

<u>Unfavorable Correspondence Conditions in Burns</u>

The impression a company's letters make on the public can either win or lose business. As the respected business columnist Sylvia Porter recently said, "To get your money's worth, you must be sure every letter helps to improve public relations as well as do its special job."

Burns letters are not the good Company representative they should be. Their tone, language, and formats all show shortcomings that provide areas for improvement.

<u>Offensive expressions, other undesirable tone, and waste costly</u>

Approximately two out of five letters leaving Burns offices are probably doing as much harm as good. Yet Burns need not feel that it is exceptional in this way. Professor C. R. Sanderson reports that 40% of 1,000 photo-copies he read in a firm where he was consulting represent letters that never should have gone out (1:13-18; meaning pp. 13-18 of Item 1 of the Bibliography). Still, the fact that other firms send out bad letters does not mean that Burns should.

<u>Letters containing offensive expressions</u>.--Of the letters that Burns sends to readers, 18% contain offensive expressions (Chart 1).

CHART 1

Percentage of Letters Containing Offensive Expressions or Unanswered Questions	
2.5%	Brusque; only one sentence
16.5%	Leave questions unanswered
18%	Show undesirable tone

So Burns is spending nearly $272,000 a year to drive business away (0.18 x 212,500 x $7.11). Accusing the reader ("You failed . . ." or "neglected . . ."), implying distrust or stupidity ("You say . . .,"

4

"If so, . . .," "Obviously . . ."), and the like certainly destroy rather than build goodwill.

A short, snappish answer often seems peevish and distasteful to readers, whether intended to be or not. Every one of the 2.5% of the sample letters that were just one sentence gave that impression of brusqueness--another form of offensive expression.

No company can afford such loss of goodwill and waste of money. Burns dictators definitely need instruction in letter courtesy.

Unnecessary duplication.--About one in six (16.5%) of Burns letters leave questions unanswered. Not only does having to write again annoy customers--unless they decide to drop the subject and go elsewhere with their business--but Burns dictators waste time in preparing letters to answer questions they should have answered in the first letter.

If they have to write again for each letter leaving unanswered questions, a waste of another $249,000 a year results (212,500 x 0.165 x 7.11). This problem apparently occurs because a dictator reads the incoming mail carelessly and dictates before planning to answer what the inquirer asked.

Language in Burns letters ineffective and hurtful

Many of the Company's letters are not creating the best public image because of wordiness, trite expressions, spelling errors, and poor sentence and paragraph structure.

CHART 2

7.0%	Poor paragraphing/structure
12.5%	Poor sentence structure
20%	Spelling error(s)
24.5%	Wordiness
27.0%	Trite expressions

Though wordiness (in 24.5% of the letters) and the use of trite expressions (27%) are not the worst of English weaknesses, the fact that more than one out of four of Burns letters uses them means Burns letters often sound pompous and dull reader interest. Wordiness stems from deadwood phrasing, rather than good idea presentation, and indicates lack of careful thought or inability of the dictator. Wordiness and triteness, along with misspellings (in a fifth of the letters), reflect ignorance or lack of thought or care, none of which is good for public relations.

Worse, however, are the more serious instances of poor sentence and paragraph structure in 12.5% and 7% (respectively) of the letters. Paragraphs of 15 lines or more (in 7% of the letters) and sentences averaging 32 or more words (in 5%) do not exist in good letters. The current literature suggests an average of 16-20 words per sentence and less than eight lines per paragraph for good readability. Long paragraphs are uninviting and hard to read. Often these faults (particularly when reinforced by wordiness, triteness, and distracting misspellings) lead to difficult reading, failure to understand, or misunderstanding--if the letters get read at all.

The price is too high to waste on such ineffectiveness as an addition to the loss of respect and goodwill. Clearly Burns dictators need motivation and/or training to do better; and since the secretaries at least originate the misspellings (and perhaps some complimentary closings, though the dictators are finally responsible for both), apparently the secretaries need help too. Even the first impressions a reader gets of a letter from its greetings, format, and adieu deserve attention.

6

<u>First impressions from letter formalities and formats unfavorable</u>

Since Burns letters are often the only direct communication contact readers have with the organization, even the first impressions our letters make are important. The appearance and tone of the stationery, layout, and standard courtesy phrases create a picture of the firm. Faulty letters (such as many going out from Burns) reflect unfavorably on the Company, its dictators, and its secretaries. Since Burns stationery (paper and printed letterhead) would score well on any reasonable standard, the matters of concern are the phrasing of titles, salutations, and complimentary closings and the typing.

CHART 3	
7.5%	Nonstandard mechanical makeup
31.0%	Participial closings

<u>Participial closings</u>.--The survey of Burns correspondence reveals that the largest percentages of improper phrasings are participial and other outmoded closings. Thirty-one percent of the letters end with outmoded expressions such as "Looking to your reply . . ." and "Until such time, I remain, etc." About one out of three letters dictated indicates to a customer a lack of up-to-dateness at Burns, Inc.

<u>Nonstandard mechanical makeup</u>.--Almost one in 12 (7.5%) of the letters contain variations in mechanical makeup. These variations often result from inconsistency on the part of various typists when the dictator does not specify the form of letter. Such variations are not necessarily errors, but some of the outmoded or ultramodern forms used do characterize the writer and the company. Since the modern trend is toward simplicity, Burns could save much time and money by adopting a simple form that would suggest that Burns is neither out of date nor frivolously ultramodern.

Though the dictator is finally responsible, most secretaries have a considerable (and often a free) hand in determining the appearance and the courtesy formalities of letters they type. Since more than one out of three Burns letters goes out with some degrading blemish in these areas, apparently both the dictators and secretaries at Burns need some training or study on letter appearance. A study of the topic in the leading textbook on business communication (Wilkinson, Clarke, and Wilkinson, <u>Communicating Through Letters and Reports</u>) would probably be sufficient. To show a united front and to ease the job of a secretary who types for several dictators, Burns might well adopt one form.

XXX

Wasteful duplication, poor tone and language, and blemishes on the physical appearance show the unsatisfactory quality of Burns correspondence. The unfavorable conditions are costing unnecessary thousands of dollars yearly and are also causing a loss of goodwill and business. Only 24%, less than one in four, of the letters Burns now sends out are of top quality--clear, correct, complete, and considerate of the reader's feelings.

Correspondence improvement offers Burns a vast area for savings in both money and goodwill.

8

The Success of Correspondence-Improvement Programs

Results at companies using letter-improvement programs include improvements in letter quality, in attitudes of correspondents, and in customer relations.

The following excerpt from Printers' Week (3:377) comments on the improvement received from correspondence instruction: "Bring in an instructor who has had experience in writing letters as well as in teaching. Conduct regular classes for several weeks. Require each member of the firm connected with letter writing--from the president to the typist--to attend. Then watch your letters improve!"

The same source lists the names of 57 companies which have carried out letter-improvement programs. The 55 replies to questionnaires sent to these companies indicate favorable results from their programs.

Improvement in letter quality considerable

The first and most important question asked was "What do you believe was the effect of your program on the quality of the company's letters?" Almost three-fourths (39 of the 55) say they have received considerable satisfaction with significant improvement in quality. Twenty-seven percent see no noticeable difference, and 2% note slight improvement.

Attitude of correspondents favorable

More than three-fourths of the firms (42 of the 55) report correspondents' favorable attitudes toward their programs. Only 4% report unfavorable reactions.

One typical comment is: "On the whole, both correspondents and typists appreciate the constructive criticism of the instructor. Nearly all are enthusiastic when they realize how important their letters are in building goodwill for the company."

9

Both correspondents' approval and improvement in letter quality
indicate that the programs improve the companies' public relations.

Customer relations improved

To the inquiry "What do you believe was the effect of the program
on your company's customer relations?" more than two-thirds (69%) report
considerable improvement, whereas 20% consider the improvement slight
and 11% notice no apparent change.

A favorable comment states that "Since completion of our training
program, we have received fewer complaints than ever before; and many
customers have written letters of appreciation."

Improvement in letter quality, correspondents' favorable attitudes,
and better customer relations show that other companies' correspondence-
improvement programs are successful. The type of program which works
best, however, is more difficult to determine.

Three-Point Attacks Used in Successful Programs

Most companies which have successful correspondence-improvement programs use a correspondence manual, a permanent supervisor, and (to start)
a special instructor.

Correspondence manuals effective

A correspondence manual for reference is an important part of a letter
improvement program. The usual manual contains both instructions and
examples of approved styles for company letters to serve as a guide for
dictators and transcribers.

Of the 55 companies questioned, only a little more than half (51%)
said yes when asked "Do you have a correspondence manual?" Those
companies which use a manual, however, readily realize its importance

10

and benefits. Of those that report using one, 86% answered yes to "Do you believe it has helped to improve letter writing?"

Evidently the others (49%) do not realize the benefits that users receive from manuals--which serve both as guides to new employees and as reminders and handy references to established employees. In most cases a manual seems to be most beneficial to follow up and answer questions that arise after completion of the course of instruction.

In discussing the benefits of the correspondence manual, one respondent commented, typically, that "The correspondence manual issued at the close of our training period served to crystallize the information presented by the instructor. It is always available for quick reference."

A correspondence manual justifies itself in a letter-improvement program, however, only if its benefits outweigh its cost.

Cost of a manual about $1,000

In replies to the question concerning the cost of correspondence manuals, $750 to $1,000 is the most frequent answer (43%). One-fourth of the firms (25%) paid $900 and over for their manuals, 2% less than $600, 1% $600 to $750.

The advantages of the savings in time and money which result from the use of a correspondence manual seem to justify the cost in the thinking of most firms. Evidently, then, a good correspondence-improvement program will provide a manual.

The most successful programs, however, do not depend on a manual alone but also provide a correspondence supervisor.

Correspondence supervisors maintain effectiveness

The correspondence supervisor serves as an adviser to the employees concerning problems and as an inspector to make sure the letters maintain standards of quality. Without the supervisor, dictators and transcribers lapse into their old habits, according to companies which have tried to operate without a supervisor.

The survey reveals that 58% of the companies make use of a correspondence supervisor or someone else who assumes the duties under another title. But 42% do not have a correspondence supervisor.

A greater percentage (58%) of firms make use of a supervisor than make use of a manual (51%). And unanimously all 32 companies which have a supervisor agree that a competent one is effective in maintaining letter quality.

The following comment from one firm further illustrates the need for a correspondence supervisor:

> The letter-improvement classes we held five years ago made correspondents conscious of their responsibilities for several months. But since we had no supervisor to encourage consistent effort to make letters effective, correspondents became lax again. Our new program provides for a supervisor who will spot-check outgoing mail and hold regular classes for discussion of letter problems.

Evidently a supervisor helps to keep the letter quality up to par. The most effective letter-improvement program should make use of both a supervisor and a manual.

Still an additional element appears in the most successful programs.

All sources recommend instruction to start

All articles read, many comments interviewees and respondents made on the questionnaire, and the advice of a professional letter-writing

12

consultant point to the wisdom of an instructional program as a necessary start to a letter-improvement program.

Dr. J. H. Mensing of Del Monte, the interviewed professional consultant, says that in his varied experience few companies have been successful
in greatly improving their correspondence without a definite program of
instruction to start. Much of the job, he says, is getting employees to
recognize the importance of good letters to their companies and themselves.
Although inspiration and exhortation alone will not do much good, some
motivating along with good instruction on how to improve usually does
produce good results.

Dr. Mensing's statements are in line with specific comments heard or
read elsewhere, and he offers a program based on 25 years of successful
experience.

Dictators and transcribers would attend 10-week courses in separate
groups. Five groups with 17 dictators each and two groups with 20
secretaries each would include all of the 85 Burns dictators and 40
transcribers while keeping the classes down to effective working groups.
Dr. Mensing proposes to analyze letters dictated by each correspondent
and to give individual suggestions on the paper (or in person when necessary).
Under his professional direction, employees are practically assured of
learning the much-needed fundamentals of good letter writing. His fee for
each class is $1,500 or $9,000 for the whole instructional program.

By employing Dr. Mensing to conduct the proposed classes, Burns would
be taking a step that everyone with successful experience in attempts at
correspondence improvement seems to agree is essential.

The Program Recommended

The high cost of correspondence and the deficiencies in the quality of letters at Burns, Inc., definitely indicate that the Company should institute an improvement program as soon as possible.

Published articles, the experiences of firms that have worked at improving their correspondence, and the advice of a professional consultant all suggest that the best plan is a three-pronged attack:

1. Employ a professional teacher to motivate and instruct employees as the first step.

2. Provide a correspondence manual for ready reference.

3. Appoint a permanent correspondence supervisor to keep up the motivation, help with special problems, and spot-check outgoing mail to catch and correct any developing laxness.

To solve the letter problem at Burns, Inc., I therefore recommend that the Company take these three steps in order as soon as practicable. Specifically, I recommend Dr. J. H. Mensing of Del Monte as the professional consultant and teacher to start the program.

With the recommended program in operation, at a cost of little more than $10,000 ($9,000 + $1,000 + overhead), both Professor Sanderson's and my estimates suggest that Burns should expect to save at least ten times that much a year by writing fewer but better letters and by avoiding duplication. The biggest improvement, however, would be the better company image Burns correspondence would put in the minds of its readers.

14

Bibliography

1. Sanderson, C. R., "Correspondence Inefficiencies, "Journal
    of Business Communication, October, 1981, 18: 13-18.

2. Howard, Henry, "Cutting Correspondence Expense," U.S. Business,
    May, 1981, 33: 11-13.

3. "Letter Training Program Pays Off," Printer's Week, January,
    1983, 171: 377.

CHECKLIST FOR MAJOR ANALYTICAL REPORTS

(An asterisk means not necessary in short reports.)

PRELIMINARY PARTS AND MECHANICS (PPM)

1. If you use a *cover*, be sure it carries at least the title and author's name (or is transparent, or has a cutout so that these items on the title page are visible). Make sure it has the appearance you want and is the right size for your report.*

2. The *title page* needs at least four items: *(a)* the title (phrased for precision, interest, and conciseness), *(b)* the authorizer's name and title, *(c)* the author's name and title, and *(d)* the place and date (in that order and in centered or in some other pleasant design. It may also have the organization's name, a brief abstract, a distribution list, and/or a project- or serial-number identification, and/or a secrecy classification.

3. A *transmittal letter or memo*, in regular letter/memo form:
   a. Starts by transmitting the report and, naturally and subordinately, referring to the topic and authorization.
   b. May reveal briefly only the general decision or may synopsize the report (unless a separate synopsis comes later).
   c. Ends expressing appreciation (and perhaps willingness to help further.)

4. The *table of contents* (or simply contents) lists the later successive parts and body sections of the report, with beginning page numbers for all and (optional, but helpful) outline symbols before the body sections.*
   a. A separate synopsis (if used), as the next page following the contents table, is the first item listed (with no outline symbol, flush at the left margin, and with the first of your vertically aligned, spaced-period leader lines between items and the page number column).*
   b. The greatest part of the table of contents shows the organization/ outline of the body.
      (1) Whether you give outline symbols (preferable and helpful—in either decimal or roman form) and all levels of heads and subheads (or just the first two or three) is your option (or assignment, or the organization's SOP—standard operating procedure).
      (2) In any case the wording (not the type form) of heads here and in the report must be identical.
      (3) Break too-long lines to leave at least seven spaces between them and the page-number column, indent the carry-over(s) and subdivisions, and make leaders of at least three spaced periods, with a space before and after.
      (4) Double-space between at least the parts and major divisions, and systematically single-space elsewhere only to keep to one page.
      (5) Remember that page numbers and roman outline-symbol numbers line up on the right.

    c.   Supplementary parts (i.e., optional appendix and bibliography) do *not* have outline symbols but do continue the arabic page numbering of the text.

5. A separate *synopsis* (SY) or *informative abstract*—the report in a nutshell, reduced between 10:1 and 20:1, but preferably to *one* page—is usually single-spaced with double spacing between paragraphs.*

    a.   Make the first paragraph stress the problem solution (or its main part) and subordinately reveal enough about the authorizer, purpose, and preparer for extra copies of the synopsis alone to be clear.

    b.   Compactly and specifically present (in a paragraph for each major division, in order and preferably in proportion) your main supporting facts and figures, while subordinately interweaving any necessary background, method, and scope.

    c.   Emphasize findings, not analysis—preferably in present tense. Rely on sequence and only short transitional words for coherence.

6. Give early, careful attention to the special *report mechanics* (RM) (layout and typing and, if needed, the generally applicable points of mechanics (GM)—see TM in Appendix F):

    a.   Double-space the body and make its bottom and side margins 1–1½", top slightly less, plus extra space for the bite of any binding used.

    b.   Start a new page only to (1) start a new part (the body is all one), (2) leave a bottom margin, or (3) allow for at least two lines of copy below a heading.

    c.   Starting with the title fly, if used, count preliminary pages down through the synopsis and (beginning with the table of contents) number them in lowercase romans.

    d.   Give all later pages arabic numbers, *without decorations*, two or more spaces above the right ends of lines (except centered at the bottom on first pages of report parts).

    e.   Vary placement, spacing above and below, and type form of headings to show different levels. Underline any not in solid capitals and double-space centered heads of more than one line.

ORGANIZATION/OUTLINING (O)

1. Phrase your title to indicate the nature, purpose, and limits of your study and to provide a basis of classification; then make the text's major divisional headings on that basis.

2. The basis may point to comparison, partition of a whole, factors to be considered, or (rarely) time periods or spatial areas, but not likely to cost-benefit or before-after analyses or source or method of getting the information. In making comparisons leading to a choice, use the criteria as the main divisions, the subjects as subheads, and anything about methods as interwoven material.

3. Use no heading for your whole text and no single subhead anywhere. The

major divisions of your report (symbolized by 1.0, 2.0, 3.0 . . . or I, II, III . . .) are first the introduction, then the logical divisions of your topic (the text, in two or more parts), and your conclusions and recommendations (together or separate).

4. Phrase each heading to cover any and all of its subdivisions.

5. In phrasing, placing, and sequencing all division headings at all levels, make clear the relationship of each part to its whole and its function in your interpretation. Outline symbols may help.

6. Maintain parallelism of grammatical form among headings of the same class, using synonyms where necessary to avoid monotony of wording.

7. Try to make your headings informative (preferably "talking"—not just topical) as well as precisely indicative of what they include.

8. Use just enough headings to help show your organization.

9. Use placement and type variations in headings (and maybe outline symbols) to show their status in the outline and relations to others.

INTRODUCTION (I)

Clear presentation of the *purpose, method, scope,* and *basic plan* is the main duty of the introduction, to provide a basis for judging the report's soundness.

1. Put the exact report title at the top of the first page of the body.

2. Then, for this first major division, try to phrase a more meaningful title than the stock term "Introduction."

3. Though you may need several paragraphs to explain your *purpose* clearly enough, *(a)* be sure your purpose is compatible with your title and organizational plan and *(b)* provide one particular sentence that is a pointed, concise statement of your problem.

4. Give a short history of the problem only if needed as a lead-in to purpose (details, if helpful, can go in a later flashback—or maybe appendix).

5. Explain your *methods* of gathering data specifically enough to show thoroughness and be convincing; but significant details beyond a reader's ability to remember (like questions in a long questionnaire or settings and measurements in a laboratory experiment) can best come later with the data.

6. As part of *scope,* clearly show any limits of coverage not made in the title; but justified (not excuse-making) limits of time or money are more appropriate in the letter of transmittal.

7. You might include a glossary for a large number of necessary unusual terms; for only a few, preferably explain each parenthetically just after the first time it comes up.

8. Try to cover the required elements of the introduction without breaking

CHECKLIST FOR MAJOR ANALYTICAL
REPORTS (continued)

it into too many pieces (more than *purpose, method, scope,* and *plan*), especially if the parts are short.

9. In a "Basic Plan" section at the end of the introduction, brief the reader on the sequence of major topics coming.

10. Keep findings, conclusions, and recommendations out of the introduction. If you want to get them to the reader early, a synopsis or even the letter of transmittal is a better place.

STYLE (S)

1. Remember that a natural style is clearer, easier, and more interesting than impersonal style for both writer and reader.

2. Enliven your style and increase readability by *(a)* using commonly understood words and short, direct sentences and paragraphs, *(b)* making people (not things) subjects and/or objects of many if not most sentences, *(c)* using mostly active voice, *(d)* eliminating "It is" and "There are" sentence beginnings, *(e)* using discrete (but not overlisted) itemizations for pointed, concise statements like conclusions and recommendations, *(f)* putting the emphasis where it belongs (see Emp and Sub in Appendix F), and *(g)* presenting quantities in easily read and remembered forms (ratios, fractions, rounded numbers, simplified percentages, rankings). Remember that the relative status of something (percent, ratio, or rank) is often more significant than the absolute value.

3. To avoid seeming prejudiced, state plausible assumptions made, give immediate and specific evidence to support points, give all the same kind(s) of information about each compared subject, and avoid emotionally persuasive passages and disclaimers like "objective," "unbiased," "impersonal."

4. Use the universal present tense to indicate continuing existence for things and tendencies that existed in the past, exist now, and are likely to continue.

5. Don't use headings as antecedents of pronouns; your text should read coherently *without* the heads.

6. Make clear, by topic statement at the beginning of each big section, the topic and any subdivisions (in the order of later treatment).

7. At the end of a sizable section, sum it up with emphasis on its significance to the overall problem (and preferably with a transitional forward look to the next topic).

8. Interpret key points from graphics in relation to your objective, *emphasizing the message* and (by parenthetical, midsentence, or nonsubject mention) *subordinating the reference to the graphic and its location.*

9. By evidence, explanation, and logic lead the reader to foresee likely conclusions and recommendations coming; but (ordinarily) leave explicit statements of them until the end.

GRAPHICS (GR)

1. Use graphics whenever helpful; but omit useless ones.
2. Choose the best kind, form, and arrangement of graphic for the kind of data.
3. For reader convenience, place graphics near the discussion (small ones maybe on graph paper on the same page, larger ones on the next page).
4. Give graphics proper titles, numbers (charts and tables in separate consecutive series), labeled parts, and credit sources of published ones.
5. Give reliable dates of graphic information (not always the date of publication), maybe in parentheses after the title.
6. Lead in with discussion of the point and proper introduction of the graphic (emphasizing what to see in it), tell *subordinately* where it is if not in sight, and (usually) follow with necessary key points of emphasis or interpretation.
7. For easy reading and close relationships, consider small spot tables closely associated with different points, though they may all come from one collective source table (appendix material) that buries key points.

DOCUMENTATION (DOC)

When you use others' material (except as explained in Item 1 below), you must give credit (to avoid plagiarism) and you want to cite the source as support for your point. The usual means for published material are a bibliography and specific citations in the text, source indications on graphics, and possibly footnotes.

1. Put in your bibliography an alphabetical listing of publications from which you used an author's special ideas, facts (including graphics), or quotations. The word *special* means that the requirement does not apply to information that is *(a)* common knowledge, *(b)* obvious, or *(c)* widely available in many sources of the kind.
2. Make specific citations (at the points you used others' materials) in the simplest way. See the end of Chapter 14 for explanations, the illustrative reports for illustrations, and GR 4 above for citing sources of graphics. Remember that to promote continuity and ease of reading, interweaving citations into the text is preferable to footnotes.
3. Avoid repeating a citation (except for different page numbers) as long as you're drawing from the same source.
4. For convenience, number footnotes (if used) anew on each page.
5. Cite the basic circumstances in the text or a footnote where you use information from interviews, speeches, and letters (which do not belong in the bibliography); explain questionnaires, observations, and experiments as sources in the methods section of the Introduction (plus necessary spe-

CHECKLIST FOR MAJOR ANALYTICAL REPORTS (concluded)

cific questions, conditions, or procedures, along with the findings in the text—I-5 above).

6. Use no source citations for the synopsis, conclusions, or recommendations; they all derive from the text, where needed source citations must appear.

7. Though you have some choice of the documentation forms you use, unless restricted by assignment in school or on the job, be sure to use an established, clear, and consistent one and *get it exactly right*—in content, capitalization, sequence, and punctuation.

CONCLUSIONS AND RECOMMENDATIONS (C/R)

1. Introduce no new facts in the terminal section; it derives from, maybe quickly recaps, and interprets information presented before.

2. Put conclusions and recommendations (together or separately) in their order of logic or importance.

3. State conclusions and recommendations pointedly (specifically and concisely, with key supporting facts and figures), as firmly as your information justifies (rarely involving "prove"), and (preferably) itemized.

4. Take a stand (including "My findings prove nothing," if necessary); being wishy-washy suggests inadequacy or incompetence.

5. Make sure your conclusions and recommendations derive from facts and explanations already presented; leave surprise endings to mystery writers.

6. You may conclude and suggest action but not command.

QUESTIONS AND EXERCISES

1. Besides being longer, what are the main differences between short analytical reports and the short reports discussed and illustrated in Chapter 13?

2. Besides being shorter, what are the main differences you may make between a short analytical report you're writing and a complete analytical report?

3. Try your mind and hand at presenting graphically your answers to Question 2.

4. Give a skeletal table of contents of a short analytical report for each psychological plan of message (A–plan, B–plan, C–plan—as explained in Chapter 4).

5. What was your answer about the conciseness of the final(?) report title worked out (in the section on "Title page")? Explain.

CASES

(See p. xiii for some important explanations.)

15–1. As assistant to Professor Robert W. Boozer (University of South Alabama, Mobile) prepare a short analytical report for his presentation to the American Business Communication Association (members mostly university teachers). The two of you have acquired the following data from a survey of personnel recruiters in firms with more than 100 employees—selected by using state directories, assigning firms identification numbers, and applying a table of random numbers for the final selection. From the 280 selected, you received 81 (29 percent) completed responses to your cover letter and questionnaire.

Questions were really statements to which answers 1–7 indicated descending strength of agreement from 1 "strongly agree" to 7 "strongly disagree," an answer of 4 meaning "undecided," answers 2 and 6 meaning "moderately agree" and "moderately disagree," and answers 3 and 5 meaning "slightly agree" and "slightly disagree."

To save space, here are our incomplete-sentence restatements of the questionnaire topics with *percentages* of the responses (in 1–7 order and *rounded*, hence not always equaling 100):

1. I (meaning the recruiter responding) study the appropriate job description and specifications before evaluating application materials—55, 21, 12, 2, 5, 2, 1.
2. I also talk to applicants' prospective co-workers—38, 15, 12, 3, 10, 9, 9.
3. The application letter helps me understand the personality—8, 27, 30, 8, 12, 9, 5.
4. Letter tells me applicant's confidence in abilities—13, 27, 30, 9, 13, 5, 2.
5. Letter indicates degree of on-the-job communication skills—24, 44, 26, 1, 2, 3, 1.
6. Letter should stress accomplishments—28, 29, 21, 2, 13, 3, 1.
7. Somewhere application package should refer to career goals—43, 26, 16, 6, 5, 2, 0.
8. Most application letters and résumés are too vague—13, 27, 33, 3, 14, 8, 1.

Besides your own survey, you have results on some other points worth mentioning from an earlier study (1979) by Barron Wells, Nelda Spinks, and Janice Hargrave of the University of Southwestern Louisiana. They surveyed the *Fortune* 500, received 175 replies (35 percent), and tabulated data in five degrees (not using your groups 3 and 5).

1. I want both an application letter and résumé—26, 35, —, 7, —, 18, 11.
2. I welcome applications even when I have no suitable openings—36, 53, —, 3, —, 3, 3.
3. The tone of the letter is important—34, 56, —, 4, —, 4, 1.
4. The letter should show how education and experience fit the job—32, 40, —, 10, —, 10, 10.

5. Any scholarships, awards, and honors should be in the résumé—39, 51, —, 6, —, 3, 1.

An older (but unpublished) study by J. H. Menning (1972) still throws the best light we have (even if possibly outdated) on a few other points:

1. Recruiters' preferences for the application package are letter, résumé, and placement-office credentials, 123; letter and placement-office credentials, 106; letter and résumé, 86; letter alone, 9.
2. Most important: letter, 55; résumé, 37; both 232.
3. *a.* Reaction to follow-up letter after a month: favorable, 252; annoying, 10; neutral, 62.
    b. Reason (if favorable): 73 shows persistence, 178 indicates interest, 220 shows still available.
4. For inexperienced applicants, which background is preferable (rank 1, 2, 3, 4):
    a. Many activities, passing grades—37, 74, 114, 99.
    b. Several activities, above-average grades—102, 124, 79, 19.
    c. Worked for school expenses, above-average grades—164, 106, 36, 18.
    d. No activities, honor grades—93, 93, 106, 82.

15–2.   You and a friend want to buy a boat for pleasure and water skiing. Neither of you has storage area for the boat, and you are both away from water; so you'll have to figure the cost of a boat carrier. Neither of you has a motor either; so the motor size and cost will have to be considered. You'll have to buy a license and safety equipment. Assume that you can use public boat docks on water just 30 minutes from your homes.

Since your friend is tied rather closely to an office job (and you're a sales representative making you own schedule), you've agreed to consider qualities and prices of at least three brands for each of the various items, make recommendations, and write your findings up in the form of a short analytical report as a basis for face-to-face discussion when you're through. Get going.

Variation: Since both you and your friend are to be married soon and both plan to have families, consider buying a boat large enough that each family could take turns enjoying the boat.

15–3.   Assume that you are president of the Student Government Association at your school and that you are asked by the school's vice president for student affairs to write a report on *(a)* suggestions for improving student-faculty relationships at your university, *(b)* suggestions for improving the parking situation at your university, *(c)* ways of getting more funding for the Student Government Association, *(d)* suggestions for improving the housing on the campus, or *(e)* suggestions for campus activities. (These are *subjects*—not titles—from which to make your choice—unless your teacher does—and write your report.)

15–4. Your employer, owner of The Snack Shop, asked you to observe the activities at three to five locations of successful hamburger restaurants in your town. For your employer check (*a*) size of parking lot and restaurant, (*b*) approximate number of people the restaurant holds, (*c*) number of tables, (*d*) hours restaurant is open, (*e*) prices and sizes of hamburgers.

The Snack Shop has been dealing only in sandwiches but is considering buying a grill and adding hamburgers and the owner wants to know if there is a need for more places to serve hamburgers. After you do the research, write your employer a short analytical report giving your recommendations.

Variation: Instead of The Snack Shop, it could be a restaurant looking at the competition for starting a special fish dinner on Friday night. The researcher must analyze other restaurants in town to see what other establishments have special fish dinners, the prices, the number of people eating, the choices of fish, sizes of restaurants and parking lots. You will not need to buy additional equipment or hire other people in order to serve buffet-style fish dinners.

15–5. You are asked to do a report for X city (a city of 60,000 people, one hospital, a family-practice center, and one ambulance service). The ambulance service is privately operated with 18 employees, a president (Everett Bobo), and a dispatcher who stays on duty from 8 A.M. until 5 P.M.—then an answering service handles the calls. Of the four ambulances, two have run more than 100,000 miles and a third has run 90,000 miles. The employees have to take holidays such as Christmas and Thanksgiving with no pay. They also have to collect their own accounts for the ambulance company. The company does not insure any employee. For the last five years six paramedics at two fire stations have helped the private ambulance service. The paramedics-in-training earn $3.35 an hour while the other employees earn $5 an hour. Because of the wages and conditions, the workers are threatening to strike. If they strike, the city will have to call on neighboring towns for workers and ambulances.

The city commission wants a report on whether it should take over the job of running an ambulance service for X city and, if so, how it should be managed.

With Jim Ford, X city's hospital administrator, you worked out a plan for two paramedics at two fire stations (instead of desirable three). The hospital rescue unit will accompany the fire department units on calls requiring a third or fourth paramedic (heart, respiratory, or major trauma calls).

To adopt the city plan will cost $150,000. The city will buy three new ambulances, but the hospital will provide routine maintenance. The city will bill all users of the three rescue units $70 per run plus $1.50 per mile and the cost of medicine.

The hospital's emergency medical services project director, Dick Lamont, says he supports this plan despite the reduced number of paramedics aboard the fire department vehicles. He also says that because local intermediate and paramedic students are required to ride on rescue units for part of their clinical training, the students riding the rescue units at the fire department "will—in many instances—provide that third person" on those units.

The hospital will not enter into coach service or routine nonemergency ambulance runs. Each surrounding county has its own ambulance service; so there's no problem of serving outside the city limits.

Last year 5,000 people used the ambulance service to X city hospital. You have no record of the distance covered or the collections of the private ambulance service.

15–6.   As research analyst you are to design a questionnaire to be sent to a selected group of business people (in banking, insurance, or accounting) to determine their views on the importance of written and oral business communication. You'll want to find out what kinds of messages they send and what kinds they receive. Find out what percent of their business is done orally (and how it is done—telephone, conference, one-to-one, meetings, workshops) and what percent is done through the written word (and how it is done—by hand, by machines and if by machines what kinds). What kinds of messages do they write (memos, letters, reports) on what subjects (sales, goodwill, directives) and what kind of forms do they use, if any? All information will be kept confidential.

Based on your research, write an analytical report to your instructor evaluating what your research shows and recommending what should be taught in courses in business communication in your locality.

15–7.   The biggest chain grocery in your locality is having quite a problem nationally with various forms of larceny—$8 million of losses last year through customer shoplifting, employee theft, and so on. The management therefore issued a memo directing the manager of each store to study the situation and institute needed changes. (If you need another memo situation, here's one.) The local manager, under whom you work, tossed the directive memo (and thus the ball) to you. You are to confer for any information already known, to study the layout and procedures by on-the-spot observation and questioning, and to propose the things to be done to reduce losses. The job may or may not include a memo or other set of directions to all store employees on just what to do when they know or suspect that larceny or pilferage is going on. This could be a separate memo assignment, requiring a good knowledge of the law and/or law enforcement procedures—perhaps a talk with some police officers.

15–8.   Assume that Kermit Kilgore, owner of a successful restaurant on a well-traveled boulevard in Main City, USA (134,000 population) asks you to do a report on whether the restaurant, The Blue Max, should expand its facility. The restaurant (20 sq. ft. per seat, 6,000 sq. ft.) has the capacity to seat 300. The lounge (15 sq. ft. per seat or 2,250 sq. ft.) seats 150. You have observed that on Thursday, Friday, and Saturday customers sometimes have to wait as much as 45 minutes to be served during the peak business hours from 6:30 to 9 P.M. People have been turned away from the lounge on Wednesday, Thursday, Friday, and Saturday nights. If The Blue Max could expand 2,000 square feet, then there would be capacity for 100 additional seats in the restaurant (20 sq. ft. per seat) or 133 seats in the lounge (15 sq. ft. per seat).

Land behind The Blue Max (150' × 240', 36,000 sq. ft.) is for sale at $75,000. The land required for the expansion of the building would be 50 by 40 feet (2,000 sq. ft.). About 25,000 square feet would be needed to provide 100 parking spaces and entry/exit lanes. A parking space that leaves enough clearance for the opening of car doors measures 18 by 9 feet, so 100 parking spaces would take 16,200 square feet. Adequate entry/exit lanes usually take about half as much area as the parking spaces in a lot. So the 36,000 square feet would be adequate for all uses, including some flower beds, shrubs, and small green lawn areas.

From a local contractor, Robert Blakeney, you learn that building cost will be approximately $50 per square foot, or $100,000 ($50 × 2,000 sq. ft.). In a talk with Ora Lee Hill, interior designer and decorator, you estimate that it will cost about $100,000 for furnishings and decorating the new area. Blakeney estimated that to pave the parking lot and do the landscaping and planting you'd have to figure on $10,000.

Present sales on Sunday have run $2,000 and nothing for the lounge. On successive weekdays the restaurant brought in $3,600 and the lounge $800; $4,500 and $1,200; $4,600 and $1,400; $4,900 and $1,900; $5,000 and $2,100; $5,000 and $1,900; making a week's total of $38,900.

Competition comes mainly from the dining rooms in seven motel/hotels and nine smaller but long-established restaurants. The 122 fast-food places, two truck stops, and three cafeterias draw largely from a different clientele. There's some competition from the food service at the four country clubs, whose clientele is also mostly different (in a different direction).

Despite this competition, Kilgore (from experience) and you (from observation of customers waiting during a typical week) estimate that The Blue Max could increase business in the restaurant at least 15 percent (or in the lounge by 10 percent) through the considered expansion. Other considerations (plus that speculation) help to determine whether to expand the restaurant or the lounge (if either): (1) kitchen facilities are already capable of handling the expansion, whereas behind-the-bar facilities are not; (2) despite twice as high profit margins in the lounge as in the restaurant, the increased restaurant receipts might produce more profit; and (3) since peak lounge business comes a little later in the evening than peak restaurant business, some excess lounge customers might be more likely to be seated in available space in the restaurant than the other way around.

15–9.   As assistant research director for *Tempo* magazine you have just completed a survey of reader interest based upon 2,000 personal interviews to determine how intensely women read *Tempo*.

Equal numbers of *Tempo*-reading men and women were questioned, and your data show the breakdown of readership by sex for each *Tempo* department.

Department	Number of women readers for each 100 men
Nation	80
World	78
Religion	102
Theatre	114
Art	128
Law	60
Books	120
Medicine	93
Sports	55
Music	117
Education	97
Science	73
People	103
Economy and business	59
Cinema	122
Essay	104
Letters	97
Living	109
Press	78

A total of 2,500,000 women and 2,800,000 men read *Tempo* each week according to your statistics. Since your facts are of interest to your advertisers and would-be advertisers, you write up your investigation, interpreting the facts for your advertisers, and offering suggestions on how they may benefit from them. Write the report (as basis for promotional cover letter) to send to your advertisers and write a letter to accompany it. (Wherever possible include forms of graphic representation.)

Analysis and illustration of complete analytical reports

A capsule/reminder analysis
The illustration
Questions and exercises
Cases

16

A CAPSULE/REMINDER ANALYSIS

Because Chapters 13, 14, and 15 have said just about everything you need to know about complete analytical reports (except for an illustration), that illustration is the main function here.

Lest you have forgotten some significant points, however, we give you these capsule reminders.

1.   In the prefatory pages before Chapter 13, we explained how

a.   Reports serve six important ways that make them essential in the management of our complex society by answering three kinds of managerial questions.

b.   Learning report writing will help you while you're a student and job candidate and when you're on the job.

2.   In Chapter 13 we gave you both a standard and an expanded definition of *report* plus eight characteristics, the classes or kinds of reports, and seven pointed techniques for writing them well. You will no doubt remember the rest of Chapter 13 even better—because (before leaving it) you should have studied and written several kinds of short reports discussed there as the most widely and frequently used kinds of written business communication except letters.

3.   Even a mastery of the short reports in Chapter 13, however, does not give you the knowledge to prepare major reports (the less frequent but individually more important short analytical reports and complete analytical reports). Since they are quite similar (except for length because of problem size and/or possible omission or combination of some parts for the short analytical), we treated the preparation of both in Chapter 14.

Preparing either is necessarily a five-step process of planning, collecting data, organizing, interpreting the data, and writing the reporting in good style and form—the five stars in the crown of Chapter 14, which rules over Chapters 15 and 16.

4.   Then in Chapter 15 we explained the general content and form of each part of major reports, illustrated a short analytical report, and gave you a detailed checklist applicable (except in a few designated details) to both kinds of major reports.

Unless you remember those instructions (especially in Chapters 14 and 15), you need to review them before going further here with an illustration, questions, and cases about complete analytical reports.

THE ILLUSTRATION

The following illustration of a complete analytical report (which one of our students wrote and gave us permission to use, with our minor emendations) is on a typical business/industrial problem—a selection or choice of location. You probably know of such a case—in which some firm (retail, wholesale, or industrial) moved (or expanded) to a new site. If so you can be sure it did not do so except on the recommendation from such a report. At one university this kind of assignment—like Case 4 at the end of this chapter—was the standard major report assignment for so long that students regularly referred to it as "The Tale of Two Cities." The selection of a favorable location does, however, highlight the key principles and problems of major analytical reports.

WHY BIRMINGHAM IS A BETTER LOCATION THAN MEMPHIS

FOR F. LEE MASON TO BEGIN LAW PRACTICE

Prepared for

Mr. F. Lee Mason

by

Robert E. Norman

Director of Research

FACTSEEKERS, INCORPORATED
1127 Main Street
New York, NY 10017

November 27, 19xx

```
                    FACTSEEKERS, INCORPORATED
                         1127 Main Street
                    New York, New York  10017




RESEARCH DEPARTMENT                           November 27, 19xx


Mr. F. Lee Mason
3807 15th Avenue
Tuscaloosa, Alabama  35401

Dear Mr. Mason:

Here is the report you requested on September 6 comparing Birmingham
and Memphis as possible locations for you to begin law practice.

The report shows Birmingham is the better city for you because of
income, competitive, personal, and economic factors.  As you re-
quested, I emphasized a specialty in tax law and the partnership
form of organization.

I am glad to have the opportunity to prepare this report for you and
will be happy to serve you again.

Sincerely yours,

FACTSEEKERS, INC.
```

Robert E. Norman

```
Robert E. Norman
Director of Research
```

Contents

Synopsis

Birmingham is a better location than Memphis in which to begin law practice, according to this study prepared for F. Lee Mason by Factseekers, Inc.

Although Memphis has a higher ratio of residents to lawyers (1,218 to 1 versus 1,200 to 1), Birmingham has a higher ratio of residents to law establishments (3,068 to 1 versus 2,533 to 1) and fewer tax lawyers (2% versus 4%). Profits per partnership average 12.7% higher and total profits per establishment average 36% higher in Birmingham.

In Memphis the median age is four years lower, the land area is three times as large, the population is growing rather than declining, median school attendance is approximately one year more, and about 5.5% more of the population is in the $15,000 and above income level. Memphis's city government spends 4½ times as much as Birmingham's. Birmingham, however, has more large employers, better continuing education for lawyers, and better within-city transportation.

Birmingham has a bigger variety of better quality sports events, although Memphis does have hunting, fishing, and water sports equal to Birmingham's. UAB's medical school, Samford's law and pharmacy schools, and special programs at other schools provide better higher education in Birmingham. Health care in Birmingham has gained national recognition. The Memphis Arts Council and The Memphis Academy of Arts, on the other hand, support many programs that make cultural activities better in Memphis.

Unemployment is 0.5% lower, income of the average factory worker is 20% higher, retail sales are up 7% more, and factory workers' income is up 12.5% more in Birmingham. But Memphis's effective buying income is $4 billion as compared to Birmingham's $3.7 billion. Median household EBI in Memphis ($12,905) is growing 1.3% faster than in Birmingham, where the median is $11,958.

WHY BIRMINGHAM IS A BETTER LOCATION THAN

MEMPHIS FOR F. LEE MASON TO BEGIN LAW PRACTICE

I. <u>Problems and Procedures of the Study</u>

A. <u>Purpose and methods</u>

This report compares Birmingham, Alabama, and Memphis, Tennessee, to
select the better city for F. Lee Mason to begin law practice. Its bases
for the decision reflect the interests and concerns of the primary reader,
as agreed on in the contractual arrangement.

For a young man planning to start a tax-law career and a family, the
criteria for selecting a location are

--the demand for, competition in, and hence likely income from tax-law

   practice;

--relevant social and convenience factors such as transportation facilities

   and flow, an effective local government, and the nature and concentration

   of the populace;

--a pleasant climate and the availability of educational, recreational,

   entertainment, and health-care facilities for a pleasant family life;

   and (as an indication of the future outlook)

--the local economic situation and trends.

Information presented here comes largely from the <u>U.S. Census of</u>
<u>Business</u>, the <u>U.S. Census of Population</u>, <u>U.S. News & World Report</u>, and
various publications of the Chamber of Commerce in each city. In some
cases we developed the percentages we used from the raw data given in
the publications.

B. <u>Scope and limitations</u>

Two of the most important criteria we used in this evaluation are

1

competition and income of existing law firms. Inspection of competition
starts with how many and what kinds of lawyers now practice in each city
but, as requested, considers more carefully the number of tax lawyers
and partnerships. Income of the attorneys, a major factor in the decision,
appears in terms of profit per establishment.

Secondary factors we examined because of their important influence
on law practice include characteristics of the population, city government
spending, area employers, continuing education, and transportation.

Family life in each city gets careful attention because an attorney
usually does not change cities and will want the best circumstances for
a family.

Second in importance only to income and competition, the general state
of the economy has an influence on the legal profession, although perhaps
not as great an influence as on some industries. No matter how large the
demand for legal services, clients may forego or delay seeking the services
if they can't afford them.

As requested, we made no attempt to compare the laws of Alabama and
Tennessee. Similarly we did not consider any kinds of taxes or housing.
A choice among the many types and prices of homes depends on individual
preference.

C. Basic plan

The bases for evaluating the two cities and arriving at the conclusions
and recommendations are, therefore, income and competition, relevant
secondary factors, family life, and the economy.

II. Competition and Income More Favorable in Birmingham

Less competition and larger income are desirable factors of major
importance in choosing the better city.

3

A. Number, type, and specialties of existing law firms favor Birmingham

1. Ratio of population to lawyers.--Memphis has a higher ratio of
residents to lawyers than Birmingham. Memphis and Birmingham have 632
and 616 lawyers, respectively (12:4-34; meaning pp. 4-34 of Item 12 of the
Bibliography). Memphis's population is 770,120 while Birmingham's is
739,274. Thus Memphis has one attorney for every 1,218 residents and
Birmingham's ratio of residents to attorneys is 1,200 to 1, as shown in
Table 1.

TABLE 1

Lawyers, Population, and Persons per Lawyer

	Birmingham	Memphis
Population	739,274	770,120
Lawyers	616	632
Persons per Lawyer	1,200	1,218

Source: Census of Legal Services, 19xx, pp. 4-34.

A new attorney in Memphis would have more prospective clients to attract
than one in Birmingham. Also since Memphis has more people per lawyer, the
number of persons not already associated with a lawyer should be larger
there. But since the number of lawyers and the number of law establishments differ, the numbers and types of existing establishments warrant
examination.

2. Ratio of population to law establishments.--Birmingham has a higher
ratio of residents to law establishments (meaning "a single physical
location at which business is conducted"--not identical with "firm," which
may consist of one or more establishments). The numbers of law establishments in Memphis and Birmingham are 304 and 241 respectively (1:4, 17).
The ratio of residents to law establishments for Birmingham is therefore
3,068 to 1 and for Memphis 2,533 to 1.

4

Since people in Birmingham have fewer law offices per person to choose from, new attorneys will have a greater chance of attracting clients in Birmingham. Even though Memphis has the advantages in the ratio of population to lawyers, Birmingham's lead in the ratio of population to law establishments may be more significant. Prospective clients tend to choose between law establishments or firms rather than between lawyers within firms. Since most firms are of the type with more than one lawyer (as shown below), the ratios on establishments seem most useful.

3. Types of law establishments.--Partnerships comprise a greater percentage of law establishments in Birmingham than in Memphis. Law establishments, as the Census Bureau classifies them, are sole practitioners, partnerships, professional service organizations, and other. An establishment owned by two or more persons, each of whom has a financial interest in the establishment, is a partnership. A professional service organization is an establishment founded under state professional association or corporation statutes. Other includes establishments whose legal form is unknown or not one of those above.

The numbers and percentages of various kinds of law establishments for both Birmingham and Memphis appear in Table 2.

TABLE 2

Law Establishments by Type

	Birmingham		Memphis	
	Number of Establishments	Percentage of Total	Number of Establishments	Percentage of Total
Total	241	100	304	100
Sole Practitioners	83	34	118	39
Partnerships	100	42	89	29
Professional Service Organizations	2	1	13	4
Other	56	23	84	28

Source: Census of Legal Services, 19xx, pp. 4-17.

5

Partnerships, with which we are primarily concerned, probably exist
more frequently in Birmingham because they are the most advantageous form
of organization in terms of income (discussed later); but form of organization is most likely overshadowed. The specialty of the lawyer's practice
probably has even more significance.

4. Specialty of law practice.--Birmingham has fewer tax lawyers and
fewer in the combined specialties of tax and corporate law. Lawyers
specializing in taxation comprise 2% of the total in Birmingham and 4%
in Memphis, while corporate lawyers comprise 4% and 3%, respectively, as
shown in Table 3. Thus Birmingham has 6% of the total in these two groups
while 7% of all Memphis's lawyers are in these two groups. Although a
new lawyer in Birmingham has less competition, comparison of incomes points
up the real advantage.

TABLE 3

Number of Lawyers in Practice by Specialty

	Birmingham		Memphis	
	Number of Lawyers	Percentage of Total	Number of Lawyers	Percentage of Total
Total	616	100	632	100
Tax	13	2	27	4
Corporation	23	4	19	3
Banking and Commercial	12	2	30	5
Criminal	3	1	35	5
Domestic Relations	4	1	1	--
Insurance	18	3	19	1
Negligence	37	6	35	6
Patent, Trademark, Copyright	--	--	7	1
Real Estate	37	6	49	8
Wills, Estate Planning, Probate	19	3	15	2
Other	42	7	30	5
General	408	65	375	60

Source: Census of Legal Services, 19xx, pp. 4-34.

B. Income of law firms larger in Birmingham

   1. Gross receipts, profits, profits per establishment.--Total Birming-

ham law establishments have larger gross receipts, larger aggregate profits,

and larger profits per establishment than those in Memphis. Also Birmingham

partnerships exceed Memphis partnerships in all these areas. Profits per

establishment for all types of establishments are $56,618 and $41,586 in

Birmingham and Memphis, respectively. Partnership profits per establishment

in Birmingham are $121,120 and in Memphis $107,472, as shown in Table 4

(12:4-9, 4-17). Thus on the average partnerships make 12.7% more in

Birmingham than Memphis and total profits per establishment are 36% higher

in Birmingham, revealing one reason for Birmingham's higher income levels.

TABLE 4

Receipts and Profits by Type of Establishment

	Receipts ($1,000)		Profits ($1,000)		Profit Per Establishment	
	Birmingham	Memphis	Birmingham	Memphis	Birmingham	Memphis
Total	30,893	30,670	13,645	12,642	56,618	41,586
Sole Practitioners	4,029	5,373	593	1,904	7,144	16,135
Partnerships	24,270	17,403	12,112	9,565	121,120	107,472
Professional Service Organizations	na	2,911	na	(1,629)		125,308
Other	na	4,983	na	4,858		57,833

na -- not available

   Source: Census of Legal Services, 19xx, pp. 4-9, 4-17.

   2. Income levels.--Birmingham lawyers have a higher median income and

more Birmingham lawyers have incomes of $10,000 or more. Median incomes of

lawyers in Birmingham and Memphis are $15,000+ and $14,901, respectively.

In Birmingham 73% of the lawyers make $10,000 or more while 71% of

Memphis's lawyers are in this category. Birmingham lawyers have a slight

edge in the $15,000-and-above income level; but approximately 50% of the

7

lawyers in both cities are in this group, as shown in Table 5 (10:2-663)
(11:44-712).

TABLE 5

Income Levels of Lawyers and Judges

	Birmingham		Memphis	
	Number	Percentage of Total	Number	Percentage of Total
Total	827	100	936	100
$1-$1,999 or less	36	4	42	4
2,000-3,999	31	4	34	4
4,000-4,999	11	1	31	3
5,000-5,999	40	5	18	2
6,000-6,999	24	3	36	4
7,000-7,999	26	3	43	5
8,000-9,999	54	7	66	7
10,000-14,999	189	23	202	22
15,000 or more	416	50	464	49

Sources: Characteristics of the Population, 19xx, Part 2, p. 663
Characteristics of the Population, Part 44, p. 712.

Even though income and competition, which favor Birmingham, are probably
most important in choosing the better city, other factors which influence
law practice (such as population characteristics, city government, major
employers, continuing education, and transportation) deserve consideration.

   III. Factors Influencing Law Practice Yield No Clear Favorite

A. Population characteristics more favorable in Memphis

   1. General characteristics.--Memphis's population (770,120) is 4% larger
than Birmingham's (739,274), and it grew 25.3% during the past decade while
Birmingham's declined 11.7%. Memphis, with a land area of 217.4 square
miles, is about 3 times as large as Birmingham with 79.5 square miles.
Memphis also has a smaller population per square mile (3,542) as compared
to Birmingham (9,299).

   The growing population of Memphis is a favorable trend for law practice
and business in general. Also the larger land area should make office
facilities easier to find in Memphis and less expensive because the city

8

is more diverse. But the growing population may counter this desirable
effect by creating more demand for business facilities.

The median age in Memphis (26.2 years) is lower than in Birmingham
(30.3 years). Approximately 50% of the population of both cities is
between 18 and 65. Birmingham has a larger percentage of the population
in the 18-and-over group with 67.4% as compared to Memphis's 63.7%
(9:630, 3:762). The lower median age and the growing population of
Memphis should mean Memphis will soon have a larger percentage of the
population in the over-18 age group--the primary users of legal services.

2. Education.--Memphis's population is better educated than Birmingham's.
Thus people should be more willing to seek legal assistance with business
organization, wills, estate planning, and tax planning. The median years
of school attended in Memphis is 12; in Birmingham, the median is 11.2.
Memphis has a larger percentage of the population in the higher education
categories. As shown in Table 6, 6.1% more of the population of Memphis
has completed four years of high school or more, and 2.5% more have completed four years of college or more (3:631,763). This higher education
level is probably one reason for higher incomes in Memphis.

TABLE 6

Education of the Population

	Birmingham	Memphis
Median Years Attended School	11.2	12
Percentage of Population Having Completed:		
5 or Less School Years	8.7%	7.3%
4 Years High School or More	44.0%	50.1%
4 Years College or More	7.4%	9.9%

Source: County and City Data Book, 19xx, pp. 631, 763.

3. Income.--The median family income in Memphis ($8,646) is higher than
that in Birmingham ($7,735), and a greater percentage of the families of

9

Memphis have incomes of $15,000 or more. In Memphis 16.5% make $15,000

or more, while 11% make $15,000 or more in Birmingham, as shown in

Table 7 (3:633,765). Thus Memphis's residents can pay more readily than

Birmingham's for legal services, and they will most likely demand more

legal assistance since they tend to be wealthier unless the tax bite

removes their advantage.

TABLE 7

Income of the Population

Percentage of Families with Income	Birmingham	Memphis
$ 3,000 or less	15.5	12.9
3,000-4,999	13.7	12.1
5,000-6,999	14.7	13.4
7,000-9,999	22.9	20.8
10,000-14,999	22.2	24.4
15,000-24,999	9.2	12.4
25,000 or more	1.8	4.1

Source: County and City Data Book, 19xx, pp. 633, 675.

B. City government expenditures larger in Memphis

The city government in Memphis spends approximately $183.4 million

yearly or 4½ times Birmingham's expenditure of $40.9 million. On a per

capita basis, Memphis spends $256 as opposed to $91 for Birmingham.

Memphis spends more total dollars in each category of spending than

Birmingham, even though Birmingham spends more as a percentage in some

categories, as shown in Table 8 (13:636,768). The larger expenditures of

Memphis's city government should make Memphis a better place to work, as

well as live.

TABLE 8

City Government Expenditures

	Birmingham		Memphis	
	Total Spent ($ Millions)	Percentage of Total	Total Spent ($ Millions)	Percentage of Total
Percentage Spent for:				
Education	16.46	40	84.7	46.2
Highways	4.6	11.3	6.6	3.6
Public Welfare	0.02	0.05	0.6	0.3
Police and Fire	10.5	25.6	28.0	15.3
Sanitation	3.4	8.2	11.2	6.1
Total	40.9	100	183.4	100

Source: County and City Data Book, 19xx, p. 636; 19xx, p. 768.

C. Large employers more numerous in Birmingham

Birmingham has more large employers than Memphis. Firms with 1,000 and over employees number 19 in Birmingham as opposed to 16 in Memphis. In the 3,000-and-over employee category, Birmingham has ten firms and Memphis has nine. The larger the firm the more likely it will require some type of legal service.

Some of Birmingham's major employers in the public and private sectors are U.S. Steel, U.S. Pipe and Foundry, the University of Alabama in Birmingham, American Cast Iron Pipe, and Alabama Power. Some of the larger ones in Memphis are Firestone Tire, International Harvester, Sears, and the U.S. government (1, 6). All of these firms need varying degrees of legal aid, possibly even full-time counsel.

D. Continuing education better in Birmingham

Birmingham has better facilities for lawyers to continue their education. Cumberland School of Law, Alabama's largest law school, is in Birmingham; and the University of Alabama is a one-hour drive from Birmingham. Both of these schools have part-time programs for lawyers. Memphis, conversely, has no law school (2:4) (7:22).

11

E. <u>Transportation more suitable in Birmingham</u>

    City transportation is more favorable in Birmingham, but out-of-city
travel is more favorable to and from Memphis. The fact that Birmingham's
interstate highways go through the heart of the business district makes
transportation time to downtown from the residential areas shorter than
in Memphis, where the completed interstate highways bypass the city.
Also since three interstate highways meet in Birmingham, all sections of
the city are near one of them.

    Memphis, on the other hand, has the advantage in out-of-city travel.
Five trunk and five regional airlines serve Memphis's new international
airport with approximately 300 flights daily. Birmingham has four major
airlines and three fixed-base private aviation companies. Both cities have
the services of seven major railroads and two national bus lines. Memphis,
the second largest inland port on the Mississippi River, gets service from
six barge lines. Birmingham does not now have port facilities but has
plans to build a port nearby (7:16) (2:9).

    These factors that influence law practice in a secondary manner give
neither city an advantage. Population characteristics, city government
expenditures, and transportation to other cities favor Memphis, while
major employers, continuing education, and travel within the city are
better in Birmingham. While neither city gains a clear advantage on these
secondary factors, no choice should depend on strictly business factors,
anyway, because family life is important.

IV. <u>Family Life Better in Birmingham</u>

    The quality of family life depends on the friendliness of the climate,
the type of recreational facilities, the quality of the arts and cultural
activities, the educational opportunities, and the health-care facilities.

12

A. <u>Climate more desirable in Birmingham</u>

   Birmingham's average annual temperature is 62° with an average summer

temperature of 81.6° and an average winter temperature of 46.5°. With an

average summer temperature of 80° and an average winter temperature of

43.8°, Memphis's average annual temperature is 61.5°.

   Average annual rainfall is 53.05 and 49.78 inches, respectively, in

Birmingham and Memphis. Average monthly rainfall in Birmingham is 4.4

inches and in Memphis it is 4.1 inches. The approximate dates of the last

frost are March 2 in Birmingham and March 21 in Memphis. November 25 in

Birmingham and November 6 in Memphis are the approximate first frost

dates, as shown in Table 9 (4:4, 7:3).

TABLE 9

Climate

	Birmingham	Memphis
Average Annual Temperature	62.0	61.5
Average Summer Temperature	81.6	80.0
Average Winter Temperature	46.5	43.8
Average Annual Rainfall	53.05"	49.78"
Average Monthly Rainfall	4.4"	4.1"
Approximate Last Frost Date	March 2	March 21
Approximate First Frost Date	November 25	November 6

Sources: <u>Birmingham Magazine</u>, February 19xx.
         Memphis Area Chamber of Commerce, 19xx.

B. <u>Recreation more plentiful in Birmingham</u>

   Birmingham's spectator sports are on a bigger scale and more plentiful

than Memphis's. College football, one of Birmingham's biggest sports

attractions, draws more fans than other sports in Birmingham. The University

of Alabama and Auburn University play home games at Birmingham's Legion Field.

Memphis State University plays its home games at the Liberty Bowl Stadium

(home of the annual Liberty Bowl Classic). College basketball is available

in both cities. The University of Alabama and Auburn University play some

13

games at the Birmingham Civic Center. University of Alabama home games
are only one hour from Birmingham in Tuscaloosa. Memphis State's home
basketball games are in the Mid-South Coliseum. Samford University also
has home basketball games in Birmingham.

Birmingham's newest sport is hockey. The Birmingham Bulls of The
World Hockey Association play at the Civic Center. Memphis's professional
sport is golf. The PGA's Danny Thomas Memphis Classic is at one of ten
private golf courses in Memphis. Memphis also has ten public golf courses
and 136 baseball fields. Golf is also a big attraction in Birmingham,
partly due to the friendly climate.

Automobile racing is a huge attraction at the Alabama International
Motor Speedway only 45 minutes from Birmingham. It is the world's longest
enclosed race track.

Tennis is a growing sport in Birmingham for both participants and
spectators. The $30,000 Birmingham International Tennis Tournament brings
in top-ranked players for a week each winter. The Racquet Place is a good
indoor tennis facility, and outdoor courts are plentiful throughout the
city. Ice skating is also becoming popular in Birmingham with the opening
of a new ice skating lodge.

Participative sports such as hunting, fishing, and water skiing are
plentiful in both cities. Near Memphis many enjoy hunting for duck,
squirrel, rabbit, quail, and dove. Memphis also holds the National Bird
Dog championships.

For sightseeing, Arlington Ante Bellum Home, The Botanical and Japanese
Gardens, the Jimmy Morgan Zoo, and the Vulcan are in Birmingham. In Memphis,
Mississippi River cruises, Overton Park Zoo and Aquarium, Chucalissa Indian

14

Village, and Brooks Memorial Art Gallery are main attractions (7:24)
(2:8) (4:2).

Since participatory recreation is relatively equal in both cities,
Birmingham's edge lies in spectator sports. A city with a good combination of sports and cultural activities is difficult to find, though.

C. The arts better in Memphis

Offerings in the arts are slightly better in Memphis than in Birmingham,
but professional performers appear most in Birmingham. The Memphis Arts
Council, which is dedicated to the promotion and support of the arts as
a vital aspect of community life, enriches local cultural life. It funds
many groups and special events. Brooks Memorial Art Gallery displays an
outstanding permanent collection of paintings and schedules circulating
exhibitions of national interest. The Memphis Academy of Arts offers a
variety of services to the community, including free-lance work and
commissions by students and faculty.

The Memphis Opera Theatre presents operas with national and international stars in leading roles. The Memphis Symphony Orchestra, The
Memphis Ballet Society, and The Beethoven Club present symphonies, ballets,
and classical recitals. Theatre Memphis, one of the oldest little theater
groups in the country, produces six plays each year. Memphis also enjoys
productions by many touring companies, including Broadway plays, Metropolitan
Opera, and concert artists (7:26).

In Birmingham three civic theatre groups, campus productions, a dinner
theater, and numerous road shows provide a variety of theater productions.
In one week Liberace, Pearl Bailey, Doc Severinsen, and Hal Holbrook
played in Birmingham.

15

Birmingham's 80-member professional symphony plays a seven-month
season. Birmingham Music Club, oldest in the South, schedules outstanding
artists. Birmingham has civic opera, string quartet, civic chorus, organ
recital series, connoisseur concerts, a special symphony series, and active
college music departments. Four dance companies and a creative dance
organization perform in Birmingham. Birmingham-Southern College offers
the Southeast's only ballet degree. The Museum of Art holds many famous
works of art (4:3).

D. Higher educational opportunities better in Birmingham, but
   preparatory schools better in Memphis

   1. Higher education.--Birmingham's higher educational opportunities
allow a wider choice than Memphis's in field of study and type of institu-
tion. Birmingham's largest university, the University of Alabama-Birmingham,
trains students in its nationally recognized medical school in the fields
of medicine, dentistry, optometry, nursing, and community and allied health
resources. UAB also offers undergraduate degrees in liberal arts and
business. The graduate school awards degrees in a wide range of fields,
but most degrees are in science and medicine. Memphis State University
has long been recognized as the regional center for higher education. The
graduate and undergraduate schools at Memphis State offer a wide range of
degrees. The Southern College of Optometry and the University of Tennessee
Center for Health Sciences provide training for health careers in the
Memphis area.

   In Birmingham, Samford University, with schools of law, pharmacy, and
nursing; Birmingham-Southern College, which offers the only major in
dance in the Southeast; and the University of Montevallo, with its
extensive program to train driver-education instructors and emergency-
vehicle operators, offer programs in almost every field. The Memphis

16

Academy of Arts, LeMoyne Owen College, and The Joint University Center
round out Memphis's major institutions. Also both cities have several
community and junior colleges (7:22) (2:4) (4:2).

The larger offerings of colleges with regionally and nationally recognized programs make higher education better in Birmingham; but secondary,
elementary, and kindergarten schools are better in Memphis.

2. Elementary and secondary education.--Memphis has a better preparatory
school system than Birmingham. The Memphis public school system ranks
seventh largest in the nation. In metropolitan Memphis 197 schools employ
7,284 teachers and have an enrollment of 138,294. The ratio of pupils to
teachers in Memphis is 19 to 1. Birmingham's 210 area schools have an
enrollment of 128,890 and employ 5,394 teachers, resulting in a 24 to 1
pupil-teacher ratio, as shown in Table 10 (7:22) (5:1).

TABLE 10

Number and Size of Elementary and Secondary
Schools, Metro Area

	Birmingham	Memphis
Number of Schools	210	197
Number of Students	128,890	138,294
Number of Teachers	5,394	7,284
Pupil-Teacher Ratio	24 to 1	19 to 1

Sources: Memphis Area Chamber of Commerce, 19xx.
The League of Women Voters of Greater
Birmingham, 19xx.

For preschoolers, Memphis offers over 100 public and private kindergarten and day-care centers. The majority of students who attend pre-school
in Birmingham go to private (usually church-based) programs. A few public
programs are operating, however (7:22) (5:1).

E. Health care more advanced in Birmingham

Medically speaking, the Birmingham area is one of the most advanced
communities in the nation. Nineteen hospitals with 5,044 beds serve

17

Jefferson and Shelby counties. The medical industry employs 14,000

workers in the health services and allied fields. The University of

Alabama Medical Center, foremost in Birmingham, provides the training

ground for many doctors, dentists, and eye specialists; has cardiac-care

facilities known worldwide; and ranks in the top 5% in the nation in

specialized burn care. Virtually all the major hospitals have been

renovated within the last ten years. Birmingham is a major referral

center in the Southeast, and patients come from all over the world for

open-heart surgery (2:5).

The Memphis health-care system, which has the Memphis Medical Center

at its heart, consists of 19 hospitals with over 6,600 beds and over

15,000 physicians. The Medical Center includes the nation's largest

private hospital, the tenth largest medical school, and specialty clinics

of international reputation. The completion of Memphis's construction

program will provide the area with a network of four peripheral health-

care facilities (7:21).

Even though family life appears better in Birmingham, bad economic

conditions would reverse these good factors or lessen their enjoyment.

V. Economic Trends Point to Birmingham

A. General economic conditions more favorable in Birmingham

Retail sales, as compared with one year ago, are up 10.9% in Birmingham

and 4% in Memphis (3:C-3, C-75). Department store sales rose 3.2 percentage

points more in Birmingham than Memphis, where they were up 7.5% as compared

to one year ago, as shown in Table 11. Unemployment is 7.1% of the work

force in Birmingham as compared with 7.6% in Memphis. Nonfarm employment

is down in both Birmingham (1.3%) and Memphis (1%). Income of the average

factory worker adjusted to an annual basis is $2,106 higher in Birmingham.

18

TABLE 11

General Economic Conditions

	Birmingham	Memphis
Unemployment	7.1%	7.6%
Income of Average Factory Worker	$12,284	$10,178
The following are compared with a year ago:		
Retail Sales	Up 10.9%	Up 4%
Department Store Sales	Up 10.7%	Up 7.5%
Nonfarm Employment	Down 1.3%	Down 1.0%
Factory Workers' Income	Up 15.7%	Up 3.2%
Construction Activity	Up 1.5%	Down 15.5%

Sources: U.S. News & World Report, October 25, 19xx, pp. 85, 87.
Survey of Buying Power, July 26, 19xx, C-3, C-75.
Survey of Buying Power, July 21, 19xx, C-2, C-74.

Factory workers' income as compared to a year ago is up 15.7% and 3.2% in Birmingham and Memphis, respectively. While construction activity is up 1.5% over the last year in Birmingham, it is down 15.5% in Memphis (3:85, 87). Thus Birmingham's economy shows more favorable trends and is better than Memphis's in every category listed except nonfarm employment.

B. Effective buying income larger in Memphis

Total effective buying income, median household effective buying income, and the increase in median household effective buying income are larger in Memphis. Effective buying income (EBI) is Sales and Marketing Management's measure of disposable personal income--wages, salaries, and other income minus federal, state, and local taxes and fines, fees, and penalties. Total EBI for Memphis and Birmingham are $4 billion and $3.7 billion, respectively. Median household EBI is up 11.5% since last year, to $12,905 in Memphis. Birmingham's median household EBI is $11,958, up 10.2% since last year (8:C-3, C-75) (9:6-2, C-74). Since EBI depends greatly on current economic conditions, the trends of the economy should probably be the primary consideration. So Birmingham has the better economy.

19

VI. Birmingham--the Preferred City for F. Lee Mason

to Begin Law Practice

Since Birmingham enjoys the advantages of

--535 more residents per law establishment

--a greater number of partnerships

--fewer tax attorneys in total and as a percentage of the total

--12.7% higher partnership profits

--higher median income for attorneys

--better continuing education

--better transportation within the city

--more desirable climate

--more recreation opportunities

--better higher education and health care

--and more favorable economic trends

a new attorney interested in forming a partnership and specializing in tax
laws would likely do better there. Although Memphis does have the advantage
in population characteristics such as income and education levels, city
government expenditures, the arts, preparatory education, and effective
buying income, the factors in which Birmingham leads are more numerous
and more important in making the choice. So we recommend that Mr. Mason
begin his practice in Birmingham.

20

Bibliography

1. Birmingham Area Chamber of Commerce, _Major Employers in the Birmingham Area_, 19xx.

2. _Birmingham and You_, South O'Town Realty Co., Birmingham, Alabama, 19xx.

3. _County and City Data Book_, 19xx, U.S. Government Printing Office, Washington, D.C. 19xx.

4. "For Newcomers, and Perhaps You," _Birmingham Magazine_, February, 19xx.

5. The League of Women Voters of Greater Birmingham, _Know Your Schools_, The Birmingham Area Chamber of Commerce, Birmingham, Alabama, 19xx.

6. Memphis Area Chamber of Commerce Pamphlet 976M1000, _Memphis Major Employers_, Memphis Area Chamber of Commerce, 19xx.

7. _A Profile of Mid-America's Big New City--Memphis_, Memphis Area Chamber of Commerce, 19xx.

8. "19xx Survey of Buying Power," _Sales and Marketing Management_, July 26, 19xx.

9. "19xx Survey of Buying Power," _Sales and Marketing Management_, July 21, 19xx.

10. U.S. Bureau of the Census, _Census of the Population, 19xx, Vol. 1 Characteristics of the Population, Part 2_, U.S. Government Printing Office, Washington, D.C. 19xx.

11. U.S. Bureau of the Census, _Census of the Population, 19xx, Vol. 1 Characteristics of the Population, Part 44_, U.S. Government Printing Office, Washington, D.C. 19xx.

12. U.S. Bureau of the Census, _Census of Selected Service Industries, 19xx, Subject Series, Legal Services_, U.S. Government Printing Office, Washington, D.C. 19xx.

QUESTIONS AND EXERCISES

1. Which of these titles is best? Why?
   a. A Study of the Parking Problem at Schiller Manufacturing Company
   b. Schiller Manufacturing Company Has Parking Problems
   c. Parking Problems at Schiller Manufacturing Company and What Can Be Done
   d. What Can Be Done to Improve the Parking Situation at Schiller

2. Read the list of topics in Case 5 and write meaningful titles for two of them. Then work up a title page for one.

3. Write a one-sentence statement of the purpose of the report for which you prepared a title page in the preceding exercise.

4. What methods would you use to get information on these two report topics? Be sure your methods include primary and secondary research.

5. What do you intend to cover (scope)?

6. What criteria or standards are you using?

7. Do you have some limitations? If so, what are they?

8. What would be your basic plan for one of these topics?

9. After you read the synopsis about Savannah and Charleston in Chapter 15 and our explanation of why it is a good one,
   a. Itemize the criteria we used in our explanation.
   b. After each criterion, list facts and/or phrases relating to it.

10. Assume you are writing to a reader who does not know what you mean when you say "computerized axial tomography." Where should you explain what this term means?

11. Why is present tense better than past tense in writing about findings in reports?

12. Go back and look at the graphics in Chapter 14. Pick one and tell how you would write copy
    a. Introducing the graphic.
    b. Interpreting the graphic.

CASES

(See p. xiii for some important explanations.)

Whether you are going to use Cases 3 and 4 or not, you should read them for points that should apply to nearly any major report-writing project.

16–1.   Choose an existing science laboratory at your school (physics, chemistry, biology—one of the hard sciences). Assume that it is going to engage in highly secret government research. What must be done to make the laboratory physically secure: Fencing? Alarms? Guards (where stationed)? Identification card system? New locks (and maybe doors)? Don't forget the roof.

You should research current methods of securing such facilities by reading published articles on the subject, acquiring product literature from companies in the business, obtaining government requirements for securing research facilities, and so on. In your analytical report describe the existing laboratory (maps and diagrams would be very helpful to your readers) and make specific recommendations on how to make it secure. You should not consider budgets at this time, but be reasonable (transporting the laboratory to a satellite might be secure, but the sky is not the limit for money!).

16–2. Select an eating place in your area (or in an area you are familiar with) that does not serve alcoholic beverages and do a study on the problem of whether that restaurant should sell alcoholic drinks. You'll have to survey the present management and customers thoroughly as to their opinions on the subject. You'll have to discover how much money the restaurant is earning now without the sale of alcoholic beverages. You have to consider fixed costs (license fees, bartender's salary, cost of liquor, cost of building a bar) as well as prices to sell mixed drinks for, and so on. Investigate the competition as well. Be as complete as you can.

16–3. Subject to approval by your instructor, choose a topic for your report. Preferably it should be a real problem actually faced by a company, organization, or individual; if not, it should be a problem somebody likely faces somewhere. It should be for one reader or a very limited group of specific readers. A term-theme topic or something like a textbook chapter will not do because it is not a report. If you can't quickly give the name or title of somebody other than a teacher who might ask for such a report, your topic is unsuitable.

It should be an analytical report: the relevant facts plus interpretation and evaluation of the advantages and disadvantages (the pros and cons) of at least two alternatives and the eventual selection of one in your final conclusions and recommendations. In other words, it must be a problem which you help someone to solve. See the list in Case 5 for suggestions if you can't readily think of one—perhaps from your own work experience.

It should be a topic for which you can get information in the library *and* (not *or*) through either interviews, questionnaires, or your own observation or experimentation.

You should settle on a topic early in the term and should not change topics after midterm for any reason. The kind of problem we're talking about usually takes 10 to 20 pages for the text alone and requires most of the school term. You and your teacher will of course cover regular class work and the shorter assignments meanwhile.

As your instructor directs, be prepared to submit on one typed page

a. A tentative title (not *now* worded to show a preconception of the outcome, but clear, concise and catching).
b. A one-sentence statement of the purpose of the report.
c. An indication of who the readers are and your relationship (actual or assumed) to them.
d. Sources and/or methods of collecting data, including the titles of five items from your tentative bibliography.

e. Major divisions (with subdivisions, if you like) of the coverage or body of the report.

Be prepared at any time to give your instructor a progress report in memo form, indicating what you have accomplished, what difficulties you've encountered, what remains to be done, and your plans for finishing. (See Chapter 13.)

At the time directed by your instructor, submit the report with title page, letter of transmittal, contents listing, synopsis, body (including introduction, facts and interpretations intermingled but in two to five major divisions, conclusions, and recommendations), bibliography, and (if necessary) appendix.

As further clarification and suggestion, here are some of the better topics chosen by students in one class:

Comparative evaluation of swimming pool (or goldfish pool) disinfectants under specific conditions.

Comparative evaluation of materials and procedures to reduce black-shank damage to tobacco plants (specific conditions).

Whether X Company should expand (or restrict, or diversify) its product line (or territory).

You'll find a long list of other possibilities in Case 5.

16–4.   One of the requests coming to your desk as director of Factseekers, Inc., New York 10032, is from the president of (name of firm supplied by your instructor). The company is a chain of retail (type of store supplied by your instructor) stores with outlets in most major cities. The chain is now contemplating opening a store in either one of two cities (names of two cities supplied by your instructor).

The letter to you as director, signed by the company president, reads:

Will you please submit in report form your analysis of retail sales possibilities for (specific goods) in (names of two cities)?

Before deciding where our next branch will be, we would like the opinion of a firm of your caliber.

Naturally we want to know the story on population, buying power, retail sales—with special emphasis on (specific goods)—competition, and current business. But please include other data which will be helpful to us in making our choice.

Your problem is only to determine which city would likely bring us the larger volume of sales. Please do not attempt to cover taxes, wage scales, real estate costs, or availability of sites, and maybe crime rates that might affect us. After your determination, we will require a shorter report on each of those topics.

Since we plan to have the store in operation within a year's time, will you please confirm that you can submit the report no later than (specific date as assigned), subject to the same rates as on previous studies?

From secondary library sources you can get all the necessary comparative data: *Statistical Abstract of the United States; County and City Data Book;*

Market Guide of Editor and Publisher; Rand McNally's *Commercial Atlas and Marketing Guide; Sales Management Survey of Buying Power; Marketing/Communication's* studies like *Sales Planning Guide* and *Major American Markets;* and *Consumer Markets,* published by the Standard Rate and Data Service. The foregoing are some of your more useful sources. But they are not intended to be an exhaustive list. You will of course want to consult the censuses of population, business, and manufacturers for (respectively) breakdowns of populations, influence of wholesaling and retailing on the local economy, and the value added to the economy by manufacturing. In all cases you will want the latest reliable data; recency of information is important.

Your entire analysis should focus on the answer to the question: Which of the two towns is a better market for selling more of the specific merchandise this store sells? Population is, of course, a factor—size as well as distribution and character. The retail market area always needs examining. Income figures are significant (a person with $4 is in a better position to buy than one with only $2). Retail sales indicate whether people are willing to spend their money (total retail sales, per capita retail sales, and retail sales figures in the particular line you're investigating—if you can find them). Sources of business strength are appropriate considerations (a manufacturing town suffers more than a distribution center during a recession; a community depending primarily upon farming for its sustenance weathers economic storms more readily than one heavily dependent upon shipbuilding, for instance). And the current business picture (as measured by construction, postal figures, employment, and bank deposits) is important for its diagnostic value.

The list of topics above is merely to help you start thinking about what to include; it is not intended to be inclusive, orderly, or arbitrary. For instance, no study of this kind would ever omit competitive factors.

This is assigned: Exclude any discussion of banking facilities, communications facilities (newspapers, radio stations, advertising agencies), and transportation facilities. These are adequate in both cities and so would not affect the decision. Furthermore, the people would have done enough reading themselves to know where the cities are—and the pertinent geographical and climate features.

Once you've made the final decision of what factors to include and—just as important—the order in which to lay them out, the analysis becomes a matter of simply comparing the two cities simultaneously to show which city is the better market—more people with more money to spend, and the apparent willingness to spend it, especially for this kind of merchandise.

Do not attempt to turn out a chamber of commerce root-for-the-home team piece of propaganda. Impersonally, impartially present the facts about the two cities and make your decision on the total evidence.

An analytical report is not just a compilation of tables and labels. Your report must present the facts in statistical display (graphics primarily, for readability). Without these, your report has no base and, in the reader's mind, no authenticity. But the most significant part of the report is your own expository (analytical) comment which explains the significance of the data you have gathered.

Of course, your grade will depend partly on physical appearance and mechanical correctness (freedom from errors in spelling, punctuation, and grammar). Counting most heavily, however, will be

1. Organization (the order of points for logic and emphasis).
2. Readability (stylistic factors).
3. Complete, authentic evidence and its reliability, analysis, and documentation.

16–5.   Parts of this assignment probably are not suitable for a large class in a small community because too many students would be getting in too many business executives' hair. This danger can be less serious, however, if students work in teams, at least on the data-collecting part of report writing. Also, consider the listed topics, which are not report titles, just suggestions to start thinking about what could be an endless list of the same kind of thing.

For your choice of the following topics, assume that you can and will arrange amicably for access to, observation of, or experimentation with the obviously necessary facts (usually available only in a small local firm). Then write the kind of report (form, tone, and length) which the facts and the situation seem to require (or your instructor assigns). Assume that the appropriate person has asked you to do the report, and assume an appropriate position for yourself. In most cases you will likely be an employee; but in some, you might reasonably assume that you are a consultant on a fee basis. Each situation is to involve thorough study of existing conditions and application of well-established, up-to-date principles (learned from courses, articles, books, and/or people) leading to recommendations for wise decision about or betterment of the situation.

Should X city convert raw garbage to energy?

Should X country town have house-to-house garbage collection instead of a dumpster system?

Can X city support another hospital?

Can X city support another cemetery?

Can the town of Y support a catering service?

Should your university authorize student evaluations of teachers and/or courses and, if so, how should they be done?

Should X city attract new business, and if so how?

Should doctors X, Y, and Z incorporate their clinic?

Should the professional cleaning service in X city advertise through newspaper, TV, or direct marketing?

Should X savings and loan company give premiums to encourage new accounts?

Should X company encourage its sales force through contests?

What about a joint venture for X company?

Should X and Y merge?

Approved vacation practices in a specific local firm.

Traffic-accident "hot spots" in a town or city (or, if too large, an appropriate area).

A campus bus service? Volume? Pay? Routes? Costs/income? Franchised/school operated?

Student costs of attending your school (low/medium/high).

Causes for failure in college work (student/school viewpoint).

Justifiable improvements at a specific sorority/fraternity/dorm.

A new (or up-for-sale) riding stable in your town—prospects for success?

Student TV, magazine, or newspaper preferences/habits at your school.

Proper credit (less, same, more?) for this (or other) business communication course.

Best buy in this year's (under 10-HP outboard motors, vacuum cleaners, . . .)?

English errors students make in (first business communication course).

Training needed for writing/speaking done by local business executives in first five years out of college.

Student reasons for choosing to attend your school.

Paralegals—should X law school train them?

Paramedics—should X medical school train them?

Needed improvements in X company's employee motivation.

The absentee-worker problem at X.

Bugs in X's inventory control.

The letter writing done by a small local firm. (Only students who have studied letter writing should attempt this assignment.)

The public relations of a local firm (limited parts, if necessary).

The accounting procedures of a local firm (limited aspects, if necessary).

The advertising program and budget (not copy) of a small local firm.

The advertising copy (not program and budget) used by a local firm.

The physical layout (floor plan) of a local store (same problem a housekeeper works on by moving the furniture around).

The hiring and firing and promoting criteria (or just one criterion) and procedures in X (business firm), related to personnel turnovers.

The financing arrangements of . . . .

The stock control procedures of . . . .

The fringe benefits (or just one) or salary scales of . . . .

The materials-handling procedures of . . . .

Pilferage losses and control in . . . .

A motion-time study of some local processing or manufacturing operation.

Any other problem of this type which you think of and can get facts on, and which your instructor approves.

Proposed equipment and procedures for fire prevention and/or fighting in a certain forest, building, or operation.

Should a given company devote some of its lands/efforts to producing . . . (a kind of production or service not now emphasized).

Solution to the problem of poor growth and fruiting/flowering of certain plants on a large lot (or crops on a specific field or farm).

Critical analysis (with suggestions) of the company publications of a comparatively small local firm.

Possible computer applications in a local library (or company).

Suggestions for improving appeal and income at a small fee-charging, publicly or privately operated park and lake.

Would a proposed campground (private, specific location) be a successful business venture?

Analysis of a local company's employee relations problems, with suggestions for improvement.

Would a specific large wood products company be wise to set up a sawmill and/or paper mill in a certain locality where it has some landholdings?

To have or not to have coffee breaks for a given company's employees.

What the people of a 10,000–100,000 community think of their public schools, with emphasis on suggested improvements.

Any of these problems can generate an oral report if your instructor so directs.

16–6.   Find an organization which grows, makes, or deals in a product(s) that you think might be sold profitably outside the United States and analyze the market potential in one or more foreign markets. After a little preliminary investigation, you should discuss with your teacher (and get agreement on) the kinds of information you are to get and analyze, such as estimated size of the market, kind(s) of customers, methods and estimated costs of advertising and promoting, best ways (and costs) of distributing, and the present and/or forseeable competition.

Almost any business capable of competing domestically can export, but some products are not appropriate for certain markets and some require modification to be successful. (See Appendix C.)

You can get much useful information in various places:

United Nations' publications like *Yearbook of International Trade Statistics, Monthly Bulletin of Statistics,* and *Trade Statistics*. If these are not in accessible libraries, write the UN Sales Section, New York, NY 10017.

The U.S. Department of Commerce, *Business America, Commerce Business Daily,* and *Market Share Reports* will be available in libraries or from the Government Printing Office, Washington, DC 20402. The Department of Commerce computer system (identified as DIALOG) also helps find markets. WITS (Worldwide Information and Trade System), a Department of Commerce computerized system, gives information on potential business contacts in the United States and abroad.

Predicasts, International is published weekly, quarterly, annually.

Various state agencies may help: state world trade association, district export council, state docks (if any), chamber of commerce, departments of agriculture and industries, governor's office of international development, international departments in state banks, and centers like the International Trade Center at the University of Alabama (which publishes the *Alabama Exporting Guide*, cost $5).

16–7. The president of the small company where you work, Jerry Hughey, asks you to compare the I.R.A. and the Keogh plan for possible use for the employees' tax-sheltering retirement plan. Take a small-sized, actual company about which you can get information, assume Hughey gives you a deadline (the due date your instructor assigns you), and write the complete analytical report your president wants.

16–8. Garden homes are the new thing in your area. Managed essentially as condominiums, they are individual homes (one level) with yard in front (that the management keeps up) and yard in back (that owner keeps up or gardens). You and a friend want to develop some garden homes in your area. Your friend lives 500 miles away, so you must do the research. You need to know what would be the best buy in low-energy appliances (dishwasher, washer, dryer). What is the best heating and airconditioner unit, water heater? Since you'll be selling to some widows, divorcees, retired people, and unattached people, safety is a prime concern. What kind of windows and door locks should you purchase? What other safety precautions should you plan for? After you have gathered your facts, write a report to your friend analyzing your information and proposing (recommending) specific choices.

Oral business communication

part 4

Oral business communication

17

["*Really, now you ask me,*" *said Alice, very much*
confused, "*I don't think—*"
"*Then you shouldn't talk,*" *said the Hatter.*]

Throughout our discussion of letters, memos, and written reports, we have constantly reminded you of the important part oral communications play in business, industry, government, and other sectors of our society. Indeed, repeated studies of executives and managers show that they spend more of their communication time speaking than writing.

To manage well, then, you must be effective in both written and oral communication. Whatever the form, a skilled communicator is better able to get subordinates to follow instructions, to get useful information and ideas from others, and to report information to superiors.

For three reasons, in this book we have chosen to give you a thorough treatment of the main kinds of written business communication first and now to help you apply the important principles in effective oral communication:

1. Communication shortcomings that employers complain about in their employees nearly always concern the inability to *write* well.
2. Writing is better for teaching and learning not only the basic language skills of conciseness, correctness, and precision but also for learning to apply the important principles of organization and psychology for effective business communication.
3. The transfer of learning from written to oral application is much easier and more effective than going the other way.

Training and practice in writing, however, are not complete substitutes for training and practice in speaking. So our selective treatment here concentrates on *business speaking* and *the oral application of effective business communication principles* presented in the earlier parts of this book.

Since both written and oral business communication use the same language and should use the same principles of organization and psychology, what you have learned so far in this book will apply to oral messages. Therefore we will not repeat (but only remind you by cross-references) as we help you transfer the principles and give you additional pointers applicable to the main kinds of oral communication you are likely to need in business—oral reports, interviews, conferences, and dictation. First, however, you need to consider some basics of effective speaking applicable in all kinds of business communication.

BASIC PREPARATION FOR EFFECTIVE SPEAKING

Getting rid of bad habits

To begin with, you have been talking longer than you've been writing—and you probably have some poor speech habits which can hurt you in various ways if you don't correct them:

1.   Carelessness in validity and precision of statement, economy of wording, or grammatical propriety are all harmful to business communication. *Solution:* Practice giving them care in your speech as in your writing; improvement in each will reinforce the other.

2.   Slovenly or incorrect pronunciation and enunciation may cause misunderstanding (or *not* understanding) and (when you write) misspellings which strike most people as unsightly warts on your competence. *Solution:* Notice how well-educated speakers place accents, assign sound qualities to vowels, and say distinctly all the syllables in key words. If in doubt, check a dictionary—and follow what you find.

3.   Inattention to the principles of good organization in sentences, paragraphs, and longer statements that often causes wordiness, incoherence, and even confusion. *Solution:* Carry over into your speaking the principles of organization you have learned in becoming a good writer. Since you talk much more frequently than you write, you will both write *and* speak more clearly, concisely, and effectively if you constantly try to speak that way.

Recognizing similarities to and differences from writing

Certainly, successful speeches have central themes, adequate and reliable facts, coherent and compact organization, clarity and vividness of phrasing, and other stylistic considerations characteristic of good writing as explained in Chapter 2 and throughout this book.

Though written and oral business communications have many similarities, their major differences deserve attention too. All of them will at times influence what you say (or *should* say) and how you say it.

Written	*Oral*
A reader can (if desired) reread unclear or difficult passages.	Except in dyadic (two-person) or small-group situations, a listener must understand the first time or not at all.
A reader's immediate reaction is unknown—no direct feedback exists.	Immediate listener reaction is known—direct feedback does exist, even in large groups.
The reader sets the pace.	The speaker sets the pace.
Attention span is usually longer in reading than in listening.	An audience's attention span is limited (though usually increasing with maturity).

A reader has few physical restrictions (may move about).	An audience usually is subject to physical restrictions (must remain seated).
A written record exists (permanent).	No record exists (ephemeral) unless recorded.
Information retrieval is relatively easy.	Information retrieval from a recorded speech is more difficult.
A writer must spell, punctuate, and paragraph.	A speaker must enunciate clearly and pronounce, inflect, and pause appropriately.
Readers are quick to catch even small errors.	An audience is usually not so critical.
A writer may not know all who will read (pass-along readership).	A speaker usually knows and can see who the audience is.

Preparing the speech, the setting, and yourself

Of course your major job in making a speech is preparing what you will say and how you will say it. Both the what and the how, however, depend so much on other factors (like the purpose, topic, methodology, audience, length, and circumstances) that we shall discuss them with specific adaptation to the main kinds of business speaking as we take them up later.

Preparing the physical setting may be wholly, partly, or not at all your responsibility, though usually you will have some say about at least any audiovisual aids you need. Whether you initiate the whole thing or accept an invitation to talk, you need to know from the start at least the date, time, place, and kind and size of audience.

Also helpful is knowledge about whether your presentation is a one-shot, one-speaker affair or one on a panel or in a series. If other speakers are in the picture, certainly you need to know the general topic, theme, and purpose as well as who the others are, their parts or angles or slants, and who precedes and follows you.

Whether you are primarily responsible or not, you will be wise to check in advance on seating (adequate capacity?), stage settings, temperature controls, lighting, audiovisual facilities, amplifying system (if wanted), and even whether the doors will be open in time for you to set up.

Sometimes you can have a curtain hung on one wall (preferably the one facing the speaker) to kill echoes if the walls and ceiling are hard surfaced. Remember, however, that an audience that fills a room will do much to absorb echoes; so simply spreading out your audience's seating might be sufficient.

If you are using projection equipment or an amplifying system, who will control them? Try them out in advance—you don't want any surprises when you are speaking.

Preparing yourself for making a speech involves your voice, physical appearance, and mental attitude. Ideally, you should follow the Greek motto: moderation in all things. Look neat, clean, and properly combed and clothed for the occasion and your audience. Avoid the appearance of a truck driver just ending a long haul or a manikin modeling the flashiest new clothes.

To get yourself in the right frame of mind to give a speech successfully, you may have to remind yourself of how well you are prepared, that you *can* do it—in short, psych yourself up. Your body language—posture, gait, nuances of expression, how you hold your limbs, and so on—will signal to your audience how you really feel. And since these signals are almost impossible to control consciously, we think you will do better to remove the causes of adverse body language. So think positively.

Having prepared well, let the mental attitude you reflect by eye, posture, and gait be that of neither a whipped dog nor a bantam rooster. Instead, calmly reflect confidence and competence. You *are* prepared; perhaps you've practiced your speech before a mirror and timed yourself until any earlier feelings of insecurity are gone. You know more about the subject than the audience does or you wouldn't be speaking in the first place. Those people are there to hear what you have to say, not to hurt you; so you have no reason for stage fright. You're going to give them what they came for—and make them glad they came.

If the game plan calls for you to walk in and take over, do just that—at the scheduled time and place, confidently but not arrogantly.

Getting into speaking position favorably

If, however, you are to wait in front of your audience for an introduction, sit comfortably relaxed. You prepared both your speech and your clothing before coming in; let them alone now or you will create a bad impression that you came unprepared.

After the introduction, walk erectly and confidently to your speaking position, thank the introducer, and move right into your subject. The more poise, confidence, and efficiency you show in these short maneuvers—based on knowing your subject and having your notes ready instead of having to fumble for them—the greater audience respect and support you will get.

If you feel a little tense when you first face an audience, an excellent way to release tension is to exhale. Just empty your lungs. Don't gulp a lungful of air and then give a great sigh; merely breathe out all the way and you'll feel more easy.

We have no firm, invariable advice about whether you should sit or stand, except possibly to sit for small groups (under 10) and stand for large ones. In general, if in doubt, stand. And if you can arrange it, do not use a lectern or podium. A lectern is a crutch for many speakers. They hang on to it desperately, use it as a barrier between them and the audience, and generally hope it will hide their nervousness. It never does. A lectern is useful only for holding your notes and, if needed, a light. (Beware, by the way, of lecterns with microphones on them. Your voice will bounce off the surface of the lectern as well as go directly into the mike, sometimes causing a distracting echo.)

When the time comes to begin actually speaking, you should be feeling calm and confident, but not arrogant.

GIVING THE SPEECH

Good speaking is, of course, a combination of many elements—the thought content, the style (mainly word choice, sentence patterns, and the organization and transitions), the voice in all its manifold variations, gestures, all forms of facial expressions and other body language, and the metacommunications (the *milieu,* as the French say, meaning the total of surrounding circumstances).

Fortunately, in preparing your speech, the physical setting, and yourself, you will have taken care of the first two and the last one. You could wisely give some prior attention to the others, too, but you can't firm them up completely beforehand—even by writing out the speech with fully orchestrated markings for voice variations, gestures, and other body language. You would, at best, look and sound like a ventriloquist's puppet.

Like an accomplished conductor rehearsing an orchestra, you need to have practiced with your orchestra of words, voice, gestures, and so on, so that in your speech you can (without a musical score) call upon the various instruments to come into play at the right times and for the best effect. Here are a few specific suggestions.

Your voice

Your voice is the major instrument in your orchestra and must be well tuned and played. What voice should you use for speeches or oral reports? Try to speak naturally and easily. Your normal, natural voice is the best. If you try to change your voice without thorough practice first, you'll sound strained and unnatural and distract your audience's attention from what you are saying.

Never, never (if you can avoid it) read a speech! No one without a great deal of training reads a speech well enough to keep an audience awake. What reads well on paper is usually awful when read aloud. Instead, use notes, listing *only* the points you want to cover (perhaps with subheads) and any appropriate quotations too long to memorize easily.

When speaking to people, you have only two seconds to break eye contact to look at your notes. Any longer and you lose and must recreate rapport with your audience. We think the best notes are two- or three-word phrases, just enough to trigger your memory for what you want to say next. You'll be much more natural and far more interesting to listen to. If you are forced to read a speech (say for a speaker who couldn't come), overemphasize changes in the tone and pitch of your voice. Also exaggerate your gestures and expressions.

In short, overact a little since you want to break away from "reading aloud" to "talking" what you are reading.

When speaking to an audience, especially a large one, you must project your voice. But projection does not mean shouting. If you shout you may be heard but not understood. Your volume should be sufficient for your farthest listener to hear you without straining but should allow you some volume left over to use for emphasis. If you cannot easily make yourself heard without straining, use a public address system.

In a speech situation you will have to use more variation in the pitch of your voice than for normal conversation. What may be acceptable variation of pitch in a conversation will sound like a monotone in a speech. Be on guard, however, agaist the tendency to raise the pitch too much and become strident or screechy as you project your voice.

Oral reporting and formal speaking require more than normal attention to pronunciation and enunciation, too—no slurring and certainly no "asides." Speak slowly, and distinctly pronounce all the parts of words, especially the ends, leaving no uncertainty about what you said.

Posture and movements

When speaking, be yourself, be natural. Consciously trying to appear serious and mature usually comes across as stodgy, boring, and dull. Your posture should be erect, alert, confident, relaxed, and natural. Your shoulders should be down and loose, not hunched and tense-looking. Keep your stomach in and up—you'll look better and you'll be able to speak better. And keep your backside in; don't slouch. Your feet should be a comfortable distance apart with your weight concentrated on the balls of your feet. Bend your knees slightly; don't lock them back. Locking your knees leads to strain and quivering and may cut off circulation.

Let your hands hang naturally at your sides and don't move them unless you are going to turn a page in your notes or gesture for emphasis. Never put your hands in your pockets or clasp them in front of or behind you. That will cause you to slouch or lean forward. Standing comfortably erect may feel awkward at first, but look at yourself in a mirror. Don't you look more authoritative, commanding, and assured?

Just as you walked calmly and deliberately to a place in front of your audience, move calmly and deliberately around the stage while talking. You should use walking around for emphasis sparingly, however; like all emphatic devices, it loses its effect from overuse. Generally, the more audiovisual aids you use in giving a talk the fewer movements you should make The important thing is to direct your audience's attention to what you want. Moving around can sometimes retrieve an audience's attention, but too much distracts from what you're saying.

Keep gestures restrained and natural unless the situation requires some overacting. When you do gesture, be aware of what you're doing. Gestures are strong reinforcements to language; but the meanings of many of them are not definite, especially to people from other cultures (as explained in Appendix C). As rough rules, the more formal the occasion, the more restricted your gestures should be; and the larger your audience, the more exaggerated so that people far away from you can see them clearly.

When you describe something, hold your hands up and apart to show the size. Use your hands to help show spatial relationships, motion, and direction. You can reinforce abstract points by holding up an index finger or pounding a fist into your hand. You can emphasize something by pointing at your audience, making a punching motion, and the like. If you are making a number of points, for emphasis (and for clear transition) hold up the appropriate number of fingers as you tick off each point. You will be wise, however, to try out your gestures before a mirror before you try them out on an audience.

Keep your facial expressions under control, using them only to reinforce what you are saying. Be animated: frown, look sad, outraged, puzzled, whatever you need. You should give the impression of being warm, alert, bright, assured, animated, confident, but not arrogant. And don't forget to smile; an audience responds most favorably to a happy, confident smile. The only way to tell what reaction you are getting is to look your audence in the eye. So make eye contact with members of your audience on a random basis, moving from side to side within but not around or over the heads of your audience— and certainly not on the far wall or your notes (except for momentary glances).

Your language

In speaking as in writing, you must adapt our language to your audience. Before speaking, decide on the level of formality you want to use. But be aware that most untrained speakers use far too formal and ornate language in an effort to overcome a deficiency (usually imaginary) in position or authority. High rhetoric has long been out of style; so keep your language natural. You will get immediate feedback from your audience if your level of formality is inappropriate, and you can quickly adjust (another good reason for speaking from notes instead of a complete text).

Restrict your use of jargon. An occasional use is desirable to indicate that you are "with" the audience; but too much is hard to understand, even when your audience knows the meanings. Also avoid emotionally charged words. They are generally too highly exaggerated for a business situation, and your audience will recognize them for what they are—and mistrust you.

Nobody is perfect, and in front of an audience you may make a slip. Don't panic. If you handle the situation right, your audience can remain unaware of your problem; and if it does show, you'll have sympathy. If you make a grammatical error or mispronounce a word, ignore it and keep right on talking. If you repeat the word or phrase later, you can do it correctly.

If you forget what comes next in your speech, keep looking thoughtfully at your audience or move about the stage contemplatively until you gather your thoughts. Audiences are not as critical as you may think. In the general run of business speaking they do not expect a professional presentation unless listening to a professional speaker. Your audience will, however, expect you to know your subject, be prepared to talk intelligently about it, and come to a conclusion—requirements you should easily meet when the time comes.

If possible, keep a talk to no more than five or six major points—more are hard to assimilate. Make the transitions clear by any or all means as you shift from one point to another. (The suggestions on "Coherence" in Appendix F and in Chapter 14 may help.) To give your audience time to digest a major point, you may want to follow it with some lighter material to change pace for the moment.

Special attention tactics

At the beginning of your talk, get your audience's attention immediately. Don't begin uselessly with an egotistic expression like "I'm pleased to be here" or a plea for sympathy like "I'm not used to speaking; so I hope you'll overlook my weaknesses." The best beginning for a speech is the subject—or conclusion if you think your audience will be in favor of what you are going to say. If not, you may want to begin with your arguments before coming to the conclusion. Some specific ways of beginning a speech, roughly in order of effectiveness, are:

1. A rhetorical question.
2. An illustration that leads logically into your subject.
3. A fact or opinion that sets up the first point you want to make.
4. An apropos quotation (such as the one at the beginning of this chapter).
5. A humorous anecdote (which sometimes makes seriousness hard to achieve later).

People's attention spans are short, rarely more than 15 or 20 minutes unless stimulated. You will know when you are losing your audience by the glassy eyes. Here are some preventatives and remedies for an inattentive audience:

1. Slow down your delivery of hard-to-understand material and speed it up for more easily comprehended matter.

2. Provide clear transitions between subjects and show how they *relate* to each other ("coherence" again). One of the best ways to lose an audience is to shift topics uannounced. You will befuddle and anesthetize with what seems to be nonsense because it does not relate to the topic you *were* talking about.

3. Eliminate distractions. Curtain off windows that have attractive views, screen off any movement behind or to either side of you, ...

4. Use language your audience readily understands. When in doubt, remember to KISS (keep it simple, stupid).

5. Be animated, energetic. Don't stand like a statue, but gesture, vary your facial expressions, move around some.

6. Talk directly to individuals, changing from one to another, from side to side, and from front to back of the audience (as with eye contact).

7. Use visual aids: slides, chalkboard, an object you hold up . . . .

You can regain an audience's wandering attention by:

1. Changing the volume of your voice, keeping in mind that a low voice is better than a shout.
2. Making a change in the level of formality if it fits naturally with what you are saying and you can logically use it for effect.
3. Using attention-getting devices:
    a. Direct a question to a member of the audience you point to (and await the answer).
    b. Make a quick joke or comment that has the slow-burn effect (and stand smiling, watching as the fire spreads in the audience).
    c. Mimic somebody or something the audience knows (maybe even yourself, the way you've been droning on).
    d. Make a grossly exaggerated gesture or change of pace or volume (Kick a chair, s-p-e-l-l s-o-m-e-t-h-i-n-g o-u-t, YELL!), turn to a visual aid (which can serve other purposes than arousing a drowsy audience), say something pertinent but stupid, then pause, looking hard at your notes, throw them in the wastepaper basket, glower at them, turn back to the audience, correct the stupidity, and go on with your speech.

Audiovisual aids

Four questions determine whether you will want to use audiovisual aids:

1. Does the *occasion* justify preparing and using audiovisual aids? For instance, if you are going to sit down with one person and informally deliver your report, would slides or a flip chart be appropriate?

2. Will the benefits justify the *costs* in time and money? Does your budget have enough in it to pay for preparing audiovisual aids?

3. Do you have sufficient *time* before giving your report or speech to prepare audiovisual aids? Slides, for example, require a photography session, a photographer, subjects or objects to be photographed or charts or graphs, developing the slides, sorting to pick the best, and arranging them for projection.

4. Are the necessary *facilities* available where you will speak? Projector? Screen? Projector stand? Power source? Public address system? Chalkboard?

Use audiovisual aids only to help your audience better understand what you are saying, never simply because you have them available or just for dramatic effect (except as waker-uppers or unless the occasion calls for some entertainment along with the information). Audiovisual aids play the same part in oral reports that graphics do in written ones: they help make quantitative data clear and quickly and easily comprehensible.

Some common audiovisual aids are: slide projector, overhead (transparency) projector, motion picture projector, opaque projector, videotape player, flip chart, chalkboard, felt board, actual object, model of an object, poster (large drawing, picture, etc.).

The two basic rules for visual aids are (1) they must be clearly visible to all members of your audience, and (2) they must be quickly comprehensible to all members of your auience. The second rule gives the most trouble.

Generally, when a visual aid fails to do its job, the fault is due to either or both (1) too much information, or (2) information presented too small or too densely to be seen. Common examples are charts with too many lines on them or charts whose lines are too fine or light to be seen, and illustrations (such as photographs or detailed drawings) that even when projected are too small to show what the speaker intends.

We recommend that when preparing visual aids you constantly keep in mind that presenting information is wasted effort unless the audience can readily comprehend it. You can find more detailed information on this subject in the many books on giving talks using audiovisual aids, and especially in the fine publications of Eastman Kodak.

When you use a visual, explain it to your audience. Rarely should you read anything to people that they can see and read themselves. To do so is insulting, implying that they cannot read. Avoid the hackneyed "As this slide shows . . ." introduction to a visual aid. Simply project the next slide or expose the next chart, and keep on the subject of your speech by launching directly into *explaining* it: "The rise in snow tire sales over . . . ."

Be careful not to block the view of a visual aid from any members of your audience. If, for instance, you want to point to something on a chart or a projected image, use a pointer and keep well to the side of the screen or chart. Talk to your audience, not to the visual aid you're using. You can control your audience by breaking eye contact to look at a visual aid only when you want your audience to look at it, and reinforce this by pointing to the visual aid. Stop pointing and regain eye contact with your audience when you want to redirect attention to you.

Ending the speech

Some people have as much trouble ending a speech or oral report as they do a letter. As with a letter, the time to quit talking is when you have finished saying what you planned to say. Avoid the natural temptation to close your speech with any expression of hope that you have done well or a hesitant declaration that you think you have finished. When you are done, gather up your notes and sit down.

If a question-and-answer session is to follow, then you may have to announce that you have finished: "That concludes my report. I'll be glad to answer any questions." Here are five ways to end a talk that unmistakably signal to your audience that the end is coming:

1.   Summarize the points you covered.
2.   Challenge your audience to meet the objectives outlined in your talk.
3.   Appeal to your audience to do what you want.
4.   Wrap up the major point you want to make with an apt illustration, anecdote, or quotation.
5.   State your intention to do whatever you advocated.

ORAL REPORTS

We begin with oral reports in our application of the preceding principles for effective speaking because

1.   Oral reports vary more and make use of more of the basic guidelines than interviews, conferences, and dictation do.
2.   Early in your career, your first contact with upper management may very well be an oral report. Though you may give oral reports infrequently, such reports can be tremendously important to you and your organization.
3.   Learning to give oral reports well can give you self-confidence and poise that will help you in other forms of oral business communication and hence in both your working and private life.

Oral reports serve the same purpose as written reports: they help the receiver make a decision by providing needed facts and/or ideas. They also answer the same questions as written reports (Is something feasible? Should some action be taken? What's the best way?) and share the same characteristics (they are management tools; they are assigned jobs; they are delivered to superiors; they are directed to a specific and usually limited audience; they give more than normal attention to organization; they make use of devices for clear communication; they are expected to be accurate, reliable and objective; and they follow the form, content, and length best suited to their particular function).

An oral report may be as informal as a conversation between two people or as formal as a full-scale presentation to a large audience, complete with audiovisual aids. Where in this range a particular oral report will be depends (as with written reports) on the occasion, the kind and amount of information transmitted, the relationship between reporter and listeners, and so on. In general, oral reports tend to be shorter than written reports simply because detailed information is hard to communicate orally and because listeners have shorter attention spans than readers.

You go through exactly the same steps in preparing an oral report that you do in preparing a written one. (We describe them in Chapter 14.) You plan your attack, get the facts or evidence you need, organize your material for coherent presentation, analyze it for interpretation and solution to the problem, and then present it clearly and concisely in appropriate style.

Indeed a frequent kind of oral report is a synopsis of a long written report. The author of an important report (now speaker/reporter) may now synopsize (orally) for a group of high-level executives and answer their questions. Thus the oral report often becomes the start of a conference (discussed later) to decide on what to do about the reporter's recommendations.

If you have not already read Chapters 13–16 (especially 14), which deal primarily with written (and incidentally with oral) reports, we urge you to do so now. Virtually all of what we say there applies to oral reports—and we will point out the differences.

Planning the attack in preparing an oral report involves essentially the same six procedures as for a written one, though a few differences do arise.

1. In the second procedure, considering conditions that influence the report, the *size* of the receiving group and the *occasion* will have a bigger influence. Size of readership makes little difference in planning a written report except that increased size is likely to increase disparity of age, experience, and knowledge of and interest in the subject. Readers have the choice of reading or not reading. (Even so-called required reading sometimes is not read, as any experienced teacher knows.) But in a large audience, some members may be there against their wills; so retaining their attention may be a special burden for the speaker.

2. An even bigger difference is that in oral reporting you communicate through many more means than the content, style, and appearance of a written report. Your physical appearance and body language (including eye contact, facial expressions, gestures, stance) and your voice (quality, pitch, enunciation, pronunciation, pace and pauses, . . .) are all tools. Even the usually desirable use of audiovisual aids is a greater problem for the oral reporter (especially in large groups) than their counterparts (graphics) are for a report writer.

3. Usually a report reader provides the physical surroundings (the milieu or whole set of circumstances for the activity). However, that burden—sometimes a considerable one—falls on the oral reporter and deserves planning time.

Only in the data-collecting step do other differences between written and oral report preparation *seem* to exist—but they are mirages not there when you look carefully. Let us explain.

Our 12-page explanation of "Collecting the facts" (Chapter 14) is in a college/university textbook where part of the purpose is to teach students to research substantial business problems for several months and prepare thorough reports of 20 or more pages. We know that most business reports are not that long. Yet we give this in-depth instruction, as well as instruction on preparing the more common shorter reports, for several reasons:

1. Doing a thorough job on a sizable report-writing problem is the best

SPEECH AND ORAL REPORT CHECKLIST

1. Before the talk:
   a. Was the speaker's overall appearance attractive and suitable for the occasion?
   b. Did the speaker walk in front of the audience quietly and confidently?
   c. Was posture acceptable?
   d. If the speaker carried notes, were they inconspicuous?
2. During the talk:
   a. Was the speaker's voice natural and expressive (not montonous and dull)?
   b. Did the speaker project voice properly for everyone's clear hearing?
   c. Did the speaker announce the title of the speech or report?
   d. Did the speaker pronounce and enunciate clearly and correctly?
   e. Were the level of language and use of jargon appropriate?
   f. Did the speaker maintain erect posture?
   g. Did the speaker make effective use of gestures?
   h. Did the speaker maintain eye contact with the audience?
   i. Did the speaker keep the audience's attention?
   j. Was the speaker aware of audience reaction?
   k. Did the speech or report follow a clear and appropriate plan?
   l. Was the talk connected by effective transitions?
   m. Did the speaker make proper use of any audiovisual aids?
   n. Did the speaker do anything distracting?
3. After the talk:
   a. Did the speaker come to a logical conclusion(s)?
   b. Did the speaker summarize the points covered?
   c. Did the speaker adequately signal the end of the talk?
   d. Did the speaker exit confidently and gracefully?

way for students to learn to prepare reports (big topic or small, long or short, written or oral).

2. Those who have seen the wide range of information sources (bibliographic and other) will help improve the vision of many myopic business people who look only at company-generated data.

3. When the big report problem does come up—as it does from time to time (maybe 10 or even 20 times as long), particularly in industry and government studies—former students so trained will sail through while those who have not been through the rough waters are likely to flounder. (But when very long reports do come up, you can bet they will not be oral.) A good reporter adapts the data-collecting procedures to the problem, regardless of whether the presentation of the report is to be written or oral.

In other words, to make a good oral report, you need to (1) learn how to prepare the particular kind of report by studying Chapters 13–16 and what we've said on the present topic, "Oral reports," and (2) present the report as explained above in this chapter.

A listener sees and/or hears only your presentation of your speech or oral report and can judge it, therefore, only by what you say. We structure our checklist for speeches and oral reports from the audience's point of view, then, to help you keep your listener(s) foremost in your mind as you prepare to talk.

INTERVIEWS

Nature, importance, kinds

In turning to interviews, we take up another widely used and important tool in business and industry. Like many tools, however, interviews can be very productive or very damaging.

Four traits characterize most good interviews:

1. They are not the group communications we have been discussing but are dyadic (on a one-to-one basis).
2. They are not like a purposeless conversation but have a specific purpose and concentrate on a specific subject.
3. They are not (at least not usually) interrogations but are with the willing consent of both parties and have none of the accusatory atmosphere of an interrogation.
4. In interviews, as in good conversations—instead of monologs or long-winded pontifications—half the job of each participant is listening.

Because of that last point, therefore, we recommend that you turn now to Appendix B and see if what we say there can't help you become a better interviewer or interviewee by becoming a better listener.

The common types of interviews in business and industry are:

1. Personnel interviews
   a. Employee screening and hiring. (And now, closely related, the getting/giving of career and job information and advice through information interviews—as explained under "Surveying work opportunities" in Chapter 9.)
   b. Orientation, instruction, training of employees new to a job.
   c. Review of employee progress.
   d. Discussion of employee grievances, firings, resignations, and problems.
2. Research—making plans, determining what has been done/discovered, possible uses, next steps, and so on.
3. Exploratory—determining the existence, cause(s), and cure(s) of a problem with an employee or activity.
4. Opinion sampling—"Surveys" in Chapter 14.

Whatever type of interview you engage in, the basic structure and purposeful nature of interviews allow three general plans for conducting one:

1. Directed. A directed interview is completely planned from start to finish. Often the interviewer will have a checklist of questions to follow, especially when an interviewer is not thoroughly trained and when doing sampling. In personnel work, organizations use directed interviews when different interviewers screen different applicants for the same job or jobs. Directed interviews minimize the effects of any interviewer bias on the results and interpretations.

2. Nondirected. In a nondirected interview the interviewee can set or at least influence the subjects covered and the directions of flow in the interview. As a way of eliciting information, the interviewer plays a much more reactive role than in a directed interview. The nondirected approach is useful in grievance, counseling, and exit (resignation or termination) interviews and forms the basis of both information interviews and psychoanalysis.

3. Stress. Conducting a stress interview involves intentionally putting the interviewee in a hostile situation, under artificial stress, to see the reaction. We think that such an interview has little justification unless such stress is an essential part of a job. You may establish the interviewee's irritation or anger threshold but lose a potentially good employee, who will likely feel contempt for your questionable practices.

But because we want you to recognize immediately if someone subjects you to a stress interview, here are the six usual devices for conducting one: The interviewer will (1) criticize or ridicule your appearance at the start, (2) take and maintain a threatening, unfriendly tone, (3) deliberately interrupt you repeatedly as you are about to make a point, (4) criticize or ridicule any opinion you express, (5) ask you very personal (perhaps insulting) questions, and (6) purposefully allow long silences to develop and try to force you to end them.

The commonest kind of interview in business and industry is the directed personnel interview. Here is a guide that will help you conduct successful interviews (after which we'll give you a similar guide for being interviewed). To be specific, for both parts, interviewer and interviewee, we'll assume a job-application interview.

The employer (interviewer)

Preparing for the interview. Have available all the information you will need about the job: rank, salary, duties, location, hours . . . . Before you call in an applicant, set the stage: clear your desk, check your own appearance, alert your secretary to intercept any phone calls or visitors, close the blinds to avoid silhouetting yourself, and review the applicant's application or résumé.

Beginning the interview. To relax the applicant, be friendly and welcoming as you shake hands and offer a seat. Sitting on facing chairs or on a couch rather than behind your desk removes a physical barrier and reduces the formal office atmosphere. Taking another minute or two to review the applicant's résumé gives the applicant a chance to settle down and look around.

The first question you ask is critical since it sets the tone. Remember that you need to hire someone; so be in a positive frame of mind and treat every applicant as a potential employee. A common opening is "Tell me about yourself," but the question is so general that most applicants don't know where to start and the interview begins on a nerve-shaking basis. A better way is to begin with a shared interest—a hobby or personal or business experience. Then proceed to your first question.

To get the applicant to open up, begin with questions that the applicant should be able to answer positively. Examples are whether the applicant satisfies the job's educational requirements, whether the applicant is physically able to perform the job, or whether the working hours are acceptable.

At the beginning avoid falling into the trap of giving more information about the job than just enough to get the applicant answering you easily and naturally. Once you start giving a sales pitch on the job and your company, getting the interview back on the track with the applicant giving you information will be very hard.

Getting information.   Once the applicant has begun to open up, you can go about your task of learning whether you have a desirable prospect. Try not to ask questions answerable yes or no, which tell you little. Instead, ask questions calling for comment. For instance, rather than asking "Do you like purchasing?" ask "What activities do you like best about being a purchasing agent?" Try to make each question (or its answer) lead logically into the next.

In asking questions about former jobs, try to avoid a mere chronological listing by asking questions that bring out more important points—things like any upward progress and special likes, dislikes, and accomplishments or successes. Whatever answers you get, be sure not to show any disapproval or disbelief, even if you feel that way. Keep the applicant talking openly while you listen and watch carefully for symptoms of uneasiness, casual remarks, or lapses of memory.

When a period of silence develops, you can wait for the applicant to end it by saying something—often very revealing information—if you don't allow the silence to last too long and undo all your efforts to create a natural and relaxed atmosphere.

You'll need to take some notes—which are more accurate than memory and more encouraging to the applicant than just listening. But don't be scribbling away all the time or whenever the applicant is saying something personally unfavorable or discussing a negative topic. Even so, be sure to cover your notes so the applicant cannot see what you are writing—or better, use the item number only of a preplanned checklist and jot down by each number your coded evaluation on the point.

Interviewing people from other cultures.   As we have said earlier, people from other cultures often view a situation in their own special ways—especially in employment interviews. They bring their backgrounds with them, and unless they have been in our country for some time will act as they would in a similar situation at home.

In Japan, for instance, a person's background (family, studies) is most important. In that culture job applicants are supposed to be modest about their abilities and should outwardly show appreciation for being considered for jobs. An American interviewer's straightforward questions may embarrass a Japanese, and the answers the Japanese gives may appear evasive and suspicious. To the Japanese the American may seen crude and poorly informed by asking background questions.

Some people from India, when being intereviewed, because of their cultural background will agree with anything the interviewer says, no matter how outrageous or contradictory it may make them seem. And what to a German might seem forceful and mature may to an American appear arrogant. You can see that successfully interviewing non-Americans often requires a good deal of tact and understanding on the part of the interviewer.

Giving information.   Once you have heard all the information you need, you should have a pretty good idea whether the applicant is worthwhile. If not, terminate the interview as graciously as you can.

We recommend that you never turn down an applicant face to face. If you do, it will generate the natural question, "Why?" If you trap yourself into explaining, you may be in for an argument and possibly anger or tears. Reject the applicant later in a carefully worded, considerate B–plan letter (Chapter 7).

If, however, you have a good prospect, now is the time to sell your organization and persuade the applicant to join it. You can describe your organization's structure, what it does, and what the opportunities are for advancement (without firm promises!). You can tell more about the job: duties, promotion possibilities . . . . You may want to describe how you choose new employees, what criteria your organization uses in its selections. If necessary to persuade the applicant to sign on, you can go into fringe benefits (hospitalization, pension plan, profit-sharing, vacation policy, and the like). Otherwise leave discussion of fringe benefits until after the applicant has agreed to come to work for you.

Ending the interview.   The thing to avoid is an awkward, indefinite, and disorganized ending, especially if because of an interruption from outside (phone, visitor, . . .) that makes you look disorganized. You can maintain your image of competence if you follow a planned sequence of events to wind up the interview. A good first step is to ask if the applicant has any questions about the job, your organization, or the interview. Next, summarize what the two of you have discussed. The applicant's acceptance of or comment on the summary tells you how clear things are and signals that you are bringing the interview to a close. Both you and the applicant should be agreed on what actions each is to take following the interview.

The applicant (interviewee)

Preparing for the interview.   As a job applicant, you have only one objective in an interview: to convince the interviewer you can successfully do the job and become a desirable part of the organization. Since most employment interviewers have pretty definite ideas about the kinds of people they want to hire and the kinds they don't, preparing for the interview may well start with study of things that might hurt your chances or even disqualify you. Professor Frank S. Endicott, long-time director of placement at Northwestern University, has given us the following list (in order of frequency) from his survey of 153 companies:

WHY SOME EMPLOYMENT INTERVIEWEES AREN'T HIRED

1.   Poor personal appearance.
2.   Overbearing, conceited, or know-it-all attitude.
3.   Inability to express self clearly (poor voice, diction, grammar).
4.   Lack of planning for career (no purpose and goals).
5.   Lack of interest and enthusiasm (passive, indifferent, or lazy).
6.   Lack of confidence and poise.
7.   Overemphasis on money, best dollar offer.
8.   Poor scholastic record, just got by; marked dislike for school work.
9.   Unwilling to start at the bottom, expects too much too soon.
10.   Makes excuses, hedges.
11.   Lack of maturity and decisiveness.
12.   Lack of courtesy (ill mannered, tactless).
13.   Condemnation of past employers.
14.   Fails to look interviewer in the eye.
15.   Loafs during vacations.
16.   Friction with parents.
17.   Sloppy application.
18.   Merely shopping around.
19.   Lack of knowledge of specialty.
20.   No interest in company or in industry, or never heard of company.
21.   Emphasis on whom one knows (not what).
22.   Unwillingness to go where sent.
23.   Cynical or radical attitudes.
24.   Intolerant (strong prejudices).
25.   Narrow interests.
26.   Spends much time with movies, TV.
27.   No interest in community activities.
28.   Inability to take criticism.
29.   Late to interview without good reason.
30.   Asks no questions about the job.

To achieve your objective of getting the interviewer's favorable evaluation, you need to know three things so that you can make a good appearance and sell your qualifications.

1.   You must know exactly what you want to do (see Chapter 9). To enter an interview (presuming you get one) and tell the interviewer you aren't sure

what you want to do is a sure sign of immaturity. You are mistaken if you think because you say you want to work in a specific job that an organization will not then consider you for anything else. Remember that the organization called you in because it thinks you can fill a need. In reality, it will consider you for all the openings it has at the time.

Suppose that, between the time an organization invites you for an interview and the time you come in for it, the sales department announces it has a critical need for a representative. Human nature being what it is, the organization will look at *everyone* who comes in, regardless of speciality, as a potential sales representative. So you see, indicating exactly what you want to do often opens up opportunities that would have been closed had you made some weak, general statement about your career desires.

2. You need to know about the organization and the field it operates in before you can undergo an intelligent interview. You should already have done most of the research before sending in your résumé. When the organization invites you for an interview, you need to know much more about the organization's structure, its problems, needs, activities, plans for the future, and the like. Most of this you can get from annual reports, brokerage house reports, *Standard and Poor's* and *Moody's* manuals, and articles in periodicals (check the periodical indexes in your library). You want to build up a stockpile of facts about the organization that you can interweave into your presentation during the interview, showing the interviewer that you are interested in the organization and its activities and that you have prepared yourself for the job and the interview.

3. You must know specifically what you can do for the organization. If the interview results from your reply to an advertised job opening, you will know. But even if you come in as a result of a prospecting application, the organization will tell you before the interview what job it is considering you for.

You will therefore want to arm yourself with as much information as you can about the job in question. What are the usual duties of someone doing that job? What is the customary salary range? What career paths does the job generally lead to? You can get the answers to these questions by consulting government publications describing various jobs, talking to people who work in such jobs, and talking with professors who teach in that area.

All of this is the necessary background information you should have for the interview. But your primary objective in the interview will be to describe yourself and your qualifications so as to convince the interviewer you are the logical choice to fill the job. To do that, you'll need your information well organized in your mind and ready for prompt use. Though more recent and better validated research has discredited the long-used estimate of 4 minutes (and replaced it with 8–10 minutes) for interviewers' average decision-making time,[1] the interviewer is in process of making the favorable/unfavorable deci-

---

[1] N. L. Reinsch, "When *Does* the Interviewer Decide? A Critical Review of the Literature," *Proceedings* (Southwest ABCA Spring Conference, 1981) pp. 149–60.

sion from the first glimpse of you and from your first word. So you need to start and keep building up a favorable impression from the first by being well prepared.

First prepare a list of the points about yourself you want to cover in the interview: applicable training, important prior job experience, personal traits, and so on. Now commit these to memory. They are the absolutely essential items you must discuss with the interviewer.

Next write down and then memorize two or three success stories. These should deal with problems you met and solved, recognized successes, earned promotions, and the like. These may come from earlier jobs or from your education experience. Have them ready to use at appropriate times in the interview.

Third, project what questions the interviewer might ask. At this point you need to do some important thinking. Tough questions should not appear to you as threats designed to trip you up and cost you the job. (The interviewer may be applying some mild stress, but bear in mind that questions reflect the organization's need to learn enough about you to make an intelligent evaluation.) Look at questions as opportunities, even invitations, for you to sell yourself. Here are 25 questions that interviewers commonly ask and that many applicants have trouble handling. Go over them and work up answers that sell you (such as our suggested answers to the first few to get you started). If you have ready answers to these questions, an interviewer is not likely to unsettle you.

1. Tell me all about yourself. (Two suggested answers, depending on the atmosphere of the interview, are: "Surely. Would you like me to start with my last job, my education, my . . .?" or "On my last job I had an experience which I think shows that . . . ." Such a general question is a direct invitation for you to sell yourself; so start with your strongest point.)

2. How would you describe your personality? (This may sound like a "no win" question, but it is really an excellent opportunity for you. Remember that you will be hired for your strengths, not your weaknesses. Don't make the mistake of admitting to a small weakness just to appear human. Say something like "I believe I am ambitious, tolerant, patient, sympathetic—all qualities you would want in a . . . ," and continue selling yourself.)

3. What are your long-term/short-term career goals? (You have to have some, and they should be realistic in view of your age and present progress.)

4. Have you established any new goals recently? (A trick question, since your answer is subject to the interpretation the interviewer places on it. Not having established any goals recently can mean either you are immature for not revising your plans or unimaginative and stodgy for the same reason! You will have to answer in light of the interviewer and how the interview is progressing.)

5. What are your plans for graduate study? (The key here is to indicate a willingness to study further while clearly understanding that the job and the organization come first: "Though I expect to devote most of my time and energies to (the job), I hope I will have occasion to continue my studies.")

6. How do other people describe you? (Again, stress your strengths.)

7. What are your strongest/weakest personal qualities? (About the only "weakness" you can safely admit to is an impatience with people who repeatedly fail to do their job.)

8. Why do you think you will/will not be successful in . . . ?

9. What have been your most satisfying/disappointing work/school experiences?

10. Describe one or more situations in which your work was criticized.

11. What do you do in your spare time?

12. Why do you want to work for us? (Answering will be easy if you did your research beforehand.)

13. Why should we hire you? (*This* is what you came to the interview to tell! So tell it.)

14. What can you do for us now? (The job in question, of course. Describe those things about you that will indicate that you can perform the job right away and with a minimum of training.)

15. How long will you stay with us?

16. Give some examples that support your stated interest in the job/organization/ area of work.

17. Do you prefer staff or line work? Why?

18. What do you look for in a job?

19. What about this job interests you most/least? Why?

20. Why did you quit your present/previous job?

21. What supervisory or leadership positions have you held? (If you are a new graduate, don't apologize for not having been a manager in business—no one would expect you to have been one. Point proudly to whatever leadership functions you performed while in school, since they are a good indication you will achieve similar positions in the world of work.)

22. Would you prefer on-the-job training or a formal training program? Why?

23. Why did you choose your major?

24. Why are your grades so low?

25. What geographic location do you prefer? Why? (Unwillingness to move is among the major reasons otherwise qualified applicants do not get jobs with big companies.)

Armed with a knowledge of the organization and what it does, a memorized list of your strongest selling points, and ready answers to questions like those above, you are mentally well prepared for the interview. Only the physical preparation, packaging the "product," remains.

The cliché that the best physical preparation for an interview is a good night's sleep is still absolutely true. If you are well rested, you will perform at the top of your abilities, as you want to do.

You must make a good appearance. As with most situations, how you look will be the basis for the first impression; and an interviewer's unfavorable first impression will set up an obstacle you will spend most of the interview trying to overcome. The image you want to present is therefore of someone the interviewer can easily visualize successfully working for the organization.

Dress formally enough to *suit the occasion*. While for some jobs a sport coat and slacks or a sweater and skirt may be suitable, a suit is more likely to present the image you want. Bear in mind that dark, subdued colors are more sincere and serious. Coordinate your accessories to your clothing. Brown shoes do not match a blue suit, nor does a red patent leather belt match some green skirts. A well-tailored suit is a good investment for both men and women. Cheap clothes look cheap and make you look cheap too.

Good grooming is, of course, a must. You should be clean and clean-smelling. Shine your shoes, trim your nails, have your hair cut and/or styled, shave, and go easy on the after-shave or perfume. Strive for a clean, well-groomed, *natural* appearance.

Before the interview. When you go to an interview, carry an attaché case. It will give you a businesslike air and let you carry extra résumés, paper, paper clips, and anything else you find necessary.

Arrive for an interview five to ten minutes before the scheduled time, no earlier and no later. If you arrive too early you will appear overanxious. Besides, the longer you have to sit and wait, the more nervous you may become, leading you to make mistakes. Never, of course, arrive late for an interview.

You may be asked to fill out an application form while waiting for the interview (but only for a low-level job). Before filling out the form, ask if you can take it with you, fill it out later, and mail it in, explaining that you will have plenty of time to give all the information wanted. This tactic can keep you from having to scribble away in the waiting room, making you appear clerical.

When you fill out the form, do so legibly and in ink. Leave no empty spaces, writing "not applicable," "to be discussed in interview," or "see attached résumé" when you do not want to give information on the form. Do not fill out the part of the form asking for your history of jobs. People apparently design such forms to make it impossible for you to present your work experience favorably. Instead, attach your résumé to the form and refer to it.

The organization may very well interview you at lunch or invite you to lunch in the course of your visit. If so, *do not drink*, even if invited to do so and if your host does. Explain that you want to keep your head clear for this most important time. No one will criticize you for that.

Now that you are mentally and physically prepared for the interview, go in there and *sell your qualifications*.

Beginning the interview. Your guiding principle during an interview is that time is limited (most interviews do not go beyond 30 minutes) and you have to develop your sales presentation on yourself. Your job in the interview, then, is to make the points you need to make that you decided on earlier. Thus you will want to exert some control over the directions the interview takes.

Your job will be easier if you can adjust the usual superior-to-subordinate relationship of interviews to a more equal footing between you and the interviewer. You can begin to do this as soon as you enter the interviewer's office if you strive to present a confident, self-assured image—but not a cocky or arrogant one. Whether you are a man or a woman, shake hands *firmly*. You needn't crush bones, but holding out a hand as limp as a dead fish makes a poor impression. After you are seated, do not smoke. Even if the interviewer lights up and invites you to, refrain. Nobody looks good when smoking. And of course you will not chew gum.

If the interviewer follows the usual practice of beginning with small talk to put you at ease, swing the conversation onto your strong points as quickly as you can. If, for instance, the interviewer comments on your hobby of playing golf, you can remark that the game has certainly taught you patience and how to deal with frustration, and this has stood you in good stead in . . . .

That puts the interview on the track you want—dealing with you as a potentially good employee. If the interviewer submits you to a stress interview (and such tactics may be unintentional), your behavior is to remain calm, patient, reasonable, and gracious. *Never get angry!* Simply keep steering the interview back on track until the interviewer realizes you will not succumb to stress tactics.

During the interview.   To understand your attitudes and motivations, the interviewer may commence a depth interview—probing with broad, open-ended questions to get you to reveal your feelings and attitudes. Generally these will be why and how questions. "How did you get the promotion to assistant sales manager?" "How do you feel about Sanders after working for him for three years?" "Why was that experience so important to you?" If you have prepared yourself as we recommended above, such questions should not trip you up. Just keep thinking of every question as an opportunity for you to talk about yourself and your strong qualifications.

Keep your voice moderate, clear, and expressive as you talk to the interviewer. Equally important, maintain eye contact all the way through. You don't want to get into a staring contest, but to fail to look the interviewer in the eye, especially when discussing something less than favorable to you, will unavoidably make an impression of dishonesty and/or weakness. (If you have trouble looking into the interviewer's eyes, concentrate on the bridge of the nose, or look at the space directly between the eyes.)

When the interviewer asks you a question that does not let you lead into a discussion of one of your strong qualifications, answer as briefly and positively as you can. Remember that you won't have much time to present your sales pitch; so minimize time spent on (for you) nonproductive questions and answers. When you make a point, stop. Try not to ramble on, especially just to fill a silence.

Try not to brag or boast; doing so never makes a good impression. You should be able to talk positively, assuredly, and self-confidently about your successes, especially if you have prepared your answers ahead of time. Keep the interview on your good points, resisting any interviewer efforts to get you to talk about your weak ones. A reply something like this will usually do the job: "Yes, I might have handled that differently, and now I would; but the important things I accomplished then were . . . ." When confronted with a wrong interpretation on the part of the interviewer, or an untrue assertion, don't deny it; that appears argumentative and defensive. Instead, respectfully and positively correct the interviewer. Finally, never say anything bad about a past employer. You will only make yourself look bad and warn the interviewer that in the future you may bad-mouth this organization too.

Constantly during the interview you will be gauging the feedback you get from the interviewer: expressions, remarks, gestures, body language . . . . You will quickly know when things are not going well, and you can take steps to improve the tone of the interview. Above all, however, you must listen. If the interviewer ever thinks you are not listening, you may very well find the situation deteriorated beyond saving. That is why, earlier in this chapter, we suggested you study what we say about listening in Appendix B.

Talking about salary. Because salary discussion is so important in the hiring process, we give it special attention in this section.

Ideally, as an applicant you want to avoid any talk of money until after the organization has offered you a job, or at least until after you have completed your sales pitch on yourself. In any case, the longer you can postpone it, the more information you will have about the organization and the job, and the better you will be able to negotiate.

Remember that salaries are almost always negotiable. The first figure you hear from the organization should be your base for negotiating. If you state the first figure, the organization surely will see that as the base for negotiations.

You want the organization to state the first salary figure. The organization naturally will want you to be the first to quote an amount. This situation often results in a "You go first—No, you go first" routine that would be amusing if so much were not at stake.

If the interviewer asks you about your present or last salary, dodge as gracefully as possible to avoid giving it. If you cannot get out of it, give the total compensation figure, including all fringe benefits, such as vacation, medical plan, retirement or pension plan, profit sharing, and the rest.

If the interviewer brings up the question of salary too soon in the interview by asking what salary you want, reply that you think the salary basis should be what you can contribute to the organization and resume selling yourself. If the interviewer presses you, be indefinite: "The customary for this job." "Your usual range for such work." "In the 30s." If you have done your homework, you should know about what the job should pay before you go in for the interview. If you are forced to quote a dollar amount, and you think the top salary for the job is, say, about $22,000, overlap it on both sides and say, "$19,000 to $25,000." This, you hope, will begin the negotiations at the top end of the scale. If you have no real idea what the job should pay, as a last resort quote a figure 20 percent above your last salary.

When you change jobs or otherwise can choose between two, you may well get 20 to 30 percent more pay in one than in the other. Once in a job, however, you'll be lucky to get more than half that in any one increase. Your big raise, therefore, comes from negotiating at the outset. Remember, however (before bargaining too hard on salary), that many other things about two jobs may make one the better choice at several thousand dollars less, things such as—

—Doing the kind of work you enjoy

—Keeping your family together (especially if your spouse has a job)

—Living in a climate that appeals to you

—Living in a low-cost area (for which statistics are readily available)

—Saving on moving expenses and perhaps the cost and trouble of selling and buying a home

—Living in the kind of state, city, culture, or group of friends that appeals to you.

The better you have sold yourself, the stronger your bargaining position will be. Negotiate your salary based on, in order of preference, your real worth to the organization, your need for the top of the salary range, offers from other organizations, your interest in furthering your career, and your needs. We do not believe many people have ceased being considered for a job because they asked for more money than the organization first offered. If the organization is unwilling to negotiate, the answer will be "No, that is as much as we will pay," and you can then accept or refuse the offer.

Ending the interview.   When you sense the interview is approaching its close, you want to accomplish four things, in this order: (1) summarize your strongest qualifications for the job in a final statement, (2) express your enthusiasm for working for the organization, (3) thank the interviewer for an interesting interview, and (4) make sure both of you agree on what the next step will be.

After you have said goodbye, leave. Don't remain in the reception room or elsewhere around the offices, for you will appear to be indecisive or at a loss what to do next.

After the interview.   As soon as possible after leaving the organization's offices, write down the names of the people you met and any other information you learned. Don't trust this to memory—it is vital that you have everything correct and the names spelled right. Also note what strengths and weaknesses about yourself came out in the interview, what went well, and what didn't. This can help you in future interviews and will aid you in writing the thank-you letter.

You must, the day after the interview or as soon thereafter as practicable, write a thank-you letter to the person who interviewed you. We have given you recommendations on how to handle this kind of message (Chapter 10). Unless you go back for further interviews, this is your last chance to sell the organization on hiring you; so don't overlook briefly touching on your strong points.

CONFERENCES

With conferences we go from speech situations and the dyadic (one-to-one) communication situations of interviews to group communication. We did not take up conferences after speeches and oral reports because we want to emphasize that conferences are oral communication situations *between* people, not speeches *at* them. The free interchange of ideas that ideally characterizes conferences is absent in speech/report situations and the tensional seeking and giving of information in interviews.

Conferences are popular in virtually all kinds of organizations because they provide an environment for two-way communication and immediate response from both management and lower-level people.

Whether conferences are impromptu meetings or formally scheduled and conducted discussions, they share three attributes:

1. Three or more people. If less than three attend, it is a conversation or an interview.
2. A leader. Without a planned or natural leader, a conference will degenerate into a bull session or an argument.
3. A specific objective. Without a specific objective, a conference will be only an unstructured, time-wasting discussion group.

Business conferences usually fall into one of three categories. The first is information-giving upward, usually a report to superiors. The second is information-giving downward, which gives directions, instruction, or information to subordinates. The third is information-seeking, in which managemant looks for information or advice.

Any conference is a team effort and when run properly will avoid the faults of conferences that have given them a bad name in some organizations. Too many conferences are time-killers and lead only to further conferences. Others, because of ego trips or bad planning, take more time than their objectives or results justify. In the end, poorly planned conferences waste an organization's time, personnel, and money. Therefore we think proper planning is essential to successful conferences.

Planning the conference

When planning a conference, ask yourself (1) whether a need exists to justify one and (2) whether a conference is the best way to handle the situation.

If you are convinced that a conference is justified and is the best approach, your next questions are (3) how to define its objective and (4) whether the objective is attainable. If you cannot define a conference's objective, you can hardly expect others to contribute to meeting it.

Next, consider (5) what topics the conference should cover (the agenda), (6) in what order, (7) whether one conference will be sufficient to cover all of them, and (8) what kind of conference to hold (information-giving, information-seeking, brainstorming . . .).

If you have fixed the conference's objective, agenda, and type, you are ready for the next step, (9) picking the participants. Ideally you should never invite people to participate in a conference just to keep them informed or because they might be hurt or insulted if not invited. The participants in a conference should be only those directly concerned with the problem or situation under discussion. Like most ideals, this one is hard to achieve; but the more directly each participant is involved the more successful your conference is likely to be.

Next you must take up what is probably the most important question about any conference: (10) who is to lead it. Just as a good leader can stimulate participants to achieve the objectives, a poor leader can make a conference futile. We discuss the characteristics of effective conference leadership in the next section, but basically the best leader is one who talks little but stimulates others to talk. The leader should not necessarily be the highest ranking participant—who might inhibit free interaction among the other participants.

Now nearly ready, you still have two related groups of questions to answer: (11) who is going to take notes or make and distribute a record of the conference. (Don't make the mistake of the man who handed a pad of paper and a pencil to a woman at a conference with instructions to take notes, only to have her caustically inform him that she was the treasurer of the corporation!) If you plan to tape-record the conference, will the presence of the microphone inhibit anyone? Remember, too, that tape recordings must be transcribed, a lengthy and therefore costly process.

As the final step in planning, you will need to (12) consider the location, the physical setup, and interruption-control measures. Usually you will want a conference room or an office large enough to hold all the participants. In any case you will first have to reserve the room for the time you will need it. Be sure of enough chairs. And if the meeting is large, you may want to set out name cards telling everyone where to sit.

While you are arranging for the conference room, decide if you should furnish pads of paper and pencils at each seat, whether to set out ashtrays (no ashtrays serve as a useful deterrent to smoking in a closed room), and if carafes and glasses are present, remind yourself to have them filled. Now is the time to arrange for audiovisual equipment. Finally, if the conference will be long enough to justify a break, do you want to have coffee or other refreshments available?

Controlling the temperature in a meeting room is often a problem since you must compensate for the heat generated by bodies (and a lot of bodies in a room will generate a lot of heat). An overheated room makes people drowsy, while one that is too cold keeps people thinking about their discomfort instead of the conference. A good compromise, if you can arrange it, is 68° F.

Because messages and telephone calls are common disruptions to conferences and often serve only to boost the egos of the persons receiving them, ideally you should forbid any interruptions except in cases of extreme emergency. However, you will probably not be able to do more than unplug the telephone and ask everyone's secretary not to interrupt the conference unless really necessary.

For informal meetings you may simply call the participants on the phone to tell them about it. For bigger or more formal conferences, send each a memo. In either case, inform people early enough so that they will have sufficient notice to schedule time for the conference.

The more you tell participants before the conference starts, the better they will be able to prepare for it, and the more likely they will contribute successfully. To that end, announce the objective of the conference and list the agenda. This information will help participants to gather materials they will need and also serve for the leader to refer to during the conference to keep the discussion on course. Cover also the essentials of the date of the conference, the time it will begin and the projected time it will end (to help participants plan their other activities), and exactly where the conference will meet. You may, if addressing subordinates, include an admonition to be on time and, if appropriate, things you want them to review beforehand. So everyone will know who is coming, you might well include in your memo a list of all the participants.

Leading the conference

We said above and we repeat here, a successful conference depends on effective leadership. Without direction, most meetings quickly degenerate into argument at the worst and into wasted time, indecision, or inaction at the best. Though resorting to the more esoteric rules of parliamentary procedure is usually unnecessary, a leader does need to know enough to keep the conference running smoothly by giving everyone an equal chance to contribute.

To begin with, the leader must respect the participants in the conference. Otherwise, whether superiors or subordinates, they will react angrily and turn from contributors to obstructionists. A wise conference leader, then, will never threaten, embarrass, ridicule, or insult anyone.

A conference that yields useful results comes from maximum contribution by the participants. To encourage participants, the leader should try not to dominate the conference. That is one good reason for the leader to sit with the participants, not to stand looking down at them. Anything that tends to separate or elevate the leader is counterproductive. Even a U-shaped table is a poor arrangement. An oval or rectangular table is much better; but the wise leader will sit in the middle of one of the longer sides, not at an end.

Everyone in a conference should feel free to contribute; open intercommunication is what makes a meeting into a conference. A protracted monolog or dialog that excludes others discourages them from getting into the discussion. In fact, the leader who allows such a monolog or dialog to develop implies approval of it.

Basically, then, leading an effective conference is a matter of successfully dealing with people. Here are some of the more common problem types and situations you may run into and some suggestions for handling them as a conference leader:

The nonparticipant.   Unless you think it will overly embarrass the person, try directing a question to the nonparticipant to break through the shell and bring out a contribution to the conference.

The violent argument.   When two or more participants get into an argument, allow one side to finish stating its case, then give the other side equal time. Do not allow interruptions; your goal is to help each side clearly understand the other side's position.

The private conference on the side.   Ask the people involved to share their conference with the rest of the group. If this doesn't work, ask them nicely to hold their own conference later so that you can get this one back to its task.

Leader of the revolution.   If a participant tries to take over your leadership job, a useful technique is to place the revolutionist on your immediate right or left where your eyes won't meet. If this person tries to interrupt other participants, you can effectively squelch such interruptions by a hand motion or whispering a request to be quiet until recognized.

The timid soul.   Place a shy or introverted participant directly opposite you, thus allowing responses to you rather than to the entire group.

The uninvited guest.   The best remedy for people who join your conference without being asked is to tell them to leave. If an uninvited guest is your superior, however, you may be able to do little about it except try to prevent undue interruptions.

The late arrival.   Regardless of your precautions, someone will usually come late. You can minimize the disruption by making sure that the empty chair is nearest the door. (Unless you're a very close friend and on bantering terms, snide remarks before the group are—as doctors say—contraindicated.)

The chronic arguer.   If one of those people who disagree with everything gets going, don't make the mistake of reacting directly yourself. You will split the conference into two sides, yours and the arguer's, effectively destroying your all-important neutrality. Instead, get the other participants to react to the arguer, using your position as a leader to keep the conference progressing by making the arguer the devil's advocate.

The contemplative ones.   When participants go into glassy-eyed reveries, direct questions specifically to them. If you get no reaction, just sit there a few moments until the silence does get through.

The tongue-tied participant.   When someone can't seem to get to the point or is unable to make a point, tactfully state the point back as best you understand, preferably in the form of a question, "You think the cost of the new pump is too high, right?" If you get agreement, you have helped over a rough spot.

The surprise package. If a participant brings up a point outside the scope or agenda of your conference (usually in an attempt to impress a superior or embarrass a competitor), interrupt and firmly get your conference back on the agenda (promising to discuss the point after the conference is over, if willing).

Ending the conference

Before you dismiss the participants, summarize what the conference accomplished so that everyone understands the conclusions(s) or agreement(s) reached.

Afterwards, you may want to distribute a summary or the minutes of the conference to the participants and others who should be informed. Put these in outline form, stripped of all the frills (it's no time to editorialize). Distributing the minutes serves to: (1) create a written record of what the conference accomplished; (2) assure that all the participants agree with the result(s) of the conference (you will hear if anyone doesn't!); and (3) clarify the participants' assignments, if any.

Participating in a conference

Your progress in an organization may depend heavily on how you show up in conferences. They may be the best means you have to bring yourself to upper management's (your bosses') favorable attention.

As a start, do your homework: be prepared to discuss *all* the items on the agenda, especially the interesting and important ones. A little study of the background of a major problem (causes, losses, past attempts to solve, reasons for failure, proposals for solution) can make you look good in the eyes of everybody—some of whom may not have done their homework so well. Take some time to consider carefully any ideas you may have before presenting them to a group.

As a good participant, you will want to both speak and listen; but above all, listen well. In fact, a useful and common technique is to wait until most of the others have said something before speaking yourself since you will then have more information to work from.

Even if everyone at the conference seems to be employing the technique, you can still turn it to your advantage by waiting until the silence just begins to become embarrassing and then relieving it (and the conference leader) by starting the discussion. The best entering wedge is a question rather than a statement of opinion, since a statement may unintentionally put you into opposition to other participants as they react to you. Beginning with a question is more likely to force them to make statements, which can then be to your advantage.

ELECTRONIC CONFERENCES

When people gather for conferences, in today's electronic world they no longer need to be at the same location. By telephone and by television you can set up conferences to include almost any number of people scattered virtually all over the world.

When you connect participants by telephone you are *teleconferencing*. When you connect them by television you are *videoconferencing*. Both teleconferences and videoconferences are available through the Bell System and other services or, for large organizations, through privately owned or leased equipment.

Teleconferences

At the time we write this you can set up a conference call to almost any number of participants in up to 58 separate locations. All you need do is tell the telephone operator the names and telephone numbers of the other participants and the operator will do the rest—contact the participants and notify you when they are all on the line.

For you and two or three other people, if they are available, you can have a teleconference set up in minutes. For a larger number of participants, a day or two in advance you should give the operator a list of participants and their numbers and the date and time when you want to hold the conference. The operator will contact the participants in advance (Bell does this at no charge), notify them of the conference, and make sure they will be available. Then, when it is time for the conference, the operator will link everyone together.

This convenient means of group discussion among geographically separated people is very common and you will likely take part in your first teleconference early in your career.

The two drawbacks to teleconferences are lack of visual contact among the participants and the need for the leader to exercise strict control, especially to cut off unwanted conversations between participants.

When people communicate by telephone, they cannot of course see each other nor can they show things to each other. While this means that they have none of the visual cues to communication we rely on when talking face-to-face, virtually everyone in our society has learned to deal with telephone conversations—though they require that we *listen* harder than in face-to-face situations.

The inability to show things is a more serious drawback to the telephone. Most people in business overcome this by planning, by making sure that all participants have a copy of whatever they will talk about. Even when the need to supply a document to one person on the other end of the line comes up during a telephone conversation, you can send the document in a minute or two by facsimile transmission over another line.

The second drawback to teleconferencing, the need for strict control by the leader, is not really a drawback. As we pointed out earlier, the better control you exercise over a conference the more successful your conference is likely to be. The main danger is that two or more participants will get involved in a miniconference of their own, holding a private conversation and leaving everyone else in the teleconference to listen. If you are leader, you will want to break up such private conversations as quickly as they get started. Fortunately, since people do listen harder on the telephone, you will find it easier to interrupt and regain control. Just break in and continue breaking in until everyone has stopped speaking, then reassert your control.

A lesser danger is that of participants' interrupting you and others while they are speaking. We say this is a lesser danger because most people have learned that interruptions in telephone conversations are never as productive as in face-to-face conversations. As conference leader, your job will be easier if you set the rules at the start: no one speaks without your permission. This may sound heavy-handed, but it is essential to successful teleconferencing, especially when many participants are on the line together. (Incidentally, as a general rule the more participants there are in a teleconference, the less participants talk and the more they listen.)

The advantages of teleconferencing are fairly obvious. The first is, of course, cost versus physically gathering the participants together. Even a long teleconference in the middle of a business day (when telephone rates are highest) will not come close in cost to the expense of having participants travel to a common location, incur food and lodging expenses, and return (including the hidden expense of nonproductive time while traveling).

To extend the use of teleconferences (and further reduce costs), you can gather a number of people together at each location and use Speakerphones to allow them to share the telephone. Where there are too many people to listen to and speak over a Speakerphone, the Bell System can supply special conference telephones with multiple microphones (which can even hook up to a public address system).

Videoconferences

Videoconferences are the same as teleconferences except that the participants can see each other over television as well as hear each other. At the present time videoconferencing is extremely expensive and enjoys limited use.

A few very large corporations have installed their own videoconferencing facilities, but most organizations use the Bell System's Picturephone service. As of this writing Picturephone is available in only 12 major cities, and participants must go to a Picturephone meeting center to use it.

Picturephone is a technologically advanced service incorporating a number of things. Basically each group of participants is in a room with a conference table, a camera and microphones, television screens, a graphics station, and a conference easel.

You can talk normally to the group in the other meeting center, watching them on one screen and monitoring what you are sending them on a second screen. You have complete privacy since the cameras are voice-actuated, automatically switching to the person speaking, and need no operators. You also have manual control over them and can switch at will to a wide-angle shot of all your participants.

A separate camera lets you present 35 mm transparencies, artwork, photographs, documents—even zoom in to show small objects. Facsimile machines are available to transmit documents to and from the other meeting center during a conference. And of course you can videotape your conference if you wish.

Videoconferencing is a very flexible tool and, even at its present high cost, is more economical than having participants physically travel long distances to a central location. The other drawbacks to videoconferencing in addition to cost are the limitation to a few large cities and the necessity to go to a Picturephone meeting center to use the service.

Because of the cost, the need for planning, the relatively small size of the meeting center conference rooms (more than five or six people can crowd the table), and the novelty, most participants behave themselves pretty well at videoconferences. If you have to lead a videoconference you will find that you can easily adapt the suggestions we give in the preceding section.

DICTATION

Dictation, the fourth and last of our major oral business communication forms, is easy to learn. Without some study and practice, however, you probably will not make the most effective use of this common office procedure. (You should be aware that dictating by machine is four times as fast as writing in longhand and twice as fast as dictating one-to-one to a secretary.) So what we say here is to help you be more efficient and effective in dictation. Whether you dictate directly or through a telephone and/or dictation equipment to your secretary or a typist in a stenographic pool makes few significant differences in procedure (which we shall point out).

First, however, we want to make two big points:

1. To your secretary you may dictate; to your customer, never.
2. Efficiency in dictating bad business messages is no virtue. You must know *how* to write effective letters, memos, and reports before you can dictate them (and the preceding chapters in this book will teach you).

Getting ready to dictate

Besides learning how to compose good business messages before you start dictating, you have some other preparations to make. Don't put yourself in the position of having to stop dictating (especially if directly to a secretary) to get something you should have had at hand to begin with. Get together all the information you will need: letters you need to answer, invoices you have to write about, files on matters you want to cover . . . .

Plan what you are going to say and how you will say it in each letter, memo, or other piece you are going to dictate. Make notes to yourself (perhaps right on the papers you are going to talk about), work up outlines . . . in other words, organize first. (An increasing practice that saves time for everybody involved stems from making notes on papers to be answered. Often by expanding the note a little you can really give all the answer you need to, especially in internal communications. All your secretary has to do is make a photocopy to file and return the original as an answer.) But never make the juvenile mistake of writing out your dictation in longhand and then reading it to a secretary or dictation machine!

If you are going to use a dictation machine, know what its capabilities and limitations are. Learn where all the controls are and what they do. Spend some time practicing with the machine, at home if necessary, so that when you begin to dictate you will feel relaxed and comfortable. You might well play back some of your dictation so you will know how you sound.

Dictating

Whether you dictate direct or use a telephone and/or dictation machine, dictation is dyadic communication; it involves two people, you and a secretary or typist. Regardless of the setup for your dictation, remember that a live human being will be on the other end whether you can see the person or not.

If you work with a secretary, you and your secretary must respect each other and know each other well enough to work calmly and efficiently together. You can help your secretary by setting aside a period for dictation at about the same time each day. Making it routine will help your secretary more efficiently plan a day's activities. Dictating in the morning is the best since your secretary will have the remainder of the day to transcribe the dictation, rather than waiting until the next day when shorthand notes may have cooled off.

Minimize interruptions while you're dictating. Cut off your phone and close the door if you need to. To further conserve your secretary's time, minimize your use of rough drafts. Rough drafts double or triple the time spent on a piece of writing. If, however, you have access to word processing equipment, you can often have as many rough drafts as you desire, making changes all along the way—especially useful when preparing long, involved reports.

The time to give a secretary or typist instructions is *before* you begin to dictate a message, not after you have finished. Nothing enrages a secretary more than to type a three-page message only to find at the end that you wanted a letter instead of a memo! So here's a list of things you may want to give instructions about before beginning to dictate:

1. Identify yourself if you are dictating to a machine in a word processing center or stenographic pool or in any other situation where the transcriber might not know who you are.
2. Give any special instructions, such as rush job, airmail, certified mail, and the like.
3. Specify the form of message you want: letter, memo, draft, whatever.
4. Specify the stationery: letterhead, memorandum form . . . .
5. Specify the number of carbons or photocopies.
6. Specify the names and addresses of those your message is to go to. (An efficient system in answering correspondence is to number the incoming messages with matching numbers on the dictation, letting the transcriber get the names and addresses from the messages you answer.)
7. Fully describe any enclosures.

Much of the success of your dictation will depend on how well the transcriber hears and understands you. To begin with, talk directly toward your secretary or the microphone—not to a window or to the top of your desk.

Talk naturally. If you're acquainted with the person you're writing to, try to visualize the face. Even if you are not personally acquainted, a careful look at a letter you're answering will often enable you to visualize the face behind it. Your dictation will just naturally sound more empathetic if you do. But remember that you're dictating a written message. Using natural speech patterns will help to signal pauses for punctuation, clauses, sentences, and so on. Natural speech will also help you avoid dictating in a monotone; it's deadly to listen to and can cause your transcriber's mind to wander, resulting in mistakes.

Enunciate clearly to the point of exaggeration (it won't sound exaggerated to the transcriber). Spell out words that sound alike, such as *accept* and *except,* and the names of people, places, and products unless the spelling is obvious or you are sure the transcriber knows. Spell out any unusual words and especially jargon or technical terms. Taking a few seconds to spell out something is far easier than making your secretary or typist question you about it or try to guess what you meant.

Your secretary can take your dictation easier, too, if you remain seated and resist the temptation to pace around your office, smoke, or chew gum. Some people dictate too fast and some dictate at almost a snail's pace. You can make it easier for your transcriber if you vary your speed, slowing down for difficult parts. And try not to be nervous about dictating. Nervousness is contagious.

While you should try not to dictate what the typist doesn't need (because dictating simple spelling and punctuation, for example, would imply ignorance), too much is better than not enough. If you know who will transcribe your dictation, you will know, for instance, how much punctuation to dictate. If you are unsure, play it safe and dicate any punctuation that is complex or doubtful. Do not assume that whoever types your messages will take care of spelling, punctuation, grammar, diction, and syntax for you; you will seldom have such a paragon working for you, especially early in your career.

Don't include jokes and extraneous comments when dictating. They often leave the transcriber wondering whether they belong in your message—and slow down the transcription process.

Most authorities say you should dictate paragraph breaks, and we agree. Paragraphing is an integral part of the writing process, and as an author (even of a memo) you should bear the responsibility for it. Signal a paragraph break by saying "paragraph" or "new paragraph." Many successful dictators number each paragraph when dictating to help the transcriber and to provide clear references. (The numbers do not appear on the final document, of course.)

When you want to capitalize a word, such as *computer,* say "capital computer" or "cap computer." If you want something typed all in capital letters, say "all capitals" or "all caps."

If you dictate a quotation, indicate the quotation marks by dictating "quote" and "unquote." You know the names of all the punctuation marks, and we have already advised you to dictate punctuation when the proper punctuation is not obvious. Two marks that often present problems to transcribers are the question mark (?) and exclamation point (!). To avoid uncertainty, we recommend that you always dictate these two. (Incidentally, a useful abbreviation for exclamation point is "bang.")

While dictation direct to a secretary is still in use, most people recognize that dictation equipment is more efficient and economical because (1) interruptions don't waste time while a secretary waits for the dictator to resume dictating after looking up something or answering the telephone, (2) recorded dictation doesn't cool off as shorthand notes may overnight or over a weekend, (3) a secretary can do other things in time otherwise spent taking dictation, and (4) most people dictate faster to a machine than to a person.

If you use dictation equipment, make regular use of the indicator so your transcriber will know the approximate length of your messages. A practiced transcriber who is familiar with your dictation style will know roughly how much typed copy a given spread between your indicator marks will make and can turn out a centered, balanced letter on the first try.

When you make a mistake, correct it immediately. Otherwise you may mislead your transcriber or forget to make the correction. Announce that you are going to make a correction by saying "correction," use the correction indicator to further alert your transcriber, identify what you are correcting, and dictate the corrected matter.

You can also help your transcriber by announcing the end of a message with "end of letter," "end of memo," or whatever is appropriate, as well as marking it on a machine indicator.

After dictating

First of all, turn off your machine when you are finished. You don't want it to record anything embarrassing or confidential.

When you get back your transcribed message, *read everything carefully before you sign it*. Remember, as dictator you, not the typist, are responsible for any errors.

When you must correct a typing error, be diplomatic and considerate: even the best of secretaries (or word processing machines) have off days now and then. Try to make it a learning experience for both you and the typist. Don't unnecessarily mark up a letter or memo so that it requires retyping. Use a pencil *lightly* so that the typist can erase your marks and white-out the errors without having to retype the whole page.

And—in the same vein of being a diplomatic and considerate (and wise) employer—when your secretary or typist does good work, give the deserved compliment. A compliment or a thank you may not replace a salary raise, but it does wonders for morale.

QUESTIONS

1. Of the three categories of bad speaking habits, of which are you most guilty?
2. Based on your experiences listening to speeches, do you agree with our suggestions about reading from a manuscript versus talking from memory or notes? Why or why not?
3. Of the special attention tactics we discuss for speakers, which one appeals to you most/least as a speaker/listener?
4. *a.* In Professor Endicott's list of reasons why some interviewees aren't hired, which three surprise you most by their frequency ranking?
   b. Which three do you think might have tripped you if not thus forewarned?
5. Do you wholly agree with our suggestions on talking about salary? If not, wherein and why?
6. How should you respond if a job interviewer
   a. Asks you to talk about your former employer?
   b. Asks you to tell about yourself?
   c. Allows a long pause in the conversation?
7. Of the five categories of oral business communications we discuss, which two do you expect to be the most important (not necessarily most frequently used) in your career? Which the least important?

CASES

(See p. xiii for some important explanations.)

17–1. For any of the cases for long or short written reports, prepare instead an oral report, following your instructor's directions regarding length, visual aids, and so on.

17–2. After receiving your graded analytical report (or before if time makes it necessary), assume that *(a)* your class is the board of directors which will make a decision on your recommendations, *(b)* you will have 10–15 minutes to make your report to them orally, *(c)* you will use at least one visual aid, and *(d)* the board will be judging you as an employee as well as on your report.

17–3. Read a current article on some aspect of business communication and write (as your instructor directs) a review or condensation of the article. In two or three minutes, tell your class about the review or condensed version of the article, using your jottings as speech notes, not a script.

17–4. Review the résumé checklist in Chapter 9 and prepare a well-organized written list of incomplete-sentence jottings about yourself for a stranger who is to introduce you as an expert on a topic you are to speak about (this may be you in the future, but be realistic). At random, and with only a few minutes for preparation, have a classmate introduce you using your notes.

17–5. As an alternative, assume the person who was to introduce you in the preceding case could not come. Using your notes, introduce yourself.

17–6. Individually or in groups, as your instructor directs, visit a bank, a savings and loan association, and a credit union. Give an oral report on which is the best source of a loan of several hundred dollars to tide you over for a while.

17–7. Individually or in groups, as directed, visit one each of a jewelry, sporting goods, clothing, hardware, and drugstore. Report on the differences and reasons for one of the following:
   a. Main points in their credit policies.
   b. Their furnishings and fixtures.
   c. Other areas as your instructor specifies.

17–8. When you are a half to three quarters finished with your analytical report, give an oral progress report to your classmates. Is your project on schedule? Why or why not? What will you do next? What obstacles have you encountered and how have you handled them? Will you finish on time?

17–9a. With one student playing the role of interviewer and the other playing that of applicant, conduct an employment interview before the class. For realism this should be for the job the applicant hopes to get upon graduation.
   b. Instead of an employment interview, conduct an information interview.

17–10. In a conference made up of a suitable number of students, consider any problem of national, local, or school scope, coming up with realistic solutions if possible. The student chosen as leader should be responsible for as much organizing of the conference as is appropriate. Participants may be as cooperative or obstructive as the instructor directs.

Appendixes

Appendix A: The communication process and semantic principles

THE COMMUNICATION PROCESS

Whether you are writing or talking, reading or listening, you are doing one half (sending or receiving) of the two-way process of communication.

Essential to this process are symbols—usually words. (We are not concerned here with smoke signals, smiles, gestures, winks, and other forms of nonverbal communication—though they are all parts of the whole communication story.) When you have an idea to convey to somebody, you cannot just hand it over; you necessarily use symbols of some kind. In oral communication, these are sounds; written, they become words, figures, charts, and other marks on paper. The first step in communication, then, is to formulate your ideas into symbols.

These sounds or written symbols do not communicate, however, until they go through some channel from you to the receiver.

Then, to complete the communication process, the receiver has to interpret these symbols back into an idea.

This simple-sounding three-step process of symbolizing, transmitting, and interpreting nevertheless involves many possibilities for breakdown. If the person with the idea or concept has not learned to talk or is mute, or the would-be receiver is deaf, for example, they obviously cannot communicate orally. If the sender does not know how to write, or the receiver to read, they cannot use written symbols. (Similarly, we leave to the postal service, telephone, telegraph, radio, TV, and satellite communications the manifold problems of transmitting symbols from sender to receiver with a minimum of interference (called noise in those areas).

But if the person with an idea has not learned the English language (a system of symbols) well enough to express ideas according to the system (called encoding), or if the receiver cannot interpret according to the system (called decoding), they cannot communicate effectively—and they are our problem.

SOME BASIC SEMANTIC PRINCIPLES[1]

Fundamental to communication is this general principle: *The symbols used must stand for essentially the same thing in the minds of the sender and the receiver.*

Just as our money is a medium of exchange for goods and services, our language has developed as a medium of exhange for ideas. Just as you cannot pay a bill for 35 cents by offering a quarter, you cannot convey the idea of localism by offering the word *colloquialism.* Good diction—choice of the proper word to represent the sender's idea—is thus a minimum essential in oral or written communication.

The fact that the sender's chosen words must also be in the receiver's vocabulary complicates the diction problem. You can't use perfectly good Greek to communicate to a person who knows only English. You can't use the highly technical language of medicine, law, engineering, insurance, or accounting to communicate with people who don't know the terms. They're all Greek to the nonspecialist. If you want to communicate, then, you must *estimate your receiver's vocabulary and adapt your own accordingly.* In general, you are justified in using unusual words or the special language of any field only if you're sure all your receivers know the terms or you explain them as you go along.

Even words which properly name a broad group of things for both sender and receiver, however, may still not reproduce the sender's specific concept. If you write *machine* while thinking *typewriter,* your reader is likely to envision some other machine. To communicate well, then, you must *use words specific enough* for the necessary precision.

Even then, words alone are far from the whole of the English language; *the way they're put together, punctuated, and even spelled can make a vast difference.* A bear does not have a bare skin.

To a reader who follows the English system of placing modifiers as close as possible to the things they modify, "Only three men passed the first screening" does not mean the same as "Three men passed the first screening only."

To a reader who knows anything about the punctuation of essential and nonessential clauses, "The prices which are higher than those last year for the same items are simply too high" does not mean the same as "The prices, which are higher than those last year for the same items, are simply too high."

To get the right idea, the reader has to assume that the writer didn't know

---

[1]The bibliography of semantics is extensive, and the books vary greatly in difficulty. If you want to read further on the subject, we suggest that you see the following books in the order listed: David K. Berlo, *The Process of Communication: An Introduction,* Holt, Rinehart & Winston, New York, 1960; William V. Haney, *Communication and Organizational Behavior,* Richard D. Irwin, Homewood, Ill., 1973; Stephen Ullman, *Semantics: An Introduction to the Science of Meaning,* Barnes & Noble, New York, 1978; Irving J. Lee, *Handling Barriers in Communication* (2d ed.), International Society for General Semantics, 1978; S. I. Hayakawa, *Language in Thought and Action* (4th ed.), Harcourt Brace Jovanovich, New York, 1978; Alfred Korzybski, *Science and Sanity* (4th ed.), Institute of General Semantics, Lakeville, Conn., 1958; Noam Chomsky, *Studies on Semantics in Generative Grammar,* Mouton, The Hague, 1972.

how to handle participles when writing "Having hung by the heels in the 30-degree temperature overnight, we found the venison made an excellent breakfast." That writer tried to pass a lead nickel in our medium of exchange, the English language. Remember the fundamental principle: *The symbols used must stand for essentially the same thing in the minds of the sender and the receiver.*

Here are eight specific principles as subheads of the general principle.

1. A statement is never the whole story. Even in reporting the simplest event, you omit some details. Usually you report only on the macroscopic level, omitting additional details that microscopic or submicroscopic examinations would reveal.

But you also omit much of the macroscopic. Even if you think you cover the standard *who, where, when, why, what,* and *how,* another reporter could easily add more details and more specifics on each of them. By way of illustration, consider how infrequently you see, in other reports, certain details standard in police reports of traffic accidents: mental and physical condition of the driver(s), weather conditions, condition of the car(s) and roadway, etc.

Whether you are sending or receiving the facts and arguments in a court case, you do not have the whole story. Even the witness who takes an oath to tell the truth, the whole truth, and nothing but the truth never can. Even an application letter of 10 pages cannot tell the whole life story of the applicant.

This concept of inevitable incompleteness—often called "abstracting" (calling attention to some details while neglecting others)—is basic in the thinking of semanticists. The International Society for General Semantics has therefore titled its journal *ETC.,* thus stressing Korzybski's suggestion that writers use the abbreviation as warning that their statements are incomplete.

The importance of the incompleteness concept stems from the dangers of ignoring it—the "allness" fallacy. If you consider only parts of a whole and judge the whole, you're in danger of the logical fallacy of hasty generalization and unsound conclusions. Remember the six blind men who each described an elephant so differently because each had felt a different part? If you forget that you do not have all the facts, you are in danger of closing your mind to other facts and points of view. You may think your way is the only way. You thus may become unteachable, intolerant, dogmatic, and arrogant.

Recognizing that you never have the whole story, on the other hand, helps to keep you open-minded, tolerant, and humble. That's one of the values of travel and of a broad education: to open the mind and replace the provincialism of the person who knows only a small area. The Italians have a proverb which makes the point: *Assai sa chi sa che non sa,* freely translated as "He knows a lot who knows that he doesn't know."

2. Perception involves both the perceived and the perceiver. Since you never tell the whole story, you *select those things which seem to you important.* What you say, then, depends as much on you (the kind of person you are, different from anybody else) as on what a thing really is. Your special interests, values, tastes, and attitudes cause what you say or how you react to a statement to differ from what anybody else would say or do. You are a special filter. Another filter (person) would filter out different things. Hence neither of you can be strictly objective.

When we claim to be objective, we delude ourselves—and others if they believe us. And when we expect others to be objective, we are simply being unrealistic. Constant recognition of this point will help to keep you reasonably tolerant.

A famous French movie aptly illustrates the point. The movie gives a life history (selected, of course) of each juror. It then shows different votes in the jury room, though all jurors had the same evidence.

Thorough recognition of the point can prevent disagreements by making you cautious about using *is* dogmatically. When you use *is* to connect a noun and adjective ("Harry Smith is honest"), you are saying that honesty belongs to or exists in Smith.

This predicate-adjective construction (the *"is* of predication") actually misrepresents reality and seems dogmatic if the receiver knows different facts about Smith or defines honesty differently. "Harry Smith *seems* to me . . ." might avoid an argument or even a fight.

Two subpoints about the perceiver and the perceived deserve special attention.

a. By the psychological principle of projection, we attribute to others our own characteristics and feelings. People who pay their bills assume that others will too. The reverse is also true. A credit manager—and anybody else who wants to avoid being duped—needs to realize that views of things depend heavily on the kind of person involved and that others may have different views. The wise credit manager will use the statistician's rather than the psychologist's meaning of *projection:* Get information about a credit applicant's past reputation for paying bills, project the trend line, and approve or disapprove the application accordingly.

b. Psychologists also say we resist the unpleasant. Facts and ideas contrary to our preconceptions, wishful thinking, and other selfish interests are unpleasant things we must face because they stimulate us to change our comfortable old ways. A semantically sound person will avoid the comfortable but antisemantic idea in "Don't confuse me with facts; my mind's made up."

3. Statements or actions based on whims, feelings, imaginings, preconceptions, customs, traditions, and platitudes are questionable. Although you never get all the relevant facts, and although you can never be strictly objective in evaluating those you do get, you should get what facts you can and evaluate them as objectively as you can. Ignoring observable facts will almost certainly lead you into conflict with reality.

A reasonable approach to problem solving involves two beginning questions: *(a)* What are the facts? *(b)* How do you know? Because of the importance for survival of instantaneous response in some simple situations, we have certain reflex mechanisms (blinking the eyes, sneezing, etc.) that do not involve thinking. But you are courting real trouble if you make reflex responses to complex situations. Fortunately, as situations become more complex, the allowable time for decision lengthens, and reactions become voluntary. A reasonable person will use that time to collect and consider the significant facts—as some semanticists say, will look at the territory before drawing a map; will look outside the skin for some facts instead of relying wholly on internal feelings and cogitations. To do otherwise is to act on prejudices, preconceptions, and whims.

While considering the collected data, you need to ask, "How do you know that this information is reliable?" Many platitudes, prejudices, customs, and the like stem from assumptions that simply do not line up with reality. Even well-established teachings of science changed after the discovery of new evidence by such researchers as Harvey, Pasteur, and Reed. The atom that could not be split, according to authoritative books not many years ago, has been split. More recently, discoveries in outer space are bringing into question many of the established principles astronomers and physicists have followed for years.

If scientists—who generally pride themselves on being careful in collecting data and in drawing conclusions, and who usually have good equipment—can be so wrong and so dogmatic as they have been on some of these things, should we all not learn the lesson of humility and caution? Should we not all be careful about the adequacy and the reliability of what appears to be information, and about the validity of our conclusions?

Surely we should all see the dangers of accepting information from old books. And the disagreements among authorities in almost every field should warn us to question authoritative statements or at least to check them against our own experience. Even then, reasonable humility would seem to warn that we rarely prove anything well enough to justify saying such and such *is true*.

If the careful research methods of scientists still lead to questionable results and probable truths, what of the statements of people who do not bother to get the facts at all and, without thinking or checking, act on the bases of prejudices, preconceptions, whims, etc.? A semanticist would warn you to take what they say with a few grains of semantic salt.

4. Facts, inferences, and value judgments are not the same thing. If you have ever heard a court trial, you have probably heard a judge order some testimony stricken from the record because the witness was stating opinions or conclusions (inferences) rather than things seen, heard, felt, etc. (sense data). The fact that our legal procedures do not allow inferences as evidence (except inferences by experts in the field) reflects society's faith in our sense data and its lack of faith in our inferences. Most of us would do well to be more skeptical of the mouthings of people who have not bothered to get the facts—and especially of nonexperts talking on complex topics.

You can see why if you consider the nature of sense data, inferences, and value judgments. Sense data usually approach certainty, inferences vary all the way from near certainty to slight probability (usually depending mainly on how many verifiable facts form the basis for them), and value judgments are nearly always debatable.

For example, you see a friend in a store on December 20. She tells you that she wants to buy a tie for her husband Joe and asks your help in selecting a pretty one. After she disapproves three ties you suggest and then you disapprove three she is considering, you see that the two of you don't agree (value judgments). On December 27 you see Joe wearing a tie that seems to be new and looks like one Jane suggested and you disapproved. More courteously than sincerely, you say, "That is a pretty tie Jane bought you." (Note the dogmatic *is*, discussed in Item 2 above.) Joe says he thinks it's ugly and Jane didn't buy it. You see that your value judgment matches Joe's better than Jane's; and when Joe tells you that a friend gave him the tie, you see that you took a calculated risk with your inference—and lost. (Note that to make this decision, you have to assume that Joe is reporting facts.)

Not even the courts rule out inferences completely, however. Judges make them, and jurors' votes are pure inferences. As a matter of practicality, we make and act on inferences all the time. We have to. We cannot always know with the near certainty of sense data; many times we have to act on inferences and thus take calculated risks. Even *calculated* risks, however, have *some* data base and are safer than wild guesses or hunches.

The danger in inferences is not in acting on them but in acting on them *as if* they were completely reliable. By recognizing the risks, we can reduce the danger considerably because otherwise unexpected turns of events will not surprise us.

To avoid deluding ourselves and others with whom we communicate, then, we will do well to remind ourselves and forewarn others of the *bases* on which our statements rest. A statement, like a ladder, is no more secure than its foundation. *Our readers and listeners have a right to know about the foundations if they are going to risk their necks on our ladders.*

Still, we need not make ourselves as ridiculous as the skeptical farmer who, when asked to observe a black sheep in the pasture, remarked, "At least it is black on this side." He did seem a bit ridiculous, but he was semantically no sucker.

5. *No two things are exactly alike.* Even things so much alike that they appear identical always reveal differences under close inspection. To be absolutely precise in naming things would require a different word or other symbol for each. Obviously, such precision is impractical—and unnecessary for most purposes.

General words, naming whole groups of things similar in one or more aspects, help us in classifications. Thus we can save words by talking about somewhat similar things collectively instead of individually. If what we say or do with the group applies equally well to all members of the group, we operate efficiently.

Trouble arises quickly, however, when we group things on the basis of a few similarities and then act as if all things in the group were identical. Such a situation exists when colleges try to treat all freshmen alike because all are first-year students, ignoring the great variety of interests and abilities in the individuals.

Some ugly results of ignoring differences and stressing similarities are faulty categorizing (or labeling or pigeonholing) and faulty analogy making. Thus we get the unsound, unyielding, and prejudicial stereotyping so often seen in fiction. Not all cowboys, politicians, professors, business people, delinquent credit customers, Russians, or blacks are alike—although they may have some similarities that justify the grouping *for a particular purpose*.

As a communicator, you can help solve the problem. You can *use symbols (usually words) that are specific enough for your purposes*. When you intend your statement to apply equally to a number of somewhat similar things (perhaps all new customers), be efficient and use the group name but don't lump together as delinquent accounts the good customer who got behind because of a temporary misfortune and the marginal risk who tried to skip by moving and leaving no address. And if what you say applies only to typewriters, don't say machines. If it applies only to portables, don't say typewriters. If it applies only to Royal portables, don't just say portables.

Accepting the premise of uniqueness, and recognizing the fallacy of identity, some semanticists recommend using the "which index." To distinguish individuals, they suggest using subscript numbers after the name, typewriter$_1$ being different from typewriter$_2$. Carried to extremes, this system is as impractical as the limitless vocabulary necessary to name each individual thing; but used in moderation, it can help. A little use of it will remind you of an important point: If significant differences exist in the group, make clear which members of the group you are talking about. "Businessmen who do such and such things are unethical" is quite different from "Businessmen are unethical."

You can also *consider significant differences along with similarities*. Analogies, similes, and other metaphors pointing to the similarities between two things help greatly in explanations. Indeed, they become almost necessary, because teaching and learning involve explanation of the unknown in terms of the known. Dictionaries explain words in terms of other words presumably known to the dictionary user. You often hear and read explanations in terms of a football game, which you presumably understand. Because you know English verbs generally go like *stay, stayed, stayed,* you can usually form the past tense and the past participle of a verb you have just learned. But if the new verb is *think*, the analogy misleads you.

That misleading analogy points to three warnings to make analogies helpful rather than harmful.

a. Since no two things are exactly alike, no analogy can be complete. Although *stay* and *think* are both English verbs, they belong to different classes. Although we speak of synonyms, they are alike only in some ways and are not always interchangeable.

b. Because two or more things always have some differences, *an analogy never proves anything.* The truth may slip through one of the holes of difference between the two analogous things. Stock-market and weather forecasters often err because they fail to consider significant differences in generally similar background conditions.

c. You must be sure your reader understands the supposedly known side of your analogy. Otherwise, you are, in effect, explaining a Russian word in Chinese terms to a person who knows neither language.

6. *Some either-or, black-white classifications are legitimate, but most are not.* The question is *whether your two-part classifications are mutually exclusive.* A person is either married or not; no one can be both married and not married at the same time. But you cannot say with equal validity that the same person is tall, intelligent, honest, and the like. Where do you draw the line between intelligent and not intelligent, honest and not honest?

You are being true to reality when you use either-or, black-white, *two-valued logic for mutually exclusive things*—things that cannot exist simultaneously. But most things are continua, with gradations, shadings, or degrees between the extremes. For them you need a "how-much index." Applying black-white logic to them ignores the gray. It is similar to the false dilemma in logic. And like the false dilemma, it comes mostly from the unthinking, intolerant, and dishonest among us. The results are delusions of self and others, intolerance, and hard feelings if not fights.

As a communicator, you can do several things to avoid the undesirable consequences of two-valued (polarized) thinking. First, you must recognize the difference between legitimate (mutually exclusive) two-pole classifications and continua. Then you can use the readily available facilities of English to show the proper gradations in continua. English contains not only somewhat similar nouns of varying degrees of specificity and strength but a large supply of adjectives and adverbs with similar variations. Moreover, the adjectives and adverbs have three standard degrees of comparison like *good, better, best* and *speedily, more speedily,* and *most speedily.* If you still feel the need for better indication of the degree of grayness in a continuum, you can always *add* specific details, as in "Quickly (3.2 seconds) the operator turned the heavy (5-ton) crane around and . . . ."

7. *Things change significantly with time.* Nature is a dynamic process. As part of nature, Joe Smith today is not exactly the same as Joe Smith yesterday, much less 10 years ago. Significant aspects of a present situation may not have existed in the past and may not continue in the future. To be true to reality, you need to *consider the date* in connection with statements sent or received. Some semanticists refer to this principle as the necessity for the "when index." Ignoring it produces what some call the "frozen evaluation."

Most universities recognize the point (consider the date) in readmitting students, after specified lengths of time, after dropping them for poor scholarship or infraction of rules. On the other hand, we have many instances of frozen evaluations. Most homes would run more smoothly if parents would recognize that their teenagers are no longer babies. Exconvicts could readjust to normal living much more easily if their neighbors would at least give them a chance to show whether they have changed, instead of pinning permanent labels on them after they've paid their penalties. We should rescind many of the blue laws on statute books.

To unfreeze some of our thinking, we may as well get used to reinterpretations of the Constitution—and to changed usages and new dictionaries of English. Our language is not static. Fighting new English textbooks and new dictionaries (which do not make but merely *record* current usage) is more futile than fighting city hall; it's fighting the whole country. Surely a credit manager should know that the facts which force refusal of requested credit may change in a few months—and should hold open the possibility of reconsidering them.

8. Words are not identical to the objects they represent. Words are just symbols of concepts that exist only in the mind. They do not have meanings themselves but only the power to represent or evoke meanings in our minds.

Concrete objects stimulate our various senses to give us our concepts of those things. We then use words to represent those concepts. Only the physical objects are real; our concepts and the symbols (words) to represent them are the first and second levels of abstraction in the "ladder of abstraction" or "structural differential" which semanticists talk about.

In this scheme, clearly the names we give are not the things themselves—even names that have referents (concrete, tangible objects to which they refer). If you question this statement, try eating the word *candy* the next time you get hungry for something sweet. Or since a word is to its referent as a map is to its territory, just take a walk on your map the next time you want to take a trip. As Korzybski repeatedly explains, our words merely represent the world of events and things outside our skins but are never the real things. Ogden and Richards (*The Meaning of Meaning*) present the symbolic nature of language as a triangle, the three points representing referent, thought, and symbol.

This semantic principle of the symbolic nature of language points to these suggestions for better communication:

a. Insofar as possible, use words with real physical objects or actions as referents, and make them specific enough to call to the receiver's mind the particular referent. If your receiver has seen or touched the kind of thing you are talking about, the concepts you want to convey about it are clearer than if you talk in generalities or talk about abstractions (concepts like loyalty and honesty that do not exist in the physical world but only in the mind). Even when your word has a referent, avoid equating the word with the physical object (for which it is only a symbol) or with some facet of it: "Russia *is* the Berlin Wall" or "Communism *is* . . . ."

b. Although you cannot avoid the use of some abstract words (which have no referents in the physical world), try to keep them to a minimum. Then consider the context in which you use them. If you have described several actions taken and then you commend the person for *integrity*, the context makes clear what you mean by the otherwise abstract word *integrity*. That's the best way to use abstract words—as summarizing words.

c.   Especially in reading and listening, try to look behind the words and envision the things and ideas the words represent. You can remember the thought much easier than all the exact words used to represent it. And in taking notes or answering questions about what you've heard or read, present the concepts in your own words except for key words and phrases. If you concentrate on words, you'll likely learn the words and repeat them parrotlike without understanding the thought they convey. Instead, concentrate on "What does the message sender mean by those words?"

Appendix B: Listening and reading

Speaking and writing are forms of the initiating or encoding phase of communication. Listening and reading are forms of the receiving or decoding phase. Considerable skill in each is vital for a literate individual in today's civilization.

Most work in schools deals with writing, reading, and—to a lesser extent—speaking. We can make our learning and living much easier if we develop and maintain skill in listening (to TV, radio, lectures, sermons, interviews, conferences, directives, conversations, etc.), which accounts for about three times as much of our communication time as reading does!

The task of listening[1]

Neither good reading nor good listening is easy. Both require training, either supervised or self-disciplined. Of the two, listening is the more demanding and the more difficult for most of us. The written word is always there to go back to. The spoken word, once uttered, is gone unless stored in the hearer's mind (a job that most of us do not perform well). The reader can proceed at a self-chosen speed; the listener must adapt to the speaker's pace.

Learning to be a good reader does not make you a good listener, either. Several differences explain why. Not only are the styles different (greater variety in sentence length and style, much more use of phrases, more personal references, more informality, more repetitions, and more adaptations in the oral), but the role of the nonverbal is even more significant. A speaker's gestures, facial expressions, pitch of voice, inflections, rhythm, speed, and pronunciation constantly affect the final message to listeners. The reader uses eyes alone. The listener uses eyes and ears.

We talk much more slowly than our minds can comprehend what we hear. Since our minds operate so much faster than our mouths, when someone is

---

[1] See Eastwood Atwater, *Listening Skills to Make You a Better Manager*, Prentice-Hall, New York, 1981; Ralph G. Nichols and Leonard A. Stevens, *Are You Listening?* McGraw-Hill, New York, 1957; Ralph G. Nichols and Thomas R. Lewis, *Speaking and Listening*, Wm. C. Brown, Dubuque, Iowa, 1965; and J. Sims and P. Peterson, *Better Listening Skills*, Prentice-Hall, Englewood Cliffs, New Jersey, 1981.

talking we tend to think about what we are going to say next and we cease to concentrate on what the other person is saying.

Learning to listen well is the single biggest thing you can do to improve your own personal relations. When you really listen to someone, you take a big step toward avoiding conflict by *understanding* that person. Further, when you listen well, you help others to work out their problems (listening is, after all, the basis of counseling and psychiatry). Good listening will lead others to communicate full information to you, and fuller information will help you to be more successful. Finally, as you demonstrate good listening, you will lead others to improve their listening practices, resulting in an overall improvement in communication.

Although in everyday living you will listen and learn in interviews, lectures, conferences, and conversation, the following suggestions apply primarily in listening to speeches and lectures.

Identify the subject and plan. Most speakers will deliver planned talks organized in the traditional pattern of introduction, thesis, body, and conclusion.

Many speakers will tell a story, quote from some authority, or say something startling first to secure attention. Many excellent lecturers dispense with the irrelevant beginning and start immediately with genuine subject matter, and wisely so.

The essential time for concentration is when the speaker announces the subject, why it is pertinent, and the plan of presentation. If you are not tuned in for this thesis statement, you are going to have difficulty following the rest.

Stay tuned in. The body of the speech (the longest part) includes the several points that support the speaker's thesis. The evidence may be statistics, testimony, stories, and/or explanation and logical analysis.

Major points and the evidence supporting them may come in *deductive* order (usual if the purpose is only to inform). This is, stated very simply, generalization followed by supporting detail. If the purpose is to persuade, an *inductive* order (generalization after evidence) will be better—and more likely if the speaker is a good one.

Obviously, this is the part on which you should exercise your concentration and your critical faculties. *The questions of completeness, validity, appropriateness, and recency are significant here.*

You will find this part easier to follow (and more interesting) if you check the speaker's announced plan against delivery and *stay on the alert for transitions*—those statements signaling a change of point. The points or principles (the *ideas*) fill in the blueprint of the plan and establish the final structure. The *facts* supporting the principles are subheads.

If the speaker announces no plan, try to anticipate what is coming. If your guess proves right, you'll feel pleasure—and probably reveal it in feedback to the speaker. And if you're wrong? Never mind, you'll have concentrated better and benefited from the mental exercise.

Good speakers (and good writers) build up their points or principles step by step. In an informative speech the conclusion is often very short. It may be no more than a quick recap of the main points and a brief statement of how the subject is significant. The conclusion of a persuasive speech may be a little longer. The persuasive speaker may not reveal a stand until the end. In addition to establishing the real objective, some speakers may use strong argument. Question. Challenge. But reserve judgment until you've had the time to sift and reevaluate—to review and rebuild.

When you're the trapped victim of a speaker who indulges in harangue, cajoling, or bombast (especially if backed only by scant, prejudiced, one-sided, or unsound facts or logic), tune out; you're entitled to stop listening.

Be sensible; control your note-taking. The temptation to record a speaker's words *verbatim* is too great for many listeners—unfortunately. This kind of note-taking causes listeners to lose significant ideas, to become confused, and to give up on note-taking—and usually on listening also.

Most speakers and lecturers agree that good listeners take good notes— and that those who take good notes *listen a lot and write a little*. Possibly the best piece of advice we can give you is to keep your notes brief and clear during listening (complete thoughts for major points; just words and short phrases for supporting details). You can expand and review later.

Rarely does an introduction merit recording. Even the thesis is better not written down when first stated. (Write it down after you've heard enough to state it precisely.) Even the brief outline or plan (if the speaker gives you one) is better recorded point by point as you go along. Strive to understand each main point your speaker makes. If you're preoccupied with catching errors or taking notes, you won't get the message. Withhold your judgments until you have reviewed the main ideas and thesis.

Careful distinction between fact and idea leads a listener to note-taking that is economical and efficient. Divide your paper into two columns, one for principles and one for facts. You'll have difficulty determining which is which sometimes. But the effort will help you concentrate and will provide enough useful reminders for later review. You'll have more entries in your facts column than in your principles column. If you have to slight the recording of one, slight the facts; concentrate on the principles.

The sooner you can review your notes after the speech, the better. As you listened, you should have mentally questioned for completeness, adequacy and appropriateness, authenticity, recency, and omission of data. An even more fruitful time to do this, however, is shortly after the talk—in a review of notes, supplementing and rebuilding, questioning, searching for negative evidence, and finally arriving at an evaluation.

Avoid the main stumbling blocks to good listening. Without the wish and the will to, you won't profit from anyone's suggestions. Our pointing out some common failings, however, may help you to improve.

To begin with, accept the fact that listening demands patience and an open mind—a considerate, even charitable, mind. The temptation to tune out and escape to reverie or daydreaming is ever with us.

Sometimes we are prone to pretend attention when our minds are not receiving any ideas. No speaker with much experience gets fooled by the head nodder, the glassy-eyed starer, the marbleized thinker. Such audience characters are only fooling themselves. They are no more interested in listening than the foot tapper, the pen flipper, the book slammer, etc. If you fall in one of these classes, wake up—and learn.

Another stumbling block is undue attention to the speaker's appearance, voice, or speech characteristics. A speaker's appearance is only an outward shell, not an indicator of mind; speech is only the vehicle, not the idea. Although we do respond almost automatically more to good-looking people, don't shut yourself off from learning because of a person's physiognomy, size, dress, or voice characteristics. The mind may have a lot to contribute.

All too often we abruptly reject or dismiss a speaker and subject because we consider them dull or difficult. Remember that the dull speaker is probably doing just what the assignment was—to give you facts and ideas—and refusing to insult your intelligence, or take pay under false pretenses, by entertaining you instead. Be selfish: Take for yourself what is meaningful and useful. Very few uninteresting speeches are devoid of something useful.

As for rejecting the difficult discourse, remember that this can become a pattern of progressive mental deterioration. The more you do it, the flabbier and more superficial your mind becomes. The only suggestions we can make are continually renewed determination to hear the speaker out and a planned effort to tackle uninteresting as well as difficult material.

Another stumbling block is the tendency of listeners to let physical surroundings distract them. Airplanes, buses, trains, thunder, and other outside noises are sometimes loud, and rarely can the listener do anything about them. But they are noises that most of us easily ignore when we want to (during a favorite TV program, for instance).

Many times, however, you can control physical circumstances. Windows and doors close as well as open. Heating mechanisms turn off as well as on. If you can't control the distraction, enlist the aid of the speaker. Even if neither can do anything and can't move to a more favorable place, both will have to exert extra effort to concentrate on effectively sending and receiving the message.

A reminder of something we already said will summarize the key point: In your listening, concentrate on principles, not detailed facts presented in support of principles. Emphasis on facts makes you lose principles, which are the most significant parts of speeches; emphasis on principles makes you not only get the principles or ideas but also helps you remember many of the facts that support them.

Efficient reading

Much of what we've said about listening also applies to reading. We shall therefore discuss this form of the receiving phase of communication in much less detail.

If reading only for pleasure, you can relax and be almost passive as you proceed at whatever pace you please. If you are not satisfied with your reading pace, you may want to enroll for one of the reading-improvement courses offered by many schools and counseling services or clinics. The aim of these courses is to increase the reader's rate and comprehension. If no such work or counseling is available, you may want to read some of the excellent books on the subject.[2]

If you are reading for information and instruction (as opposed to pleasure or entertainment), you can profit even more from such courses and books. The following brief suggestions give you only the main points of some of them.

When you read an informative publication (book, section, chapter, or article):

1. Understand the scope and limitations of the subject as shown in the title and often in a subtitle, the preface, and introductory comments.

2. Determine the primary purpose, which may be only implied. Phrase it in your own words.

3. Take advantage of mechanical aids (indentions, paragraphing, outline symbols, change of type, etc.) and transitions as you read through the first time *rapidly*. Don't ponder over phrases or even whole sentences; don't look up definitions. *Read through and read fast!*

4. When you've finished, try to recall as much as you can. Check the theme or central idea you have formulated againt the author's expression of it either in the ending or in the beginning.

5. Reread the material paragraph by paragraph. (The first rapid reading will decrease your reading time at this stage, and much that was foggy the first time will be clear.) If you own the material (but not in library or borrowed materials, please!), underscore key words and topic sentences, often at the beginning or end.

Then you can take further steps:

1. If you are reasonably certain of the meaning of a word from the context, you are probably safe in not looking it up. Otherwise, look it up and pencil the appropriate definition in the margin.

2. When the article or chapter is fairly short and not formally organized, you're probably better off simply to write a short précis.

3. When the article or chapter is formally organized, you may want to write a formal outline. Such outlining is another step in remembering and is vital if you need to submit an oral or a written report.

These suggestions apply if you want or need to do more than record and possibly transmit what some author wrote. If you want or need to evaluate (as for a review), you will have to answer such questions as the following:

---

[2]We suggest that you start with these books in this order (some of them have bibliographies to direct you further): Mortimer J. Adler, *How to Read a Book,* Simon & Schuster, New York, 1940; A. L. Raygor and D. M. Wark, *Systems for study,* (2d ed.), McGraw-Hill, New York, 1979; George D. Spache and Paul C. Berg, *The Art of Efficient Reading,* Macmillan, New York, 1978; and A. L. Raygor and G. B. Schick, *Reading at Efficient Rates,* (2d ed.), McGraw-Hill, New York, 1980.

1. About the author:
   Who? Position or status? Authority? Biased?
2. About the treatment:
   a. Are generalizations supported by evidence? Ample? Secondary or primary? Based on sound research?
   b. Is coverage of major points adequate? Significant omissions?
   c. What is the announced or apparent intended audience? Is treatment adapted to this audience?

You can add to this list. Certainly we do not intend it to be exhaustive.

Appendix C: Intercultural business communication

Few people or organizations in America, whatever sector of our economy they occupy, are not involved in some way with other countries (and hence their cultures). In fact, 2 million Americans now work within the borders of the United States for foreign employers (14:9).[1]

Because contact with people in other cultures is common today in so many jobs, we offer the information in this appendix to help you prepare yourself for effective communication in the rapidly growing international business, where (as a likely future business manager) you will almost certainly need to be informed to be effective.

The area of international business communication is so vast that we cannot, of course, cover all of it. But we can help you better understand the problem areas and suggest ways to hurdle language barriers. The selected bibliography at the end of this appendix contains sources of information that in turn will lead you to much more information.

Main problem areas and approaches to solutions

Distance no longer presents the barrier to transportation and communication it once did. Well-established worldwide transportation facilities (and freight forwarders as intermediaries) are available almost everywhere. Though surface mail is relatively slow, wordwide airmail is almost as fast as our domestic service; and telex and facsimile transmission are nearly instantaneous and becoming quite economical, thanks to satellites. World banks in major countries provide essentially all the services for international trade that local banks do for domestic—especially for collections through letters of credit.

Language problems in international business are only a little greater than those within America (the concern of most of this book)—and they have various solutions. Either party to a transaction may know the other's language or employ an interpreter or other bilingual intermediary (say a freight forwarder or the international branch of a bank). If you are dealing with someone from another culture who knows a little English, you can negotiate for it as the common language and adapt as we explain in a later part of this appendix.

---

[1]Meaning page 9 of Item 14 in this section's bibliography.

Cultural differences cause the main problems and are therefore the main concern of this appendix. A few embarrassing instances will show the need for attention to the explanations there—to avoid stepping in potholes. Taboos (such as not serving liquor to Muslims) are probably overrated as problems because they are so obvious. But faux pas or potholes demand attention.

> For instance an American businessman invited to a formal dinner while in Saudia Arabia noticed his hosts were ignoring him. If he had known about Middle Eastern culture, he would have realized that he insulted the hosts by using his left hand (the toilet hand to them) for eating from a communal serving platter.

> A soft-drink company named a new product Three Stars and put three six-pointed stars on the label. Because of the similarity to the Israeli Star of David, Libya banned the product.

> The Hopi Indians protested when a distillery put its bourbon in bottles similar to the kachina dolls that represent Hopi holy spirits.

> A U.S. petroleum engineer in Bangladesh started a plantwide walkout by insisting (nastily) that a Bengali assistant come to work early the next morning (in the emergency) even after the assistant objected because it was Eid (the major Muslim holiday).

> An American organizational specialist started turmoil in a formerly peaceful family business in India by instituting a new organization chart that placed the youngest male member of the family (because he had an MBA) above two older cousins (contrary to the Indian deference to age).

Understandable English for nonnative receivers

The world has approximately 3,000 languages, though estimates run as high as 10,000 with the inclusion of dialects—India alone counting 15 languages and 200 dialects (10:3). Obviously you aren't going to learn (or need to learn) all of them. For the relatively few areas where you'll be operating—minus the number where the other party knows English—you can, however, be a better communicator (even with an interpreter) by mastering some useful phrases and reading about the local culture. Books, articles, monographs, films, tapes, visitors, immigrants, and other informants can help.

Even when the other party knows only a little English, you may be able to operate better (with or without an interpreter) by making your English easily understandable. Since the choice of language for intercultural business is usually a point in preliminary negotiations, try to get agreement on English. (It is the most widely used.) Since you will probably have to write many reports to your home company in the United States, superiors in other countries, and superiors in your adopted country—some of whom will not know English as their native tongue—these 10 suggestions will help you to write understandably.

1. Use simple, precise words. Be sure every word used means exactly what the dictionary says it means. When you mean *think*, do not say or write *feel*. For precision and their usual similarity in various languages, even technical words may help. Still you may have trouble with some semitechnicals. For example, we have seven names for the colors in the spectrum; but Bassa (Liberian) has only two—*hui* for the cool colors and *ziza* for the warm.

2. *Use concrete words* insofar as possible (words naming things you can see, feel, hear, taste, or smell—not abstractions like *idea, concept, belief*).

3. *Avoid slang, jargon, buzz words* like the current use of *impact* as a verb and made-up words like acronyms and product names (unless explained or clear from context, easy to pronounce, and free from undesirable denotations and connotations).

In general such terms are useful only between native speakers of the same language, and then only in appropriate circumstances. Alphabet soup surrounds us—FBI, IRS, AACSB. We assume you know AACSB stands for American Assembly of Collegiate Schools of Business. Could we also assume that you know the acronyms DOS (disk operating system), UNESCO (United Nations Educational, Scientific and Cultural Organization)? Since that's doubtful, we should avoid them in intercultural business.

Product names and advertisements also require attention. The long name that is not easily pronounceable and is specifically American is not suitable. Some of the names that travel well abroad are Ford, Kodak, Coca-Cola, and Sears. Esso even got that name partly because in most languages it is easy to pronounce. When General Motors advertised "Body by Fisher" in Belgium, however, it appeared in Flemish as "Corpse by Fisher." "Come Alive with Pepsi" nearly appeared in the Chinese translation of *Reader's Digest* as "Pepsi Brings Your Ancestors Back from the Grave."

Denotations and connotations can cause trouble too. A manufacturer planned to market a new leather-care product in Europe under the name Dreck (because that sounded virile) but changed the name quickly on discovering that in German the word means dung. Similarly, Pepsi-Cola changed its name for a new noncola drink from Patio to Mirinda because of the connotation in Spanish (25:24).

As we move from considering simple, precise, concrete, standard words to putting them together in phrases, sentences, paragraphs, and whole messages, we find another group of helpful suggestions. Even the great Dr. Samuel Johnson (author of the famous first English dictionary, 1755) recognized the problem: "Ask me the meaning of any English word and I'll tell you; but put two of them together and God knows what they mean."

4. *Avoid idioms and figurative expressions.* We native speakers learn idioms and figurative expressions largely by the osmosis of growing up hearing them. Other people, not having had that chance, find that learning the vocabulary, grammar, and syntax of English does not serve the purpose. Indeed therein lies the basic definition of idioms, of which English is full. For example, try to explain to anyone of another culture what you mean by "take that with a grain of salt," or "left holding the bag," or "has ants in the pants."

Similarly, our numerous figurative expressions do not mean what the words, grammar, and syntax say literally. They depend on analogy or parallelism to something else the reader or listener supposedly knows. By making a "Duke's mixture" of this sentence, we can illustrate (with the four quotes) how it would cause a nonnative speaker of English to "fumble the ball" and be caught "out in left field" because it "throws a curve."

As a side note you'll see that we've illustrated with terms from games because in our culture you'll find many references to games—as is true of the French, German, and Swiss cultures too (7). But mostly they play different games, on the field and on the page. People in the United States write and talk a lot about team play and good or bad team players. We have war games like "Gettysburg," video games, and best sellers like *Games People Play*. But to use these national (not international) idioms and figurative terms to someone in another culture adds confusion.

5. *Lower your Fog Index.* Because the percentage of hard words (three or more syllables) and the average sentence length (in words) determine the Fog Index, use short words and sentences instead of long ones. While Robert Gunning gives specific directions for figuring the index (in *The Technique of Clear Writing*, explained in our Chapter 2), general guidelines for native users of English are *(a)* no more than 1.5 times as many syllables as words and *(b)* an average below 19 words for sentence length. For export, both counts should be a little lower.

6. *Keep paragraphs short and unified*—to no more than 8–10 lines (with a lower average). How could a business representative from Korea understand a message written in long, compound-complex sentences with wildly digressive paragraphs?

7. *Organize what you say*—each sentence, paragraph, and whole message. Lay out a plan (in outline or other form), with the major divisions in order and clear indications of their subdivisions (again in order). You have to decide on the order, based on a principle such as importance, logic, reader psychology, chronology, or dramatic effect. The direct message that has related ideas grouped together with logical sequencing (avoiding all nonsense or haphazard sequencing) will be easy to read and understand.

8. *Guide your reader (or, even more important, your listener)* with adequate, clear coherence and transition devices. Within sentences the simple conjunctions and prepositions plus unity of topic and purpose are the glue that holds the sentence together coherently. For the several sentences in a paragraph, a good topic sentence and a summarizing one need only a little help from proper sequencing and (possibly) a few gluing words like *moreover* and *furthermore*.

Topic and summarizing sentences plus strong transitional words like *conversely* and *nevertheless* also help as reader guides to transitions between paragraphs and between even longer sections. For the last, however, divisional and subdivisional headings may be necessary. An important point is to give the reader or listener a clear signal, before going down the road too far, when making a major change of direction. Strong direction-changing words like "on the contrary" are exceptions to the generally sound objection (because of overemphasis) to transitional words as sentence beginnings.

9. *Avoid distortions of truth in all forms.* U.S.-style *exaggerations* are misleading or confusing and hard to explain in other cultures. For example, when an American said "I have cooked all day and there are tons to eat," she quite confused her Japanese friends. The Japanese hostess (in reverse exaggeration, because the Japanese hostess prefers to humble herself) would more likely say "Nani mo gazaimasen," which means literally "There is nothing to eat."

Similarly, Americans have to watch that they don't talk in *superlatives* (which surround us and don't give us the best image in other countries)—superlatives like when a sales manager says "We make the best junction boxes you can buy" and others brag about the busiest airport, the largest state, the tallest building, the richest dessert.

Also avoid unnecessary and inaccurate *qualifiers* (such as *maybe, probably, almost, always, never, often, frequently*). If a person goes too far and skips necessary qualifiers, or uses such categorical ones as *always* and *never*, the result is exaggeration. Speakers and writers from different cultures may use qualifiers with different frequencies and for different reasons. An English speaker will say "It will rain tomorrow." A Japanese will say, "It probably (maybe) will rain tomorrow." To the Japanese the *will* is too cocksure for a mere prediction.

10. *Whenever helpful, use numbers, graphics* (pictures, drawings, tables, graphs, charts), and forms to supplement words. In general they have the great advantage of knowing no language or geographical boundaries.

For this reason standard printed forms play a large role in international trade. Except for the space they would take (increasing the price of this book) and the fact that they don't teach you how to phrase business messages well (our main purpose), we would show you a dozen or more. Here are, however, brief descriptions of eight forms (out of 13, plus many letters) used in a comparatively small transaction ($16,000—a U.S. manufacturer who found a market and sold the first 1,000 fire extinguishers to a Brazilian agent/distributor).

(1) The natural start was to use the U.S. Department of Commerce (US-DOC) form "Request for Agent/Distributor Service." Besides small blocks for date, name, address, telephone, foreign country, it asks for kind of company and qualifications needed, related products, signature(s), and brief description of products for sale.

(2) Naturally, USDOC would have a reply form (Agent/Distributor Service Telegraphic Reply). The reply listed three "Following firms interested corresponding" and added "Comment: No manufacturers of chemical extinguishers in Brazil. Favorable market for U.S. manufacturers."

(3) Pro forma invoice to selected agent/distributor: usual invoice information (names, addresses, date; table of number, description, packaging, charges,

terms), irrevocable letter of credit in dollars confirmed by seller's bank for full CIF (cost, insurance, freight) value.

(4) Banco do Brasil's standard letter of credit and order (with specifications) by telex.

(5) USDOC form "Shipper's Export Declaration"—shipper and buyer names, addresses, shipping arrangements (loading/unloading ports, freight forwarder, description of goods, packing, weight, value).

(6) Freight forwarder's "Certificate of Origin"—identifications of self, seller, buyer; description of goods; import permit number; certification.

(7) Signed Bill of Lading with covering in-transit insurance policy: names and addresses; vessel (flag, voyage number, loading port); description of cargo (product, packaging, weight), verified loading data, import permit number, freight prepaid.

(8) Invoice to buyer and forms bankers use in settling a letter-of-credit collection are essentially the same as in domestic transactions.

The oral counterparts to written numbers, graphics, and forms are gestures and other forms of body language. They have *some* of the same advantages of universal meanings—but not all. A smile is a smile and a frown a frown— worldwide; but in intercultural communications you do have to be wary of significant differences in attitudes, procedures, customs, and meanings of the many thousands of possible gestures in different cultures.

Awareness of cultural differences

When you try to relate effectively to anyone, within or outside your own culture, you realize that you need to empathize with the other person and to understand verbal and nonverbal communication. You have a tremendous challenge to understand (and be understood by) even those closest to you; so you can realize the challenge of intercultural communication.

Easiest among your problems will be your writing or speaking about products and procedures (including the specific terms of contractual agreements). As Hall says (11), they are largely on the "technical" level and involve little emotion and few intercultural misunderstandings.

Your necessary relations and responses to your host country's (or countries') rituals such as marriages, births, burials, and holidays (particularly church and state) will be more difficult and dangerous. They are Hall's "formal" level and are filled with emotions and hence potholes for the unwary. To be safe, you need to study the various local systems—religious, political, societal, educational, economic, recreational, health, transportation, and entertainment (as host or guest).

Even more numerous (though individually less serious—but still deserving some prior study plus constant alertness) are Hall's "informal" relations, where good manners call for almost automatic proper responses. An example is recognizing the roles local people play with others of different rank or sex. In these informal relations, particularly, body language and other nonverbal communications are especially important. Though too varied and numerous to treat in detail here, a few examples will help to clarify.

Gestures and body language.   The human body is capable of over 270,000 different gestures (10:182)—and meanings of quite similar ones vary with where you are. Snapping the fingers of both hands and slipping an open palm over a closed fist are vulgar gestures (thus meanings) to the French. They also consider a firm and pumping handshake uncultured (14:225). When dealing with Arabs, don't cross your legs so that the sole of your foot points toward someone—it is impolite. Don't turn your back on an Iranian—that, too, is impolite.

Head shaking in some cultures has nothing to do with saying yes or no, as Joan Rubin points out. She says that Turks signal no by moving the head backwards while rolling the eyes upwards. In parts of India, rolling the head slowly from side to side means something like "Yes, go on; I'm listening" (22:73).

Attitudes toward time.   Americans generally view time as money, a resource to be saved or wasted; Mexicans regard time in relation to other priorities. In Mexico standards of punctuality are less strict (Mañana—why not—the future inevitably comes). Interviews, meetings, and letters begin with an exchange of personal greetings before business discussions—with discussions being much longer than is customary in the United States. Americans seem preoccupied solely with getting the job done. Africans view time as flexible and not rigid or segmented. People may arrive several hours late. The term *African time* means the same as the *hora Peruana* in Spanish. In contrast, Germans are precise about the clock.

Personal space.   Americans prefer about 30 inches for face-to-face impersonal conversation while Arabs want a distance of half that (14:227). Latin Americans and Vietnamese want to be closer when talking than do Americans. Polynesian men embrace and rub each other's backs. Some Europeans kiss the sides of the face. Americans seem to prefer to be individually cased in an imaginary bubble that protects them and keeps them from breathing down the other person's neck.

Dress and appearance.   The type of climate and kind of culture influence the way the people dress. We're all aware of the Japanese kimono, African headdress, English bowler and umbrella, and the Polynesian sarong. Keep in mind that you (as a representative from your company and country) should dress to make a positive impression.

Some top managers from America (dressed in plaid suits and white buck shoes) lost a big deal with some Japanese business people because the Japanese said they didn't trust these Americans because of the kind of dress they wore.

Food and eating habits.   Americans enjoy beef, but Hinduism forbids it. Chinese and others enjoy pork, the forbidden food in Moslem and some Jewish cultures. Eating habits differ from eating with hands to eating with silverware to eating with chopsticks. Even the way of holding the silverware varies between Americans and Europeans.

You can learn something about the culture of a country by enjoying the food. So, when in Germany try their stollen (Christmas bread); in Italy, panettone (coffee cake); in Russia, kulich (Easter bread); in Ireland, barmbrack (fruit bread); in Yugoslavia, potica (coffee cake); or try a Swedish coffee ring or a Danish kringle—all different—all good. Taste the Irish coffee, Syrian coffee, and Chinese tea.

Adaptations to cultural differences (beliefs and attitudes)

Religion affects people's views of life, death, hereafter, superstitions, and even their holidays and work attitudes. Religion is the heart of a country's culture (25).

One of the explanations of the American attitude of honoring work is our Puritan/Calvinist/Judeo-Christian background. Judaism emphasizes work and achieving. To the Roman Catholics, however, work is not so important as it is to people of other faiths. The numerous religious holidays in most of Europe and Central and South America can play havoc with work and time schedules.

The Hindus and Buddhists are less attached to worldly goods than the Judeo-Christians. Buddhism, Confucianism, Taoism, and Hinduism dominate the Oriental cultures.

Religion expresses the philosophy of a people about many important facets of life—such as the role of women. Some societies enshrine women, others treat them like equals, and others treat them like chattel.

Not only the treatment of women but of elders and children varies from one culture to another. The hierarchy in other cultures as well as the patrilineal (male line of the family) plays a part in business throughout the world.

Where Americans regard change as an improvement, Chinese revere tradition; Latin Americans are fatalistic.

With all these many different angles, you might think about viewing different cultures as you would look at a beautiful diamond. Hold up this diamond of different cultures and see the different lights so that you can better appreciate the beauty of human variations and capabilities.

We must emphasize that to characterize the style of a culture does not mean that all its members, all the time, in all social circumstances, manifest the same attributes. We have touched on just some of the similarities and differences of some of the cultures. To understand any other country, you must study many facets—and thereby see many lights in those diamonds.

The key point in *having an awareness* of these cultural differences is this: In communicating with people of any different culture, you do not need to *adopt* their ways and beliefs, but you do need to *adapt* to them. You *must* avoid (whether because of ignorance or intent) *belittling* or *showing contempt or disdain*. Or, most important of all, you must *neither flaunt your own ways and beliefs nor flout theirs*.

BIBLIOGRAPHY

1. *Alabama Exporting Guide*, The International Trade Center, University of Alabama, University, Alabama, 1980.
2. Asante, Molefi K., Eileen Newmark, and Cecil A. Blake (ed.), *Handbook of Intercultural Communication*, Sage Publications, Beverly Hills, Calif., 1979.
3. Boulding, Elise, *Women: The Fifth World*, Foreign Policy Association, New York, 1980.
4. *The Bridge,* Systron Corporation, Denver, Colo. (quarterly).
5. Condon, John C., and Fathi S. Yousef, *An Introduction to Intercultural Communication*, Bobbs-Merrill, Indianapolis, Ind., 1975.
6. _____,and M. Saito (eds.), *Communicating across Cultures for What?* Simul Press, Tokyo, 1976. Distributed by International Scholarly Book Services, Beaverton, Oregon.
7. Craig, JoAnn, *Culture Shock!* Time-Life Books, Signapore, 1979.
8. Desatnick, R. L., and M. L. Bennett, *Human Resource Management in the Multinational Company*, Nichols Publishing Co., New York, 1978.
9. Dynsza, William A., *Multinational Business Strategy*, McGraw-Hill, New York, 1972.
10. Eisenberg, Abne, and Ralph R. Smith, *Nonverbal Communication*, Bobbs-Merrill, Indianapolis, Ind., 1971.
11. Hall, E. T., *The Silent Language*, Anchor-Doubleday, New York, 1973.
12. _____, "How Cultures Collide," *Psychology Today*, 10:66–7, July, 1976.
13. Hamelink, Cees, *The Corporate Village*, International General, Rome, Italy, 1977.
14. Harris, Philip R., and Robert T. Moran, *Managing Cultural Differences*, Gulf Publishing, Houston, 1979.
15. Hoopes, D. S. (ed.), *Readings in Intercultural Communication*, vols. I–II, Regional Council for International Education, University of Pittsburgh, 1971–1973.
16. Mason, R. Hal, Robert R. Miller, and Dale R. Weigel, *International Business* (2d ed.), John Wiley & Sons, New York, 1981.
17. Morris, Desmond, Peter Collett, Peter Marsh, and Marie O'Shaughnessy, *Gestures*, Stein & Day, New York, 1979.
18. _____, *Manwatching: A Field Guide to Human Behavior*, Jonathan Cope, London, 1978.
19. Palmquist, B., and K. Darrow (eds.), *Transcultural Study Guide*, 2d ed., Volunteers in Asia, Stanford, Calif., 1975.
20. Prosser, M. H., *Intercommunication among Nations and Peoples*, Harper & Row, New York, 1973.
21. Raban, Jonathan, *Arabia: A Journey through the Labyrinth*, Simon & Schuster, New York, 1979.
22. Rubin, Joan, "How to Tell When Someone Is Saying 'No'," *Research in Culture Learning*, East-West Center, University of Hawaii, 1980, pp. 73–77.

23. Scarbaugh, L. E., *Intercultural Communication*, Hayden Book Co., Rochelle Park, N. J., 1978.

24. Smith, Elise C., and Louise Fiber Luce (eds.), *Toward Internationalism: Readings in Cross-Cultural Communication*, Newbury House, Rowley, Mass., 1979.

25. Terpstra, Vern, *The Cultural Environment of International Business*, South-Western Publishing., Cincinnati, 1978.

26. _____, *International Marketing* (2d ed.), Dryden Press, Hinsdale, Ill., 1978.

27. Wilce, H., "How to Ease the Culture Shock," *International Management*, June, 1971, pp. 18–22.

28. Yousef, Fathi S., "Communication Patterns: Some Aspects of Nonverbal Behavior in Intercultural Communication," *Interethnic Communication*, E. Lamar Ross (ed.), University of Georgia Press, Athens, Ga., 1978.

Appendix D: Writing proposals

A proposal is a written offer to satisfy a customer's need, plus facts and reasons designed and presented to convince the customer to pick the proposer as the winning supplier. Thus it is basically a sales presentation—with differences.

Since a good proposal must present verifiable information to convince the customer, it also usually applies many of the methods (and some of the parts and formats) of reports. And because a successful proposal will become a part of the purchase contract, it needs the specifics and precision of statement necessary in a legal instrument.

As with other sales presentations, a proposal may be *unsolicited* (like the sales letters discussed in Chapter 8 and the justification reports in Chapter 13) or *solicited* (like the invited sales discussed in Chapter 5). Most unsolicited proposals are about comparatively small matters, whereas the solicited ones usually involve large projects—and competitors.

Because we know you can handle the small fry if you learn how to handle the big fish, we shall further concern ourselves only with solicited (and big) proposals. Since the U.S. government is the biggest customer in the world and has developed and tested a rigorous system of calling for proposals before large purchases, mostly we shall refer specifically to its procedures.

Don't forget, however, that essentially the same procedures exist in state and local governments and in industrial and commercial firms. Likewise, universities and other scholarly, professional, and scientific organizations now advertise so many available research grants that the art of writing proposals for them has become known (in academic circles) as the "art of grantsmanship"—despite the sexist wording.

The U.S. government seldom does its own research and development, especially for manufactured goods. Instead, it usually relies on industrial/commercial firms for this function. So-called specifications for a new armored personnel carrier, for instance, may be more a list of what the vehicle should be capable of doing than specifications of how to manufacture it.

Rather than asking for a bid, therefore, the government (like other big customers) usually issues an RFP (request for proposals—the government's published in the *Commerce Business Daily* and the *Federal Register*). The notices include the department issuing the RFP and identifying numbers or other information. They also indicate contractors (if any) who have already won a bid and plan to subcontract portions of the work.

Planning your response to an RFP

Writing a proposal in response to an RFP is a complicated business with a great deal of art to it.[1] Your aim is to build reader confidence in your organization and get the contract you're applying for and offering to fulfill as specified in the RFP.

In showing how you as the supplier will meet the specifications, the proposal should show that you completely understand the customer's needs, know how to satisfy those needs, and are qualified to do so (in terms of facilities, equipment, and personnel). Finally, but frequently of less importance to the customer, the price should be reasonable. We say price is less important because ability to fulfill the contract is more important to most customers. Especially in dealing with the federal government, the most successful organizations are not necessarily those best equipped to meet needs but those which best convince the potential customer of their competence and dependability.

The proper style for a proposal is positive, confident, and sales-oriented without being hard sell. Your language should be clear, simple, and easy to read. Your aim is to build reader confidence in your organization and get you the contract.

Studying the solicitation package

When a government agency needs something done and announces an RFP, it will also issue a solicitation package (sometimes called a "bid set"). The package usually contains a statement of work (SOW) specifying exactly the wanted product or service, copies of applicable federal regulations or references to them, checkoff forms for the proposer to certify compliance with the rules and regulations, a contract (usually Standard Form 33) for the proposer to sign, special clauses that are a part of the contract, and a letter with instructions about when the proposal is due, who is to receive it, the criteria for evaluating proposals, and anything else the issuing authority thinks is necessary.

You must study these documents very carefully. You cannot expect to write a winning proposal unless you know as much as possible about what the customer wants. The criteria for evaluating proposals are especially important.

Your proposal must be complete. Respond specifically to *every* specification in the RFP. Provide *all* the information asked for. Establish that you can meet the schedule or deadline for completing the project. Make sure that

---

[1]The art is rare and much in demand. Indeed a prestigious accounting firm (Coopers & Lybrand) is desperate for people who can write effective proposals. The firm is even considering hiring English majors and teaching them accounting.

your staff of people meets the RFP's specifications and (if specified) that they are permanent employees. Show that you can solve the customer's problem, but do not do it in the RFP's words—*don't quote the customer's language in your proposal*. To neglect anything, to fudge on a specification, or fail to meet any requirement will make your proposal "nonresponsive"—a government term that equates with "kiss of death."

While you're thinking about writing your response, also remember that good writing will help your cause. Despite the government's propensity for unintelligible bureaucratic pomposity, most proposal evaluators respond to clear, concise, correct English. Not only does clear, correct language make their job easier, it makes the proposing organization appear professional, which is what you want.

Present facts, not claims. Do not say you can do something; instead say how you propose to do something. A proposal may be a sales presentation, but hold off on the superlatives and explain specifically how you propose to solve the customer's problem or fill the need described in the RFP.

Good organization is the necessary starting point for good writing. You certainly won't look good if your proposal wanders around the subject, and evaluators won't appreciate having to find their way through it.

ORGANIZING YOUR PROPOSAL

Understanding the need

Despite the information in the RFP, you still have to define the customer's need. In fact, as Holtz and Schmidt point out, the RFP may very well describe *symptoms*, leaving it up to you to determine what the *problem* is.[2]

You cannot count on some RFPs to be helpful. Writing them is a rare art. Stating a problem so that someone else can understand it requires that the writer not only understand the problem but be able to describe it clearly—abilities not everyone possesses.

Writing a successful proposal requires that you study the RFP and solicitation package intensely to glean all the information you can to demonstrate that you understand the problem the customer wants solved or the need you are to satisfy.

Making your plan or program to satisfy the need

Once you have identified the customer's need, you can develop your program or plan to satisfy it. This is usually the major step in preparing to write a proposal. (If you cannot devise a good plan, you logically cannot submit a proposal.)

---

[2]Herman Holtz and Terry Schmidt, *The Winning Proposal . . . How to Write It*, McGraw-Hill, New York, 1982.

Your plan or program must address the problem and be feasible—possible to carry out. If what you propose does not promise to solve the problem *or* is something that nobody can carry out, it is nonresponsive. Either case will cost you any chance at getting the business.

Analyzing your capabilities

Once you have shown you understand the customer's need and have presented a feasible plan to satisfy it, you must take the next step: show the customer that you have the capabilities to carry out the plan you proposed. You demonstrate your capabilities by describing your staff, facilities, experience, and financial resources—all the things about your organization that will convince the proposal evaluators that you should get the contract.

Provide résumés on all the members of your organization who will do important work if you get the contract. Be sure that each résumé emphasizes the person's experience necessary for this particular job.

Describe your buildings and equipment if appropriate. Show that you have the necessary physical plant to do the job. If what you propose requires specialized equipment, say you have it or prove that you can get it. Don't overlook transportation: can you efficiently ship things if that is part of the job?

Does your organization have the experience to carry out what you propose? You want to indicate in terms of personnel, facilities, and other resources that you do indeed have the necessary experience.

If you have experience satisfying similar needs for other customers, this is a very strong selling point. Describe such experience as much as possible in terms of a current customer's needs, stressing how similar they are to this customer's to make your experience as directly applicable as you can.

You also need to show that you have the necessary financial resources. Describe your finances in such a way as to prove that you have the money to buy needed raw materials and special equipment—or have the credit standing to borrow needed funds—and the capacity to repay the loans. Provide assuring evidence that if you get the contract the customer will not be involved in any outside financial entanglements.

All of this—proving that you understand the customer's need, that you have a plan to satisfy it, that you have carried out similar plans in the past, and that you have the means to carry out your plan—is designed to demonstrate that your firm is the logical one to get the contract to do the job.

You see that we have described above a four-part organization plan, and that is the conventional plan for proposals. Unless the customer tells you what plan to use (mandates one, as federal agencies often do), we think you will find it a good one. The four parts are usually listed as Introduction, Discussion, Proposed Plan, and Qualifications. Whatever you name them, their functions will be the same.

WRITING THE MAJOR PARTS

A proposal strikes a balance between the marketing effort of a sales letter (Chapter 8) and the authority/believability of a report (Chapters 13–14). If you have studied the applicable sections in this book, you will be prepared to strike this balance.

Introduction

The Introduction to a proposal is crucial since it sets the tone for the rest of the proposal. A poorly written Introduction can ruin the image of capability you need to get the contract ("If they can't write clear English, how can they be qualified to do what we need?"). Remember that you have competition (other organizations will be submitting proposals), and you want your proposal to get the best reading.

As with a sales letter, a good start is to promise a benefit, in this case to satisfy the customer's need. This idea you can best convey not necessarily by stating the promise but by stating the customer's problem to show that you understand it. *Do not repeat the wording in the RFP!* That is nonresponsive. Instead describe the problem as you see it in good, clear, simple English. Doing that is ample evidence that you understand the problem (especially if the RFP, as is usual, gave only the symptoms of the problem). And it is an attention-getter for it addresses the evaluators' immediate concern—the problem.

Though you may have identified the problem as the first step in preparing to write the proposal, you will be wise to write the Introduction after you have finished the other three parts of the proposal. (The Introduction is usually an abridgment of the next section, the Discussion.)

Clear, easy-to-understand writing is necessary in a proposal and absolutely essential in the Introduction. Consider this: the evaluator who reads your proposal probably reads many similar to yours submitted in hopes of getting the contract. Or, perhaps it's late in the afternoon and the evaluator has been reading proposals all day. Yours will have to be good to get attention through the fog of fatigue, but you will definitely get appreciation for a well-organized, easy-to-read proposal.

First of all you must identify clearly what RFP you are responding to (a customer may have a large number of them out). To avoid wasting your first paragraph for the identification, you may wish to use a header at the top of the first page of the Introduction, something like "A proposal in response to RFP AB-12-345-6789-CDE to prepare documentation for 'Project Fountain,' a new database management system."

Most proposals begin the Introduction by explaining who the proposing organization is. If you choose this approach, quickly show how you are the logical firm to do the job; don't just say that you are the "C. W. Jones Division of Proposers, Inc., a subsidiary of Gigantic Corporation, who can do anything." Much better would be something like

> Arcus Company is an experienced group of writers, most of whom (as documented later) are familiar with programming and software through ownership of personal computers. This broad experience means that not only have we the personnel capabilities to prepare superior documentation for the CP/M version of "Project Fountain" but can later write alternate versions for other computers and operating systems as needed.

Whether you begin with the problem or who you are, remember to be extra careful to write as clearly as you can. The easier you make it for the evaluator to read your Introduction, the better acceptance you will get for the rest of your proposal.

Discussion

While Introduction might do as the title for that section (but we bet you will think of a better one), Discussion is not what you want to call the second major section of your proposal. In the Discussion you will present the logical arguments to convince the customer to award you the contract.

If what we have said so far reminds you of the AICA formula for sales letters (attention, interest, conviction, action), you are right. A proposal, as we have said, is a sales effort; and as such it follows the logic of all good sales efforts. The Introduction should get the evaluator's attention and the Discussion should arouse interest.

The problem or need is the first item for discussion. In your Discussion be sure you completely convince the customer that you understand the need or problem and all its ramifications. Now you can develop your definition of the problem in detail, showing that you have considered it in all its aspects and possibly understand it better than the customer. Now is the time to explore all the side effects and secondary problems.

Next discuss what is required to solve the problem or satisfy the need. Again be complete, cover everything you can think of. You want to demonstrate that you have thoroughly thought through what needs to be done and how to do it.

Go into anticipated problems (usually you can see some) and suggest ways to avoid them or solve them. Don't be afraid of making the job sound too difficult or of sounding defeatist. The customer will take your foresight as evidence of your thorough planning, and suggesting solutions in positive language will prevent any hint of defeatism.

List and discuss the possible different ways of solving the problem. Show the good and bad points of each. This analysis should lead you logically into the next part (like conclusions and recommendations in a report), the heart of your proposal.

Proposed plan

Your program for solving the problem is the heart. Now that you have introduced yourself, defined the problem, discussed it in depth, and said what you think needs to be done, you need to *show exactly how you propose to carry out your recommended program*.

Whatever you call this section (Our Program is obviously unsuitable), it should show that your program is feasible and that your planning is complete. It should also protect you against possible future disputes, especially over changes by the customer after you have begun the contracted work (often a troublesome point).

What you want to do is prove that yours is the best plan to satisfy the defined need and/or that your organization is the logical one to do the job. How you organize the elements of your discussion will depend on the circumstances. Most successful proposal writers begin their thinking with the plan or program to be presented, *then* construct a chain of logical arguments to prove that the plan or program is the best one. Frequently the nature of the problem and the proposed plan to solve it will provide the organizational framework for this section.

Perhaps the most important part of any program is the people who will carry it out. This section of your proposal should thus contain *résumés* of all the *key* people who will work on carrying out your proposed program. Don't get into support personnel (clerks, technicians, artists, and the like); stay with directors, managers, supervisors, and professional personnel.

Anyone who has worked a number of years has probably developed a number of specialities. A COBOL programmer may also be proficient in RPG II and ADA, just as a professor may teach in several related areas. Thus a standard or boiler-plate résumé designed to fit all proposals fits none of them well. Each proposed program requires a different set of specialities, and you will profit if you take the time to write new résumés for each proposal— emphasizing the specialities your people have that qualify you for that specific program.

An RFP may specify the format for résumés or list the information wanted, and in such a case you will follow the customer's wishes. Otherwise take advantage of the opportunity to sell by presenting each person in descriptive writing. Avoid giving education and personal details (or put them at the end if you have to include them), unless the RFP makes it clear these details are important to the customer. (As people progress in their careers, education usually becomes less important and evidence that they can perform becomes more important.) Likewise, try not to list jobs held. That forces you into a chronological listing of experience and makes it difficult to emphasize the points you need to for a particular program.

Give the person's name, title, proposed position if you get the contract, and a description of the person's experience emphasizing what applies to this proposal. List things successfully done that are similar to what the person will do for your program, and show what the person now does for your organization. Remember that résumés are like sales brochures bound into your proposal. You don't want to get into hard selling or hucksterism, but you can certainly present your people in the best light as qualified to carry out your proposed program.

Often the RFP will contain *a schedule* for solving the problem or satisfying the need, and at least it will specify an end date for completion of the project. You should present in this section your *schedule* for carrying out your plan or program. It will of course fit into the framework of the schedule specifications in the RFP, but usually it should be much more detailed.

Supplying your own schedule is further evidence of your thorough planning. It shows the customer exactly when you plan to accomplish each step and corrects any deficiencies or unrealities in the customer's schedule. If you do vary from the customer's schedule, be sure to sell your version by giving your good reasons for doing so. (You should have laid the groundwork for this in the previous section.)

You can avoid future trouble by (1) being clear whether you mean calendar days or working days and (2) scheduling completion of each step a certain number of days after completion of the preceding step. This second device will protect you against, say, the customer's taking a month for a one-week review period (during which you suspend work until the review is done) and still insisting on completion by the contracted end date.

If your program requires *special facilities or equipment*, now is the time to announce you have them and to describe them. For instance, manufacturing battle tanks for the Army could require high-capacity overhead cranes to move the heavily armored parts of the vehicles. You might want to list them, say whether they are operator controlled or remote controlled, and tell how modern they are. Similarly, if you will need a computer, you would want to show you have the necessary size and the software to run it.

Qualifications

The *qualifications* part of your proposal should show that your organization has the experience to carry out the program you propose. Essentially you want to show that you are the best choice for the contract and that you are dependable with *a record of success in similar projects*.

Whether the RFP requires it or not, plan to include here a list of past contracts on which you have performed well. As with résumés, don't prepare a standard list to tack onto every proposal you write. Instead, do it right and review your list for each proposal so that you can list jobs similar to the one you are seeking and so that you can emphasize the points important for this proposal.

Give the names of past customers, names of references at each customer, and a history of what you did. In these histories describe exactly what you did, the dollar amount of the contract, whether you completed the job within the budget or not, and anything else that will show your organization's dependability. You may want to itemize everything but the description, making that a narrative paragraph. Keep the history fairly short—you don't want to run on and on extolling your virtues through past job after past job.

This section of your proposal is also where you can point with pride to any special accomplishments.

If you didn't fully describe your facilities and equipment earlier in the proposal, do it now. And if you are a division or subsidiary of another organization, explain it here. Such information leads logically to talk about *your financial picture,* especially your soundness and responsibility, if you didn't adequately cover this subject earlier.

Something else you might include in this section is letters of appreciation from satisfied customers. Such testimonials are powerful selling tools.

Providing good format and special parts

Many proposals, especially big ones, use appendixes to contain matter that is not essential to every reader and might slow down reading. Examples are tables of statistics, drawings, and other supporting material, and documentation from previous successful contracts. (By cross-references at appropriate places, you can point attention to these supplements for readers who want to see them.)

In *appearance* your proposal should be as professional as you can make it. Submit each copy in a quality binder or other container (unless the RFP prescribes how the customer wants it). The typing should be clean—no erasures, white out, or strikeovers. In these days of word processors, poor typing stands out. Take the time to make yours perfect. If you are using photocopied documents, clean and adjust your copier to get the highest quality copies. Technical and engineering drawings, likewise, should be clean and smudge-free, with well-defined lines and shadings. Any other graphics (graphs, charts, etc.) should look professional. Hire a commercial artist if necessary; it will pay off.

The *cover* should carry some identification of your organization as well as at least the RFP your proposal answers—as a convenience for the customer who has proposals coming in on a number of RFPs.

Include a *title page* that identifies you and the RFP as well as the date you are submitting your proposal. You may also want to put a statement on it that information in the proposal is proprietary and may not be released for any use unless you get the contract. (You may need to see a lawyer for the appropriate wording.)

Some proposals include an *abstract* of the proposal (sometimes called Summary or Executive Summary) for people who want a quick summary of the major points of your proposal. If you provide one, make sure your abstract sells persuasively. The people who make the final decision commonly don't read proposals but rely on evaluators to weed out the bad ones and recommend the potential winner or winners. Desirably, you should keep your abstract to one page, but telling your story well is more important. Take whatever space is needed (but keep it concise).

A useful item in a proposal is a *response matrix* (a table of the things the RFP specified for the proposal, and where to find them—*much* as a contents table does). The usual format is the name of the item ("Equipment," "Personnel," etc.) followed by a page reference to the RFP, then the page the item begins on in the proposal, and perhaps some remarks. The primary purpose of a response matrix is to help evaluators find the points they want to go over in your proposal. Anything that makes the evaluators' job easier deserves your consideration.

A *letter of transmittal* is mandatory. Proposal readers expect it, and it gives you a fine opportunity to do some initial selling. The letter of transmittal goes to the contracting officer as a separate document accompanying the proposal, but you should bind a copy into the proposal for other readers. The contracting officer is usually concerned primarily with cost; so make your quoted cost and its justification a part of the letter unless the RFP specifies a separate cost proposal. You might also want to say that the signer is authorized to enter into a binding contract, tell who else might answer questions (if the signer is not available), and say how long your offer is good for (though the RFP may have specified this).

Unless your proposal is very short, also put in a *table of contents* and, if justified, a *list of illustrations*. Remember that you want to make your proposal as easy to read as possible, and a table of contents is a big help.

If your proposal is extraordinarily large, you might consider including an *index*. Preparing one is a big job, but it can pay off by helping evaluators find the items they want.

For more information on format, and especially on using heads, subheads, graphics, and special parts, see the chapters on report writing (especially Chapters 14 and 15).

SETTING YOUR PRICE

You can say what you will charge for the proposed work anywhere in your proposal, but the sooner the better. Many writers do it in the letter of transmittal—especially in the copy to the contracting officer. If your price is high, you might be inclined to delay quoting your price (for reasons you learned in letter writing) until you have made your big selling points; but evaluators of proposals won't stand still for this. They want to know (up front) what the cost is, and you have to cater to them.

RFPs from government agencies and numerous commercial firms specify that a separate "cost proposal" accompany your proposal, and the federal government supplies special forms for this.

Basically, break your cost down and show how you arrived at it. Give your direct labor costs, your overhead rate, other direct costs, administrative costs, and your profit. Account for material costs, subcontractors, travel, testing time and costs, and anything else that influences your price to the customer. A cost proposal can be very complicated, and most organizations have their accountants prepare them. (Perhaps that is why—as mentioned earlier—Cooper & Lybrand is desperately trying to find accountants who can write good proposals.)

Appendix E: Case series

I. THE INTERCULTURAL SERIES

A. As vice president of the International Department (Telex: 587650, telephone: 205-398-8765, and cable: ALBANC) of the First National Bank of Birmingham, Alabama, USA, P.O. Box 10106, Birmingham 35276, write Banco do Brasil S.A., Foreign Trade Department, P.O. Box 30.345, Rio de Janeiro, Brazil, asking it for names and addresses of companies in Brazil that might be interested in selling fire extinguishers for a reliable customer of yours (Ever-Ready Manufacturing Company, P.O. Box 776, Tuscaloosa, Alabama 35401). These are portable, red metal extinguishers pressure charged for dry chemicals, carbon dioxide, pressurized water, or Halon $^{12}/_{11}$—charged weight from 2½ to 20 pounds. Furnished with wall brackets. About 250 people work at this plant under direction of Vernon P. Slater, president. They have been making reliable fire extinguishers for 20 years.

B. As Director–Industrial, Sergio Souza Soares Sobral, Foreign Trade Department, Banco do Brasil, S.A., P.O. Box 30.345, Rio de Janeiro, Brazil, write the First National Bank (preceding case). For the Ever-Ready Manufacturing Company you have found one of your dependable clients which wants to do business with Ever-Ready. You recommend Comercio Y Industria Brasileiro Ltda., Avenida Rio Branco, 645-11 Rio de Janeiro, Brazil, a wholesaler, retailer, and importer of commercial and industrial supplies and equipment (founded in 1948). You are enclosing a confidential status report.

C. Over the signature of Francisco Escobar Melendrez, vice president of Comercio Y Industria Brasileiro Ltda. (two preceding cases), write Ever-Ready Manufacturing company asking it to quote you prices CIF (cost, insurance, freight to port of destination) for delivery two months from now for 1,000 Model 987, 6 kgs, dry chemical powder fire extinguishers.

Because you will have to get an import license for importing fire extinguishers, ask Ever-Ready to send you quotation as a pro forma invoice giving export factory prices, packing costs, inland and ocean freight costs, and other applicable charges as separate items. Ask Ever-Ready to confirm your commission of 10 percent on the FOB factory price (FOB means generally that the seller is required to place the goods sold on board a ship at the port of shipment, transportation costs prepaid. Legally, the rail of the ship forms the dividing line with respect to the responsibilities of the buyer and seller.)

D. Using the letterhead stationery of the Ever-Ready Manufacturing Company, write Comercio Y Industria Brasileiro Ltda., and attach your pro forma invoice No. 10/023/1089 giving CIF Rio de Janeiro prices. Assure the firm that the fire extinguishers would be packaged according to the standard method for export shipping. Your quotation does not include any taxes, licenses, or consul fees. Terms must be an irrevocable letter of credit payable in U.S. dollars confirmed by the First National Bank of Birmingham for 100 percent CIF value. To expedite shipment, suggest the Brazil firm open a letter of credit with either Banco do Brasil or Banco del Norte. It should take about three weeks for the Tuscaloosa firm (assuming the letter of credit is acceptable) to get the fire extinguishers to Rio de Janeiro. Shipment is made subject to prior sale of space, strikes, interruptions of manufacture, acts of God, all U.S. governmental regulations, and all conditions beyond your control. Ask for acceptance of this offer before the close of business one month from now.

II. THE HAGELIN SERIES

A. Assume that you are V. A. Hagelin, director of Executive Course Development for Eastinghouse Electric Corporation, Bayard Road, Pittsburgh, PA 15213. You have just received instructions from the corporate policy committee to develop a course for new and near-term general managers. Top management is concerned about the ratio of general manager replacements due to poor performance and the nonavailability of trained general manager candidates. The corporate policy committee specifies that the new course must be different from and better than any existing management development models, and it must be tailored to developing Eastinghouse managers. At the national convention of the American Society for Training and Development several months ago you heard Professor Robert Lemelin, Department of Management, Pennsylvania State University, University Park, PA 16802, make a presentation on andragogy; and you want to explore the possibility of adapting Lemelin's model to Eastinghouse's specifications. Write a letter explaining your need for Lemelin to come to Pittsburgh as soon as possible. Your company will pay the usual consulting fee and expenses.

B. Lemelin accepted V. A. Hagelin's proposal (preceding case) and came for an all-day session. Both agreed that the starting point would be to ask Eastinghouse top management (with the help of the executive vice presidents and general managers) to develop a list of essential compentencies required to perform the role of Eastinghouse general manager. They generated a list of 125 items which were grouped into six traditional areas: marketing, engineering, manufacturing, finance, personnel, and general management. The next step is to have these managers divided into task forces. Each task force will be chaired by an experienced and successful senior general manager and consist of general managers, an executive vice president as adviser, one or more staff specialists as resources, and an assigned writer to record and report task force deliberations. The task forces are to determine what and how much a general manager needs to know in the specific functional areas. Write a memo from Hagelin to possible members of the task forces suggesting that they attend these meetings. If their work is too pressing at this time, or if they simply are not interested, they'll be excused.

C. After reading the two preceding cases for background, write a memo to Hagelin for H. A. Coyle, director of marketing. You have an overload of work (have been doing all-night stands just to keep up); therefore you cannot take on participation in task forces. Also, you will be on the committee on design changes (all very hush, hush right now).

D. After reading Cases A and B, assume that you are Susan R. Drennan, personnel department. You simply are not interested in getting involved in any more task force work or workshops. You have just returned from a national convention where you got worn out with forums, workshops, and task forces. Gracefully and politely turn down Hagelin's invitation.

E. Three weeks after the program started, Hagelin must write a progress report to all key personnel and has tried to organize thoughts and get the message across in a clear and concise manner. But as you can see by the following, Hagelin needs help. See if you can rewrite the memo for Hagelin, as requested.

Because of the functional orientation of the task forces, their outputs (except for the general management task force) were, for the most part, too detailed and cumbersome. They tended to describe competencies required of specialists in the respective categories, rather than competencies for general managers. Thus, after the task forces had completed their work, the course developers faced the challenge of refining the task force outputs into a model of the functions uniquely involved in performing the role of the general manager.

The planning group designed a three-week residential "course" later named Executive Forum. The framework included assumptions about adult learning and about the management process as involving: measuring how business is doing and modifying to correct, if necessary; probing details to accumulate relevant experience and information; getting the "big picture" and developing strategic plans, goals, and objectives; pervading plans down through the organization.

But first we organized the required functions into performance-related sets and constructed a "learning unit module" (LUM) for each set.

Finally, the LUMs were grouped into four competency-development units called organizational understanding, mission and planning, people management, and operations (including measurement and control). Almost 100 executives were recruited to serve as resources for these units, and they were assembled for a one-day orientation seminar to make certain that they understood how to perform the role of resources to self-directed learners. The basic design of the course was pretested with 24 potential general managers.

F. Now that you have rewritten the memo for V. A. Hagelin, you have the job of writing the participants in the three-week Executive Forum asking them to evaluate the sessions. Was the forum worth their time? "Since attending the Executive Forum, what are the two most significant improvements or changes in your managerial skill and /or knowledge?"

G. Write a sincere and meaningful memo to V. A. Hagelin for Katharine T. Luft, management. You are to make up some things that you liked about the course, and just one little touch of vinegar.

H. Unlike Katharine T. Luft, you thought the Executive Forum was a waste of time. You do not have time to read the recommended management books. Make up any plausible explanation of why you thought it was a waste of time. Should you consider finding something nice (and realistic) to say as well?

III. THE MUENNINK SERIES

A. This has not been a good year for Mrs. Edna C. Muennink, who retired last year from the state's Department of Children and Family Services. On May 14 an executive at the state retirement system found a serious error leading to sizeable overpayments made to Mrs. Muennink over the past six years.

When Mr. Muennink retired from working for the state 10 years ago and died later that same year, Mrs. Muennink (designated by him as his beneficiary) was listed on the records to receive his benefits for her lifetime ($371.41 a month at that time). The trouble began when the state legislature started a series of cost-of-living raises for retirees but did not include beneficiaries of retirees.

You (because it's your job) have the unpleasant duty of writing Mrs. Muennink (make up an address) and asking her to refund the money overpaid her as a beneficiary. (Nothing here will have any effect, however, on her monthly check as a retiree herself.) To be convincing and clear, you'll need to give the details, including exact dates and figures. (Remember that you're writing on May 14 of this year.) Mrs. Muennink received the correct amount of $371.41 for 23 months (November and December nearly 10 years ago plus all the next year and through September the following year). Then there was a raise of $94.96 a month (erroneously sent for the next three months). For the next two years and nine months (33 months) another raise brought the overpayments to $129.41 per month. Still other raises brought the monthly overpayments to $159.41/mo. for the next two years, and then to $199.41/mo. for the next seven months (after which you write the letter and stop the overpayments).

You realize that Mrs. Muennink may not be prepared to repay the whole $9,777.12 at once. Therefore you ask that she repay in 60 days or you will stop the beneficiary checks until they amount to the repayment due.

B. When Mrs. Muennink got the letter you wrote May 14 about refunding the overpayments the state had made her (preceding case), she was horrified at the thought of repaying $9,777.12; but she had to admit that your explanations, figures, and proposed plans were clear, reasonable, accurate, and considerate. She wants to repay by having you stop the beneficiary checks, starting with the one for May. At $371.41/mo., repaying will take 26 months plus $120.46 out of the 27th month. Write the letter for her signature.

C. Now in November Mrs. Muennink (two preceding cases) has changed her mind and wants to pay (this year, primarily for income tax reasons) the remainder of the refund due the state retirement system. When she and her second husband filed 1040X forms (amended tax returns) to get refunds of income taxes paid on the overpayments she had received, IRS said no refunded tax from us except in years you repay the undeserved money on which the taxes were due. Since tax rates are higher this year than for the coming two years (according to action Congress has already taken), she wants to pay up this year (in December) and take the whole $9,777.12 as a tax deduction at the highest rates and get her tax refunds of $850.31, $871.50, $703.00, and $973.10. (Yes, her husband—and tax man—has learned how to recover excess tax the fourth year back, though IRS usually will not consider refunds for more than three years back.) Write the letter for her signature.

D. As the executive in the state retirement system office, reply favorably to Mrs. Muennink's proposal (preceding), giving all necessary dates and amounts for clarity and legality.

E. As Mr. Otto Muennink write the explanatory letter you and your wife will send to IRS (Internal Revenue Service, at the address for your region). Assume that you're enclosing copies of letters for the four preceding cases and completely filled-out copies of Forms 1040X (amended income tax forms) for the past four years.

IV. THE TECHNICAL EMPLOYMENT SERVICE SERIES

A. Your organization has been hiring lower-level personnel through a local employment agency. After you hire a person through the agency, you pay the fee within one week. Unfortunately, new employees sometimes quit or you have to fire them. As personnel director for Cannon Electric Company, 5220 Carlingford Ave., Riverside, CA 92504, write to Aurora Ignacio, president, Technical Employment Service, 3859 Main St., Riverside, CA 92501. You'll write rather than telephone because negotiating a new agreement makes putting everything in writing a good idea. You want Technical to agree to a sliding scale whereby you will pay half the fee after an employee works six months with Cannon, another quarter after nine months, and the final quarter when the employee has been with you a full year. What arguments can you think of that might help persuade Technical to accept your proposal (and lose some money)?

B. As Aurora Ignacio, politely refuse to alter the agreement with Cannon (preceding case). You have been doing a successful and necessary service for Cannon. You have to screen at least a dozen applicants to find one to pass on; so you are saving Cannon a lot of time, effort, and money. As far as you know, very few of the applicants hired through you have quit or been fired soon after being employed, fewer (you think) than is true for people hired without your screening. Some immediate turnover in personnel is just part of doing business. You have the same problem at your agency. Waiting for an employee to complete a full year's employment before you receive your fee is unfair, since there are simply too many variables that can affect an employee's success. Suppose a firm fires people because of a retrenchment or closing a branch office, as Cannon has done recently? Plug as hard as you can for keeping the status quo, marshaling all the good arguments you can think of. But don't agree to any changes.

C. Surely Ignacio (preceding case) can see some injustice in your paying the full screening fee for an employee that works only two weeks and quits. So, as personnel director for Cannon, you're going to try again. When Paul Morton came to you two weeks ago (after TES screening), you assigned him to bench work during the afternoon shift (2 P.M.–10 P.M.)—close to your most experienced worker, for the breaking-in period—and all went well. When your every-two-weeks shifting of shifts came today (Monday) and Paul found himself on the graveyard shift (10 P.M.–6 A.M.), he stormed into your office and insisted on one of the other shifts. As his temper rose and you stuck to your calm no, he came out with another argument—the guy who is assigned to the adjoining bench on that graveyard shift is Paul's bitterest enemy for stealing (during high school days) the best girl he ever had, for winning the first-string quarterback position on the football team, for this, for that, and the other. Your still firm but calm no brought a huffy resignation on the spot.

You can't tolerate such emotional, must-be-pampered people in your shop—you have a business to run. Does Ignacio think you should pay the full TES fee for two weeks of breaking-in work you got out of Paul? Try to persuade him to make an adjustment.

D. As Ignacio, agree to (and explain why) a 50 percent reduction in the fee in this unusual, specific case—but don't welsh on the stand you took earlier in Case B. (Case B also gives you some information for your explanation.)

V. THE KOFSHUR SERIES

A. Last year when Trinity County (212 County Office Building, Coalville, WV 24999) negotiated a new contract with the Amalgamated Public Service Workers Union, the union asked for and got a provision for up to a year's maternity leave (without pay, of course) for its members. Now you (Mrs. Sophie Kofshur) and your husband are going to adopt a baby, and one of the conditions of the adoption is that you take a year off from your job to care for the child. Write the county manager of Trinity County and ask for a one-year leave of absence under the provisions of your union's contract so that you can satisfy the adoption agency's requirements.

B. As the county manager of Trinity County, answer the request of Mrs. Sophie Kofshur for a year's leave of absence so that she and her husband can adopt a baby (preceding case). The county's contract with the union representing Mrs. Kofshur does call for up to a year's maternity leave for employees having babies, but it does not cover adoptive parents. So refuse her request, and remind her that if she takes a leave of absence without permission she will lose all seniority rights when—and if—she returns to work.

C. One of your members, Mrs. Sophie Kofshur (two preceding cases) has called on you—the president of Local 512, Amalgamated Public Service Workers Union—for help. As a prospective adoptive parent and a dues-paying member, she wants you to make Trinity County, her employer, grant her a one-year leave of absence, a maternity leave. The county has refused her request. The applicable clause in the contract says that "Any member who is a prospective mother shall be granted up to one year of maternity leave without salary. The employee shall lose no rights, benefits, or status as a result of such leave." Write the county manager and request a leave for Mrs. Kofshur. Point out that the contract does not specifically differentiate between natural and adoptive mothers, and therefore the clause about maternity leave applies to both.

D. As the county manager of Trinity County, you have to reply to the letter from Sam Nuccio, president of Local 512, Amalgamated Public Service Workers Union, 505 Main St., Coalville, WV 24999. You have reread Mrs. Kofshur's request and also the maternity leave clause in the county's contract with the union. Clearly the clause is meant to cover only natural parents, and that was obviously the intent of both the county and the union when negotiating the contract. Since Mrs. Kofshur is to be an adoptive parent, she is not entitled to a maternity leave. Refuse the request.

E.   Mrs. Kofshur won't take no for an answer and has brought her request for a maternity leave to arbitration. As the county manager of Trinity County, comply with the request of the federal arbitrator (Anna Haase, 403-A-6 Department of Labor, 500 Quarrier Ave., Charleston, WV 25301) and send her a letter detailing the history of Mrs. Kofshur's claim and the county's reasons for refusing her maternity leave. As one of your arguments, you might point out that your dictionary defines a mother as one who has borne a child.

F.   Now put yourself in the shoes of the president of the Amalgamated Public Service Workers Union, Local 512, and tell your side of the story to the federal arbitrator. Support Mrs. Kofshur's claim. Since you know that the county is quoting a dictionary definition of *mother,* quote one of your own that defines maternity as "the state of being a mother." Use any other arguments that you think might help your—and Mrs. Kofshur's—case.

G.   As the federal administrator rule in favor of Trinity County and against Mrs. Kofshur. The basis for your ruling is that since the contract does not specifically differentiate between natural and adoptive parents, the generally accepted meaning of *mother* is held to apply, and the clause dealing with maternity leave applies only to natural mothers. Write a letter announcing and explaining your decision to the president of the union. In compliance with directives from the Secretary of Labor, you will avoid bureaucratese and excessively legal language and endeavor to use clear, easily understood English. Assume that you send copies of your decision letter to Mrs. Kofshur, the county, and the union.

VI. THE MAKANI KAI SERIES

A.   In planning for your retirement, you (a captain for a major airline) bought as an investment several luxurious apartments in a condominium on the ocean front of the island of Maui in the Hawaiian islands. Nine other pilots with your airline invested in this condo, called Makani Kai, 129 Paokalani Ave., Paia, HI 96779. Besides elegant lobbies, meeting rooms, and game rooms, the building has a heated swimming pool, hot tub, sauna, well-lighted parking areas, 24-hour security, ground maintenance, and building maintenance. All apartments are furnished with linens, dishes, pans, and utensils (for light housekeeping).

At the organization meeting after the purchase, the group elected you coordinator of the project. As part of the job you have to write to the other owners and call a board meeting in the meeting room near the east exit of the condo two months from now. Some of the problems that have come up (such as disappearance of the linens, dishes, pans, and utensils) require discussion. The groundskeeper, Robinson Kepaa, is having trouble with the underground sprinkler system. Charges for the apartments also must be discussed because inflation is making all the expenses run higher than you first estimated. Of course you'll write basically the same letter to all nine owners, but for this assignment assume that this first letter goes to Captain and Mrs. A. L. Lee, 67 Woodapple Rd., Barrington, IL 60010.

B. You have sublet a three-bedroom apartment from A. L. Lee, 67 Woodapple Rd., Barrington, IL 60010, for January and February. Apartment No. 40 in the Makani Kae condominium, 129 Paokalani Ave., Paia, HI 96779, was beautifully decorated, had a good view of the ocean, but it did not have enough pots or pans or enough dishes to do any kind of cooking. When you asked Ernie Shea (the person in charge of housekeeping) about more kitchen furnishings, he told you that the supply was limited because people were stealing, breaking, or misplacing things. You don't want to load up on pots, pans, and dishes because of the problem of hauling them back home (where the house is full of such). The price for rent is high enough that it should include adequate supplies (as the agreement said).

Also, Robinson Kepaa has not been on the job of keeping the grounds. You're afraid that the plumeria, royal poinciana, anthurium, hibiscus, and bird of paradise will dry up. The grass around the walks needs clipping and mowing. Someone had a wild party in the east game room last Saturday; and although Ernie Shea saw to it that the room was cleaned up, the walls are marked with magic markers. The room looks like a graffiti-covered New York City subway car. It will take several coats of paint to cover the artist's work. Also, you've had some disturbing trouble with the woman next door whom you think has a drug or alcohol problem. She sleeps all day but goes full steam at night, all night. The loud voices, stereo, sounds (like banging doors) keep you awake. You came to Maui for peace and quiet and to get away from your hectic pace back home. Can't Lee do something about all these problems?

C. As Captain A. L. Lee, after reading the request from your good friend (Case A), write an acceptance letter. You and your wife, Mary Louise, look forward to a trip back to Maui and to the Makani Kai condominium. Mary Louise keeps her clothes for Hawaii ready so that she can quickly fly the friendly skies. Comment appropriately on the problems as suggested in the request letter (and some you have encountered—preceding and following cases) and make up the name and address of the person you are writing to.

D. For background information read Cases A and B. As Captain A. L. Lee, write a letter to M. P. Evans, 225 E. Michigan Ave., Milwaukee, WI 53202, who has rented your apartment for two months in Maui. You are aware of the disappearance of furnishings that is going on and have not yet found a way of stopping it. This very subject was discussed two weeks ago at a board of directors meeting and the only things that were recommended were to (1) put positively worded messages in all apartments urging the renters to take better care of your things and (2) spend more money for replacements (which of course will increase the operating costs eventually). Last year the board had to spend $5,000 to replace missing furnishings. Robinson Kepaa was ill for three weeks and did not tell any member of the board but all board members live on the mainland. Also there was a slight problem with the underground sprinkler system, but it is fixed now. You had a long talk with Kepaa, and he promises to do better. A painter has been hired to redecorate the east game room. No one seems to know how all that damage came about. The room was supposed to have been used for a bridge party the night it got creatively painted. As for Ms. Yvonne Delbridge, former actress from New York, and next-door neighbor to Evans, you have no easy solution. She maintains that the TV next door keeps her awake in the daytime. She's an owl— not a lark. Generally she limits her parties to weekends so that she can study acting during the week. She admits to having lots of friends, some of whom have good voices (voices that carry) and friends who like to drink and to live it up. She suggests more insulation, but the walls already have the prescribed amount of insulation for this type of building. She has a year's lease and very likely will extend her stay since she is opening in a new play next month. There's no way that you can move Delbridge or Evans.

E.   As A. L. Lee (Cases A–D) you have the job (assigned by the other board members) of writing a positively worded message that will be framed and placed on the back of the entrance door of each apartment. Many of your linens, dishes, pots, pans, waste baskets, ice buckets, draperies, and just about everything that isn't nailed down have disappeared from the apartments. The replacement costs continue to go up and up. Most of your renters are from wealthy backgrounds and can well afford the high rent you charge. But many of them are careless and the linens, pots, and pans wander off to the beach and to luaus—or are damaged, broken, or taken. If the losses aren't stopped, you'll have to do something to cover the replacement costs. The board is now considering the problem. This message is the first step in the solution (along with a more careful check on the disappearance or undue damaging of furnishings in each apartment). Depending on the results of this step, the board may consider raising rents or requiring a damage/loss deposit.

VII. THE GENERAL AUTOMOTIVE SERIES

A.   Business has been bad for giant General Automotive, the world's largest automobile manufacturer. Environmental restrictions have necessitated hugely expensive redesign and retooling. Repeated concessions to the union over many years have raised workers' salaries to the highest in the world but not increased productivity concomitantly. Inflation has eroded customers' purchasing power while forcing frequent raises in new car prices. Soaring interest rates have made new car loans prohibitively expensive for most people. Foreign competition has increased, causing a further erosion of General

Automotive's position in a shrinking global market. And fuel costs have sky-rocketed, causing customers to demand smaller, more fuel-efficient, simpler and more trouble-free (but less profitable) cars.

Last year the company lost $763 million, its first deficit since 1921. This year so far is only marginally profitable. The sharp deterioration in new car sales that began in October has continued. General Automotive has canceled or delayed new-car projects and the construction of six new assembly plants. The company is laying off 13,000 white-collar workers worldwide. It is making further cutbacks and is asking the union to agree to similar cuts for blue-collar workers. It is asking the federal government for help, specifically for relief on interest rates, amendments to the Clean Air Act, and other steps; the government has as yet made no specific commitments.

General Automotive is taking the following steps to cut back benefits for its remaining white-collar employees.

1. Eliminate the 10 special paid holidays beyond the usual holidays and vacation time. These are the equivalent of the "paid personal holidays" the union negotiated two years ago, which the company will seek to eliminate if the union agrees to renegotiate the contract.

2. Reduce regular vacation time by 50 percent. An employee with 20 years of service will get 2½ weeks vacation each year instead of the present 5 weeks, for instance.

3. Eliminate the present cost-of-living adjustments for time not worked. The adjustments, which now total $2.04 per hour, will henceforth not apply to vacation, holiday, and sick pay but only to regular hourly pay.

4. General Automotive will increase its contribution to medical insurance. The current contribution of $1.30 per month for family coverage will increase to $7.70 per month. This increase will leave General Automotive substantially below most companies. At the same time, annual deductibles for medical coverage will increase. For a family the deductible will rise from $100 to $250.

5. The company's top 4,000 executives will take cutbacks equivalent to those imposed on the white-collar workers, but specifics vary.

6. The freeze on merit raises, lifted last spring, is now reimposed.

The steps outlined above should save the company about $500 million a year. For the chief executive officer (CEO), compose a letter to all remaining white-collar (clerical) employees in the United States announcing these cutbacks and the reasons for them.

B. For the signature of the CEO of General Automotive (preceding case), draft a letter to go to all stockholders of the corporation informing them of the steps you are taking to assure that their company will survive this crisis. Since in the last two years General Automotive's stock has plummeted from 81 to 22, and you reduced the dividend from $2 per year to $.40, you may not have a particularly friendly audience. What you want to avoid is stockholders selling their shares in disgust, further depressing the price per share, and making borrowing even more difficult and costly.

C.   Using the information in the Cases A and B, write a letter or memo announcing the cutbacks to General Automotive clerical employees in one of the following countries: Singapore, India, France, England.

D.   Based on the information in Case A, write a letter or memo to go out over the chief executive officer's signature telling 8,100 U.S. clerical employees that General Automotive is laying them off indefinitely. Be realistic in adding details (severance pay, rehiring preference, and so on).

E.   As in the preceding case, use the information provided in Case A and write a letter or memo for the CEO's signature. This one will announce layoffs in one of these countries: Malaysia, Kenya, Norway, Ireland.

F.   For the CEO of General Automotive, draft a letter or memo to go to the corporation's top 4,000 executives announcing that instead of the customary annual bonus, they will suffer cutbacks similar to those imposed on clerical employees. What cutbacks would you impose on the executives if *you* were CEO of General Automotive? (Be reasonable.)

G.   Write a letter for the CEO of General Automotive to send to each U.S. senator and representative asking for relief on interest rates, amendments to the Clean Air Act, and any other realistic steps you think Congress should take to help the beleaguered automobile industry. You can find basic information in Case A and much more in the current events files in your library. What arguments can you use to sway congressmen? (Bribery is frowned upon.)

H.   This case is the same as F, but this time draft the letter or memo for executives in one of the following countries: Australia, Saudi Arabia, Israel, Italy.

VIII. THE SOFTWARE SERIES

A.   As a part-time free-lance author you are working on a magazine article on dressing up titles and other written information that appear on a computer's video monitor screen. Your article will include programs in Basic to make words move across the screen and to add moving borders to words on the screen. These techniques will add some pizazz to programs written for microcomputers, especially games. Your six little programs are the shortest you know of for producing moving title and marquee effects (which is what they're called), and your article should fit into two and not more than three conventional magazine pages. You will have the article, including the six computer programs, ready in a week or two. Write *Software Magazine,* 12 North St., Ford's Mill, NH 03055. Address your letter to Maurice Frank, the editor, and ask if *Software Magazine* would be interested in your article.

B. As the editor of *Software Magazine,* tell Kenneth Pfeiffer (1624 17th St., Two Rivers, WI 54241) you definitely would be interested in seeing his article. So ask him to submit it—but make no promises, implied or otherwise, that you will accept it. Remind him that while the article may be typewritten, the programs should be submitted recorded on a mini-floppy disk so that you can run them on your computer to see what they look like and (if you accept his article) so that you can print out the programs from the disk, thus assuring that they will appear in the magazine without editorial or typesetting errors. Also remind him you can't return his disk unless he encloses a suitable mailing container, stamped and addressed.

C. Your article and programs are ready; so as the author write a letter to Maurice Frank at *Software Magazine* to accompany the typescript of your article and the disk with the programs recorded on it. Do some mild selling. You are not enclosing a stamped container because you do not necessarily want the disk back.

D. Two months have gone by since you submitted your article and programs about moving titles and marquees to *Software Magazine,* and you have had no response. Write the editor and inquire about the status of the article and programs you submitted. Watch your tone.

E. As editor of *Software Magazine,* reply to the letter from Kenneth Pfeiffer inquiring about his submission. You are the new editor of the magazine, replacing Maurice Frank. You are catching up (as quickly as you can) with the work he left. In addition, Pfeiffer's disk requires DOS 4.4 (DOS means disk operating system), and you do not have this version yet. You can use only disks with DOS 4.3 or earlier. However, you expect to have DOS 4.4 up and running in a week or two, and at that time you will review his and all the other disks awaiting arrival of the new DOS.

F. Another two months have gone by and still no decision from *Software Magazine* on the article you submitted four months ago. Since DOS 4.4 has been available in computer stores for more than eight months, *Software* (as a leading magazine in the field) seems to you to be using a weak excuse. Apparently the magazine does not want your article; so write to *Creative Software Magazine,* 5000 N. Dawn Dr., Peoria, IL 61614, and ask the editor, Bonnie Sanders, if she would like to see it. Because *Creative Software Magazine* is a bigger and more prestigious magazine than *Software Magazine,* you had better do a little selling. Your very short programs in Basic easily allow programmers to make text scroll across the screen, or to give text moving borders (marquees). With marquees, the text may or may not scroll, as the programmer specifies. Moving titles and marquees provide desirable animation to what is otherwise unmoving textual matter in most microcomputer programs, especially games.

G. Kenneth Pfeiffer has written offering to send you (as editor of *Creative Software Magazine*) his article on moving titles and marquees; and you think the article, if it is as described, will fit into your "Small Programs" section. Payment for material published in this section is two thirds your regular rate for major articles. Invite Pfeiffer to submit his material to you, with the programs on a mini-floppy disk, and to include a stamped, addressed container if he wants the disk returned. Don't make or imply any promises.

H. Since *Creative Software Magazine* would like to see your article on moving titles and marquees, and since you submitted the article to *Software Magazine* almost five months ago but have no answer, write to *Software Magazine* acknowledging its implied rejection of your article and withdrawing your submission, explaining that another magazine has formally accepted it. Thus *Software Magazine* is under no obligation to you. Don't burn any bridges. As a free-lance writer you can't afford to make any enemies in the computer publishing business (where everyone knows everyone else) or the magazine publishing business (where everyone seems to know everyone else). You can assume that on the same day you send your article and programs to *Creative Software Magazine*.

I. The turnover in editors at *Software Magazine* in the last five months has been furious. You are the fourth editor since Maurice Frank, but you expect to stay a while. Among your other problems, you have to reply to Kenneth Pfeiffer, an author your publication has not treated very well. When his letter came in, you immediately got his mini-floppy disk and article out of the pile of submissions you have been trying to get to and ran his programs. They are clever and well done. What you would like to do is run them in various places throughout an issue of *Software Magazine* rather than as a single article, though you will pay your standard article rate for them.

Now you must convince Pfeiffer to let you have the programs rather than give them to another (competitive) publication. To try to sell him, you can argue that despite the delay in replying to him (not intentional, but a result of the unforseen turnover in your personnel), he submitted to you first and you should have first rights of acceptance or refusal. Further, your magazine can give his programs the best presentation to readers, etc. Add what arguments you can think of that will help do the job, but remember to stay within the bounds of reality.

J. That letter from Gerald Urban, the new editor of *Software Magazine*, is not only very persuasive; but he makes a good case. So, since he has accepted your article and *Creative Software Magazine* has not yet made a decision, with some qualms you write a letter to Bonnie Sanders at *Creative Software Magazine* to tell her you are withdrawing your submission to her magazine. Explain as much of the history of all this as you think appropriate to persuade her to release your article and programs, but keep the channels open so you can send her other material in the future.

K. *Creative Software Magazine* has reluctantly agreed to release your article and programs on moving title and marquees, although Bonnie Sanders had decided to accept them for publication but had not yet notified you (contract in preparation stage). Despite Ms. Sander's skill as a writer, you can sense from her letter that she is not too happy about all this—and you can't blame her. Write Gerald Urban at *Software Magazine* and tell him that the other magazine has released your article and programs and that he is free to publish them.

L. You are the new editor of *Software Magazine,* having replaced Gerald Urban. In reviewing material accepted for publication, you came across Pfeiffer's programs for moving titles and marquees. While nice little programs, they do not fit in with your concept of what *Software Magazine* should be. Write Pfeiffer and tell him that you are rejecting his submission, but do it in a such a way that he will continue to submit articles to you.

M. As the editor of *Personal Software Magazine,* write a letter of sympathy to the widow of Kenneth Pfeiffer on his suicide. Kenneth was a good author for you and you published several of his submissions. Would this be a good time to ask if before his death he had completed any articles that Mrs. Pfeiffer could send to you?

Appendix F: Concise writer's handbook

This alphabetical list of short, easy-to-remember **symbols** will save teachers time in marking papers and will help students by giving brief explanations of many usual problems.

The **symbols** (the boldfaced part of each entry) are nearly all abbreviations of already familiar grading or proofreading terms. Even the few abstract, unalphabetized ones at the end are mostly standard proofreader's marks.

The list includes everything teachers and students of business writing are likely to need for improving the English in their papers. Although it is much more concise than the usual English handbook, it omits only those points college students already know or don't need to know. We based our selection of the included items on a combined 90 years of experience in observing the good and the unacceptable in the writing of students in 23 colleges and universities.

The explanations of points of grammar and usage derive from the studies of linguists and philologists—the true authorities.

A, an   Use *a* as the indefinite article if the next word begins with a consonant sound (including the now pronounced *h* in *hotel* and *historical*—and combined consonant and vowel sounds, as in *European, usage, unit,* and *eulogy*); use *an* if the next word begins with a vowel sound, including words beginning with silent *h (hour, honor, honest)*.

Ab   Before using an abbreviation, make sure it is appropriate, understood, and in a standard form (including capitalization, spacing, and punctuation—though *Webster's New Collegiate* allows some choices). Ordinarily, you should not abbreviate dates and states (except that the U.S. Postal Service has a complete system of state abbreviations for envelope addresses—listed in Chapter 1—to adapt to electronic mail sorting). Mr., Mrs. Dr., A.M., P.M., COD, FOB, and EOM most commonly appear as abbreviations. Also, abbreviation is preferable for many specialized terms in almost every professional field of work or study—as illustrated in Appendix C on intercultural communication. Though general practice may call for a period after the abbreviation of a word (except in groups of words making acronyms or other forms of alphabet soup), recent dictionaries are very permissive on both the form(s) and

punctuation of abbreviations. Your best guide is an up-to-date dictionary or specialty handbook if in doubt about an abbreviation.

Accuracy   Get facts, names, addresses, and statements right. If your reader
may misunderstand your statement, restate it so that it is clear.

Accussations   See Chapter 3.

Adapt   to your reader's interests, reading ability, and experience. A message
that seems to fit somebody else, or nobody in particular, is less effective than one which seems to fit the reader. See Chapter 4.

Adj/Adv   Be sure you use the right form of a word for its function in the
sentence. Many English words may, with or without change of form,
play different roles in sentences. For example, in "a quick decision"
quick is an adjective modifying the noun *decision;* but in "decided
quickly" the *quickly* is an adverb (in the usual *-ly* form) modifying a
verb. (For the comparative and superlative forms, see **Cpr** 3.)

Agreement of subjects with their verbs and of pronouns with their antecedents is essential to clear, inconspicuous communication. Don't be confused by other words that come between two that are supposed to
agree.

1. Notice that the first sentence about agreement is an illustration of
the first point: *agreement* (singular) is the subject of the verb *is;*
but between them is a prepositional phrase with four plurals. As
other illustrations, consider

Selection of topics *depends* on the reader's knowledge and interests.

Lee also tells how important the arrangement of the records
offices *is.*

Part, series, type, and other words usually followed by plural phrases
are frequently pitfalls to the unwary writer:

The greatest part of their investments *is* in real estate.

A series of bank loans *has* enabled the firm to stay in business.

2. *Any, anyone, each, every, everyone, everybody, either,* and *neither* all point to singular verbs (and pronouns)—except that in an
either-or situation, with one noun singular and one plural, verbs
and pronouns agree with the closer noun.

Any of the women in the group *is* willing to give some of *her*
time to helping the group when asked.

Either board members or the president *has* power to act on the
point.

Neither the mayor nor the council members *are* allowed to use
city-owned automobiles in transacting *their* own business.

3. Two separate singular subjects combined by *and* require a plural verb or pronoun; but when combined by *besides, either-or, together with,* or *as well as,* they take a singular:

> Mrs. Davis and her secretary *do* the work in the central office.

> Considerable knowledge, as well as care, *is* necessary in good writing.

But note:

> The honorary president and leader of this group *is* Mr. Anderson (one person, two titles).

4. Be sure your pronouns agree in number and gender with their antecedents (words they stand for).

> Find out whether Coronal Supermarkets is dissatisfied—without emphasizing its (not *their*) possible dissatisfaction.

> The company plans to move *its* main operations closer to *its* major source of raw materials.

> The benefits students get from studying the practical psychology, writing skills, and ways of business in good courses like letter writing and report writing will help *them* throughout life.

5. Relative clauses beginning with *who, that,* or *which* require verbs agreeing with the antecedents of those words.

> The manager is one of those *persons who* expect unquestioning loyalty.

> The *actions* in the life of any animal *which* interest a biologist are those concerned with food, shelter, protection from enemies, and procreation.

6. Plural-sounding collective subjects take singular verbs and pronouns when the action is that of the group but plural verbs when the action is that of two or more individuals in the group:

> The board *is* having a long meeting.

> The board *have* been arguing and disagreeing on that point for months.

> Twenty-five dollars *is* a reasonable price in view of . . . .

> The faculty *are* allowed almost complete freedom in the conduct of *their* classes while the administration *plays its* part by providing the facilities, general policy, and record keeping. (The collective faculty acting as individuals, the administration acting as a group.)

7. Beware of letting the complement tempt you to make the verb agree with it instead of the subject:

> Our main difficulty *was* errors in billing.

The biggest cost item *is* employees' salaries and wages. (In most such situations, however, rewriting would be better, to avoid equating a subject with a predicate noun of different number.)

8. Certain words deserve careful attention because their form is an uncertain or misleading indication of their number:

    a. The meaning of the whole context determines the number of *any, all, more, most, some,* and *none.*

    b. *Acoustics, economics, genetics, linguistics, mathematics, news, physics,* and *semantics* are all singular despite their look and sound; *deer* and *fish* are both singular and plural; and *mice,* like *men,* is a plural word despite the singular smell.

9. Beware of words whose forms are in transition, like *data.* The original forms, from Latin, were singular, *datum,* and plural, *data.* In modern usage, *datum* is disappearing and *data* is coming into use as both the singular and plural form.

    All the data are in.

    All the data is in (commonly seen in modern usage).

Ambiguous—more than one possible meaning and hence not clear. Usually you can clear up the temporary confusion by (1) correcting a faulty pronoun reference (see **Ref**) or (2) rewording to straighten out a modifier so that it can modify only what you intend (see **Mod**).

He took over the management of the business from his father when he was 55. (When his father reached 55, Carl took over management of the business.)

We agreed when we signed the papers that you would pay $100. (When we signed the papers, we agreed that you would pay $100 *or* We agreed that you would pay $100 when we signed the papers.)

And is a strong coordinating conjunction—one of the most useful and most troublesome of words.

1. It should connect (in the sense of addition) only things of similar quality and grammatical form. Used otherwise, it produces faulty coordination between an independent and a dependent clause, misparallelism, or sentence disunity. See **Sub, Para,** and **Unit.**

    The plans call for a new four-story building, and which will cost $4.5 million. (Omit *and;* it can't connect an independent clause to a dependent one.) See **Coh.**

    In this course you learn the ways of the business world, the principles of practical psychology, and to write better. (The infinitive *to write* is not parallel with the nouns *ways* and *principles*. Make them all the same form before connecting them by *and*.) See **Para.**

We feel sure that the saw will serve you well, and we appreciate your order. (The two ideas are not closely enough related to appear in the same sentence—probably not even in the same paragraph.) See **Unit.**

2. *And* is properly the most-used connective, but don't overuse it to connect a series of independent clauses into a long, stringy sentence. If the clauses deserve equal emphasis, you can make separate sentences. If not, subordinate the weaker ones. See **Sub.**

    The consultant first talked with the executives about their letter-writing problems *and* then took a sample of 1,000 carbon copies *and* classified them into two groups *and* 45 percent of them were for situations that could just as well have been handled by forms. (After talking with the executives about their letter-writing problems, the consultant classified a sample of 1,000 carbon copies from the files. Forty-five percent of them were for situations that could just as well . . . .)

3. *And* may properly begin a sentence, but only if you want to emphasize it.

4. *And* is not proper before *etc*.; the *et* in *et cetera* means *and*.

5. Except in formal writing *and/or* is acceptable to mean either or both of two mentioned possibilities.

Ap   The appearance of a letter, as of a person, should be pleasant but unobtrusive and should suggest that the writer is competent, accurate, neat, and alert. Check Chapter 1.

Apostrophes (usually considered with punctuation, although they belong with spelling) should appear in:

1. Possessives (except *its* and the personal pronouns): before *s* in singulars (*man's*); after the *s* in plurals if the *s* or *z* sound is there to make the word plural (*ladies'* but *women's*).

2. Contractions: to mark the omission of a letter (*isn't, doesn't, it's*—meaning "it is," quite different from the possessive *its*).

3   Plurals of symbols: figures (illegible *8's*), letters of the alphabet (one *o* and two *m's*), and words written about as words (too many *and's* and *but's*), though some authorities now restrict this use to avoiding confusion.

Appropriateness to the situation is an important test of good English. Is your statement too slangy, colloquial, or formal for the occasion? See **Adapt** and p. 52 for a discussion of levels of usage.

Assign   Follow the facts and directions in the assignment. Although you should fill in with necessary details of your own invention, you are not to go contrary to the facts or the spirit of the assigned case; and you are to make only reasonable assumptions. See p. xiii.

BB   Browbeating the reader is redundant and insulting.

Clark plans to use two approaches to attack the fast-food market. These approaches are: (1) capture the shopper who wants a more convenient way to prepare and eat meals at home and (2) lure the lunchtime shoppers into the store. (Put the colon after *market* and omit *These approaches are*.) See also **P10**.

Capitalization is pretty well standardized (except that newspapers set their own practices and hence are not guides for other writing).

1.   Capitalize the names of specific things, including the titles of people, but not general words. For instance, you capitalize the name of any specific college, university, or department; but you write:

A university education may well cost $12,000, regardless of the department in which one studies.

L. W. Wilson, president of the University of . . . . When President Wilson came . . . .

You capitalize any specific course, room, lake, river, building, etc., but not the general words. So you might write:

I am taking Economics 215.

I am majoring in engineering.

Now I must go to a history class in the Liberal Arts Building, after stopping to see a professor in Room 115.

Next summer I may fish mostly in Portage Lake and some in the Ausable River, although I prefer river to lake fishing.

Of course, you capitalize *English, French, German*—all the languages, because they derive from the names of countries.

2.   In titles of books and articles capitalize the first word and (though library materials don't) all others except articles (*a, an, the*), prepositions (like *of, to, in, on, for*), and conjunctions (like *and, but, or, nor, although*).

3.   Capitalize the seasons (spring, summer) only when you personify them (rare except in poetry).

4.   Capitalize sections of the country (the South, the East Coast) but not directions (east, west).

5.   Capitalize people's titles (*Mr., Mrs., Ms., Miss, Dr., Colonel, Professor, Judge, Governor, President*) and terms of family relations (*Uncle Jim*) when used before names but only to show unusual respect when used in place of or after names:

Yes, Son, ...

The Senator then went . . . .

After Mother had seen . . . .

6. Capitalize the first word after a colon only if it starts a complete sentence. (In an itemized listing, you may capitalize the first words of items even though they are incomplete sentences.)

Cardinal numbers (*one, two, three; 6, 7, 9*) are preferable to ordinals (*first, second, third; 1st, 2d, 3d, 4th,* or *2nd, 3rd*) in dates except in very formal invitations and legal documents, or when you separate the day from the month. Since the simple ordinal forms may be either adjectives or adverbs, they need no *-ly* endings, ever.

On October 7 . . . ; sometime in November—probably about the 7th.

Case in modern English is a problem only with personal pronouns. One form serves for all cases of nouns except the possessive, and the only problem there is remembering correct use of the apostrophe.) For pronouns:

1. Use the nominative case (*I, we, he, she, they, who*) for the subject of a verb (other than an infinitive) and for the complement of a linking verb (any form of *to be* except the infinitive with a subject).

2. Use the objective case (*me, us, him, her, them, whom*) as the object of a verb or preposition and as the subject or object of an infinitive (except *to be* without a subject). In informal speaking and writing, however, *who* is acceptable as the object of a preposition (especially if it is in the usual subject position) unless it immediately follows the preposition:

   Who was the letter addressed to?

3. Use the possessive case to show possession and to serve as the subject of a gerund (a verb form ending in *ing* and used as a noun):

   His accusing me of dishonesty . . . .

   My thinking that a . . . .

4. The case of an appositive (an immediately following, and usually parenthetical, explanation like this) is that of the thing explained.

5. Watch case particularly after *than* and *as* and in compounds with a name and a personal pronoun:

   He is better informed on the subject than I (*am informed* implied).

   I am a more cautious man than he (*is* understood).

   He is not so cautious as I (*am* understood).

   Virginia and she went . . . (subject).

I am to pick up Virginia and her . . . (object of verb).

He told the story to Virginia and her (object of preposition).

Choppy, jerky, short sentences are slow and awkward. Usually the trouble is (1) incoherence (the sentences don't follow each other naturally—see **Coh**); (2) poor control of emphasis (all the ideas in independent clauses, although of different importance—see **Sub**); or (3) lack of variety (all the sentences of the same pattern, usually all beginning with the subject or nearly the same length—see **Var**). Try combining several of the sentences, subordinating the less important ideas and stressing the important ones in the independent clauses.

Cl Immediate clearness is a fundamental of good writing. Make sure your reader can get your meaning quickly and easily.

Coherence means clearly showing your reader *the relationships between ideas*. It comes best from a logical sequence with major emphasis on the important ideas, with less on the related but less important ones, and with any necessary conjunctions to indicate what relationships exist. Incoherence comes from mixing unrelated ideas together in the same sentence or paragraph, but particularly from (*a*) using a causative word when the named cause is not the whole cause of the named effect and (*b*) linking unrelated ideas or ideas of different importance by *and*.

1. Plan ahead—get your ideas in logical sequence *before* you write. You can group seemingly unrelated ideas with a topic sentence such as "Three factors deserve special consideration." Such a sentence will clearly show that the three following sentences or paragraphs are related.

2. Give your ideas proper emphasis (see **Emp** and **Sub**). Important ideas should be in independent clauses or separate sentences. Two closely related and equally important ideas can be together in a compound sentence. Put a less important idea in a dependent clause attached to an independent clause, making a complex sentence.

3. Carefully choose transitional words or phrases if you need them to smooth the natural sequence of ideas (see **Tr**). Consider the following as examples:

    And . . . moreover, besides, in addition, also, furthermore.

    But . . . however, nevertheless, yet, still, athough, while.

    Either-or . . . neither-nor, else, whether.

    Therefore . . . consequently, hence, as a result, accordingly, so, ergo, thus. (Check for *true* cause-effect relation.)

    Because . . . since, as, for, the reason is.

    Then . . . after that, afterward, later, subsequently.

    Meanwhile . . . during, simultaneously, concurrently, while.

Before . . . preceding, previously, prior to.

If . . . provided, assuming, in case, unless.

4. In papers longer than a page or two—and even more so in similar oral presentations—you probably will need even more than the three preceding means of showing the relationships of ideas and thus keeping the reader on the track (See "Topic and Summary Sentences" and "Headings and Subheads" in the Index.)

Conciseness (which is not necessarily brevity) depends on leaving out the irrelevant, leaving unsaid what you can adequately imply (see **Imp**), and cutting out deadwood. See Chapter 2 for explanation and illustration of techniques.

Connotations—the overtones or related meanings of words—are often as important as the denotations, or dictionary meanings. Be sure that the words you use are appropriate in connotations as well as in denotations. Consider, for example, the connotations in the following: *cheap, inexpensive, economical; secondhand, used, previously owned; complaint department, customer service department; basement store, thrift store, budget floor.*

Copying from the assignment or from other people produces writing that doesn't sound like you. Put your ideas in your own words. You won't learn much about writing by copying other people or the phrasing of illustrations in the text. Read them for ideas, approaches, and psychology; then express your ideas in your own phrasing.

Cpr   Comparisons require special attention to these points:

1. Things compared must be comparable. Usually the trouble is omission of necessary phrases like *that of, that on, other,* or *else.*

    The markup on Schick shavers is higher than *that on* Remingtons. (You can't omit *that on* or you'll be comparing the height of a Remington—measured in inches—with the markup on Schicks—a percentage.)

    Frank Mosteller sells more Fuller brushes than any *other* salesperson. (Without *other,* the statement is illogical if Frank is a salesperson; he can't sell more than he himself sells.)

2. Incomplete comparisons mean nothing; complete them.

    You get more miles per dollar with XXX. (More than with what?)

    This material has a higher percentage of wool. (Higher than what?)

3. Be sure to use the correct form of comparison words. Comparisons involving two things usually call for adding *-er* (the comparative) to the simple form (*cold, slow*). Those involving more than two usually require the *-est* (or superlative) form (*coldest, slowest, fastest*).

For words of three syllables or more—and for many with two and some with only one—the better form is *more* plus the simple form (for the comparative) or *most* plus the simple form (for the superlative): *more frequently, most hopeful.* Some words can go either way: *oftener* or *more often; oftenest* or *most often.*

4. Watch these idioms: Complete the *as much as* phrase and use *to* after *compare* when pointing out similarities only, *with* when pointing out any differences:

Price increases may be worth as much *as,* if not more than, the dividends on a common stock purchase.

Comparison of X *to* Y shows that they involve the same principles.

Comparison of sales letters with application letters shows that they have minor differences.

5. Some words (*unique, empty, final,* for example) are logical absolutes and hence cannot take comparative or superlative forms.

CS Comma splice—a serious error. Except when they are in series or are short and parallel, two or more independent clauses require separation by a period, a comma and a coordinating conjunction, or a semicolon (which may or may not require a following transition like *that is* or one of the conjunctive adverbs). See **SOS2** and **P2.**

CSP Select a central selling point (in a sales or application letter) and give it the major emphasis by position and full development. Scattering your shots over too many points leaves the major ones weak. See **Emp** and **Dev.**

Date Date all letters and reports in the standard form (*November 2, 1985*) unless you have good reason to do otherwise. Your most likely good reasons could be: (1) You are in the armed services, where the form *2 November 1985* is standard; or (2) you're writing a formal notice, where you use words with no figures, or (3) you're writing an informal note and may well use the form *11/2/85.* Modern business writing usually does not abbreviate months and does not use the ordinal forms. See **Card.**

DC Dramatized copy would be more effective here. See pp. 36, 119.

Deadwood phrases add nothing to the meaning but take writing and reading time. See **Conc** and the list of frequent deadwood expressions in Chapter 2.

Develop your point more thoroughly with more explanation, definition, specific details, classifications, comparisons, or examples to make it clearer, more interesting, more convincing, or more emphatic. See **Spec.**

Diction   Use a more suitable word. The big test, of course, is whether the word, including its connotations, conveys your thought accurately. Consider whether your words are easy for your reader to understand; whether they give a sharp, vivid picture by being natural and fresh instead of pompous, jargonistic, or trite; whether they give a specific, concrete meaning instead of a fuzzy or dull concept because they are general or abstract; and whether they are appropriately informal, formal, standard, technical, or nontechnical—according to the topic and reader. See Chapter 2.

Watch especially the following often-confused pairs: *accept, except; adapt, adopt; affect, effect; almost, most; amount, number; already, all ready; altogether, all together; beside, besides; between, among; capital, capitol; complement, compliment; disinterested, uninterested; farther, further; fewer, less; formerly, formally; imply, infer; it's, its; loose, lose; marital, martial; maybe, may be; moral, morale; oral, verbal; personal, personnel; principal, principle; respectfully, respectively; stationary, stationery; sometime, some time; with regards to, in regard to; your, you're;* and *too, to, two*.

Others (not always in pairs and sometimes requiring more than usual dictionary distinction) bother Howard G. Sawyer, *Advertising Age*, June 29, 1981:

Activate (externally stimulated reaction)/*actuate* (internal motive).

Agenda (Latin plural; English singular—plural is *agendas*).

Balance (means "remainder" or "rest" only in bookkeeping; use other terms elsewhere).

Behalf (*in behalf* means for the benefit of; *on behalf* means as the agent of).

Bi- (meaning either two, as in bifocal or bilingual, or every two as in biennial. Bimonthly means both—twice a month and every other month. Suggestion: use *semi-* or *every other* for the second meaning).

Dilemma (restrict use to a choice between two undesirables).

Disinterested (having no monetary or other biasing interest, or impartial)/*uninterested* (simply not being interested).

Equable (steady)/*equitable* (just, fair).

Evident (recognizable by external signs)/*apparent* (seemingly, based on evidence and reason).

Flaunt (to show something off)/*flout* (to disregard contemptuously).

If (introduces a possibility)/*whether* (introduces alternatives).

Instigate (incite)/*initiate* (begin or originate).

Literally (truly)/*figuratively* (metaphorically—one thing in terms of another).

Momentarily (*for* a short time, not *in* a short time).

Myself (first person reflexive, which is never the subject but refers back to the speaker or writer).

Renown (noun—quality of being widely acclaimed or famous)/*renowned* (adjective—having renown, being famous).

Try and (try *to* is correct).

Directness saves words, speeds up reading, and makes your ideas clearer. Don't waste words by beginning too far back in the background of the subject, by stating what the reader already knows, or by expressing what you will clearly imply if you begin with the key thought. Write direct, active-voice sentences beginning with the important word as the subject. The expletives "It is . . ." and "There are . . ." are indirect, passive, and wordy (see **Exp**).

Dng Dangling modifier. See **Mod 1**.

Documentation, or telling your sources, is necessary when you use the ideas of others—to avoid plagiarism and to convince your reader by showing that you have the backing of cited authorities for what you say. See end of Chapter 14.

Emphasis, divided among your ideas according to their relative importance, is basic to good communication.

1. When you state important ideas, give them deserved emphasis by methods explained in Chapter 2.

2. When you have negative, unimportant, already known, or other ideas that don't deserve emphasis, avoid overemphasizing them (as explained in Chapter 2).

    Spring is just around the corner. You'll be needing . . . . (With spring just around the corner, you'll . . . .)

    On October 3 you asked me to write a report on . . . . I have finished it and am . . . . (Here is the report requested in your letter of October 3 . . . .)

    I have your letter of April 20 in which you ask for quotations on X. I am glad to give you our prices. Our present prices on X are . . . . (Just omit the first two sentences. They're implied in the third.)

3. Transitional words like *and, but,* and *however* usually do not deserve the emphasis they would get at the beginning of a sentence; and prepositions usually do not deserve end-of-sentence emphasis. Indeed, this point of emphasis is the only legitimate reason for objection to such words in these positions.

Enclosures. See pp. 19, 38, 122, 123(5).

Etc. An abbreviation of Latin *et cetera,* meaning *and so forth,* is appropriate only when the reader can easily fill out the incomplete list (as in "Please take even-numbered seats 2, 4, 6, etc."). Otherwise, it can mean only "Reader, you guess what else I mean to include." Because *etc.* is an abbreviation, it takes a period. In no case should you write "and etc." (*et* means *and*) or "etc. . . . ." (the middle three dots mean the same as etc. here).

Expletives (*it is, there are*) always slow up the reader's getting to significant information. They also nearly always make your writing unnecessarily wordy, weak, and passive. They often improperly dodge writer responsibility for statements.

Expletives usually result from a *misguided* attempt to write an impersonal style. If you write them in first drafts, revising to remove them will make better sentences at least nine times out of ten. In general, then, you should avoid them, although sometimes they may help to soften a command or avoid presumptuousness in a recommendation, or ease reader acceptance of bad news.

It was thought that you would prefer . . . . (I thought you would . . . .)

There are four important factors involved. These are: . . . . (The four important factors are . . . .)

It will be necessary to have your . . . . ("You must send . . ." might be too commanding.)

FI The Fog Index is too high here. See Chapter 2 and make your writing easier to read.

Figures are better than words (except at the beginning of a sentence) for serial, telephone, page, chapter, chart, catalog, and street numbers; for money, dimensions, and dates and time (except in formal announcements); for all quantities when several are close together (but not adjoining) in a sentence or paragraph; and for other isolated quantities requiring more than two words. (As an acceptable replacement for the two-word rule, your teacher may authorize usual newspaper practice: Use figures if the quantity is above ten.)

1. If a quantity comes at the first of a sentence, write it in words or recast the sentence.

2. When a sentence involves two different series of quantities, use figures for one and words for the other to avoid confusion; if more than two, use a table.

On the qualifying exam, ten percent of the applicants scored 90–100, thirty percent 80–89, ...

Please make six 2" × 3" and three 5" × 7" black-and-white prints.

3. The old longhand practice of stating quantities twice—in figures followed parenthetically by words—is unnecessary and undesirable in type or print, although it still sometimes appears in legal

documents, and always in checks, for double certainty and security.

4. Except in dates, street numbers, and serial numbers, use a comma between groups of three digits, counting from the right.

5. Except in tables involving some cents, periods and zeros after money quantities are wasted typing and reading.

6. Two-word quantities between 20 and 100 require the hyphen (*twenty-six*).

7. Cardinal numbers (*1, 2, 3, 4,* etc.) are preferable to ordinals (*1st, 2d, 3d, 4th*) in dates except when the day is separate from the month. See **Card** and **Date.**

8. Since ordinals are either adjectives or adverbs, an *-ly* ending is never necessary or desirable.

Flattery, especially if obvious, is more likely to hurt than help. See Chapter 3.

Fragments (phrases or subordinate clauses posing as sentences) are serious errors (because they show ignorance of sentence structure) except when perfectly clear and intentional. Attach them to the independent clauses to which they belong (see **P3**) or change their wording to make them the complete, independent sentences they pretend to be.

The latter being the better way. (This is a phrase fragment which should be attached by comma to the preceding sentence. Or you could simply change *being* to *is*.)

One job in revising any paper is checking for and correcting any fragments. Which is easy to do. (The second "sentence" is a dependent clause and hence a fragment unless attached—by a comma—to the preceding.)

Gobbledygook is big-wordy, roundabout, long-winded, or stuffed-shirt language. Avoid it like poison.

Graphic devices of various kinds can often supplement words to make the information clearer, easier, or more interesting. Use them where they will help, but only if they will. See Chapter 14 and the checklist in Chapter 15.

Gw Goodwill, a basic requirement of a business letter, is lacking or poorly handled here. See Chapter 3.

HS Heads and subheads could improve coherence and transitions.

Idiom violated. Follow the natural, customary (idiomatic) way of expressing your idea. Usually an error in idiom is use of the wrong preposition. Consider *possibility of, possible to, necessity of, need for,* and *ability to*. See **Prep.**

Imply rather than express the idea, to save words or avoid overemphasis. See **Emp** and **Conc.**

Italic print, indicated by underscoring in typewritten and handwritten copy, can emphasize occasional words, or mark the title of a book or journal, or mark a word, letter, or figure used as an illustration or typographical unit (instead of for its meaning). It is also the way to indicate an un-anglicized foreign-language expression used in English context.

> Italics are *not* the *preferable* way to mark titles of *parts,* such as the title of an article in a journal or a chapter in a book. Quotation marks are preferable for that purpose.
>
> Chapter 2, "Style: What the Reader Reads," stresses clear, natural style and general linguistic *savoir faire*.
>
> Many people misspell *convenience* and *questionnaire*. Use of fewer *I*'s and more *you*'s would improve many letters.

Item   Itemize complex series and lists (like this) to (1) emphasize the points, (2) avoid complex punctuation, (3) force yourself to state your points more precisely and concisely, and (4) grab your reader's attention. This point is particularly important in oral communication.

Jargon is fuzzy or inappropriate writing attributable to pompousness, circumlocution, deadwood, abstractness, big words, technical terms (written to nontechnical readers), or hackneyed expressions. It is the opposite of simple, natural, clear writing. Avoid it.

Juxtapose (put side by side) facts and ideas that the reader needs to consider together. For instance, wholesale and retail prices need to appear together (with the difference and percentage of markup figured) if they are to mean as much as they should to the retailer being asked to stock the product.

K   Awkwardness in expression calls attention to itself, and it may confuse the reader. Reconstruct your sentence or change word order for a more natural flow.

> A so-called split infinitive (putting a modifier between *to* and a verb) is usually undesirable only because it is usually awkward.

K/S   Known to the reader. Omit or **Sub**ordinate.

lc   Lowercase needed here, instead of capital. See **Cap.**

Logic   Avoid statements which will not stand the test of logic or for which the logic is not readily clear. Perhaps you need to supply a missing step in the logic. Maybe you need to state your idea more precisely. Or maybe you need to complete a comparison to make it logical. (If the last, see **Cpr** for fuller explanation.)

Mechanics   See **TM.**

Modifiers should come in the sentence where they fit most naturally and make the meaning clearest. To avoid awkwardness and write clearly, you have to make sure that each modifier relates clearly to the thing it is supposed to modify. As a general rule, the two should be as close together as natural sentence construction will allow.

1. Participles (usually phrases including a verb form ending in *-ing* or *-ed*, and usually at the beginning of a sentence) require careful attention lest you relate them to the wrong word (or nothing at all).

> Smelling of liquor, I arrested the driver. (The officer did not intend to report drinking on duty—but the words do.)

> After soaking in sulphuric acid over night, I set the specimen up to dry. (The scientist didn't really soak, either.)

Infinitives can be "misrelated modifiers" the same way:

> To enjoy the longest, most dependable service, the motor must be tuned up about every 500 hours of operation.
> (The motor cannot enjoy dependable service.)

> In order to assist you in collecting for damages, it will be necessary to fill out a company blank. (The two infinitives dangle because they do not relate to any proper doers of the actions indicated.)

But absolute phrases (a noun plus a participle) and participles, gerunds, and infinitives naming an accepted truth rather than the action of any particular person or thing do not need to relate to any subject:

> The sun having set, the fish began to bite.

> All things considered, Steve is the better man.

> Counting all costs, the little X is not an inexpensive car.

> To judge from results, that was an effective method.

2. Watch where you put such limiting qualifiers as *only, almost,* and *nearly*. Consider the varied meanings from placing *only* at different spots in "I can approve payment of a $30 adjustment" or in "He mourned for his brother."

Monotonous   See **Var.**

Mood   The usual indicative (for statements of fact) and imperative (commanding) moods give little trouble. But be careful with the subjunctive (for verbs after commands and wishes) and the conditional (for uncertainties or conditions contrary to fact), especially in formal writing. Consider: "Let it be said . . . ," "I wish he were . . . ," and "If I were in your place . . . ." See **SW.**

Natural writing avoids triteness, awkwardness, and pomposity. Clichés, trite and hackneyed expressions, and jargon suggest that you are not thinking about your subject and your reader; awkwardness suggests carelessness; and big words and pomposity suggest that you are trying to make an impression. Think through what you want to say and put it simply, smoothly, and naturally. Although you cannot write exactly as you talk, try to write with the same freedom, ease, simplicity, and smoothness. See Chapter 2.

Negative in letter and memo writing means anything unpleasant to your reader. Since you want the reader's goodwill, you should avoid the negative when you can and subordinate it when you can't avoid it. Insofar as possible, stress the positive by telling what you have done, can do, will do, or want done instead of their negative opposites. See Chapter 4; and for methods of surbordinating, Chapter 2, **Emp,** and **Sub.**

Objectivity Use of emotional or feverish words (especially if extensive) suggests a prejudiced rather than an objective view of the situation and therefore causes the reader to lose faith in the writer—especially a report writer. See pp. 467 and 477.

Obvious statements—when they are unnecessary as bases for other statements—at least waste words; and when they appear in independent clauses, they show poor control of emphasis and may insult the reader's intelligence. When you need to establish an obvious fact as the basis for something else, put it in a dependent clause or imply it and use the independent clause for the new idea. (See **Emp** and **Sub.**)

New York is America's biggest city. Therefore . . . . (Since New York is America's biggest city, ...)

Punctuation which follows the conventions of written English is a *helpful device for both reader and writer in communicating clearly, quickly, and easily*. But when it goes contrary to the understood conventions, it does not help and may even confuse.

You should not try to use even good punctuation, however, as a crutch for bad writing. Heavy punctuation cannot make a bad sentence into a good one; the need for it suggests revising the sentence rather than trying to punctuate the involved statement. The best style is so direct and simple that it requires little punctuation except periods at the ends of sentences. Still, you cannot write much without need for some internal punctuation. Here are the conventions most commonly violated. For convenience and clarity in explanation, we divide punctuation into two categories—end-of-sentence marks (with parts **Pa, b,** and **c**) and internal punctuation (with parts **P1–P13**). Since **Pa, b,** and **c** are all sentence-end marks, they all interact with quotation marks and parentheses as explained for quotation marks in **P9.**

Pa Use a period at the end of a sentence unless it is a question, is questionable (see **Pb**), or is an exclamation (see **Pc**). Less than full-sentence expressions used as outline items may end with periods or remain open-ended. Remember, however, that a period can do double duty as the end of an abbreviation *and* of the sentence ending at the same place.

Pb Use a question mark at the end of a question and (in parentheses) after a spelling or statement about which you feel unsure.

> Though I've heard of Mrs. Muennink's (?) varied interests and accomplishments, I've never met the lady. (The question mark means only that I'm not sure of the spelling.)
>
> When Colby first moved to Miami in January, 1981 (?), I thought . . . .

Pc Use an exclamation mark after a sentence or (in parentheses) after a lesser expression which you want to give dramatic emphasis.

> He said he wanted (!) to be the first to . . . .
>
> The General's succinct reply was "Nuts!"

Pl Use a comma between two independent clauses connected by *and, but, or,* or *nor* if no other commas are in the sentence; but be sure you are connecting two clauses rather than a compound subject, verb, or object.

> You may buy the regular Whiz mixer at $78.75, but I think you would find the Super Whiz much more satisfactory (two clauses).
>
> We make two grades of Whiz mixers and sell both at prices lower than those of our competitors' products (compound verb; one subject).

Be sure, too, that you don't use obtrusive commas before the first or after the last item in a series or between a subject and its verb, a verb and its object, or a noun and its adjective. Also you do not usually need a comma after a transitional word (*and, but, however, therefore*), but using one emphasizes the word.

P2 The semicolon is a pivotal mark; avoid using it between expressions unless they are of equal grammatical structure (usually two independent clauses or two items in a complex series). Use a semicolon between two independent clauses unless connected by *and, but, or,* or *nor;* and even then, use a semicolon if the sentence already has a comma in it (as in this one). Typical weaker connectives requiring the semicolon between two independent clauses are *therefore, so, moreover, hence, still, accordingly, nevertheless, furthermore, consequently,* and *however.* When these words are simple connectors not between two independent clauses, however (as right here), set them off by a pair of commas unless they fit so smoothly into the sentence that they require no marks.

> New developments in office machines have made maintenance workers relearn their jobs; the new manuals are twice as thick as those of only a few years ago (no connective).
>
> The preceding sentence could be two, of course; but because the

ideas are closely related, it is better as one. (Commas elsewhere in this sentence require a semicolon before even a strong conjunction.)

Good business writing requires proper punctuation; therefore you must know how to use the semicolon (weak connective).

The proper style for letters is simpler and less involved than for most other writing, however, and therefore does not require very complex punctuation procedures. (*However* is a simple transition, *not* used between two clauses here and *not* close-knit into the phrasing the way *therefore* is; so it needs commas while *therefore* goes unmarked. Note, too, that the weak connective *so* requires the semicolon because it connects two clauses.)

P3   Use a comma after all first-of-sentence dependent clauses, long phrases, or other phrases containing any form of a verb. But when these forms or appositives or transitional words appear elsewhere in a sentence, use commas only with nonrestrictive (nonessential) ones. Nonrestrictive statements add descriptive detail about an already identified word and are not necessary to the logic or grammatical completeness of the sentence; restrictive ones define, limit, or identify and are necessary to convey the intended meaning or complete the sentence. If, on reading aloud, you naturally pause and inflect your voice, the statement is nonrestrictive and requires the comma(s).

Because the dependent clause comes at the beginning, we have to use a comma in this sentence.

We do not need a comma in a complex sentence if the dependent part comes at the end or in the middle and restricts the meaning the way this one does.

Having illustrated the two points about dependent clauses at the beginning and restrictive clauses elsewhere in the sentence, we now use this sentence to illustrate the use of a comma after a long phrase at the first of a sentence. (Because it includes a verb form, it would require a comma even if it were short, like "Having illustrated the point, we now leave the topic.")

The three points already illustrated, which are certainly important, are no more important than the point about using commas to set off nonrestrictive clauses anywhere, which this sentence illustrates. (In fact, it illustrates twice: you could omit both the *which* clauses; they are nonrestrictive because they merely give added information unnecessary to either the meaning or the grammar of the basic sentence.)

Sometimes you need a comma to prevent misreading—especially after a gerund, participle, or infinitive:

In the office, files were scattered all over the floor.

By shooting, the man attracted the attention of the rescue party.

Thinking that, he was unwilling to listen to reason.

Seeing the foreman's unwillingness to help, the men gave up.

P4 Use *pairs* of commas, parentheses, or dashes as needed to mark off parenthetical expressions within sentences. The "as needed" in the preceding sentence is a reminder that some parentheticals need no surrounding punctuation. Like dependent clauses, some appositives are restrictive or so closely related that they require no punctuation, while others are nonrestrictive or so loosely related that they do.

Our starting point that good punctuation is a matter of following the conventions has not had enough attention.

Our second point—the importance of writing letters so smoothly and naturally that they require little internal punctuation—would preclude most punctuation problems.

1. Commas are normal for short, unemphatic, and otherwise unpunctuated direct addresses like "Yes, Mr. Thomas, you may . . . ," tucked-in transitions like *however* and *on the other hand,* and brief appositives.

2. As the length increases in a side comment or an appositive (a restatement like this one, following immediately to explain a term), the call for stronger marks like parentheses becomes more likely. Commas within a parenthetical (as in the preceding) or a desire to de-emphasize it also make parentheses necessary around it.

3. If you want to emphasize a parenthetical expression—or if it contains complicated punctuation or is long—a pair of dashes such as we're using here will be your best punctuation to fence it in. Also see **P13.**

4. People in business often use ellipses in the place of dashes to emphasize parenthetical expressions . . . or if they contain complicated punctuation or are long . . . as we do here. Since this use of ellipses has not yet become a convention, we cannot recommend it; but to use ellipses in this manner is no longer absolutely wrong. (See **P13.**)

P5 Use commas to separate coordinate adjectives. As two tests for coordinacy, see if you can put *and* between the adjectives or invert their order without producing awkwardness. If so, they are coordinate and require a comma.

Proper punctuation can help greatly in writing a clear, easy-to-read style.

Fairly heavy white paper is best for letterheads.

P6 A comma is the usual punctuation *between* (but not before or after) items in a series (preferably including one before the *and* with the last item, because it is sometimes necessary for clearness and is always correct). But if any item except the last has a comma *within* it, use semicolons at all points *between* items. (Suggestion: If only one of a series requires an internal comma, consider putting it last and using commas between the items.)

Make your writing clear, quick, and easy to read.

Use commas between independent clauses connected by *and, but, or,* or *nor;* semicolons between independent clauses with other connectives or no connecting words; commas for dependent clauses and verbal or long phrases at the beginnings of sentences, for nonrestrictive ones elsewhere, and for simple series; and semicolons for complex series like the one in this sentence.

P7   Dashes (like commas and parentheses—as explained in **P4**) are all acceptable (in pairs) around parenthetical expressions that interrupt the main part of the sentence.

If the parenthetical part contains internal parentheses, dashes must surround it; if it contains commas, then dashes *or* parentheses must surround it. (Of course, only a pair of parentheses can surround a sentence giving explanations, relatively unimportant additional detail, or side information, as this sentence does. In that case the period comes inside the closing parentheses, although it comes outside otherwise.)

Except as explained in the preceding paragraph, the choice depends on the desired emphasis and on the other punctuation.

1.   Two dashes (called "bridge dashes") emphasize most:

   Your main weaknesses in writing—misspelling, faulty punctuation, and incoherence—deserve attention before you write letters.

2.   A single dash—made by two hyphens without spacing before, between, or after—may mark an abrupt change in the trend of a sentence or precede an added statement summarizing, contrasting, or explaining the first part. In this second function, it is the "pickup dash."

Errors in spelling, punctuation, or coherence—all these mar an otherwise good letter.

A letter writer must avoid the common errors in writing—misspelling, bad punctuation, and incoherence. (Of course, a colon could replace the dash here; but ordinarily it should not unless the preceding statement is a formal introduction, usually indicated by the word *following,* or unless it is an introduction to an itemized list.)

P8   Hyphenate two or more words (unless the first ends in *-ly*) used to make a compound adjective modifying a following noun.

   Fast-selling product, wrinkle-resistant material, long-wearing soles, never-to-be-forgotten experience

Note that you do not hyphenate when the adjectives follow the noun.

The material is highly wrinkle resistant and long wearing. Certainly it does not apply when the adjectives modify the noun separately. See **P5**.

These slacks are made of a hard, durable material.

The compound-adjective principle does apply, however, to double compounds made with one element in common, where the "suspension hyphen" follows the first: three- and five-pound cans; only light- and middle-weight boxers.

The hyphen also marks the break in a word at the end of a line. See **Syl**.

Other less-frequent uses of the hyphen include (1) spelling of fractions as modifiers (*three-fourths* majority) and two-word quantities between 20 and 100, and (2) prefixing words or syllables to names (*post-Hitler* Germany), to other words beginning with the same vowel as the end of the prefix (*re-entry, pre-established*), or to any word that might otherwise be confusing (*re-collect*, not *recollect; re-cover*, not *recover*).

P9 Quotation marks are primarily for short, exact quotations (not paraphrasings) of other people's words and for titles of *parts* of publications, such as magazine and newspaper stories or book chapters. (Italicize the titles of whole journals and books—underlined in typed copy. See **Ital**.) If a quotation is more than two or three lines long, you should indent it from each side, single-space it, and omit quotation marks.

When closing quotation marks and other marks seem to come at the same place, the standard *American* practice is as follows: Place commas or periods *inside* the closing quotes; place semicolons or colons *outside;* and place question or exclamation marks inside or outside depending on whether they belong to the quotations or only to your sentence encompassing it.

P10 The colon is either an anticipating or a separating mark. As an anticipator, it appears after introductory lead-ins to explanations or quotations, especially if the lead-in includes such formalizing terms as the word *following* or if the explanation is lengthy or itemized.

The X Company's ink was even redder: its third-quarter loss of . . . .

Three main benefits deserve your attention: . . . . (Enumeration follows. Notice that you do not need—indeed should not use—a browbeating, word-wasting expression like "these benefits are" before or after the colon! See **BB**.)

On the use of the colon, Perrin says: . . . . (Long quotation follows.)

Because the colon is also a separating mark, however—used to separate hours from minutes and volume numbers from pages, for example—it should not serve as an anticipating mark when the lead-in phrasing fits well as an integral part of a short, informal statement. Some people call this misuse the "obtrusive colon."

> The three main advantages are (colon would be obtrusive here) speed, economy, and convenience.

> Perrin reports that (no colon; not even a comma) *"Will* has practically replaced *shall* in . . . ."

Almost invariably words like *namely, that is, for example,* and *as follows* are wasted (and browbeating) when used with a colon. The introductory phrasing and the colon adequately anticipate without these words.

> We have several reasons for changing: namely the . . . . (Omit *namely*.)

> We had several reasons for changing. These reasons are: . . . . (This is worse. Omit *These reasons are;* put the colon after *changing*.)

Although practice varies, usually you should capitalize the first word after a colon only if it begins a complete sentence; but if itemizations follow, you may capitalize even though each item depends on the introductory statement for completeness.

The same idea applies to the end punctuation of items following a colon. If the items make complete sentences, put a period after each; but if all are to be considered one sentence, use comma or semicolon at the end of each (except the last, of course) as in other series—or you may use no end punctuation.

P11 Underlining in typed or handwritten copy specifies italic type when printed. Its main uses are to mark titles of books and journals, to emphasize, and to indicate unanglicized words. In copy not to be printed, underlining should go with any heading not written in solid capitals. Otherwise the heading, which is really a title for the copy over which it stands, does not stand out sufficiently. (A printer would make it stand out by using big or boldface type.)

Typed underlining is preferably continuous, rather than broken by individual words, because it is easier both to type and to read that way.

P12 Besides its well-known use at the end of a question, the question mark (in parentheses) immediately following a statement or spelling indicates that the writer is uncertain and unable to determine. Obviously, it should not be an excuse for laziness; but if you have only heard a difficult name, for example, and have to write to that person, you'd better use the mark than unconcernedly misspell the name.

A question mark should not appear after indirect questions and is unnecessary after commands softened by question form, but some writers feel that it further softens commands.

> We need to know what your decision is. (This is an indirect question.)

> Will you please ask the secretary in your office to change my mailing address. (This is a softened command, with or without the question mark.)

P13 Ellipsis (three *spaced* periods) means that you have left out something. You *must* use this mark when giving an incomplete quotation. Note that if an omission comes at the end of a sentence, you need to add the appropriate end-of-sentence punctuation—a fourth dot for the period, or a question mark or an exclamation point. Ellipses are also coming into wide use, especially in business, as an additional way to mark parenthetical expressions; but this practice has not yet achieved total acceptance (see **P7**).

> "We the people of the United States . . . do ordain and establish this Constitution . . . ."

Paragraphs in letters and reports are the same as in other writing—unified and coherent developments of topics—except that they tend to be more compressed and shorter for easier readability. (The symbol ¶ may replace **Par** to indicate an impropriety on paragraphing.)

1. Keep your paragraphs reasonably short. Long ones are discouragingly hard to read. Especially the first and last paragraphs of letters and memos should be short (rarely more than three or four lines). Elsewhere, if a paragraph runs to more than about eight lines, you should consider breaking it up for easier readability. Certainly you should ignore any idea that a paragraph has to be more than one sentence.

2. But develop your paragraphs adequately to clarify and support your points—by explanation, detail, facts and figures, or illustrations and examples.

3. Make each paragraph unified and coherent by taking out elements irrelevant to the topic, by organizing carefully, and by showing the interrelationship of the ideas. Consider beginning with a topic sentence and/or ending with a summary. See **Unit** and **Coh** for further tips.

4. (**Coh**) Show the relation of the paragraph to the preceding (by following logical sequence, carrying over key ideas, and/or using transitional words) and to the purpose of the whole paper or section (by pointing out the significance and/or using transitional words or sentences).

   Paragraph unity also includes . . . . (*Also* means some of the explanation has preceded.)

   Carrying over key words and using transitional words are both means of providing unity between paragraphs as well as within them. (As *well as* means we've discussed unity *in* paragraphs and now will discuss it *between* them.)

5. **Par** with **No** before it means "No new paragraph needed here because you are still on the same topic and within reasonable paragraph length."

Parallelism means using the same kind of grammatical structure for ideas that you use coordinately, as in pairs, series (including lists), comparisons, and outlines. These structures state or imply relationships usually indicated by *and, but,* or *or* and hence should relate only full sentences to full sentences, nouns to nouns, verbs to verbs, active voice to active voice, plural to plural—indeed *any* grammatical form only to the same grammatical form in the related part. Watch for parallelism with *not only . . . but also, as well as, larger, less expensive,* and the like. (See Item 5 under "Organizing the findings" in Chapter 14 for parallelism in outlines.)

> One of the duties of the flight attendant is to offer customers magazines, pillows, and hang their coats (two plural nouns and a verb improperly connected by the coordinating conjunction *and*).
>
> The No-Skid knee guard is long wearing, washable, and stays in position (two adjectives improperly connected by *and* to a verb).
>
> John Coleman is 39, married, and a native (two adjectives and a noun).
>
> If we fair each side of the arc, we produce a more practical airfoil section and an increase in performance is attained. (Active voice related to passive. Rewrite the last part as "increase performance.")
>
> The next step is baking or catalyzation. (Use "baking or catalyzing.")
>
> Swimming is better exercise than to walk (a gerund compared with an infinitive).

Parallelism in pairs, series, and comparisons is largely a question of logic; you can add together and compare only like things. See **Log.**

Passive voice (in which the subject receives rather than does the action indicated by the verb) is usually wordy, awkward, and weak. Most of your sentences should therefore use the active voice. It makes important words (usually persons or products in letters) the subjects and objects of your verbs, as they should be.

Writers often use passive constructions in a misguided effort to avoid *I* and *we* as the subject. If you feel that you must avoid them to prevent monotony of sentence pattern, Chapter 2 explains better ways. If you feel that you must avoid them to increase objectivity, you are working under a false impression; you can be just as biased without them. But you can avoid the first person and the passive at the same time, as explained in the first illustration below.

Still, you may find appropriate use for passives to convey unwelcome information, to meet a thesis director's or company executive's unsound requirement that you write impersonally, to avoid a direct accusation, to put emphasis on something other than the doer of the action, or to weaken an otherwise rankling command or recommendation.

Your Long-Flight skis were shipped this morning by our mailing department. (Can be made active and impersonal, as "Two Long-Flight skis are on their way; they left the mailing department this morning.")

The subject has been considered from the following viewpoints: . . . . (The requirement of impersonal style may justify the passive here.)

The mower apparently has not been oiled adequately (avoids accusing the user).

Careful attention should be given to . . . (weakens a possibly rankling command).

It is recommended that . . . . (Though this weakens and avoids egotism in a recommendation, surely you can find a better way. This deserves criticism for both a **Passive** and an **Expl**etive.)

PD Psychological description (interpreting facts and physical features of a product in terms of reader benefits) is the real heart of selling. Unless your reader readily makes the interpretation, pure physical description is ineffective in selling. So when you name a physical feature of a product you're selling, show the reader what it means in terms of benefits—as explained in Chapters 5 and 8.

The Bostonian Sporty shoe has Neolite soles and triple-stitched welt construction. (Better with **PD**: The Neolite soles and triple-stitched welt construction cause the Bostonian Sporty to last long and keep your feet dry.)

Personalized messages written for and adapted to specific readers are more effective than mass broadcasts. What seems to be for everybody has less interest to anybody. Even form letters should be worded to give the feeling that the message is directed to each reader. Expressions such as "Those of you who . . ." and "If you are one who . . ." give just the opposite impression. (See Chapter 4.)

Plan your message more appropriately for the circumstances as an **A–**, **B–**, or **C–plan**. (See Chapter 4.)

Pompous   Try to express the thought simply, not to impress the reader.

Pr   Follow more generally acceptable business practice.

PR   Personal references (names of people or pronouns referring to them) not only help to keep the reader in the picture and produce you-attitude (**YA**); they help to avoid the passive (**Pas**), to make your writing specific and concrete instead of general and abstract (**Spec**), and to make your writing easier and more interesting to read. Naming or referring to persons—Flesch suggests at least 6 percent of your words—is an important element in readability.

Prepositions indicate relationships within a sentence.

1. Be sure to use the right one for your construction. Some words require certain prepositions; others vary prepositions for different meanings. See **Id.**

   Ability *to;* agree *to, with,* or *in;* compare *to* (for similarities only) or *with* (for likeness and differences); different *from* (not different *than.*)

2. When you use two words that require different prepositions, use both:

   Because of your interest *in* and aptitude *for. . . .*

3. Don't use many of the .45-caliber group prepositions (*according to, in regard to, by means of, in connection with, on the part of*) for squirrel-size ideas or your prepositions will "bulk too large," as Perrin says.

PV Insofar as possible, keep the same point of view in a sentence, a paragraph, or a whole letter. Make only logically necessary shifts, and let your reader know by providing the necessary transitional words. Watch carefully for shifts in time, location, and those whose eyes you seem to be looking through. For effective you-attitude, look through the reader's eyes whenever possible. See **YA.**

R Bring your reader into the picture early—and don't forget later. The reader is the most important person involved with your letter. See **Per, PR, PV,** and **YA.**

Redundancy includes not only useless repetition but wasting words saying things that are obvious or clearly implied. Avoid it.

Ref The references of your pronouns must be immediately certain and clear to your reader—not ambiguous, too far away, or merely implied. Except for the few indefinite pronouns (*one, everybody, anybody,* and *it* referring to the weather), a pronoun confuses or distracts a reader unless it refers clearly to a preceding noun and agrees with it in number and gender. *Each, every, any,* and their combinations *anybody* and *everybody* are singulars requiring singular verbs and pronouns; but see **Agr** for further explanation of agreement.

1. Often the trouble with a pronoun reference is that the antecedent is just too far away. Ordinarily a pronoun tends to "grab onto" the closest preceding noun as its antecedent. So construct (or reconstruct) your sentences with that tendency in mind—lest you mislead your reader. Repeat the antecedent or change the word order so that the reader knows immediately what the antecedent is

2. Guard particularly against *this, that, which, it,* and *they* making

vague reference to ideas of whole preceding clauses instead of clear, one-word antecedents.

Dayton adopted the plan in 1914 and has kept it ever since, which is a good example of the success of the council-manager form of government. (What does *which* refer to?)

After reading a book about television engineering, the young man wanted to be one of them. (One of what? The antecedent is only implied.)

3. Don't use the same pronoun with different meanings in the same sentence:

The directions say that it is up to the owner to change the filter whenever it needs it.

Repetition of words or ideas seems wordy and monotonous unless it serves a justified purpose. Restatement of important ideas deserving emphasis, however, is often desirable; but even then, the restatement usually should be in somewhat different words to avoid monotony.

Resale material—reassuring a customer that a choice of goods and/or firm was a good one—not only shows your service attitude (**SA**); it helps keep incomplete orders and delayed shipments on the books, rebuilds reader confidence in adjustment situations, and serves as a basic idea in collections. Look it up in the Index and read about it in connection with the particular type of message involved.

SA Service attitude—showing a genuine desire to give the kinds and quality of goods and services wanted, favorable prices, and various conveniences, plus unselfish reassurance of appreciation for business—can go a long way toward overcoming a reader's feeling that you are indifferent. Your basic techniques are to interweave into your letters some sales promotion material (**SPM**) and resale talk (**Res**). See Chapter 3.

SC Show more success consciousness (self-confidence, Chapter 4).

Selfish interest (yours) is something both reader and writer assume, but it does not help your cause and therefore is best not mentioned. For more interest and persuasion, show what's in the situation for *the reader*. See **YA** and Chapter 4.

Shifting of tense (time), voice (active-passive), mood (indicative, imperative, subjunctive), or person (first, second, third) should come only when the logic of the situation dictates it; otherwise it leads to incoherence and loses or confuses readers. See **PV**.

Simplify. Needlessly big words or involved sentences are hard to read.

Sincerity is essential if you are to be believed. Don't pretend or overstate your case. See Chapter 3.

Slow movement is desirable only in a B–plan message where you must reason calmly with the reader to justify the unpleasant point you are preparing to present; otherwise it is objectionable.

1. Don't use too many words before getting to an important point. Starting too far back in the background, giving too many details, or saying things that you should imply are the most frequent faults.

2. Don't use too many short, choppy sentences and thus slow up a message that should move fast.

SOS Errors in sentence organization and structure are sometimes serious enough to justify the distress signal.

1. Don't present a phrase or dependent clause as a sentence. Usually correction requires only attaching the dependent element to the preceding or following sentence (on which it depends). See **Frag.**

   In answer to your request concerning what the company is like, what has been accomplished, and the future prospects. Here is the information I have been able to acquire. (Replace the period with a comma.)

2. Don't use a comma—or no punctuation at all—between two independent clauses unless a strong conjunction (*and, but, or,* or *nor*) is there. The error is not basically one of punctuation (as discussed in **P1** and **P2**) but the more serious failure to recognize what a sentence is. You need a period if the two statements are not so closely related that they ought to be in the same sentence, or a semicolon if they are.

   The credit business is big business some people estimate that it is as much as 86 percent of American business (period needed before *some*).

   Running two sentences together without punctuation is about the worst error a writer can make, however it is little worse than using a comma where a semicolon is required, as in this sentence. See **P2.**

3. Don't put words together in unnatural, confusing relationships that the reader has to ponder to get the intended meaning. (See **K** and **Mod.**)

   Just because you want to sell I don't want right now to buy. (The fact that you want to sell doesn't mean I want to buy.)

4. Don't put ideas together with connectives that falsely represent their relationship. See **Coh** and **Unit.**

Spelling errors rarely confuse or mislead, but they nearly always have an equally unfavorable effect—they cause bad spellers to lose face and their readers' faith. So here are the most important tips on spelling and a list of words frequently misspelled in business writing. If you have spelling problems, study both—carefully.

1. *Ie* or *ei*: When pronounced like *ee*, write *ie* except after *c*, as in *achieve, believe; receive, deceive, perceive*. The exceptions are *either, neither, leisure, seize*, and *weird*. When pronounced otherwise, write *ei* (as in *freight, height, forfeit*) except in *die, lie, pie, tie, vie*, and *science*.

2. Double a final single consonant preceded by a single vowel (*a, e, i, o, u*) in an accented syllable when you add a suffix (*-ing, -ed, -er*) beginning with a vowel (*plan, planning; shop, shopping*). Note that if the word already ends in two consonants, or one preceded by two vowels, you do not double the last consonant (*holding, helping; daubing, seeded*). Note, too, that you usually do not double the consonant unless in an accented syllable (*refer, referred, references*). Two new exceptions, *benefitted* and *travelled*, can now go either way.

3. Drop a final unpronounced *e* preceded by a consonant when you add a suffix beginning with a vowel (*hope, hoping; owe, owing*); but retain the *e* after *c* or *g* unless the suffix begins with one of the front vowels, *i* or *e* (*noticeable, changeable, changing, reduced*).

4. Change final *y* to *i* and add *es* for the plural if a consonant precedes the *y* (*ally, allies; tally, tallies*); otherwise, just add *s* (*valley, valleys*).

5. Add *'s* for the possessive of all singulars and of plurals which do not end in *s* (*man's, men's, lady's*); add only apostrophe for *s*-ending plurals (*ladies', Davises', students'*).

6. Hyphenate double-word quantities between 20 and 100 (*twenty-one, thirty-two, forty-four, ninety-eight*) and fractions used as modifiers (*nine-tenths* depleted) but not fractions used as nouns (increased by one fourth).

7. Most words ending with the sound of *seed* are like *concede, precede*, and *recede*; but three require *ee exceed, proceed*, and *succeed*; and one takes an *s* instead of a *c* (*supersede*).

8. Get somebody to pronounce for you while you try to spell the following words commonly misspelled in business. Then study those you miss (along with others from whatever source which give you trouble).

a lot	explanation	prejudiced
accessible	faze	prepare
accidentally	forty	principal
accommodate	gauge	principle
accurate	government	privilege
achievement	grammar	probably
acquaintance	guarantee	proceed
acquire	height	procedure
affect (to influence)	hindrance	prominent

among	imagine	psychology
analyze	immediately	pursue
apparent	incidentally	quantity
appropriate	interest	questionnaire
argument	interpret	realize
attorneys	it's (its)	receive
basically	laboratory	recommend
beginning	led	referring
believe	lose (loose)	renowned
calendar	maintenance	repetition
category	moral (morale)	sense
choose (chose)	mortgage	separate
comparative	necessary	stationary
conscientious	noticeable	stationery
conscious	occasionally	succeed
consensus	occurrence	surprise
consistent	offered	temperament
convenience	omitted	than (then)
decision	original	their (there)
definitely	paid	thorough
description	parallel	transferred
disastrous	passed (past)	tries
effect (result)	perform	too (to, two)
efficiency	permissible	undoubtedly
embarrass	personal	unnecessary
environment	personnel	until
equipped	possession	using (useful)
exaggerate	practical	varies
excellence	precede	whether (weather)
existence	preferred	writing (written)
experience	preference	

Specific wording, like a sharp photograph, helps the reader get a clear idea; general words give only a hazy view.

1. If you are inclined to use the general word for a class of things, consider the advantages of giving the specific kind in that class (machine—mower; office equipment—files, desks, chairs, and type-writers; employees—salesclerks, janitors, secretaries, and others).

2. Another kind of specificness is giving supporting details, illustrations, examples, and full explanations for general statements made. If you use generalities to gain conciseness in topic and summarizing statements, be sure to provide necessary supporting explanations or further details; otherwise, your unsupported statements may not be accepted, even if understood. See **Dev.**

3. Still another important kind of specificness is giving the evidences of abstract qualities you may use. If you are inclined to say that something is a bargain, an outstanding offer, of the highest quality, revolutionary, best, ideal, or economical, give the concrete evi-

dences for these qualities instead of the abstract words. In an application letter, if you want to convey the idea that you are intelligent, industrious, honest, dependable, and sociable, give the evidence and let the reader draw the conclusions. You will sound too cocky if you apply these words to yourself, and your reader will not believe them anyway unless you give the supporting concrete facts.

SPM Sales promotion material (when appropriate and unselfish) not only shows a service attitude (see **SA**) and produces some additional sales; it helps to take the sting out of early collection letters and provides a pleasant ending for essentially bad-news letters, provided that the situation is not too seriously negative. See Chapter 3.

Style See Chapter 2 and (especially for reports) Chapter 14.

Subordinate Don't overstress negative ideas, facts the reader knows, or insignificant points. If you must say them, put them in the middle of the paragraph or letter, devote little space to them, and/or put them in dependent clauses or phrases. Since dependent clauses are particularly useful in subordinating, here are some of the main beginning words that make clauses dependent: *after, although, as, because, before, if, since, though, till, unless, until, when, where, while.*

SW Shall-will; should-would. General usage differs so much from formal usage of *shall* and *will* that formal practice now sounds old-fashioned and stiff in most letters and reports. In general usage (which is appropriate for business writing), *will* has almost completely replaced *shall*. (Formal usage calls for *shall* with the first person and *will* with other persons to indicate the simple future, and for the reverse to indicate firm promise or determination.)

More important for business writers is the distinction between the simple futures and their conditional forms, *should* and *would*. Using the simple future sometimes seems presumptuous.

I will appreciate your giving me your answer by November 20 so that . . . . (*Would*, in place of *will*, would remove the presumption that the reader will answer, by using the conditional mood and saying, in effect, "*If* you will answer . . . I will appreciate it.")

SX Sexist language or viewpoint. Phrase your message for equal treatment of females and males. See p. 56 for common errors and means of avoiding or correcting them.

Syl Divide words at the ends of lines only at syllable breaks, and then only if each part has at least two letters and is pronounceable. If in doubt about where to divide a word, check your dictionary.

T & S Topic and summary statements would help coherence and transitions here.

TM Typing mechanics. If you are an untrained typist, these tips may help:

1. Standard within-line spacings are *(a)* five for paragraph indention; *(b)* two after a colon or end-of-sentence punctuation (including an enclosing end parenthesis); *(c)* one after all other punctuation except as explained below; *(d)* none after an opening parenthesis or before or after a hyphen or dash.

2. Abbreviations pose a spacing problem: some (like our governmental alphabet soup—HEW, IRS, SEC, CAB, for example) are solid; others (even with the same meaning) go various ways. Learn the main ones; look up the others in your dictionary.

3. Dashes (not at all the same as hyphens—see **P7** and **P8**) are preferably two hyphens with no spacing.

4. For quotations of more than four lines, space above and below, indent from each side, single-space, and use no quotation marks.

T-t-t A tea-table turn is an abrupt shift from the pleasant to the unpleasant. Typically, the statement is sweet for a few sentences. Then the next begins, "However, ..." The situation is quite like that of several friends already at a tea-party table when they see X arriving a little late. One of those at the table makes a very favorable remark about X and adds "but . . ."—and everybody has the sinking feeling, "Poor X!"

Tabulate or itemize when you have lots of figures to present or a series of distinct points to make. Itemization will make you think more sharply and state your ideas more precisely and concisely. Thus you produce clearer, quicker reading and more emphasis. Furthermore, **itemization** grabs readers' or hearers' attention.

Telegraphic style (omitting subjects, connective words, and articles, as in telegrams and newspaper headlines) is not acceptable practice in letters, memos, and reports—except in headings or subheads.

Tense Watch the tense (time indicated by your verbs) for appropriateness in the individual verb and logic in the sequence of verbs.

1. Normally you use the present, past, or future according to the time of the action you are reporting.

2. The tense of the key verb in an independent clause governs a sentence. So the tenses of other verbs or verbals should indicate time *relative to* the time of the main verb:

    I will do it as soon as I am able (a future and relative present).

    I had hoped that I would be able to go (a past perfect and relative future).

3. A special use of the present tenses deserves careful attention, however, for some situations: You use the present (called the "universal present") for statements that were true in the past, are true now, and will be true later. We say the sun *sets* in the west (universal present) even though it may have set hours earlier. Any statement you might make about what a book *says* fits the conditions. If you now read a book written even in 1620, it still *says*. . . . Similarly in reporting on your research findings (which presumably are still true), you use the universal present tense. To do otherwise would imply doubt about the present validity of your results.

The law of supply and demand *means* . . .

The 1983 edition *says* . . .

4. Do not shift tenses unless the logic of the situation requires.

5. Be sure to spell the appropriate verb form correctly. Remember that English has two classes of verbs. The Old English weak verbs became our regular verbs whose principal parts go like *plow, plowed, plowed*. Old English strong verbs became our irregular ones that change internally (*think, thought, thought; throw, threw, thrown; lead, led, led;* and *meet, met, met*).

Tone   Watch out for a tone of distrust, indifference, undue humility, flattery, condescension, preachiness, bragging, anger, accusation, sarcasm, curtness, effusiveness, or exaggeration. See Chapter 3.

Since salutations and complimentary closes are the first and last indications of your feelings about the formality of your relationship to your reader, be sure they represent those feelings accurately. See Chapter 1.

Transitions between sentences in a paragraph, between paragraphs, and between sections in longer presentations must show their relationships. Your best method is use of a thread of logic (based on careful organization) that will hold your thoughts together like beads on a string. When the logical thread does not make the relationship clear, however, you need to do so by repeating a key word or idea from the preceding or by using a connecting word, phrase, sentence, or heading that shows the relationship. See **Coh** and **Unit**.

Trite expressions (a form of **Jargon**) are usually overused and hence worn-out figures of speech that dull your writing. The remedy is to state your idea simply in natural, normal English or to use an original figure of speech.

Unity (of sentences, paragraphs, or whole pieces of writing) requires that you show how each statement fits in or belongs (is not irrelevant). Applied to a sentence or paragraph, **Unit** means that the statement seems irrelevant or that the several ideas are not closely enough related to be in one sentence or paragraph. When applied to a whole letter or report, it means that the content seems so varied as to lack a central theme and you should put it in two or more separate papers. Often, however, the writer sees relationships that justify putting things together as they are, and the fault is in not showing the reader the relationships—an error of coherence (see **Coh**).

> Please put your answers in ink and have your signature witnessed by two people. One of our envelopes is enclosed for your convenience. (The envelope is not a convenience in doing what is requested in the first sentence. The two unrelated ideas should not be in the same paragraph. Or adding "in returning your answers" would help.)

Usage refers to the appropriateness of the language to the situation. A passage or expression marked with the symbol may be too formal and stiff, literary, flashy, or highbrow; or too slangy, familiar, crude, or lowbrow. The normal, natural English of educated people conducting their everyday affairs is neither formal nor illiterate but informal and natural. That's what you should use for most letters, memos, and reports.

Be on guard against the following illiterate forms (mostly the result of bad pronunciation): "He is prejudice" (*prejudiced*), "He is bias" (*biased*), "usta" or "use to" (*used to*), "had of" (*had*), "would of" (*would have*), "most all" (*almost all*), "a savings of" (*a saving of*), "She lead the meeting" (*led*).

Variety (of diction and of sentence pattern, type, and length) is necessary to avoid monotony, which puts readers to sleep. Achieving variety should be a part of the revision process, however, and should not distract your thoughts from saying what you want to say in writing a first draft.

In your revision, see that you haven't begun too many successive sentences the same way (especially not with *I* or *we*). If you have repeated yourself, cut out the repetition unless you need it for emphasis; and then change the wording if the two statements of the same idea are close together.

The usual English sentence pattern is subject-verb-complement; in revision, vary the pattern to avoid a dull sameness.

Good style also requires variety in sentence type. Some of your sentences should be simple (one independent clause); some should be compound (two independent clauses stating two closely related ideas of nearly equal importance); and some should be complex (at least one independent clause and one or more dependent, all expressing related ideas but of unequal importance). Especially avoid too many successive simple sentences for ideas not deserving equal emphasis or too many compound sentences connected by *and*. (See **Sub**.)

Although most of your sentences should be relatively short (averaging 17–20 words for easy readability), you will produce a monotonous choppiness if all your sentences are in that range. See **Sim** and **Chop,** and revise accordingly.

Wordy   See Chapter 2.

YA   You-attitude. The you-attitude is certainly one of the three most important points about letter writing. People do things for their own benefit, not yours. If you want to persuade them to act, you have to show them the advantages to themselves. Both your reader and you know that you're interested in yourself. To deny that would be insincere and disbelieved. But you need not put your selfish interests in the letter; the fact that you want something is no reason for the reader to act. The benefits going the other way are. Write about *them*. See **Self** and Chapter 4.

To show readers what is in the situation for them, you have to visualize their ways of life and show how your proposal fits in. See **Adapt.**

✕   Obvious error. Proofread carefully and correct such errors.

∾   Invert the order or sequence of words or ideas.

◡   Close up the unnecessary space.

¶   New paragraph needed. See **Par.**

Additional space needed here.

ϑ or **⅄**   Delete (take out); unnecessary.

←↕→   Move in the direction pointed.

Index

This book has been set Merganthaler 202 in 10 and 9 point Caledonia, leaded 2 points. Part numbers and titles are 16 point and 18 point Helvetica Medium. Chapter titles are 20 point Helvetica. The size of the text page is 28 by 47 picas.